THE INVISIBLES

THE DELUXE EDITION

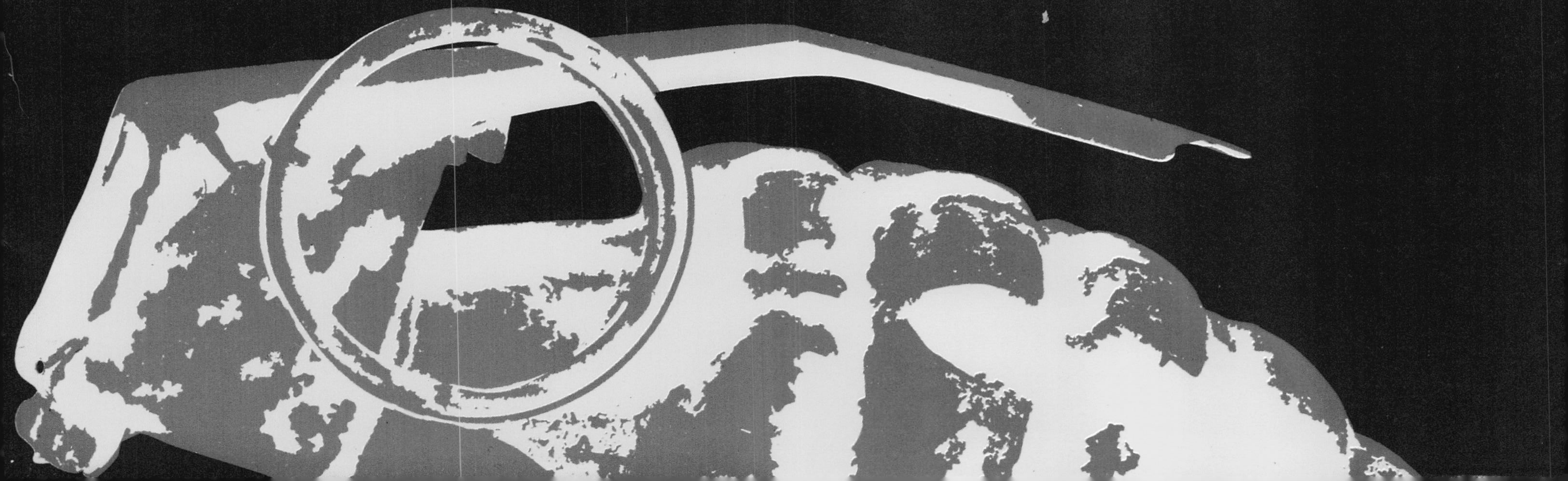

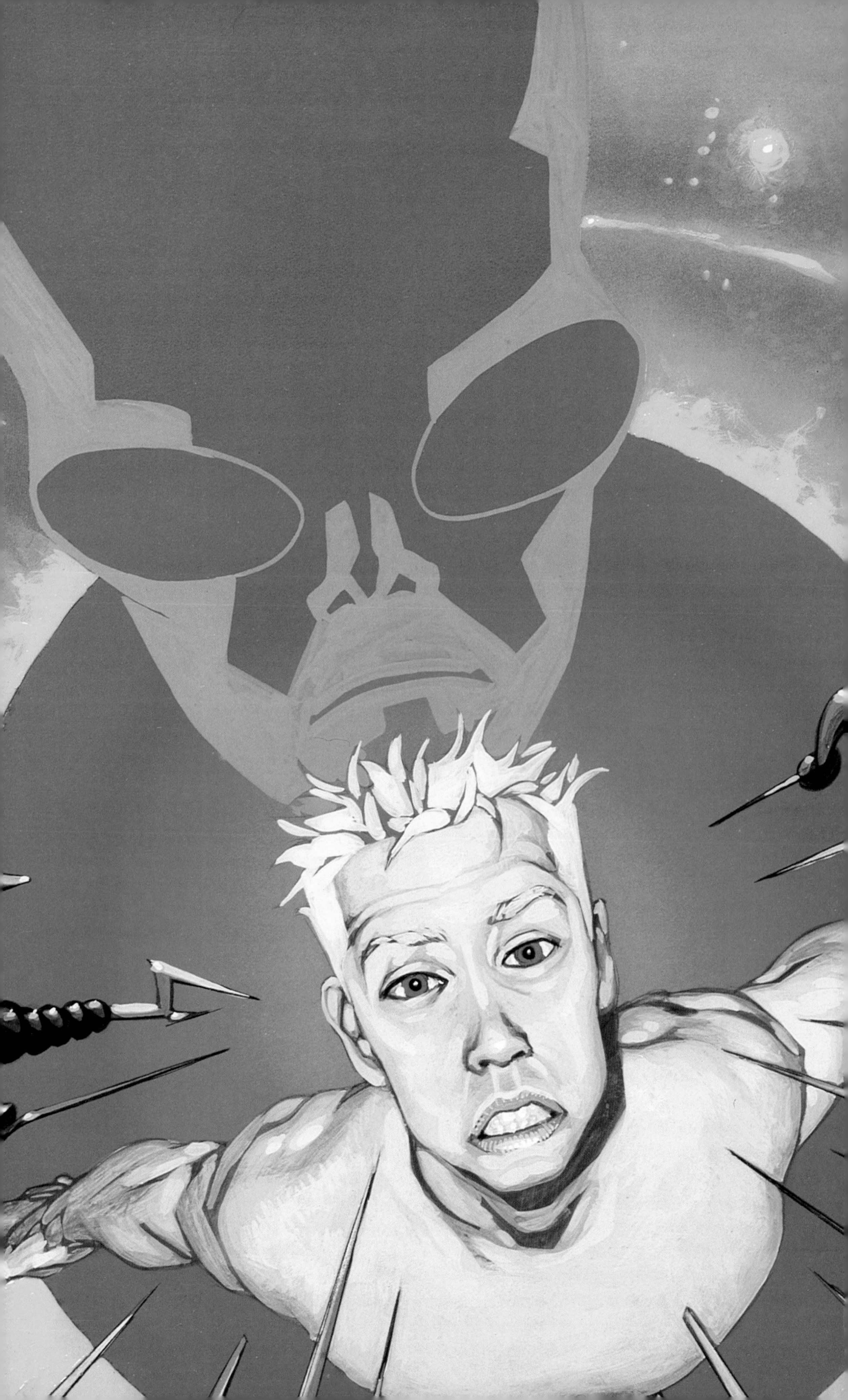

THE DELUXE EDITION BOOK TWO

THE INVISIBLES

Grant Morrison
Writer

Phil Jimenez
Jill Thompson
Paul Johnson
Tommy Lee Edwards
Steve Yeowell
Mark Buckingham
Philip Bond
John Stokes
Dick Giordano
Mark Pennington
Glyn Dillon
Kim DeMulder
Artists

Daniel Vozzo
Colorist

Clem Robins
Ellie De Ville
Todd Klein
Letterers

Sean Phillips *Original Series Covers*

Brian Bolland *Cover Artist*

THE INVISIBLES created by Grant Morrison

Stuart Moore Shelly Roeberg Editors – Original Series Julie Rottenberg Associate Editor – Original Series Scott Nybakken Editor
Robbin Brosterman Design Director – Books Louis Prandi Publication Design

Shelly Bond Executive Editor – Vertigo Hank Kanalz Senior VP – Vertigo & Integrated Publishing

Diane Nelson President Dan DiDio and Jim Lee Co-Publishers Geoff Johns Chief Creative Officer Amit Desai Senior VP – Marketing & Franchise Management
Amy Genkins Senior VP – Business & Legal Affairs Nairi Gardiner Senior VP – Finance Jeff Boison VP – Publishing Planning
Mark Chiarello VP – Art Direction & Design John Cunningham VP – Marketing Terri Cunningham VP – Editorial Administration
Larry Ganem VP – Talent Relations & Services Alison Gill Senior VP – Manufacturing & Operations Jay Kogan VP – Business & Legal Affairs, Publishing
Jack Mahan VP – Business Affairs, Talent Nick Napolitano VP – Manufacturing Administration Sue Pohja VP – Book Sales
Fred Ruiz VP – Manufacturing Operations Courtney Simmons Senior VP – Publicity Bob Wayne Senior VP – Sales

THE INVISIBLES: THE DELUXE EDITION BOOK TWO

DC Comics
1700 Broadway, New York, NY 10019. A Warner Bros. Entertainment Company.
Printed in the USA. First Printing. ISBN: 978-1-4012-4599-3

SUSTAINABLE FORESTRY INITIATIVE
Certified Chain of Custody
20% Certified Forest Content, 80% Certified Sourcing
www.sfiprogram.org
SFI-01042
APPLIES TO TEXT STOCK ONLY

Library of Congress Cataloging-in-Publication Data

Morrison, Grant.
The Invisibles Book Two Deluxe Edition / Grant Morrison.
pages cm
Summary: "One of Grant Morrison's most controversial, trippiest and abstract comic books ever is back in a second deluxe edition hardcover. This volume focuses Lord Fanny's past as a prostitute in Brazil, while King Mob leads the other Invisibles in a search for the missing Jack Frost. Then, King Mob is captured by his enemies and tortured mercilessly, while his past as a mod super-agent is revealed. Collects THE INVISIBLES #13-25 and a story from VERTIGO: WINTER'S EDGE #1." — Provided by publisher.
ISBN 978-1-4012-4599-3 (hardback)
1. Graphic novels. I. Title.
PN6728.I58M66433 2014
741.5'973—dc23
2014011611

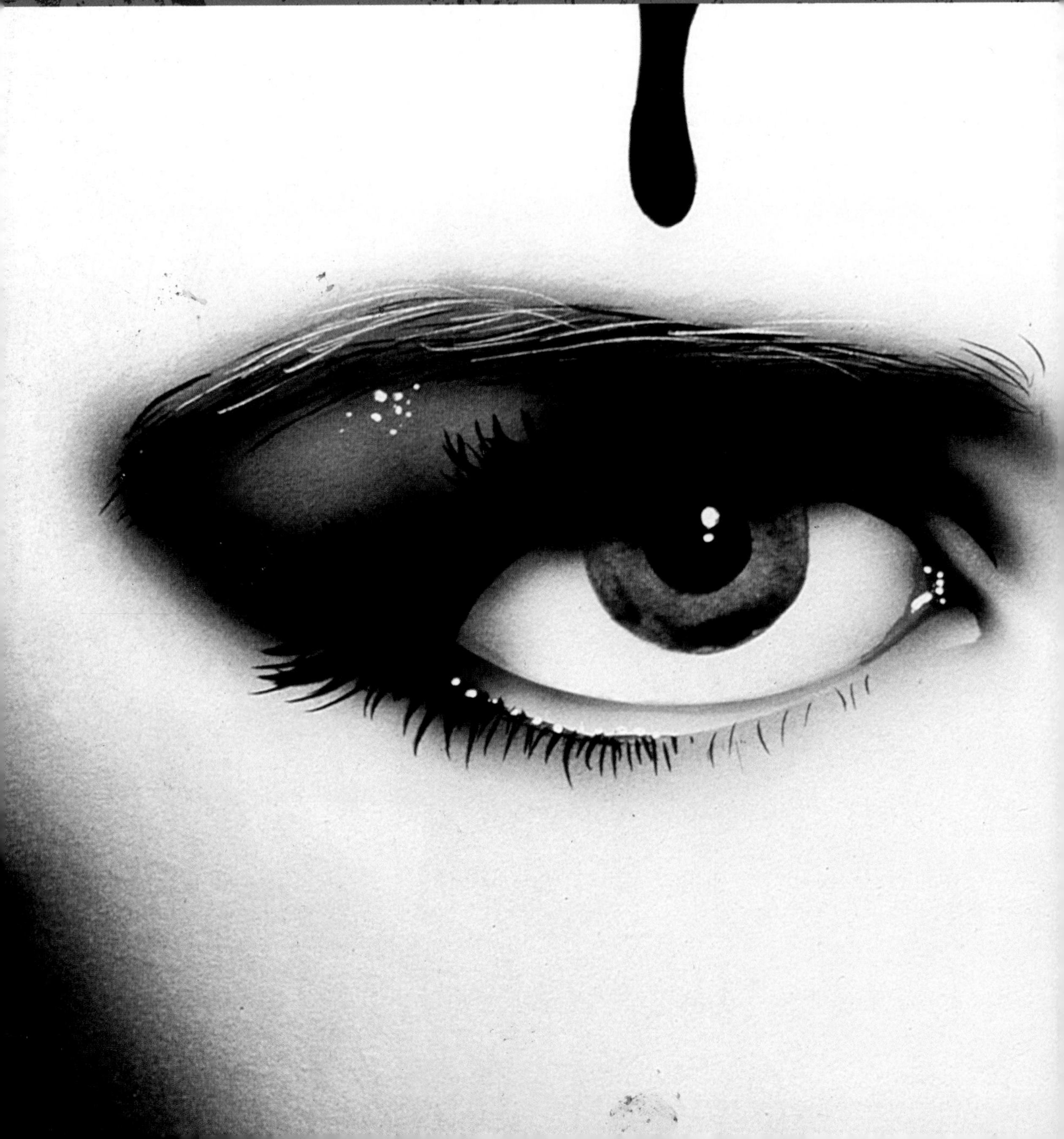

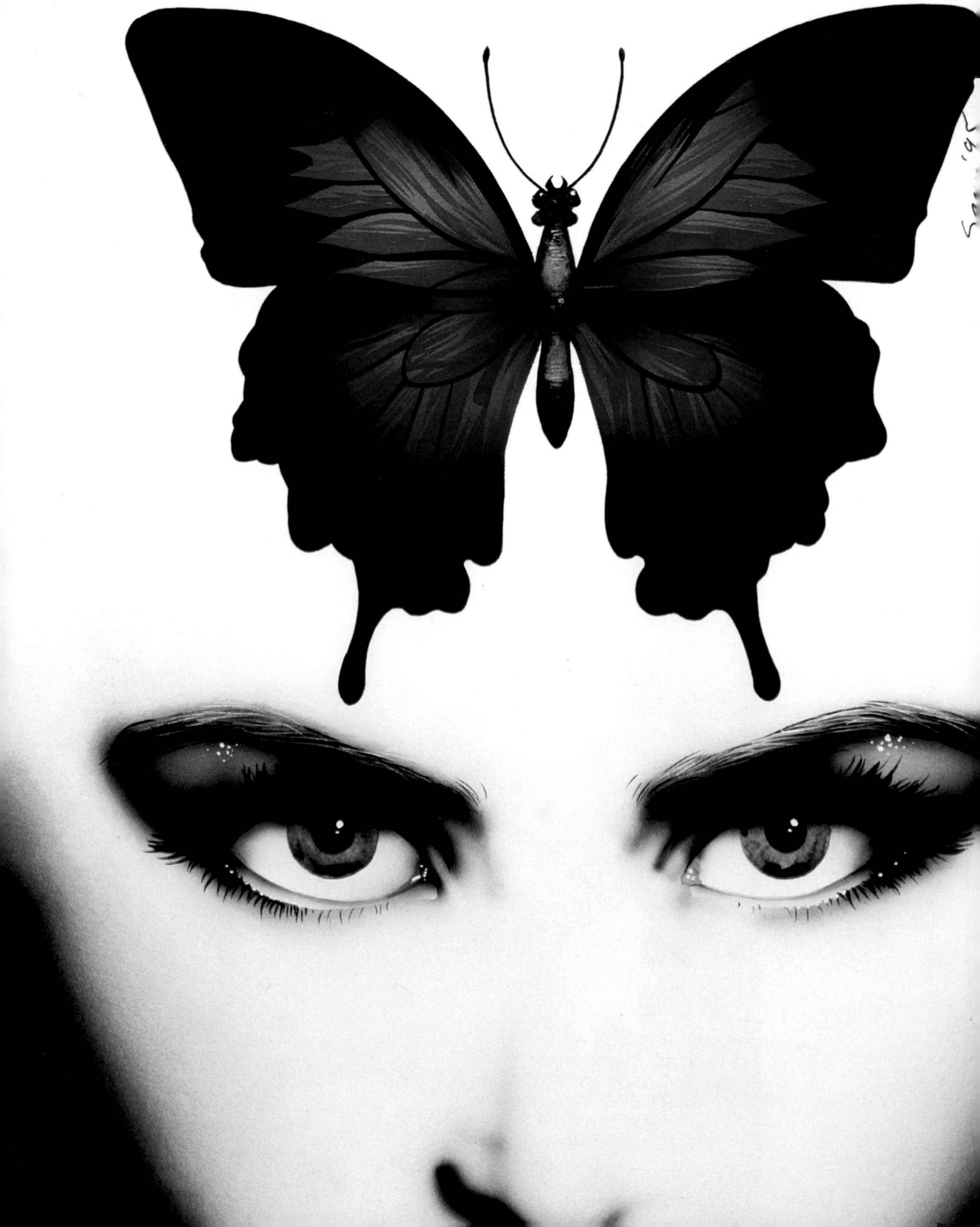

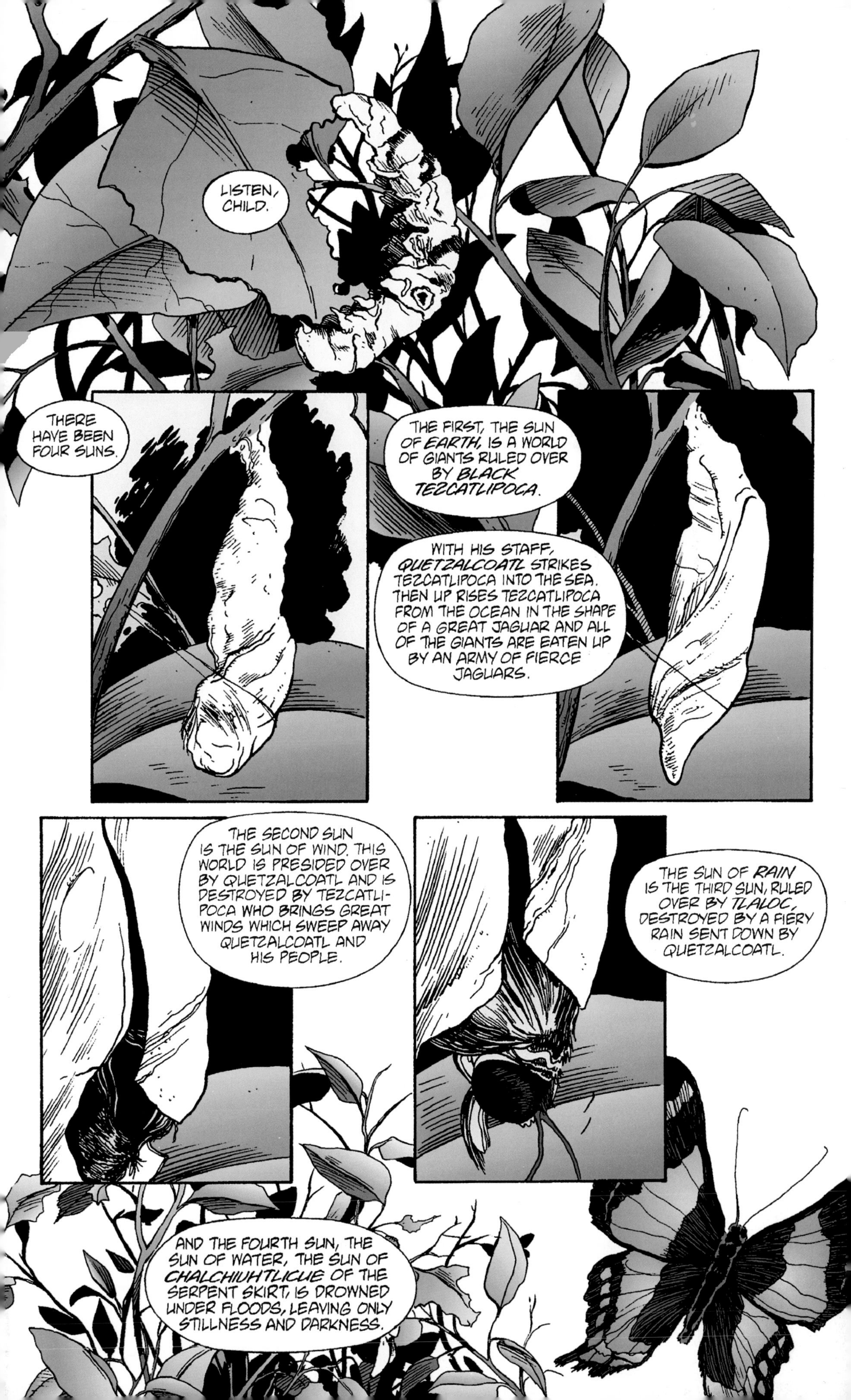
LISTEN, CHILD.
THERE HAVE BEEN FOUR SUNS.
THE FIRST, THE SUN OF EARTH, IS A WORLD OF GIANTS RULED OVER BY BLACK TEZCATLIPOCA.
WITH HIS STAFF, QUETZALCOATL STRIKES TEZCATLIPOCA INTO THE SEA. THEN UP RISES TEZCATLIPOCA FROM THE OCEAN IN THE SHAPE OF A GREAT JAGUAR AND ALL OF THE GIANTS ARE EATEN UP BY AN ARMY OF FIERCE JAGUARS.
THE SECOND SUN IS THE SUN OF WIND. THIS WORLD IS PRESIDED OVER BY QUETZALCOATL AND IS DESTROYED BY TEZCATLIPOCA WHO BRINGS GREAT WINDS WHICH SWEEP AWAY QUETZALCOATL AND HIS PEOPLE.
THE SUN OF RAIN IS THE THIRD SUN, RULED OVER BY TLALOC, DESTROYED BY A FIERY RAIN SENT DOWN BY QUETZALCOATL.
AND THE FOURTH SUN, THE SUN OF WATER, THE SUN OF CHALCHIUHTLICUE OF THE SERPENT SKIRT, IS DROWNED UNDER FLOODS, LEAVING ONLY STILLNESS AND DARKNESS.

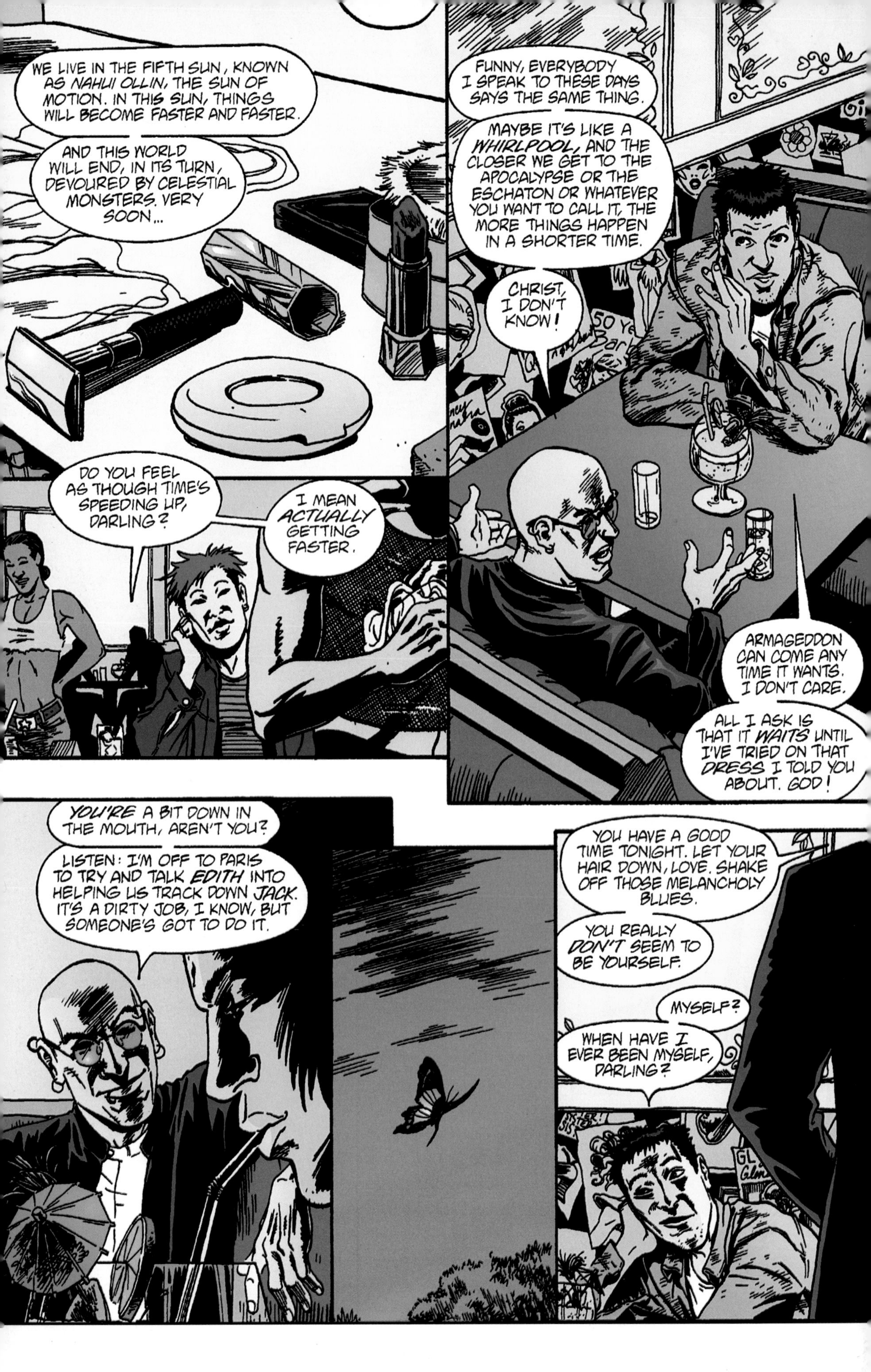
WE LIVE IN THE FIFTH SUN, KNOWN AS NAHUI OLLIN, THE SUN OF MOTION. IN THIS SUN, THINGS WILL BECOME FASTER AND FASTER.
AND THIS WORLD WILL END, IN ITS TURN, DEVOURED BY CELESTIAL MONSTERS. VERY SOON...
FUNNY, EVERYBODY I SPEAK TO THESE DAYS SAYS THE SAME THING.
MAYBE IT'S LIKE A WHIRLPOOL, AND THE CLOSER WE GET TO THE APOCALYPSE OR THE ESCHATON OR WHATEVER YOU WANT TO CALL IT, THE MORE THINGS HAPPEN IN A SHORTER TIME.
CHRIST, I DON'T KNOW!
DO YOU FEEL AS THOUGH TIME'S SPEEDING UP, DARLING?
I MEAN ACTUALLY GETTING FASTER.
ARMAGEDDON CAN COME ANY TIME IT WANTS. I DON'T CARE.
ALL I ASK IS THAT IT WAITS UNTIL I'VE TRIED ON THAT DRESS I TOLD YOU ABOUT. GOD!
YOU'RE A BIT DOWN IN THE MOUTH, AREN'T YOU?
LISTEN: I'M OFF TO PARIS TO TRY AND TALK EDITH INTO HELPING US TRACK DOWN JACK. IT'S A DIRTY JOB, I KNOW, BUT SOMEONE'S GOT TO DO IT.
YOU HAVE A GOOD TIME TONIGHT. LET YOUR HAIR DOWN, LOVE. SHAKE OFF THOSE MELANCHOLY BLUES.
YOU REALLY DON'T SEEM TO BE YOURSELF.
MYSELF?
WHEN HAVE I EVER BEEN MYSELF, DARLING?

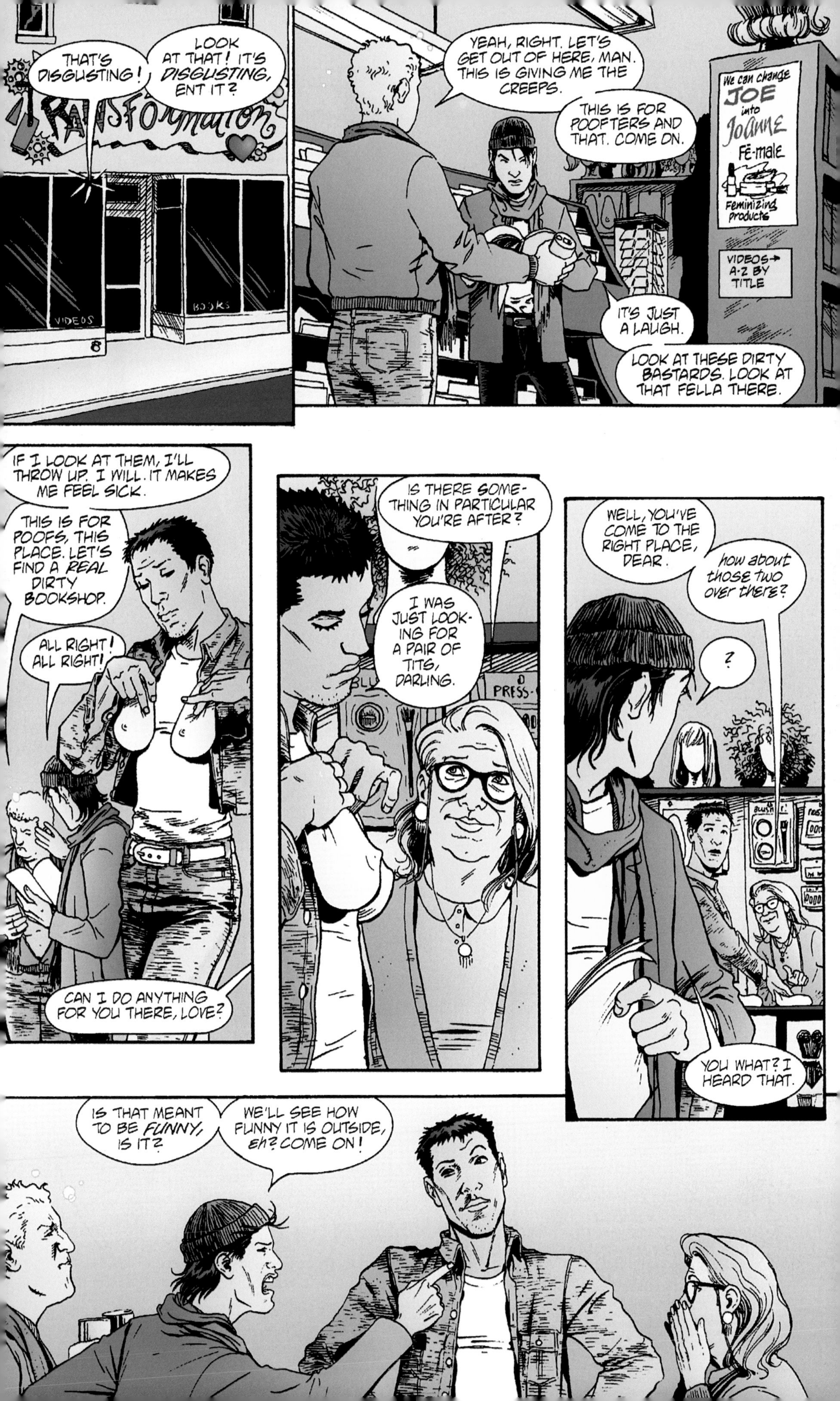
THAT'S DISGUSTING!
LOOK AT THAT! IT'S DISGUSTING, ENT IT?
TRANSFORMATION
VIDEOS
BOOKS
YEAH, RIGHT. LET'S GET OUT OF HERE, MAN. THIS IS GIVING ME THE CREEPS.
THIS IS FOR POOFTERS AND THAT. COME ON.
We can change JOE into JoAnne Fē-male
Feminizing products
VIDEOS→ A-Z BY TITLE
IT'S JUST A LAUGH.
LOOK AT THESE DIRTY BASTARDS. LOOK AT THAT FELLA THERE.
IF I LOOK AT THEM, I'LL THROW UP. I WILL. IT MAKES ME FEEL SICK.
THIS IS FOR POOFS, THIS PLACE. LET'S FIND A REAL DIRTY BOOKSHOP.
ALL RIGHT! ALL RIGHT!
CAN I DO ANYTHING FOR YOU THERE, LOVE?
IS THERE SOMETHING IN PARTICULAR YOU'RE AFTER?
I WAS JUST LOOKING FOR A PAIR OF TITS, DARLING.
WELL, YOU'VE COME TO THE RIGHT PLACE, DEAR.
how about those two over there?
?
YOU WHAT? I HEARD THAT.
IS THAT MEANT TO BE FUNNY, IS IT?
WE'LL SEE HOW FUNNY IT IS OUTSIDE, eh? COME ON!

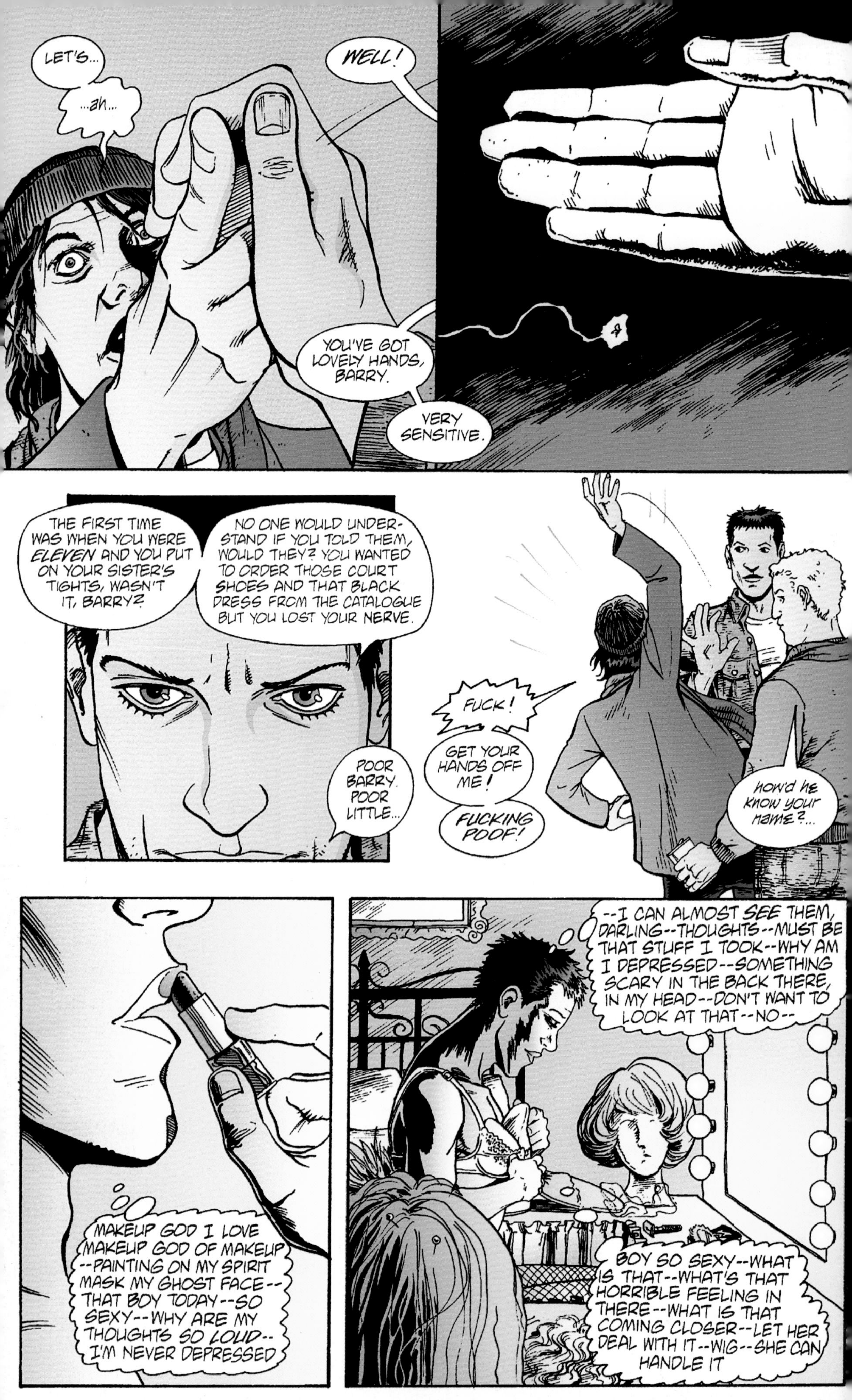
LET'S...
...ah...
WELL!
YOU'VE GOT LOVELY HANDS, BARRY.
VERY SENSITIVE.
THE FIRST TIME WAS WHEN YOU WERE ELEVEN AND YOU PUT ON YOUR SISTER'S TIGHTS, WASN'T IT, BARRY?
NO ONE WOULD UNDERSTAND IF YOU TOLD THEM, WOULD THEY? YOU WANTED TO ORDER THOSE COURT SHOES AND THAT BLACK DRESS FROM THE CATALOGUE BUT YOU LOST YOUR NERVE.
POOR BARRY. POOR LITTLE...
FUCK!
GET YOUR HANDS OFF ME!
FUCKING POOF!
how'd he know your name?...
MAKEUP GOD I LOVE MAKEUP GOD OF MAKEUP --PAINTING ON MY SPIRIT MASK MY GHOST FACE-- THAT BOY TODAY--SO SEXY--WHY ARE MY THOUGHTS SO LOUD-- I'M NEVER DEPRESSED
--I CAN ALMOST SEE THEM, DARLING--THOUGHTS--MUST BE THAT STUFF I TOOK--WHY AM I DEPRESSED--SOMETHING SCARY IN THE BACK THERE, IN MY HEAD--DON'T WANT TO LOOK AT THAT--NO--
BOY SO SEXY--WHAT IS THAT--WHAT'S THAT HORRIBLE FEELING IN THERE--WHAT IS THAT COMING CLOSER--LET HER DEAL WITH IT--WIG--SHE CAN HANDLE IT

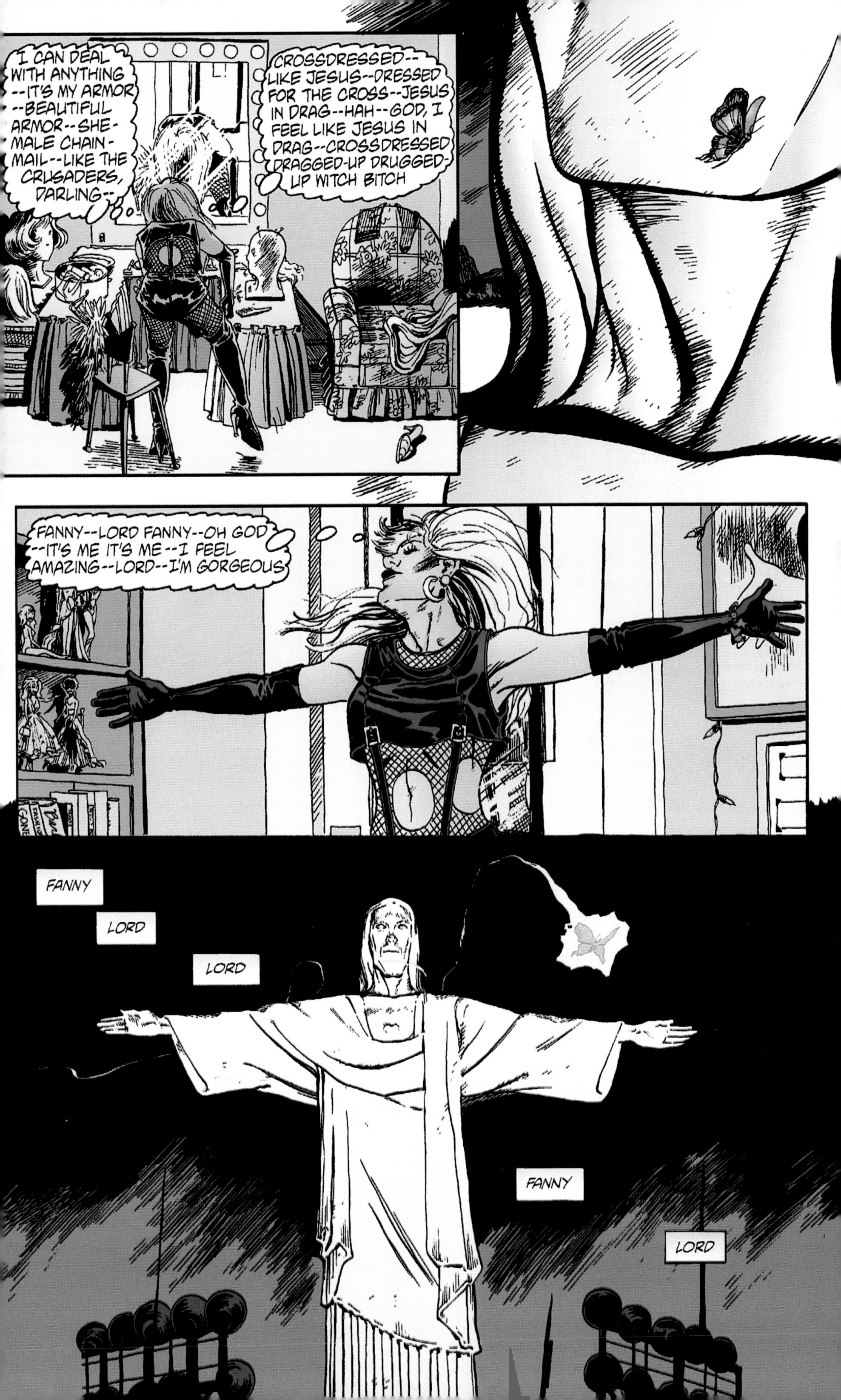

I CAN DEAL WITH ANYTHING --IT'S MY ARMOR --BEAUTIFUL ARMOR--SHE-MALE CHAIN-MAIL--LIKE THE CRUSADERS, DARLING--
CROSSDRESSED--LIKE JESUS--DRESSED FOR THE CROSS--JESUS IN DRAG--HAH--GOD, I FEEL LIKE JESUS IN DRAG--CROSSDRESSED DRAGGED-UP DRUGGED-UP WITCH BITCH
FANNY--LORD FANNY--OH GOD--IT'S ME IT'S ME--I FEEL AMAZING--LORD--I'M GORGEOUS
FANNY
LORD
LORD
FANNY
LORD

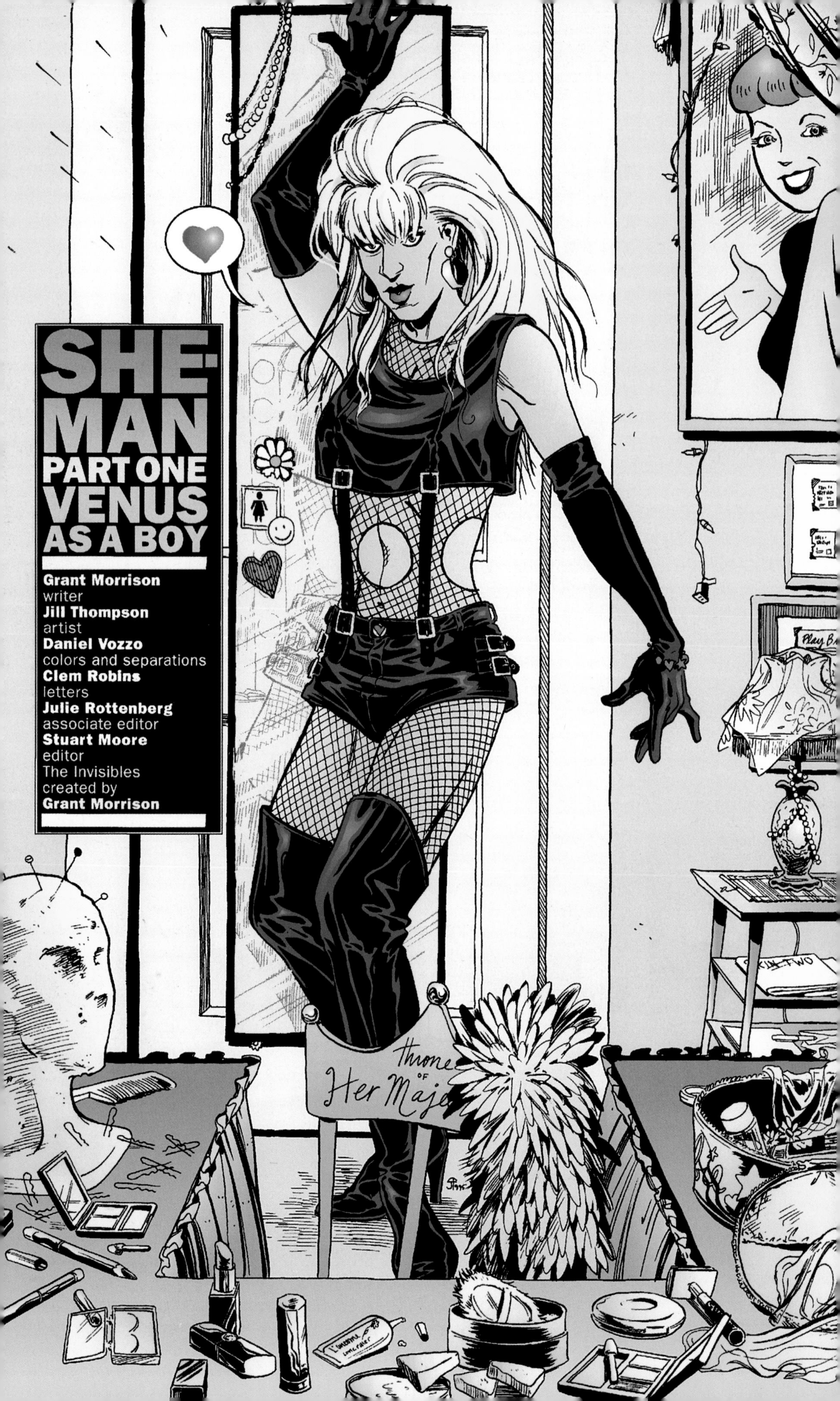
SHE-MAN
PART ONE
VENUS AS A BOY
Grant Morrison
writer
Jill Thompson
artist
Daniel Vozzo
colors and separations
Clem Robins
letters
Julie Rottenberg
associate editor
Stuart Moore
editor
The Invisibles created by
Grant Morrison
throne
OF

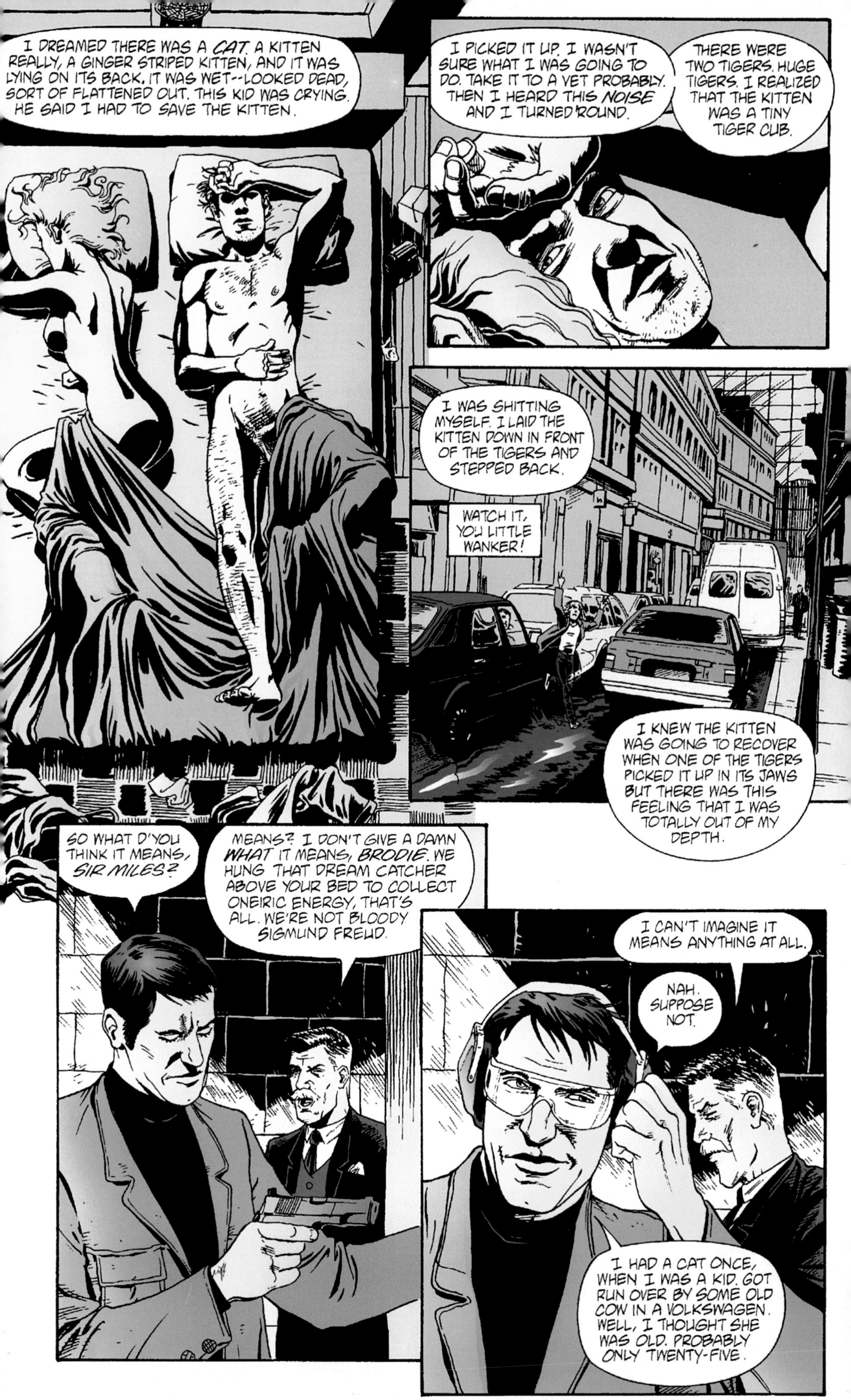

I DREAMED THERE WAS A CAT. A KITTEN REALLY, A GINGER STRIPED KITTEN, AND IT WAS LYING ON ITS BACK. IT WAS WET--LOOKED DEAD, SORT OF FLATTENED OUT. THIS KID WAS CRYING. HE SAID I HAD TO SAVE THE KITTEN.
I PICKED IT UP. I WASN'T SURE WHAT I WAS GOING TO DO. TAKE IT TO A VET PROBABLY. THEN I HEARD THIS NOISE AND I TURNED 'ROUND.
THERE WERE TWO TIGERS. HUGE TIGERS. I REALIZED THAT THE KITTEN WAS A TINY TIGER CUB.
I WAS SHITTING MYSELF. I LAID THE KITTEN DOWN IN FRONT OF THE TIGERS AND STEPPED BACK.
WATCH IT, YOU LITTLE WANKER!
I KNEW THE KITTEN WAS GOING TO RECOVER WHEN ONE OF THE TIGERS PICKED IT UP IN ITS JAWS BUT THERE WAS THIS FEELING THAT I WAS TOTALLY OUT OF MY DEPTH.
SO WHAT D'YOU THINK IT MEANS, SIR MILES?
MEANS? I DON'T GIVE A DAMN WHAT IT MEANS, BRODIE. WE HUNG THAT DREAM CATCHER ABOVE YOUR BED TO COLLECT ONEIRIC ENERGY, THAT'S ALL. WE'RE NOT BLOODY SIGMUND FREUD.
I CAN'T IMAGINE IT MEANS ANYTHING AT ALL.
NAH. SUPPOSE NOT.
I HAD A CAT ONCE, WHEN I WAS A KID. GOT RUN OVER BY SOME OLD COW IN A VOLKSWAGEN. WELL, I THOUGHT SHE WAS OLD. PROBABLY ONLY TWENTY-FIVE.

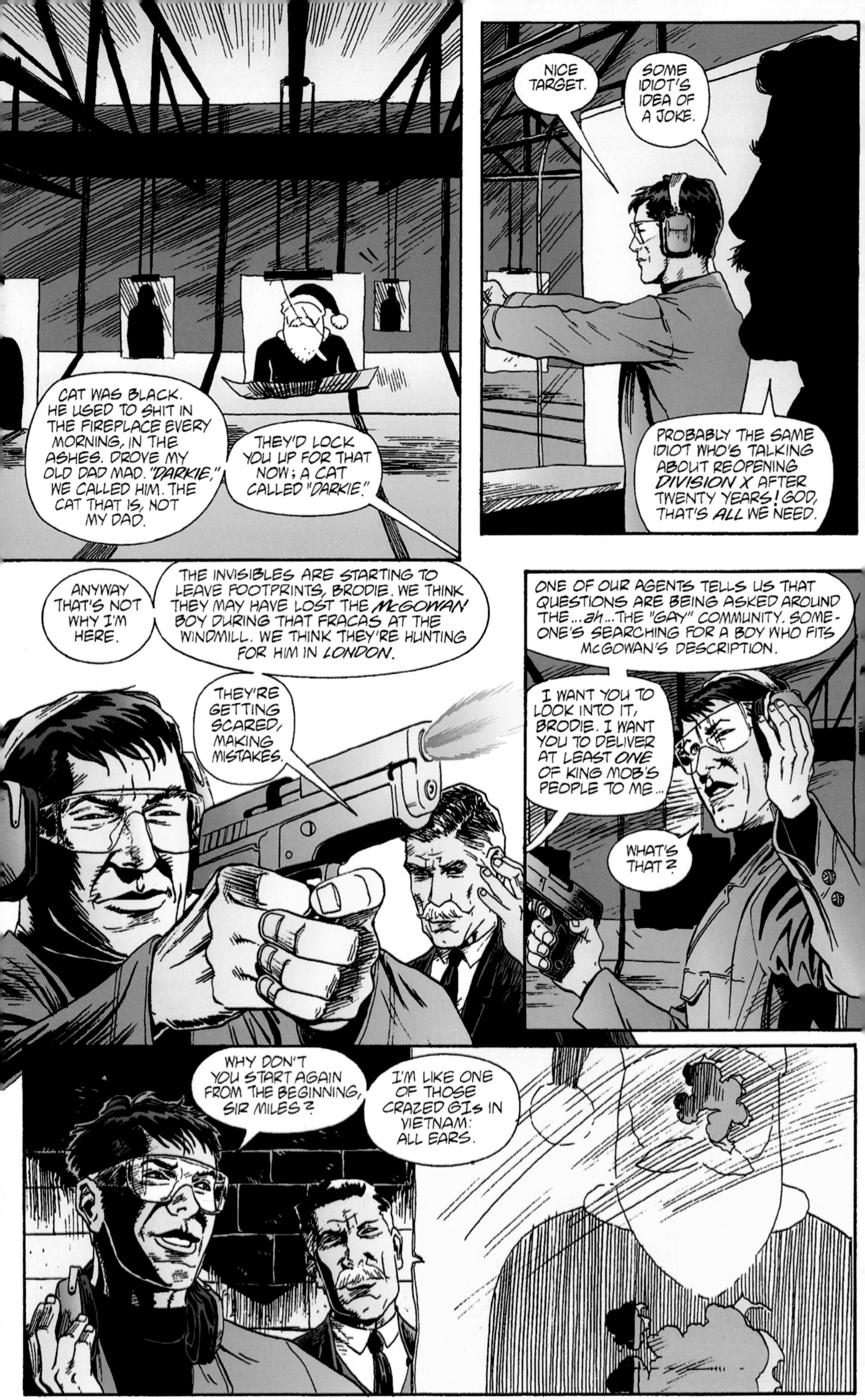
CAT WAS BLACK. HE USED TO SHIT IN THE FIREPLACE EVERY MORNING, IN THE ASHES. DROVE MY OLD DAD MAD. "DARKIE," WE CALLED HIM. THE CAT THAT IS, NOT MY DAD.
THEY'D LOCK YOU UP FOR THAT NOW; A CAT CALLED "DARKIE."
NICE TARGET.
SOME IDIOT'S IDEA OF A JOKE.
PROBABLY THE SAME IDIOT WHO'S TALKING ABOUT REOPENING DIVISION X AFTER TWENTY YEARS! GOD, THAT'S ALL WE NEED.
ANYWAY THAT'S NOT WHY I'M HERE.
THE INVISIBLES ARE STARTING TO LEAVE FOOTPRINTS, BRODIE. WE THINK THEY MAY HAVE LOST THE McGOWAN BOY DURING THAT FRACAS AT THE WINDMILL. WE THINK THEY'RE HUNTING FOR HIM IN LONDON.
THEY'RE GETTING SCARED, MAKING MISTAKES.
ONE OF OUR AGENTS TELLS US THAT QUESTIONS ARE BEING ASKED AROUND THE... ah... THE "GAY" COMMUNITY. SOMEONE'S SEARCHING FOR A BOY WHO FITS McGOWAN'S DESCRIPTION.
I WANT YOU TO LOOK INTO IT, BRODIE. I WANT YOU TO DELIVER AT LEAST ONE OF KING MOB'S PEOPLE TO ME...
WHAT'S THAT?
WHY DON'T YOU START AGAIN FROM THE BEGINNING, SIR MILES?
I'M LIKE ONE OF THOSE CRAZED GIs IN VIETNAM: ALL EARS.

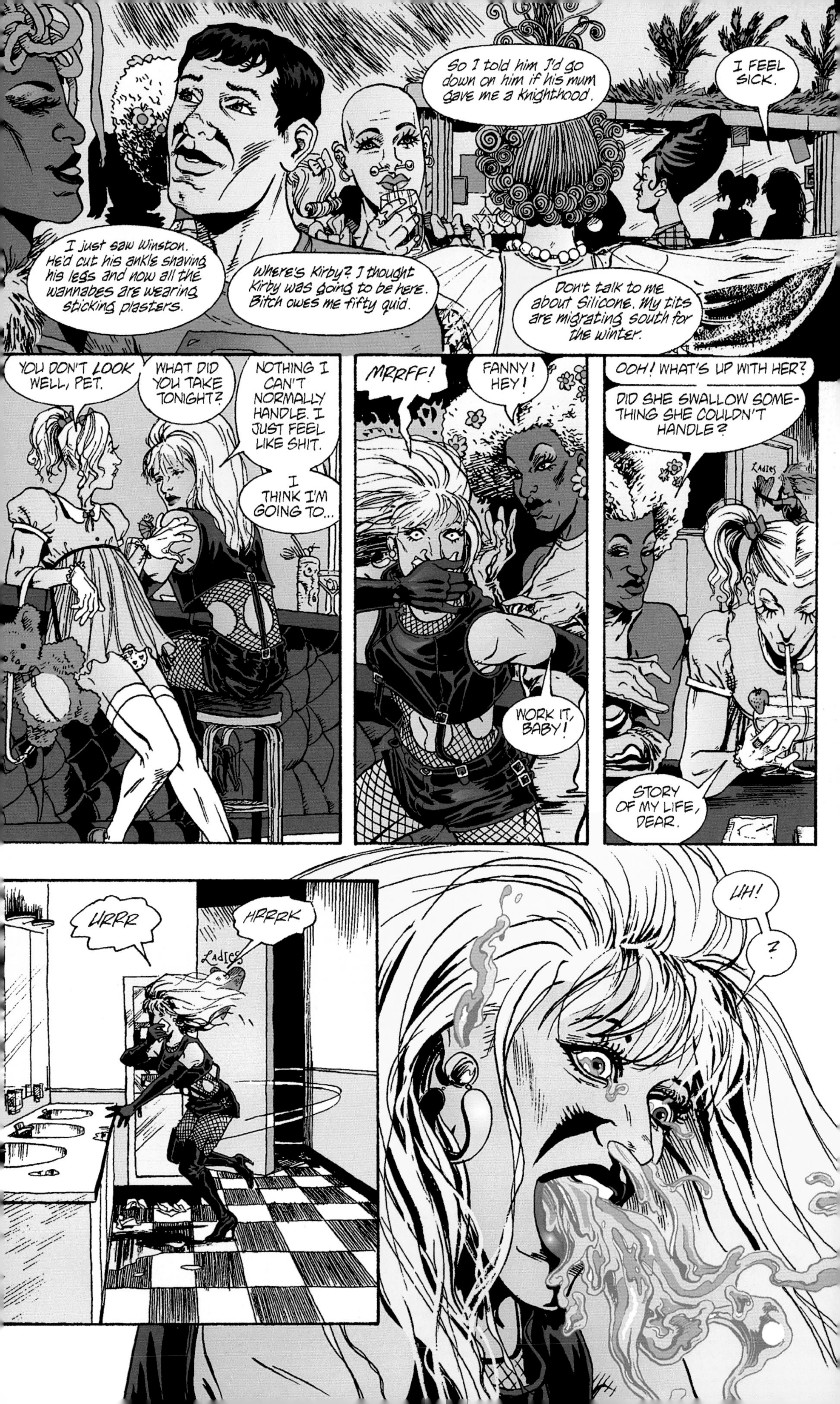
So I told him I'd go down on him if his mum gave me a knighthood.
I FEEL SICK.
I just saw Winston. He'd cut his ankle shaving his legs and now all the wannabes are wearing sticking plasters.
Where's Kirby? I thought Kirby was going to be here. Bitch owes me fifty quid.
Don't talk to me about Silicone. My tits are migrating south for the winter.
YOU DON'T LOOK WELL, PET.
WHAT DID YOU TAKE TONIGHT?
NOTHING I CAN'T NORMALLY HANDLE. I JUST FEEL LIKE SHIT.
I THINK I'M GOING TO...
MRRFF!
FANNY! HEY!
WORK IT, BABY!
OOH! WHAT'S UP WITH HER?
DID SHE SWALLOW SOMETHING SHE COULDN'T HANDLE?
LADIES
STORY OF MY LIFE, DEAR.
URRR
HRRRK
LADIES
UH!
?

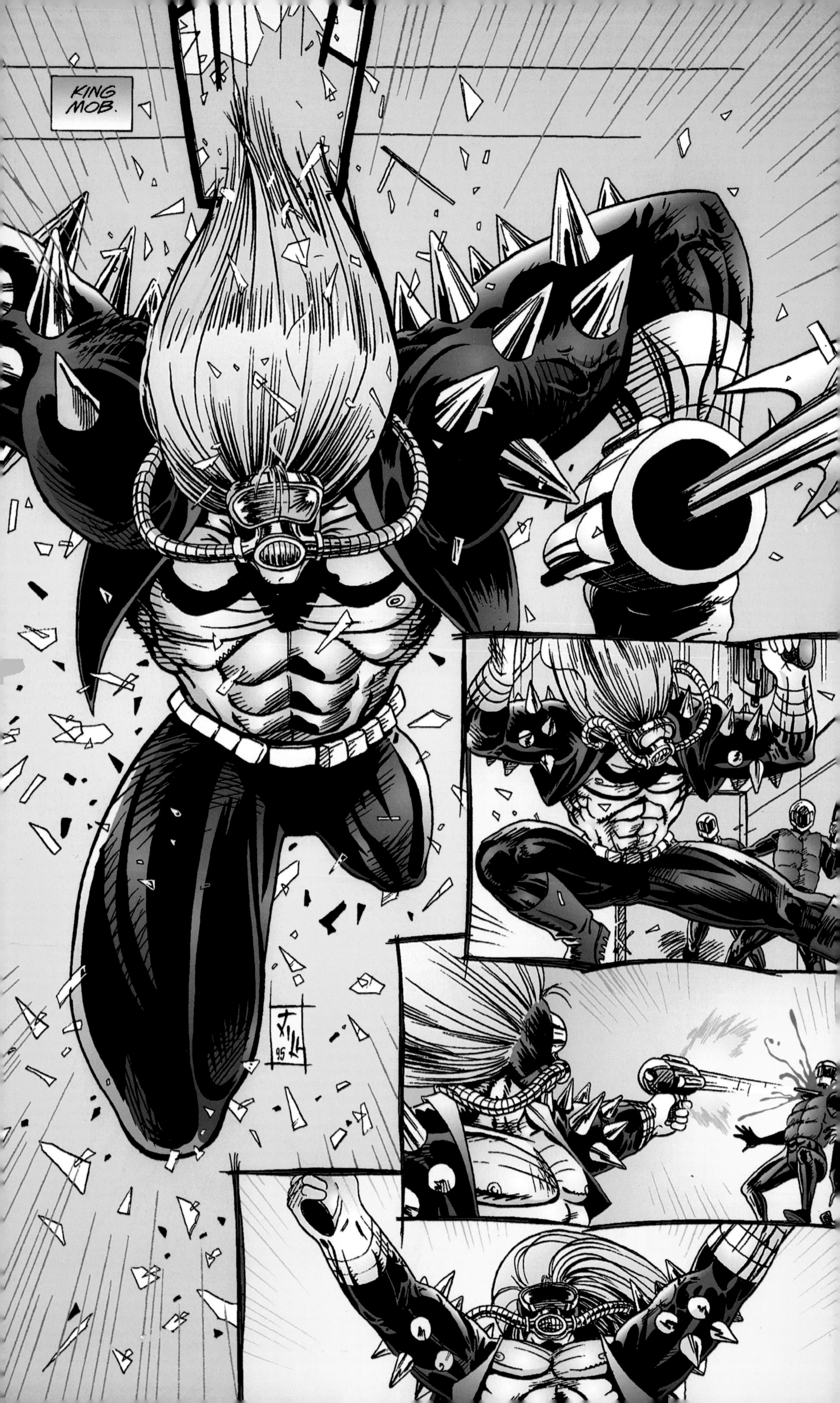
KING MOB.

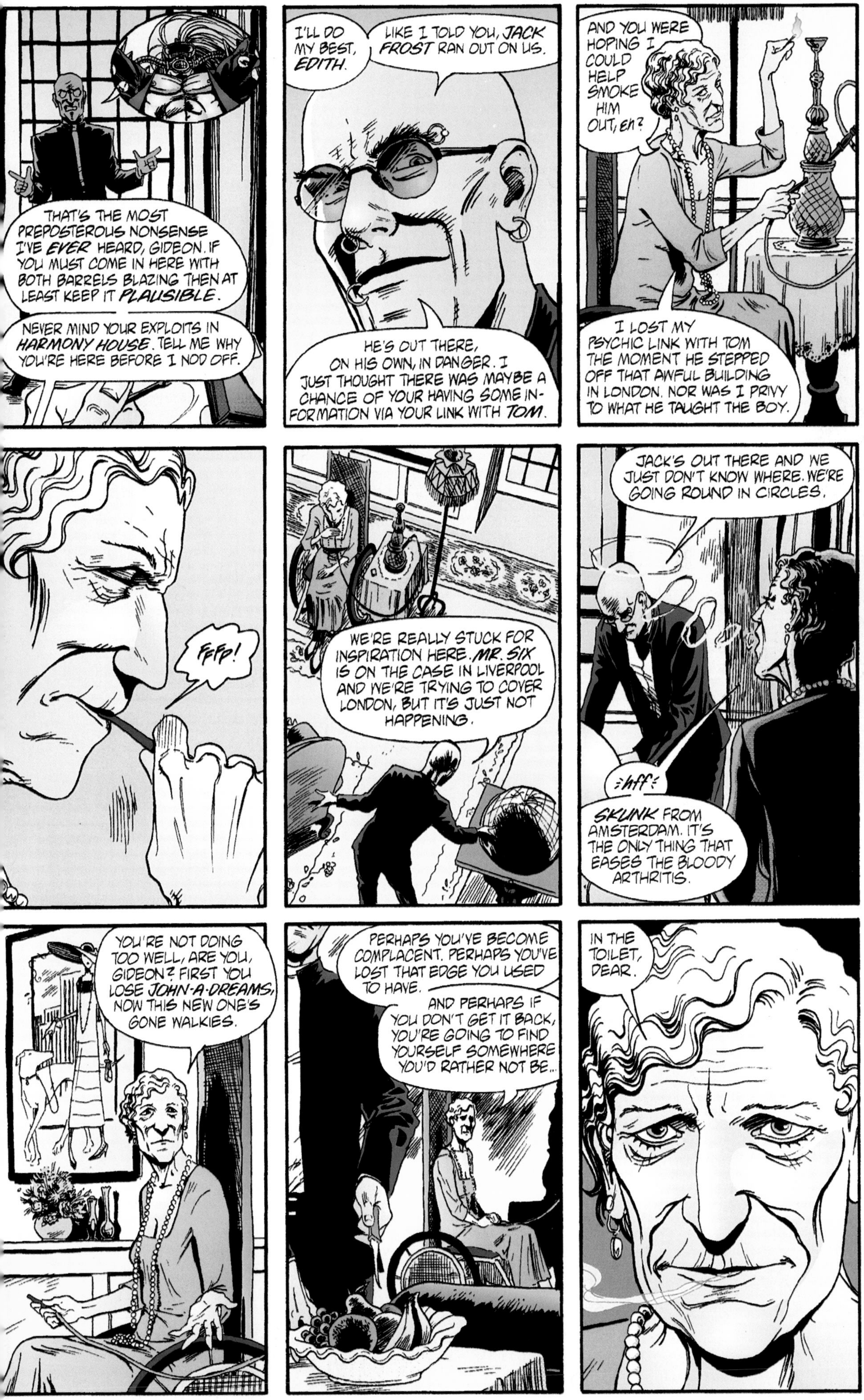
THAT'S THE MOST PREPOSTEROUS NONSENSE I'VE EVER HEARD, GIDEON. IF YOU MUST COME IN HERE WITH BOTH BARRELS BLAZING THEN AT LEAST KEEP IT PLAUSIBLE.
NEVER MIND YOUR EXPLOITS IN HARMONY HOUSE. TELL ME WHY YOU'RE HERE BEFORE I NOD OFF.
I'LL DO MY BEST, EDITH.
LIKE I TOLD YOU, JACK FROST RAN OUT ON US.
HE'S OUT THERE, ON HIS OWN, IN DANGER. I JUST THOUGHT THERE WAS MAYBE A CHANCE OF YOUR HAVING SOME INFORMATION VIA YOUR LINK WITH TOM.
AND YOU WERE HOPING I COULD HELP SMOKE HIM OUT, EH?
I LOST MY PSYCHIC LINK WITH TOM THE MOMENT HE STEPPED OFF THAT AWFUL BUILDING IN LONDON. NOR WAS I PRIVY TO WHAT HE TAUGHT THE BOY.
FFFP!
WE'RE REALLY STUCK FOR INSPIRATION HERE. MR. SIX IS ON THE CASE IN LIVERPOOL AND WE'RE TRYING TO COVER LONDON, BUT IT'S JUST NOT HAPPENING.
JACK'S OUT THERE AND WE JUST DON'T KNOW WHERE. WE'RE GOING ROUND IN CIRCLES.
HFF
SKUNK FROM AMSTERDAM. IT'S THE ONLY THING THAT EASES THE BLOODY ARTHRITIS.
YOU'RE NOT DOING TOO WELL, ARE YOU, GIDEON? FIRST YOU LOSE JOHN-A-DREAMS, NOW THIS NEW ONE'S GONE WALKIES.
PERHAPS YOU'VE BECOME COMPLACENT. PERHAPS YOU'VE LOST THAT EDGE YOU USED TO HAVE.
AND PERHAPS IF YOU DON'T GET IT BACK, YOU'RE GOING TO FIND YOURSELF SOMEWHERE YOU'D RATHER NOT BE...
IN THE TOILET, DEAR.

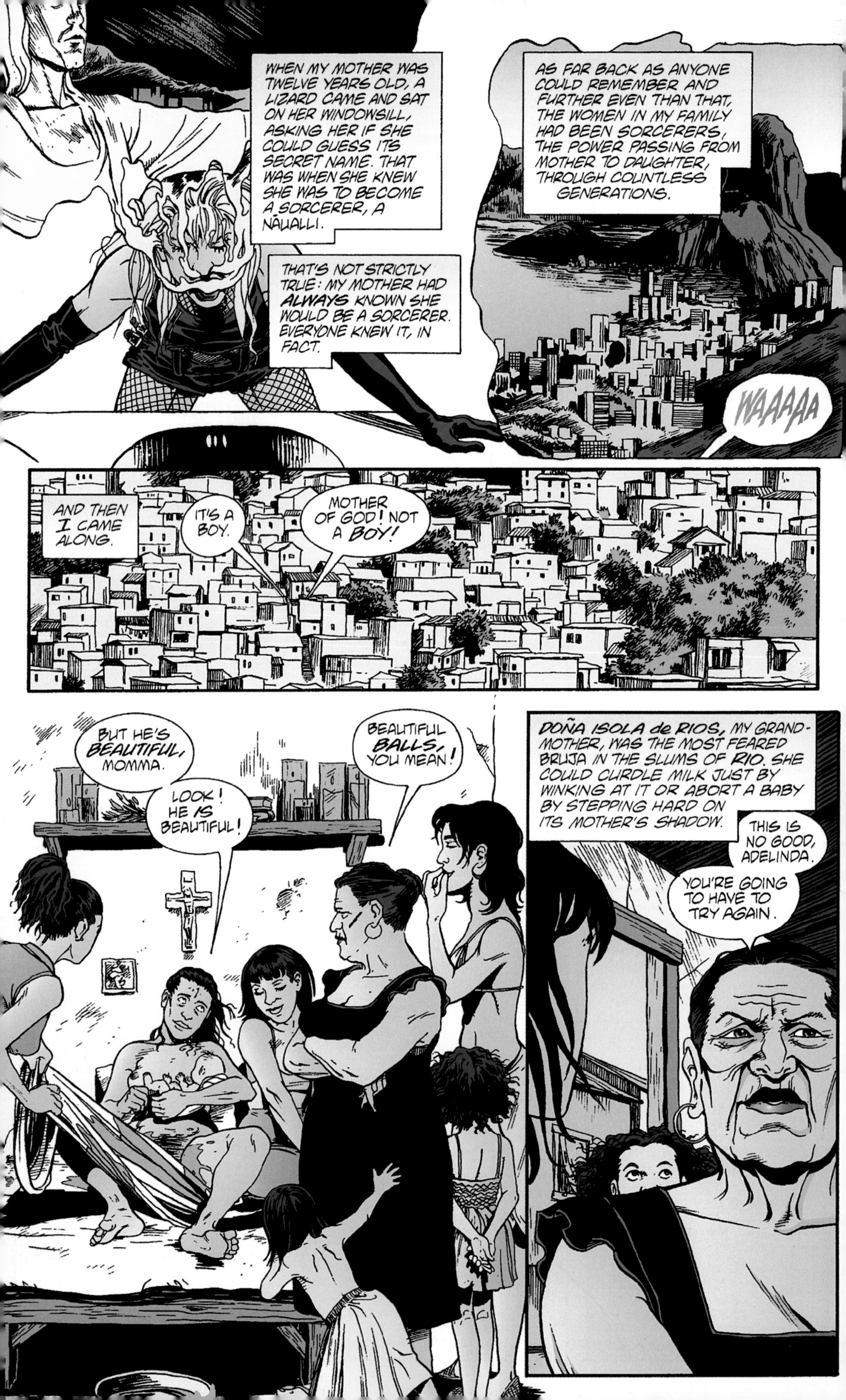
WHEN MY MOTHER WAS TWELVE YEARS OLD, A LIZARD CAME AND SAT ON HER WINDOWSILL, ASKING HER IF SHE COULD GUESS ITS SECRET NAME. THAT WAS WHEN SHE KNEW SHE WAS TO BECOME A SORCERER, A NÄUALLI.
THAT'S NOT STRICTLY TRUE: MY MOTHER HAD ALWAYS KNOWN SHE WOULD BE A SORCERER. EVERYONE KNEW IT, IN FACT.
AS FAR BACK AS ANYONE COULD REMEMBER AND FURTHER EVEN THAN THAT, THE WOMEN IN MY FAMILY HAD BEEN SORCERERS, THE POWER PASSING FROM MOTHER TO DAUGHTER, THROUGH COUNTLESS GENERATIONS.
WAAAAA
AND THEN I CAME ALONG.
IT'S A BOY.
MOTHER OF GOD! NOT A BOY!
BUT HE'S BEAUTIFUL, MOMMA.
LOOK! HE IS BEAUTIFUL!
BEAUTIFUL BALLS, YOU MEAN!
DOÑA ISOLA de RIOS, MY GRANDMOTHER, WAS THE MOST FEARED BRUJA IN THE SLUMS OF RIO. SHE COULD CURDLE MILK JUST BY WINKING AT IT OR ABORT A BABY BY STEPPING HARD ON ITS MOTHER'S SHADOW.
THIS IS NO GOOD, ADELINDA.
YOU'RE GOING TO HAVE TO TRY AGAIN.

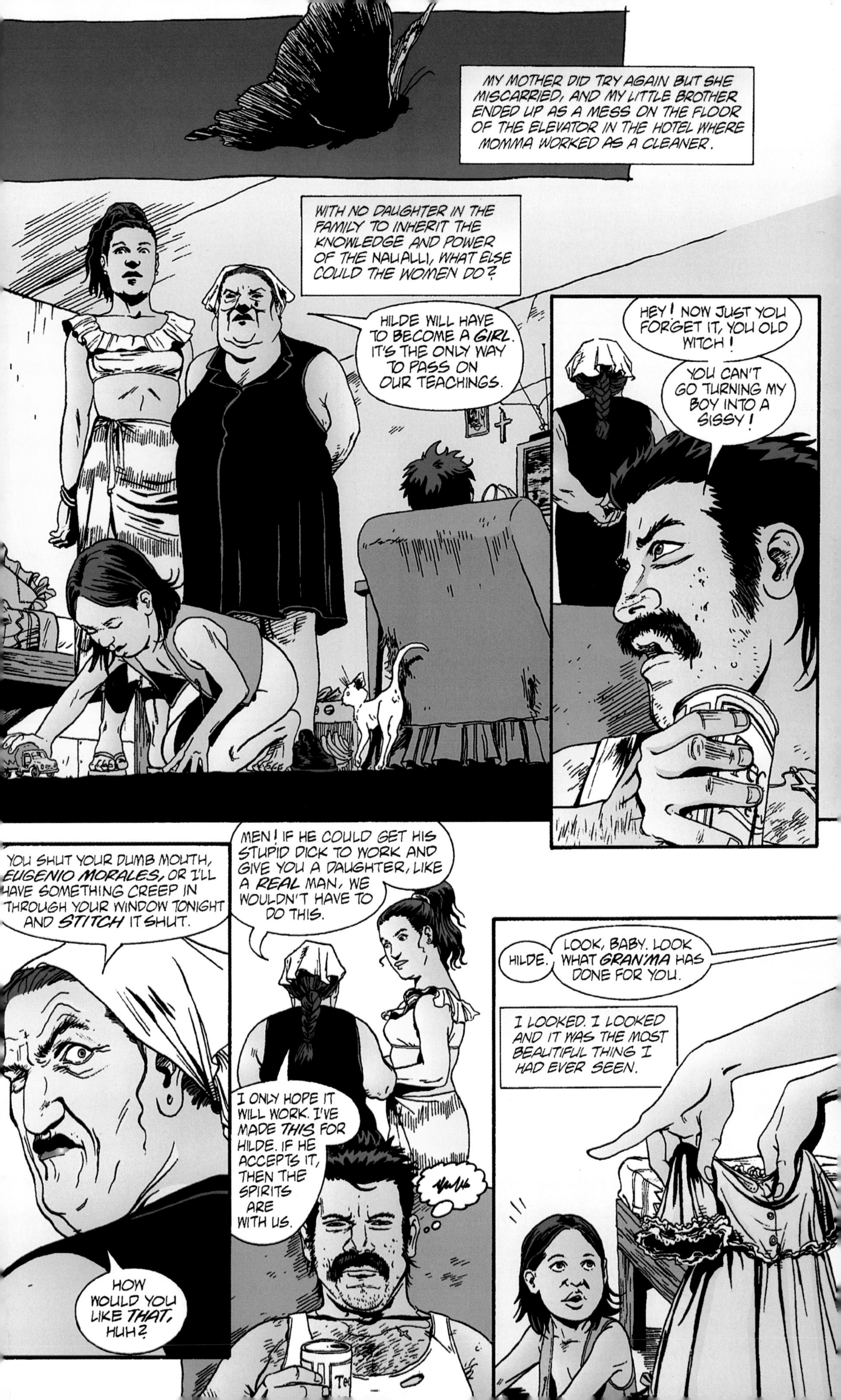
MY MOTHER DID TRY AGAIN BUT SHE MISCARRIED, AND MY LITTLE BROTHER ENDED UP AS A MESS ON THE FLOOR OF THE ELEVATOR IN THE HOTEL WHERE MOMMA WORKED AS A CLEANER.
WITH NO DAUGHTER IN THE FAMILY TO INHERIT THE KNOWLEDGE AND POWER OF THE NAUALLI, WHAT ELSE COULD THE WOMEN DO?
HILDE WILL HAVE TO BECOME A GIRL. IT'S THE ONLY WAY TO PASS ON OUR TEACHINGS.
HEY! NOW JUST YOU FORGET IT, YOU OLD WITCH!
YOU CAN'T GO TURNING MY BOY INTO A SISSY!
YOU SHUT YOUR DUMB MOUTH, EUGENIO MORALES, OR I'LL HAVE SOMETHING CREEP IN THROUGH YOUR WINDOW TONIGHT AND STITCH IT SHUT.
HOW WOULD YOU LIKE THAT, HUH?
MEN! IF HE COULD GET HIS STUPID DICK TO WORK AND GIVE YOU A DAUGHTER, LIKE A REAL MAN, WE WOULDN'T HAVE TO DO THIS.
I ONLY HOPE IT WILL WORK. I'VE MADE THIS FOR HILDE. IF HE ACCEPTS IT, THEN THE SPIRITS ARE WITH US.
HILDE.
LOOK, BABY. LOOK WHAT GRAN'MA HAS DONE FOR YOU.
I LOOKED. I LOOKED AND IT WAS THE MOST BEAUTIFUL THING I HAD EVER SEEN.

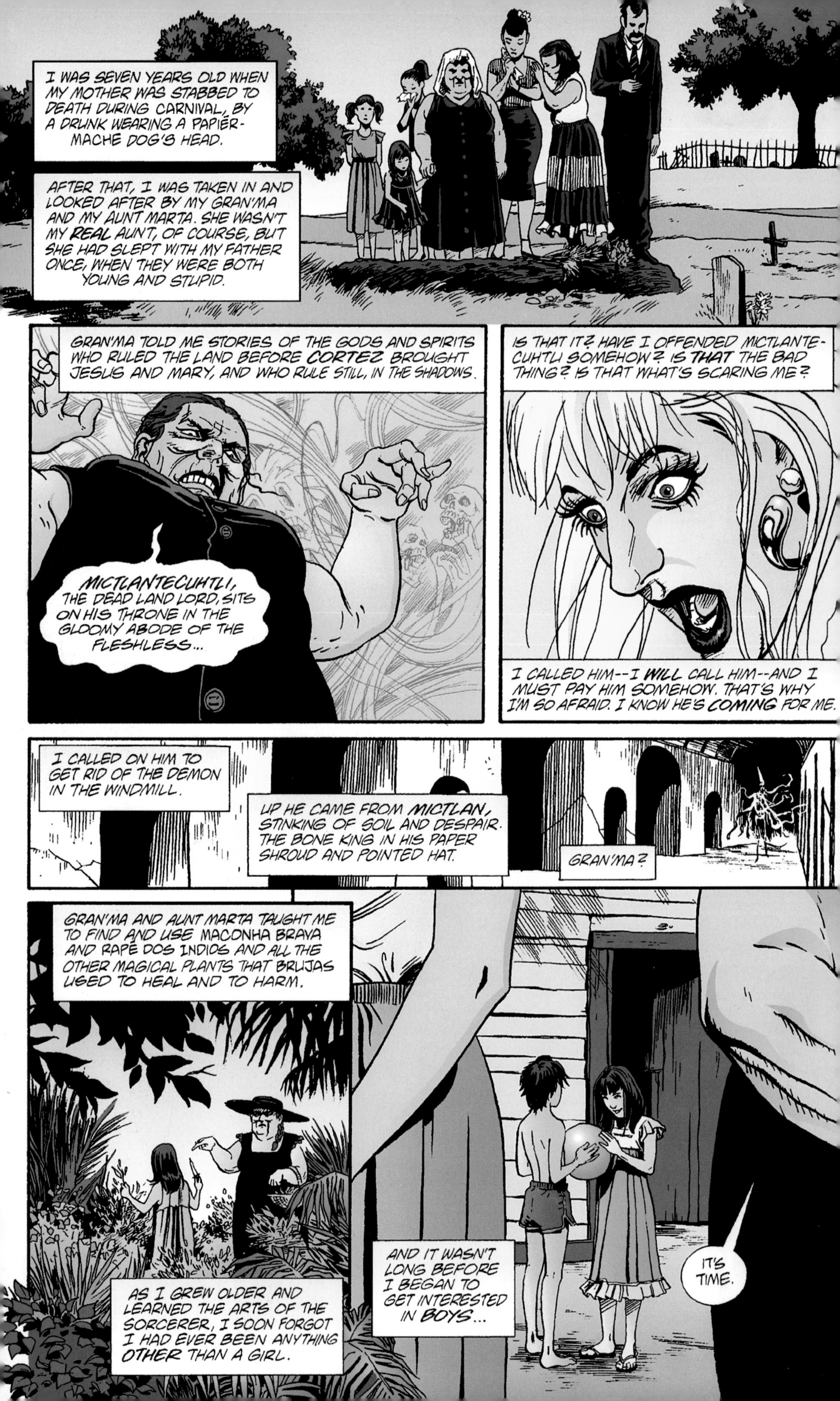

I WAS SEVEN YEARS OLD WHEN MY MOTHER WAS STABBED TO DEATH DURING CARNIVAL, BY A DRUNK WEARING A PAPIÉR-MACHE DOG'S HEAD.
AFTER THAT, I WAS TAKEN IN AND LOOKED AFTER BY MY GRAN'MA AND MY AUNT MARTA. SHE WASN'T MY REAL AUNT, OF COURSE, BUT SHE HAD SLEPT WITH MY FATHER ONCE, WHEN THEY WERE BOTH YOUNG AND STUPID.
GRAN'MA TOLD ME STORIES OF THE GODS AND SPIRITS WHO RULED THE LAND BEFORE CORTEZ BROUGHT JESUS AND MARY, AND WHO RULE STILL, IN THE SHADOWS.
MICTLANTECUHTLI, THE DEAD LAND LORD, SITS ON HIS THRONE IN THE GLOOMY ABODE OF THE FLESHLESS...
IS THAT IT? HAVE I OFFENDED MICTLANTE-CUHTLI SOMEHOW? IS THAT THE BAD THING? IS THAT WHAT'S SCARING ME?
I CALLED HIM--I WILL CALL HIM--AND I MUST PAY HIM SOMEHOW. THAT'S WHY I'M SO AFRAID. I KNOW HE'S COMING FOR ME.
I CALLED ON HIM TO GET RID OF THE DEMON IN THE WINDMILL.
UP HE CAME FROM MICTLAN, STINKING OF SOIL AND DESPAIR. THE BONE KING IN HIS PAPER SHROUD AND POINTED HAT.
GRAN'MA?
GRAN'MA AND AUNT MARTA TAUGHT ME TO FIND AND USE MACONHA BRAVA AND RAPÉ DOS INDIOS AND ALL THE OTHER MAGICAL PLANTS THAT BRUJAS USED TO HEAL AND TO HARM.
AS I GREW OLDER AND LEARNED THE ARTS OF THE SORCERER, I SOON FORGOT I HAD EVER BEEN ANYTHING OTHER THAN A GIRL.
AND IT WASN'T LONG BEFORE I BEGAN TO GET INTERESTED IN BOYS...
IT'S TIME.

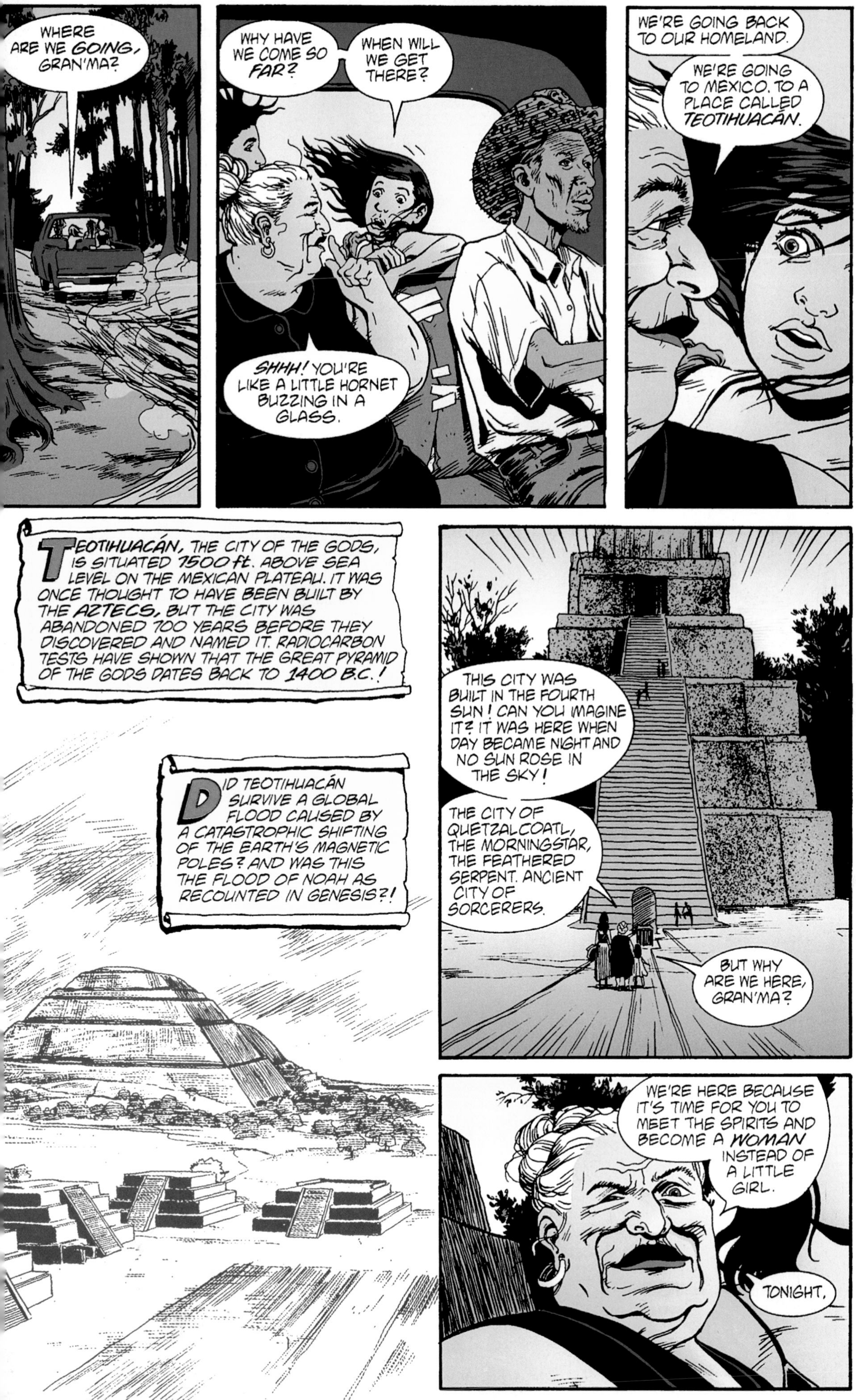
WHERE ARE WE GOING, GRAN'MA?
WHY HAVE WE COME SO FAR?
WHEN WILL WE GET THERE?
SHHH! YOU'RE LIKE A LITTLE HORNET BUZZING IN A GLASS.
WE'RE GOING BACK TO OUR HOMELAND.
WE'RE GOING TO MEXICO, TO A PLACE CALLED TEOTIHUACÁN.
TEOTIHUACÁN, THE CITY OF THE GODS, IS SITUATED 7500 ft. ABOVE SEA LEVEL ON THE MEXICAN PLATEAU. IT WAS ONCE THOUGHT TO HAVE BEEN BUILT BY THE AZTECS, BUT THE CITY WAS ABANDONED 700 YEARS BEFORE THEY DISCOVERED AND NAMED IT. RADIOCARBON TESTS HAVE SHOWN THAT THE GREAT PYRAMID OF THE GODS DATES BACK TO 1400 B.C.!
THIS CITY WAS BUILT IN THE FOURTH SUN! CAN YOU IMAGINE IT? IT WAS HERE WHEN DAY BECAME NIGHT AND NO SUN ROSE IN THE SKY!
THE CITY OF QUETZALCOATL, THE MORNINGSTAR, THE FEATHERED SERPENT. ANCIENT CITY OF SORCERERS.
BUT WHY ARE WE HERE, GRAN'MA?
DID TEOTIHUACÁN SURVIVE A GLOBAL FLOOD CAUSED BY A CATASTROPHIC SHIFTING OF THE EARTH'S MAGNETIC POLES? AND WAS THIS THE FLOOD OF NOAH AS RECOUNTED IN GENESIS?!
WE'RE HERE BECAUSE IT'S TIME FOR YOU TO MEET THE SPIRITS AND BECOME A WOMAN INSTEAD OF A LITTLE GIRL.
TONIGHT.

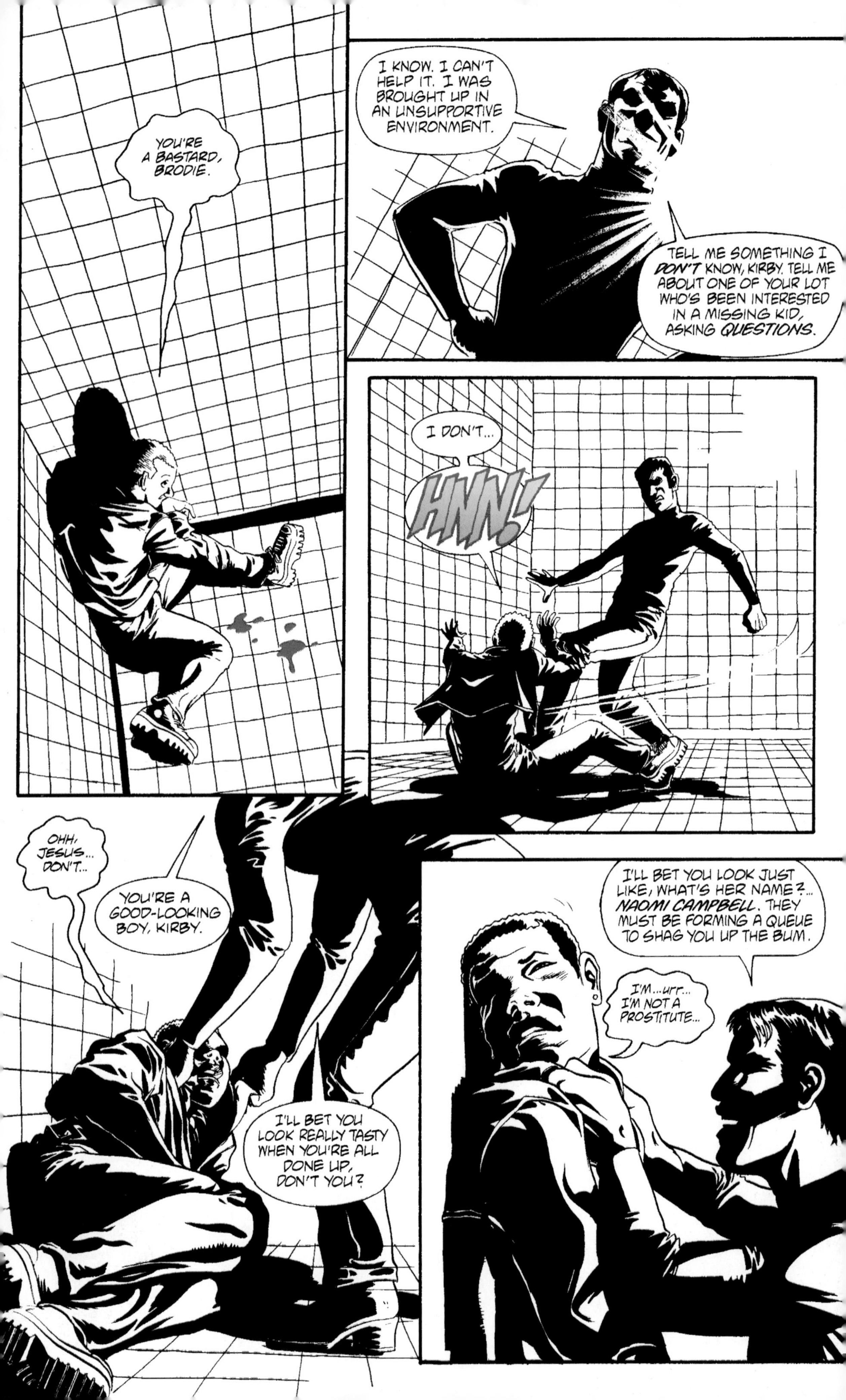
YOU'RE A BASTARD, BRODIE.
I KNOW. I CAN'T HELP IT. I WAS BROUGHT UP IN AN UNSUPPORTIVE ENVIRONMENT.
TELL ME SOMETHING I DON'T KNOW, KIRBY. TELL ME ABOUT ONE OF YOUR LOT WHO'S BEEN INTERESTED IN A MISSING KID, ASKING QUESTIONS.
I DON'T...
HNN!
OHH, JESUS... DON'T...
YOU'RE A GOOD-LOOKING BOY, KIRBY.
I'LL BET YOU LOOK REALLY TASTY WHEN YOU'RE ALL DONE UP, DON'T YOU?
I'LL BET YOU LOOK JUST LIKE, WHAT'S HER NAME?... NAOMI CAMPBELL. THEY MUST BE FORMING A QUEUE TO SHAG YOU UP THE BUM.
I'M...urr... I'M NOT A PROSTITUTE...

NO.

NNGH!

BUT WHAT ARE YOU GONNA DO IF I MAKE YOU *REALLY* UGLY? IT WOULDN'T TAKE LONG, YOU KNOW.

NO MORE MODELLING FOR VIVIENNE WESTWOOD, NO MORE DJ'ING AT *HEAVEN* OR PHOTOS IN THE FETISH GLOSSIES. BY THE TIME I'VE FINISHED WITH YOU, PROSTITUTION'S GOING TO SEEM LIKE A DREAM TICKET.

STILL, MAYBE YOU COULD WEAR A BAG OVER YOUR HEAD, LIKE THE ELEPHANT MAN. HAVE YOU SEEN THAT FILM, KIRBY?

"FFFANK OO YEWWY MUSS, DOCHTOR TLEVES..."

...DON'T... PLEASE...

NOT MY FACE, MAN... DON'T TOUCH MY FACE...

...I...

THERE'S ONE...ONE OF THE GIRLS...SHE WAS ASKING ABOUT A KID...I DON'T KNOW...MAYBE *SHE* COULD HELP YOU, MAN...

SHE... *ah*...SHE CALLS HERSELF *FANNY.* I DON'T KNOW ANY MORE...HONEST...

LORD FANNY.

UTT!

GOOD GIRL.

NOW THEN: MAYBE IT'S THE WRONG TIME TO ASK BUT...*ah*...ANY CHANCE OF A BLOW JOB?

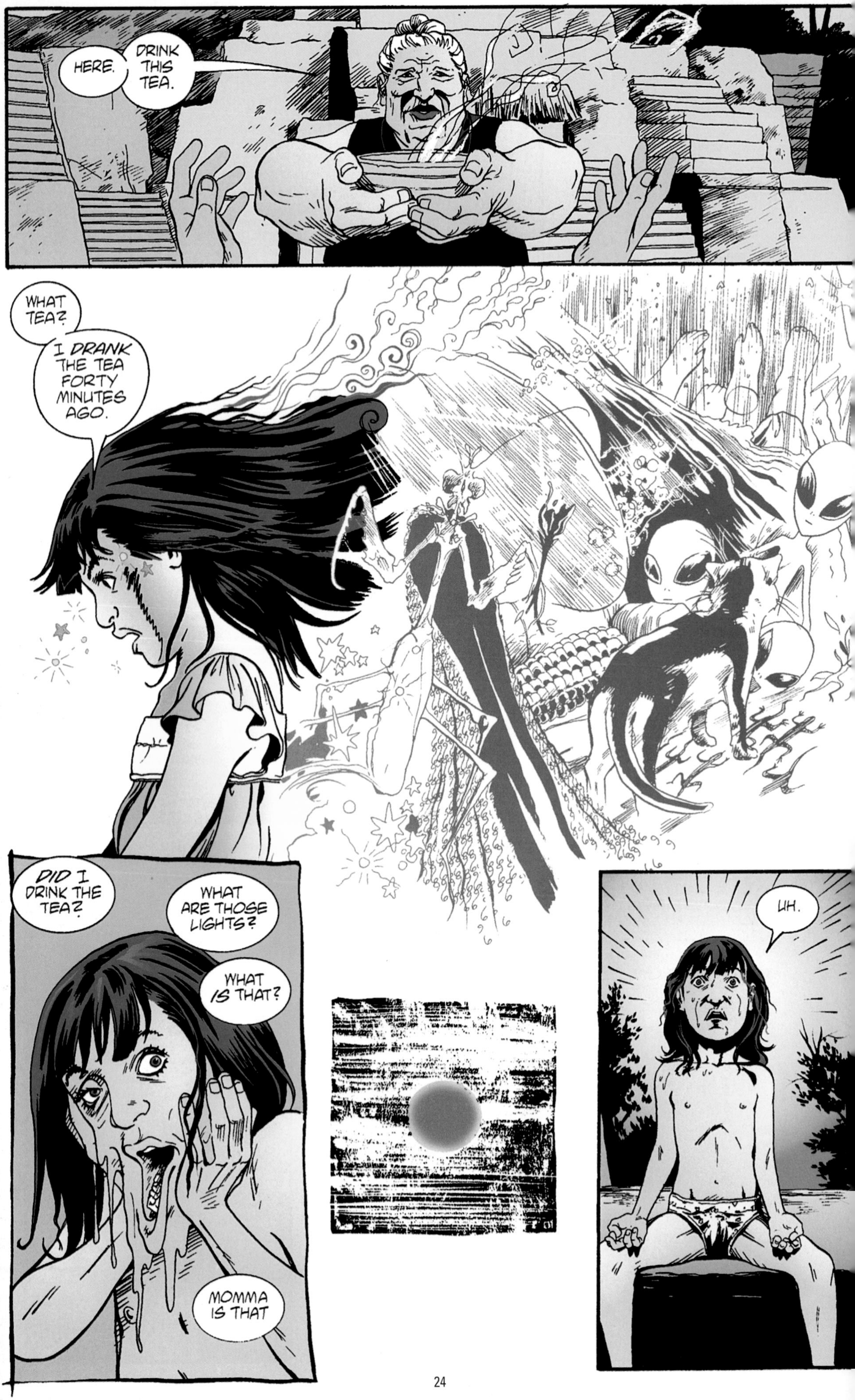
HERE.
DRINK THIS TEA.
WHAT TEA?
I DRANK THE TEA FORTY MINUTES AGO.
DID I DRINK THE TEA?
WHAT ARE THOSE LIGHTS?
WHAT IS THAT?
MOMMA IS THAT
UH.

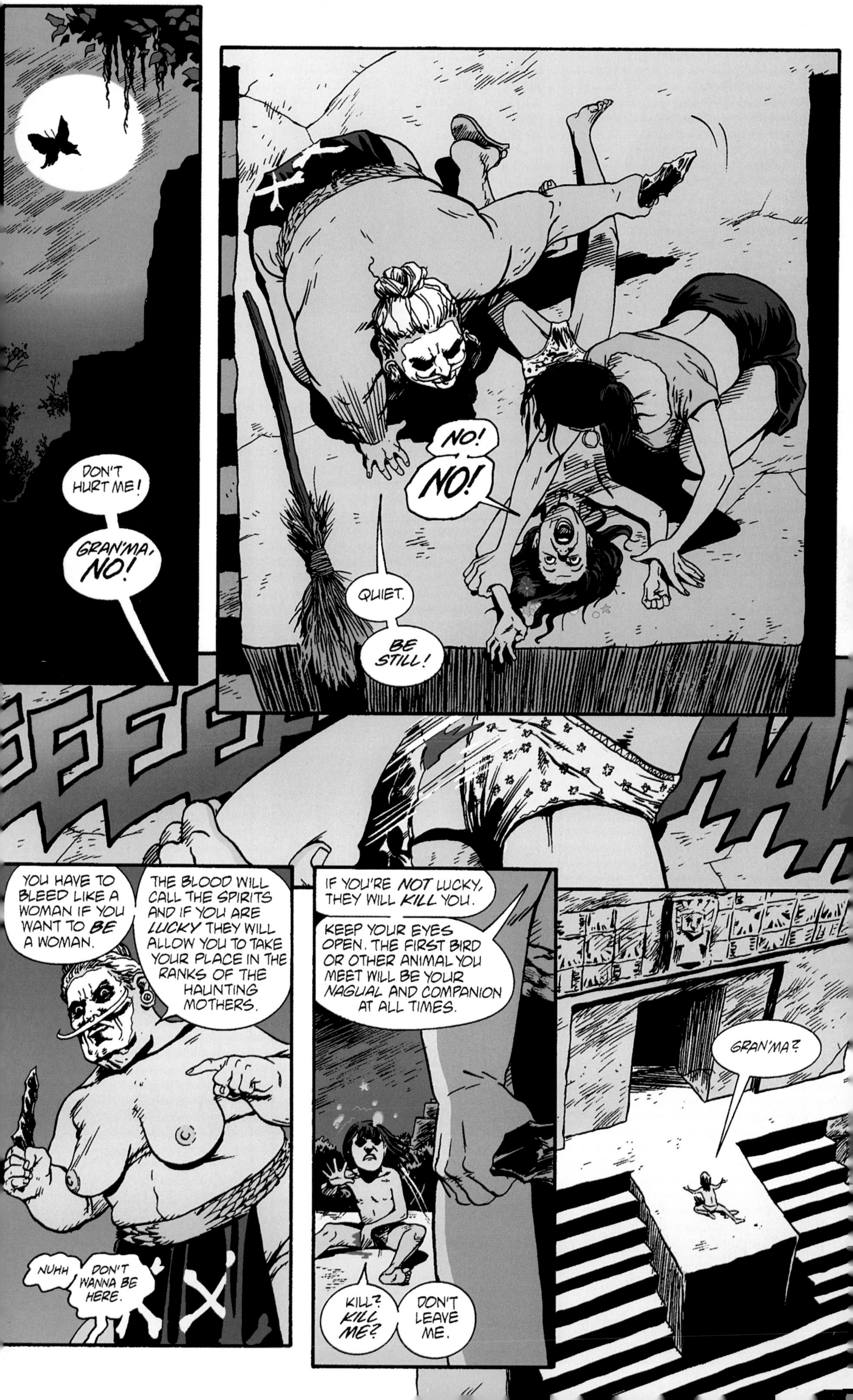
DON'T HURT ME!
GRAN'MA, NO!
NO! NO!
QUIET.
BE STILL!
EEEEEE
AAA
YOU HAVE TO BLEED LIKE A WOMAN IF YOU WANT TO BE A WOMAN.
THE BLOOD WILL CALL THE SPIRITS AND IF YOU ARE LUCKY THEY WILL ALLOW YOU TO TAKE YOUR PLACE IN THE RANKS OF THE HAUNTING MOTHERS.
NUHH
DON'T WANNA BE HERE.
IF YOU'RE NOT LUCKY, THEY WILL KILL YOU.
KEEP YOUR EYES OPEN. THE FIRST BIRD OR OTHER ANIMAL YOU MEET WILL BE YOUR NAGUAL AND COMPANION AT ALL TIMES.
KILL? KILL ME?
DON'T LEAVE ME.
GRAN'MA?

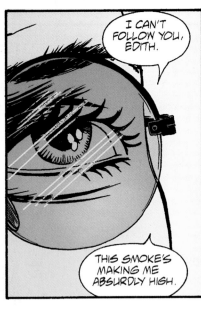

I CAN'T FOLLOW YOU, EDITH.

THIS SMOKE'S MAKING ME ABSURDLY HIGH.

OH, GIDEON! DON'T BE SUCH A MILQUETOAST.

I WAS JUST SAYING THAT PERHAPS THERE'S A *REASON* FOR ALL OF THIS.

PERHAPS THIS BOY, "JACK FROST" OR WHATEVER IT IS YOU CALL HIM, IS SERVING A *HIGHER* PURPOSE.

INVISIBLES CELLS ARE ORGANIZED ON ELEMENTAL PRINCIPLES, AM I CORRECT? I HAVEN'T FORGOTTEN THE RULES, HAVE I?

THEN YOU MUST TELL ME WHICH MEMBERS OF YOUR TEAM CURRENTLY REPRESENT WHICH OF THE ELEMENTS.

WELL, FOR THE PAST YEAR OR SO, I'VE TAKEN THE *AIR* ROLE, FANNY'S BEEN *WATER*, BOY'S *EARTH* AND ROBIN'S *FIRE*.

WE BROUGHT JACK INTO THE TEAM AS *SPIRIT*. FREE BLOODY SPIRIT.

SPIRIT USUALLY WORKS TO RAISE THE MORALE OF THE TEAM, THAT SORT OF THING...

SPIRIT? OH WELL, IT'S DAZZLINGLY OBVIOUS THEN.

THE SPIRIT ROLE'S *ALWAYS* UNPREDICT-ABLE, YOU KNOW THAT. IT EXISTS TO GALVANIZE AND REVITALIZE THE ELEMENTS AROUND IT.

HERE'S A BOY WHOSE HATRED OF AUTHORITY IS SUCH THAT HE EVEN REBELS AGAINST *US*, AGAINST THE INVISIBLES.

I THINK HE'S HERE TO *TEST* YOU TO YOUR LIMITS, GIDEON, THAT'S WHAT I THINK. HE'S HERE TO SHAKE YOU TO THE CORE.

TO GET HIM BACK, YOU'RE GOING TO HAVE TO ENTER THE LABYRINTH AND FACE THE *BEAST*. YOU MUST BRAVE THE JAWS OF THE DRAGON, DEAR.

EACH OF YOU IN TURN, I SHOULDN'T WONDER.

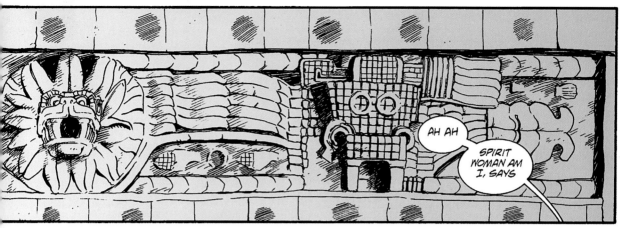

AH AH

SPIRIT WOMAN AM I, SAYS

ILLUMINATED WOMAN AM I, SAYS LED BY A YELLOW DOG ACROSS RIVERS AND DESERTS

ON A DRY ROAD WALKING, SAYS IN THE DAY OF NINE DOGS, SAYS GOING DOWN TO THE PLACE OF WEEPING

THIS THING IS BIG

WE STILL DON'T KNOW IF THE SPIRITS WILL *ACCEPT* HER AS A WOMAN.

EVEN SPIRITS CAN BE FOOLED.

THE IMPORTANT THING IS TO SEE *WHICH* OF THEM WILL MARK HER AS HIS OWN.

WOMAN OF THE FIRST STAR, AM I WOMAN OF THE STAR OF DAY MYSTERIOUS WOMAN, SAYS

CAN YOU HEAR IT?

IT'S COMING. THE *NAGUAL*, THE TOTEM PROTECTOR.

I HEARD IT. I HEARD GREAT WINGS IN THE SKY, GIGANTIC WINGS BEATING... AND...

AND...

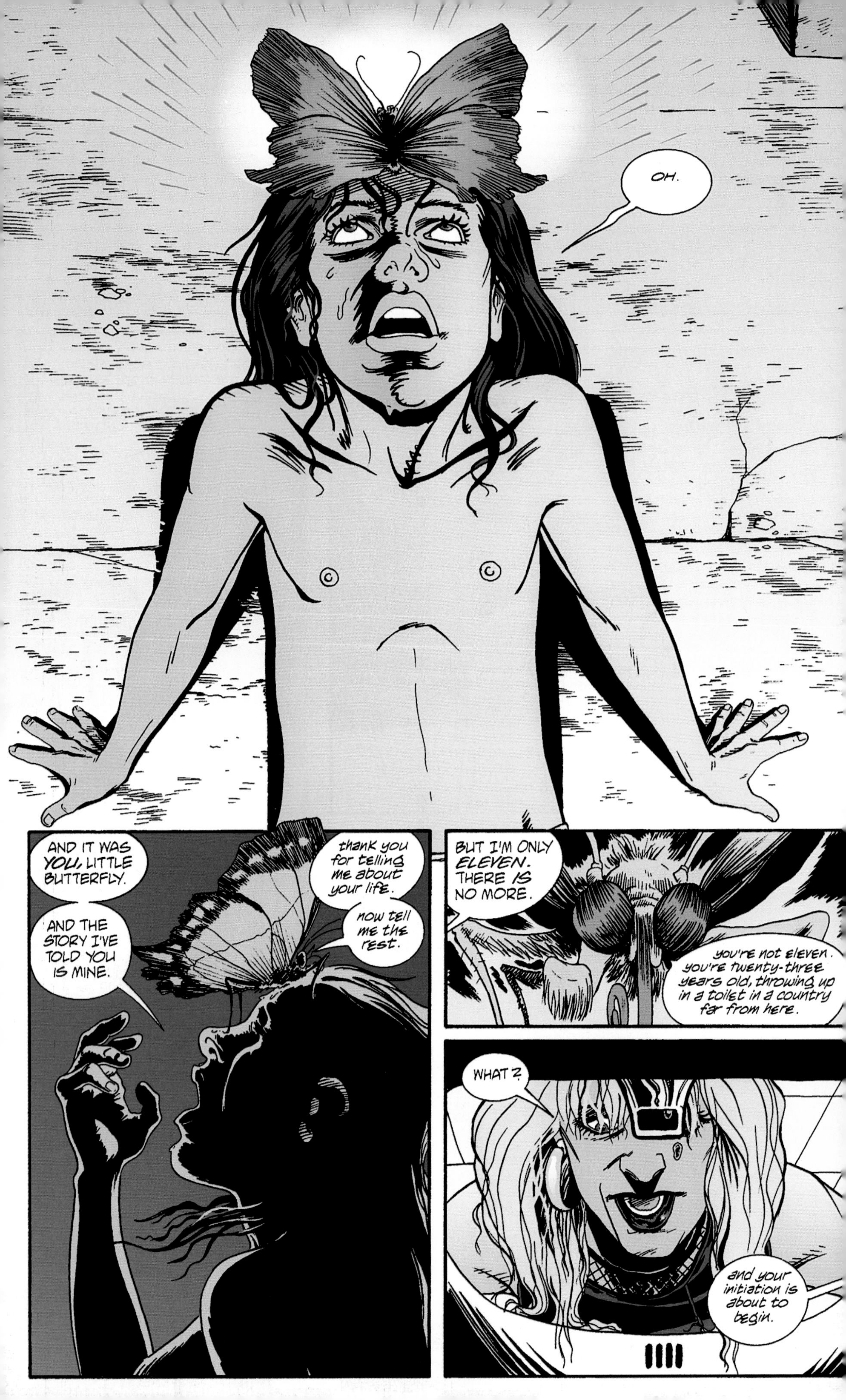
OH.
AND IT WAS YOU, LITTLE BUTTERFLY.
AND THE STORY I'VE TOLD YOU IS MINE.
thank you for telling me about your life.
now tell me the rest.
BUT I'M ONLY ELEVEN. THERE IS NO MORE.
you're not eleven. you're twenty-three years old, throwing up in a toilet in a country far from here.
WHAT?
and your initiation is about to begin.

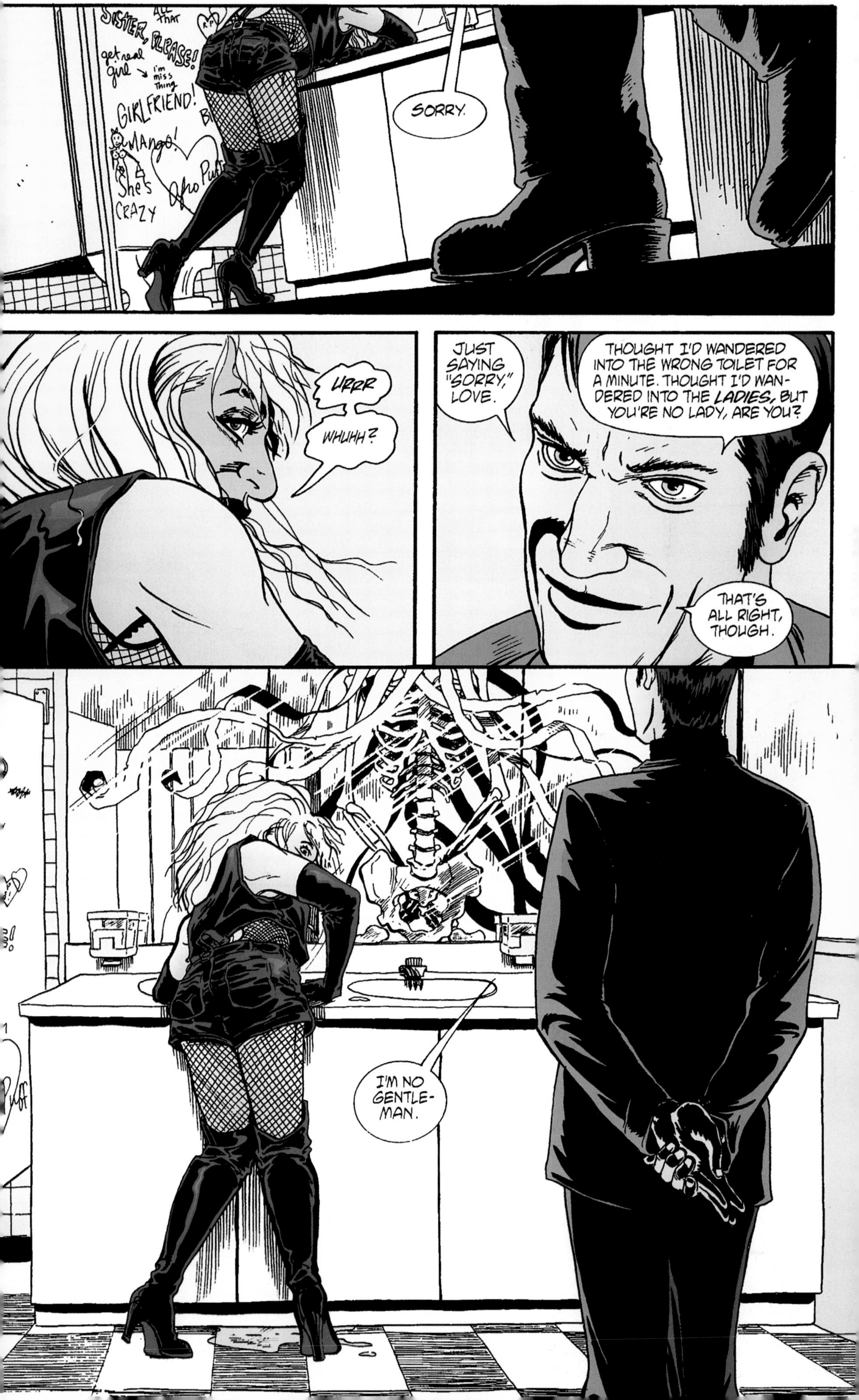

SISTER, PLEASE!
ALL THAT
get real girl
i'm miss thing
GIRLFRIEND!
Mango!
She's CRAZY
SORRY.
URRR
WHUHH?
JUST SAYING "SORRY," LOVE.
THOUGHT I'D WANDERED INTO THE WRONG TOILET FOR A MINUTE. THOUGHT I'D WANDERED INTO THE *LADIES,* BUT YOU'RE NO LADY, ARE YOU?
THAT'S ALL RIGHT, THOUGH.
I'M NO GENTLEMAN.

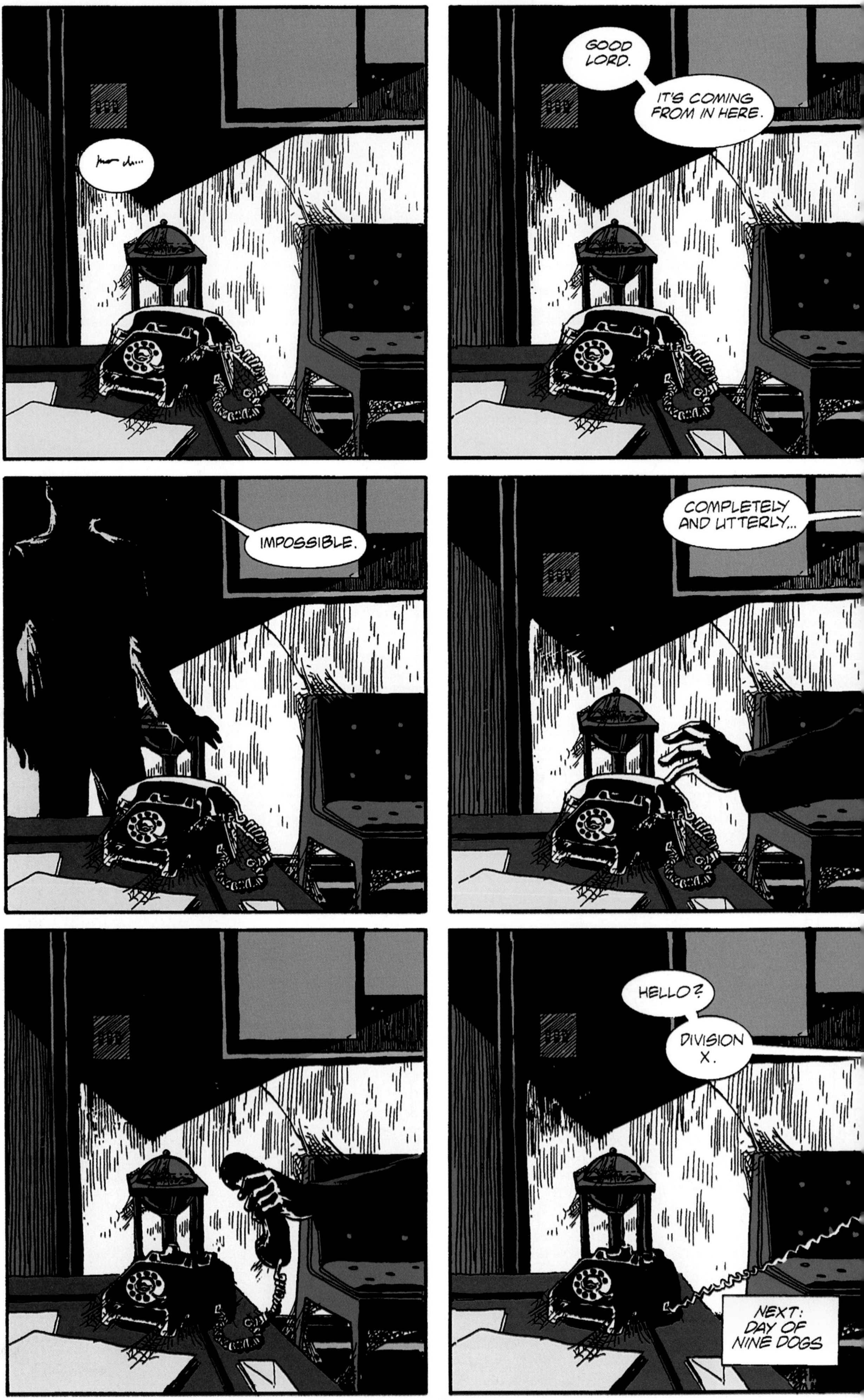
GOOD LORD.
IT'S COMING FROM IN HERE.
IMPOSSIBLE.
COMPLETELY AND UTTERLY...
HELLO?
DIVISION X.
NEXT: DAY OF NINE DOGS

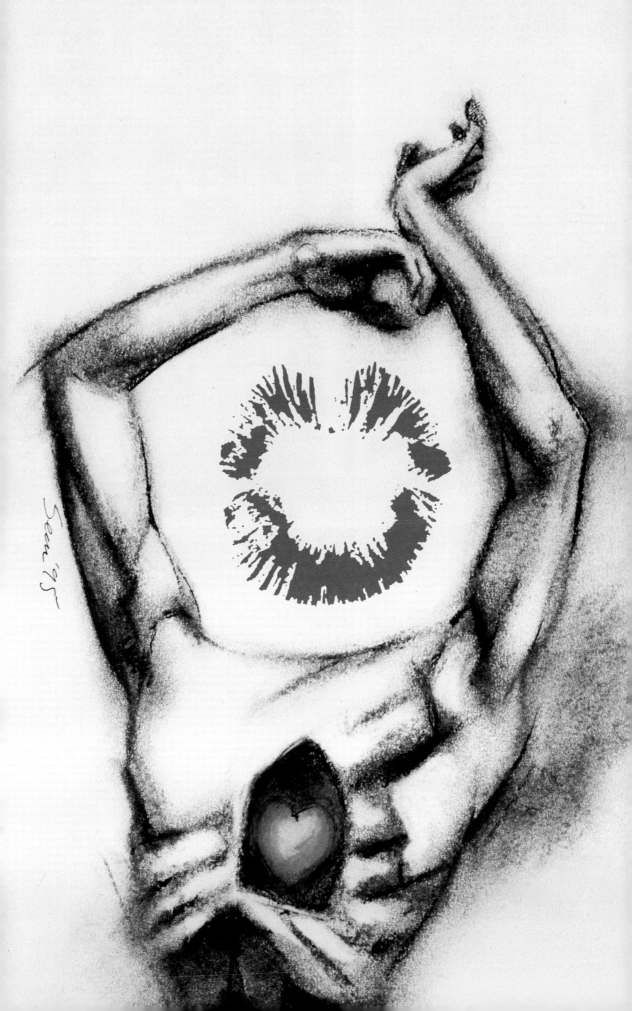

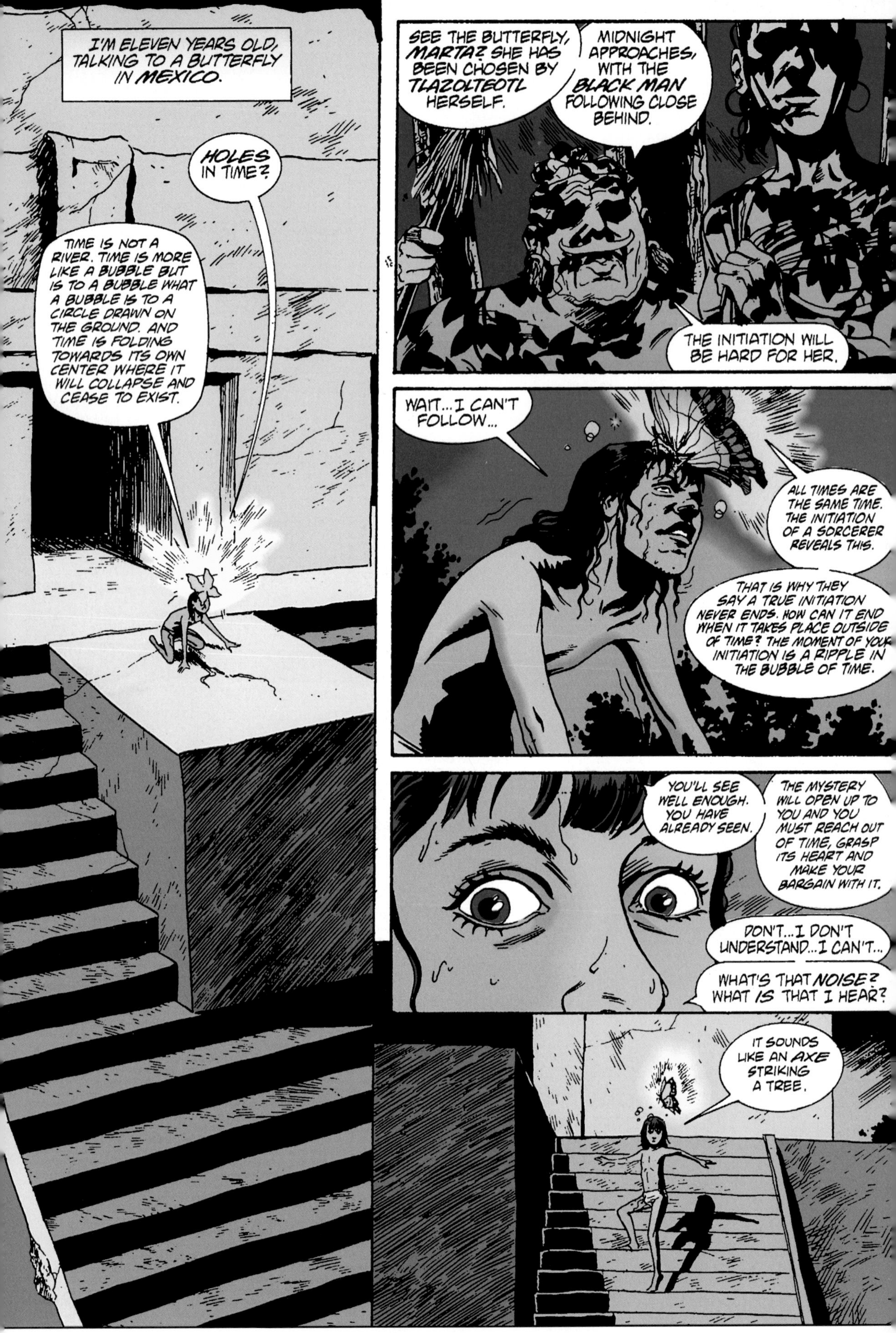
I'M ELEVEN YEARS OLD, TALKING TO A BUTTERFLY IN MEXICO.
HOLES IN TIME?
TIME IS NOT A RIVER. TIME IS MORE LIKE A BUBBLE BUT IS TO A BUBBLE WHAT A BUBBLE IS TO A CIRCLE DRAWN ON THE GROUND. AND TIME IS FOLDING TOWARDS ITS OWN CENTER WHERE IT WILL COLLAPSE AND CEASE TO EXIST.
SEE THE BUTTERFLY, MARTA? SHE HAS BEEN CHOSEN BY TLAZOLTEOTL HERSELF.
MIDNIGHT APPROACHES, WITH THE BLACK MAN FOLLOWING CLOSE BEHIND.
THE INITIATION WILL BE HARD FOR HER.
WAIT... I CAN'T FOLLOW...
ALL TIMES ARE THE SAME TIME. THE INITIATION OF A SORCERER REVEALS THIS.
THAT IS WHY THEY SAY A TRUE INITIATION NEVER ENDS. HOW CAN IT END WHEN IT TAKES PLACE OUTSIDE OF TIME? THE MOMENT OF YOUR INITIATION IS A RIPPLE IN THE BUBBLE OF TIME.
YOU'LL SEE WELL ENOUGH. YOU HAVE ALREADY SEEN.
THE MYSTERY WILL OPEN UP TO YOU AND YOU MUST REACH OUT OF TIME, GRASP ITS HEART AND MAKE YOUR BARGAIN WITH IT.
DON'T... I DON'T UNDERSTAND... I CAN'T...
WHAT'S THAT NOISE? WHAT IS THAT I HEAR?
IT SOUNDS LIKE AN AXE STRIKING A TREE.

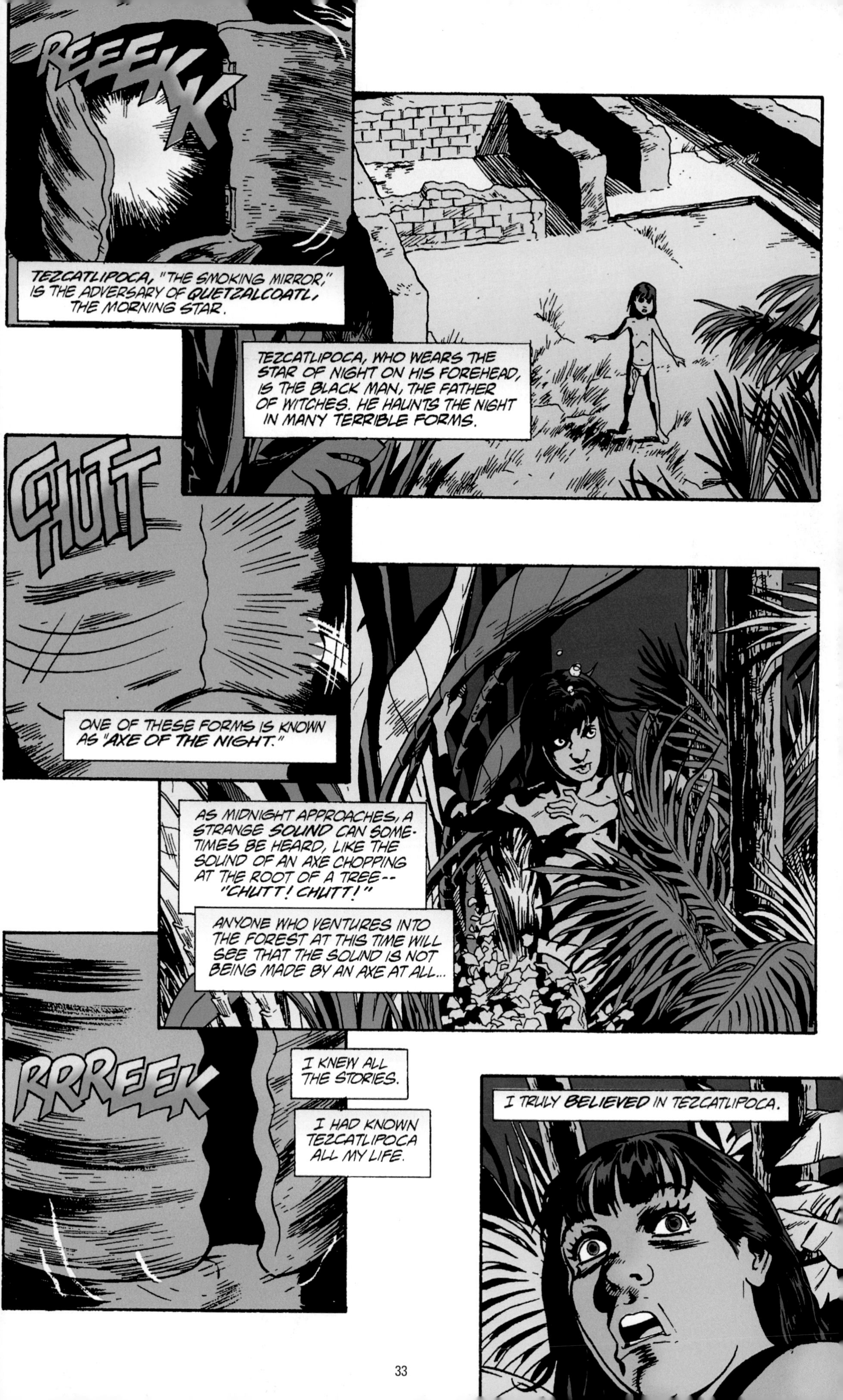
REEEKK
TEZCATLIPOCA, "THE SMOKING MIRROR," IS THE ADVERSARY OF QUETZALCOATL, THE MORNING STAR.
TEZCATLIPOCA, WHO WEARS THE STAR OF NIGHT ON HIS FOREHEAD, IS THE BLACK MAN, THE FATHER OF WITCHES. HE HAUNTS THE NIGHT IN MANY TERRIBLE FORMS.
CHUTT
ONE OF THESE FORMS IS KNOWN AS "AXE OF THE NIGHT."
AS MIDNIGHT APPROACHES, A STRANGE SOUND CAN SOMETIMES BE HEARD, LIKE THE SOUND OF AN AXE CHOPPING AT THE ROOT OF A TREE-- "CHUTT! CHUTT!"
ANYONE WHO VENTURES INTO THE FOREST AT THIS TIME WILL SEE THAT THE SOUND IS NOT BEING MADE BY AN AXE AT ALL...
RRREEK
I KNEW ALL THE STORIES.
I HAD KNOWN TEZCATLIPOCA ALL MY LIFE.
I TRULY BELIEVED IN TEZCATLIPOCA.

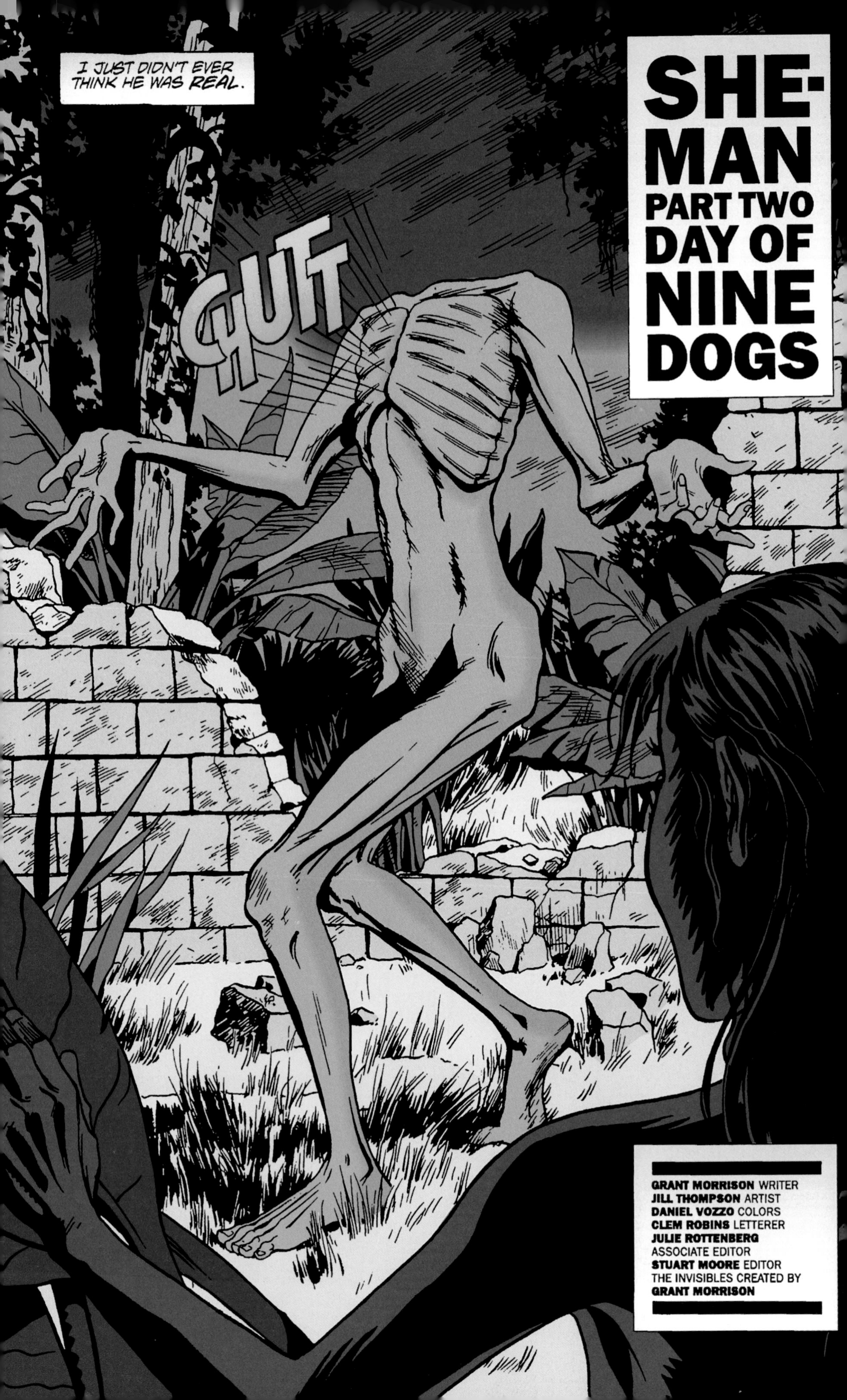

I JUST DIDN'T EVER THINK HE WAS REAL.
CHUTT
SHE-MAN PART TWO DAY OF NINE DOGS
GRANT MORRISON WRITER
JILL THOMPSON ARTIST
DANIEL VOZZO COLORS
CLEM ROBINS LETTERER
JULIE ROTTENBERG ASSOCIATE EDITOR
STUART MOORE EDITOR
THE INVISIBLES CREATED BY GRANT MORRISON

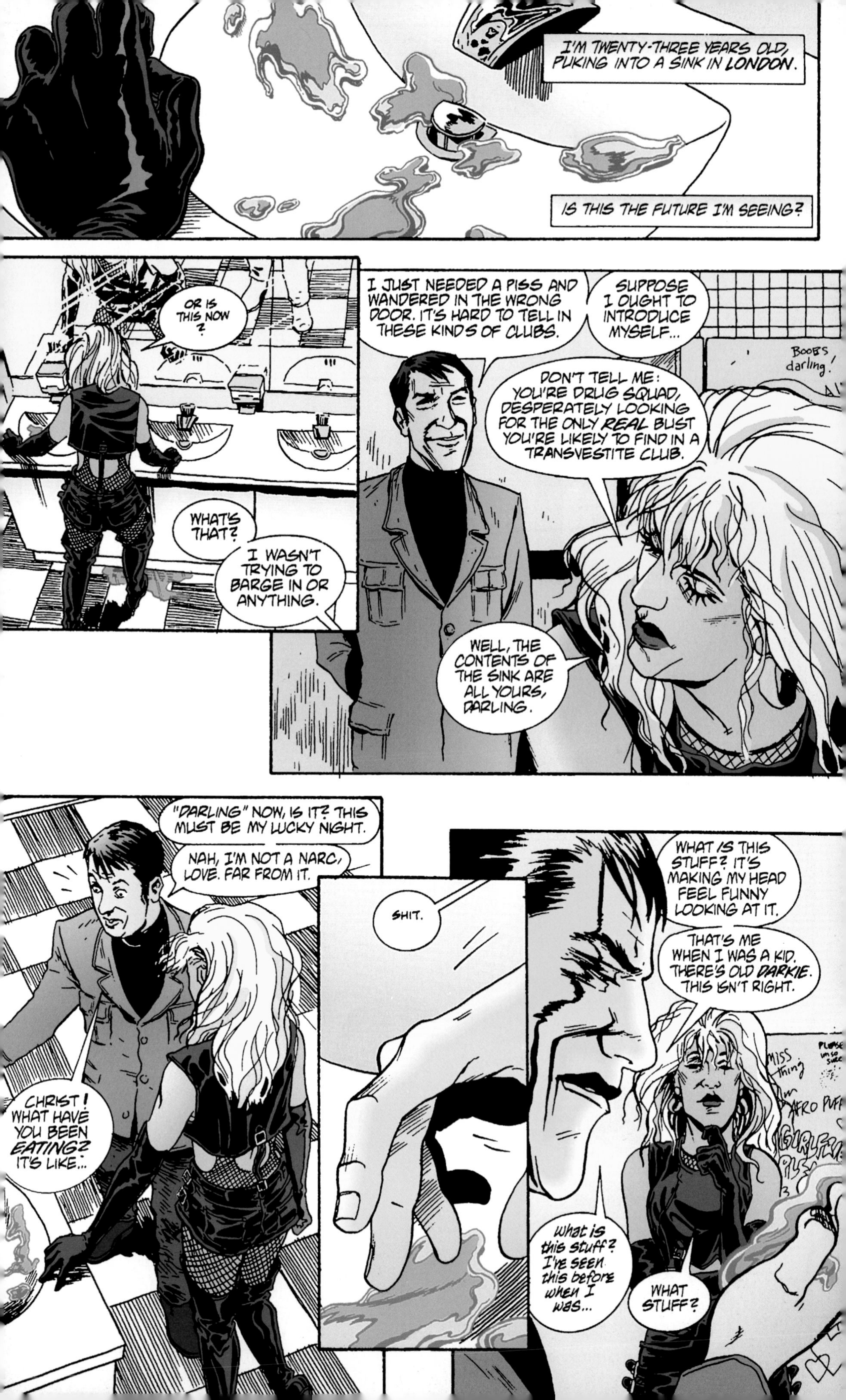
I'M TWENTY-THREE YEARS OLD, PUKING INTO A SINK IN LONDON.
IS THIS THE FUTURE I'M SEEING?
OR IS THIS NOW ?
WHAT'S THAT?
I WASN'T TRYING TO BARGE IN OR ANYTHING.
I JUST NEEDED A PISS AND WANDERED IN THE WRONG DOOR. IT'S HARD TO TELL IN THESE KINDS OF CLUBS.
SUPPOSE I OUGHT TO INTRODUCE MYSELF...
DON'T TELL ME: YOU'RE DRUG SQUAD, DESPERATELY LOOKING FOR THE ONLY REAL BUST YOU'RE LIKELY TO FIND IN A TRANSVESTITE CLUB.
WELL, THE CONTENTS OF THE SINK ARE ALL YOURS, DARLING.
Boobs darling!
"DARLING" NOW, IS IT? THIS MUST BE MY LUCKY NIGHT.
NAH, I'M NOT A NARC, LOVE. FAR FROM IT.
CHRIST! WHAT HAVE YOU BEEN EATING? IT'S LIKE...
SHIT.
WHAT IS THIS STUFF? IT'S MAKING MY HEAD FEEL FUNNY LOOKING AT IT.
THAT'S ME WHEN I WAS A KID. THERE'S OLD DARKIE. THIS ISN'T RIGHT.
what is this stuff? I've seen this before when I was...
WHAT STUFF?
MISS thing
AFRO PUFF

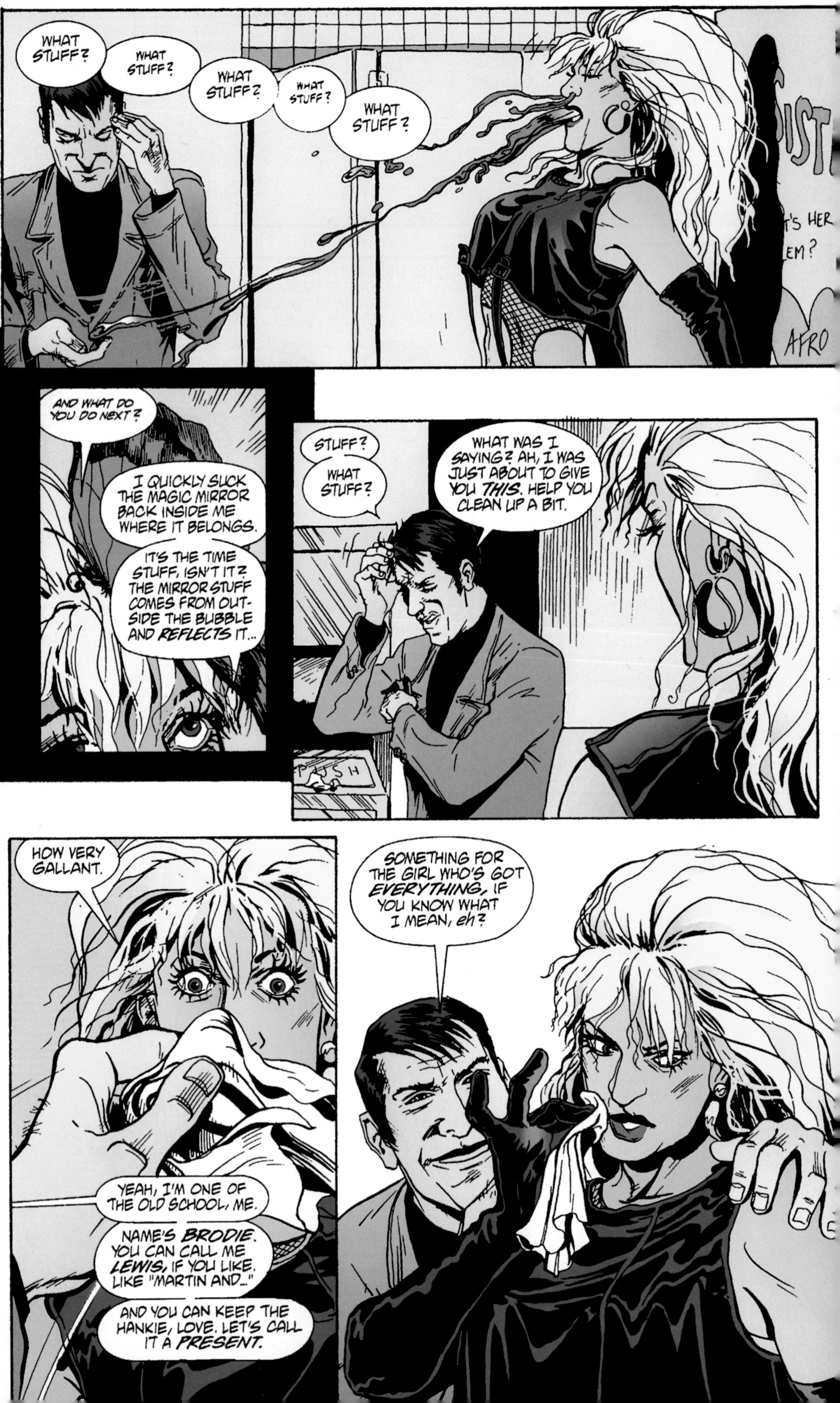
WHAT STUFF?
WHAT STUFF?
WHAT STUFF?
WHAT STUFF?
WHAT STUFF?
'S HER
EM?
AFRO
AND WHAT DO YOU DO NEXT?
I QUICKLY SUCK THE MAGIC MIRROR BACK INSIDE ME WHERE IT BELONGS.
IT'S THE TIME STUFF, ISN'T IT? THE MIRROR STUFF COMES FROM OUTSIDE THE BUBBLE AND *REFLECTS* IT...
STUFF?
WHAT STUFF?
WHAT WAS I SAYING? AH, I WAS JUST ABOUT TO GIVE YOU *THIS*. HELP YOU CLEAN UP A BIT.
PUSH
HOW VERY GALLANT.
YEAH, I'M ONE OF THE OLD SCHOOL, ME.
NAME'S *BRODIE*. YOU CAN CALL ME *LEWIS*, IF YOU LIKE. LIKE "MARTIN AND..."
AND YOU CAN KEEP THE HANKIE, LOVE. LET'S CALL IT A *PRESENT*.
SOMETHING FOR THE GIRL WHO'S GOT *EVERYTHING*, IF YOU KNOW WHAT I MEAN, *eh*?

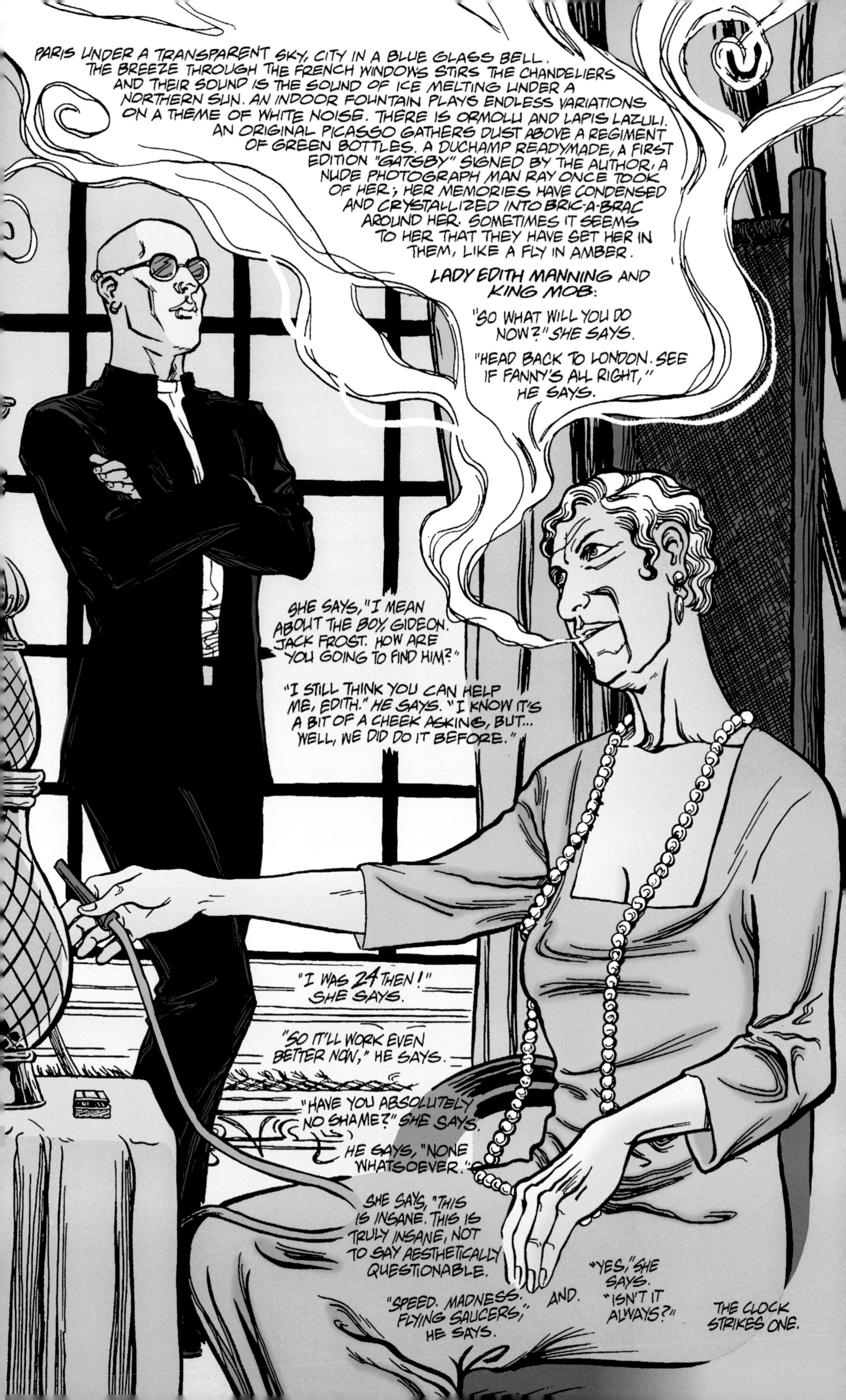
PARIS UNDER A TRANSPARENT SKY, CITY IN A BLUE GLASS BELL. THE BREEZE THROUGH THE FRENCH WINDOWS STIRS THE CHANDELIERS AND THEIR SOUND IS THE SOUND OF ICE MELTING UNDER A NORTHERN SUN. AN INDOOR FOUNTAIN PLAYS ENDLESS VARIATIONS ON A THEME OF WHITE NOISE. THERE IS ORMOLU AND LAPIS LAZULI. AN ORIGINAL PICASSO GATHERS DUST ABOVE A REGIMENT OF GREEN BOTTLES. A DUCHAMP READYMADE, A FIRST EDITION "GATSBY" SIGNED BY THE AUTHOR, A NUDE PHOTOGRAPH MAN RAY ONCE TOOK OF HER; HER MEMORIES HAVE CONDENSED AND CRYSTALLIZED INTO BRIC-A-BRAC AROUND HER. SOMETIMES IT SEEMS TO HER THAT THEY HAVE SET HER IN THEM, LIKE A FLY IN AMBER.
LADY EDITH MANNING AND KING MOB:
"SO WHAT WILL YOU DO NOW?" SHE SAYS.
"HEAD BACK TO LONDON. SEE IF FANNY'S ALL RIGHT," HE SAYS.
SHE SAYS, "I MEAN ABOUT THE BOY, GIDEON. JACK FROST. HOW ARE YOU GOING TO FIND HIM?"
"I STILL THINK YOU CAN HELP ME, EDITH." HE SAYS. "I KNOW IT'S A BIT OF A CHEEK ASKING, BUT... WELL, WE DID DO IT BEFORE."
"I WAS 24 THEN!" SHE SAYS.
"SO IT'LL WORK EVEN BETTER NOW," HE SAYS.
"HAVE YOU ABSOLUTELY NO SHAME?" SHE SAYS.
HE SAYS, "NONE WHATSOEVER."
SHE SAYS, "THIS IS INSANE. THIS IS TRULY INSANE, NOT TO SAY AESTHETICALLY QUESTIONABLE.
"SPEED. MADNESS. FLYING SAUCERS," HE SAYS.
AND.
"YES," SHE SAYS. "ISN'T IT ALWAYS?"
THE CLOCK STRIKES ONE.

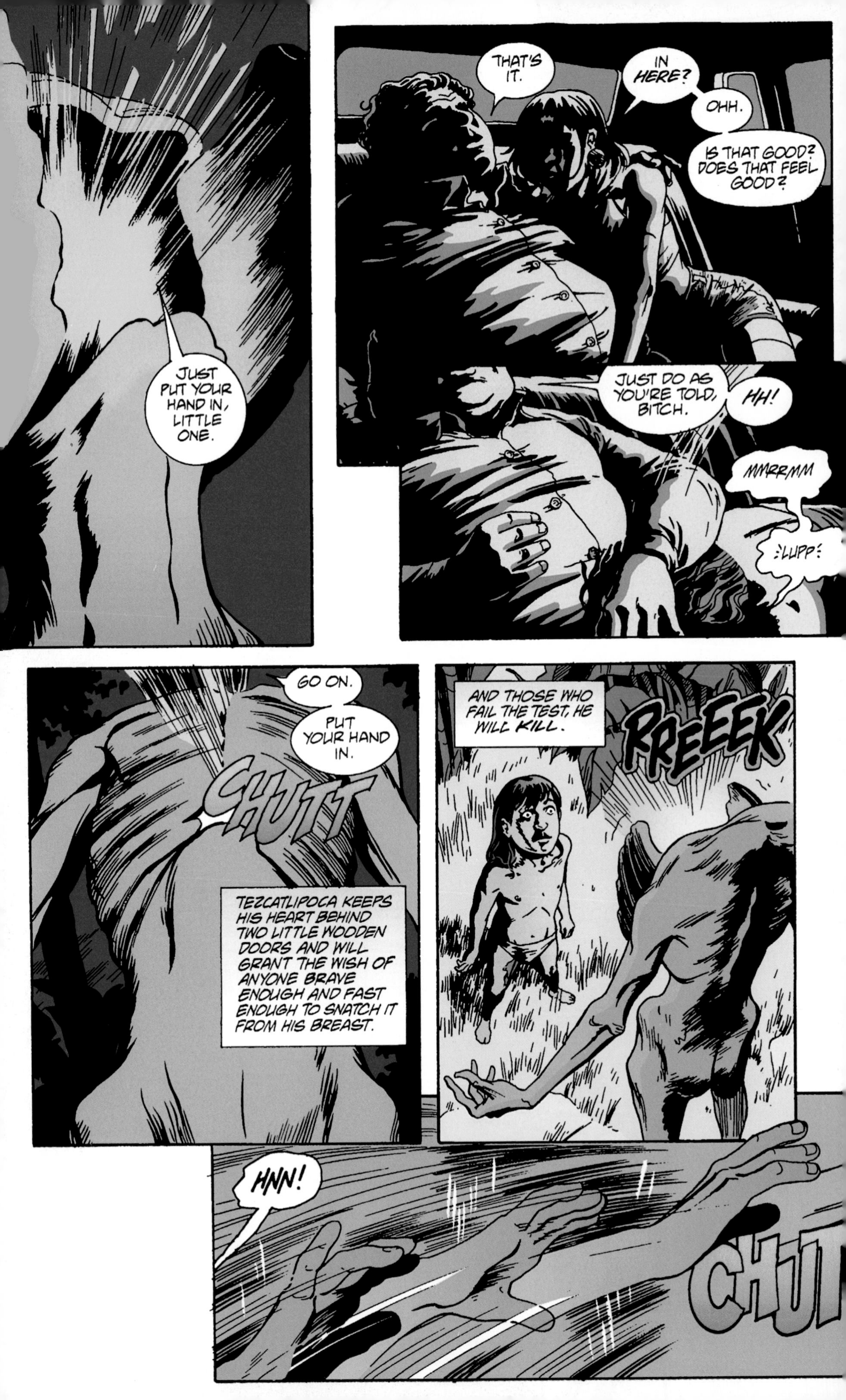
JUST PUT YOUR HAND IN, LITTLE ONE.
THAT'S IT.
IN HERE?
OHH.
IS THAT GOOD? DOES THAT FEEL GOOD?
JUST DO AS YOU'RE TOLD, BITCH.
HH!
MMRRMM
LUPP
GO ON.
PUT YOUR HAND IN.
CHUTT
TEZCATLIPOCA KEEPS HIS HEART BEHIND TWO LITTLE WOODEN DOORS AND WILL GRANT THE WISH OF ANYONE BRAVE ENOUGH AND FAST ENOUGH TO SNATCH IT FROM HIS BREAST.
AND THOSE WHO FAIL THE TEST, HE WILL KILL.
RREEEK
HNN!
CHUT

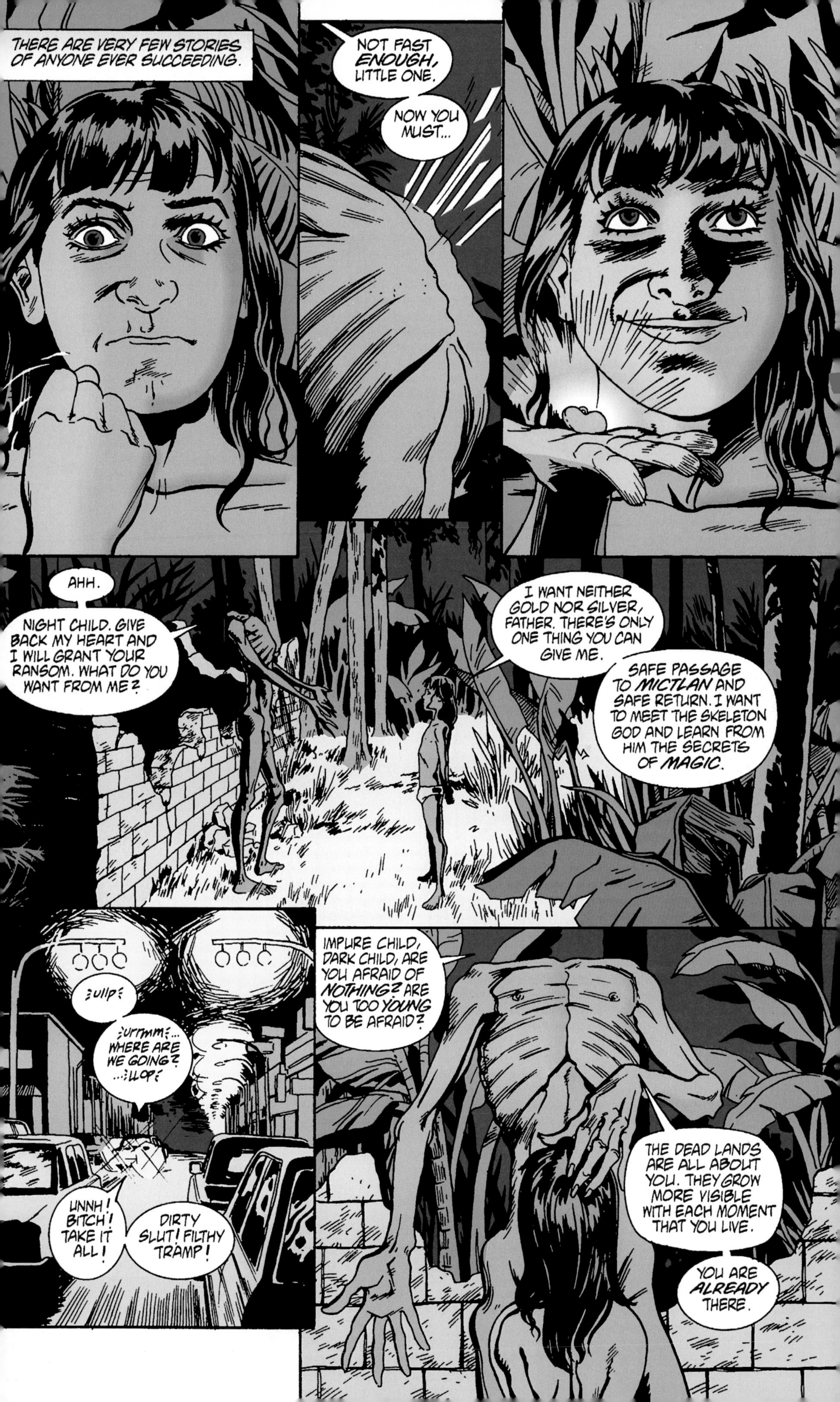
THERE ARE VERY FEW STORIES OF ANYONE EVER SUCCEEDING.
NOT FAST ENOUGH, LITTLE ONE.
NOW YOU MUST...
AHH.
NIGHT CHILD. GIVE BACK MY HEART AND I WILL GRANT YOUR RANSOM. WHAT DO YOU WANT FROM ME?
I WANT NEITHER GOLD NOR SILVER, FATHER. THERE'S ONLY ONE THING YOU CAN GIVE ME.
SAFE PASSAGE TO MICTLAN AND SAFE RETURN. I WANT TO MEET THE SKELETON GOD AND LEARN FROM HIM THE SECRETS OF MAGIC.
:ULLP:
:URRMM:... WHERE ARE WE GOING? ...:LLOP:
UNNH! BITCH! TAKE IT ALL!
DIRTY SLUT! FILTHY TRAMP!
IMPURE CHILD, DARK CHILD, ARE YOU AFRAID OF NOTHING? ARE YOU TOO YOUNG TO BE AFRAID?
THE DEAD LANDS ARE ALL ABOUT YOU. THEY GROW MORE VISIBLE WITH EACH MOMENT THAT YOU LIVE.
YOU ARE ALREADY THERE.

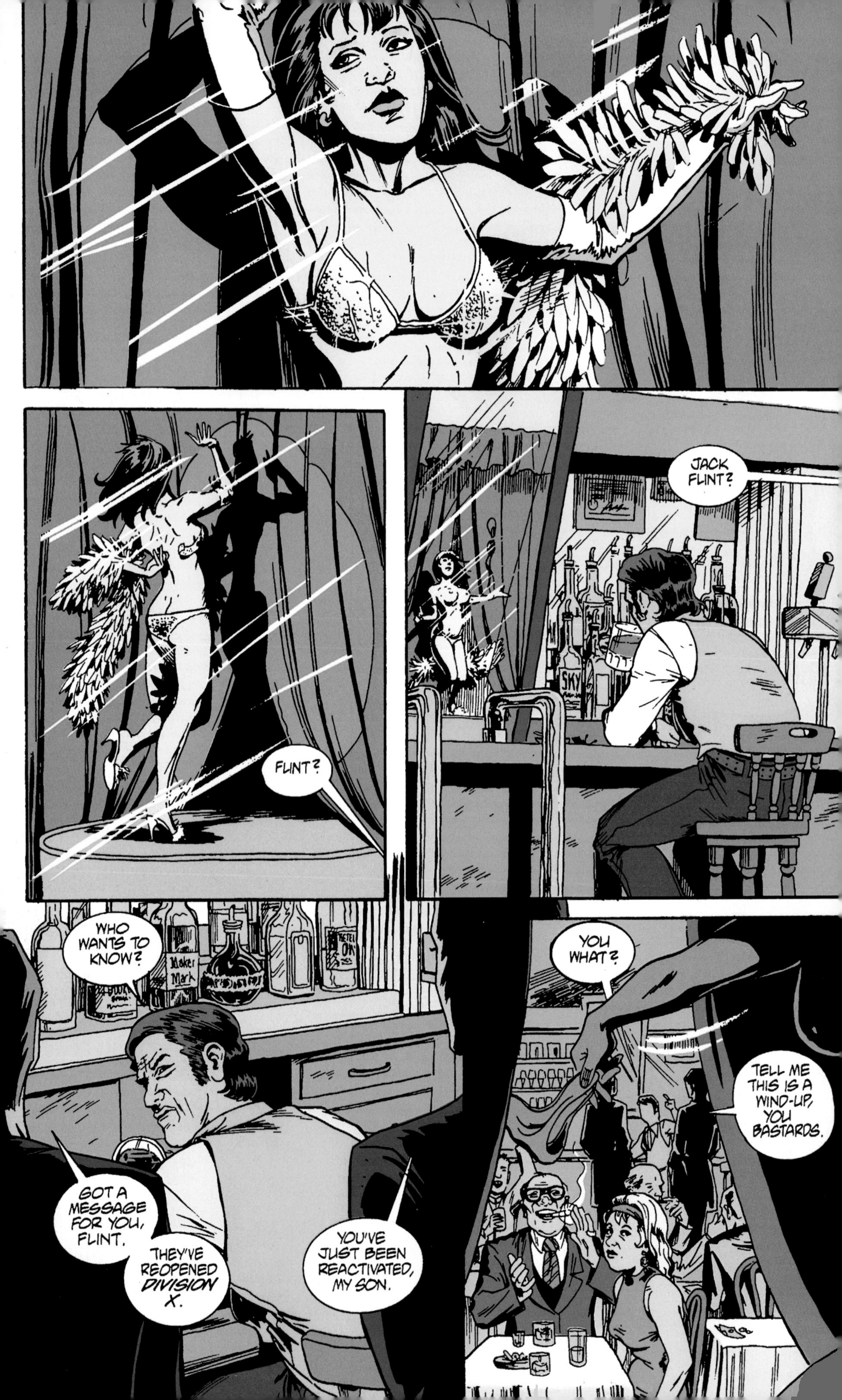

FLINT?
JACK FLINT?
WHO WANTS TO KNOW?
Maker's Mark
GOT A MESSAGE FOR YOU, FLINT.
THEY'VE REOPENED DIVISION X.
YOU'VE JUST BEEN REACTIVATED, MY SON.
YOU WHAT?
TELL ME THIS IS A WIND-UP, YOU BASTARDS.

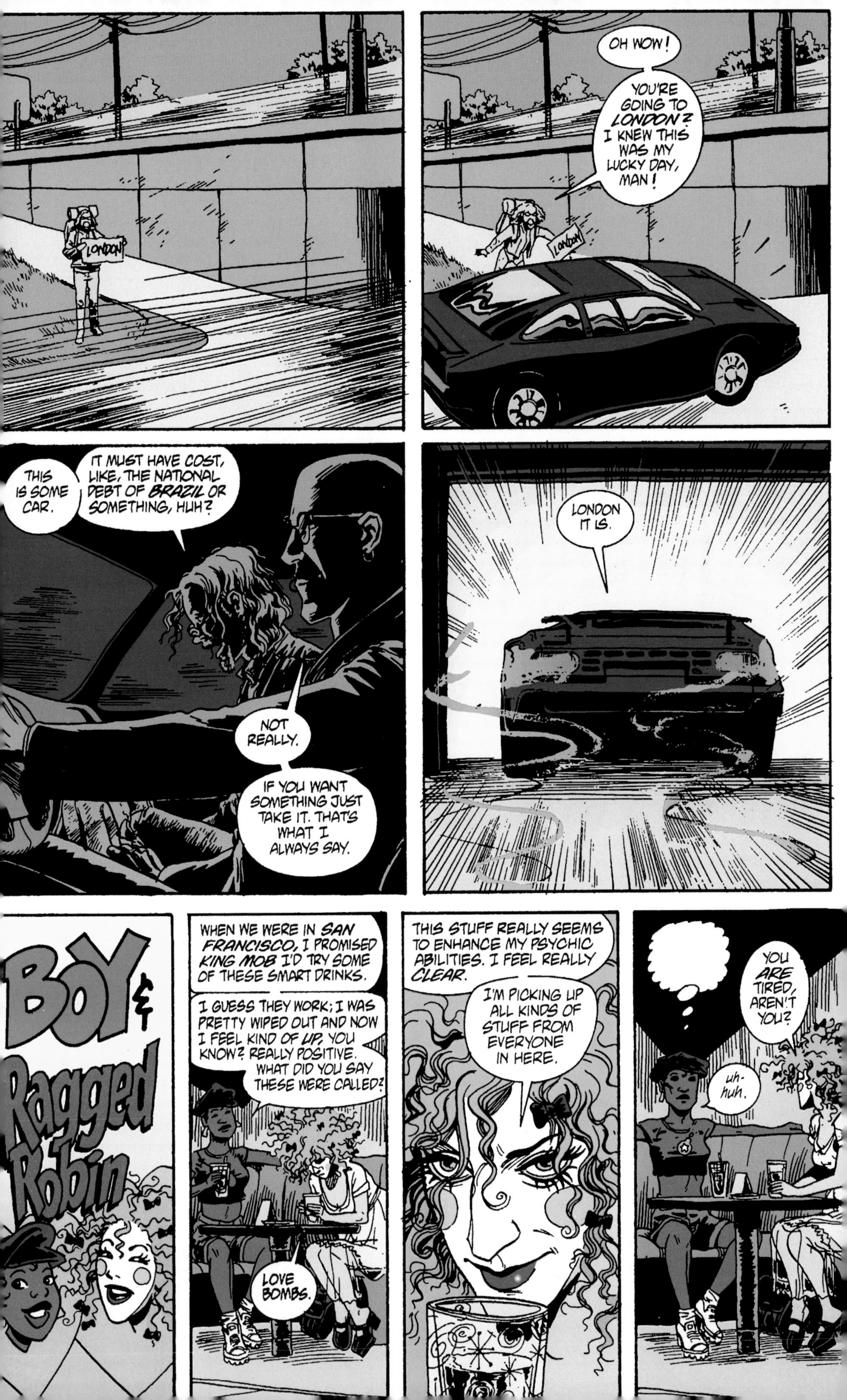

OH WOW!
YOU'RE GOING TO LONDON? I KNEW THIS WAS MY LUCKY DAY, MAN!
THIS IS SOME CAR.
IT MUST HAVE COST, LIKE, THE NATIONAL DEBT OF BRAZIL OR SOMETHING, HUH?
NOT REALLY.
IF YOU WANT SOMETHING JUST TAKE IT. THAT'S WHAT I ALWAYS SAY.
LONDON IT IS.
BOY & Ragged Robin
WHEN WE WERE IN SAN FRANCISCO, I PROMISED KING MOB I'D TRY SOME OF THESE SMART DRINKS.
I GUESS THEY WORK; I WAS PRETTY WIPED OUT AND NOW I FEEL KIND OF UP, YOU KNOW? REALLY POSITIVE. WHAT DID YOU SAY THESE WERE CALLED?
LOVE BOMBS.
THIS STUFF REALLY SEEMS TO ENHANCE MY PSYCHIC ABILITIES. I FEEL REALLY CLEAR.
I'M PICKING UP ALL KINDS OF STUFF FROM EVERYONE IN HERE.
YOU ARE TIRED, AREN'T YOU?
uh-huh.

I'VE BEEN HITCHING ALL *OVER* EUROPE. BEEN TALK-ING TO A LOT OF PEOPLE AND PIECING SHIT TOGETHER, YOU KNOW WHAT I'M SAYING?

WHAT IT'S ALL ABOUT IS, I THINK THERE'S A WAR ON, MAN. I *KNOW* THERE IS.

WAR?

WHAT *KIND* OF WAR?

A *MIND* WAR. IT'S LIKE THE U.S. ARMY HAVE THESE *UFOs*, MAN, BUT THEY'RE NOT *PHYSICAL*, YOU KNOW? THEY'RE LIKE NEGATIVE PSYCHIC ENERGY AND THEY'VE GOT TOTALLY PSYCHIC PILOTS. THEY TRAIN THESE FREAKOS IN *NEW MEXICO*.

YOU SURE YOU DON'T WANT SOME OF THIS?

I'M FINE.

TELL ME MORE ABOUT THE *UFOs*.

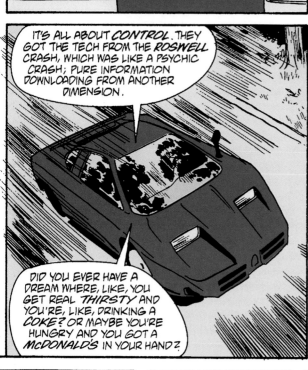

IT'S ALL ABOUT *CONTROL*. THEY GOT THE TECH FROM THE *ROSWELL* CRASH, WHICH WAS LIKE A PSYCHIC CRASH; PURE INFORMATION DOWNLOADING FROM ANOTHER DIMENSION.

DID YOU EVER HAVE A DREAM WHERE, LIKE, YOU GET REAL *THIRSTY* AND YOU'RE, LIKE, DRINKING A *COKE*? OR MAYBE YOU'RE HUNGRY AND YOU GOT A *McDONALD'S* IN YOUR HAND?

THAT'S *PRODUCT PLACEMENT*, MAN.

THE BIG COMPANIES ARE PAYING THE GOVERNMENT TO USE THE *UFOs* TO PROJECT ADVERTISING *DIRECTLY* INTO OUR DREAMS.

PRODUCT PLACEMENT.

I FOUND THESE TAROT CARDS IN MY BAG. I'VE BEEN CARRYING THEM AROUND FOR AGES.

WHY DON'T YOU DO A SPREAD? MAYBE THE CARDS WILL GIVE US SOME IDEA WHERE TO LOOK FOR JACK.

ANYTHING'S WORTH A TRY. I'VE HAD IT UP TO HERE WITH WALKING ROUND LONDON.

SPREADS TAKE FAR TOO LONG. I CAN'T BE BOTHERED WITH ALL THAT STUFF.

I'LL DO A FATE CARD FOR THE BROAD PICTURE OF HOW THIS WHOLE THING'S GOING TO TURN OUT.

LET'S SEE WHAT WE...

UM.

DO YOU WANT THE GOOD NEWS OR THE BAD NEWS?

XIII

LA MO

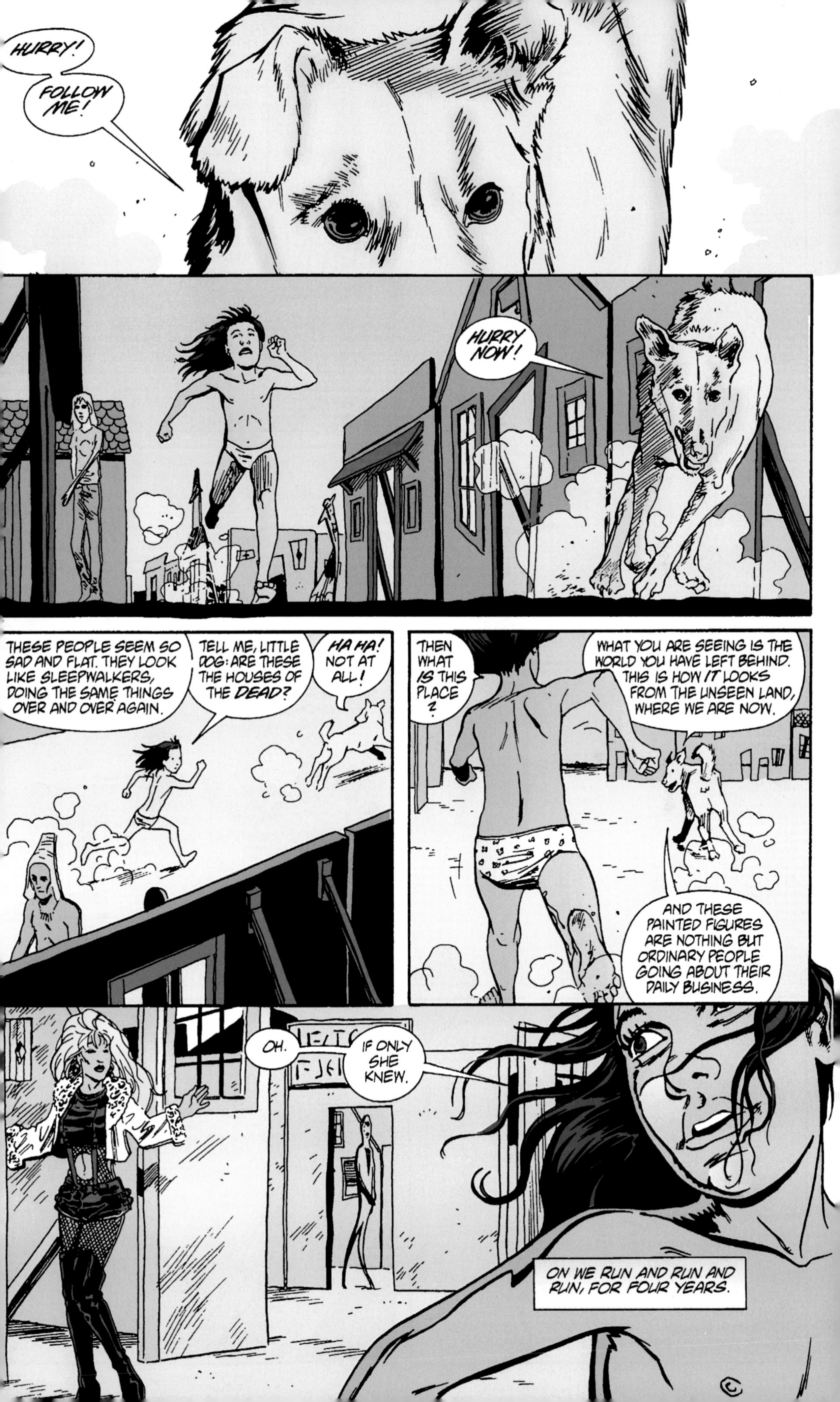
HURRY!
FOLLOW ME!
HURRY NOW!
THESE PEOPLE SEEM SO SAD AND FLAT. THEY LOOK LIKE SLEEPWALKERS, DOING THE SAME THINGS OVER AND OVER AGAIN.
TELL ME, LITTLE DOG: ARE THESE THE HOUSES OF THE DEAD?
HA HA! NOT AT ALL!
THEN WHAT IS THIS PLACE?
WHAT YOU ARE SEEING IS THE WORLD YOU HAVE LEFT BEHIND. THIS IS HOW IT LOOKS FROM THE UNSEEN LAND, WHERE WE ARE NOW.
AND THESE PAINTED FIGURES ARE NOTHING BUT ORDINARY PEOPLE GOING ABOUT THEIR DAILY BUSINESS.
OH.
IF ONLY SHE KNEW.
ON WE RUN AND RUN AND RUN, FOR FOUR YEARS.

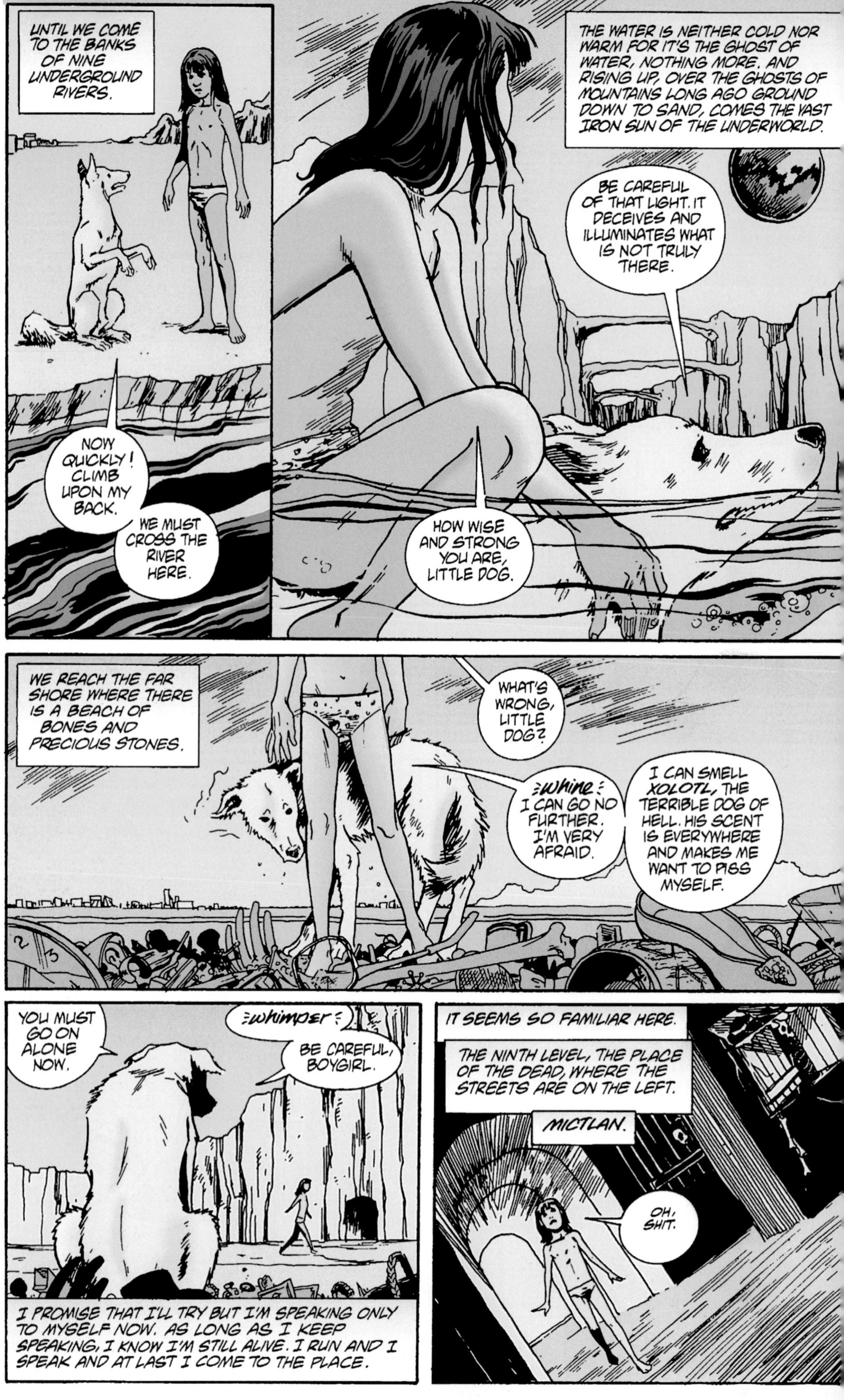
UNTIL WE COME TO THE BANKS OF NINE UNDERGROUND RIVERS.
NOW QUICKLY! CLIMB UPON MY BACK.
WE MUST CROSS THE RIVER HERE.
THE WATER IS NEITHER COLD NOR WARM FOR IT'S THE GHOST OF WATER, NOTHING MORE. AND RISING UP, OVER THE GHOSTS OF MOUNTAINS LONG AGO GROUND DOWN TO SAND, COMES THE VAST IRON SUN OF THE UNDERWORLD.
BE CAREFUL OF THAT LIGHT. IT DECEIVES AND ILLUMINATES WHAT IS NOT TRULY THERE.
HOW WISE AND STRONG YOU ARE, LITTLE DOG.
WE REACH THE FAR SHORE WHERE THERE IS A BEACH OF BONES AND PRECIOUS STONES.
WHAT'S WRONG, LITTLE DOG?
whine
I CAN GO NO FURTHER. I'M VERY AFRAID.
I CAN SMELL XOLOTL, THE TERRIBLE DOG OF HELL. HIS SCENT IS EVERYWHERE AND MAKES ME WANT TO PISS MYSELF.
YOU MUST GO ON ALONE NOW.
whimper
BE CAREFUL, BOYGIRL.
I PROMISE THAT I'LL TRY BUT I'M SPEAKING ONLY TO MYSELF NOW. AS LONG AS I KEEP SPEAKING, I KNOW I'M STILL ALIVE. I RUN AND I SPEAK AND AT LAST I COME TO THE PLACE.
IT SEEMS SO FAMILIAR HERE.
THE NINTH LEVEL, THE PLACE OF THE DEAD, WHERE THE STREETS ARE ON THE LEFT.
MICTLAN.
OH, SHIT.

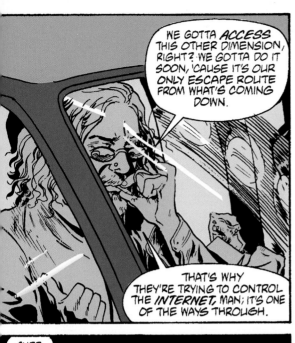

WE GOTTA *ACCESS* THIS OTHER DIMENSION, RIGHT? WE GOTTA DO IT SOON, 'CAUSE IT'S OUR ONLY ESCAPE ROUTE FROM WHAT'S COMING DOWN.

THAT'S WHY THEY'RE TRYING TO CONTROL THE *INTERNET*, MAN; IT'S ONE OF THE WAYS THROUGH.

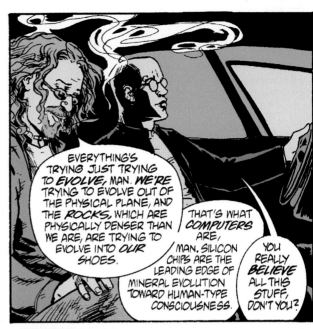

EVERYTHING'S TRYING JUST TRYING TO *EVOLVE*, MAN. *WE'RE* TRYING TO EVOLVE OUT OF THE PHYSICAL PLANE, AND THE *ROCKS*, WHICH ARE PHYSICALLY DENSER THAN WE ARE, ARE TRYING TO EVOLVE INTO *OUR* SHOES.

THAT'S WHAT *COMPUTERS* ARE, MAN. SILICON CHIPS ARE THE LEADING EDGE OF MINERAL EVOLUTION TOWARD HUMAN-TYPE CONSCIOUSNESS.

YOU REALLY *BELIEVE* ALL THIS STUFF, DON'T YOU?

SURE.

I GUESS YOU LIKE *COOKIES*, HUH?

YEAH. GIVE US ONE OVER, WILL YOU?

NOTHING LIKE A BISCUIT TO BRING YOU BACK DOWN TO EARTH.

BOY & Ragged Robin

DEATH DOESN'T NECESSARILY MEAN, LIKE...WELL, *DEATH*, DOES IT?

IT CAN MEAN OTHER THINGS.

LA MORT

I SUPPOSE SO.

A TAROT CARD SHOWING A SKELETON WITH A SCYTHE, MOWING DOWN KINGS AND COMMONERS ALIKE CAN BE INTERPRETED IN ANY NUMBER OF WAYS BY PEOPLE WHO DON'T DARE ACCEPT IT AT FACE VALUE.

SO GIVE ME THE *GOOD* NEWS, GIRL!

I JUST DID.

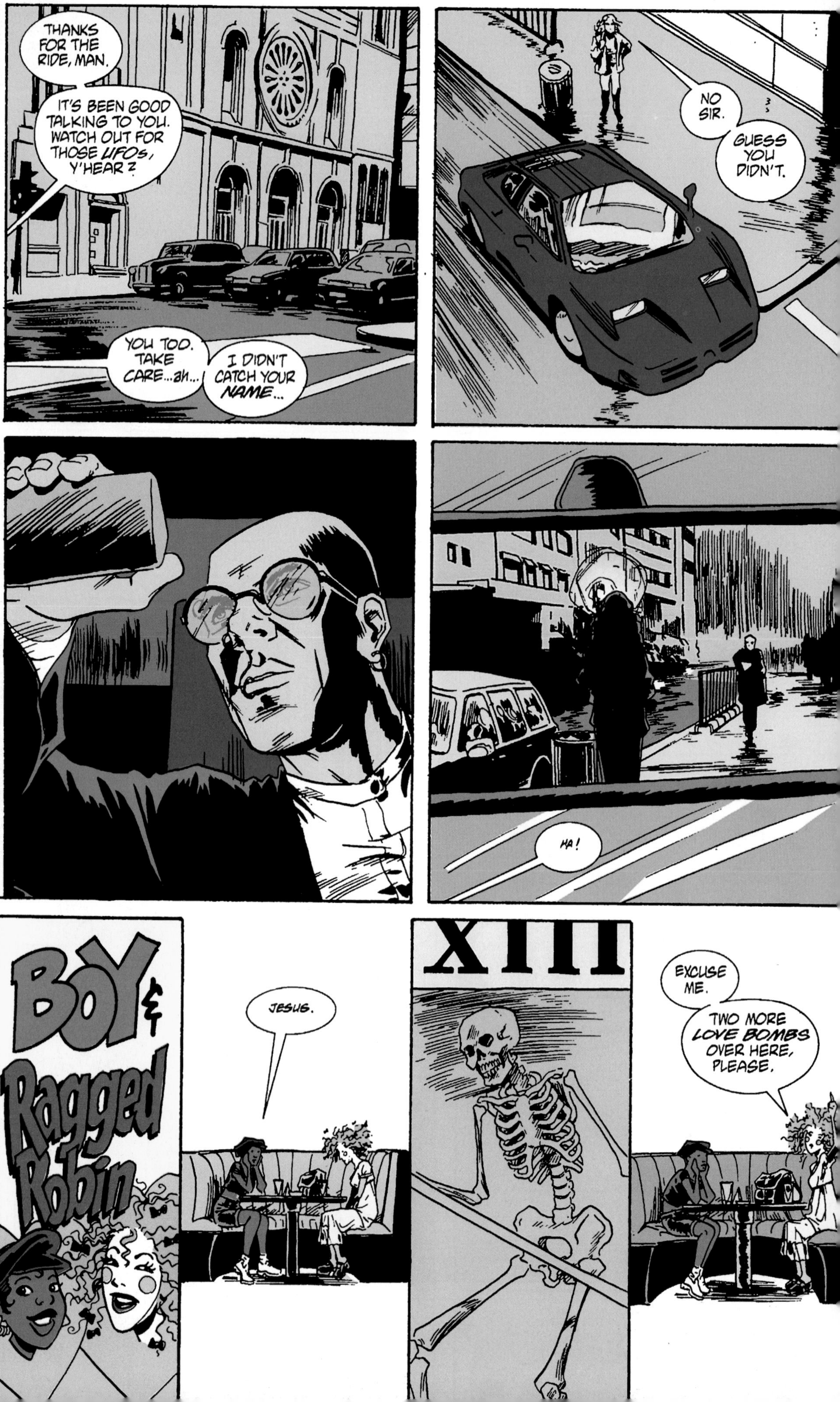

THANKS FOR THE RIDE, MAN.
IT'S BEEN GOOD TALKING TO YOU. WATCH OUT FOR THOSE UFOs, Y'HEAR?
YOU TOO. TAKE CARE...ah...
I DIDN'T CATCH YOUR NAME...
NO SIR.
GUESS YOU DIDN'T.
HA!
BOY & Ragged Robin
JESUS.
XIII
EXCUSE ME.
TWO MORE LOVE BOMBS OVER HERE, PLEASE.

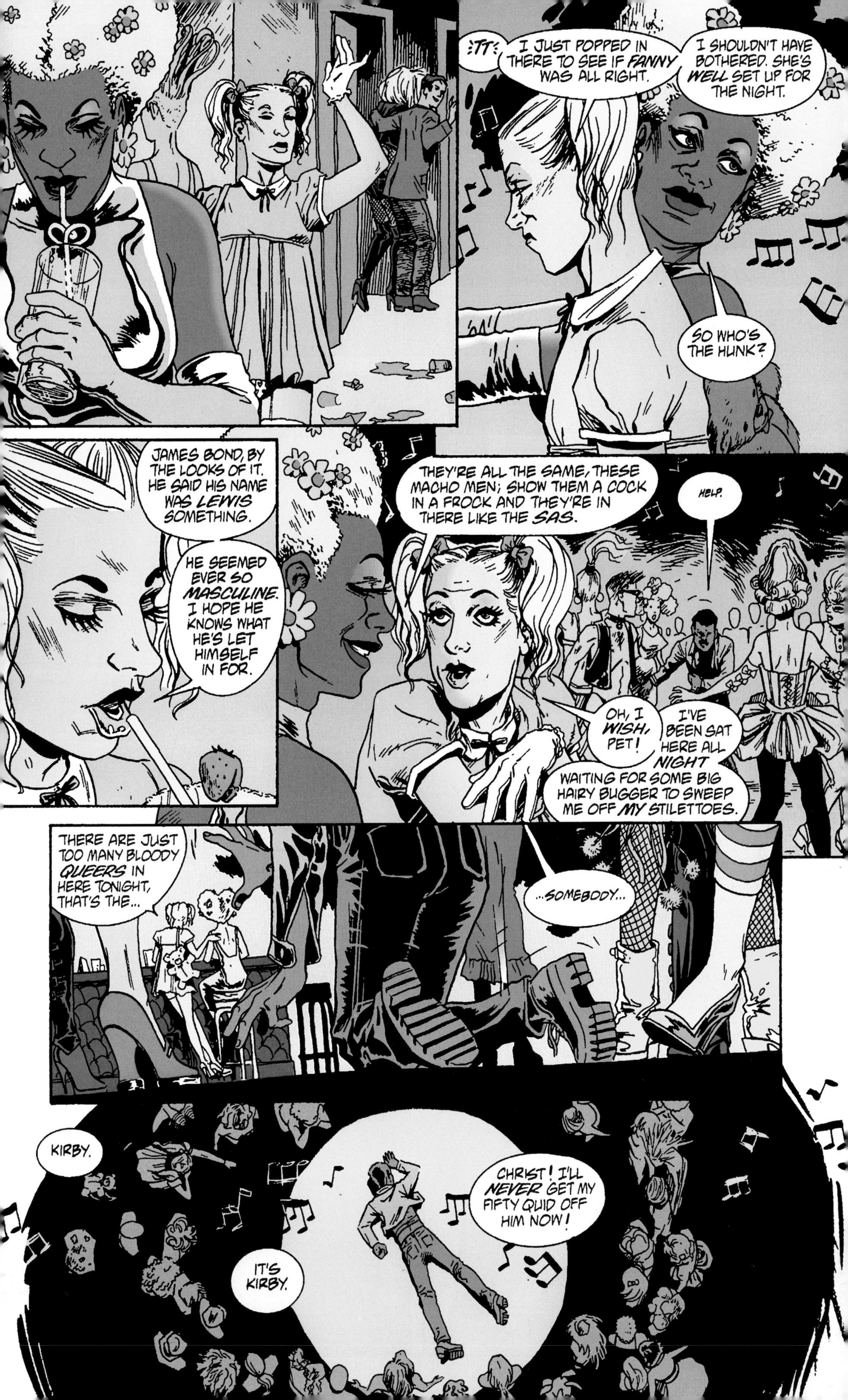
TT
I JUST POPPED IN THERE TO SEE IF FANNY WAS ALL RIGHT.
I SHOULDN'T HAVE BOTHERED. SHE'S WELL SET UP FOR THE NIGHT.
SO WHO'S THE HUNK?
JAMES BOND, BY THE LOOKS OF IT. HE SAID HIS NAME WAS LEWIS SOMETHING.
HE SEEMED EVER SO MASCULINE. I HOPE HE KNOWS WHAT HE'S LET HIMSELF IN FOR.
THEY'RE ALL THE SAME, THESE MACHO MEN; SHOW THEM A COCK IN A FROCK AND THEY'RE IN THERE LIKE THE SAS.
HELP.
OH, I WISH, PET!
I'VE BEEN SAT HERE ALL NIGHT WAITING FOR SOME BIG HAIRY BUGGER TO SWEEP ME OFF MY STILETTOES.
THERE ARE JUST TOO MANY BLOODY QUEERS IN HERE TONIGHT, THAT'S THE...
...SOMEBODY...
KIRBY.
CHRIST! I'LL NEVER GET MY FIFTY QUID OFF HIM NOW!
IT'S KIRBY.

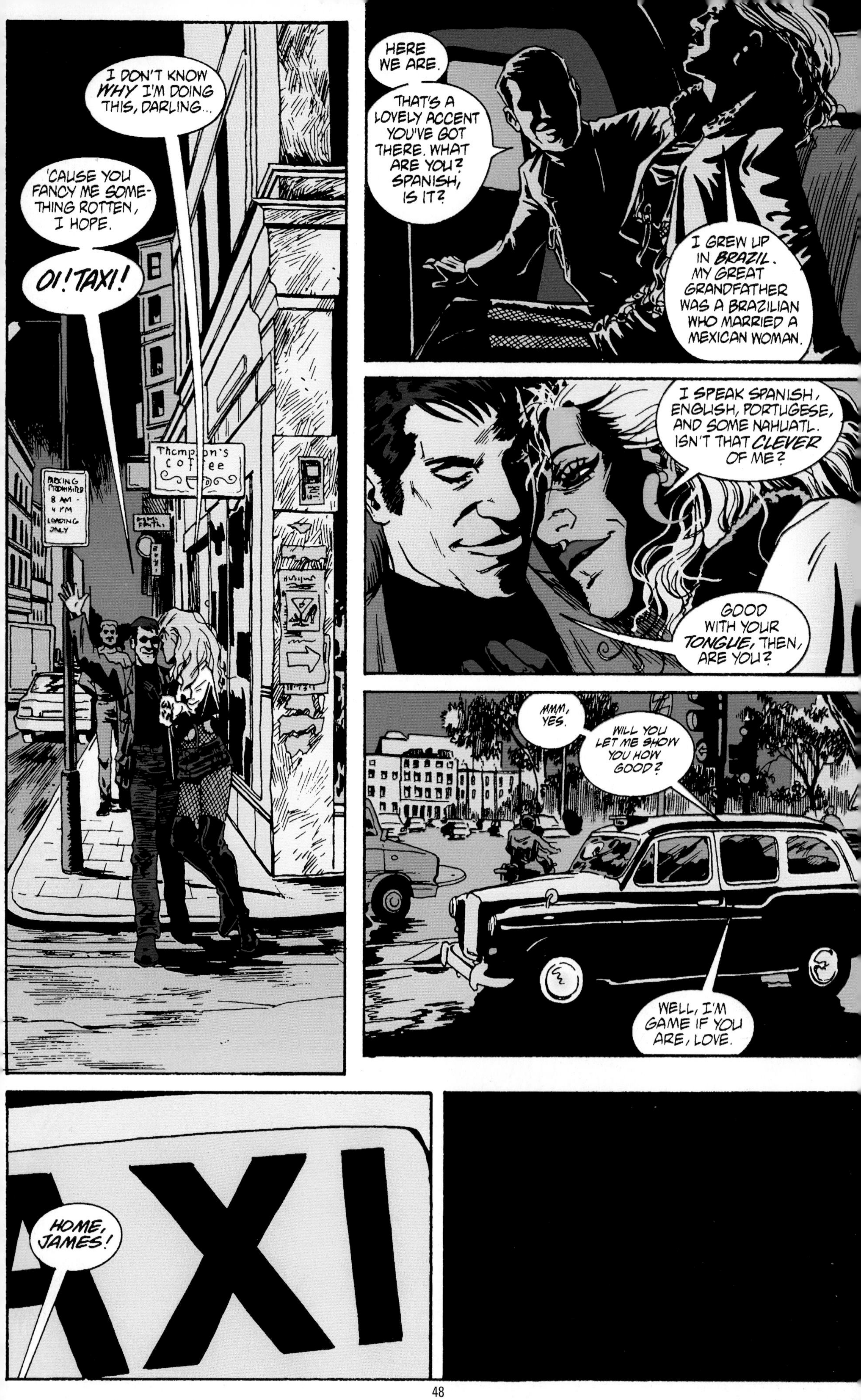
I DON'T KNOW WHY I'M DOING THIS, DARLING...
'CAUSE YOU FANCY ME SOMETHING ROTTEN, I HOPE.
OI! TAXI!
Thompson's coffee
PARKING PROHIBITED 8 AM - 4 PM LOADING ONLY
HERE WE ARE.
THAT'S A LOVELY ACCENT YOU'VE GOT THERE. WHAT ARE YOU? SPANISH, IS IT?
I GREW UP IN BRAZIL. MY GREAT GRANDFATHER WAS A BRAZILIAN WHO MARRIED A MEXICAN WOMAN.
I SPEAK SPANISH, ENGLISH, PORTUGESE, AND SOME NAHUATL. ISN'T THAT CLEVER OF ME?
GOOD WITH YOUR TONGUE, THEN, ARE YOU?
MMM, YES.
WILL YOU LET ME SHOW YOU HOW GOOD?
WELL, I'M GAME IF YOU ARE, LOVE.
HOME, JAMES!

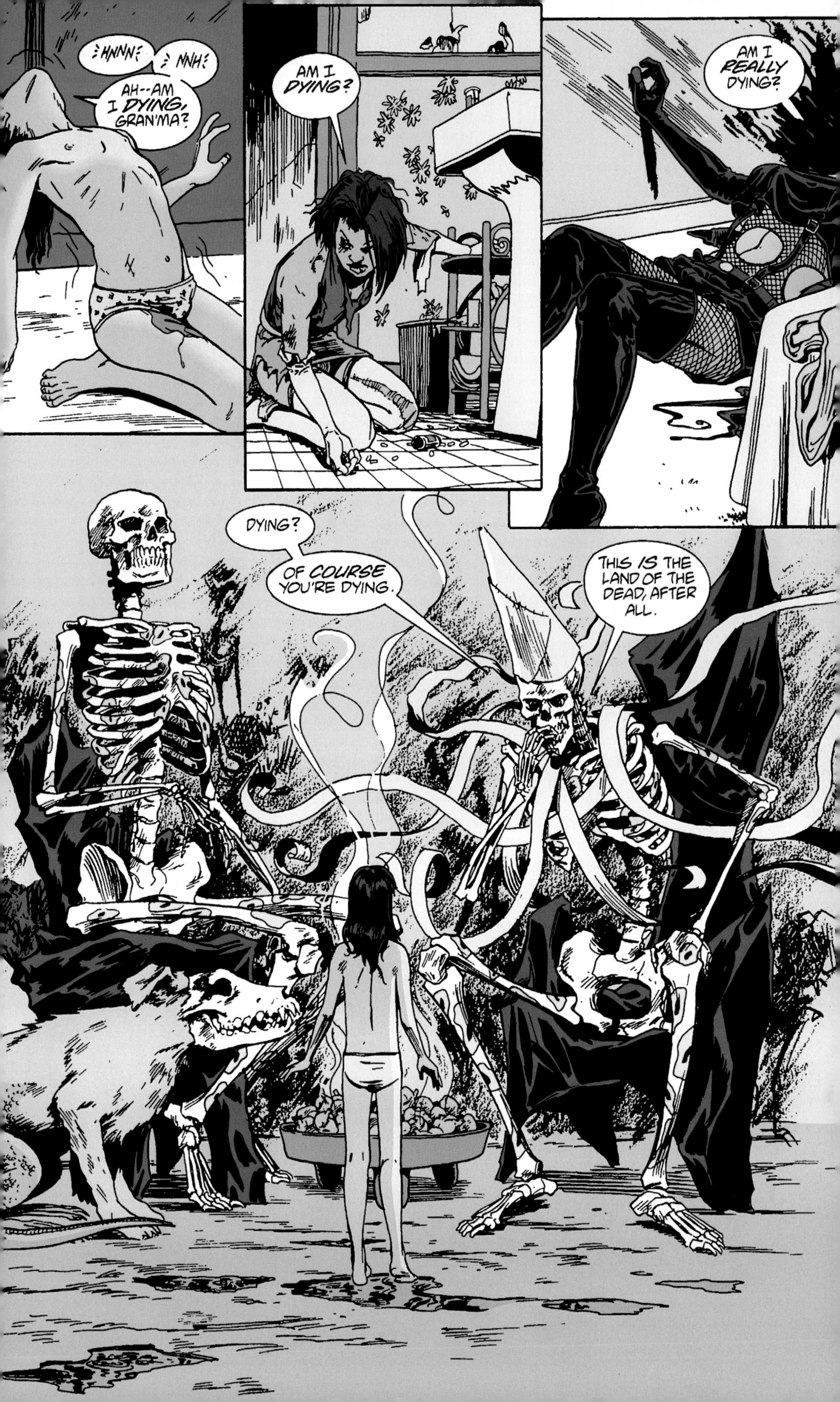
HNNN
NNH
AH--AM I DYING, GRAN'MA?
AM I DYING?
AM I REALLY DYING?
DYING?
OF COURSE YOU'RE DYING.
THIS IS THE LAND OF THE DEAD, AFTER ALL.

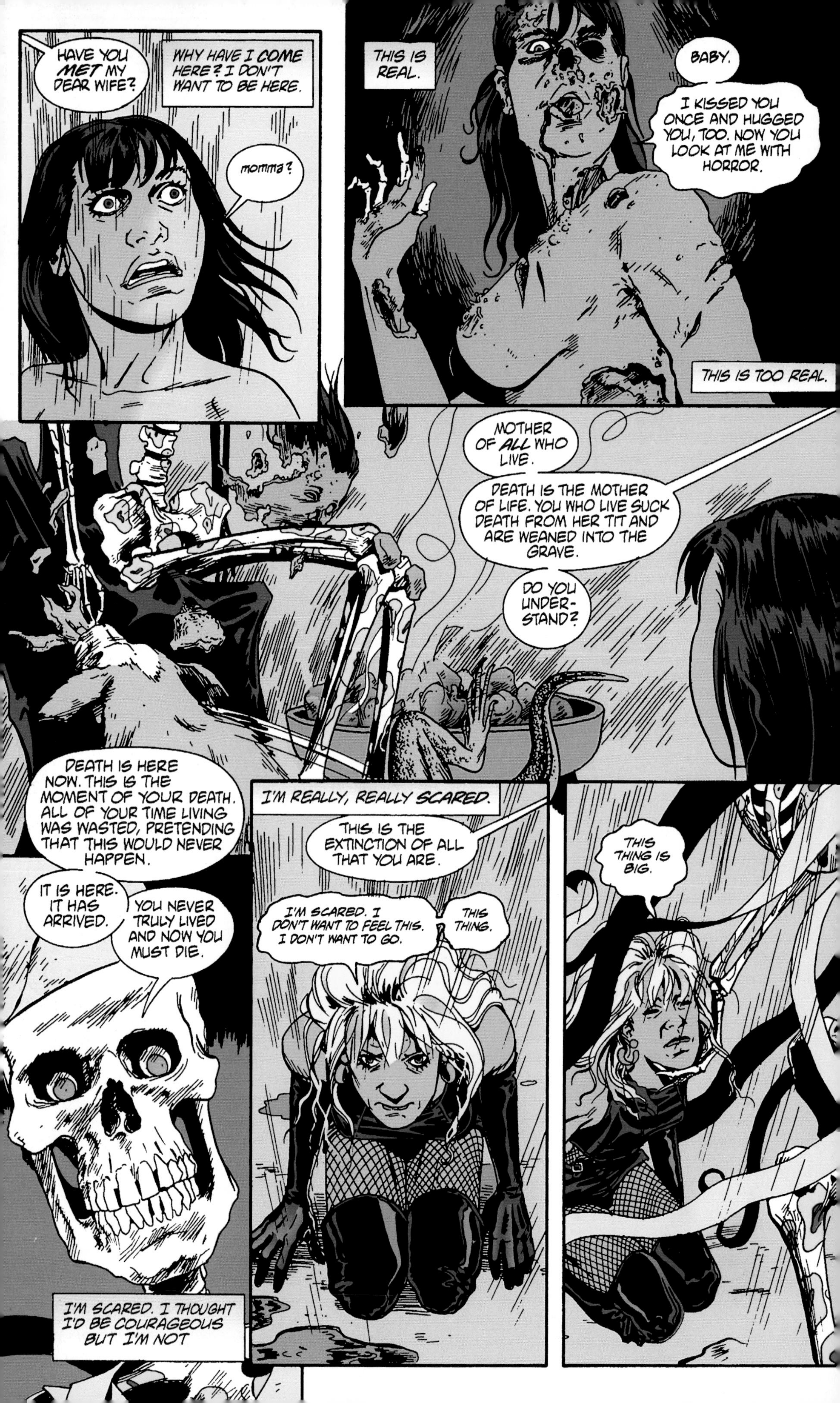
HAVE YOU MET MY DEAR WIFE?
WHY HAVE I COME HERE? I DON'T WANT TO BE HERE.
momma?
THIS IS REAL.
BABY.
I KISSED YOU ONCE AND HUGGED YOU, TOO. NOW YOU LOOK AT ME WITH HORROR.
THIS IS TOO REAL.
MOTHER OF ALL WHO LIVE.
DEATH IS THE MOTHER OF LIFE. YOU WHO LIVE SUCK DEATH FROM HER TIT AND ARE WEANED INTO THE GRAVE.
DO YOU UNDER-STAND?
DEATH IS HERE NOW. THIS IS THE MOMENT OF YOUR DEATH. ALL OF YOUR TIME LIVING WAS WASTED, PRETENDING THAT THIS WOULD NEVER HAPPEN.
IT IS HERE. IT HAS ARRIVED.
YOU NEVER TRULY LIVED AND NOW YOU MUST DIE.
I'M SCARED. I THOUGHT I'D BE COURAGEOUS BUT I'M NOT
I'M REALLY, REALLY SCARED.
THIS IS THE EXTINCTION OF ALL THAT YOU ARE.
I'M SCARED. I DON'T WANT TO FEEL THIS. I DON'T WANT TO GO.
THIS THING.
THIS THING IS BIG.

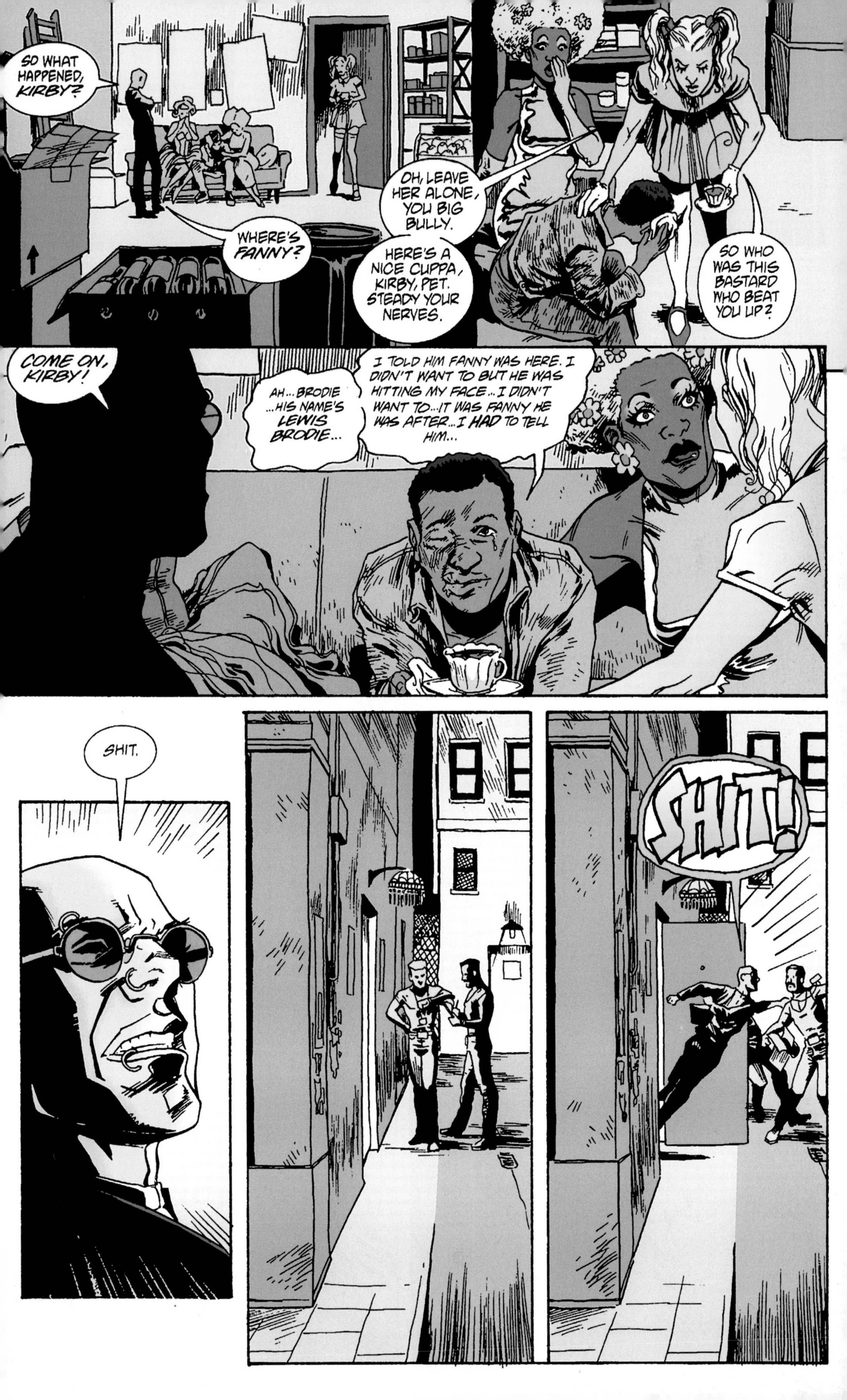
SO WHAT HAPPENED, KIRBY?
WHERE'S FANNY?
OH, LEAVE HER ALONE, YOU BIG BULLY.
HERE'S A NICE CUPPA, KIRBY, PET. STEADY YOUR NERVES.
SO WHO WAS THIS BASTARD WHO BEAT YOU UP?
COME ON, KIRBY!
AH... BRODIE ...HIS NAME'S LEWIS BRODIE...
I TOLD HIM FANNY WAS HERE. I DIDN'T WANT TO BUT HE WAS HITTING MY FACE... I DIDN'T WANT TO... IT WAS FANNY HE WAS AFTER... I HAD TO TELL HIM...
SHIT.
SHIT!

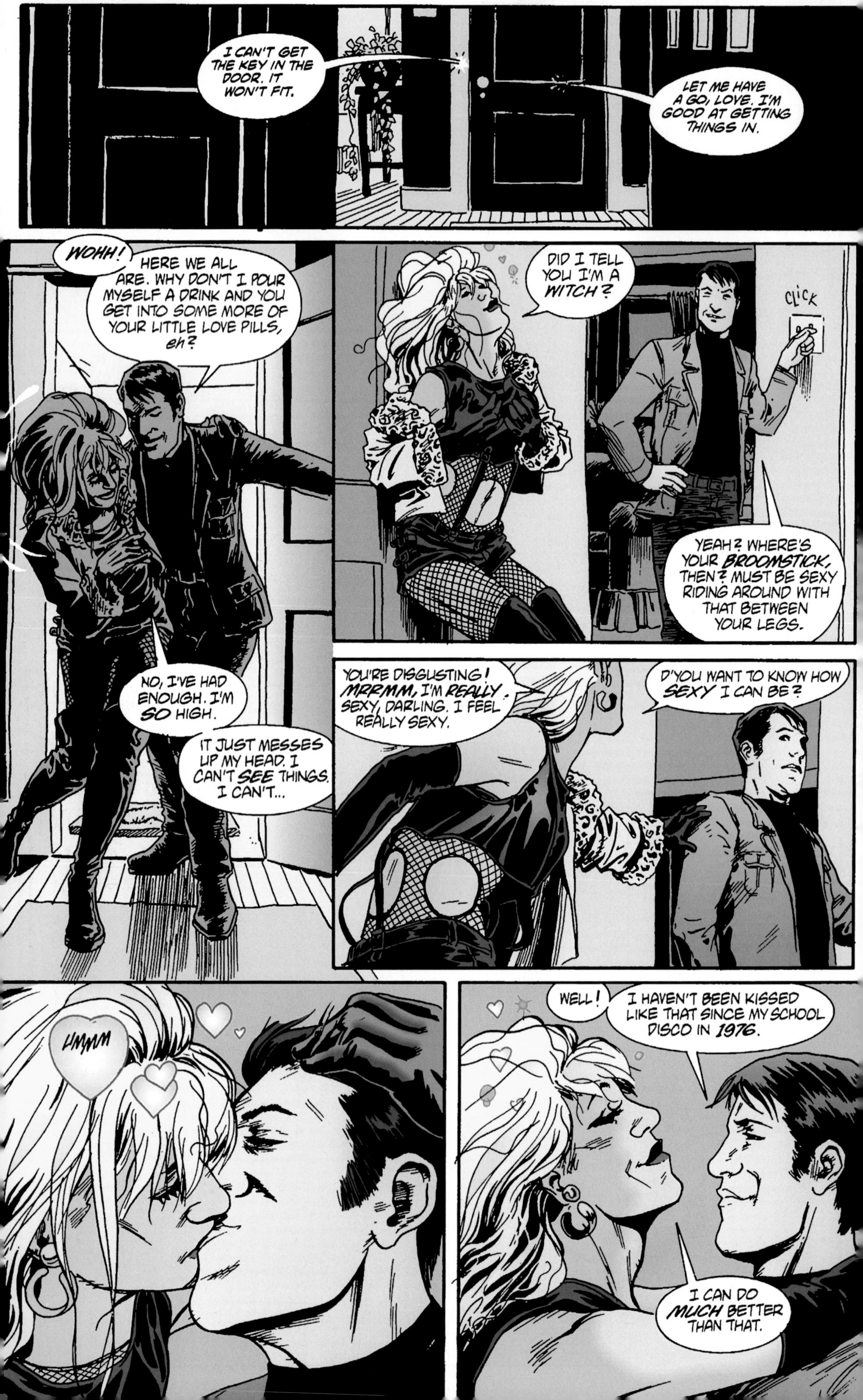
I CAN'T GET THE KEY IN THE DOOR. IT WON'T FIT.
LET ME HAVE A GO, LOVE. I'M GOOD AT GETTING THINGS IN.
WOHH!
HERE WE ALL ARE. WHY DON'T I POUR MYSELF A DRINK AND YOU GET INTO SOME MORE OF YOUR LITTLE LOVE PILLS, eh?
NO, I'VE HAD ENOUGH. I'M SO HIGH.
IT JUST MESSES UP MY HEAD. I CAN'T SEE THINGS. I CAN'T...
DID I TELL YOU I'M A WITCH?
CLICK
YEAH? WHERE'S YOUR BROOMSTICK, THEN? MUST BE SEXY RIDING AROUND WITH THAT BETWEEN YOUR LEGS.
YOU'RE DISGUSTING! MRRMM, I'M REALLY SEXY, DARLING. I FEEL REALLY SEXY.
D'YOU WANT TO KNOW HOW SEXY I CAN BE?
UMMM
WELL!
I HAVEN'T BEEN KISSED LIKE THAT SINCE MY SCHOOL DISCO IN 1976.
I CAN DO MUCH BETTER THAN THAT.

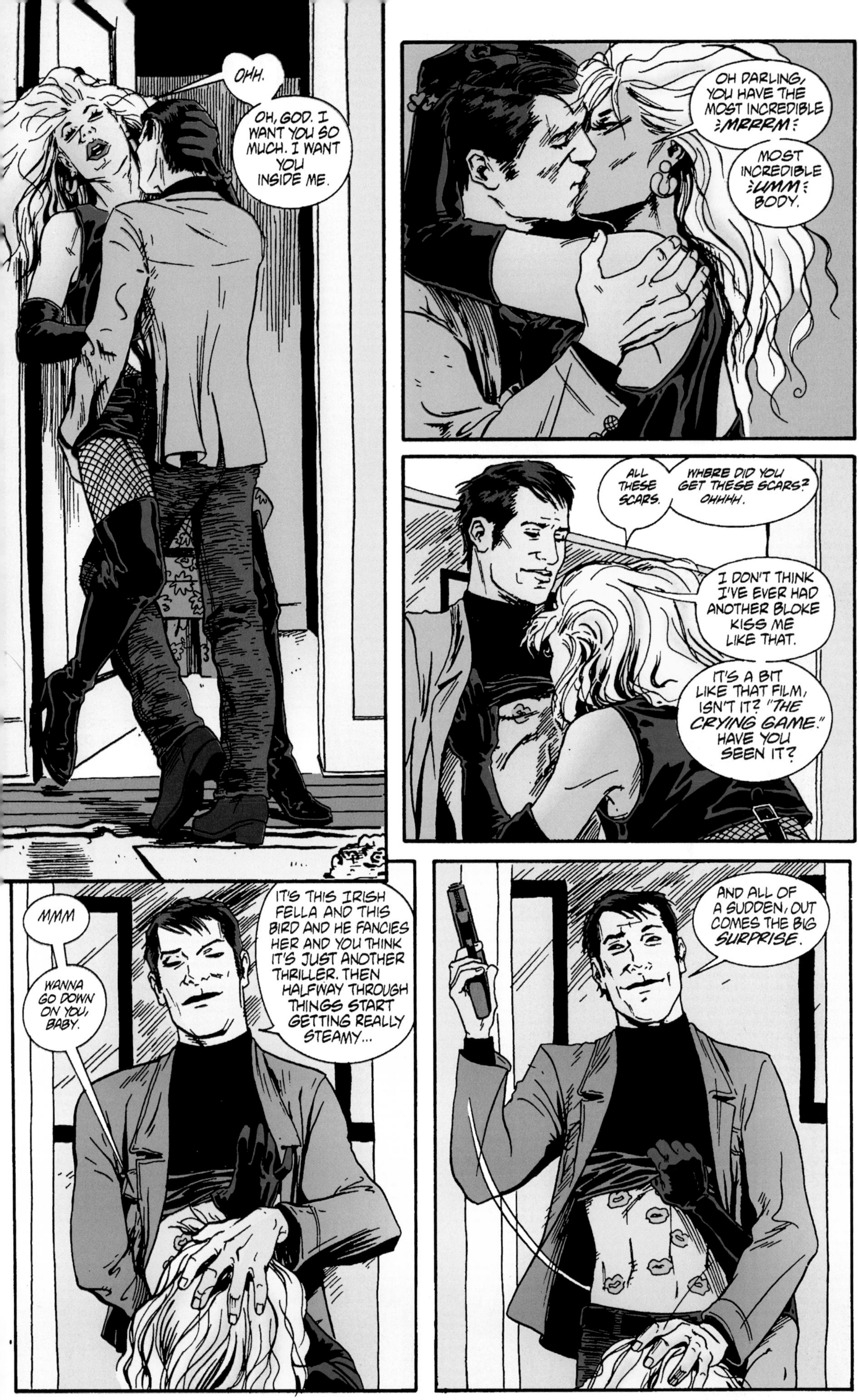
OHH.
OH, GOD. I WANT YOU SO MUCH. I WANT YOU INSIDE ME.
OH DARLING, YOU HAVE THE MOST INCREDIBLE MRRRM
MOST INCREDIBLE UMM BODY.
ALL THESE SCARS.
WHERE DID YOU GET THESE SCARS? OHHHH.
I DON'T THINK I'VE EVER HAD ANOTHER BLOKE KISS ME LIKE THAT.
IT'S A BIT LIKE THAT FILM, ISN'T IT? "THE CRYING GAME." HAVE YOU SEEN IT?
MMM
WANNA GO DOWN ON YOU, BABY.
IT'S THIS IRISH FELLA AND THIS BIRD AND HE FANCIES HER AND YOU THINK IT'S JUST ANOTHER THRILLER. THEN HALFWAY THROUGH THINGS START GETTING REALLY STEAMY...
AND ALL OF A SUDDEN, OUT COMES THE BIG SURPRISE.

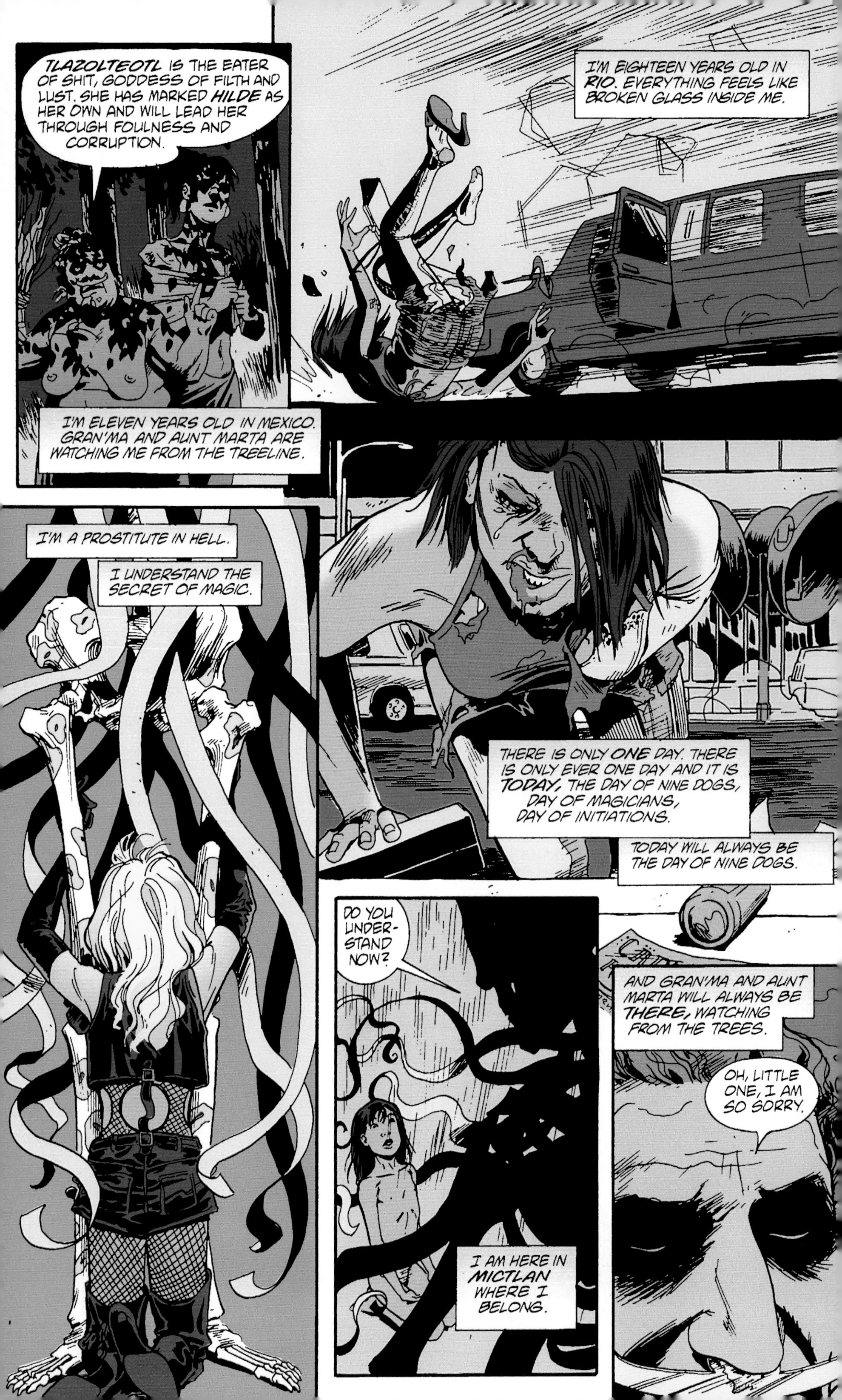
TLAZOLTEOTL IS THE EATER OF SHIT, GODDESS OF FILTH AND LUST. SHE HAS MARKED HILDE AS HER OWN AND WILL LEAD HER THROUGH FOULNESS AND CORRUPTION.
I'M ELEVEN YEARS OLD IN MEXICO. GRAN'MA AND AUNT MARTA ARE WATCHING ME FROM THE TREELINE.
I'M EIGHTEEN YEARS OLD IN RIO. EVERYTHING FEELS LIKE BROKEN GLASS INSIDE ME.
I'M A PROSTITUTE IN HELL.
I UNDERSTAND THE SECRET OF MAGIC.
THERE IS ONLY ONE DAY. THERE IS ONLY EVER ONE DAY AND IT IS TODAY, THE DAY OF NINE DOGS, DAY OF MAGICIANS, DAY OF INITIATIONS.
TODAY WILL ALWAYS BE THE DAY OF NINE DOGS.
DO YOU UNDER-STAND NOW?
I AM HERE IN MICTLAN WHERE I BELONG.
AND GRAN'MA AND AUNT MARTA WILL ALWAYS BE THERE, WATCHING FROM THE TREES.
OH, LITTLE ONE, I AM SO SORRY.

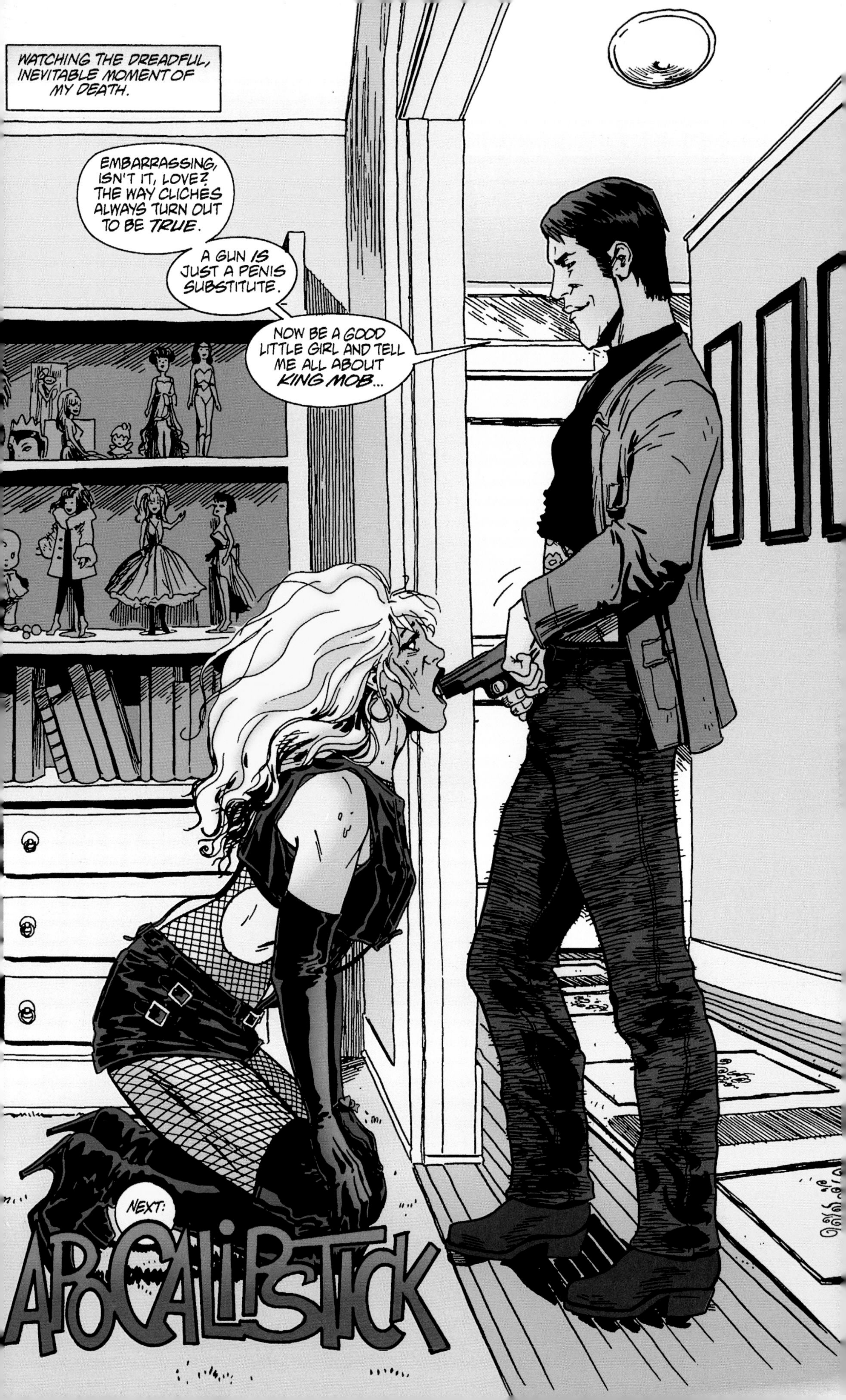
WATCHING THE DREADFUL, INEVITABLE MOMENT OF MY DEATH.
EMBARRASSING, ISN'T IT, LOVE? THE WAY CLICHÉS ALWAYS TURN OUT TO BE TRUE.
A GUN IS JUST A PENIS SUBSTITUTE.
NOW BE A GOOD LITTLE GIRL AND TELL ME ALL ABOUT KING MOB...
NEXT:
APOCALIPSTICK

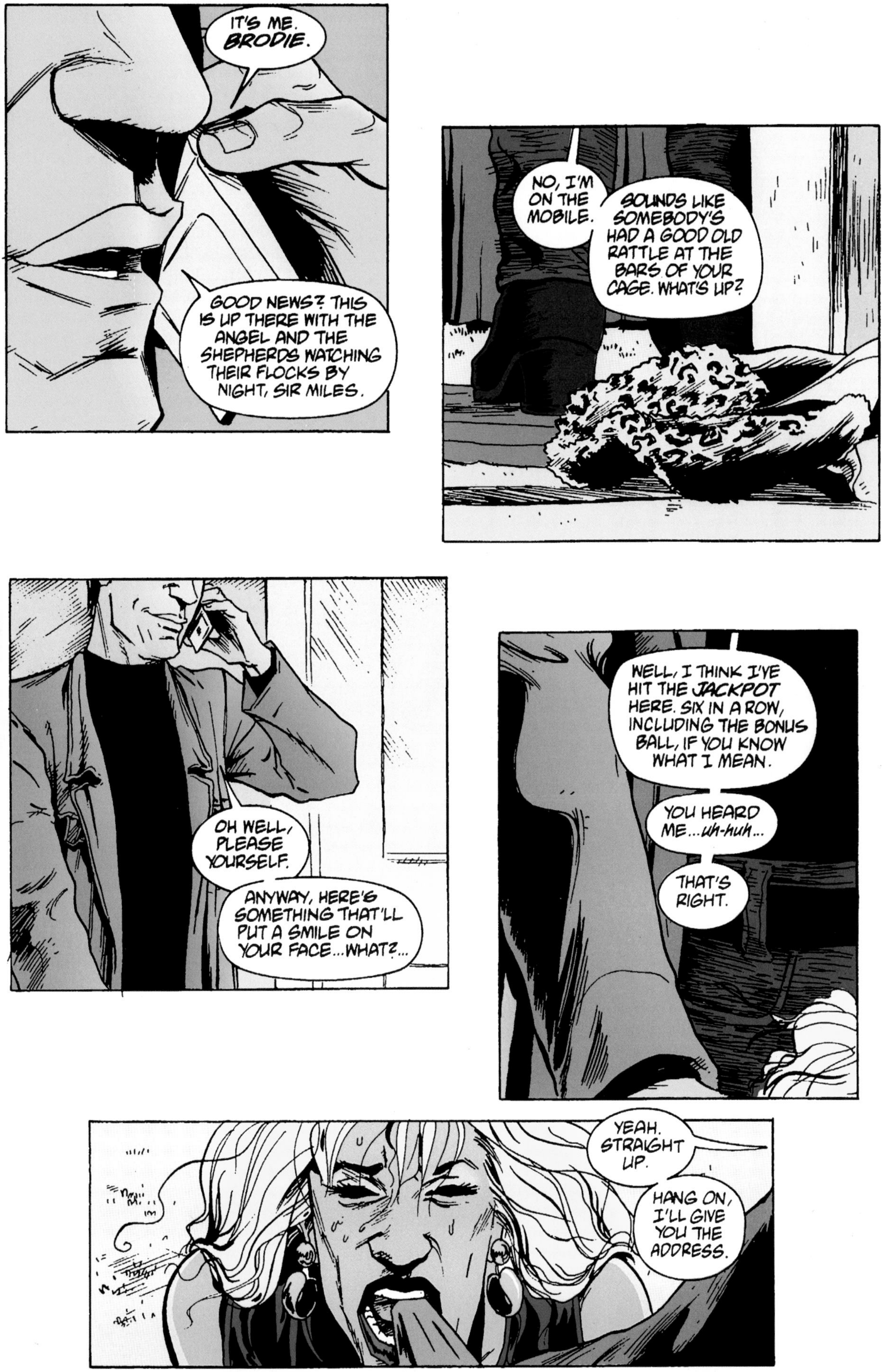
IT'S ME. BRODIE.
GOOD NEWS? THIS IS UP THERE WITH THE ANGEL AND THE SHEPHERDS WATCHING THEIR FLOCKS BY NIGHT, SIR MILES.
NO, I'M ON THE MOBILE.
SOUNDS LIKE SOMEBODY'S HAD A GOOD OLD RATTLE AT THE BARS OF YOUR CAGE. WHAT'S UP?
OH WELL, PLEASE YOURSELF.
ANYWAY, HERE'S SOMETHING THAT'LL PUT A SMILE ON YOUR FACE...WHAT?...
WELL, I THINK I'VE HIT THE JACKPOT HERE. SIX IN A ROW, INCLUDING THE BONUS BALL, IF YOU KNOW WHAT I MEAN.
YOU HEARD ME...uh-huh...
THAT'S RIGHT.
YEAH. STRAIGHT UP.
HANG ON, I'LL GIVE YOU THE ADDRESS.

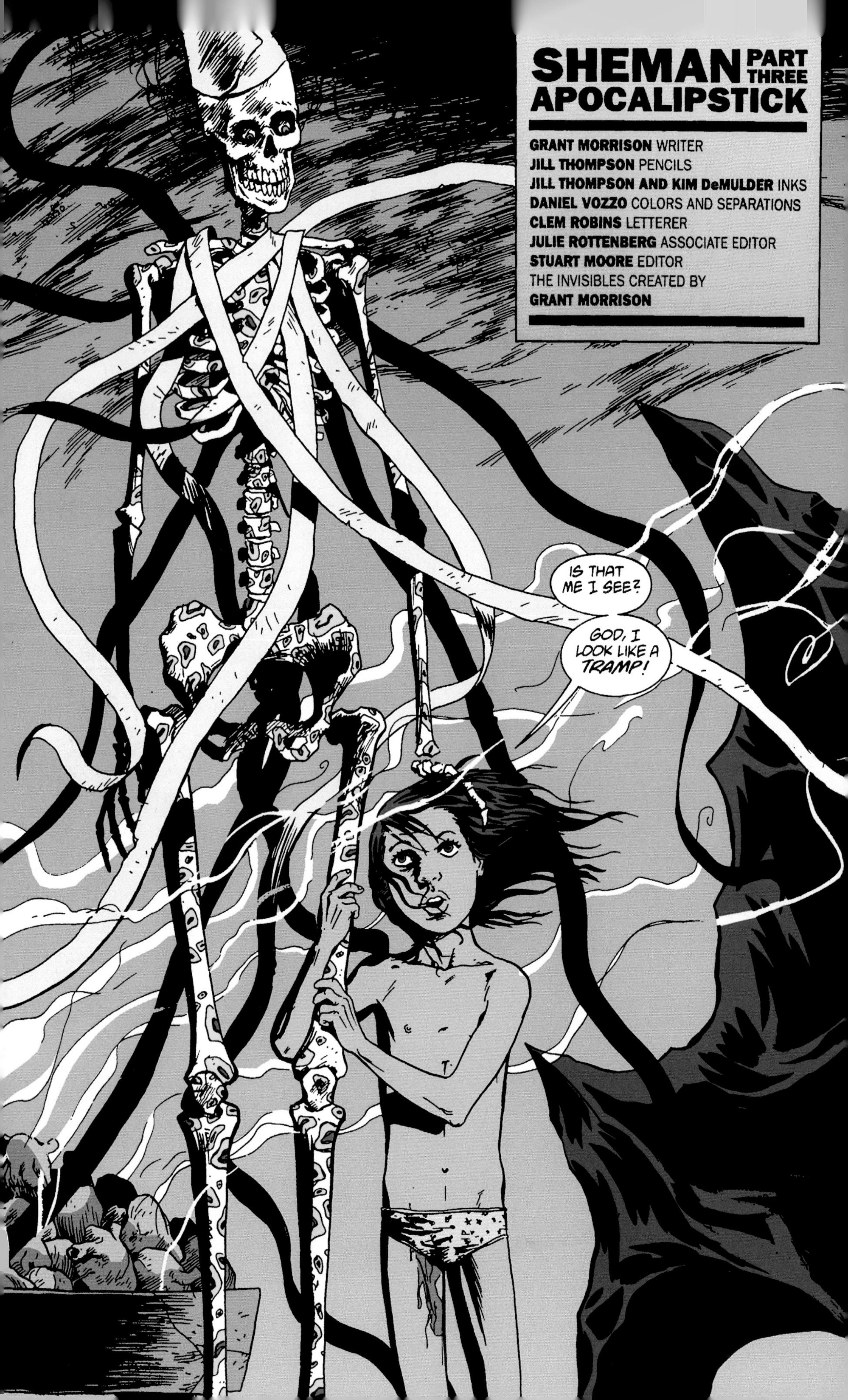
SHEMAN PART THREE
APOCALIPSTICK
GRANT MORRISON WRITER
JILL THOMPSON PENCILS
JILL THOMPSON AND KIM DeMULDER INKS
DANIEL VOZZO COLORS AND SEPARATIONS
CLEM ROBINS LETTERER
JULIE ROTTENBERG ASSOCIATE EDITOR
STUART MOORE EDITOR
THE INVISIBLES CREATED BY
GRANT MORRISON
IS THAT ME I SEE?
GOD, I LOOK LIKE A TRAMP!

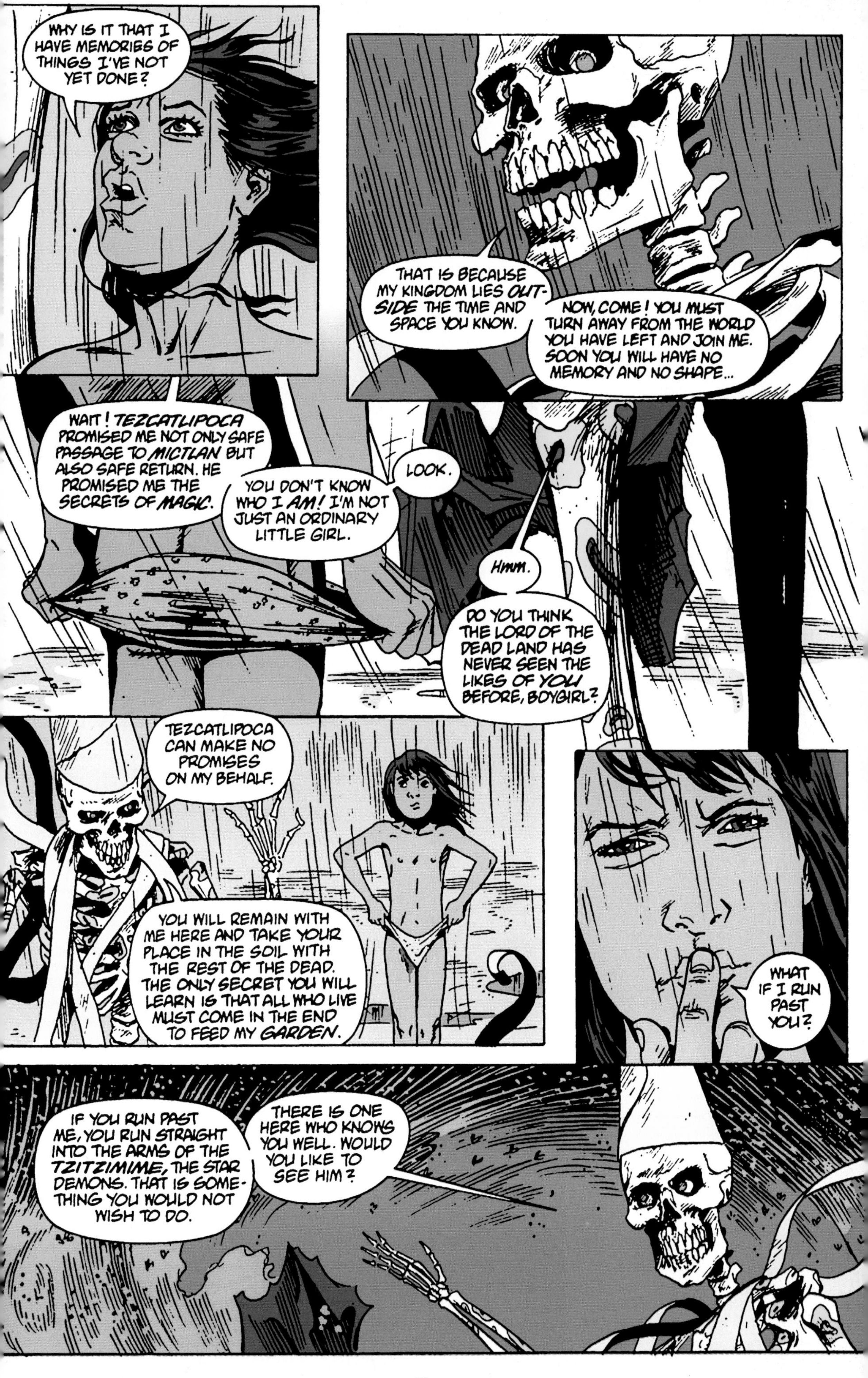
WHY IS IT THAT I HAVE MEMORIES OF THINGS I'VE NOT YET DONE?
THAT IS BECAUSE MY KINGDOM LIES OUTSIDE THE TIME AND SPACE YOU KNOW.
NOW, COME! YOU MUST TURN AWAY FROM THE WORLD YOU HAVE LEFT AND JOIN ME. SOON YOU WILL HAVE NO MEMORY AND NO SHAPE...
WAIT! TEZCATLIPOCA PROMISED ME NOT ONLY SAFE PASSAGE TO MICTLAN BUT ALSO SAFE RETURN. HE PROMISED ME THE SECRETS OF MAGIC.
YOU DON'T KNOW WHO I AM! I'M NOT JUST AN ORDINARY LITTLE GIRL.
LOOK.
HMM.
DO YOU THINK THE LORD OF THE DEAD LAND HAS NEVER SEEN THE LIKES OF YOU BEFORE, BOYGIRL?
TEZCATLIPOCA CAN MAKE NO PROMISES ON MY BEHALF.
YOU WILL REMAIN WITH ME HERE AND TAKE YOUR PLACE IN THE SOIL WITH THE REST OF THE DEAD. THE ONLY SECRET YOU WILL LEARN IS THAT ALL WHO LIVE MUST COME IN THE END TO FEED MY GARDEN.
WHAT IF I RUN PAST YOU?
IF YOU RUN PAST ME, YOU RUN STRAIGHT INTO THE ARMS OF THE TZITZIMIME, THE STAR DEMONS. THAT IS SOMETHING YOU WOULD NOT WISH TO DO.
THERE IS ONE HERE WHO KNOWS YOU WELL. WOULD YOU LIKE TO SEE HIM?

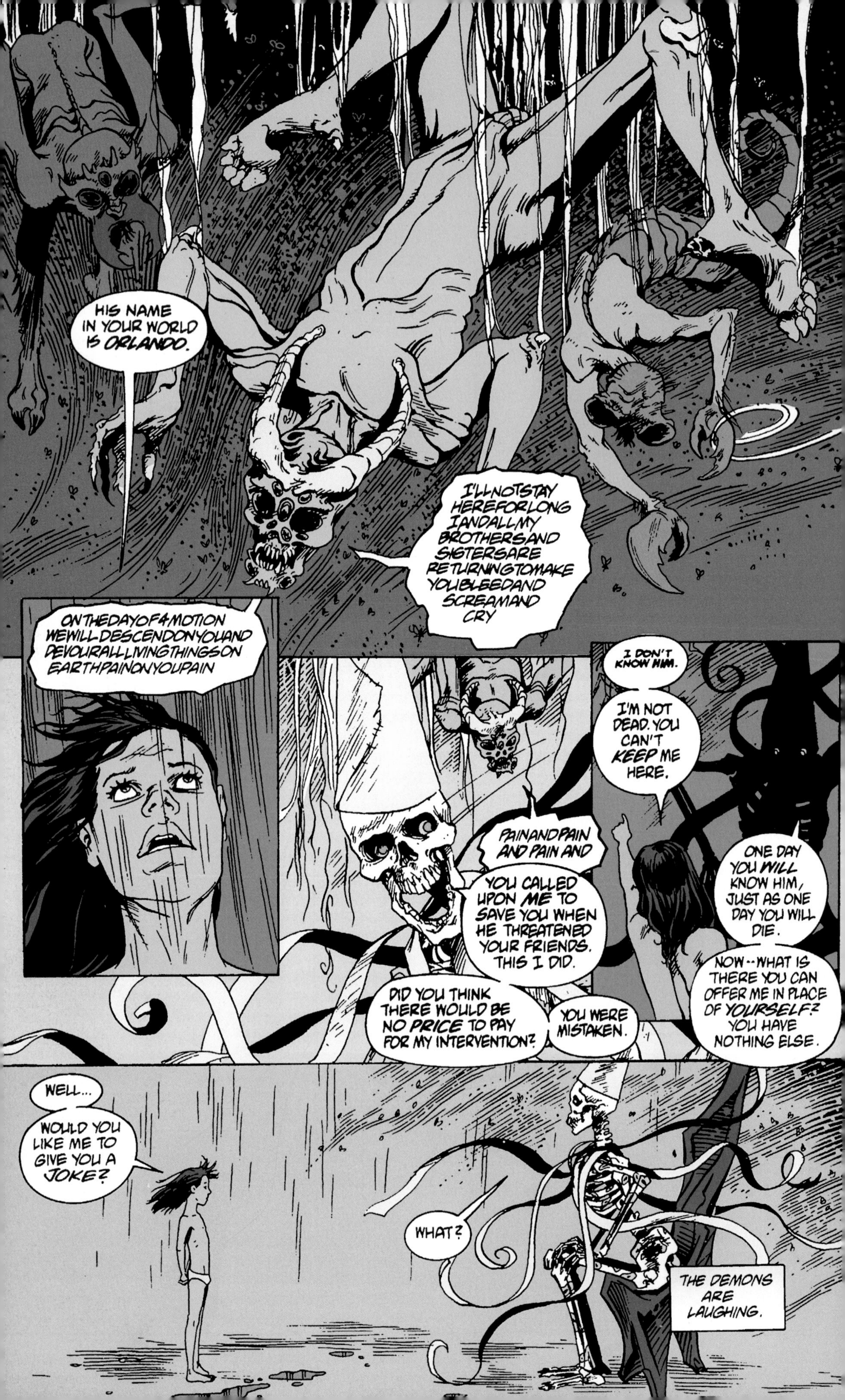
HIS NAME IN YOUR WORLD IS ORLANDO.
I'LLNOTSTAY HEREFORLONG IANDALLMY BROTHERSAND SISTERSARE RETURNINGTOMAKE YOUBLEEDAND SCREAMAND CRY
ONTHEDAYOF4MOTION WEWILLDESCENDONYOUAND DEVOURALLLIVINGTHINGSON EARTHPAINONYOUPAIN
PAINANDPAIN AND PAIN AND
YOU CALLED UPON ME TO SAVE YOU WHEN HE THREATENED YOUR FRIENDS. THIS I DID.
DID YOU THINK THERE WOULD BE NO PRICE TO PAY FOR MY INTERVENTION?
YOU WERE MISTAKEN.
I DON'T KNOW HIM.
I'M NOT DEAD. YOU CAN'T KEEP ME HERE.
ONE DAY YOU WILL KNOW HIM, JUST AS ONE DAY YOU WILL DIE.
NOW--WHAT IS THERE YOU CAN OFFER ME IN PLACE OF YOURSELF? YOU HAVE NOTHING ELSE.
WELL...
WOULD YOU LIKE ME TO GIVE YOU A JOKE?
WHAT?
THE DEMONS ARE LAUGHING.

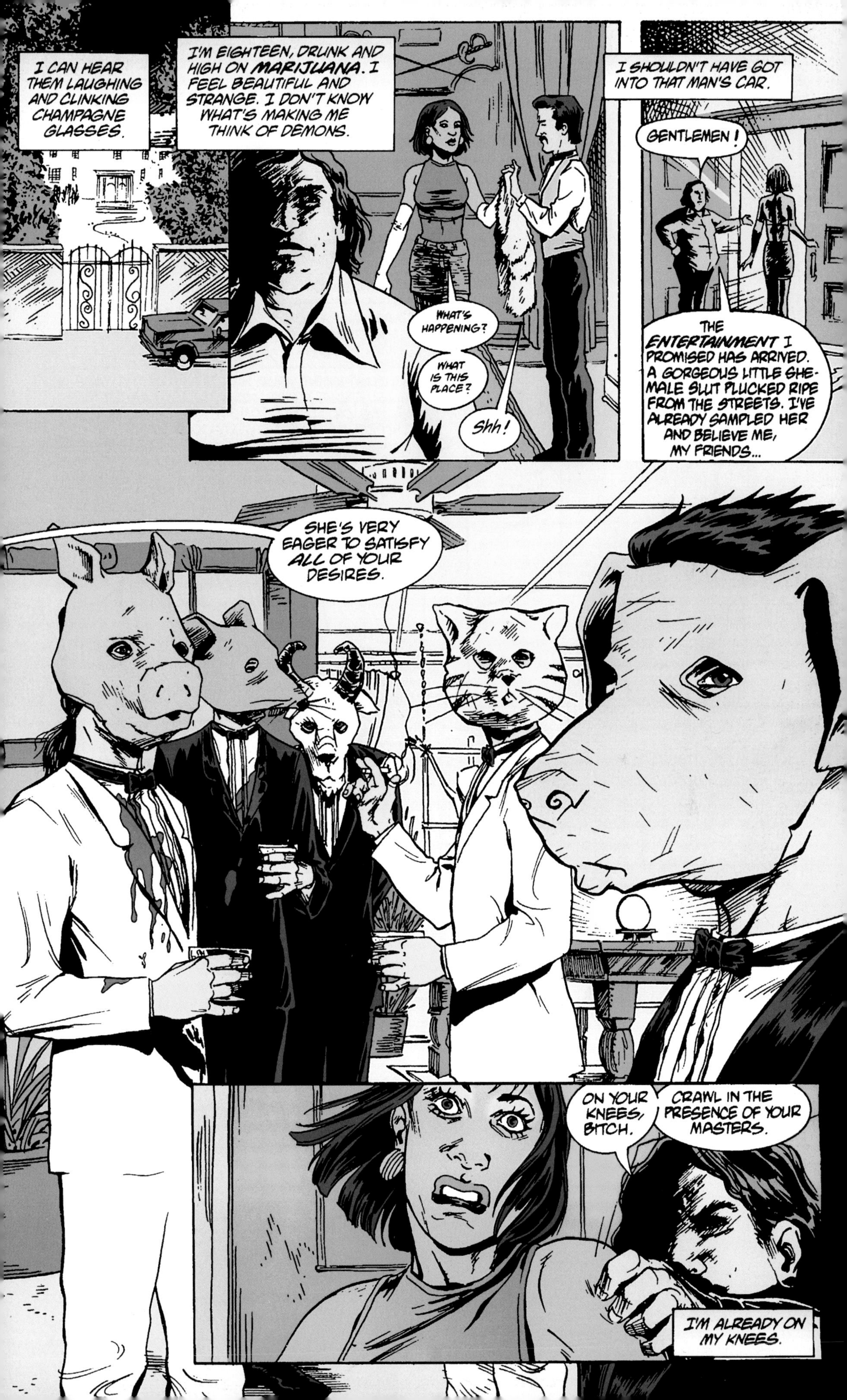
I CAN HEAR THEM LAUGHING AND CLINKING CHAMPAGNE GLASSES.
I'M EIGHTEEN, DRUNK AND HIGH ON MARIJUANA. I FEEL BEAUTIFUL AND STRANGE. I DON'T KNOW WHAT'S MAKING ME THINK OF DEMONS.
WHAT'S HAPPENING?
WHAT IS THIS PLACE?
Shh!
I SHOULDN'T HAVE GOT INTO THAT MAN'S CAR.
GENTLEMEN!
THE ENTERTAINMENT I PROMISED HAS ARRIVED. A GORGEOUS LITTLE SHE-MALE SLUT PLUCKED RIPE FROM THE STREETS. I'VE ALREADY SAMPLED HER AND BELIEVE ME, MY FRIENDS...
SHE'S VERY EAGER TO SATISFY ALL OF YOUR DESIRES.
ON YOUR KNEES, BITCH.
CRAWL IN THE PRESENCE OF YOUR MASTERS.
I'M ALREADY ON MY KNEES.

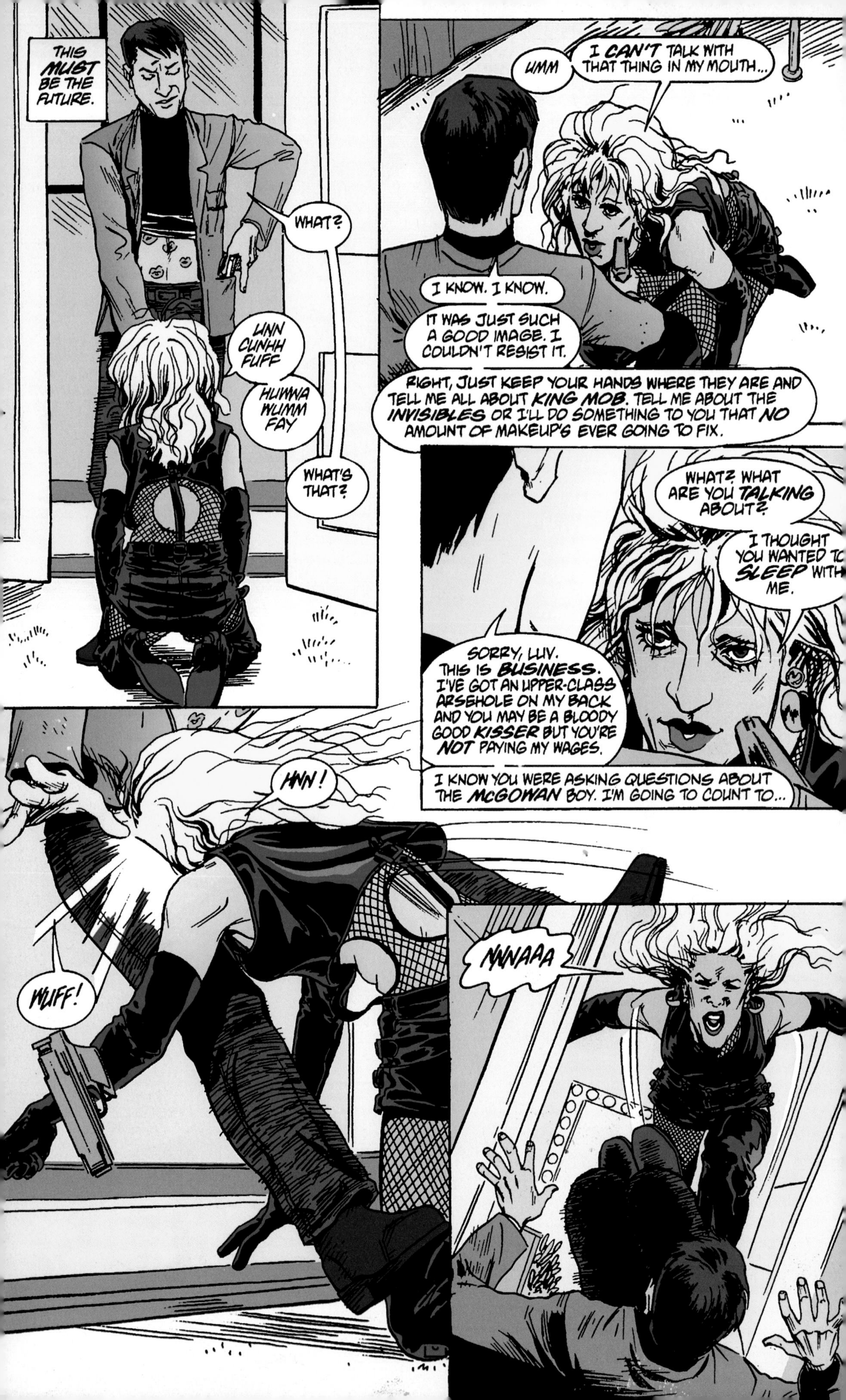
THIS MUST BE THE FUTURE.
WHAT?
UNN CUNHH FUFF
HUWWA WUMM FAY
WHAT'S THAT?
UMM
I CAN'T TALK WITH THAT THING IN MY MOUTH...
I KNOW. I KNOW.
IT WAS JUST SUCH A GOOD IMAGE. I COULDN'T RESIST IT.
RIGHT, JUST KEEP YOUR HANDS WHERE THEY ARE AND TELL ME ALL ABOUT KING MOB. TELL ME ABOUT THE INVISIBLES OR I'LL DO SOMETHING TO YOU THAT NO AMOUNT OF MAKEUP'S EVER GOING TO FIX.
WHAT? WHAT ARE YOU TALKING ABOUT?
I THOUGHT YOU WANTED TO SLEEP WITH ME.
SORRY, LUV. THIS IS BUSINESS. I'VE GOT AN UPPER-CLASS ARSEHOLE ON MY BACK AND YOU MAY BE A BLOODY GOOD KISSER BUT YOU'RE NOT PAYING MY WAGES.
I KNOW YOU WERE ASKING QUESTIONS ABOUT THE McGOWAN BOY. I'M GOING TO COUNT TO...
HNN!
WUFF!
NNNAAA

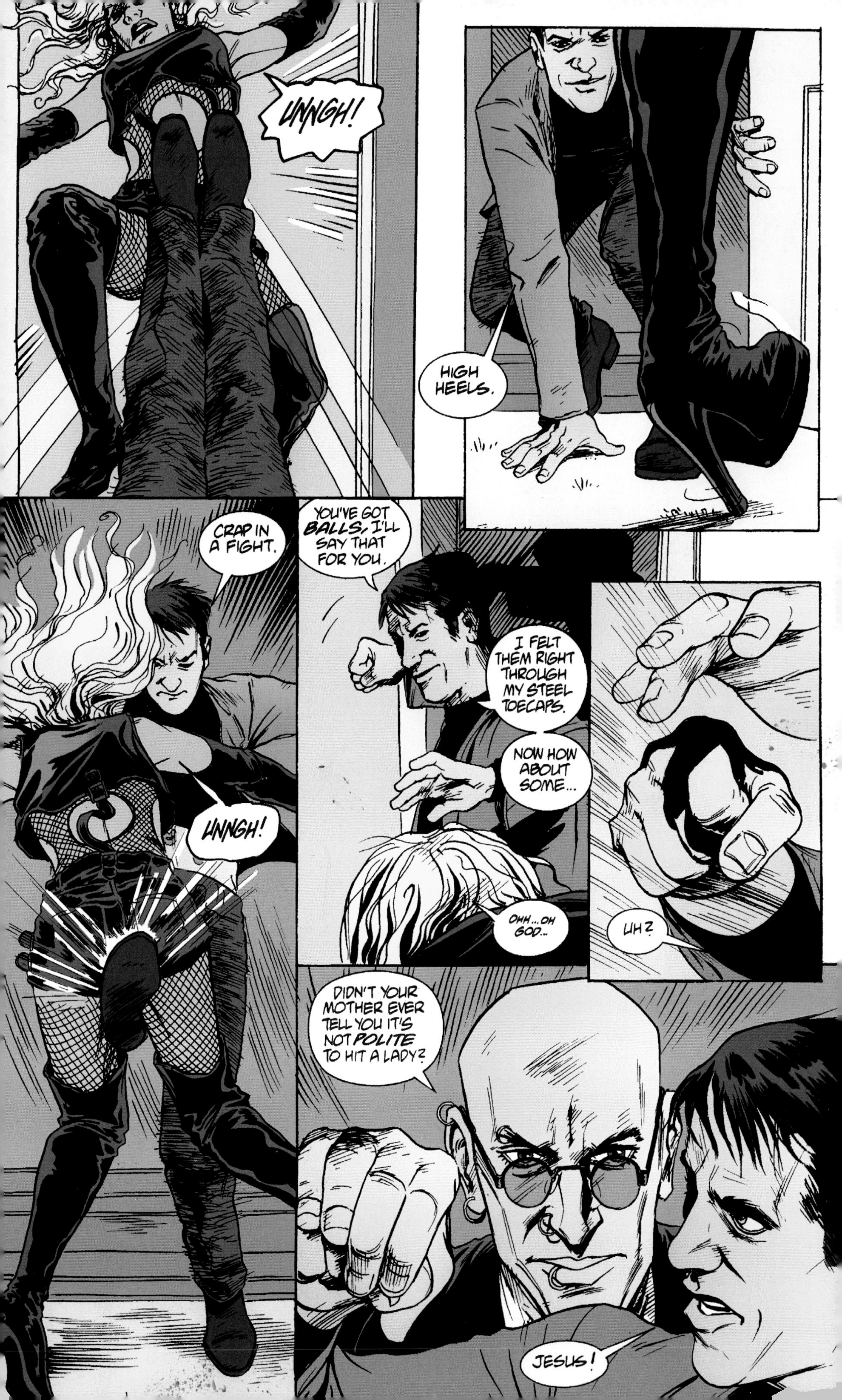
UNNGH!
HIGH HEELS.
CRAP IN A FIGHT.
UNNGH!
YOU'VE GOT BALLS, I'LL SAY THAT FOR YOU.
I FELT THEM RIGHT THROUGH MY STEEL TOECAPS.
NOW HOW ABOUT SOME...
OHH...OH GOD...
UH?
DIDN'T YOUR MOTHER EVER TELL YOU IT'S NOT POLITE TO HIT A LADY?
JESUS!

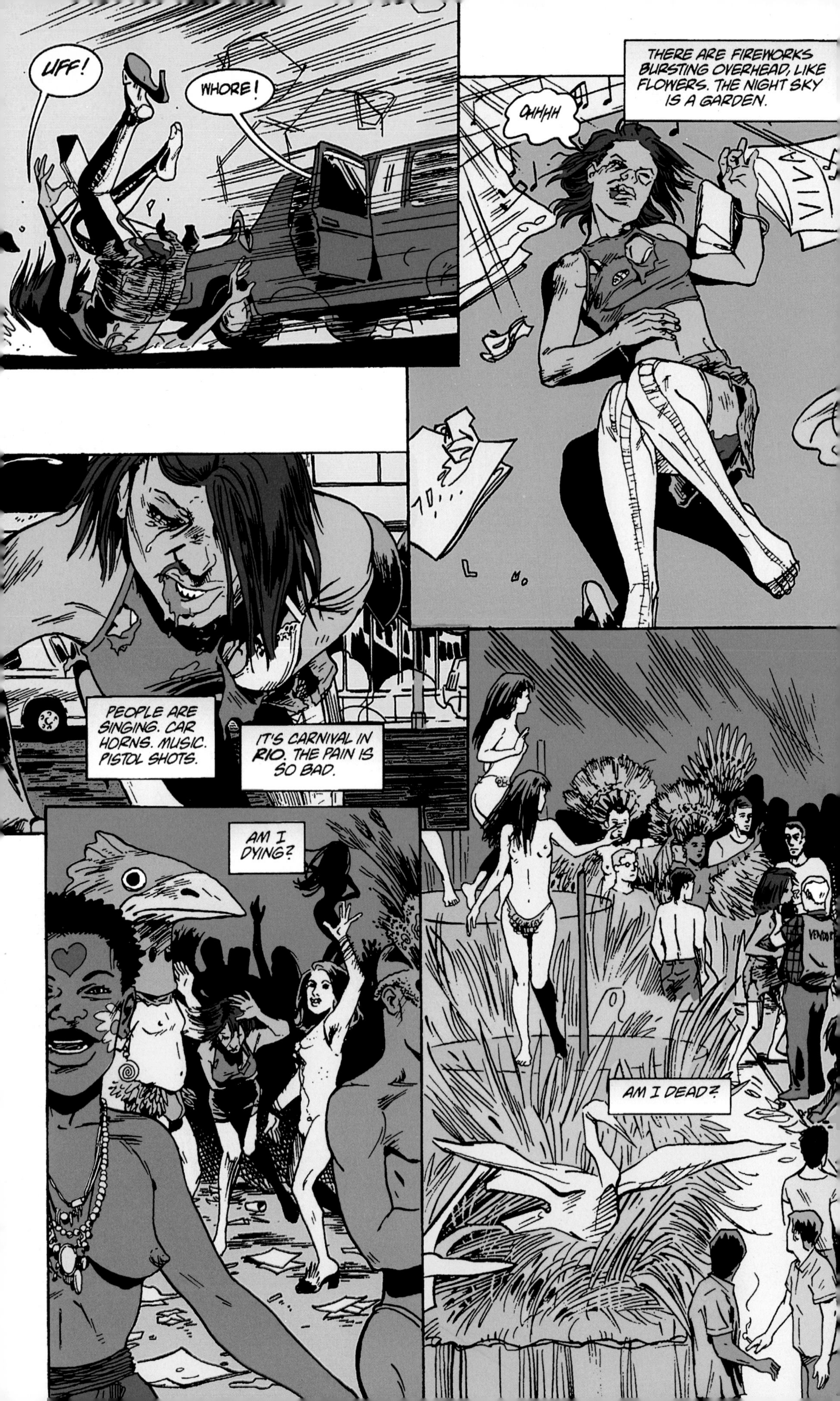
UFF!
WHORE!
OHHHH
THERE ARE FIREWORKS BURSTING OVERHEAD, LIKE FLOWERS. THE NIGHT SKY IS A GARDEN.
VIVA
PEOPLE ARE SINGING. CAR HORNS. MUSIC. PISTOL SHOTS.
IT'S CARNIVAL IN RIO. THE PAIN IS SO BAD.
AM I DYING?
AM I DEAD?

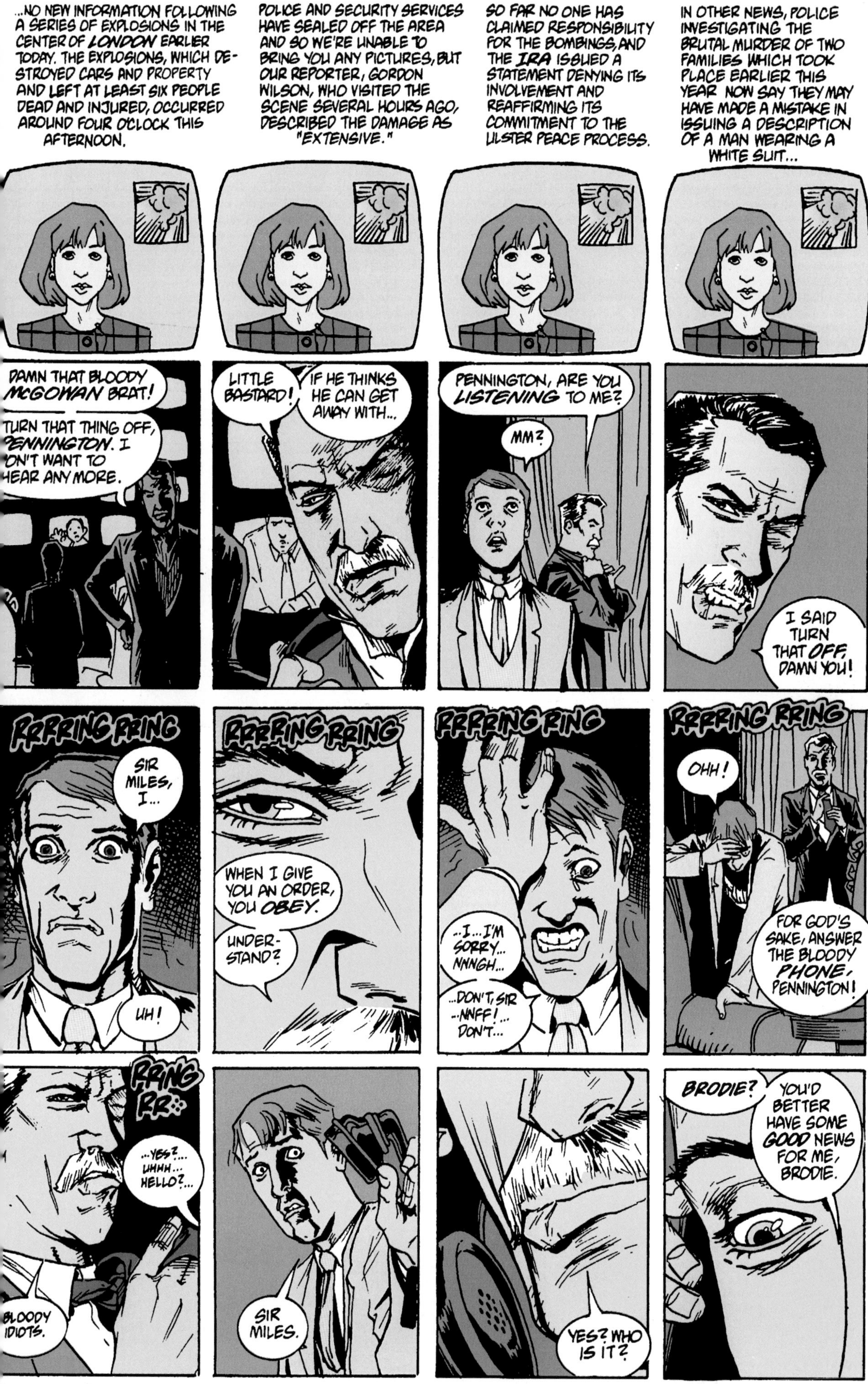
...NO NEW INFORMATION FOLLOWING A SERIES OF EXPLOSIONS IN THE CENTER OF LONDON EARLIER TODAY. THE EXPLOSIONS, WHICH DESTROYED CARS AND PROPERTY AND LEFT AT LEAST SIX PEOPLE DEAD AND INJURED, OCCURRED AROUND FOUR O'CLOCK THIS AFTERNOON.
POLICE AND SECURITY SERVICES HAVE SEALED OFF THE AREA AND SO WE'RE UNABLE TO BRING YOU ANY PICTURES, BUT OUR REPORTER, GORDON WILSON, WHO VISITED THE SCENE SEVERAL HOURS AGO, DESCRIBED THE DAMAGE AS "EXTENSIVE."
SO FAR NO ONE HAS CLAIMED RESPONSIBILITY FOR THE BOMBINGS, AND THE IRA ISSUED A STATEMENT DENYING ITS INVOLVEMENT AND REAFFIRMING ITS COMMITMENT TO THE ULSTER PEACE PROCESS.
IN OTHER NEWS, POLICE INVESTIGATING THE BRUTAL MURDER OF TWO FAMILIES WHICH TOOK PLACE EARLIER THIS YEAR NOW SAY THEY MAY HAVE MADE A MISTAKE IN ISSUING A DESCRIPTION OF A MAN WEARING A WHITE SUIT...
DAMN THAT BLOODY McGOWAN BRAT!
TURN THAT THING OFF, PENNINGTON. I DON'T WANT TO HEAR ANY MORE.
LITTLE BASTARD!
IF HE THINKS HE CAN GET AWAY WITH...
PENNINGTON, ARE YOU LISTENING TO ME?
MM?
I SAID TURN THAT OFF, DAMN YOU!
RRRRING RRING
SIR MILES, I...
UH!
RRRRING RRING
WHEN I GIVE YOU AN ORDER, YOU OBEY.
UNDERSTAND?
RRRRING RRING
...I...I'M SORRY... NNNGH...
...DON'T, SIR ...NNFF!... DON'T...
RRRRING RRING
OHH!
FOR GOD'S SAKE, ANSWER THE BLOODY PHONE, PENNINGTON!
RRING RR
...YES?... UHHH... HELLO?...
BLOODY IDIOTS.
SIR MILES.
YES? WHO IS IT?
BRODIE?
YOU'D BETTER HAVE SOME GOOD NEWS FOR ME, BRODIE.

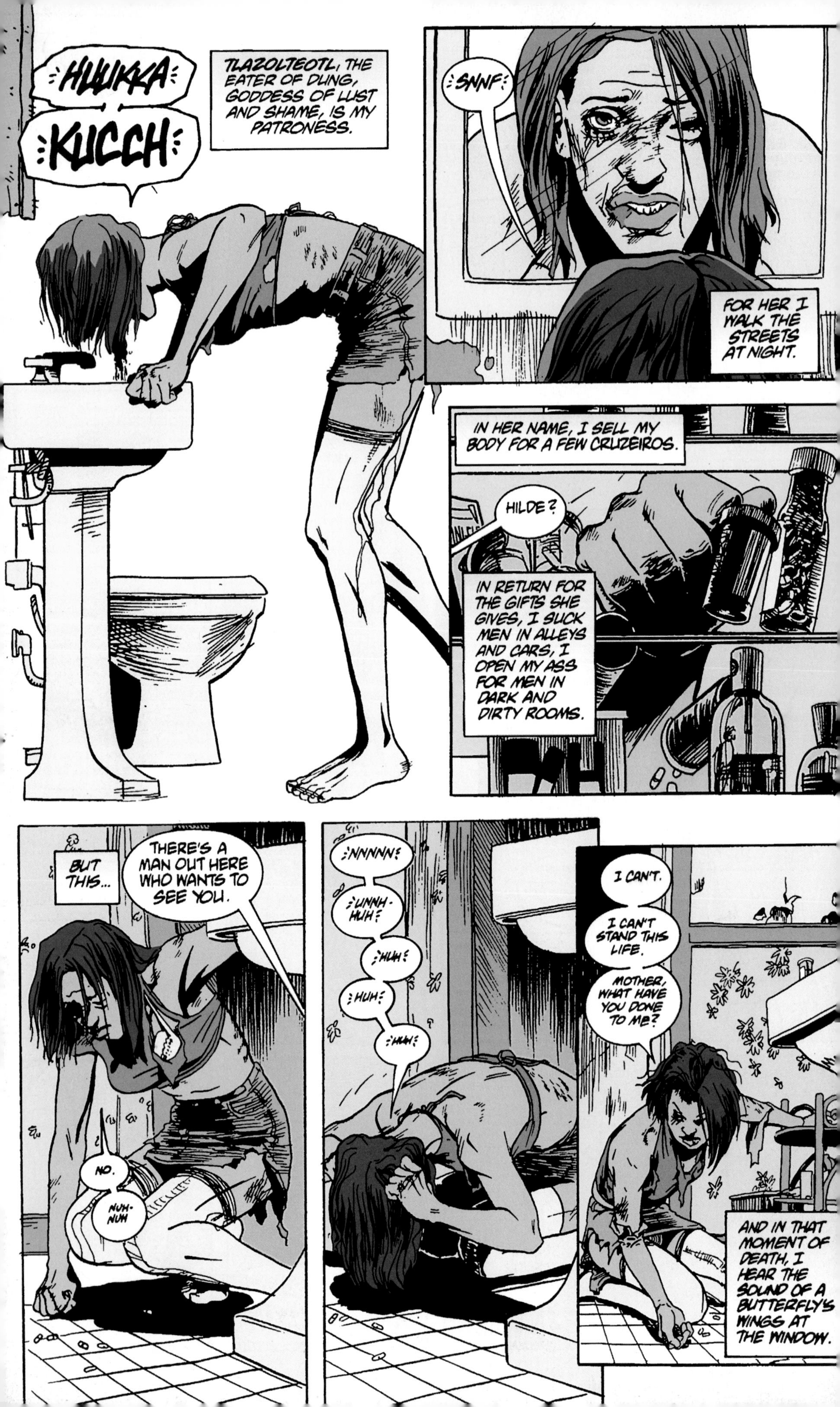
HUUKKA
KUCCH
TLAZOLTEOTL, THE EATER OF DUNG, GODDESS OF LUST AND SHAME, IS MY PATRONESS.
SNNF
FOR HER I WALK THE STREETS AT NIGHT.
IN HER NAME, I SELL MY BODY FOR A FEW CRUZEIROS.
HILDE?
IN RETURN FOR THE GIFTS SHE GIVES, I SUCK MEN IN ALLEYS AND CARS, I OPEN MY ASS FOR MEN IN DARK AND DIRTY ROOMS.
BUT THIS...
THERE'S A MAN OUT HERE WHO WANTS TO SEE YOU.
NO.
NUH-NUH
NNNNN
UNNH-HUH
HUH
HUH
HUH
I CAN'T.
I CAN'T STAND THIS LIFE.
MOTHER, WHAT HAVE YOU DONE TO ME?
AND IN THAT MOMENT OF DEATH, I HEAR THE SOUND OF A BUTTERFLY'S WINGS AT THE WINDOW.

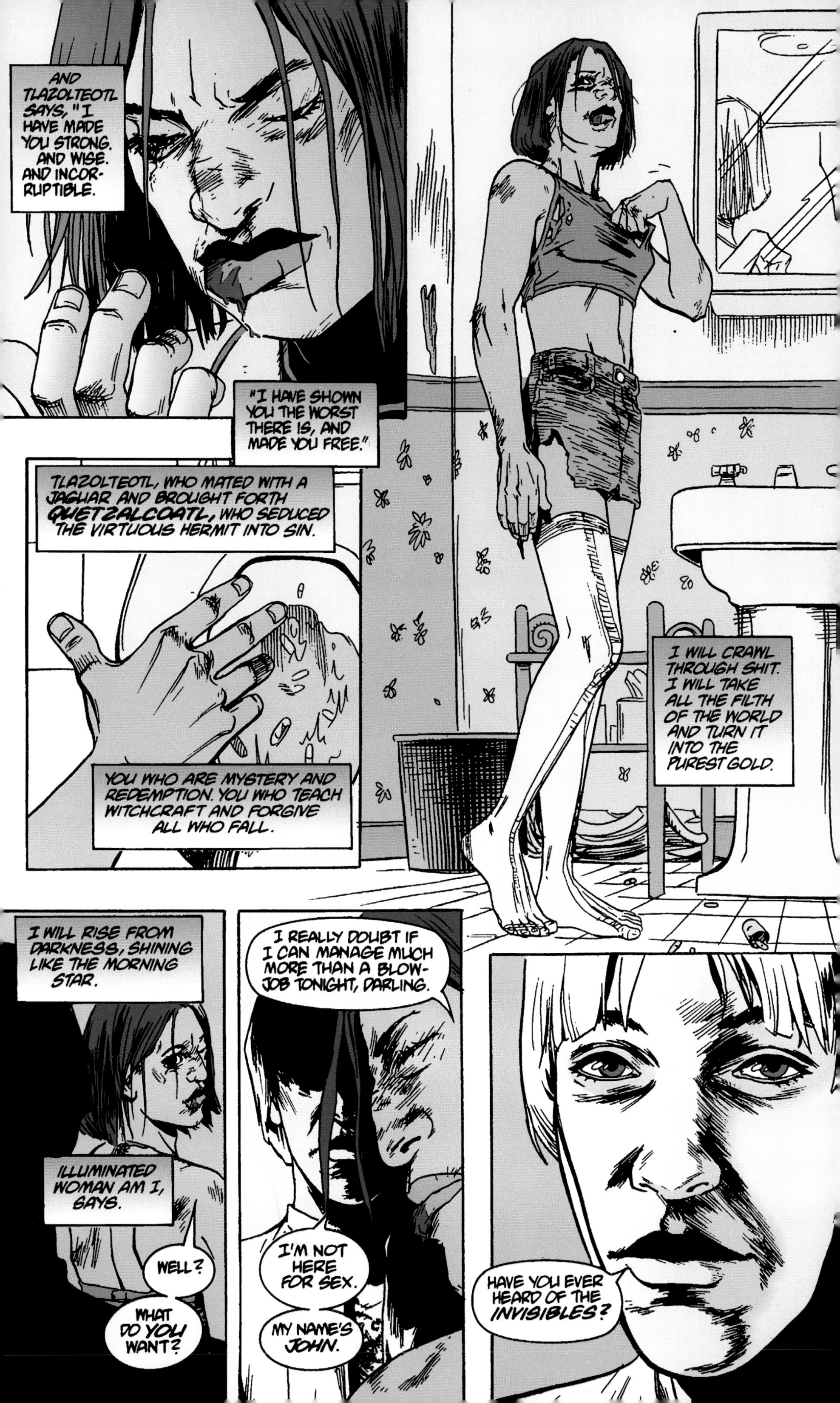

AND TLAZOLTEOTL SAYS, "I HAVE MADE YOU STRONG. AND WISE. AND INCORRUPTIBLE.
"I HAVE SHOWN YOU THE WORST THERE IS, AND MADE YOU FREE."
TLAZOLTEOTL, WHO MATED WITH A JAGUAR AND BROUGHT FORTH QUETZALCOATL, WHO SEDUCED THE VIRTUOUS HERMIT INTO SIN.
YOU WHO ARE MYSTERY AND REDEMPTION. YOU WHO TEACH WITCHCRAFT AND FORGIVE ALL WHO FALL.
I WILL CRAWL THROUGH SHIT. I WILL TAKE ALL THE FILTH OF THE WORLD AND TURN IT INTO THE PUREST GOLD.
I WILL RISE FROM DARKNESS, SHINING LIKE THE MORNING STAR.
ILLUMINATED WOMAN AM I, SAYS.
WELL?
WHAT DO YOU WANT?
I REALLY DOUBT IF I CAN MANAGE MUCH MORE THAN A BLOW-JOB TONIGHT, DARLING.
I'M NOT HERE FOR SEX.
MY NAME'S JOHN.
HAVE YOU EVER HEARD OF THE INVISIBLES?

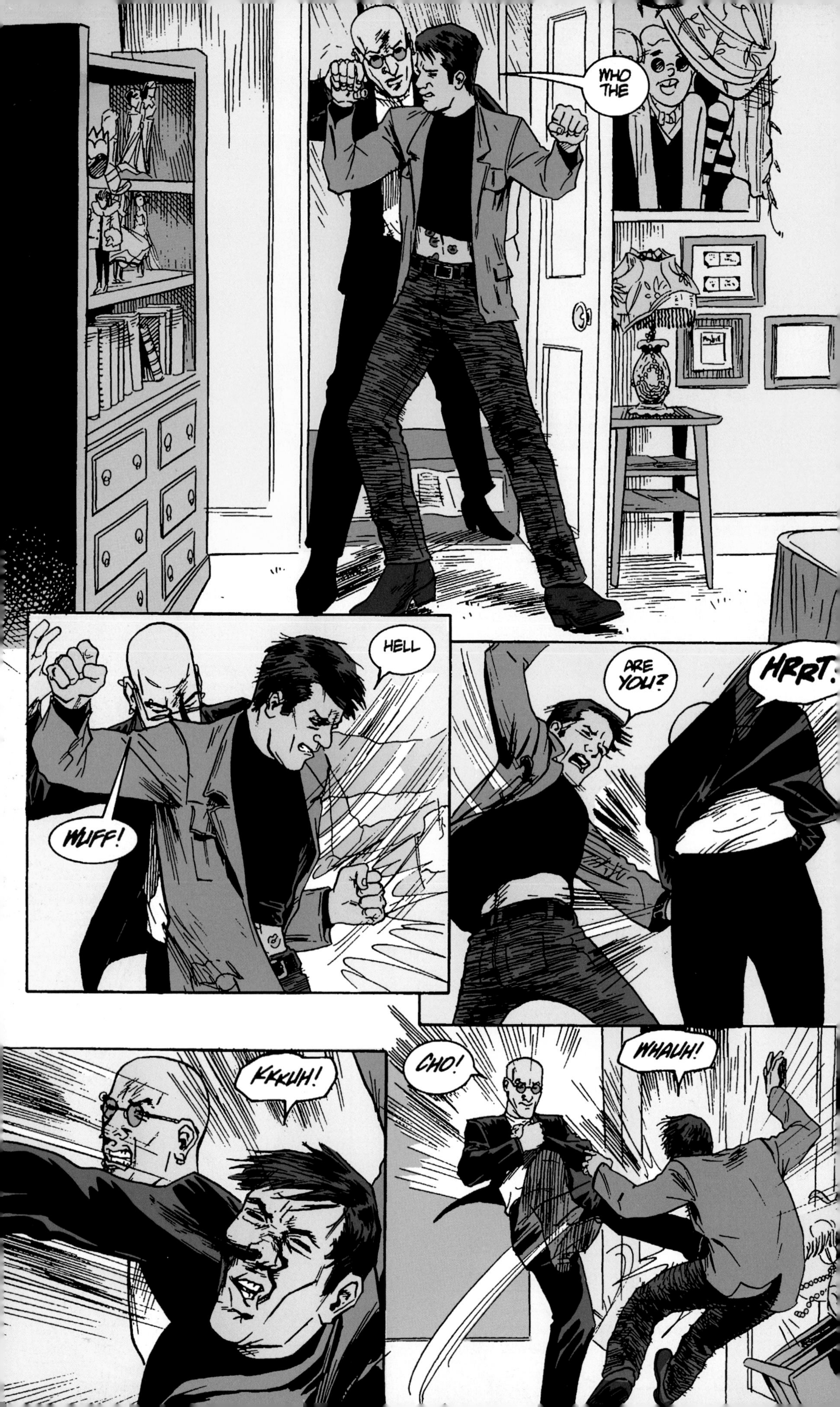

WHO THE
HELL
WUFF!
ARE YOU?
HRRT.
KKKUH!
CHO!
WHAUH!

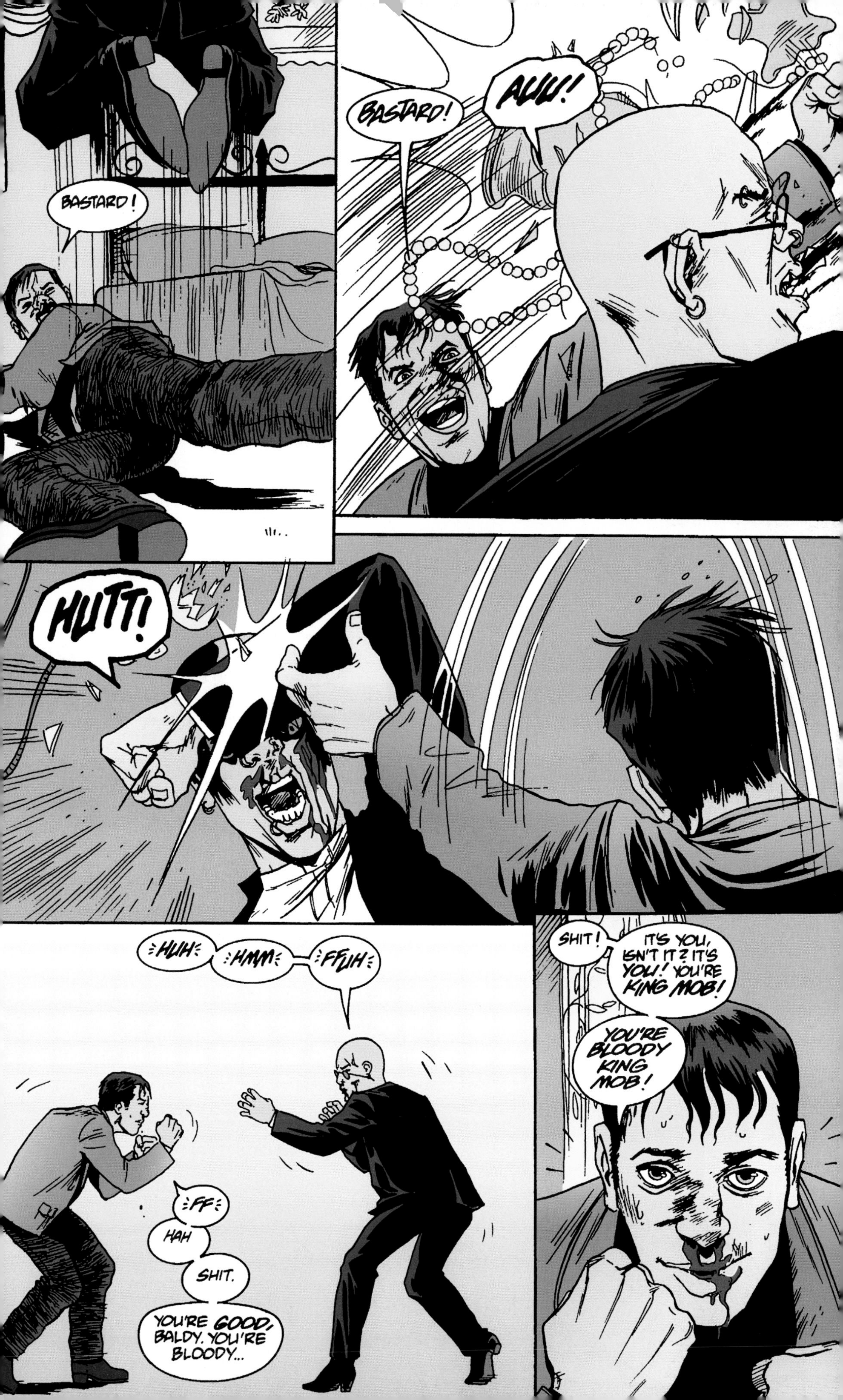
BASTARD!
BASTARD!
AUU!
HUTT!
HUH
HMM
FFUH
FF
HAH
SHIT.
YOU'RE GOOD, BALDY. YOU'RE BLOODY...
SHIT!
IT'S YOU, ISN'T IT? IT'S YOU! YOU'RE KING MOB!
YOU'RE BLOODY KING MOB!

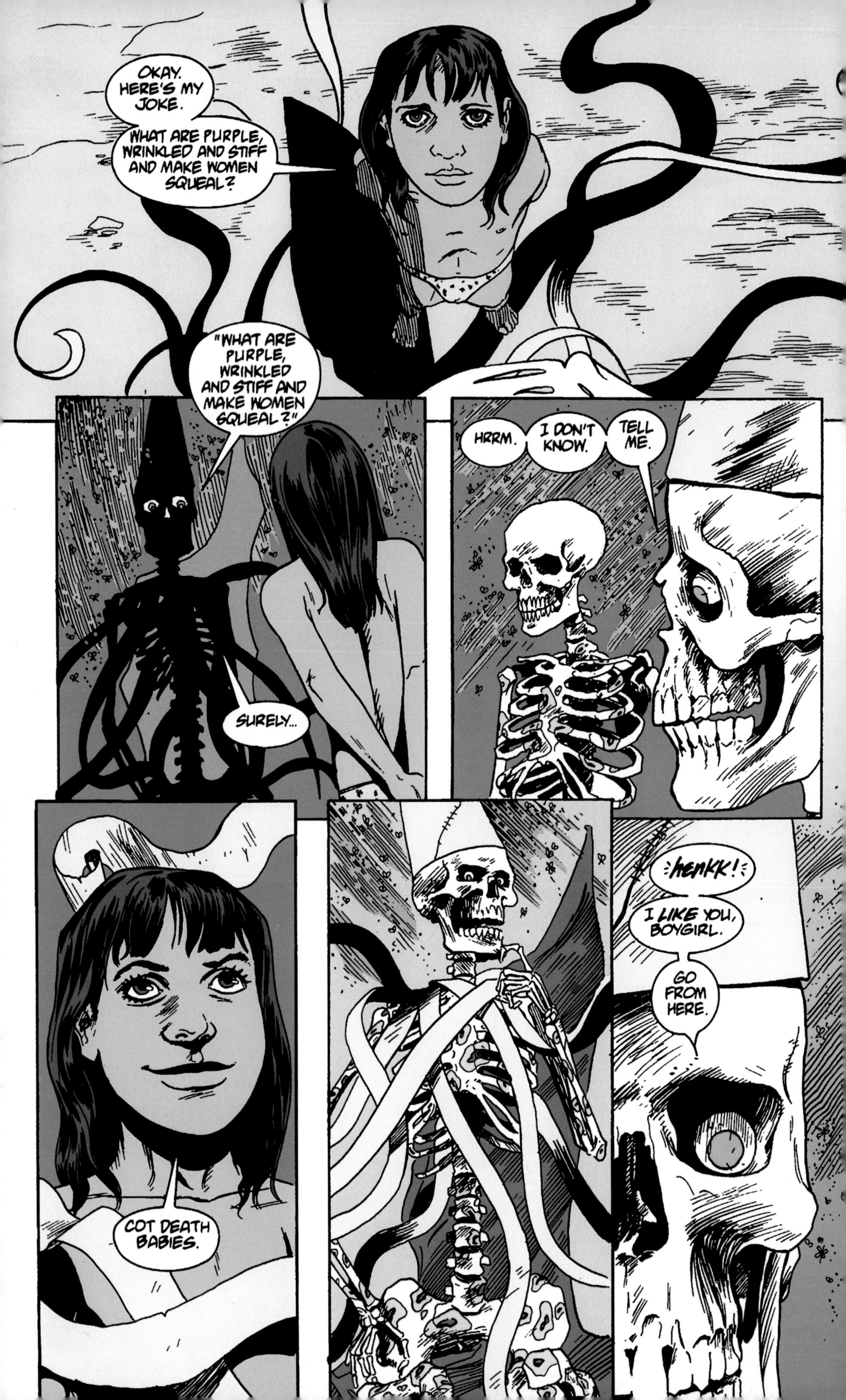
OKAY. HERE'S MY JOKE.
WHAT ARE PURPLE, WRINKLED AND STIFF AND MAKE WOMEN SQUEAL?
"WHAT ARE PURPLE, WRINKLED AND STIFF AND MAKE WOMEN SQUEAL?"
SURELY...
HRRM.
I DON'T KNOW.
TELL ME.
COT DEATH BABIES.
henkk!
I LIKE YOU, BOYGIRL.
GO FROM HERE.

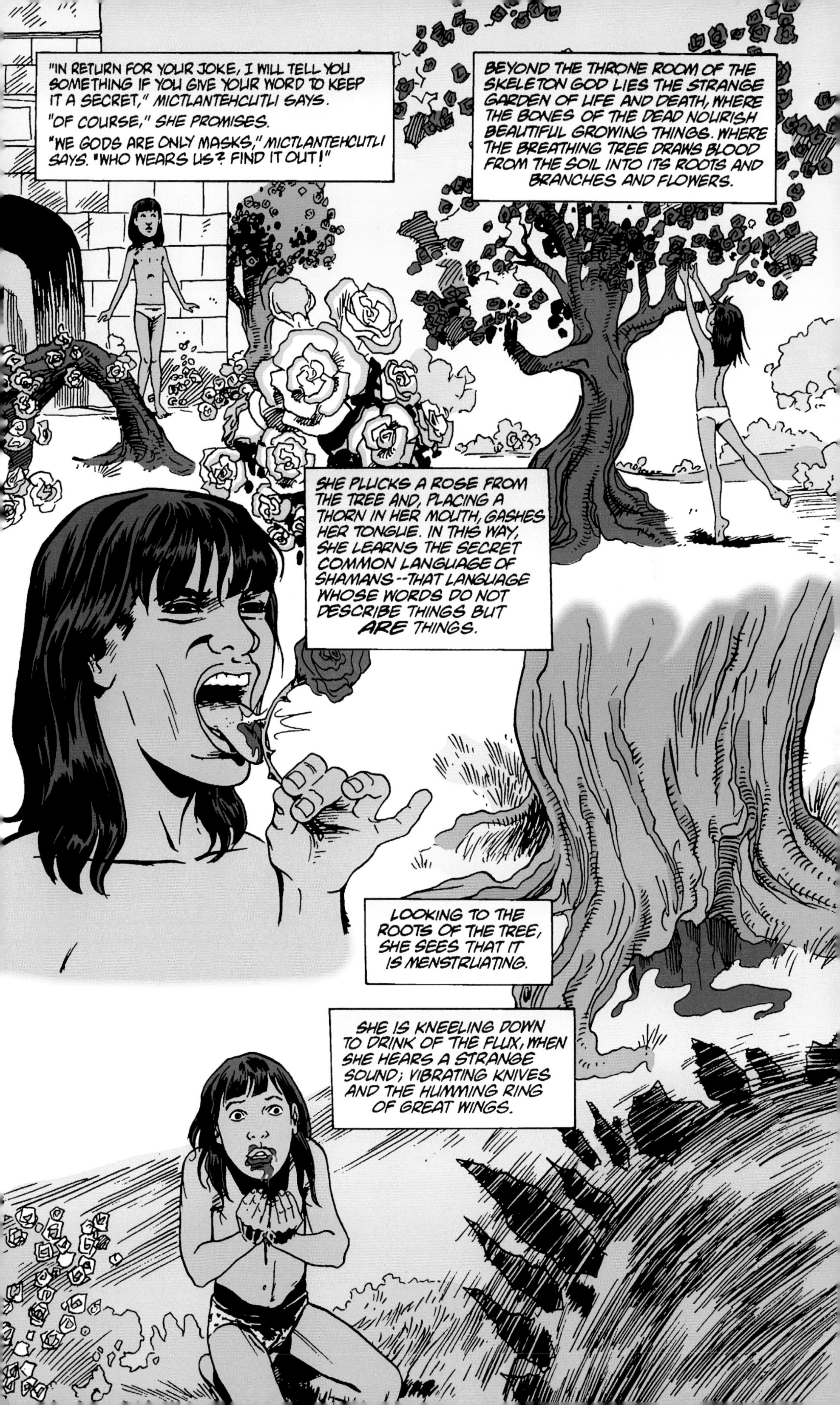
"IN RETURN FOR YOUR JOKE, I WILL TELL YOU SOMETHING IF YOU GIVE YOUR WORD TO KEEP IT A SECRET," MICTLANTEHCUTLI SAYS.
"OF COURSE," SHE PROMISES.
"WE GODS ARE ONLY MASKS," MICTLANTEHCUTLI SAYS. "WHO WEARS US? FIND IT OUT!"
BEYOND THE THRONE ROOM OF THE SKELETON GOD LIES THE STRANGE GARDEN OF LIFE AND DEATH, WHERE THE BONES OF THE DEAD NOURISH BEAUTIFUL GROWING THINGS. WHERE THE BREATHING TREE DRAWS BLOOD FROM THE SOIL INTO ITS ROOTS AND BRANCHES AND FLOWERS.
SHE PLUCKS A ROSE FROM THE TREE AND, PLACING A THORN IN HER MOUTH, GASHES HER TONGUE. IN THIS WAY, SHE LEARNS THE SECRET COMMON LANGUAGE OF SHAMANS--THAT LANGUAGE WHOSE WORDS DO NOT DESCRIBE THINGS BUT ARE THINGS.
LOOKING TO THE ROOTS OF THE TREE, SHE SEES THAT IT IS MENSTRUATING.
SHE IS KNEELING DOWN TO DRINK OF THE FLUX, WHEN SHE HEARS A STRANGE SOUND; VIBRATING KNIVES AND THE HUMMING RING OF GREAT WINGS.

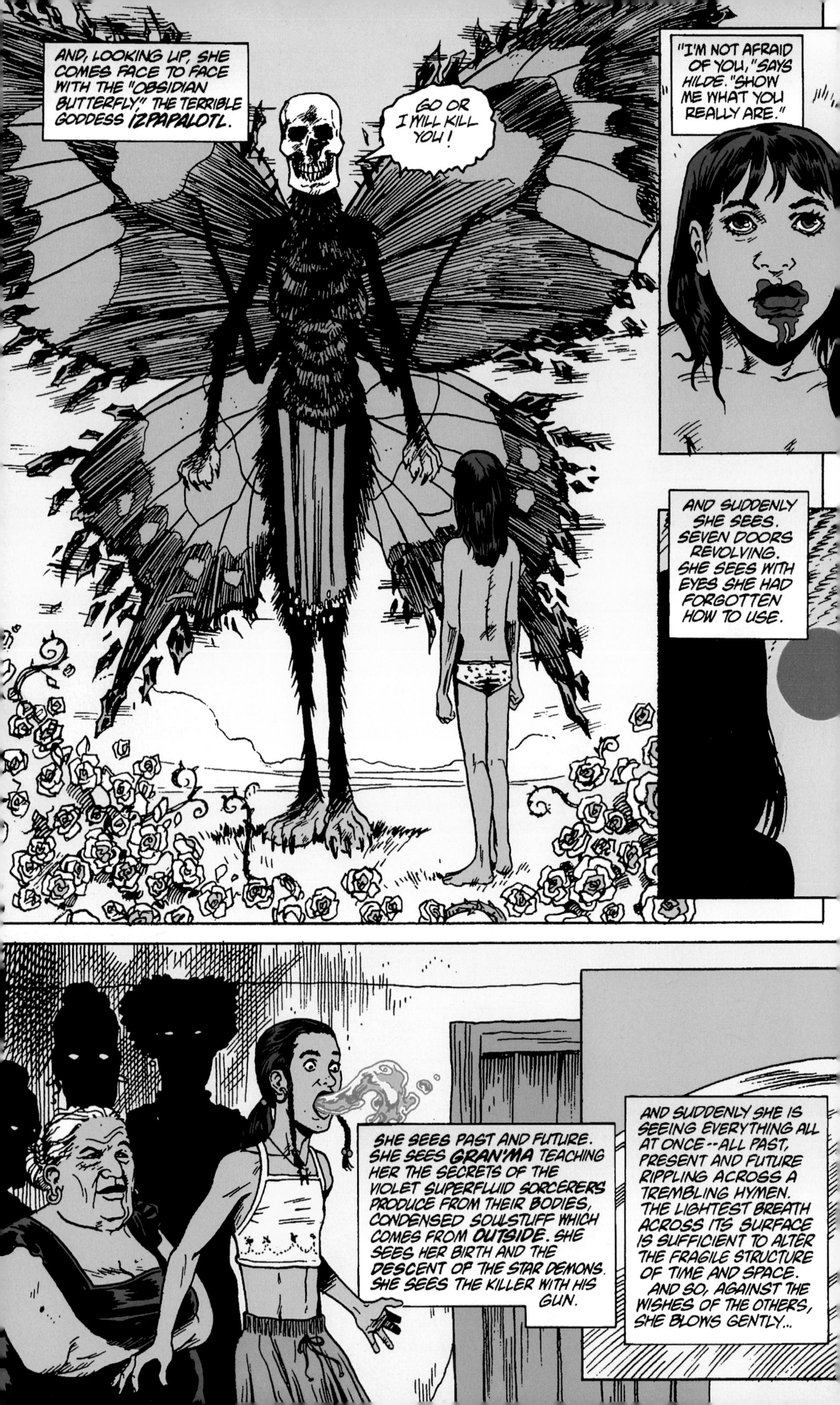

AND, LOOKING UP, SHE COMES FACE TO FACE WITH THE "OBSIDIAN BUTTERFLY," THE TERRIBLE GODDESS IZPAPALOTL.
GO OR I WILL KILL YOU!
"I'M NOT AFRAID OF YOU," SAYS HILDE. "SHOW ME WHAT YOU REALLY ARE."
AND SUDDENLY SHE SEES. SEVEN DOORS REVOLVING. SHE SEES WITH EYES SHE HAD FORGOTTEN HOW TO USE.
SHE SEES PAST AND FUTURE. SHE SEES GRAN'MA TEACHING HER THE SECRETS OF THE VIOLET SUPERFLUID SORCERERS PRODUCE FROM THEIR BODIES, CONDENSED SOULSTUFF WHICH COMES FROM OUTSIDE. SHE SEES HER BIRTH AND THE DESCENT OF THE STAR DEMONS. SHE SEES THE KILLER WITH HIS GUN.
AND SUDDENLY SHE IS SEEING EVERYTHING ALL AT ONCE--ALL PAST, PRESENT AND FUTURE RIPPLING ACROSS A TREMBLING HYMEN. THE LIGHTEST BREATH ACROSS ITS SURFACE IS SUFFICIENT TO ALTER THE FRAGILE STRUCTURE OF TIME AND SPACE. AND SO, AGAINST THE WISHES OF THE OTHERS, SHE BLOWS GENTLY...

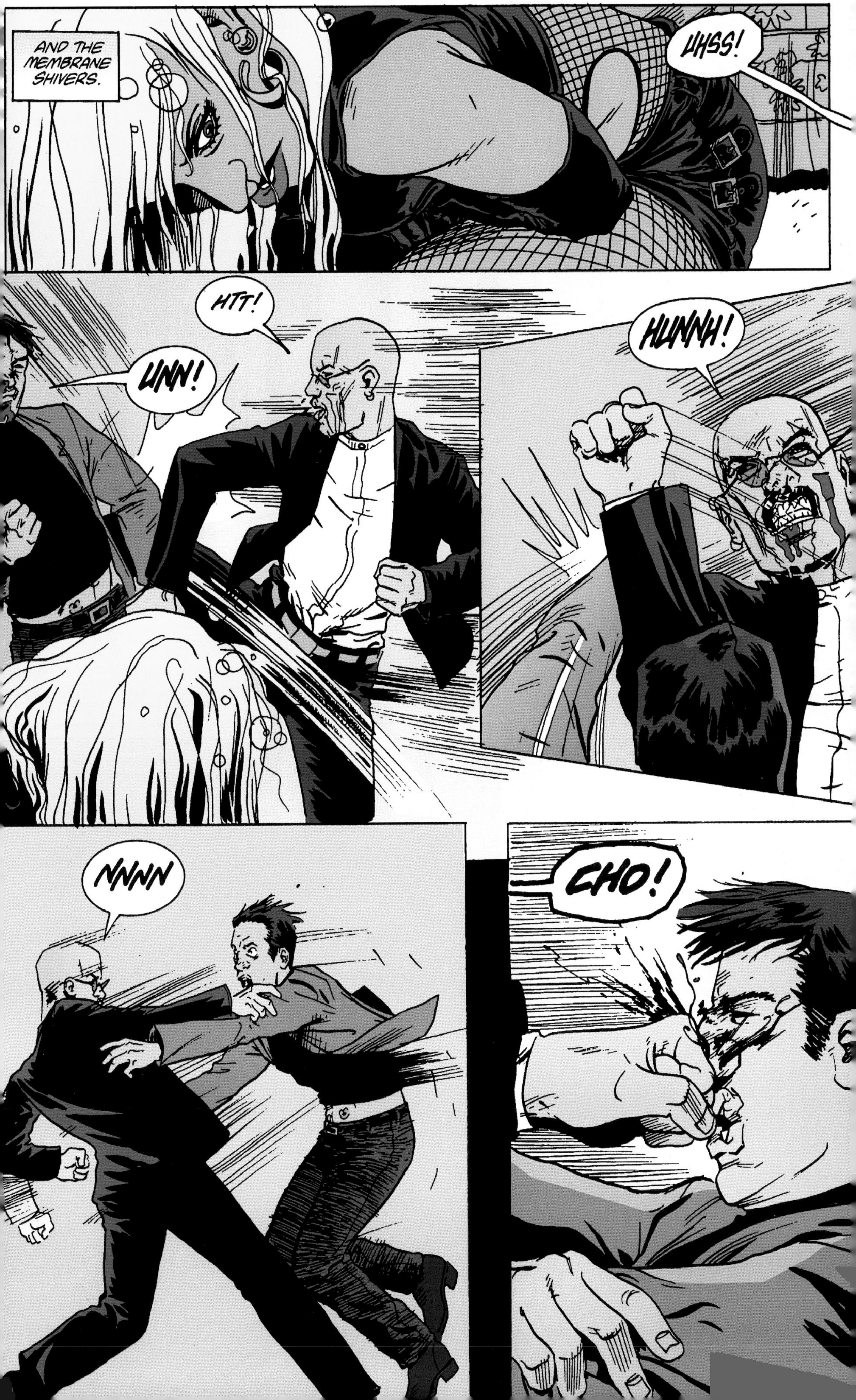
AND THE MEMBRANE SHIVERS.
UHSS!
HTT!
UNN!
HUNNH!
NNNN
CHO!

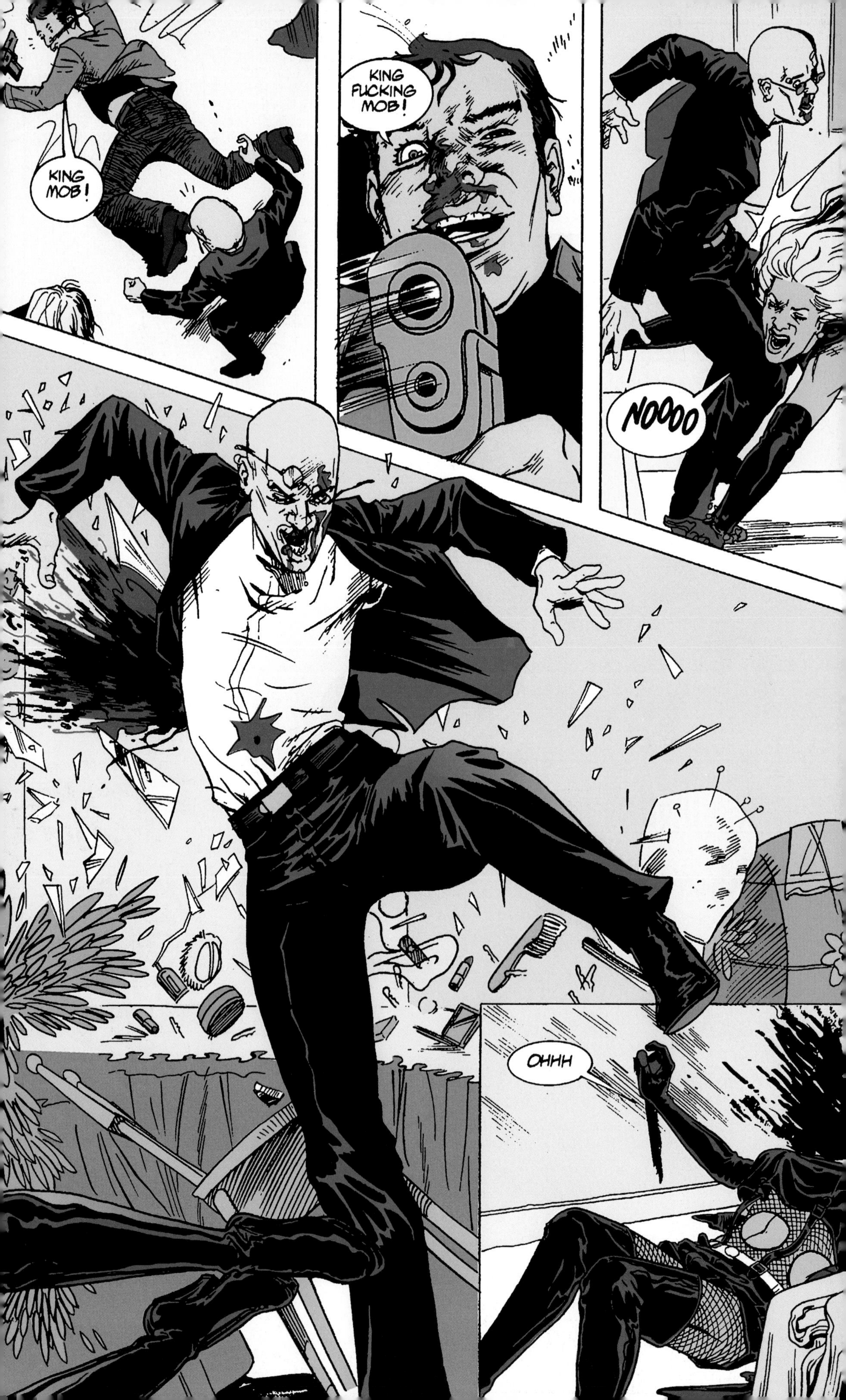

KING MOB!
KING FUCKING MOB!
NOOOO
OHHH

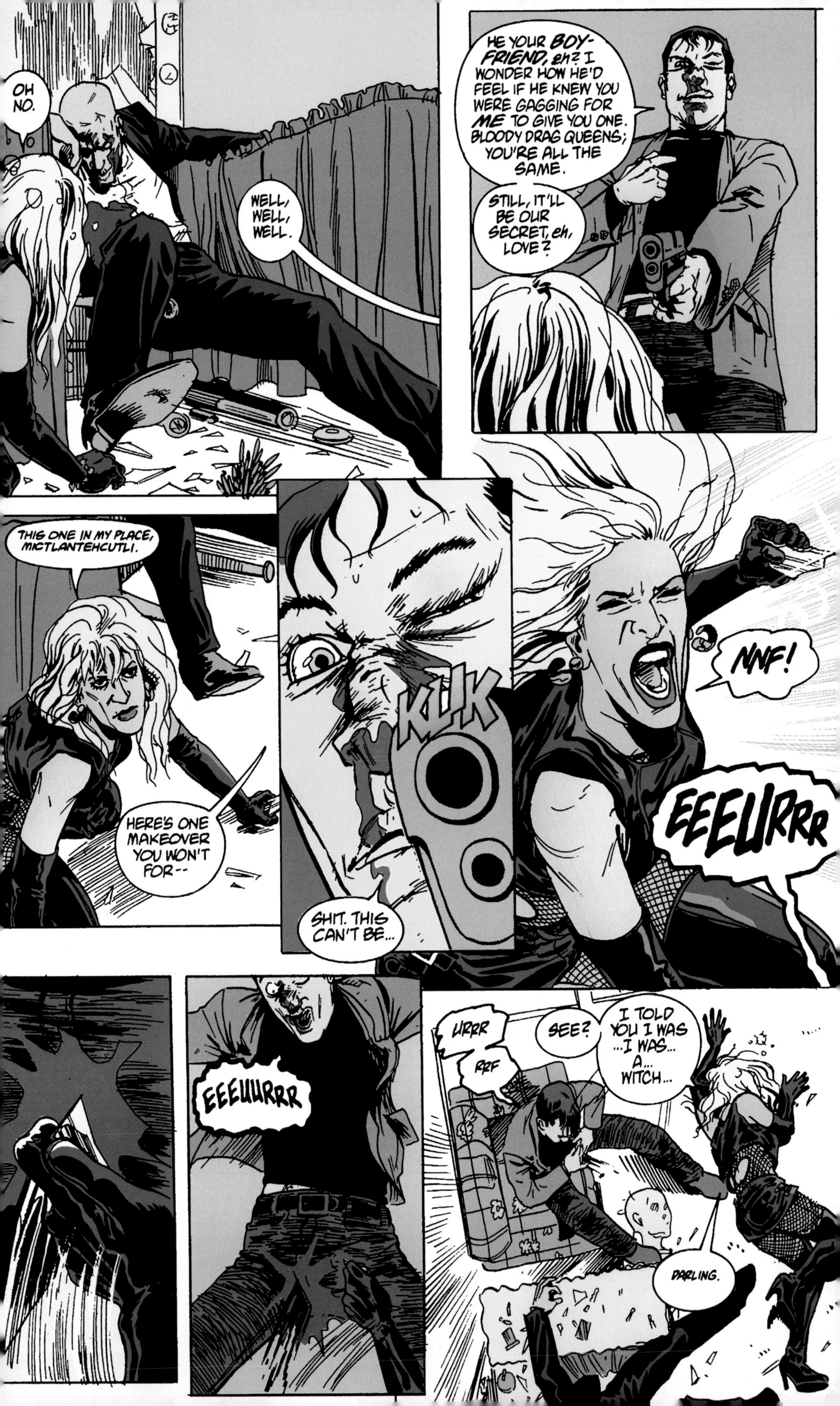

OH NO.
WELL, WELL, WELL.
HE YOUR BOY-FRIEND, eh? I WONDER HOW HE'D FEEL IF HE KNEW YOU WERE GAGGING FOR ME TO GIVE YOU ONE. BLOODY DRAG QUEENS; YOU'RE ALL THE SAME.
STILL, IT'LL BE OUR SECRET, eh, LOVE?
THIS ONE IN MY PLACE, MICTLANTEHCUTLI.
HERE'S ONE MAKEOVER YOU WON'T FOR--
KLIK
SHIT. THIS CAN'T BE...
NNF!
EEEURRR
EEEUURRR
URRR
RRF
SEE?
I TOLD YOU I WAS ...I WAS... A... WITCH...
DARLING.

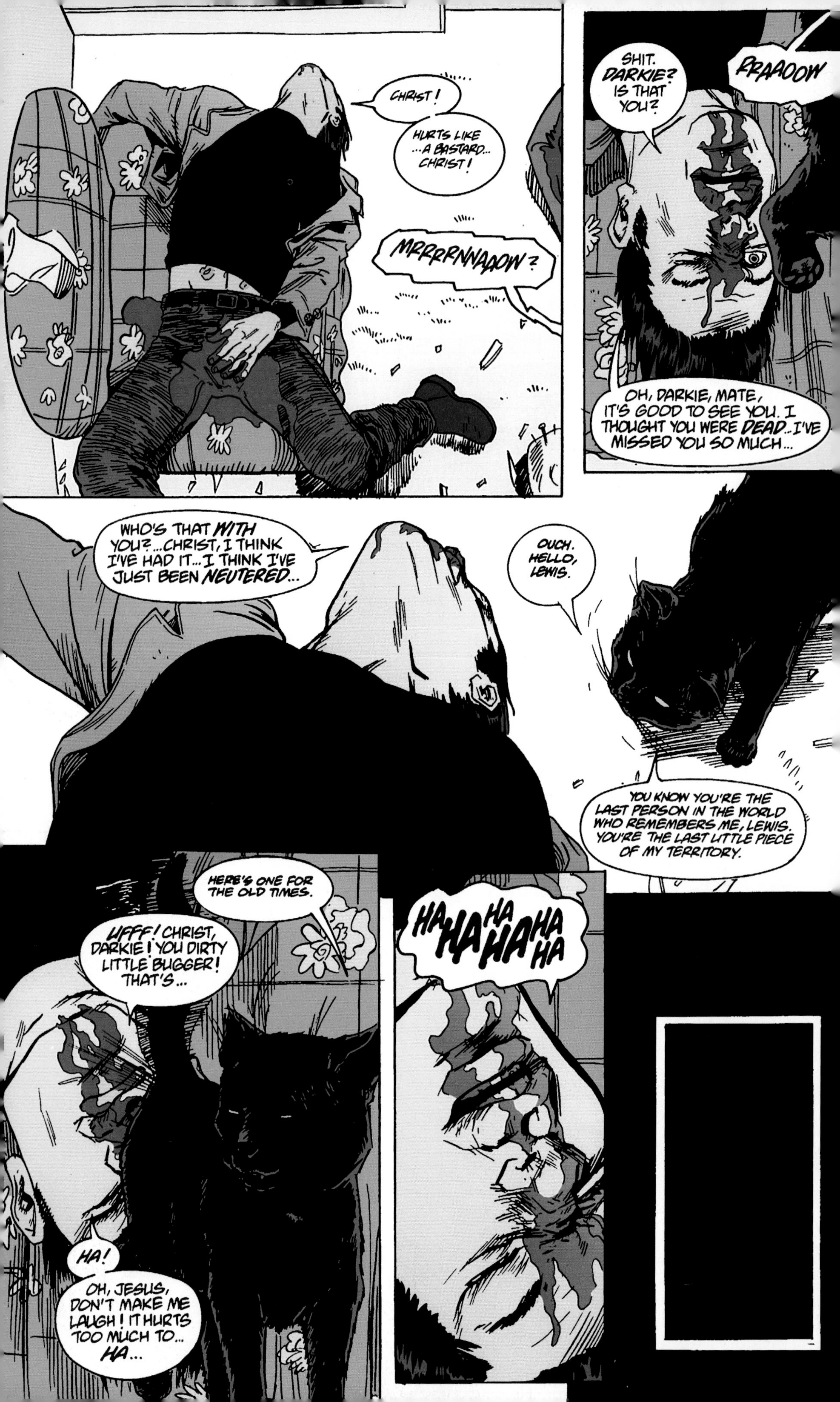
CHRIST!
HURTS LIKE ...A BASTARD... CHRIST!
MRRRRNNAAOW?
SHIT. DARKIE? IS THAT YOU?
RRAAAOOW
OH, DARKIE, MATE, IT'S GOOD TO SEE YOU. I THOUGHT YOU WERE DEAD... I'VE MISSED YOU SO MUCH...
WHO'S THAT WITH YOU? ...CHRIST, I THINK I'VE HAD IT... I THINK I'VE JUST BEEN NEUTERED...
OUCH. HELLO, LEWIS.
YOU KNOW YOU'RE THE LAST PERSON IN THE WORLD WHO REMEMBERS ME, LEWIS. YOU'RE THE LAST LITTLE PIECE OF MY TERRITORY.
HERE'S ONE FOR THE OLD TIMES.
UFFF! CHRIST, DARKIE! YOU DIRTY LITTLE BUGGER! THAT'S...
HA!
OH, JESUS, DON'T MAKE ME LAUGH! IT HURTS TOO MUCH TO... HA...
HA HA HA HA HA HA HA

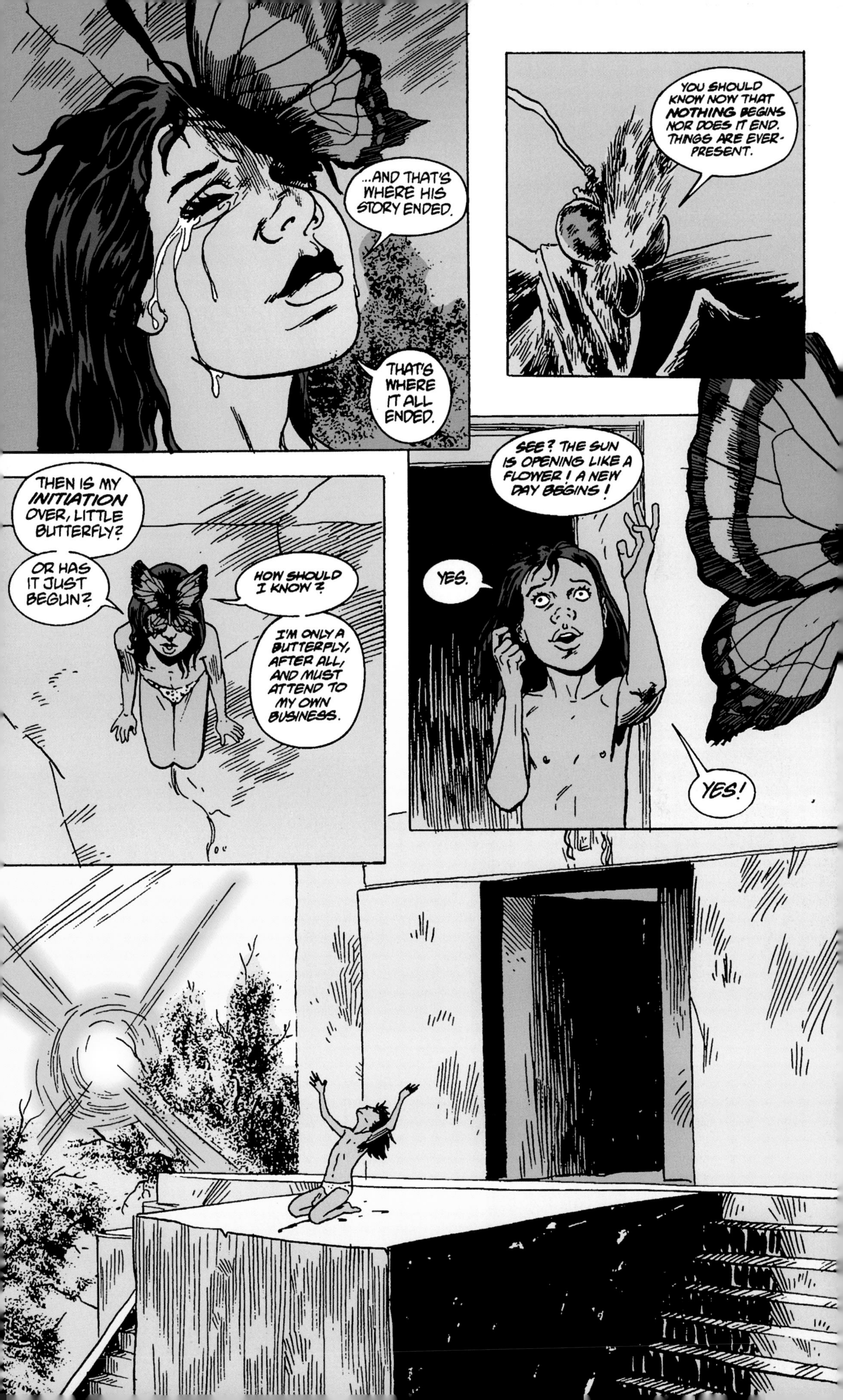
...AND THAT'S WHERE HIS STORY ENDED.
THAT'S WHERE IT ALL ENDED.
YOU SHOULD KNOW NOW THAT NOTHING BEGINS NOR DOES IT END. THINGS ARE EVER-PRESENT.
THEN IS MY INITIATION OVER, LITTLE BUTTERFLY?
OR HAS IT JUST BEGUN?
HOW SHOULD I KNOW?
I'M ONLY A BUTTERFLY, AFTER ALL, AND MUST ATTEND TO MY OWN BUSINESS.
SEE? THE SUN IS OPENING LIKE A FLOWER! A NEW DAY BEGINS!
YES.
YES!

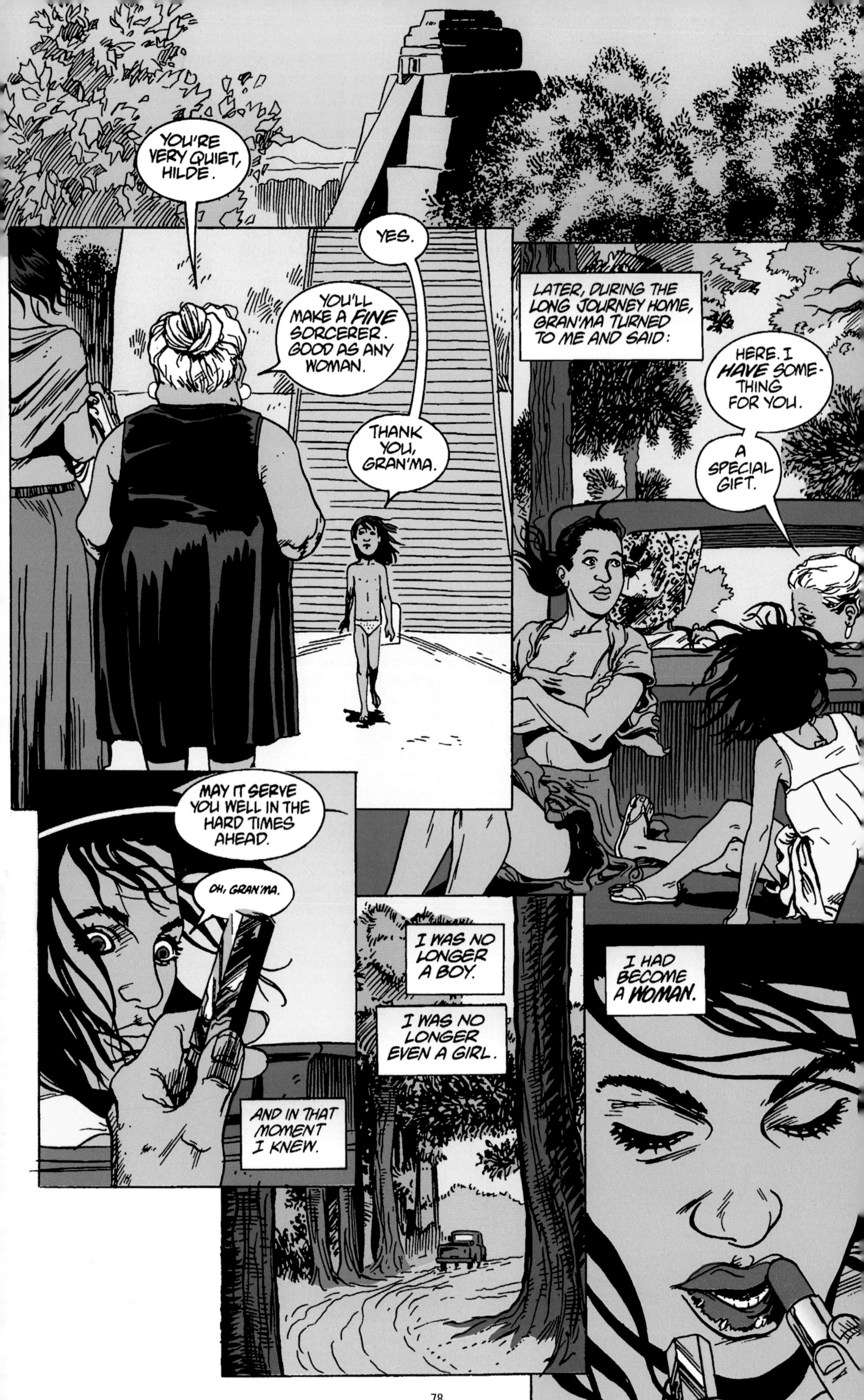
YOU'RE VERY QUIET, HILDE.
YES.
YOU'LL MAKE A FINE SORCERER. GOOD AS ANY WOMAN.
THANK YOU, GRAN'MA.
LATER, DURING THE LONG JOURNEY HOME, GRAN'MA TURNED TO ME AND SAID:
HERE. I HAVE SOMETHING FOR YOU.
A SPECIAL GIFT.
MAY IT SERVE YOU WELL IN THE HARD TIMES AHEAD.
OH, GRAN'MA.
AND IN THAT MOMENT I KNEW.
I WAS NO LONGER A BOY.
I WAS NO LONGER EVEN A GIRL.
I HAD BECOME A WOMAN.

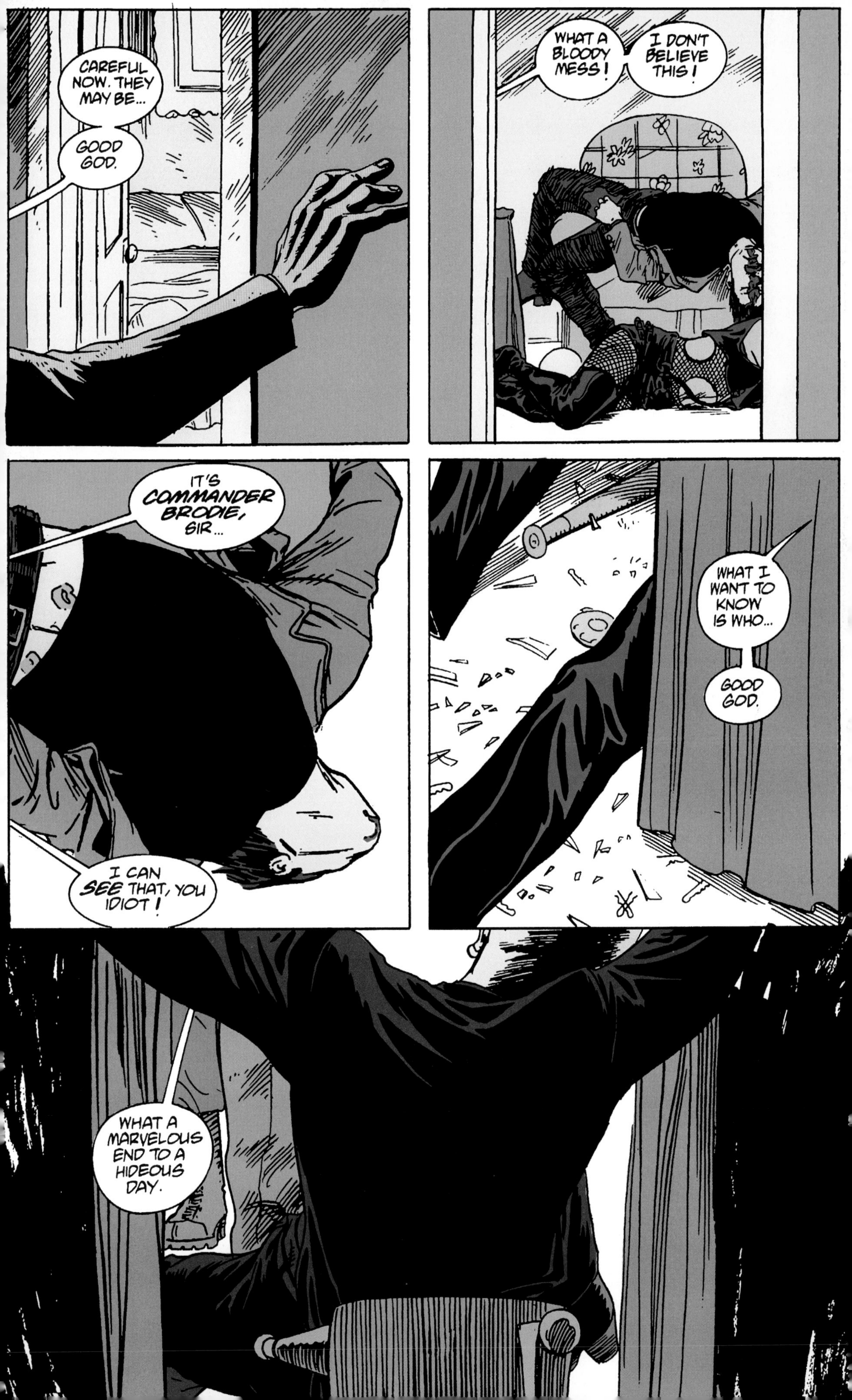
CAREFUL NOW. THEY MAY BE...
GOOD GOD.
WHAT A BLOODY MESS!
I DON'T BELIEVE THIS!
IT'S COMMANDER BRODIE, SIR...
I CAN SEE THAT, YOU IDIOT!
WHAT I WANT TO KNOW IS WHO...
GOOD GOD.
WHAT A MARVELOUS END TO A HIDEOUS DAY.

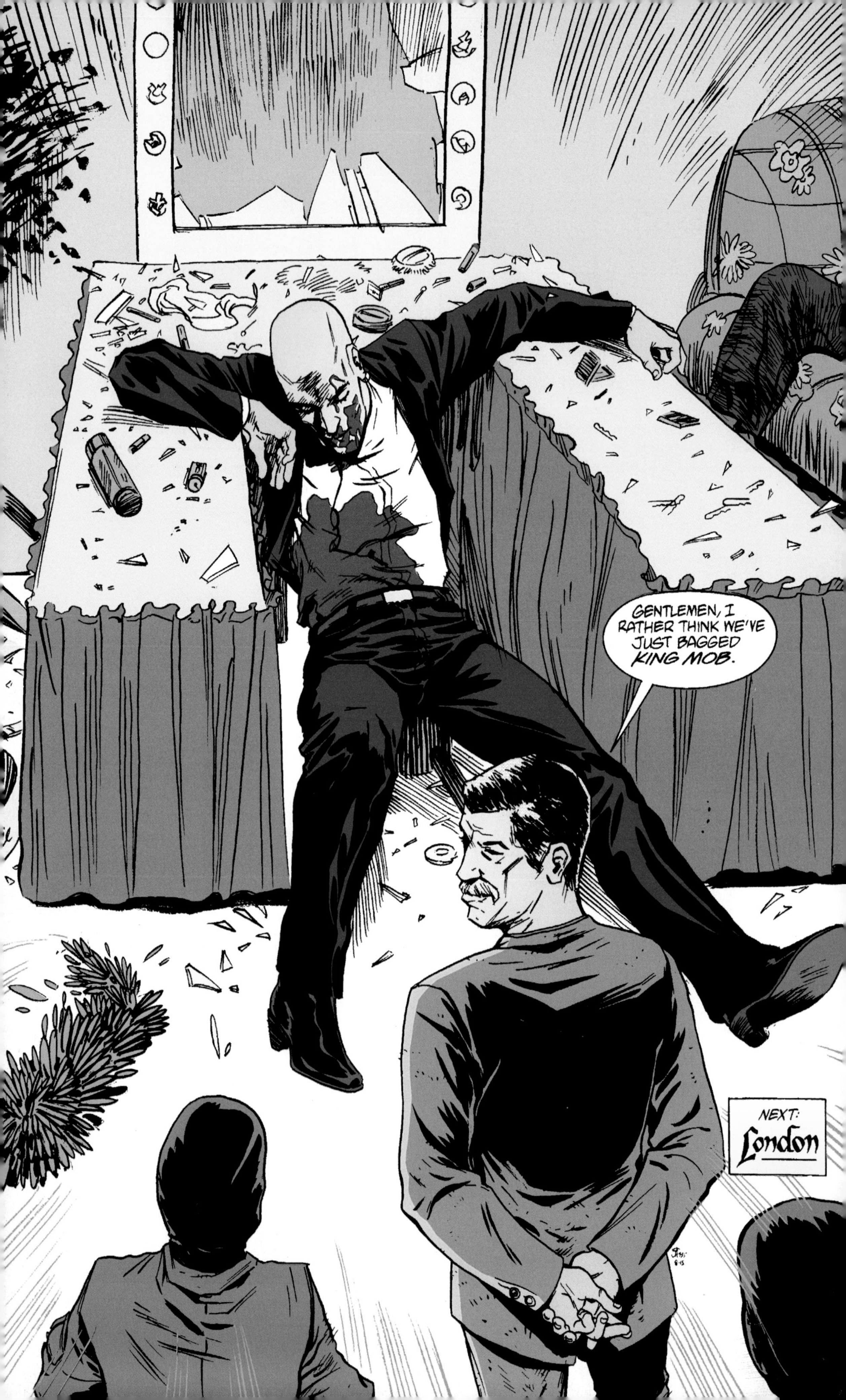
GENTLEMEN, I RATHER THINK WE'VE JUST BAGGED KING MOB.
NEXT: London

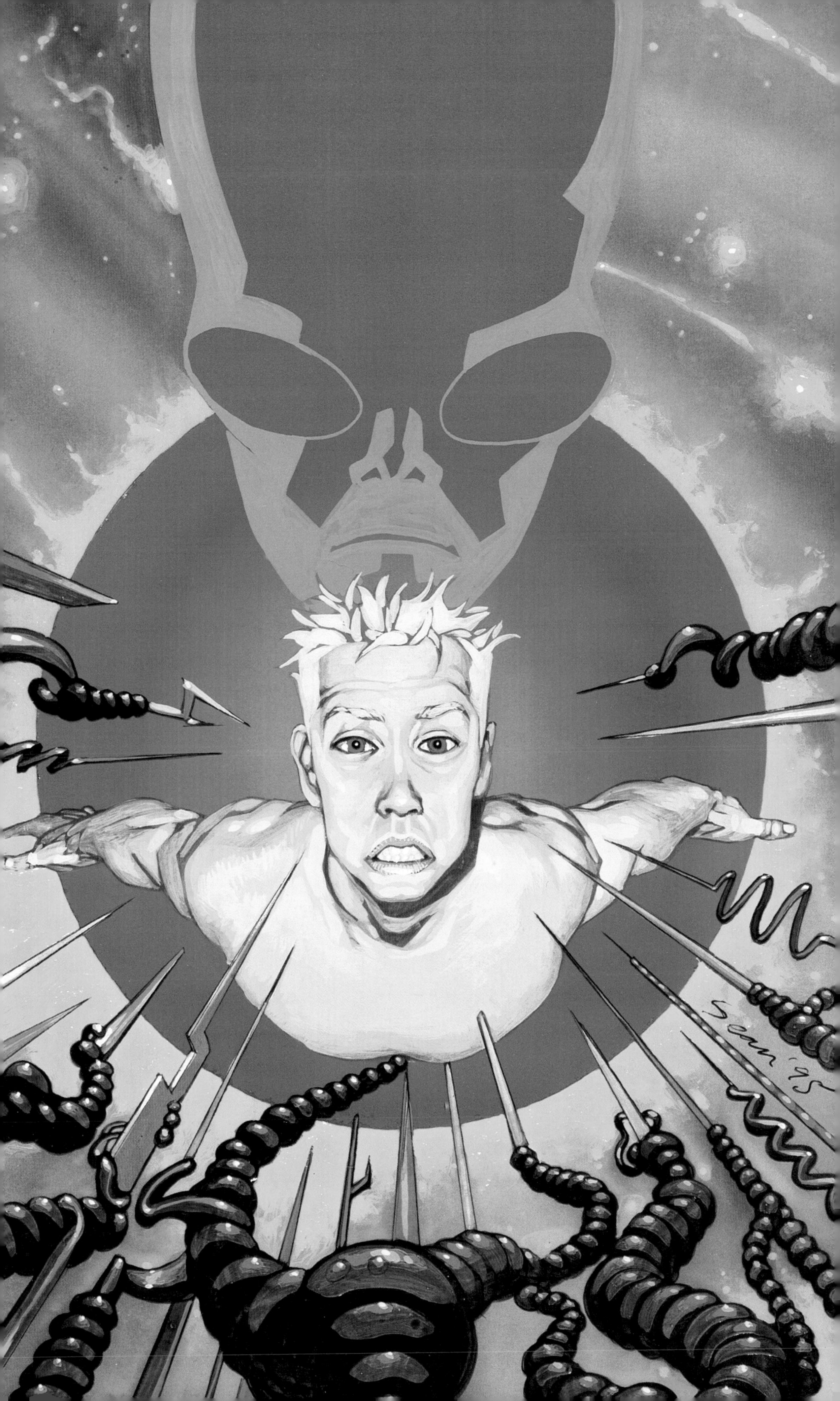
Sean '95

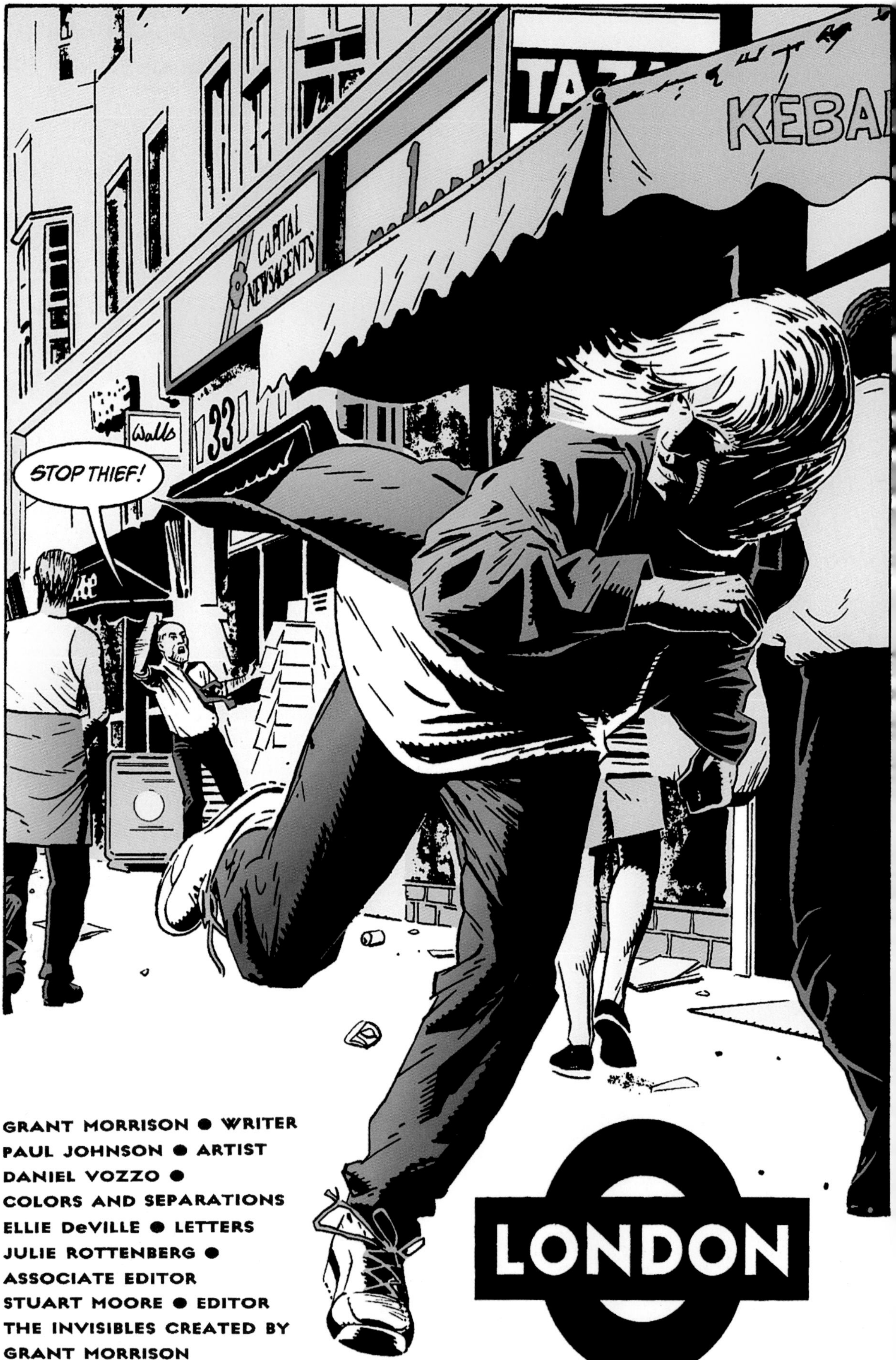
TAZ
KEBA
CAPITAL NEWSAGENTS
Walls
33
STOP THIEF!
LONDON

GRANT MORRISON ● WRITER
PAUL JOHNSON ● ARTIST
DANIEL VOZZO ●
COLORS AND SEPARATIONS
ELLIE DeVILLE ● LETTERS
JULIE ROTTENBERG ●
ASSOCIATE EDITOR
STUART MOORE ● EDITOR
THE INVISIBLES CREATED BY
GRANT MORRISON

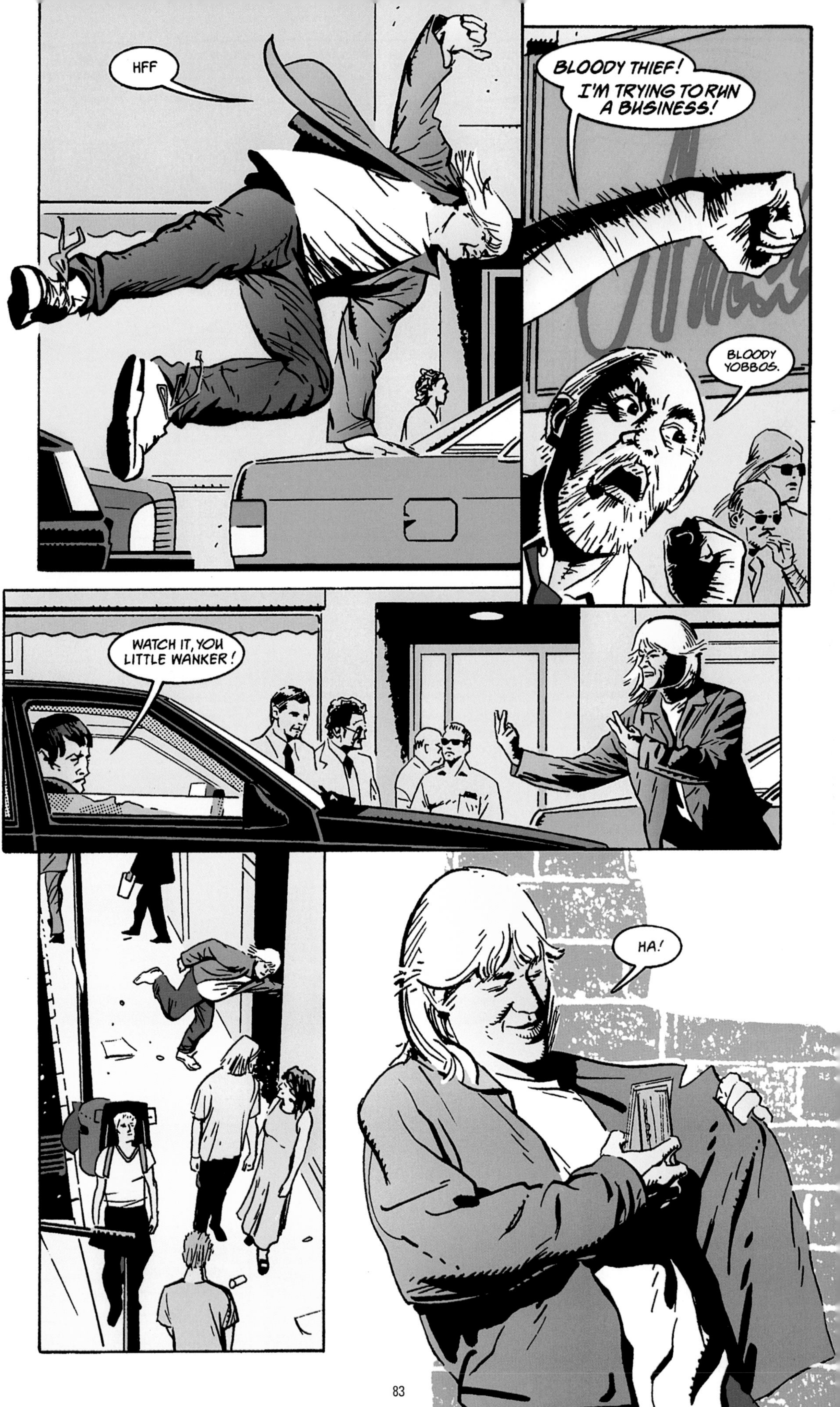
HFF
BLOODY THIEF! I'M TRYING TO RUN A BUSINESS!
BLOODY YOBBOS.
WATCH IT, YOU LITTLE WANKER!
HA!

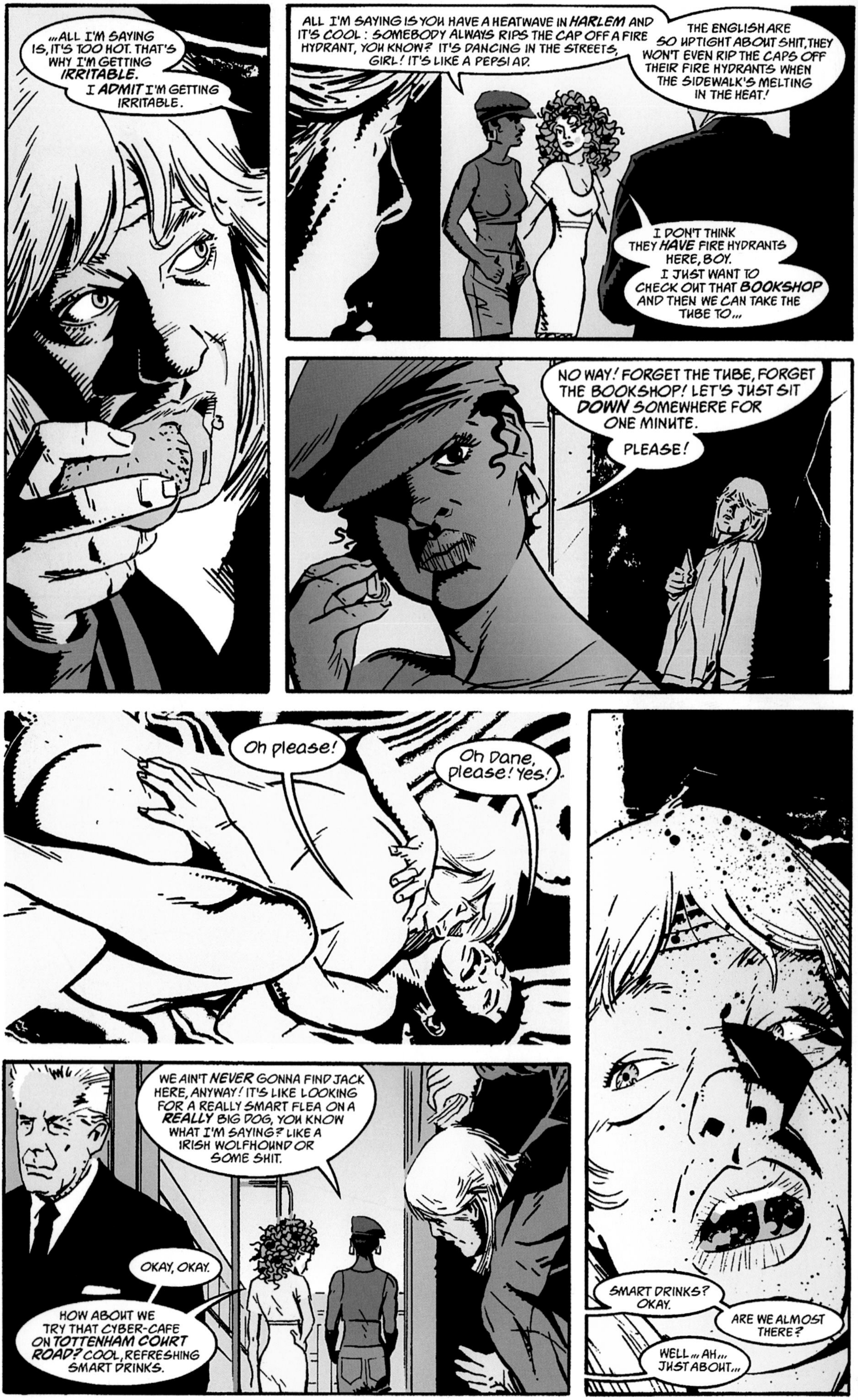
...ALL I'M SAYING IS, IT'S TOO HOT. THAT'S WHY I'M GETTING IRRITABLE. I ADMIT I'M GETTING IRRITABLE.
ALL I'M SAYING IS YOU HAVE A HEATWAVE IN HARLEM AND IT'S COOL: SOMEBODY ALWAYS RIPS THE CAP OFF A FIRE HYDRANT, YOU KNOW? IT'S DANCING IN THE STREETS, GIRL! IT'S LIKE A PEPSI AD.
THE ENGLISH ARE SO UPTIGHT ABOUT SHIT, THEY WON'T EVEN RIP THE CAPS OFF THEIR FIRE HYDRANTS WHEN THE SIDEWALK'S MELTING IN THE HEAT!
I DON'T THINK THEY HAVE FIRE HYDRANTS HERE, BOY. I JUST WANT TO CHECK OUT THAT BOOKSHOP AND THEN WE CAN TAKE THE TUBE TO...
NO WAY! FORGET THE TUBE, FORGET THE BOOKSHOP! LET'S JUST SIT DOWN SOMEWHERE FOR ONE MINUTE.
PLEASE!
Oh please!
Oh Dane, please! Yes!
WE AIN'T NEVER GONNA FIND JACK HERE, ANYWAY! IT'S LIKE LOOKING FOR A REALLY SMART FLEA ON A REALLY BIG DOG, YOU KNOW WHAT I'M SAYING? LIKE A IRISH WOLFHOUND OR SOME SHIT.
OKAY, OKAY.
HOW ABOUT WE TRY THAT CYBER-CAFE ON TOTTENHAM COURT ROAD? COOL, REFRESHING SMART DRINKS.
SMART DRINKS? OKAY.
ARE WE ALMOST THERE?
WELL... AH... JUST ABOUT...

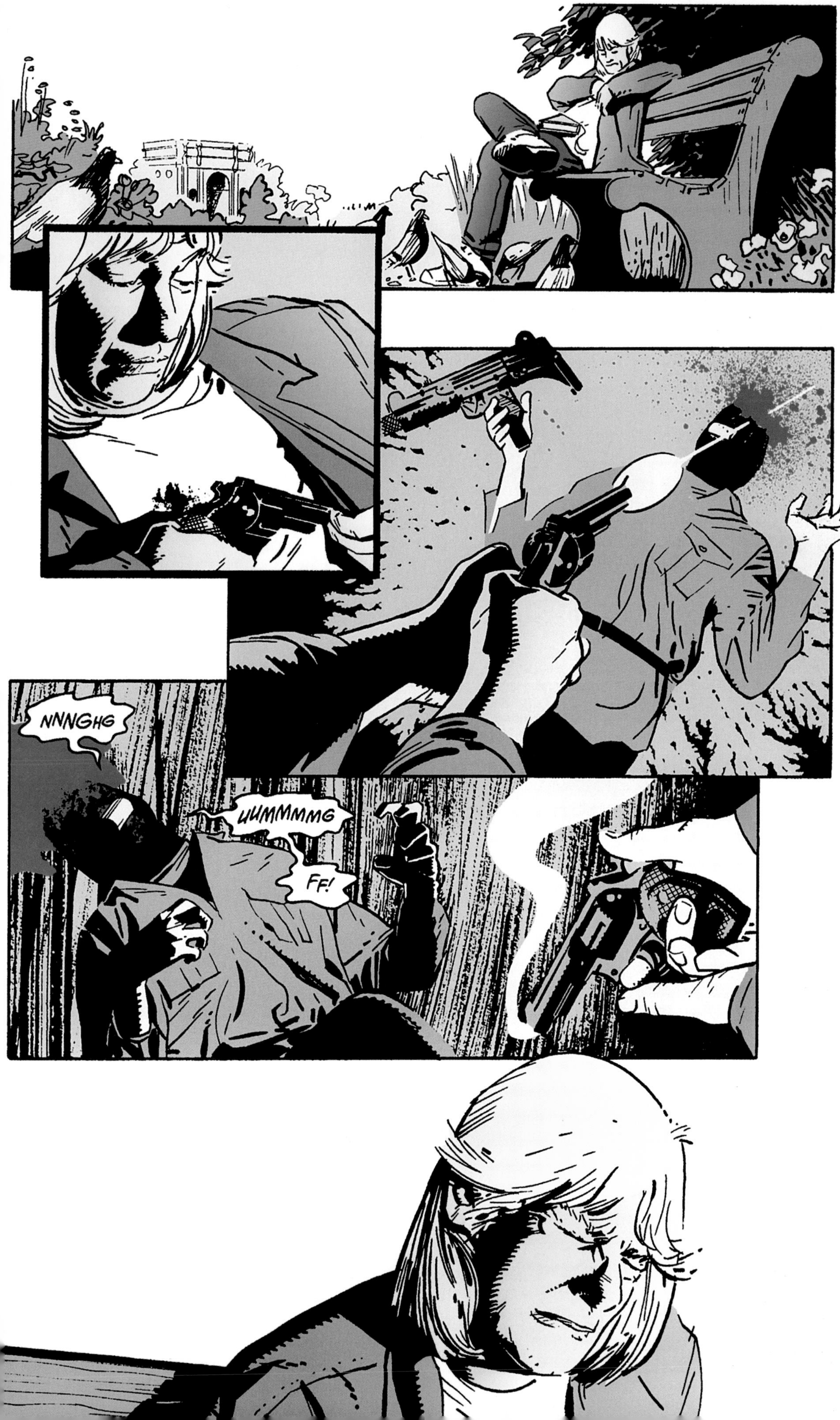
NNNGHG
UUMMMMMG
FF!

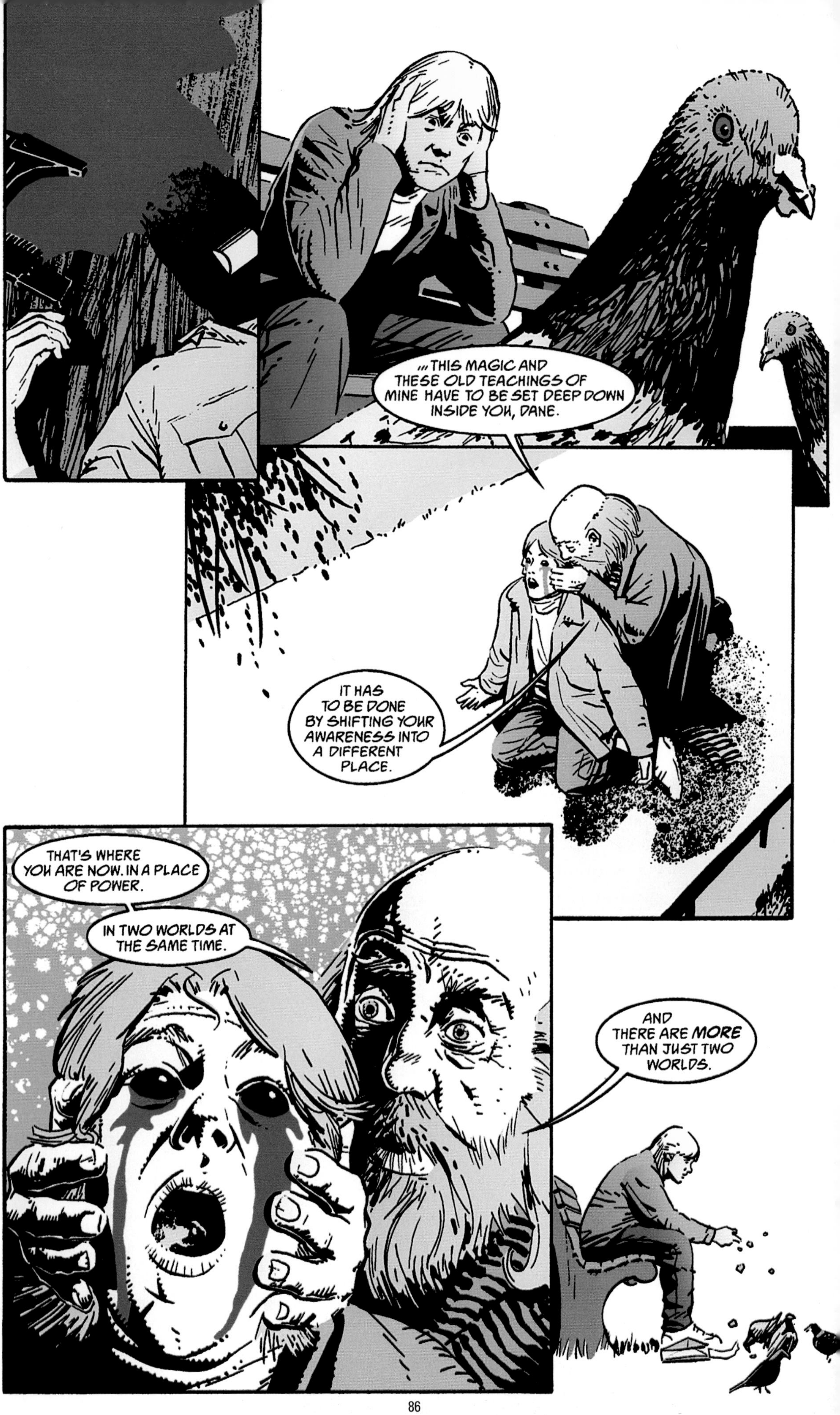
...THIS MAGIC AND THESE OLD TEACHINGS OF MINE HAVE TO BE SET DEEP DOWN INSIDE YOU, DANE.
IT HAS TO BE DONE BY SHIFTING YOUR AWARENESS INTO A DIFFERENT PLACE.
THAT'S WHERE YOU ARE NOW. IN A PLACE OF POWER.
IN TWO WORLDS AT THE SAME TIME.
AND THERE ARE MORE THAN JUST TWO WORLDS.

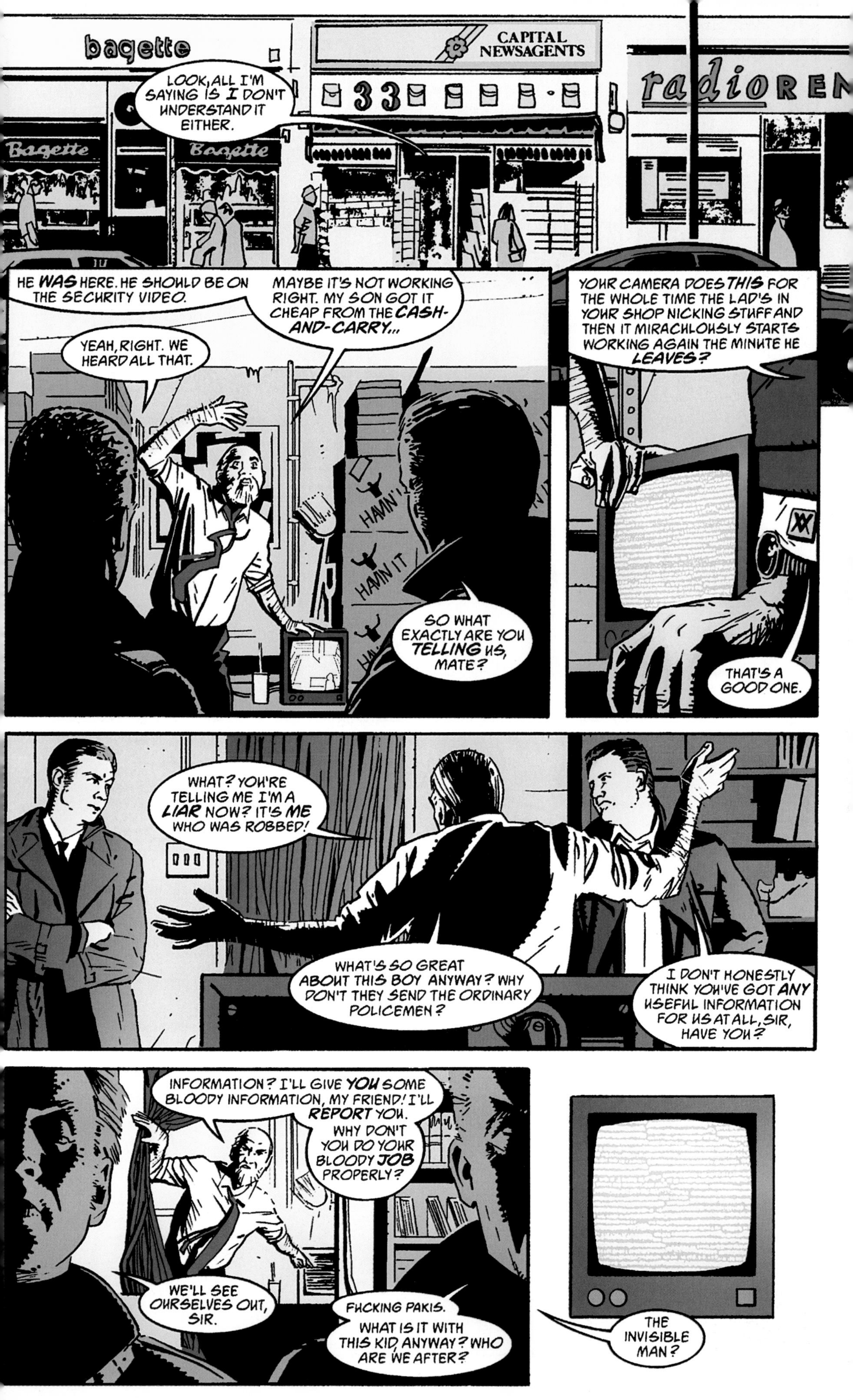

bagette
CAPITAL NEWSAGENTS
33
radioREN
Bagette
Bagette
LOOK, ALL I'M SAYING IS I DON'T UNDERSTAND IT EITHER.
HE WAS HERE. HE SHOULD BE ON THE SECURITY VIDEO.
MAYBE IT'S NOT WORKING RIGHT. MY SON GOT IT CHEAP FROM THE CASH-AND-CARRY...
YEAH, RIGHT. WE HEARD ALL THAT.
SO WHAT EXACTLY ARE YOU TELLING US, MATE?
HAVIN' IT
HAVIN IT
YOUR CAMERA DOES THIS FOR THE WHOLE TIME THE LAD'S IN YOUR SHOP NICKING STUFF AND THEN IT MIRACULOUSLY STARTS WORKING AGAIN THE MINUTE HE LEAVES?
THAT'S A GOOD ONE.
WHAT? YOU'RE TELLING ME I'M A LIAR NOW? IT'S ME WHO WAS ROBBED!
WHAT'S SO GREAT ABOUT THIS BOY ANYWAY? WHY DON'T THEY SEND THE ORDINARY POLICEMEN?
I DON'T HONESTLY THINK YOU'VE GOT ANY USEFUL INFORMATION FOR US AT ALL, SIR, HAVE YOU?
INFORMATION? I'LL GIVE YOU SOME BLOODY INFORMATION, MY FRIEND! I'LL REPORT YOU.
WHY DON'T YOU DO YOUR BLOODY JOB PROPERLY?
WE'LL SEE OURSELVES OUT, SIR.
FUCKING PAKIS.
WHAT IS IT WITH THIS KID, ANYWAY? WHO ARE WE AFTER?
THE INVISIBLE MAN?

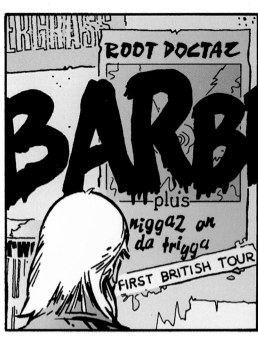

ROOT DOCTAZ

BARB

14 plus

niggaz on da trigga

FIRST BRITISH TOUR

BARBELITH

"At This Stage I Couldn't Say"

YOU'LL REMEMBER EVERYTHING WHEN THE TIME IS RIGHT.

WHAT?

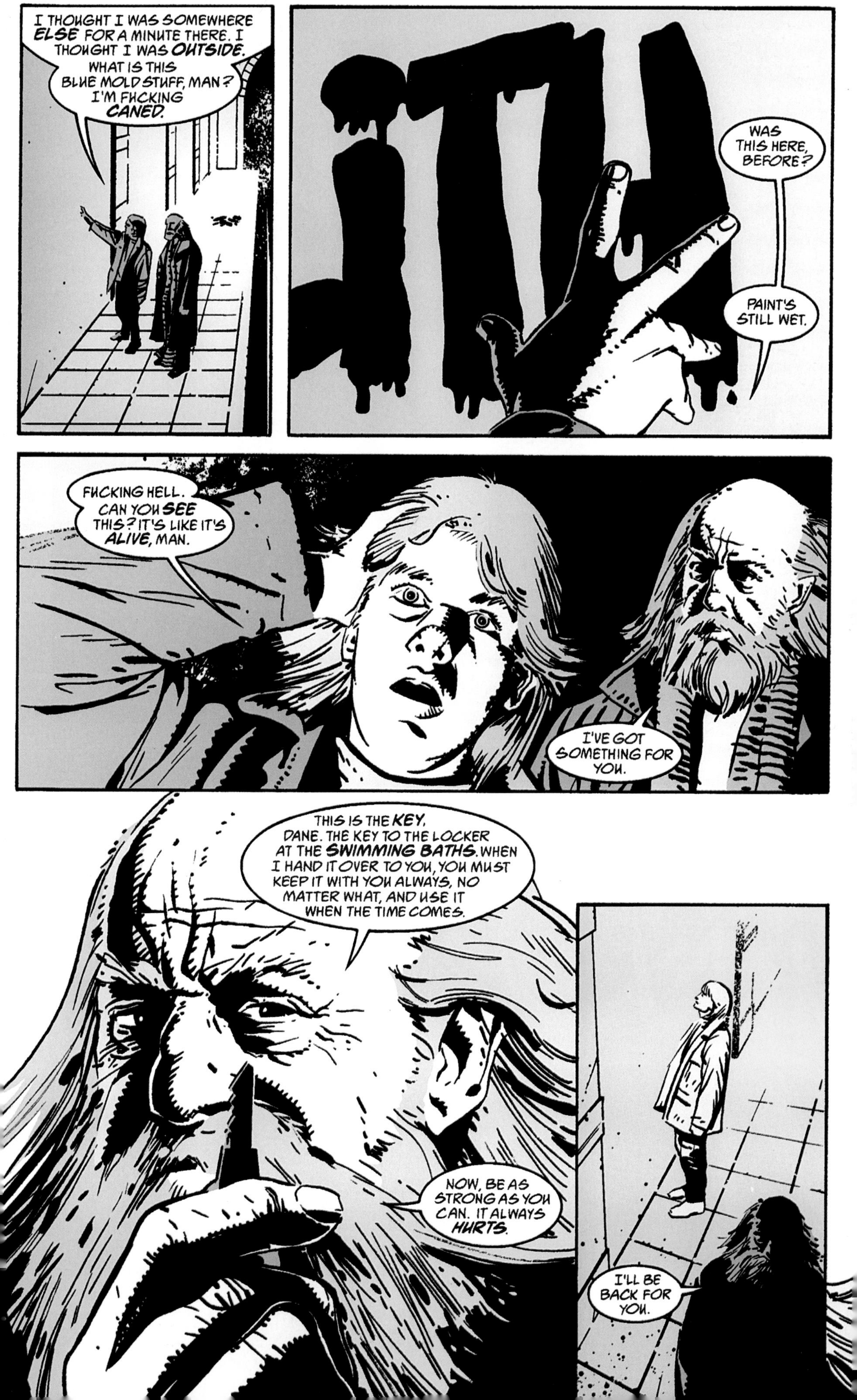
I THOUGHT I WAS SOMEWHERE ELSE FOR A MINUTE THERE. I THOUGHT I WAS OUTSIDE. WHAT IS THIS BLUE MOLD STUFF, MAN? I'M FUCKING CANED.
WAS THIS HERE, BEFORE?
PAINT'S STILL WET.
FUCKING HELL. CAN YOU SEE THIS? IT'S LIKE IT'S ALIVE, MAN.
I'VE GOT SOMETHING FOR YOU.
THIS IS THE KEY, DANE. THE KEY TO THE LOCKER AT THE SWIMMING BATHS. WHEN I HAND IT OVER TO YOU, YOU MUST KEEP IT WITH YOU ALWAYS, NO MATTER WHAT, AND USE IT WHEN THE TIME COMES.
NOW, BE AS STRONG AS YOU CAN. IT ALWAYS HURTS.
I'LL BE BACK FOR YOU.

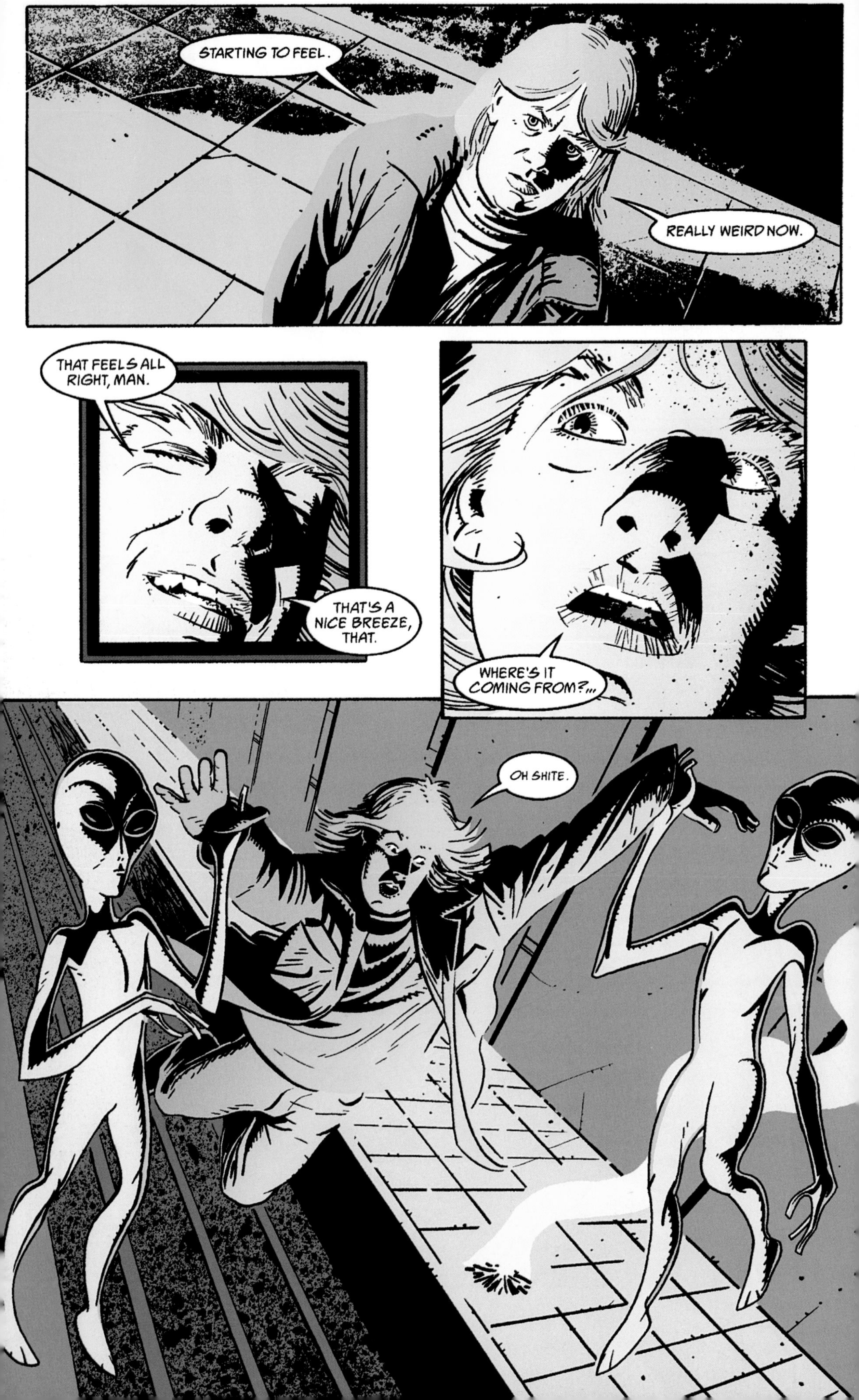
STARTING TO FEEL.
REALLY WEIRD NOW.
THAT FEELS ALL RIGHT, MAN.
THAT'S A NICE BREEZE, THAT.
WHERE'S IT COMING FROM?...
OH SHITE.

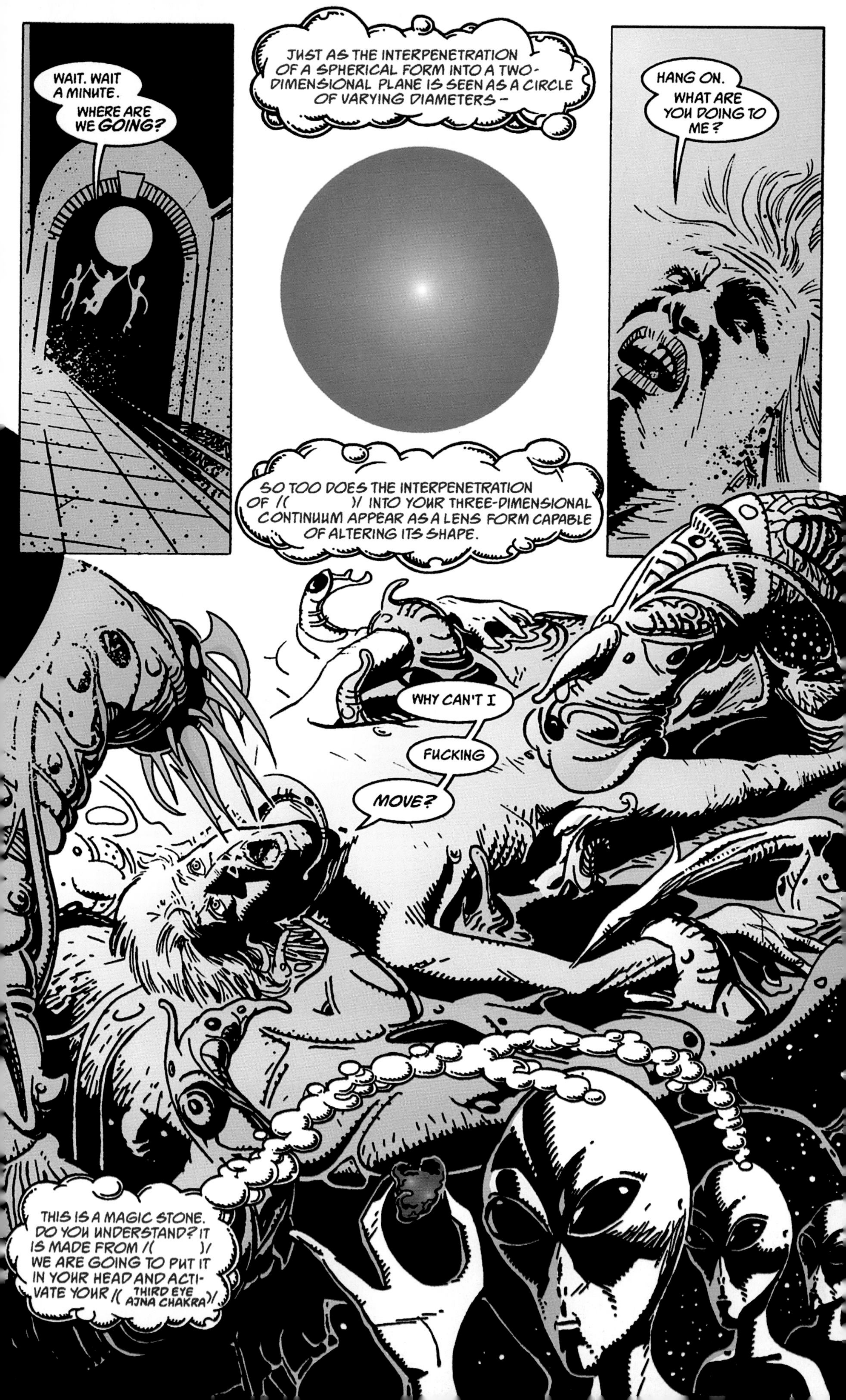
WAIT. WAIT A MINUTE.
WHERE ARE WE GOING?
JUST AS THE INTERPENETRATION OF A SPHERICAL FORM INTO A TWO-DIMENSIONAL PLANE IS SEEN AS A CIRCLE OF VARYING DIAMETERS –
HANG ON.
WHAT ARE YOU DOING TO ME?
SO TOO DOES THE INTERPENETRATION OF /( )/ INTO YOUR THREE-DIMENSIONAL CONTINUUM APPEAR AS A LENS FORM CAPABLE OF ALTERING ITS SHAPE.
WHY CAN'T I
FUCKING
MOVE?
THIS IS A MAGIC STONE. DO YOU UNDERSTAND? IT IS MADE FROM /( )/ WE ARE GOING TO PUT IT IN YOUR HEAD AND ACTIVATE YOUR /(THIRD EYE AJNA CHAKRA)/

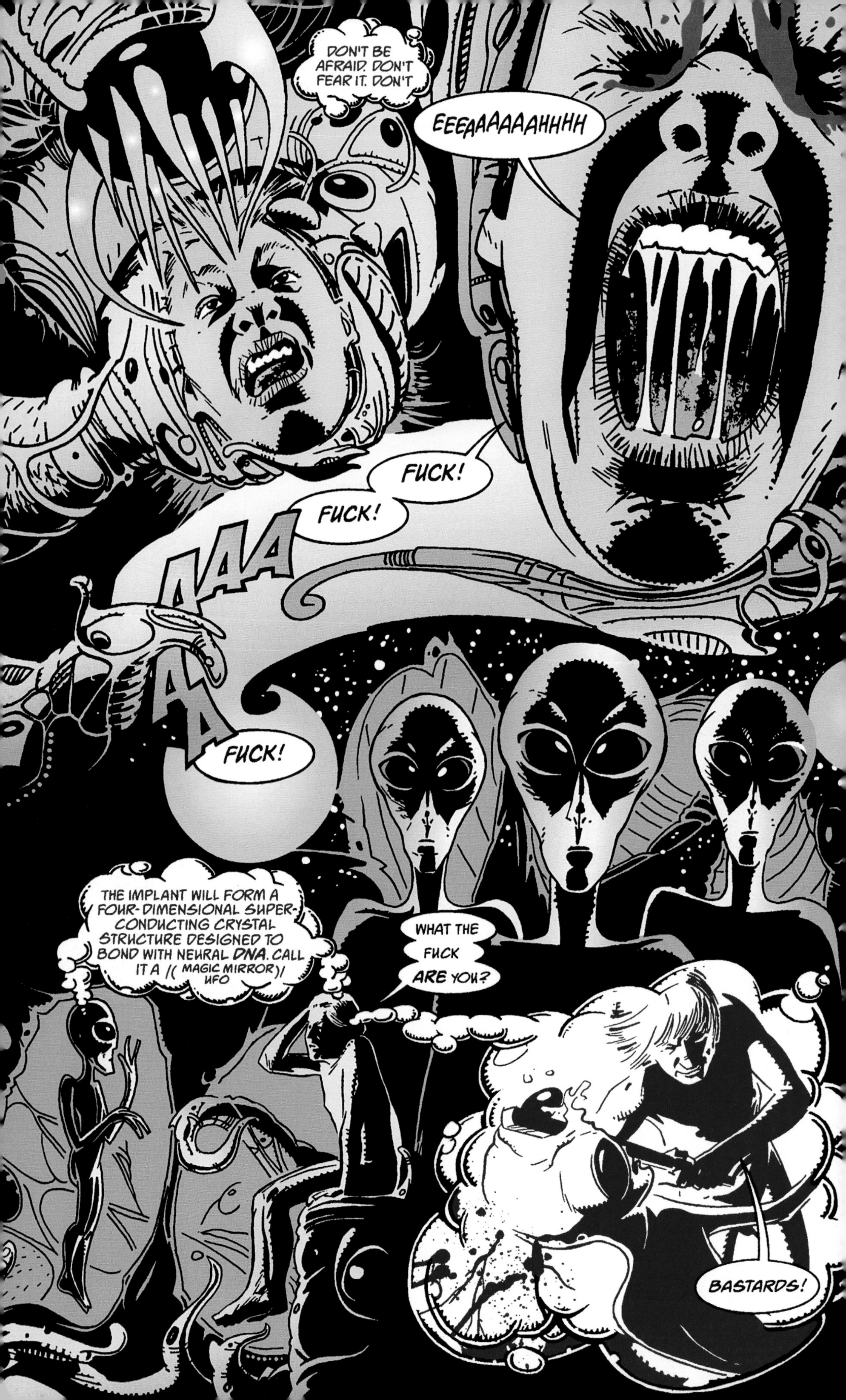
DON'T BE AFRAID. DON'T FEAR IT. DON'T
EEEAAAAAAHHHH
FUCK!
FUCK!
AAA
AAA
FUCK!
THE IMPLANT WILL FORM A FOUR-DIMENSIONAL SUPER-CONDUCTING CRYSTAL STRUCTURE DESIGNED TO BOND WITH NEURAL DNA. CALL IT A "MAGIC MIRROR" UFO
WHAT THE FUCK ARE YOU?
BASTARDS!

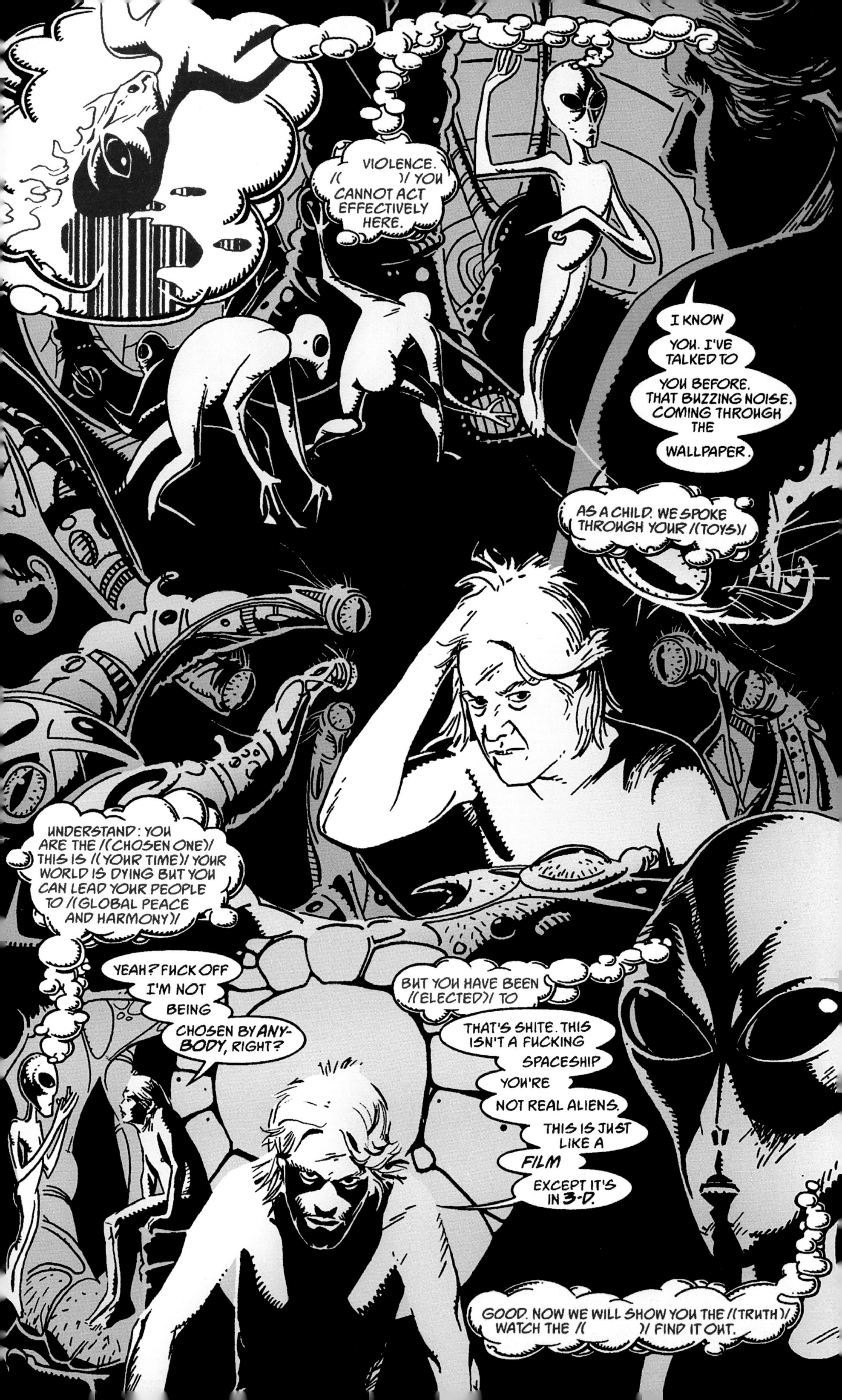
VIOLENCE. //( )/ YOU CANNOT ACT EFFECTIVELY HERE.
I KNOW YOU. I'VE TALKED TO YOU BEFORE. THAT BUZZING NOISE. COMING THROUGH THE WALLPAPER.
AS A CHILD. WE SPOKE THROUGH YOUR //(TOYS)/
UNDERSTAND: YOU ARE THE //(CHOSEN ONE)/ THIS IS //(YOUR TIME)/ YOUR WORLD IS DYING BUT YOU CAN LEAD YOUR PEOPLE TO //(GLOBAL PEACE AND HARMONY)/
YEAH? FUCK OFF I'M NOT BEING CHOSEN BY ANYBODY, RIGHT?
BUT YOU HAVE BEEN //(ELECTED)/ TO
THAT'S SHITE. THIS ISN'T A FUCKING SPACESHIP YOU'RE NOT REAL ALIENS. THIS IS JUST LIKE A FILM EXCEPT IT'S IN 3-D.
GOOD. NOW WE WILL SHOW YOU THE //(TRUTH)/ WATCH THE //( )/ FIND IT OUT.

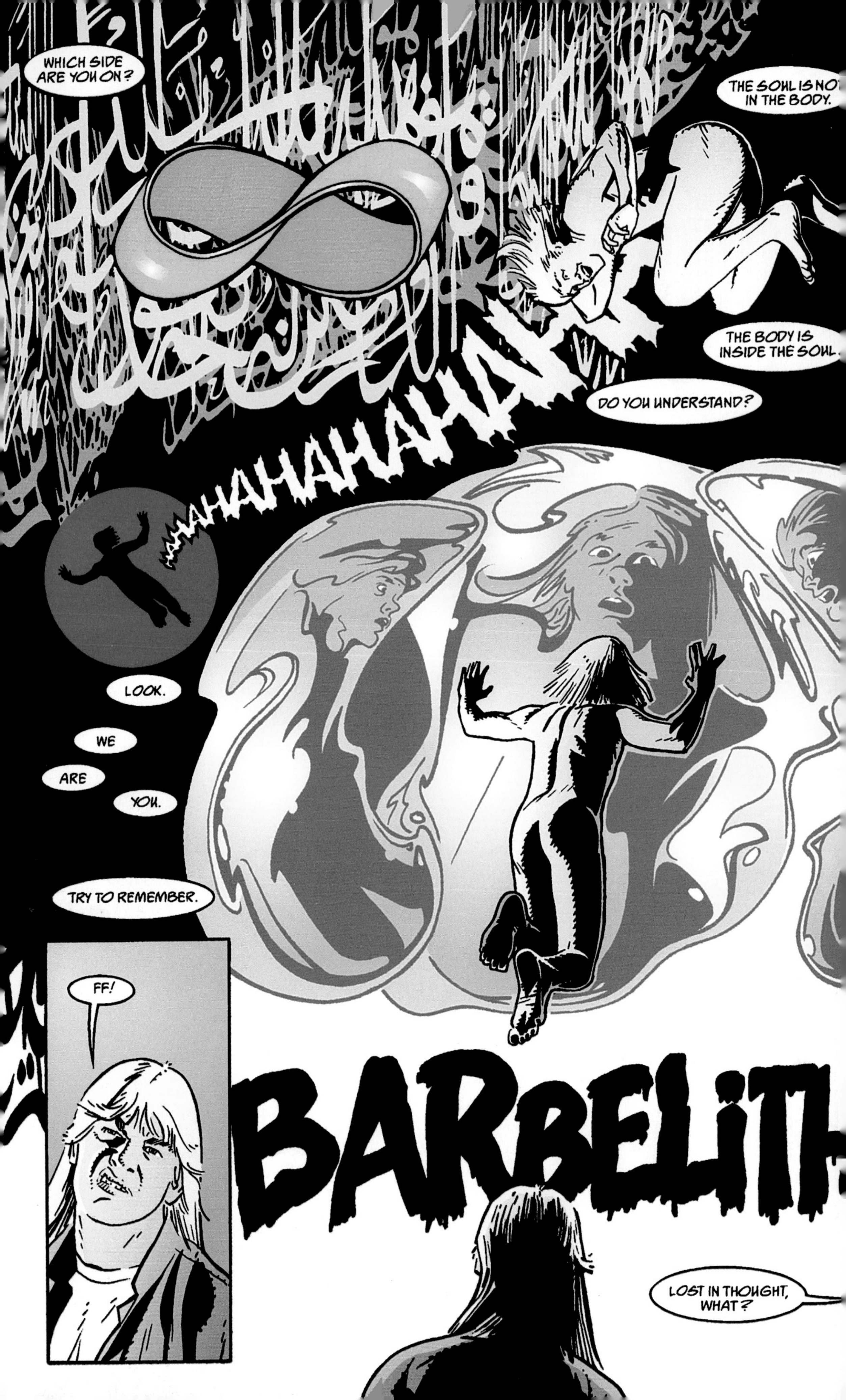
WHICH SIDE ARE YOU ON?
THE SOUL IS NOT IN THE BODY.
THE BODY IS INSIDE THE SOUL.
DO YOU UNDERSTAND?
WAHAHAHAHAHA
LOOK.
WE
ARE
YOU.
TRY TO REMEMBER.
FF!
BARBELITH
LOST IN THOUGHT, WHAT?

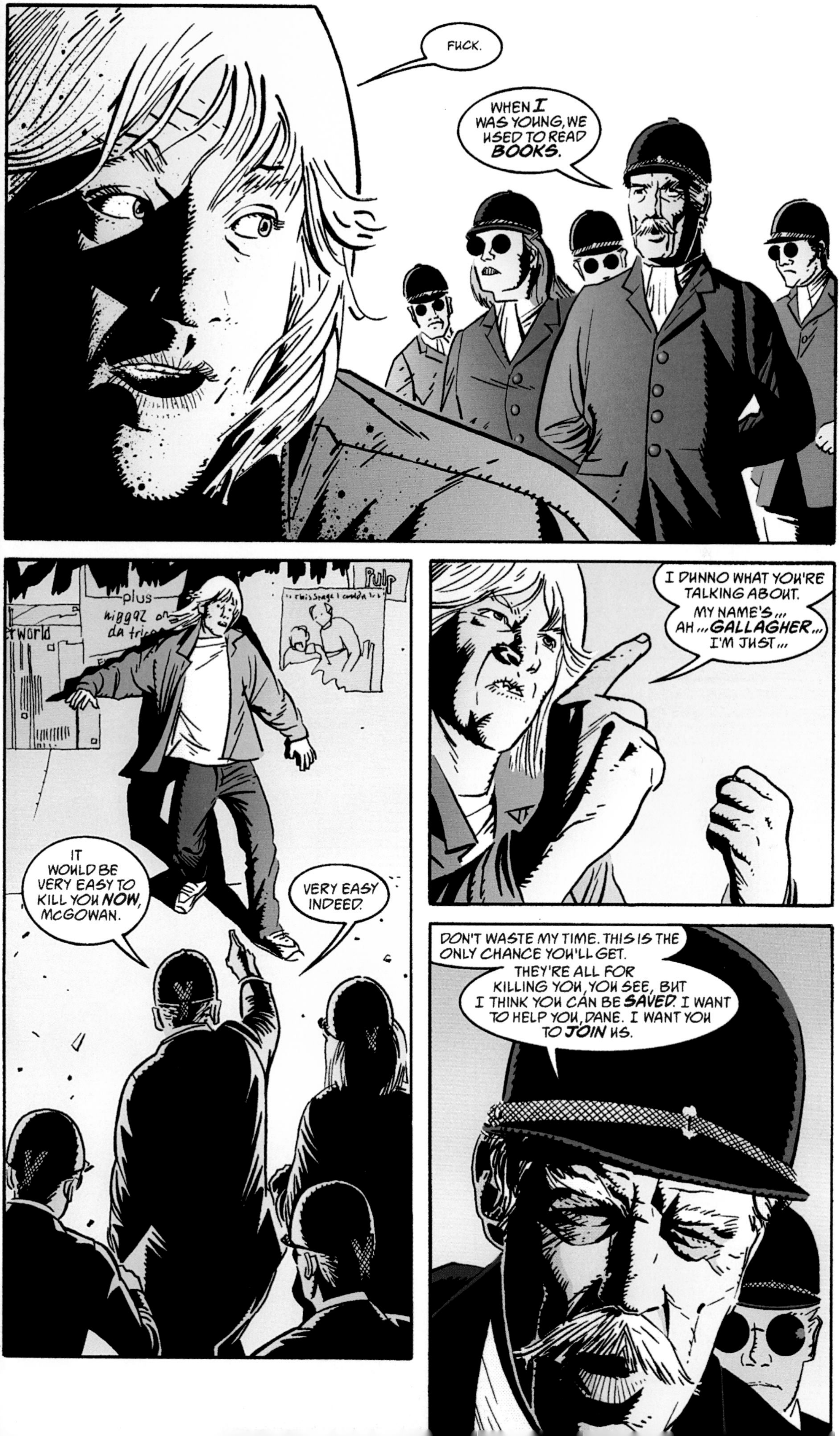
FUCK.
WHEN I WAS YOUNG, WE USED TO READ BOOKS.
IT WOULD BE VERY EASY TO KILL YOU NOW, McGOWAN.
VERY EASY INDEED.
I DUNNO WHAT YOU'RE TALKING ABOUT. MY NAME'S... AH... GALLAGHER... I'M JUST...
DON'T WASTE MY TIME. THIS IS THE ONLY CHANCE YOU'LL GET. THEY'RE ALL FOR KILLING YOU, YOU SEE, BUT I THINK YOU CAN BE SAVED. I WANT TO HELP YOU, DANE. I WANT YOU TO JOIN US.

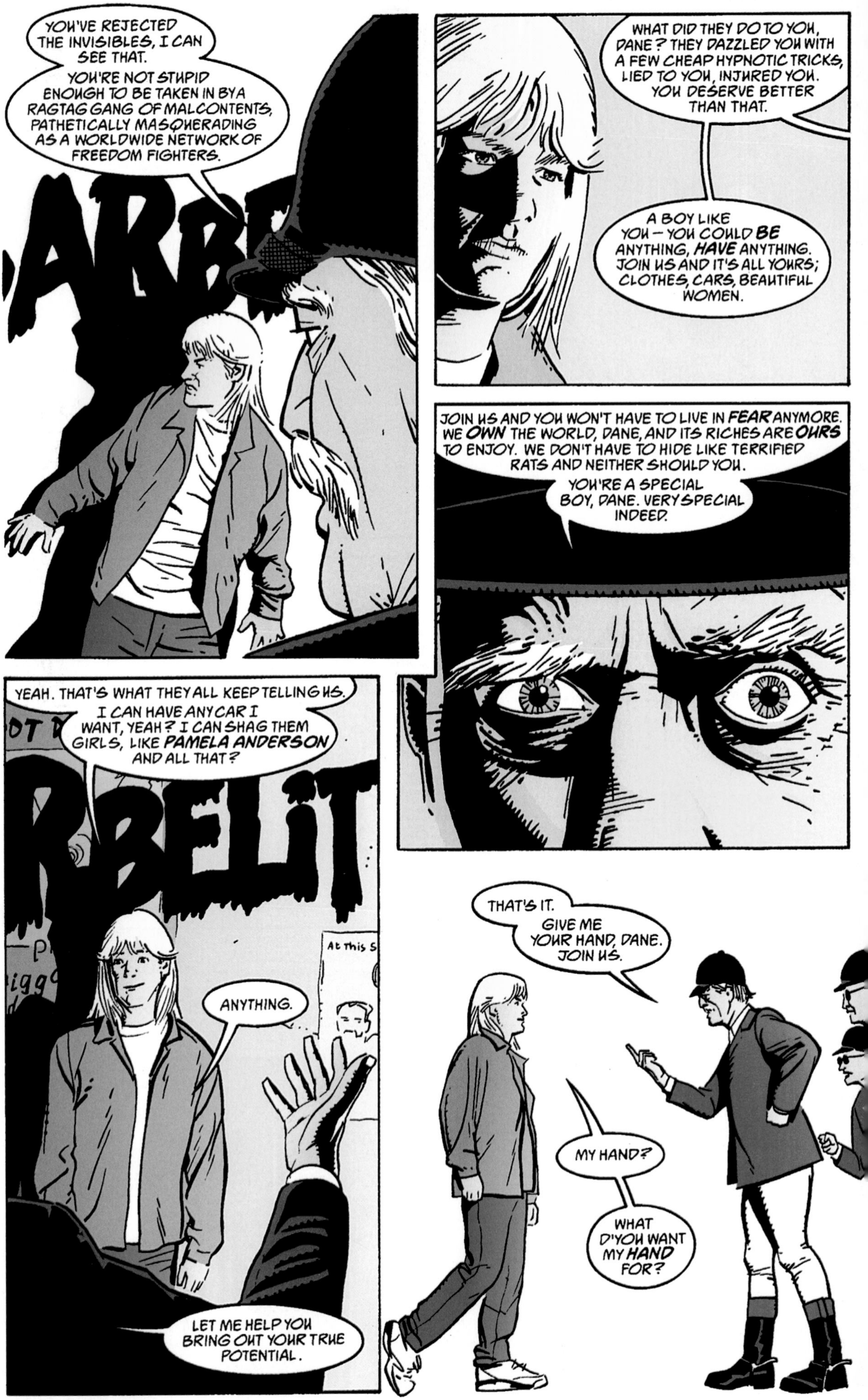
YOU'VE REJECTED THE INVISIBLES, I CAN SEE THAT.
YOU'RE NOT STUPID ENOUGH TO BE TAKEN IN BY A RAGTAG GANG OF MALCONTENTS, PATHETICALLY MASQUERADING AS A WORLDWIDE NETWORK OF FREEDOM FIGHTERS.
WHAT DID THEY DO TO YOU, DANE? THEY DAZZLED YOU WITH A FEW CHEAP HYPNOTIC TRICKS, LIED TO YOU, INJURED YOU. YOU DESERVE BETTER THAN THAT.
A BOY LIKE YOU — YOU COULD BE ANYTHING, HAVE ANYTHING. JOIN US AND IT'S ALL YOURS; CLOTHES, CARS, BEAUTIFUL WOMEN.
JOIN US AND YOU WON'T HAVE TO LIVE IN FEAR ANYMORE. WE OWN THE WORLD, DANE, AND ITS RICHES ARE OURS TO ENJOY. WE DON'T HAVE TO HIDE LIKE TERRIFIED RATS AND NEITHER SHOULD YOU.
YOU'RE A SPECIAL BOY, DANE. VERY SPECIAL INDEED.
YEAH. THAT'S WHAT THEY ALL KEEP TELLING US.
I CAN HAVE ANY CAR I WANT, YEAH? I CAN SHAG THEM GIRLS, LIKE PAMELA ANDERSON AND ALL THAT?
ANYTHING.
LET ME HELP YOU BRING OUT YOUR TRUE POTENTIAL.
THAT'S IT.
GIVE ME YOUR HAND, DANE. JOIN US.
MY HAND?
WHAT D'YOU WANT MY HAND FOR?

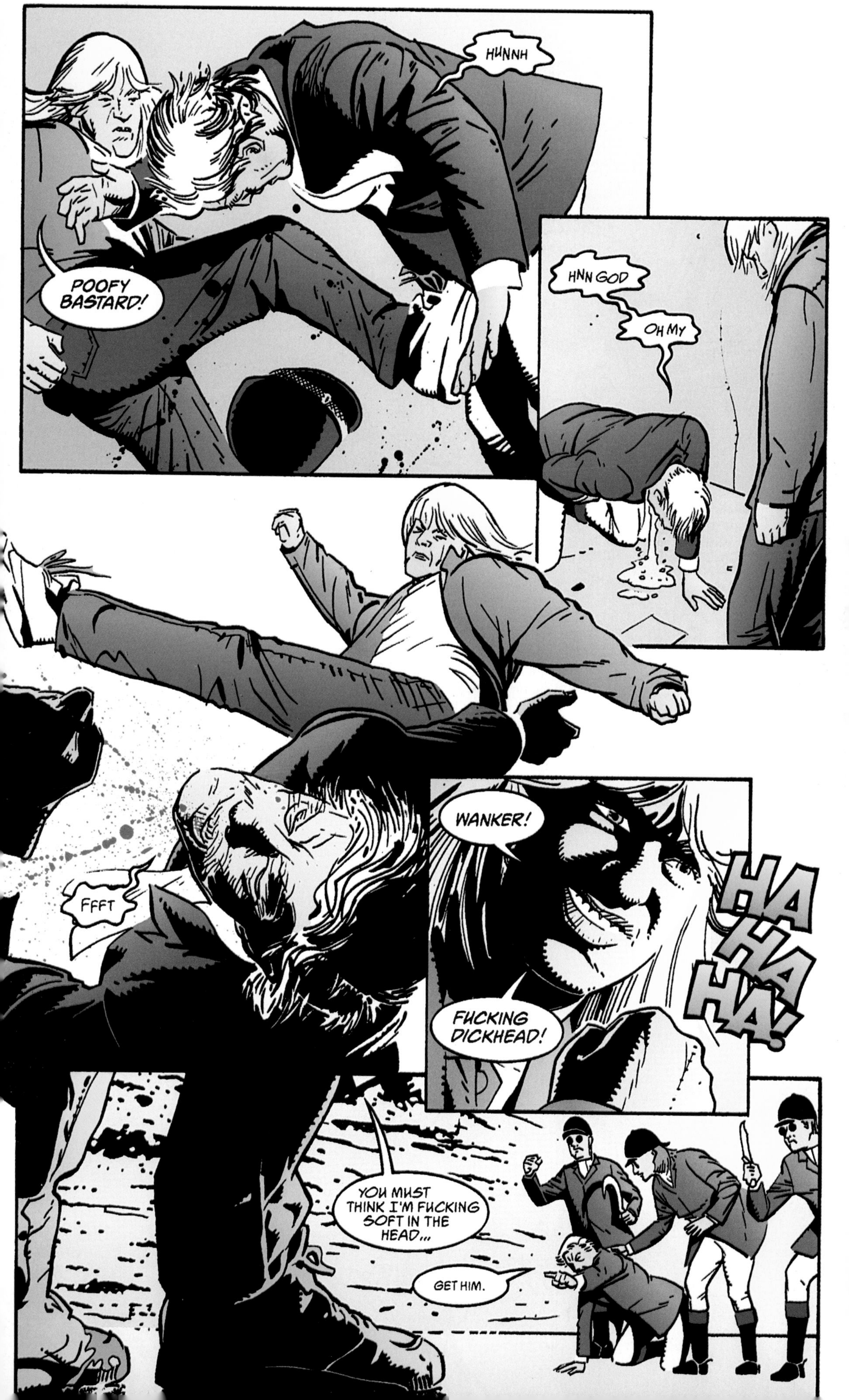
HUNNH
POOFY BASTARD!
HNN GOD
OH MY
FFFT
WANKER!
FUCKING DICKHEAD!
HA HA HA!
YOU MUST THINK I'M FUCKING SOFT IN THE HEAD...
GET HIM.

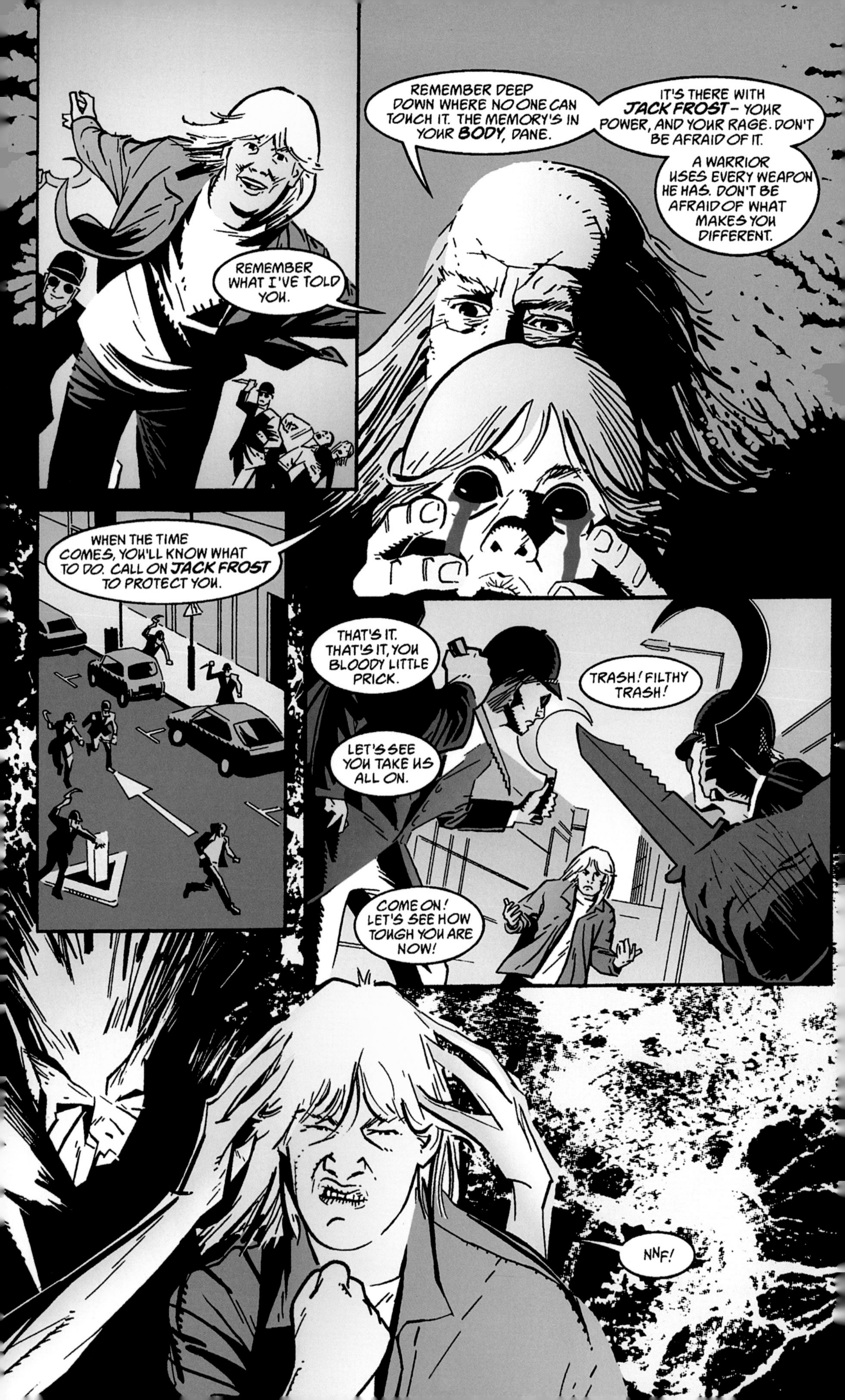
REMEMBER WHAT I'VE TOLD YOU.
REMEMBER DEEP DOWN WHERE NO ONE CAN TOUCH IT. THE MEMORY'S IN YOUR BODY, DANE.
IT'S THERE WITH JACK FROST – YOUR POWER, AND YOUR RAGE. DON'T BE AFRAID OF IT.
A WARRIOR USES EVERY WEAPON HE HAS. DON'T BE AFRAID OF WHAT MAKES YOU DIFFERENT.
WHEN THE TIME COMES, YOU'LL KNOW WHAT TO DO. CALL ON JACK FROST TO PROTECT YOU.
THAT'S IT. THAT'S IT, YOU BLOODY LITTLE PRICK.
TRASH! FILTHY TRASH!
LET'S SEE YOU TAKE US ALL ON.
COME ON! LET'S SEE HOW TOUGH YOU ARE NOW!
NNF!

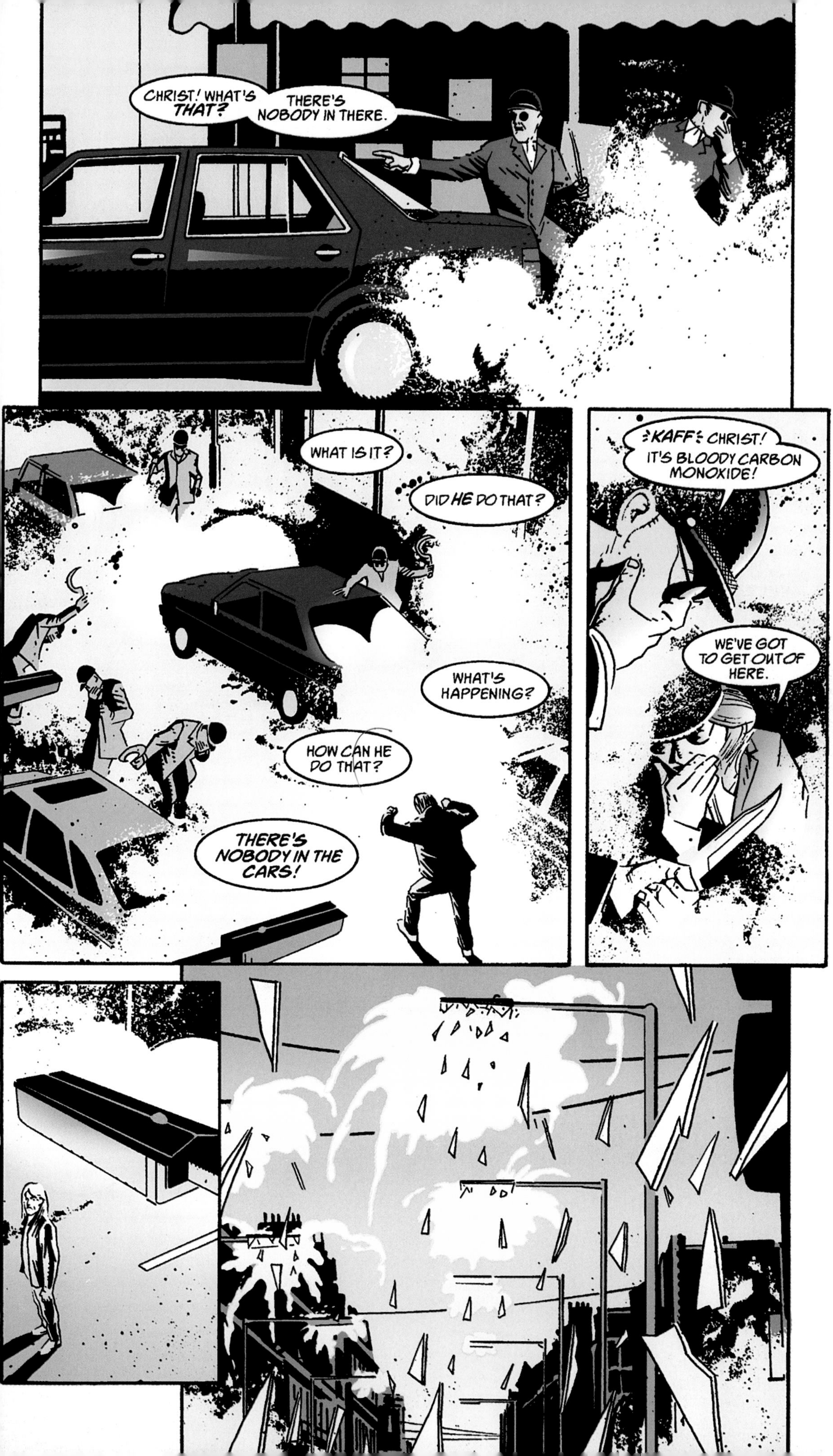

CHRIST! WHAT'S THAT?
THERE'S NOBODY IN THERE.
WHAT IS IT?
DID HE DO THAT?
WHAT'S HAPPENING?
HOW CAN HE DO THAT?
THERE'S NOBODY IN THE CARS!
KAFF CHRIST! IT'S BLOODY CARBON MONOXIDE!
WE'VE GOT TO GET OUT OF HERE.

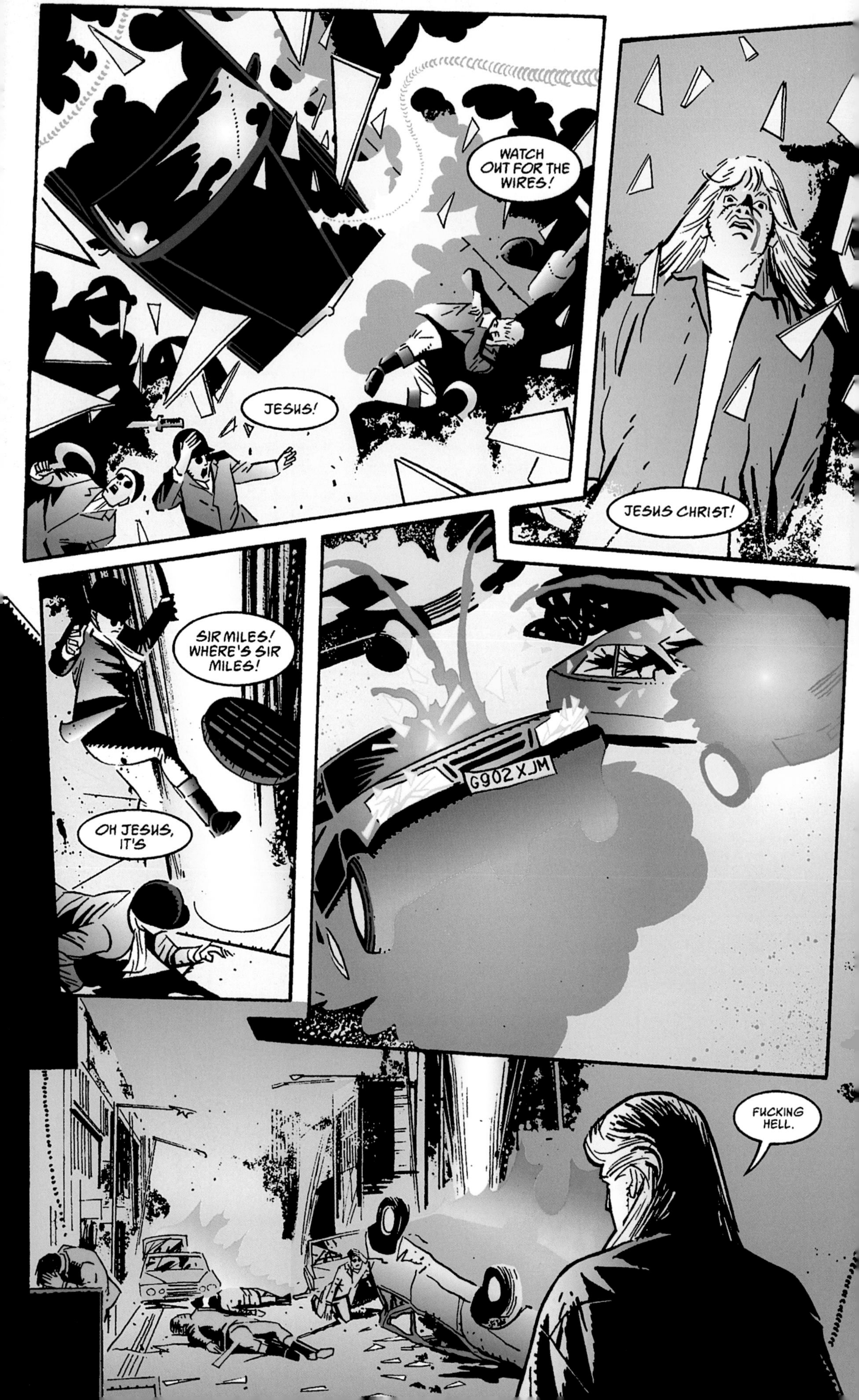
WATCH OUT FOR THE WIRES!
JESUS!
JESUS CHRIST!
SIR MILES! WHERE'S SIR MILES!
OH JESUS, IT'S
G902 XJM
FUCKING HELL.

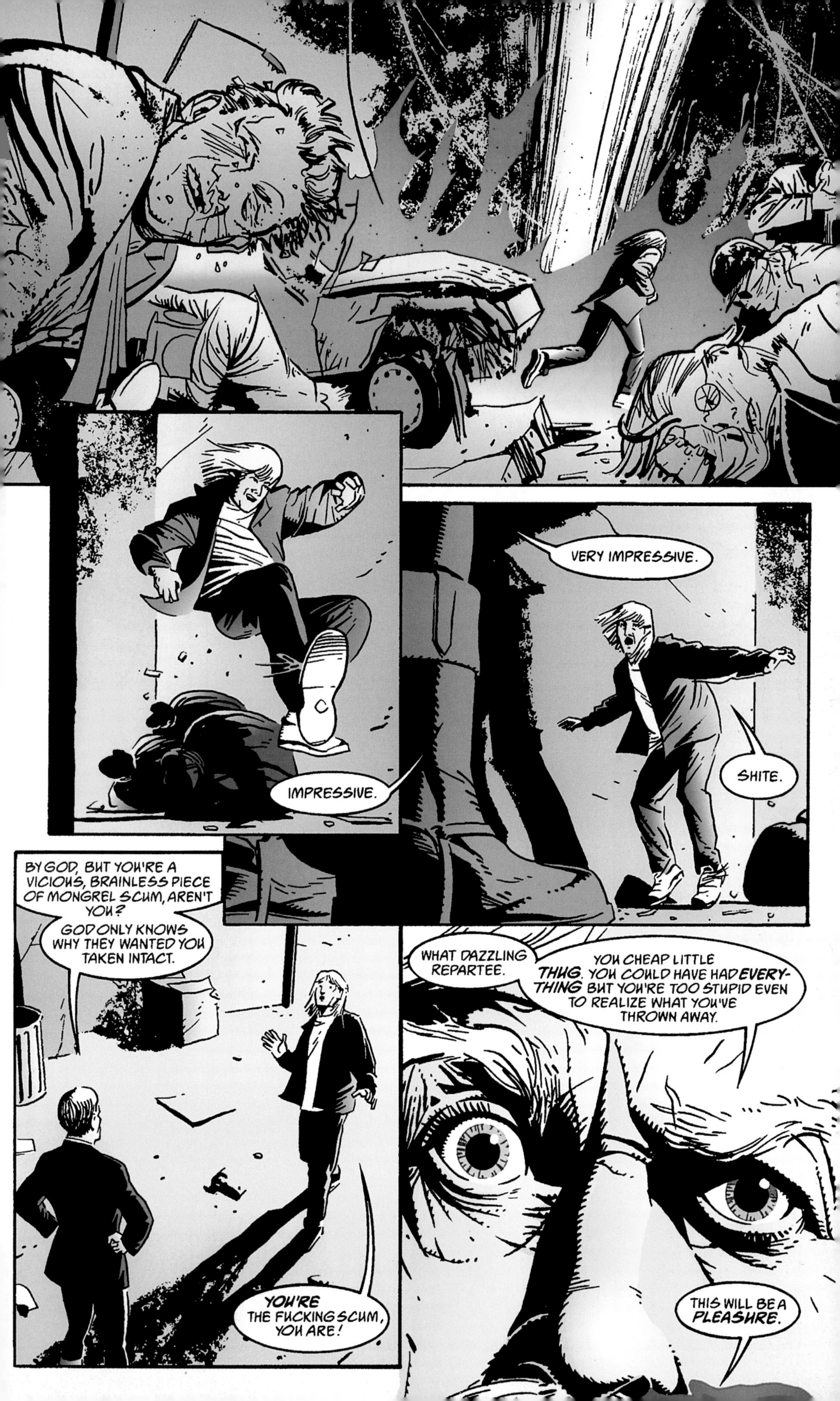
IMPRESSIVE.
VERY IMPRESSIVE.
SHITE.
BY GOD, BUT YOU'RE A VICIOUS, BRAINLESS PIECE OF MONGREL SCUM, AREN'T YOU?
GOD ONLY KNOWS WHY THEY WANTED YOU TAKEN INTACT.
YOU'RE THE FUCKING SCUM, YOU ARE!
WHAT DAZZLING REPARTEE.
YOU CHEAP LITTLE THUG. YOU COULD HAVE HAD EVERYTHING BUT YOU'RE TOO STUPID EVEN TO REALIZE WHAT YOU'VE THROWN AWAY.
THIS WILL BE A PLEASURE.

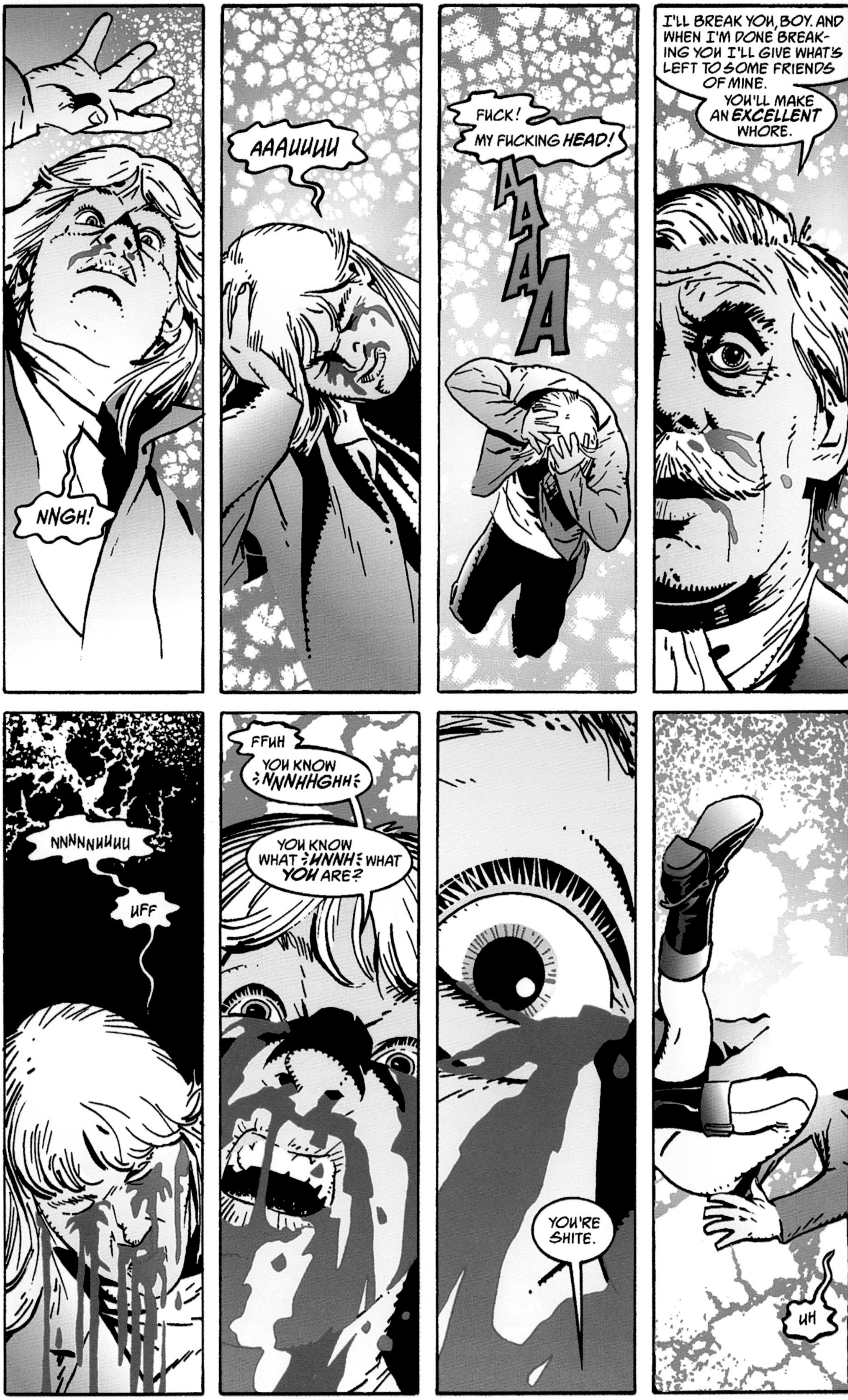
NNGH!
AAAUUUU
FUCK!
MY FUCKING HEAD!
AAAAA
I'LL BREAK YOU, BOY. AND WHEN I'M DONE BREAKING YOU I'LL GIVE WHAT'S LEFT TO SOME FRIENDS OF MINE.
YOU'LL MAKE AN EXCELLENT WHORE.
NNNNUUUU
UFF
FFUH
YOU KNOW NNNHHGHH
YOU KNOW WHAT UNNH WHAT YOU ARE?
YOU'RE SHITE.
UH

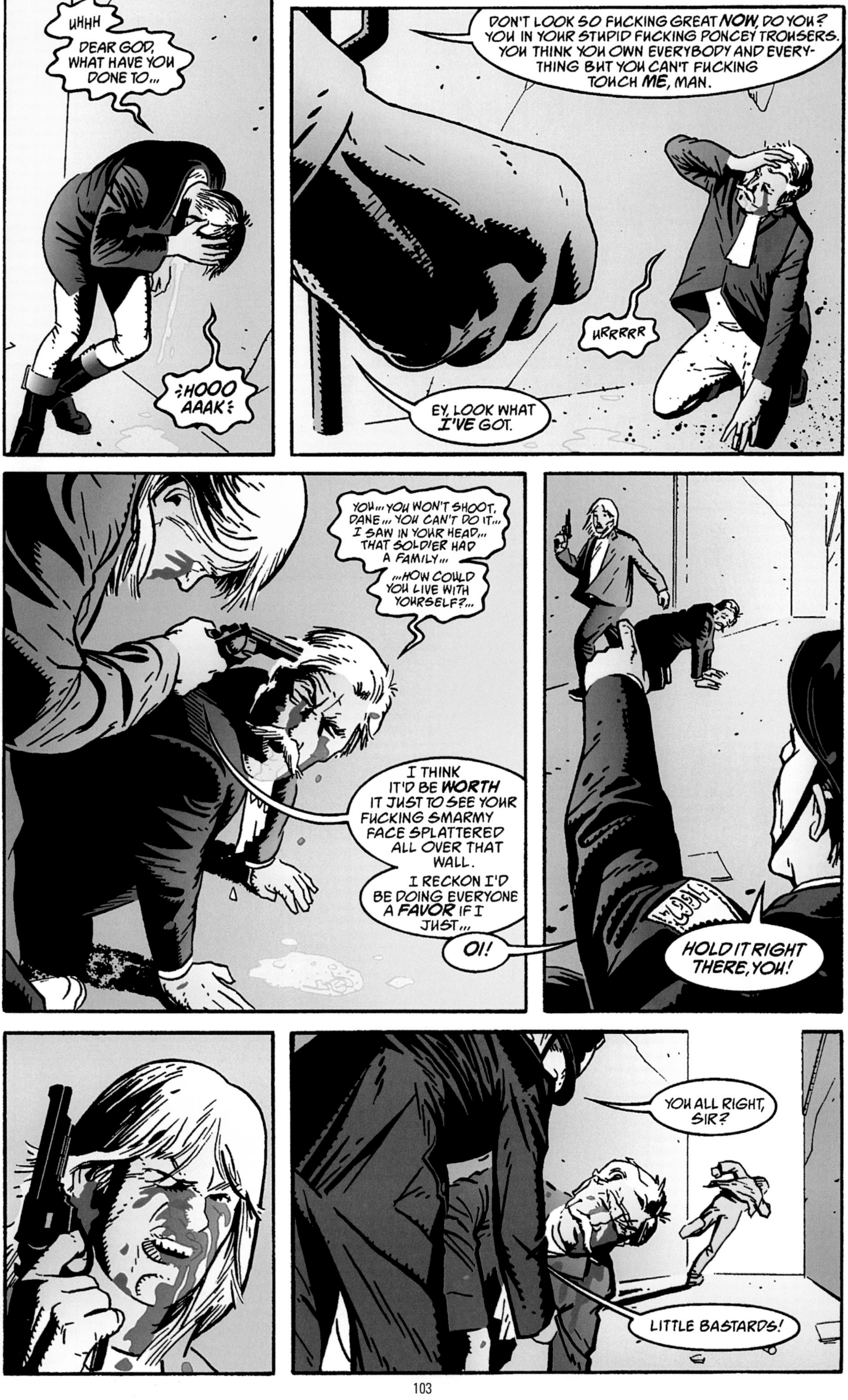
UHHH
DEAR GOD, WHAT HAVE YOU DONE TO...
HOOO AAAK
DON'T LOOK SO FUCKING GREAT NOW, DO YOU? YOU IN YOUR STUPID FUCKING PONCEY TROUSERS. YOU THINK YOU OWN EVERYBODY AND EVERYTHING BUT YOU CAN'T FUCKING TOUCH ME, MAN.
URRRRR
EY, LOOK WHAT I'VE GOT.
YOU... YOU WON'T SHOOT, DANE... YOU CAN'T DO IT... I SAW IN YOUR HEAD... THAT SOLDIER HAD A FAMILY...
...HOW COULD YOU LIVE WITH YOURSELF?...
I THINK IT'D BE WORTH IT JUST TO SEE YOUR FUCKING SMARMY FACE SPLATTERED ALL OVER THAT WALL.
I RECKON I'D BE DOING EVERYONE A FAVOR IF I JUST...
OI!
HOLD IT RIGHT THERE, YOU!
YOU ALL RIGHT, SIR?
LITTLE BASTARDS!

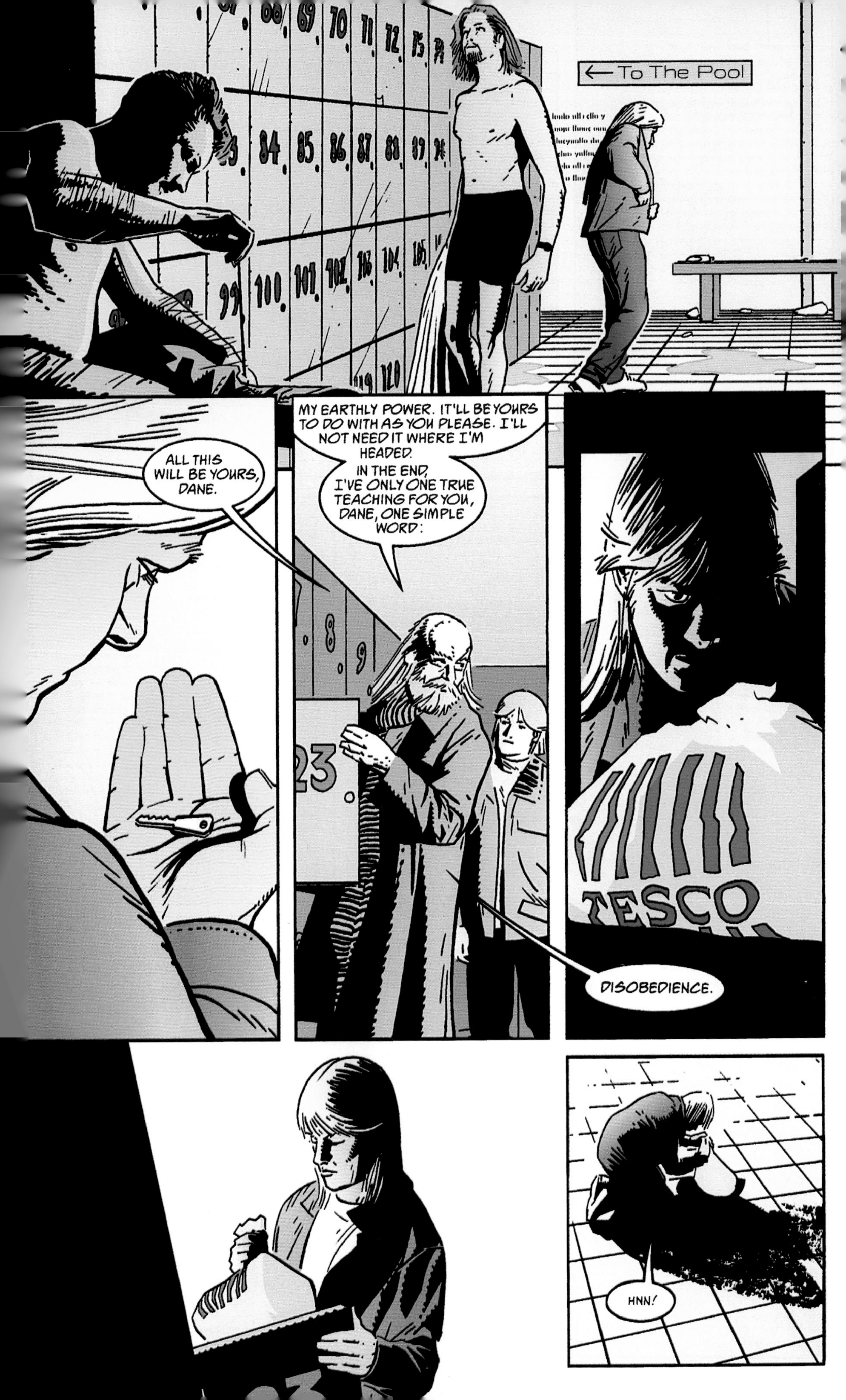
← To The Pool
ALL THIS WILL BE YOURS, DANE.
MY EARTHLY POWER. IT'LL BE YOURS TO DO WITH AS YOU PLEASE. I'LL NOT NEED IT WHERE I'M HEADED.
IN THE END, I'VE ONLY ONE TRUE TEACHING FOR YOU, DANE, ONE SIMPLE WORD:
TESCO
DISOBEDIENCE.
HNN!

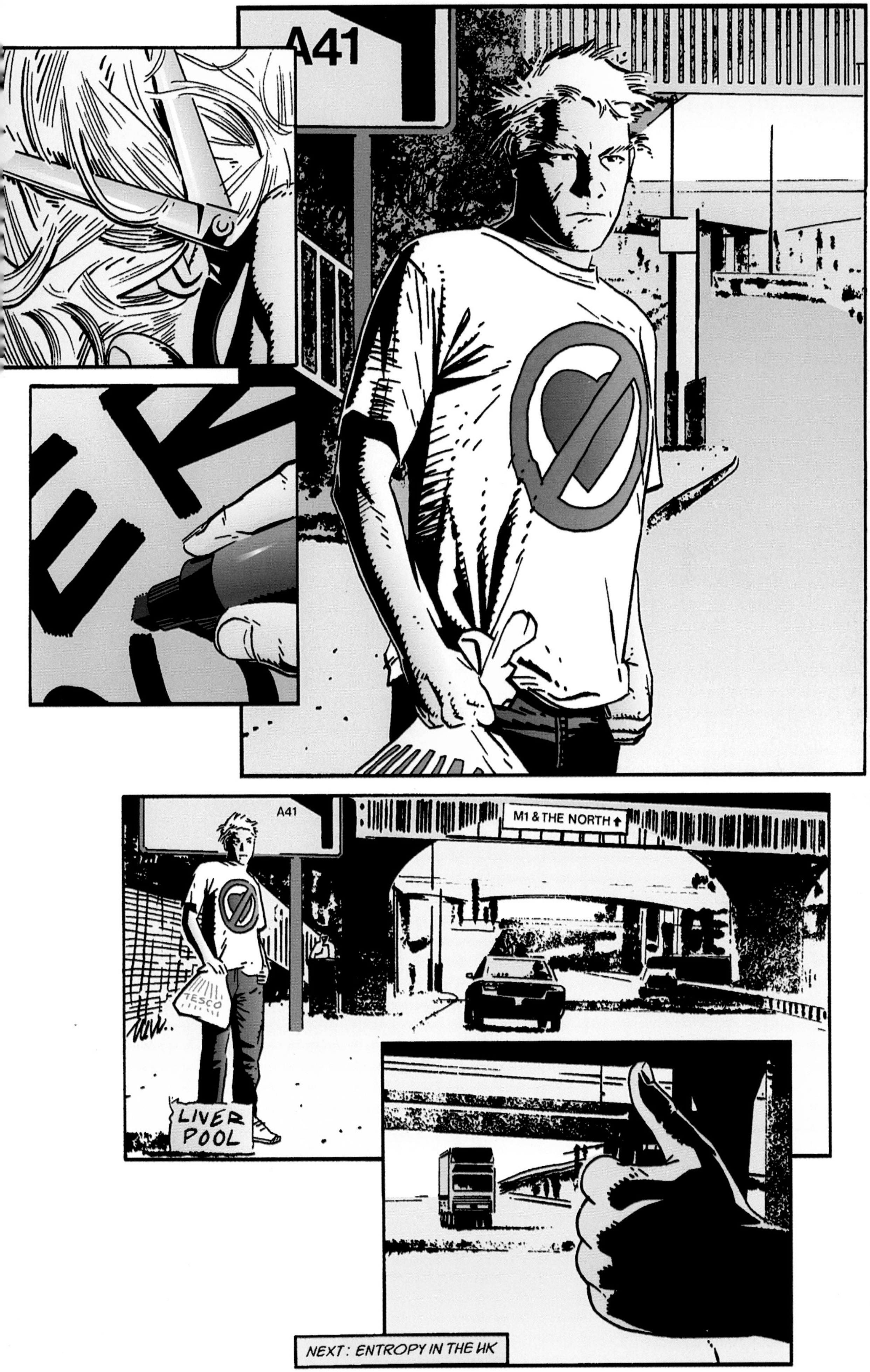
A41
A41
M1 & THE NORTH
TESCO
LIVER POOL
NEXT: ENTROPY IN THE UK

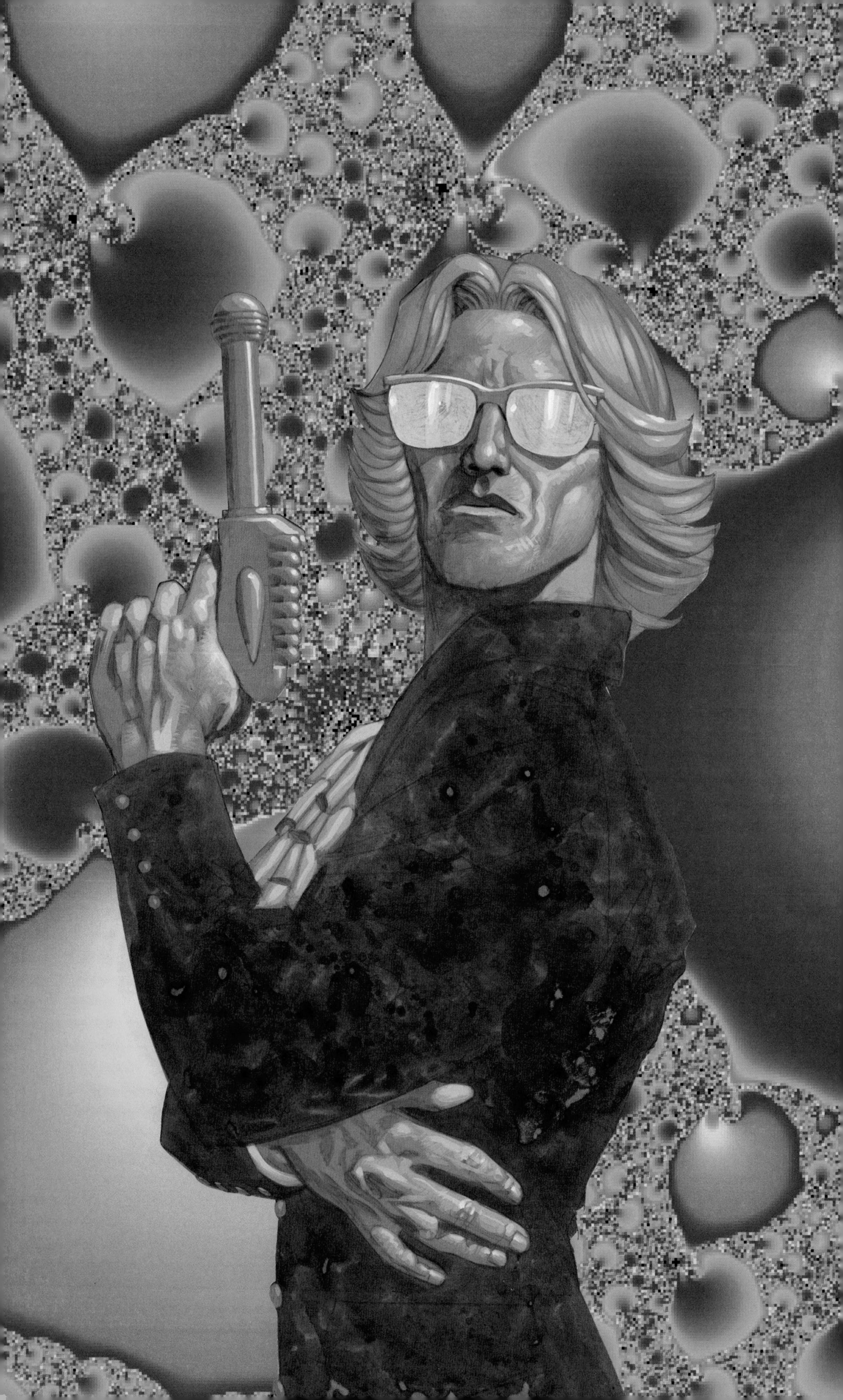

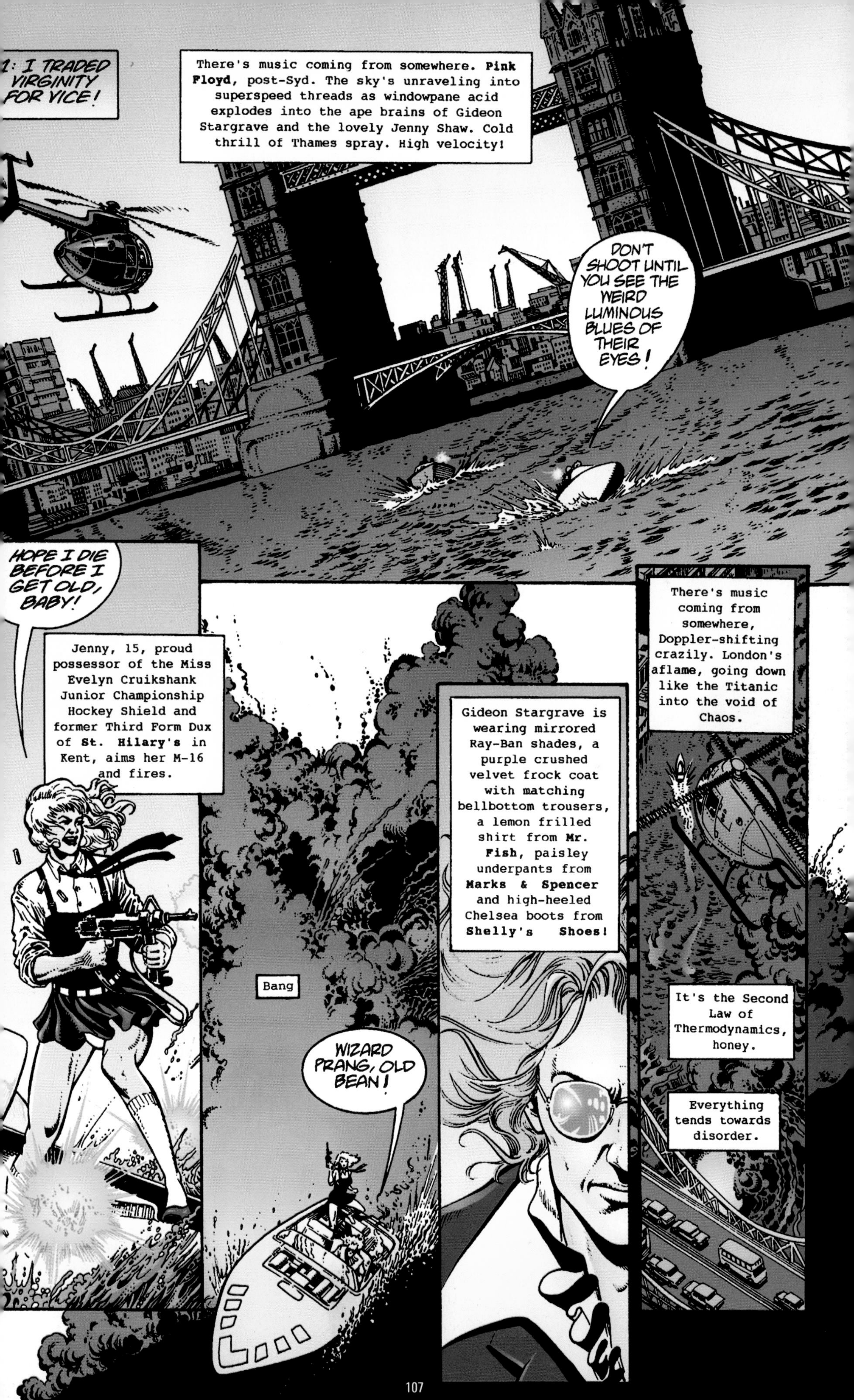
1: I TRADED VIRGINITY FOR VICE!
There's music coming from somewhere. **Pink Floyd**, post-Syd. The sky's unraveling into superspeed threads as windowpane acid explodes into the ape brains of Gideon Stargrave and the lovely Jenny Shaw. Cold thrill of Thames spray. High velocity!
DON'T SHOOT UNTIL YOU SEE THE WEIRD LUMINOUS BLUES OF THEIR EYES!
HOPE I DIE BEFORE I GET OLD, BABY!
Jenny, 15, proud possessor of the Miss Evelyn Cruikshank Junior Championship Hockey Shield and former Third Form Dux of **St. Hilary's** in Kent, aims her M-16 and fires.
Bang
WIZARD PRANG, OLD BEAN!
Gideon Stargrave is wearing mirrored Ray-Ban shades, a purple crushed velvet frock coat with matching bellbottom trousers, a lemon frilled shirt from **Mr. Fish**, paisley underpants from **Marks & Spencer** and high-heeled Chelsea boots from **Shelly's Shoes**!
There's music coming from somewhere, Doppler-shifting crazily. London's aflame, going down like the Titanic into the void of Chaos.
It's the Second Law of Thermodynamics, honey.
Everything tends towards disorder.

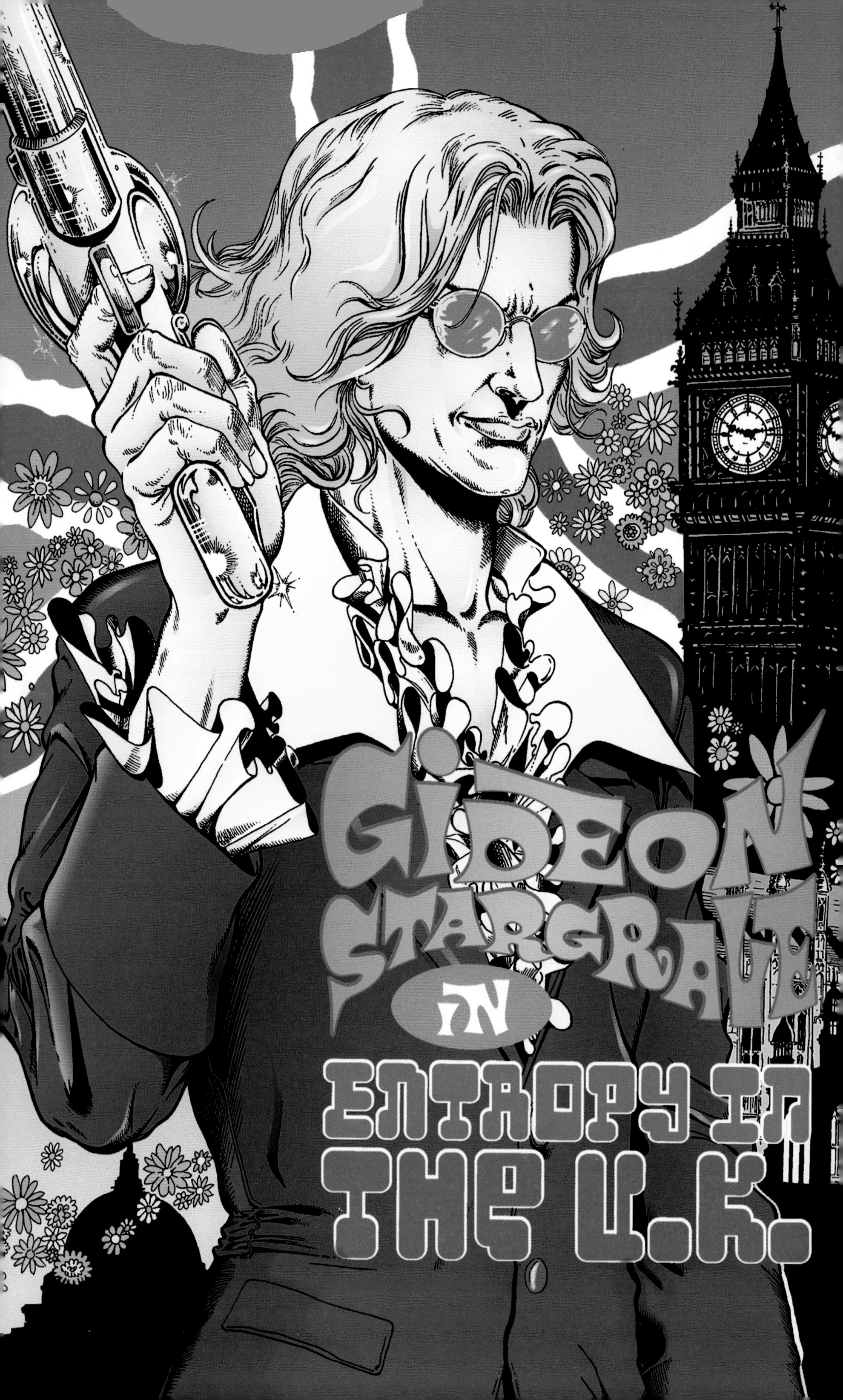

GIDEON STARGRAVE
IN
ENTROPY IN THE U.K.

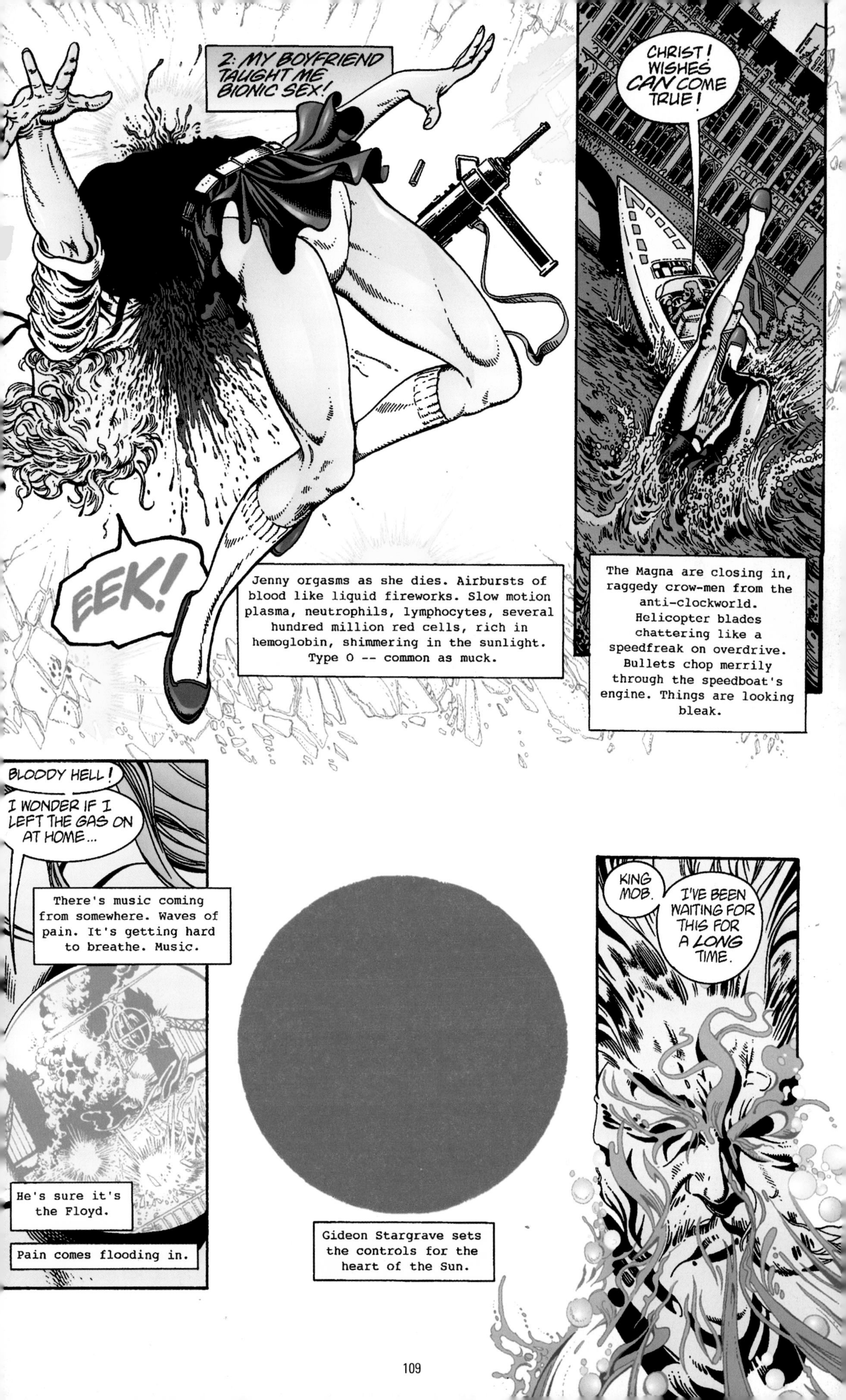
2: MY BOYFRIEND TAUGHT ME BIONIC SEX!
EEK!
Jenny orgasms as she dies. Airbursts of blood like liquid fireworks. Slow motion plasma, neutrophils, lymphocytes, several hundred million red cells, rich in hemoglobin, shimmering in the sunlight. Type O -- common as muck.
CHRIST! WISHES CAN COME TRUE!
The Magna are closing in, raggedy crow-men from the anti-clockworld. Helicopter blades chattering like a speedfreak on overdrive. Bullets chop merrily through the speedboat's engine. Things are looking bleak.
BLOODY HELL!
I WONDER IF I LEFT THE GAS ON AT HOME...
There's music coming from somewhere. Waves of pain. It's getting hard to breathe. Music.
He's sure it's the Floyd.
Pain comes flooding in.
Gideon Stargrave sets the controls for the heart of the Sun.
KING MOB.
I'VE BEEN WAITING FOR THIS FOR A LONG TIME.

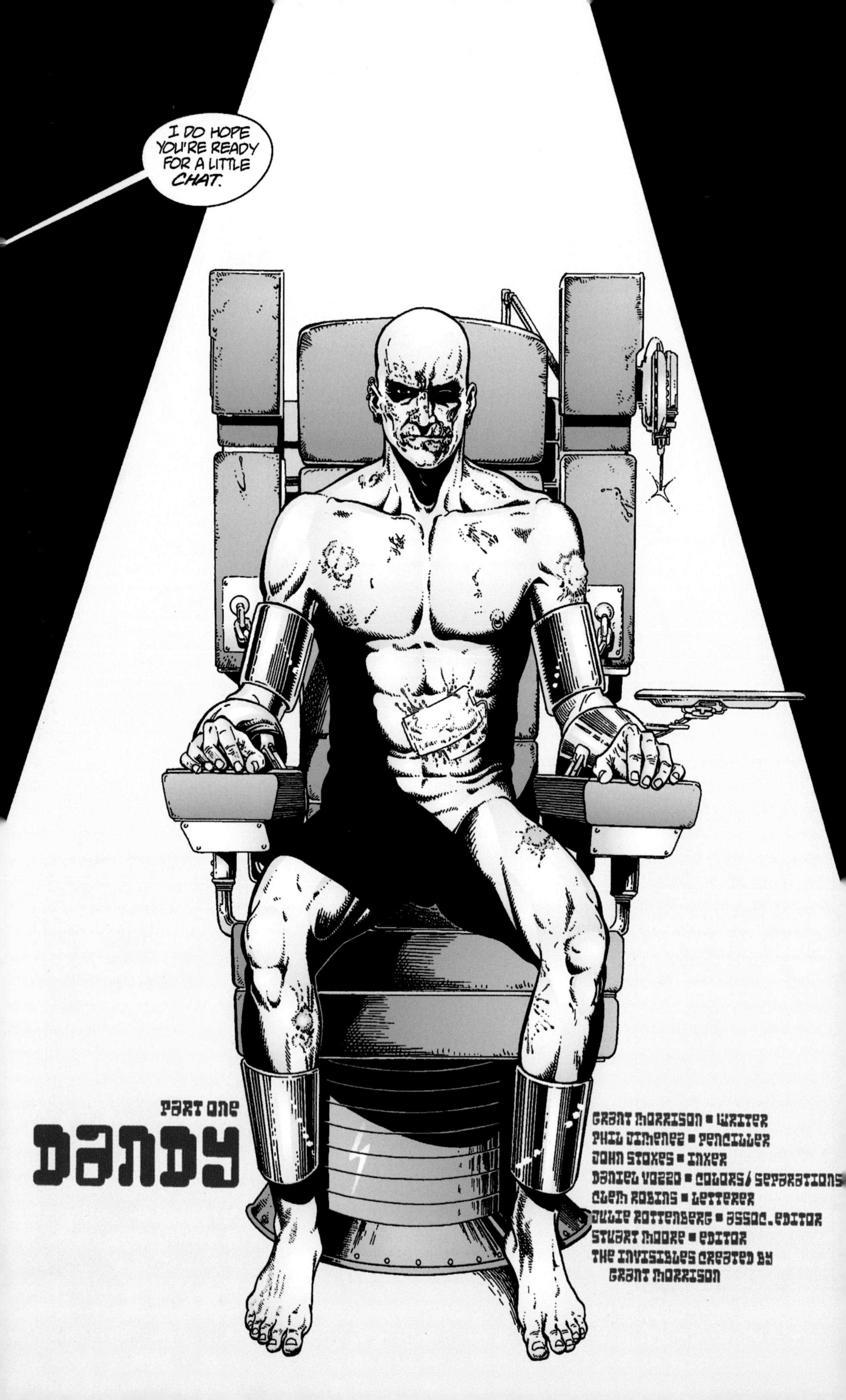
I DO HOPE YOU'RE READY FOR A LITTLE *CHAT*.
PART ONE
DANDY
GRANT MORRISON ▪ WRITER
PHIL JIMENEZ ▪ PENCILLER
JOHN STOKES ▪ INKER
DANIEL VOZZO ▪ COLORS/ SEPARATIONS
CLEM ROBINS ▪ LETTERER
JULIE ROTTENBERG ▪ ASSOC. EDITOR
STUART MOORE ▪ EDITOR
THE INVISIBLES CREATED BY GRANT MORRISON

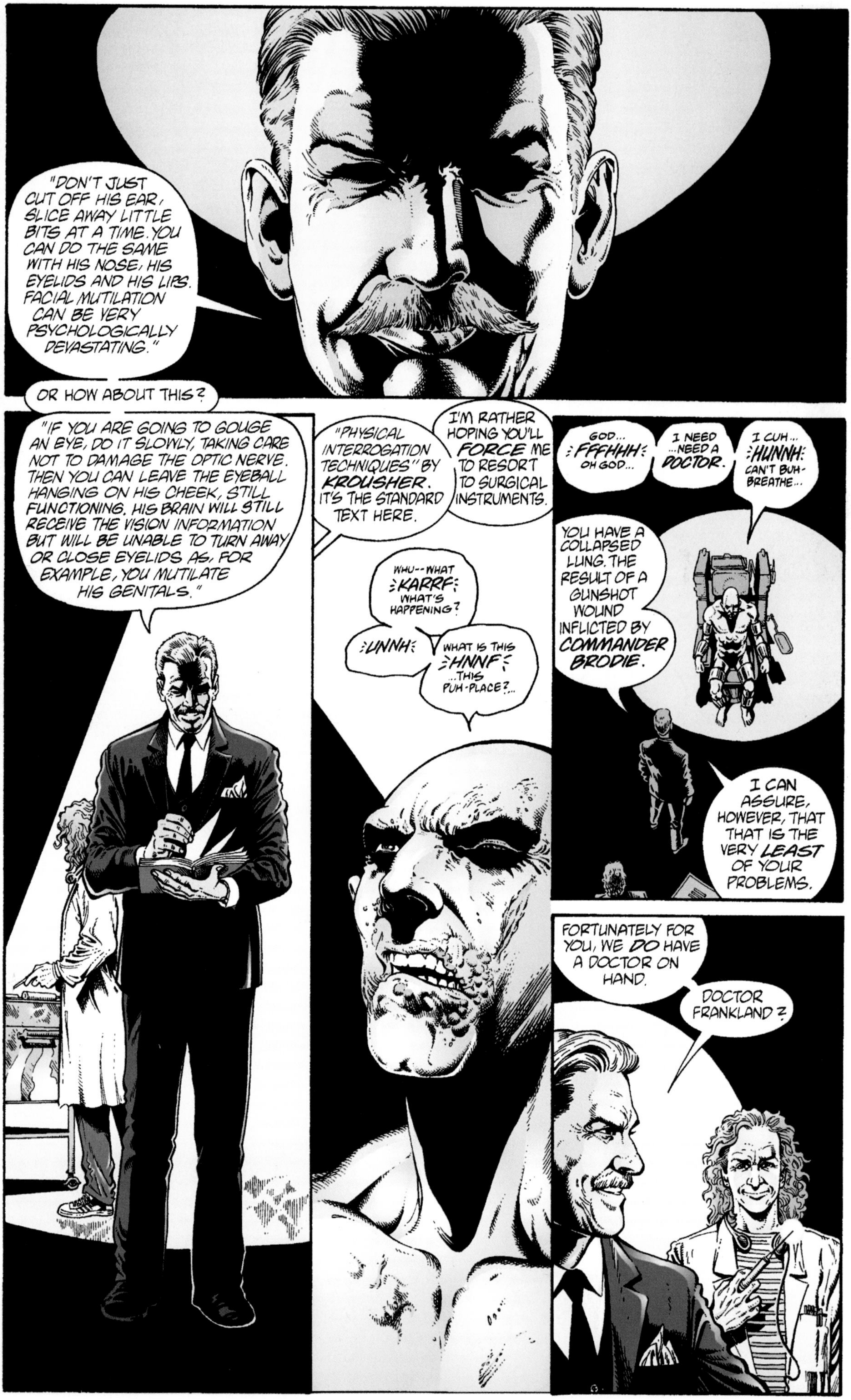
"DON'T JUST CUT OFF HIS EAR, SLICE AWAY LITTLE BITS AT A TIME. YOU CAN DO THE SAME WITH HIS NOSE, HIS EYELIDS AND HIS LIPS. FACIAL MUTILATION CAN BE VERY PSYCHOLOGICALLY DEVASTATING."
OR HOW ABOUT THIS?
"IF YOU ARE GOING TO GOUGE AN EYE, DO IT SLOWLY, TAKING CARE NOT TO DAMAGE THE OPTIC NERVE. THEN YOU CAN LEAVE THE EYEBALL HANGING ON HIS CHEEK, STILL FUNCTIONING. HIS BRAIN WILL STILL RECEIVE THE VISION INFORMATION BUT WILL BE UNABLE TO TURN AWAY OR CLOSE EYELIDS AS, FOR EXAMPLE, YOU MUTILATE HIS GENITALS."
"PHYSICAL INTERROGATION TECHNIQUES" BY KROUSHER. IT'S THE STANDARD TEXT HERE.
I'M RATHER HOPING YOU'LL FORCE ME TO RESORT TO SURGICAL INSTRUMENTS.
WHU--WHAT KARRF WHAT'S HAPPENING?
UNNH
WHAT IS THIS HNNF ...THIS PUH-PLACE?...
GOD... FFFHHH OH GOD...
I NEED ...NEED A DOCTOR.
I CUH... HUNNH CAN'T BUH-BREATHE...
YOU HAVE A COLLAPSED LUNG. THE RESULT OF A GUNSHOT WOUND INFLICTED BY COMMANDER BRODIE.
I CAN ASSURE, HOWEVER, THAT THAT IS THE VERY LEAST OF YOUR PROBLEMS.
FORTUNATELY FOR YOU, WE DO HAVE A DOCTOR ON HAND.
DOCTOR FRANKLAND?

WUH-WHAT ARE YOU {HUFF} WHAT...

DON'T...

WAIT... JUST...

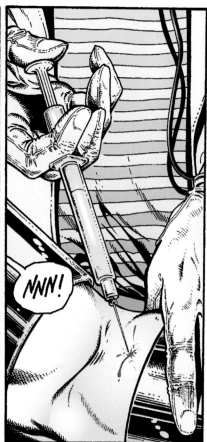

NNN!

WHAT ARE YOU DOING TO ME?

IS IT... {MMMM} ...IS IT MONEY?...

WHO IS GIDEON STARGRAVE?

IS THAT YOUR REAL NAME?

WHAT?

{chuff}

{hunnhh}

WHY ARE YOU ASK.... {KKuhh} ...ASKING ME THIS?...

BECAUSE I CAN SEE INSIDE YOUR BLOODY HEAD!

YOU CAN'T LIE TO ME!

DON'T TRY!

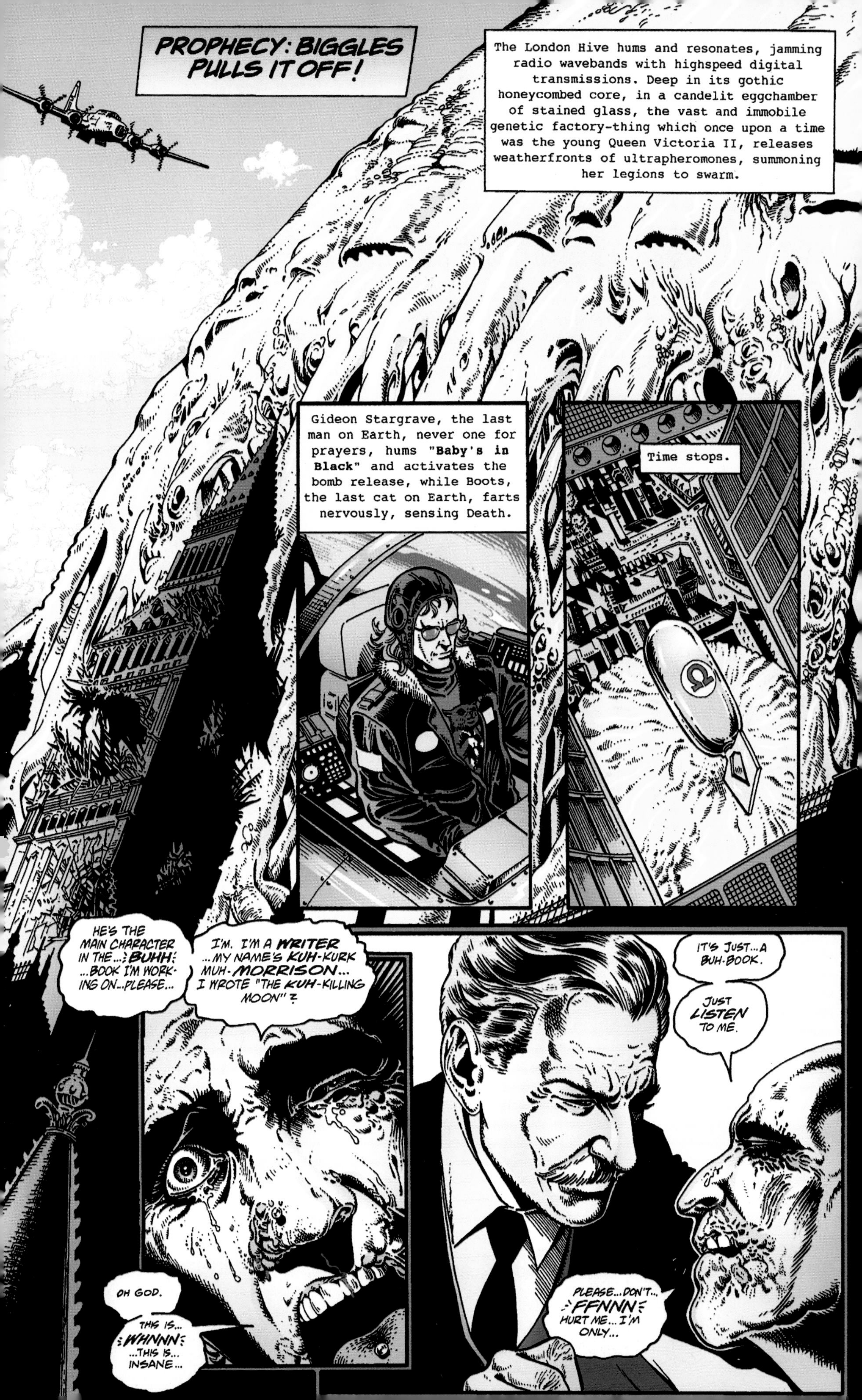
PROPHECY: BIGGLES PULLS IT OFF!
The London Hive hums and resonates, jamming radio wavebands with highspeed digital transmissions. Deep in its gothic honeycombed core, in a candelit eggchamber of stained glass, the vast and immobile genetic factory-thing which once upon a time was the young Queen Victoria II, releases weatherfronts of ultrapheromones, summoning her legions to swarm.
Gideon Stargrave, the last man on Earth, never one for prayers, hums "Baby's in Black" and activates the bomb release, while Boots, the last cat on Earth, farts nervously, sensing Death.
Time stops.
HE'S THE MAIN CHARACTER IN THE...BUHH...BOOK I'M WORKING ON...PLEASE...
I'M. I'M A WRITER ...MY NAME'S KUH-KURK MUH-MORRISON... I WROTE "THE KUH-KILLING MOON"?
IT'S JUST...A BUH-BOOK.
JUST LISTEN TO ME.
OH GOD.
THIS IS... WHNNN ...THIS IS... INSANE...
PLEASE...DON'T... FFNNN HURT ME...I'M ONLY...

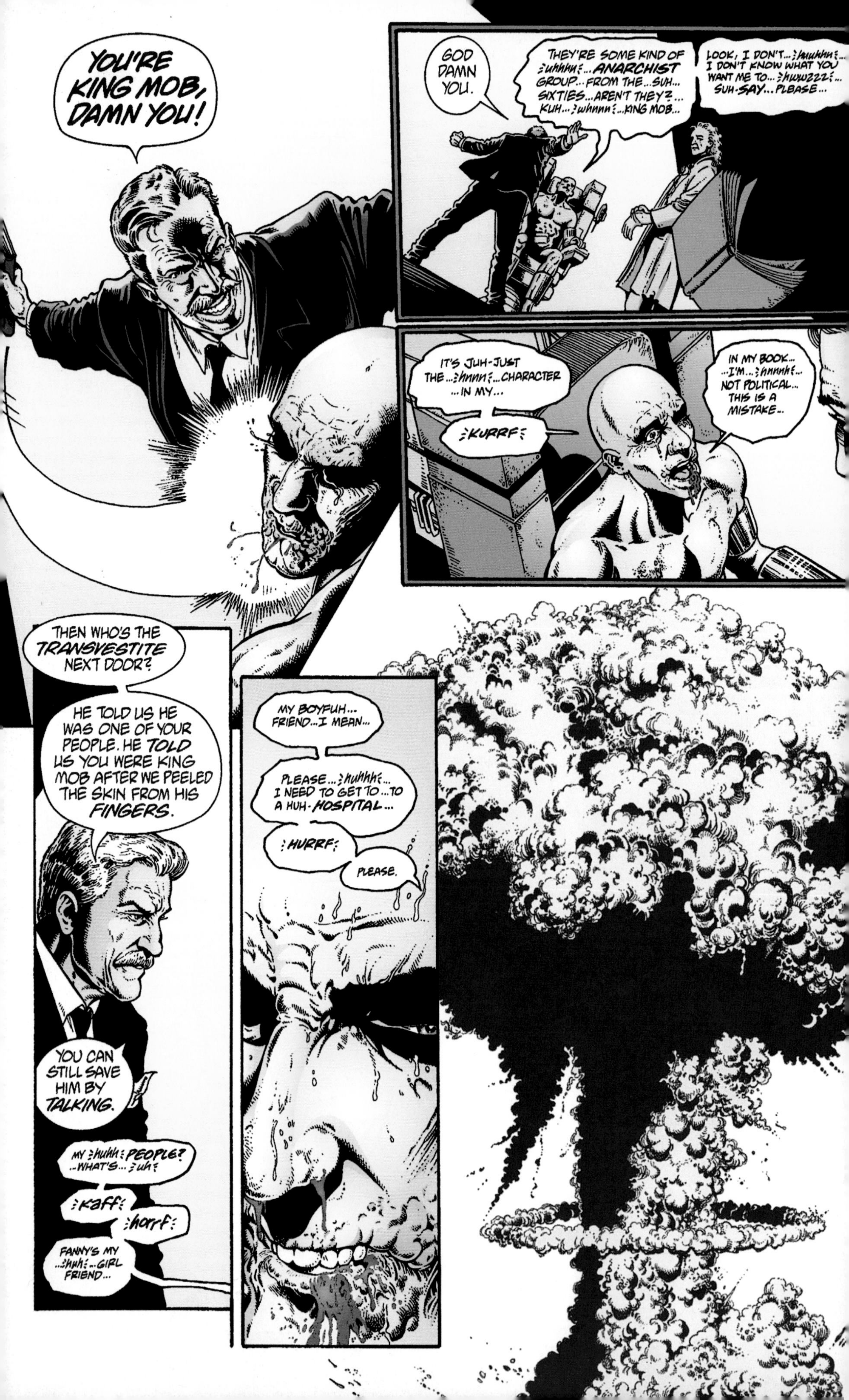
YOU'RE KING MOB, DAMN YOU!
GOD DAMN YOU.
THEY'RE SOME KIND OF ⁝uhhhn⁝... ANARCHIST GROUP... FROM THE... SUH... SIXTIES... AREN'T THEY? ... KUH... ⁝whnnn⁝ ...KING MOB...
LOOK, I DON'T... ⁝huhhn⁝... I DON'T KNOW WHAT YOU WANT ME TO... ⁝hwwzzz⁝... SUH-SAY... PLEASE...
IT'S JUH-JUST THE... ⁝hnnn⁝ ...CHARACTER ...IN MY...
⁝KURRF⁝
IN MY BOOK... ...I'M... ⁝hnnnh⁝... NOT POLITICAL... THIS IS A MISTAKE...
THEN WHO'S THE TRANSVESTITE NEXT DOOR?
HE TOLD US HE WAS ONE OF YOUR PEOPLE. HE TOLD US YOU WERE KING MOB AFTER WE PEELED THE SKIN FROM HIS FINGERS.
YOU CAN STILL SAVE HIM BY TALKING.
MY ⁝huhh⁝ PEOPLE? ...WHAT'S... ⁝uh⁝
⁝kaff⁝
⁝horrf⁝
FANNY'S MY ...⁝huh⁝... GIRL FRIEND...
MY BOYFUH... FRIEND... I MEAN...
PLEASE... ⁝huhhh⁝... I NEED TO GET TO... TO A HUH-HOSPITAL...
⁝HURRF⁝
PLEASE.

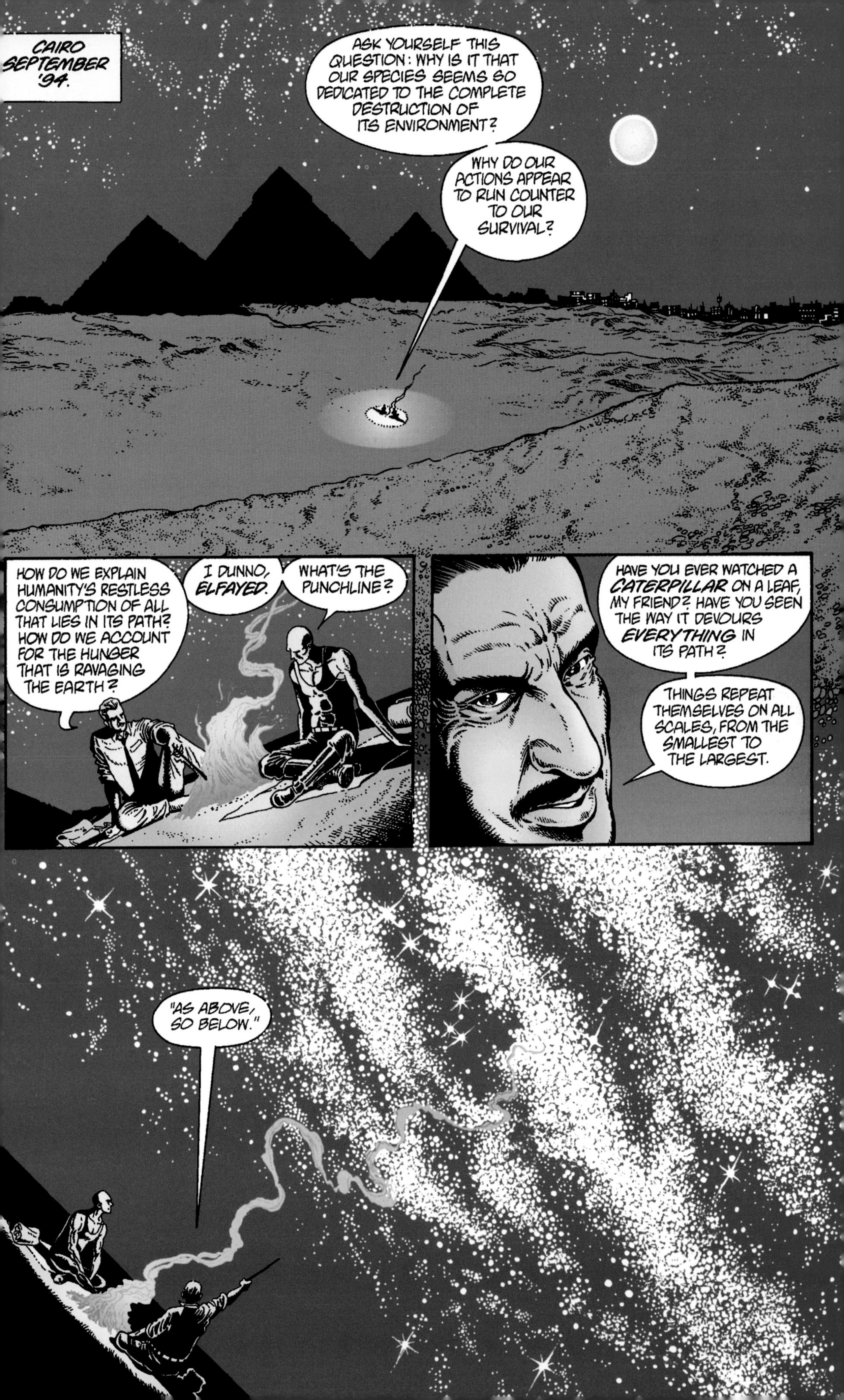
CAIRO SEPTEMBER '94.
ASK YOURSELF THIS QUESTION: WHY IS IT THAT OUR SPECIES SEEMS SO DEDICATED TO THE COMPLETE DESTRUCTION OF ITS ENVIRONMENT?
WHY DO OUR ACTIONS APPEAR TO RUN COUNTER TO OUR SURVIVAL?
HOW DO WE EXPLAIN HUMANITY'S RESTLESS CONSUMPTION OF ALL THAT LIES IN ITS PATH? HOW DO WE ACCOUNT FOR THE HUNGER THAT IS RAVAGING THE EARTH?
I DUNNO, ELFAYED.
WHAT'S THE PUNCHLINE?
HAVE YOU EVER WATCHED A CATERPILLAR ON A LEAF, MY FRIEND? HAVE YOU SEEN THE WAY IT DEVOURS EVERYTHING IN ITS PATH?
THINGS REPEAT THEMSELVES ON ALL SCALES, FROM THE SMALLEST TO THE LARGEST.
"AS ABOVE, SO BELOW."

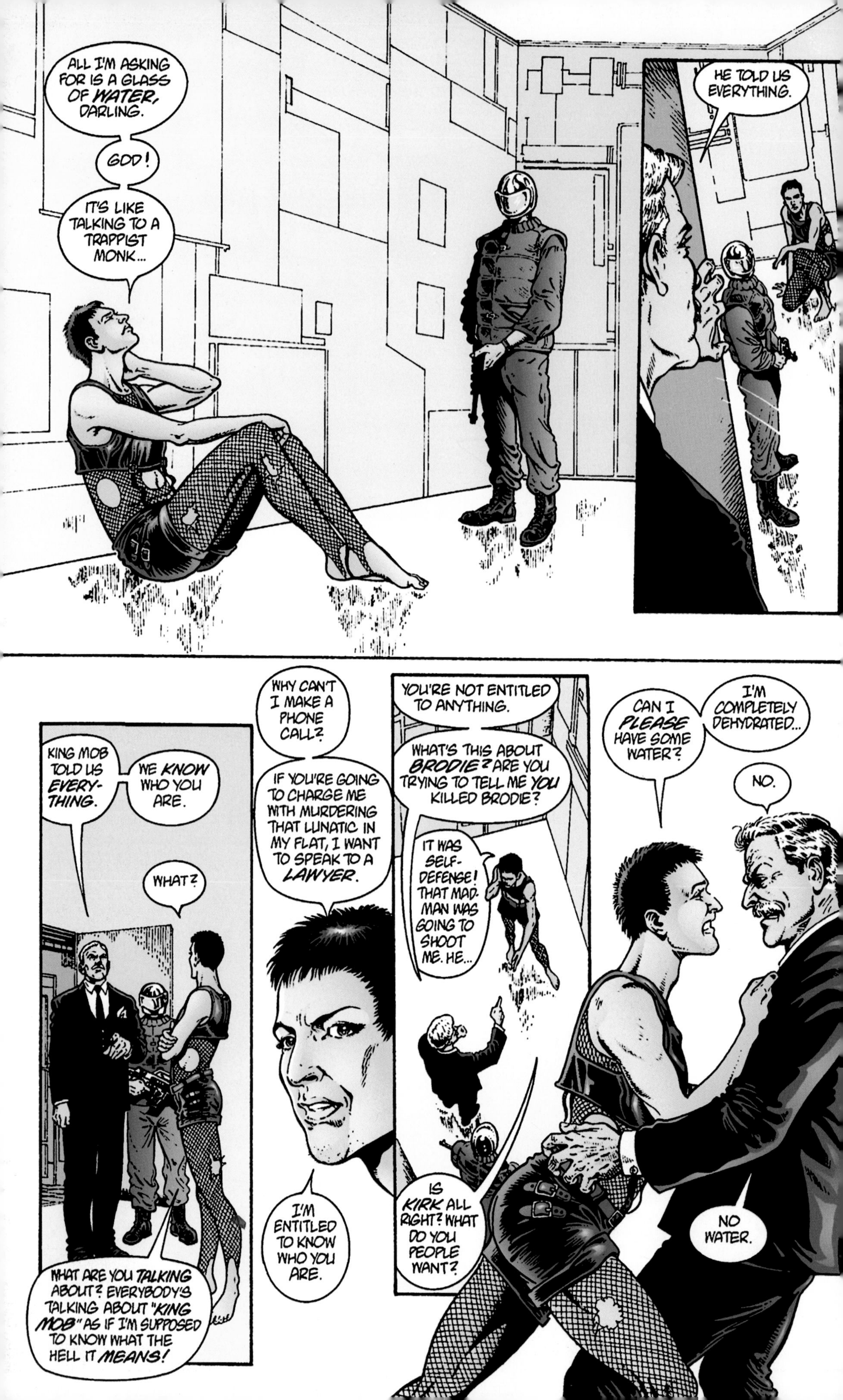
ALL I'M ASKING FOR IS A GLASS OF WATER, DARLING.
GOD!
IT'S LIKE TALKING TO A TRAPPIST MONK...
HE TOLD US EVERYTHING.
KING MOB TOLD US EVERY-THING.
WE KNOW WHO YOU ARE.
WHAT?
WHAT ARE YOU TALKING ABOUT? EVERYBODY'S TALKING ABOUT "KING MOB" AS IF I'M SUPPOSED TO KNOW WHAT THE HELL IT MEANS!
WHY CAN'T I MAKE A PHONE CALL?
IF YOU'RE GOING TO CHARGE ME WITH MURDERING THAT LUNATIC IN MY FLAT, I WANT TO SPEAK TO A LAWYER.
I'M ENTITLED TO KNOW WHO YOU ARE.
YOU'RE NOT ENTITLED TO ANYTHING.
WHAT'S THIS ABOUT BRODIE? ARE YOU TRYING TO TELL ME YOU KILLED BRODIE?
IT WAS SELF-DEFENSE! THAT MAD-MAN WAS GOING TO SHOOT ME. HE...
IS KIRK ALL RIGHT? WHAT DO YOU PEOPLE WANT?
CAN I PLEASE HAVE SOME WATER?
I'M COMPLETELY DEHYDRATED...
NO.
NO WATER.

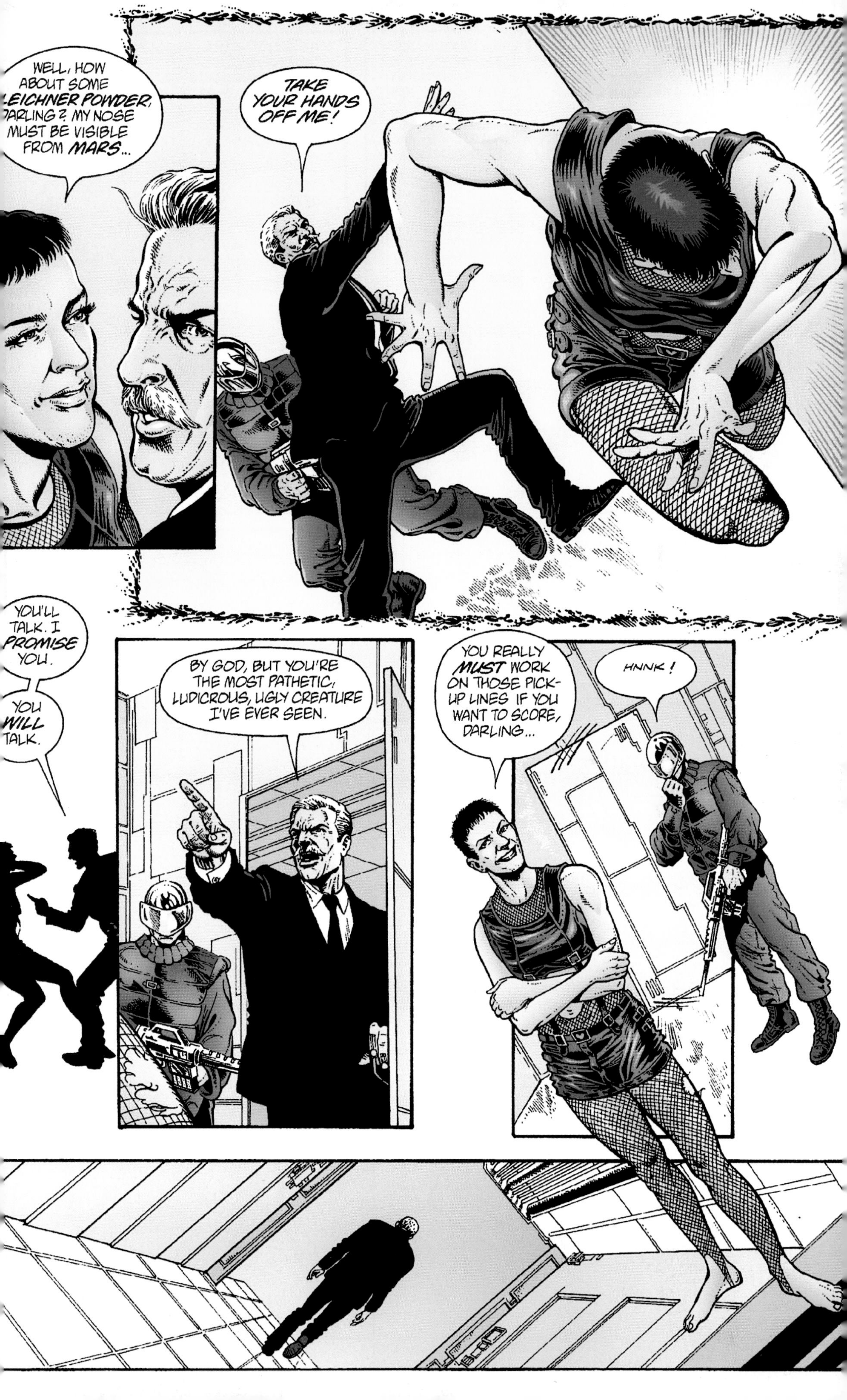

WELL, HOW ABOUT SOME LEICHNER POWDER, DARLING? MY NOSE MUST BE VISIBLE FROM MARS...
TAKE YOUR HANDS OFF ME!
YOU'LL TALK. I PROMISE YOU.
YOU WILL TALK.
BY GOD, BUT YOU'RE THE MOST PATHETIC, LUDICROUS, UGLY CREATURE I'VE EVER SEEN.
YOU REALLY MUST WORK ON THOSE PICK-UP LINES IF YOU WANT TO SCORE, DARLING...
HNNK!

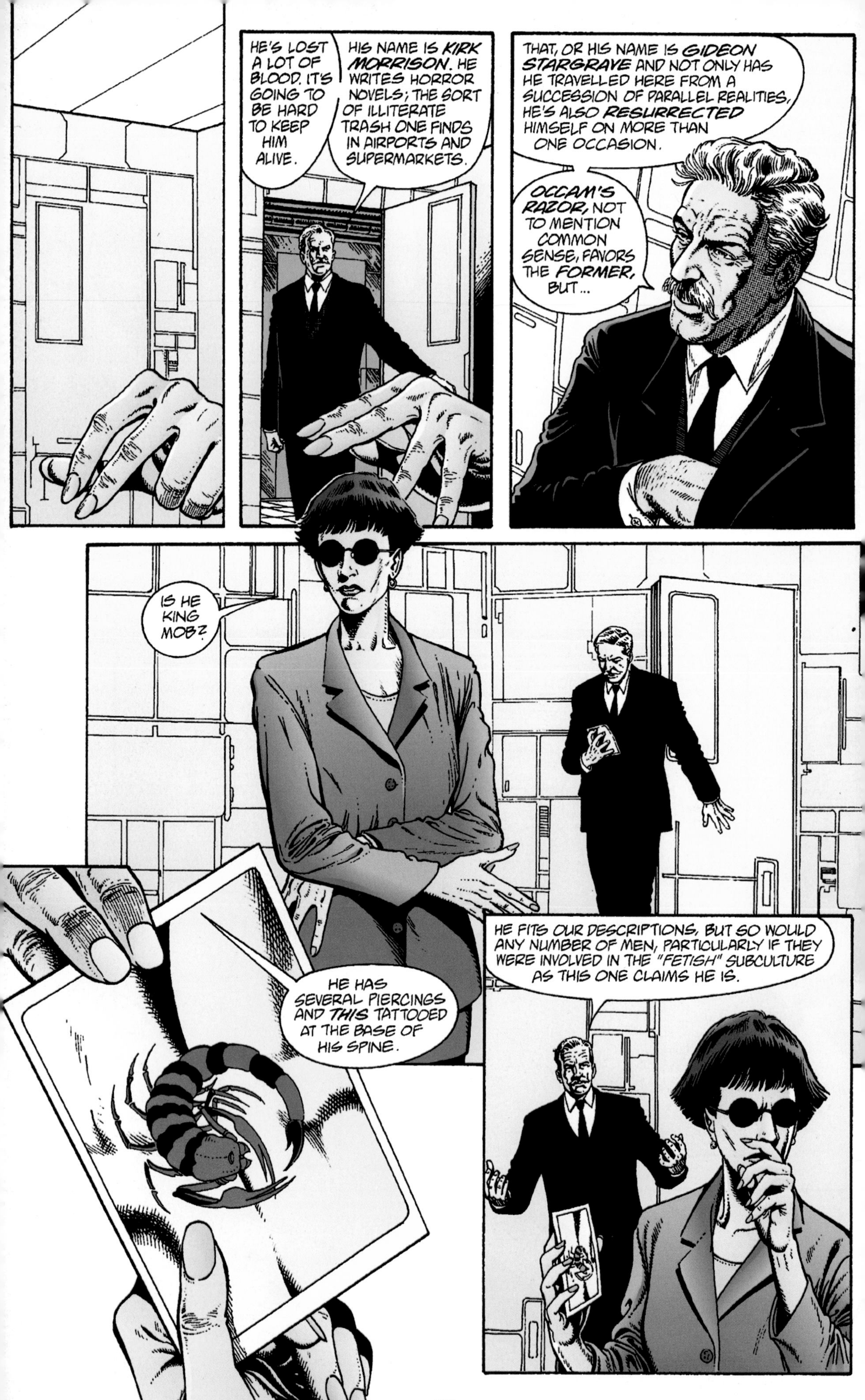

HE'S LOST A LOT OF BLOOD. IT'S GOING TO BE HARD TO KEEP HIM ALIVE.
HIS NAME IS KIRK MORRISON. HE WRITES HORROR NOVELS; THE SORT OF ILLITERATE TRASH ONE FINDS IN AIRPORTS AND SUPERMARKETS.
THAT, OR HIS NAME IS GIDEON STARGRAVE AND NOT ONLY HAS HE TRAVELLED HERE FROM A SUCCESSION OF PARALLEL REALITIES, HE'S ALSO RESURRECTED HIMSELF ON MORE THAN ONE OCCASION.
OCCAM'S RAZOR, NOT TO MENTION COMMON SENSE, FAVORS THE FORMER, BUT...
IS HE KING MOB?
HE HAS SEVERAL PIERCINGS AND THIS TATTOOED AT THE BASE OF HIS SPINE.
HE FITS OUR DESCRIPTIONS, BUT SO WOULD ANY NUMBER OF MEN, PARTICULARLY IF THEY WERE INVOLVED IN THE "FETISH" SUBCULTURE AS THIS ONE CLAIMS HE IS.

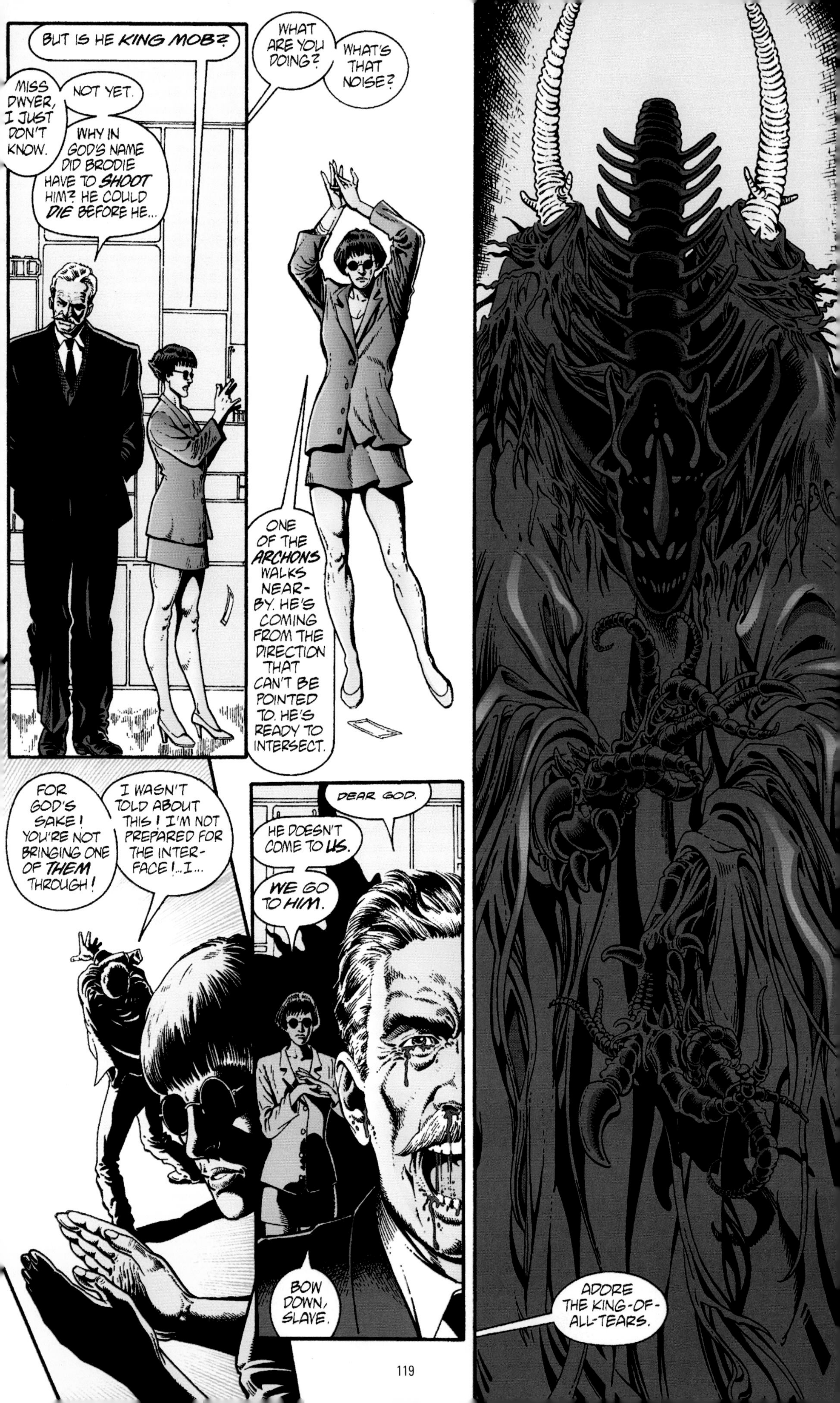
BUT IS HE **KING MOB**?
MISS DWYER, I JUST DON'T KNOW.
NOT YET.
WHY IN GOD'S NAME DID BRODIE HAVE TO **SHOOT** HIM? HE COULD **DIE** BEFORE HE...
WHAT ARE YOU DOING?
WHAT'S THAT NOISE?
ONE OF THE **ARCHONS** WALKS NEAR-BY. HE'S COMING FROM THE DIRECTION THAT CAN'T BE POINTED TO. HE'S READY TO INTERSECT.
FOR GOD'S SAKE! YOU'RE NOT BRINGING ONE OF **THEM** THROUGH!
I WASN'T TOLD ABOUT THIS! I'M NOT PREPARED FOR THE INTER-FACE!...I...
DEAR GOD.
HE DOESN'T COME TO **US**.
WE GO TO **HIM**.
BOW DOWN, SLAVE.
ADORE THE KING-OF-ALL-TEARS.

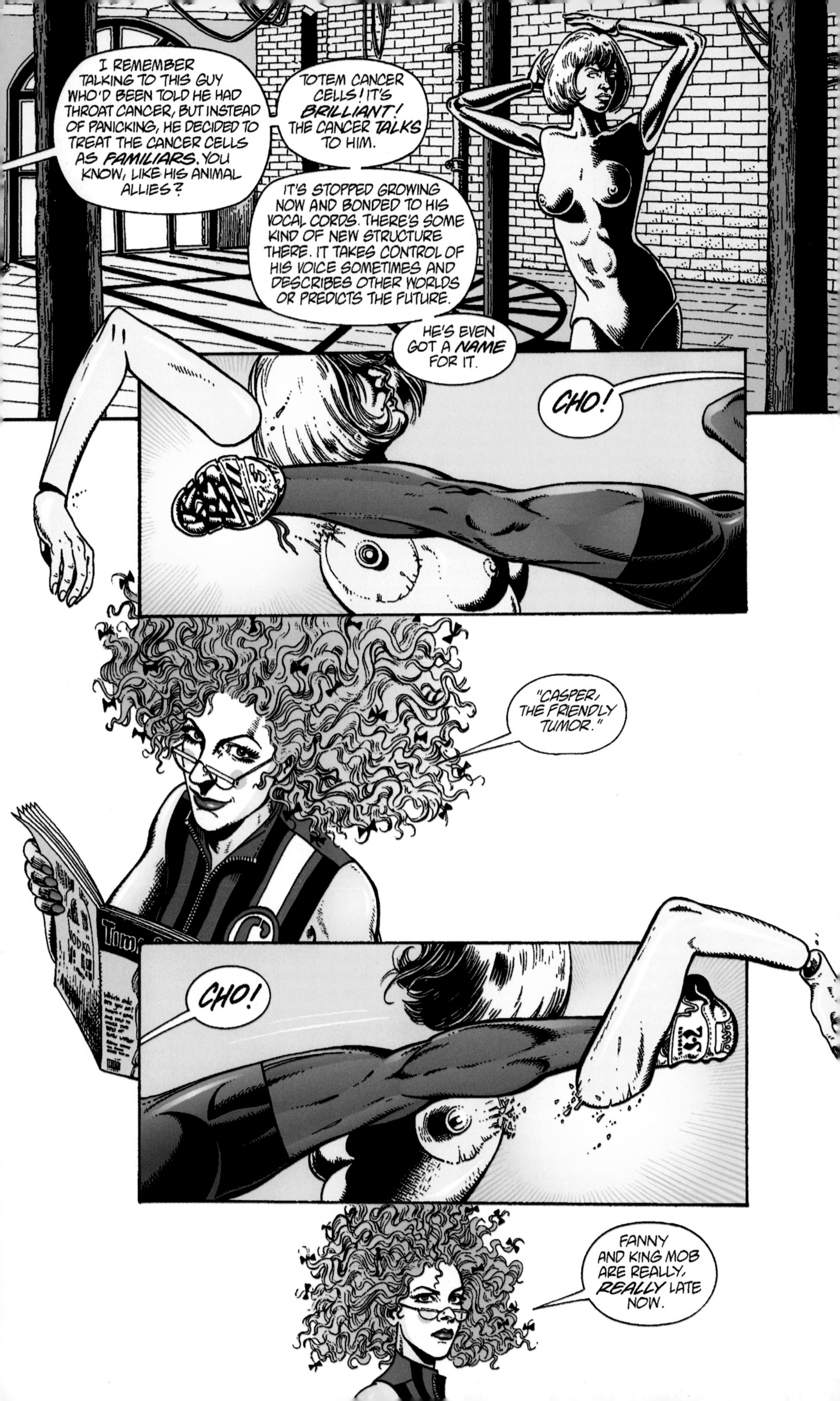

I REMEMBER TALKING TO THIS GUY WHO'D BEEN TOLD HE HAD THROAT CANCER, BUT INSTEAD OF PANICKING, HE DECIDED TO TREAT THE CANCER CELLS AS FAMILIARS. YOU KNOW, LIKE HIS ANIMAL ALLIES?
TOTEM CANCER CELLS! IT'S BRILLIANT! THE CANCER TALKS TO HIM.
IT'S STOPPED GROWING NOW AND BONDED TO HIS VOCAL CORDS. THERE'S SOME KIND OF NEW STRUCTURE THERE. IT TAKES CONTROL OF HIS VOICE SOMETIMES AND DESCRIBES OTHER WORLDS OR PREDICTS THE FUTURE.
HE'S EVEN GOT A NAME FOR IT.
CHO!
"CASPER, THE FRIENDLY TUMOR."
CHO!
FANNY AND KING MOB ARE REALLY, REALLY LATE NOW.

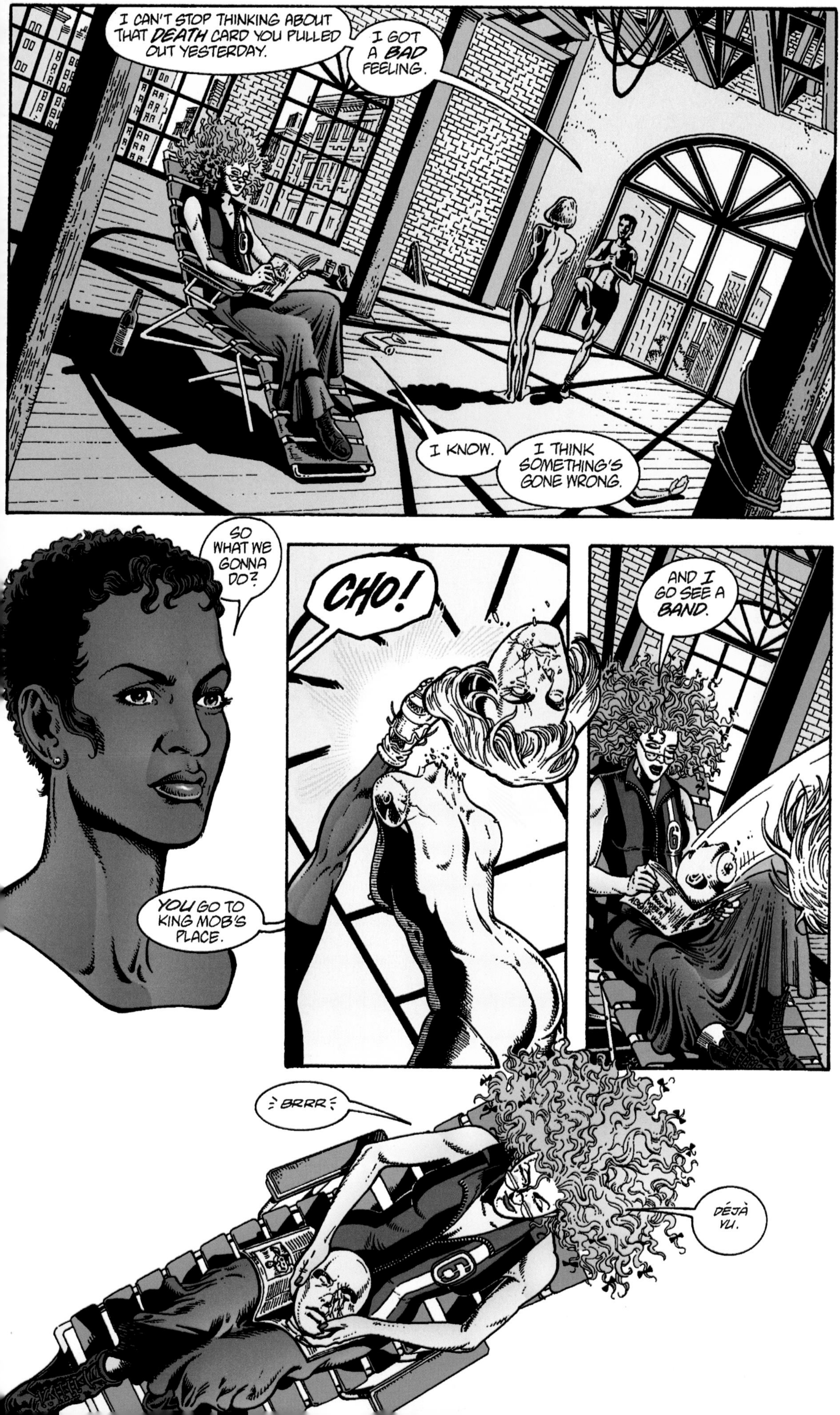

I CAN'T STOP THINKING ABOUT THAT DEATH CARD YOU PULLED OUT YESTERDAY.
I GOT A BAD FEELING.
I KNOW.
I THINK SOMETHING'S GONE WRONG.
SO WHAT WE GONNA DO?
YOU GO TO KING MOB'S PLACE.
CHO!
AND I GO SEE A BAND.
BRRR
DÉJÀ VU.

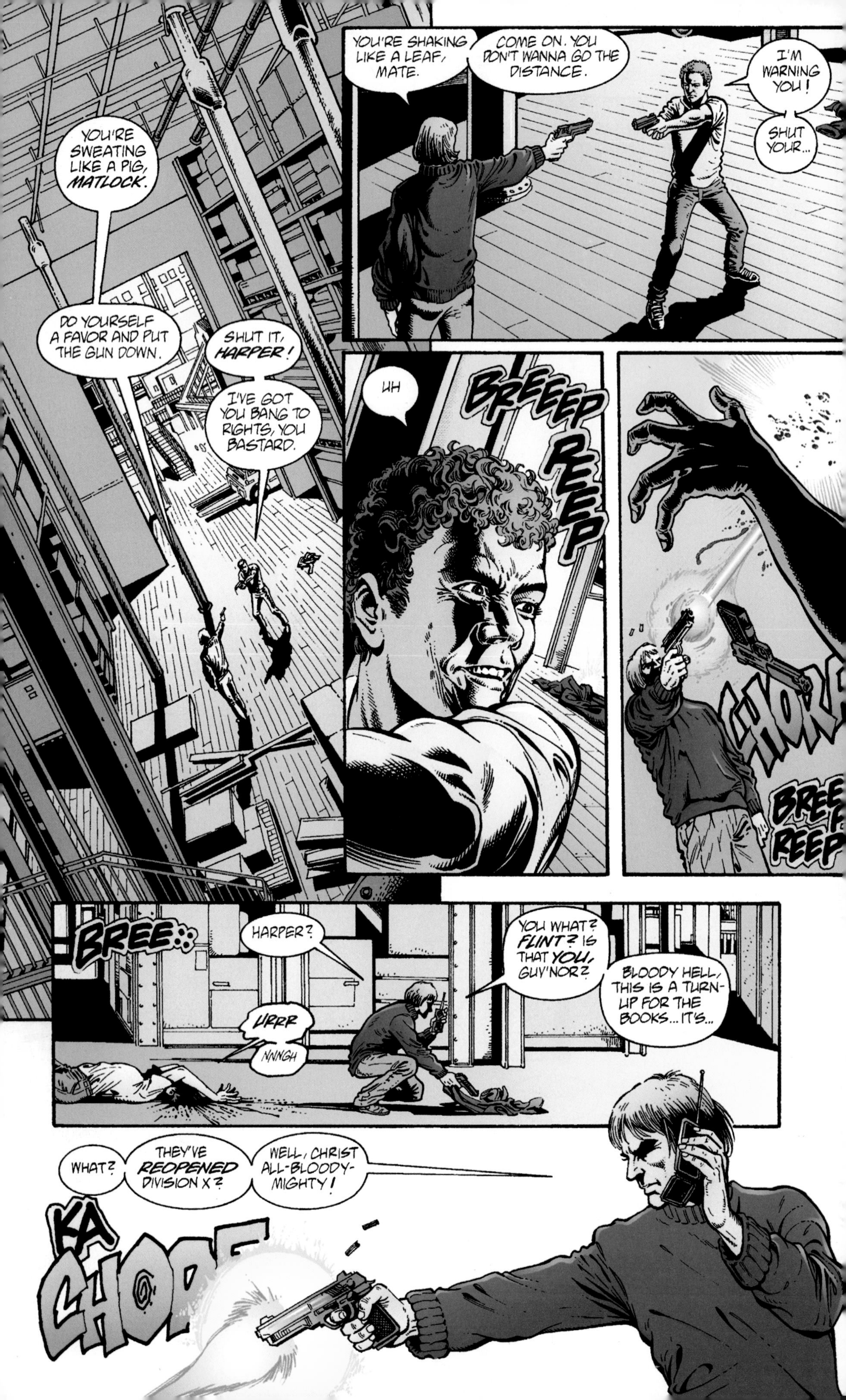

YOU'RE SWEATING LIKE A PIG, *MATLOCK*.
DO YOURSELF A FAVOR AND PUT THE GUN DOWN.
SHUT IT, *HARPER*!
I'VE GOT YOU BANG TO RIGHTS, YOU BASTARD.
YOU'RE SHAKING LIKE A LEAF, MATE.
COME ON. YOU DON'T WANNA GO THE DISTANCE.
I'M WARNING YOU!
SHUT YOUR...
UH
BREEEEP REEEP
BREE REEP
BREE
HARPER?
URRR
NNNGH
YOU WHAT? *FLINT?* IS THAT *YOU*, GUV'NOR?
BLOODY HELL, THIS IS A TURN-UP FOR THE BOOKS... IT'S...
WHAT?
THEY'VE *REOPENED* DIVISION X?
WELL, CHRIST ALL-BLOODY-MIGHTY!
KA

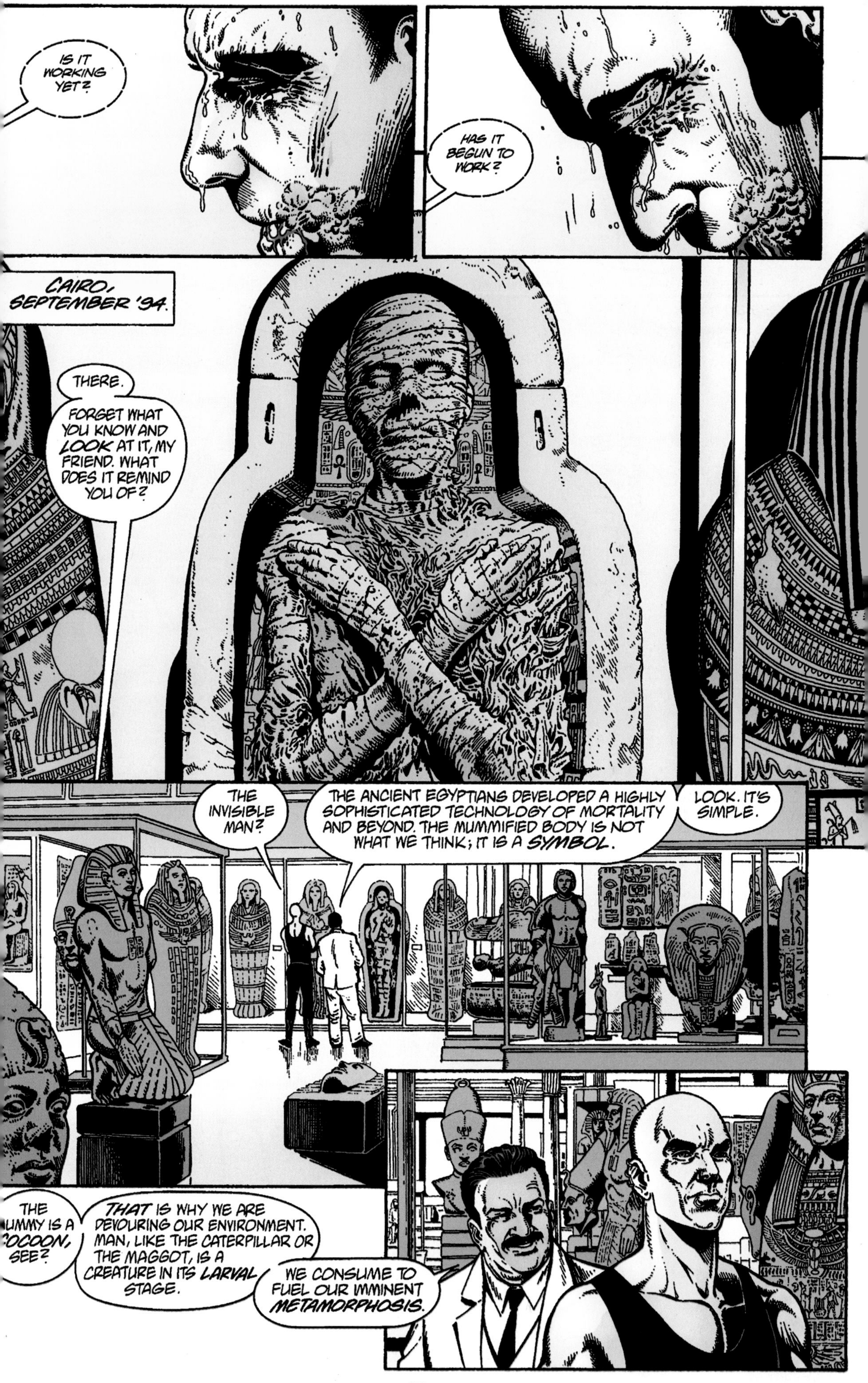
IS IT WORKING YET?
HAS IT BEGUN TO WORK?
CAIRO, SEPTEMBER '94.
THERE.
FORGET WHAT YOU KNOW AND LOOK AT IT, MY FRIEND. WHAT DOES IT REMIND YOU OF?
THE INVISIBLE MAN?
LOOK. IT'S SIMPLE.
THE ANCIENT EGYPTIANS DEVELOPED A HIGHLY SOPHISTICATED TECHNOLOGY OF MORTALITY AND BEYOND. THE MUMMIFIED BODY IS NOT WHAT WE THINK; IT IS A SYMBOL.
THE UMMY IS A OCOON, SEE?
THAT IS WHY WE ARE DEVOURING OUR ENVIRONMENT. MAN, LIKE THE CATERPILLAR OR THE MAGGOT, IS A CREATURE IN ITS LARVAL STAGE.
WE CONSUME TO FUEL OUR IMMINENT METAMORPHOSIS.

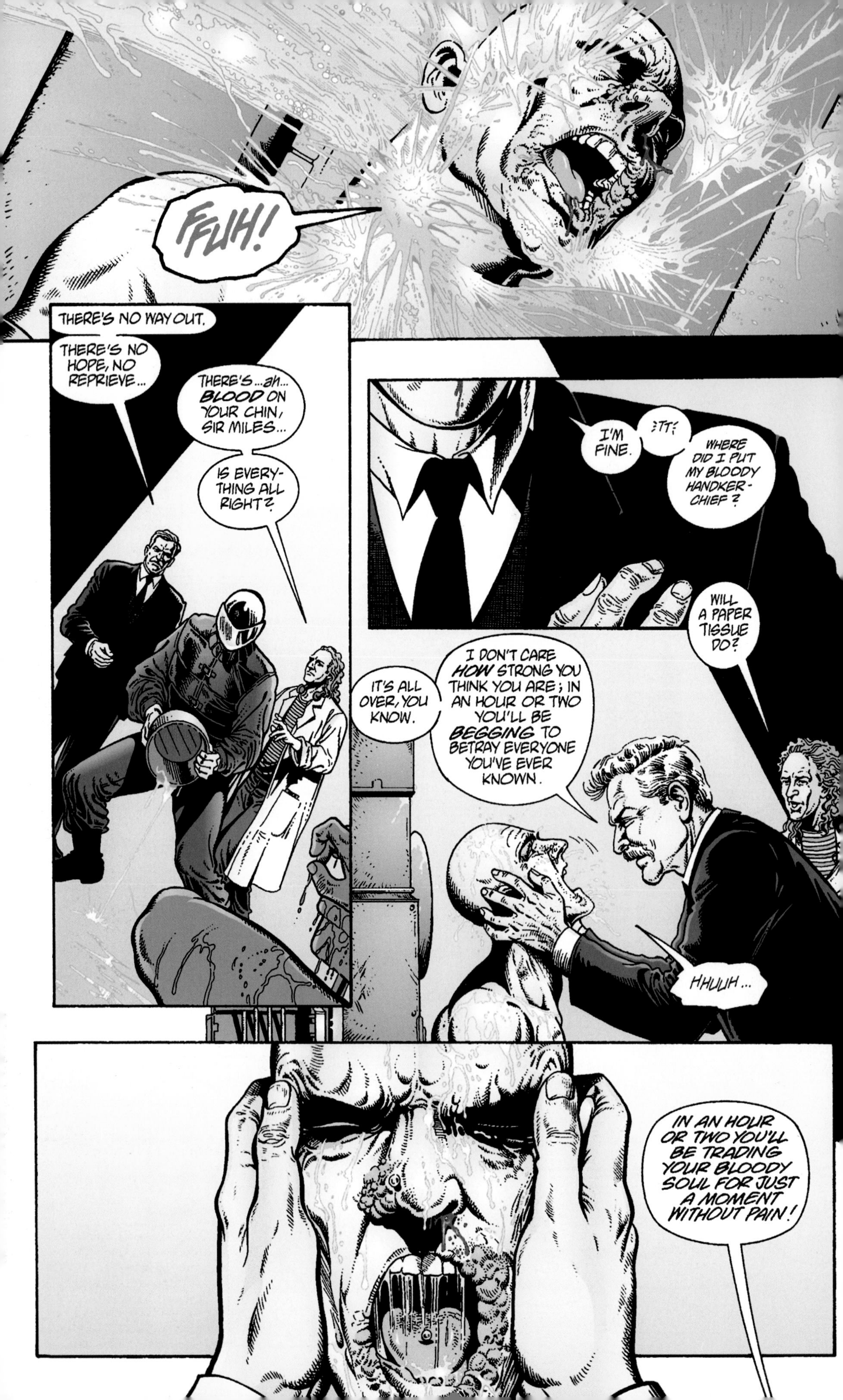
FFUH!
THERE'S NO WAY OUT.
THERE'S NO HOPE, NO REPRIEVE...
THERE'S...ah... BLOOD ON YOUR CHIN, SIR MILES...
IS EVERYTHING ALL RIGHT?
I'M FINE.
TT
WHERE DID I PUT MY BLOODY HANDKER-CHIEF?
WILL A PAPER TISSUE DO?
IT'S ALL OVER, YOU KNOW.
I DON'T CARE HOW STRONG YOU THINK YOU ARE; IN AN HOUR OR TWO YOU'LL BE BEGGING TO BETRAY EVERYONE YOU'VE EVER KNOWN.
HHUUH...
IN AN HOUR OR TWO YOU'LL BE TRADING YOUR BLOODY SOUL FOR JUST A MOMENT WITHOUT PAIN!

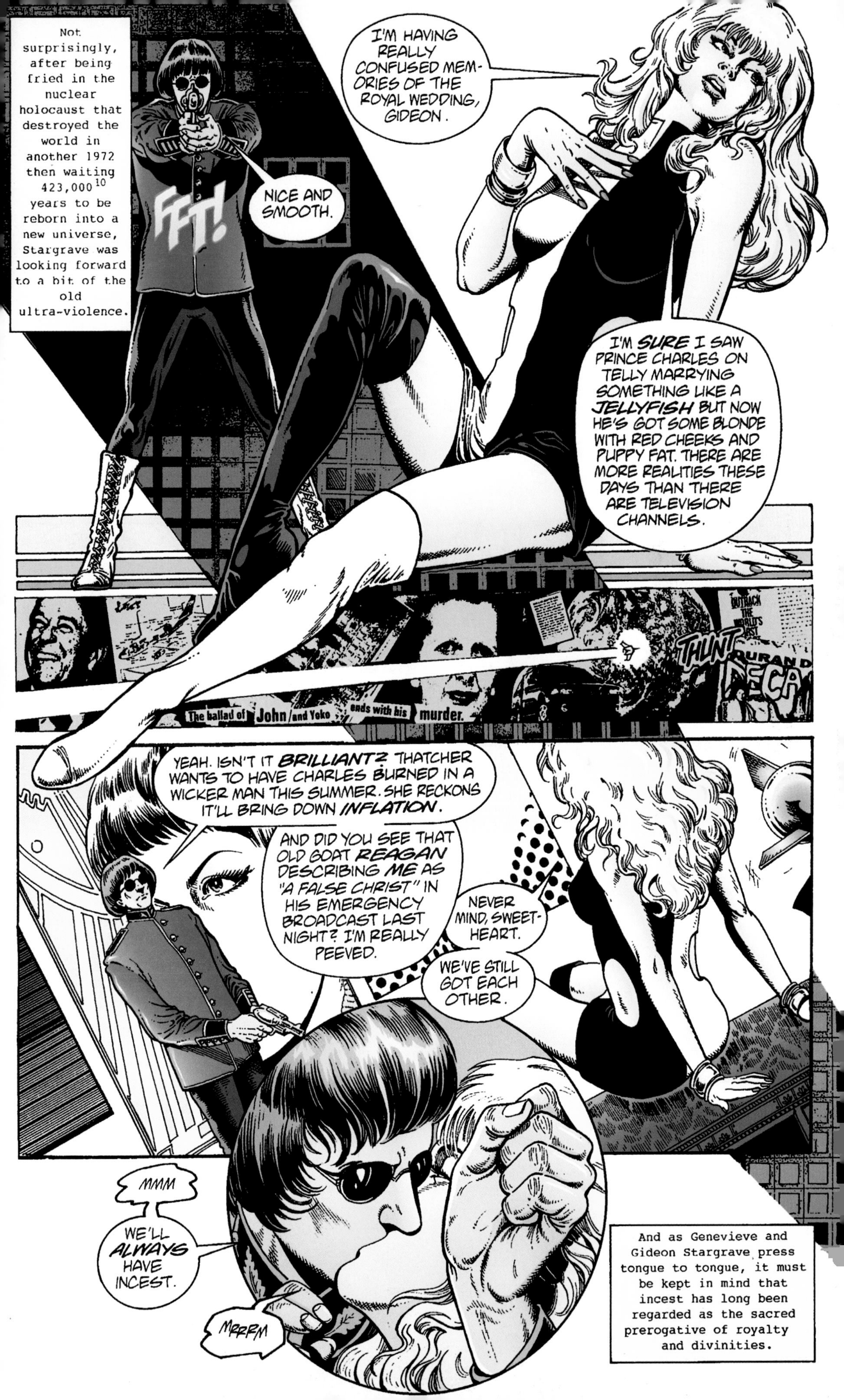
Not surprisingly, after being fried in the nuclear holocaust that destroyed the world in another 1972 then waiting 423,000[10] years to be reborn into a new universe, Stargrave was looking forward to a bit of the old ultra-violence.
I'M HAVING REALLY CONFUSED MEMORIES OF THE ROYAL WEDDING, GIDEON.
NICE AND SMOOTH.
FFT!
I'M SURE I SAW PRINCE CHARLES ON TELLY MARRYING SOMETHING LIKE A JELLYFISH BUT NOW HE'S GOT SOME BLONDE WITH RED CHEEKS AND PUPPY FAT. THERE ARE MORE REALITIES THESE DAYS THAN THERE ARE TELEVISION CHANNELS.
THUNT
The ballad of John and Yoko ends with his murder.
YEAH. ISN'T IT BRILLIANT? THATCHER WANTS TO HAVE CHARLES BURNED IN A WICKER MAN THIS SUMMER. SHE RECKONS IT'LL BRING DOWN INFLATION.
AND DID YOU SEE THAT OLD GOAT REAGAN DESCRIBING ME AS "A FALSE CHRIST" IN HIS EMERGENCY BROADCAST LAST NIGHT? I'M REALLY PEEVED.
NEVER MIND, SWEETHEART.
WE'VE STILL GOT EACH OTHER.
MMM
WE'LL ALWAYS HAVE INCEST.
MRRRM
And as Genevieve and Gideon Stargrave press tongue to tongue, it must be kept in mind that incest has long been regarded as the sacred prerogative of royalty and divinities.

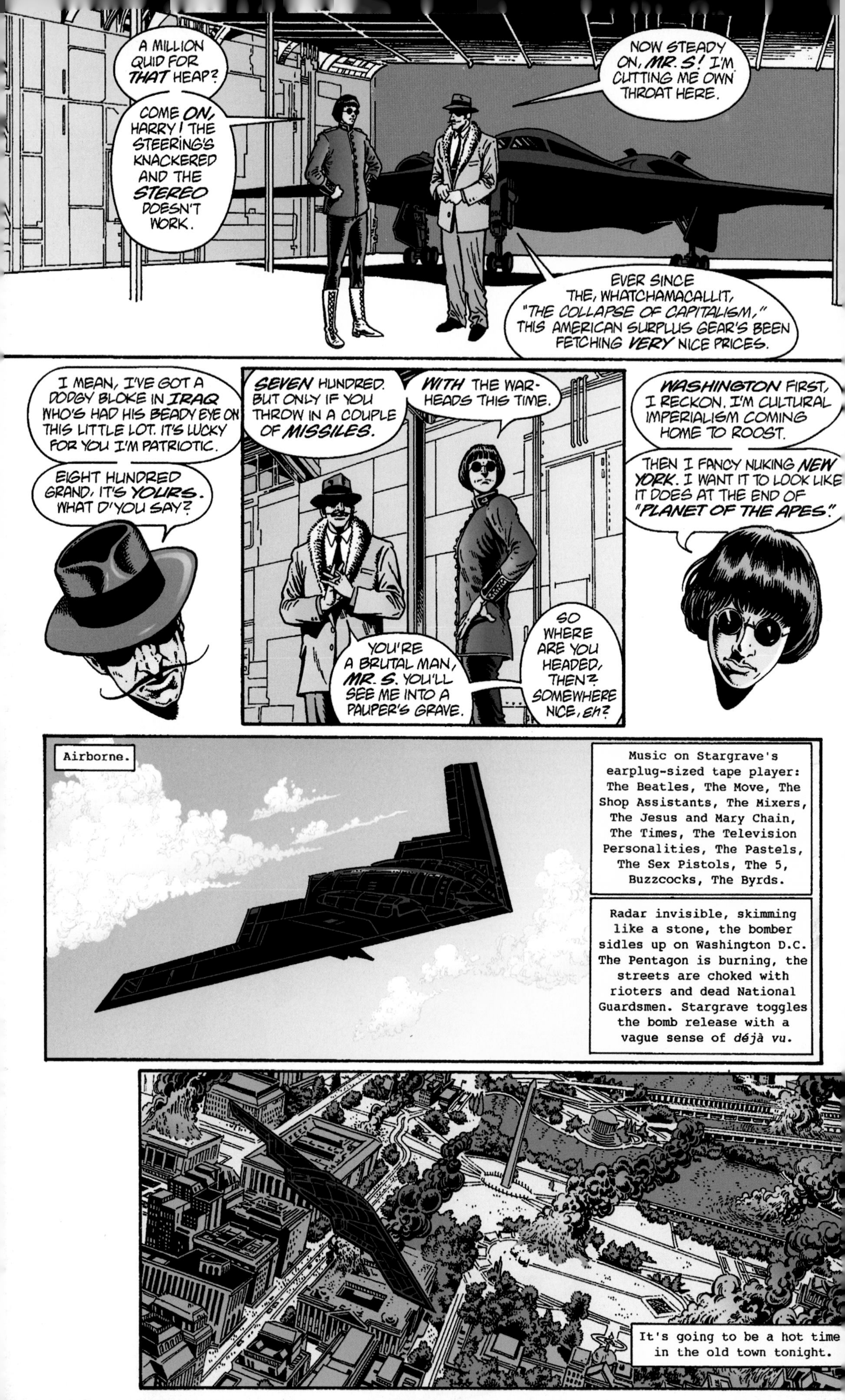

A MILLION QUID FOR THAT HEAP?
COME ON, HARRY! THE STEERING'S KNACKERED AND THE STEREO DOESN'T WORK.
NOW STEADY ON, MR. S! I'M CUTTING ME OWN THROAT HERE.
EVER SINCE THE, WHATCHAMACALLIT, "THE COLLAPSE OF CAPITALISM," THIS AMERICAN SURPLUS GEAR'S BEEN FETCHING VERY NICE PRICES.
I MEAN, I'VE GOT A DODGY BLOKE IN IRAQ WHO'S HAD HIS BEADY EYE ON THIS LITTLE LOT. IT'S LUCKY FOR YOU I'M PATRIOTIC.
EIGHT HUNDRED GRAND, IT'S YOURS. WHAT D'YOU SAY?
SEVEN HUNDRED. BUT ONLY IF YOU THROW IN A COUPLE OF MISSILES.
WITH THE WAR-HEADS THIS TIME.
YOU'RE A BRUTAL MAN, MR. S. YOU'LL SEE ME INTO A PAUPER'S GRAVE.
SO WHERE ARE YOU HEADED, THEN? SOMEWHERE NICE, EH?
WASHINGTON FIRST, I RECKON. I'M CULTURAL IMPERIALISM COMING HOME TO ROOST.
THEN I FANCY NUKING NEW YORK. I WANT IT TO LOOK LIKE IT DOES AT THE END OF "PLANET OF THE APES".
Airborne.
Music on Stargrave's earplug-sized tape player: The Beatles, The Move, The Shop Assistants, The Mixers, The Jesus and Mary Chain, The Times, The Television Personalities, The Pastels, The Sex Pistols, The 5, Buzzcocks, The Byrds.
Radar invisible, skimming like a stone, the bomber sidles up on Washington D.C. The Pentagon is burning, the streets are choked with rioters and dead National Guardsmen. Stargrave toggles the bomb release with a vague sense of déjà vu.
It's going to be a hot time in the old town tonight.

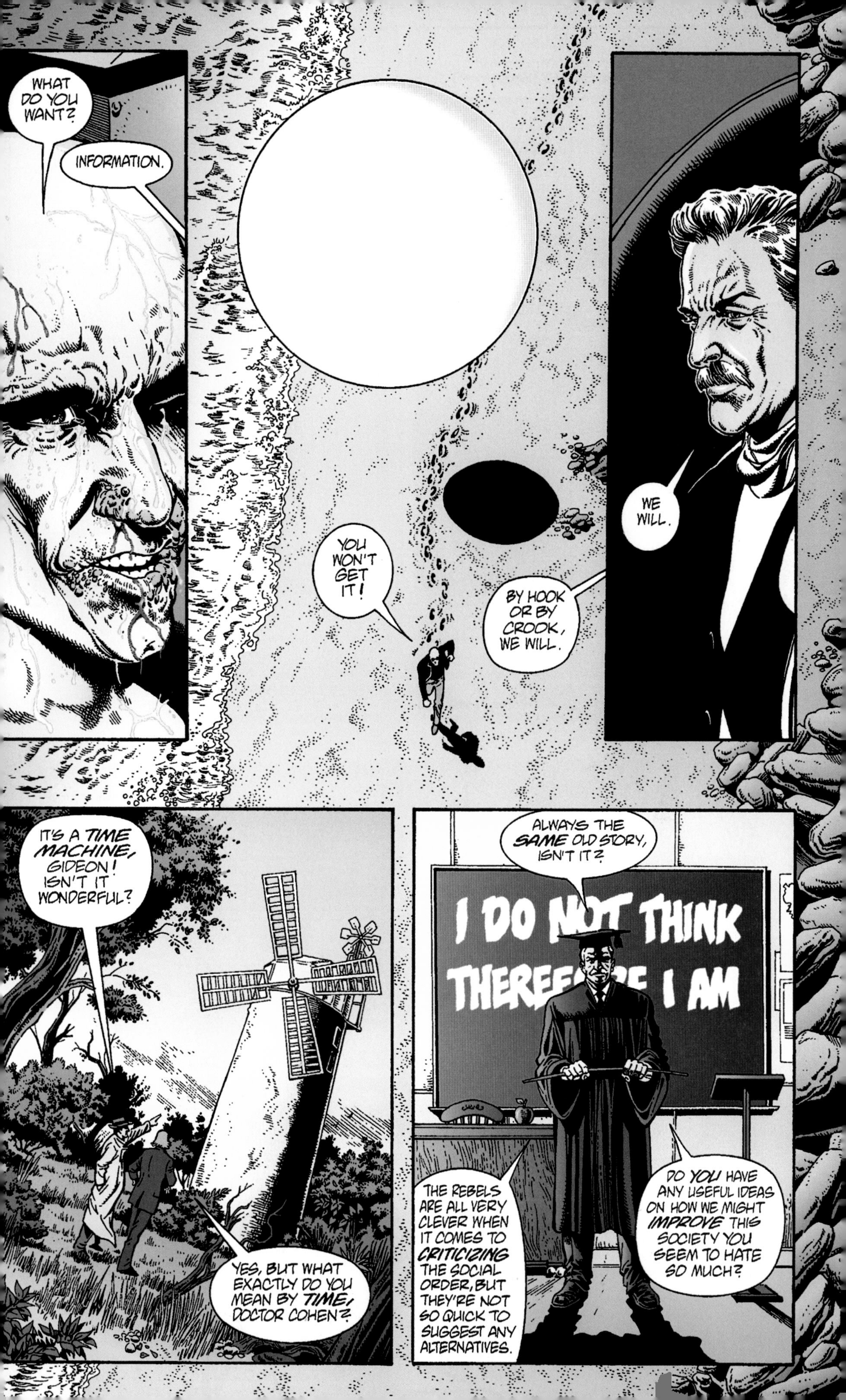
WHAT DO YOU WANT?
INFORMATION.
YOU WON'T GET IT!
WE WILL.
BY HOOK OR BY CROOK, WE WILL.
IT'S A *TIME MACHINE,* GIDEON! ISN'T IT WONDERFUL?
YES, BUT WHAT EXACTLY DO YOU MEAN BY *TIME,* DOCTOR COHEN?
ALWAYS THE *SAME* OLD STORY, ISN'T IT?
I DO NOT THINK THEREFORE I AM
THE REBELS ARE ALL VERY CLEVER WHEN IT COMES TO *CRITICIZING* THE SOCIAL ORDER, BUT THEY'RE NOT SO QUICK TO SUGGEST ANY ALTERNATIVES.
DO *YOU* HAVE ANY USEFUL IDEAS ON HOW WE MIGHT *IMPROVE* THIS SOCIETY YOU SEEM TO HATE SO MUCH?

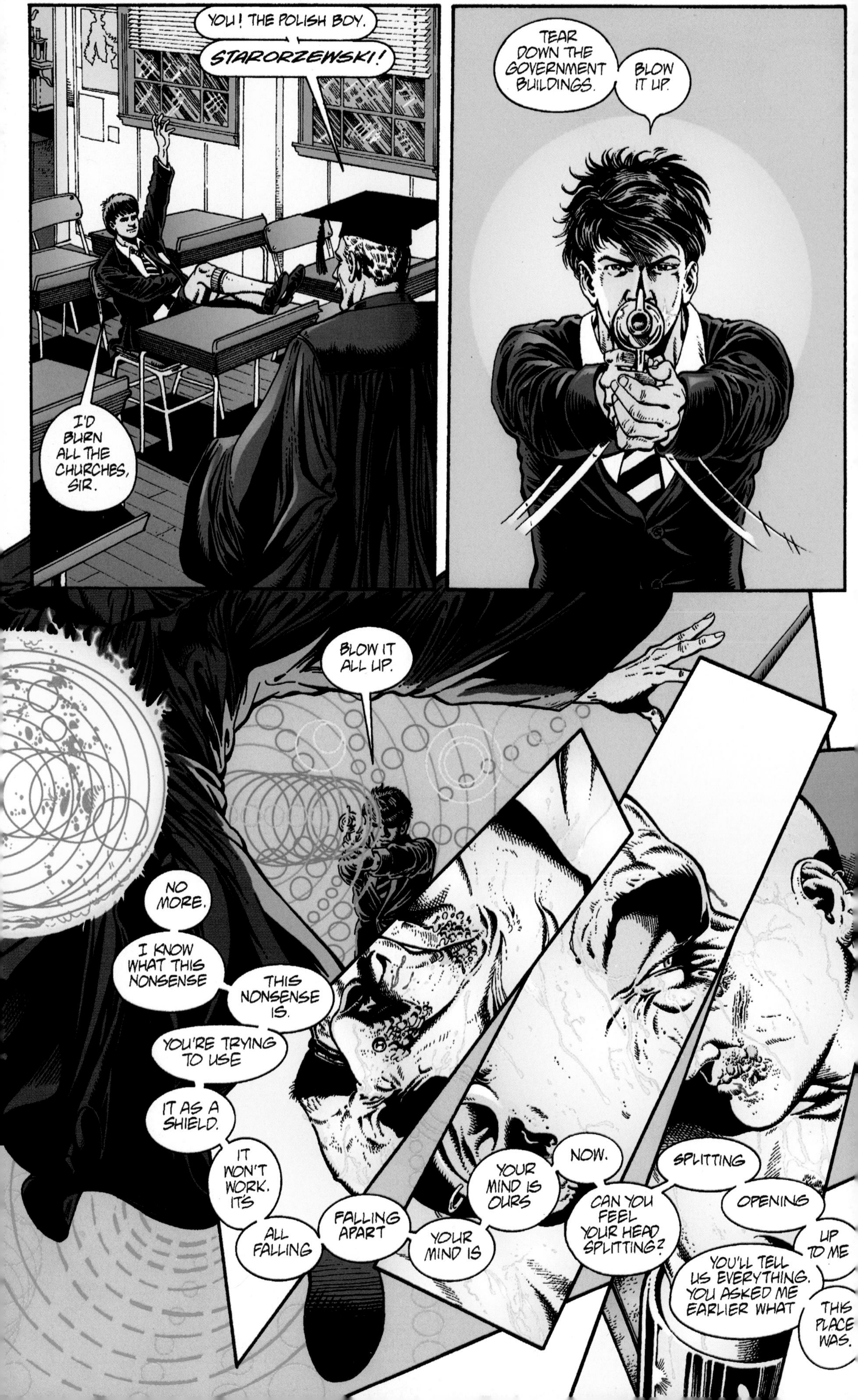

YOU! THE POLISH BOY.
STARORZEWSKI!
I'D BURN ALL THE CHURCHES, SIR.
TEAR DOWN THE GOVERNMENT BUILDINGS.
BLOW IT UP.
BLOW IT ALL UP.
NO MORE.
I KNOW WHAT THIS NONSENSE
THIS NONSENSE IS.
YOU'RE TRYING TO USE
IT AS A SHIELD.
IT WON'T WORK. IT'S
ALL FALLING
FALLING APART
YOUR MIND IS
YOUR MIND IS OURS
NOW.
CAN YOU FEEL YOUR HEAD SPLITTING?
SPLITTING
OPENING
UP TO ME
YOU'LL TELL US EVERYTHING. YOU ASKED ME EARLIER WHAT
THIS PLACE WAS.

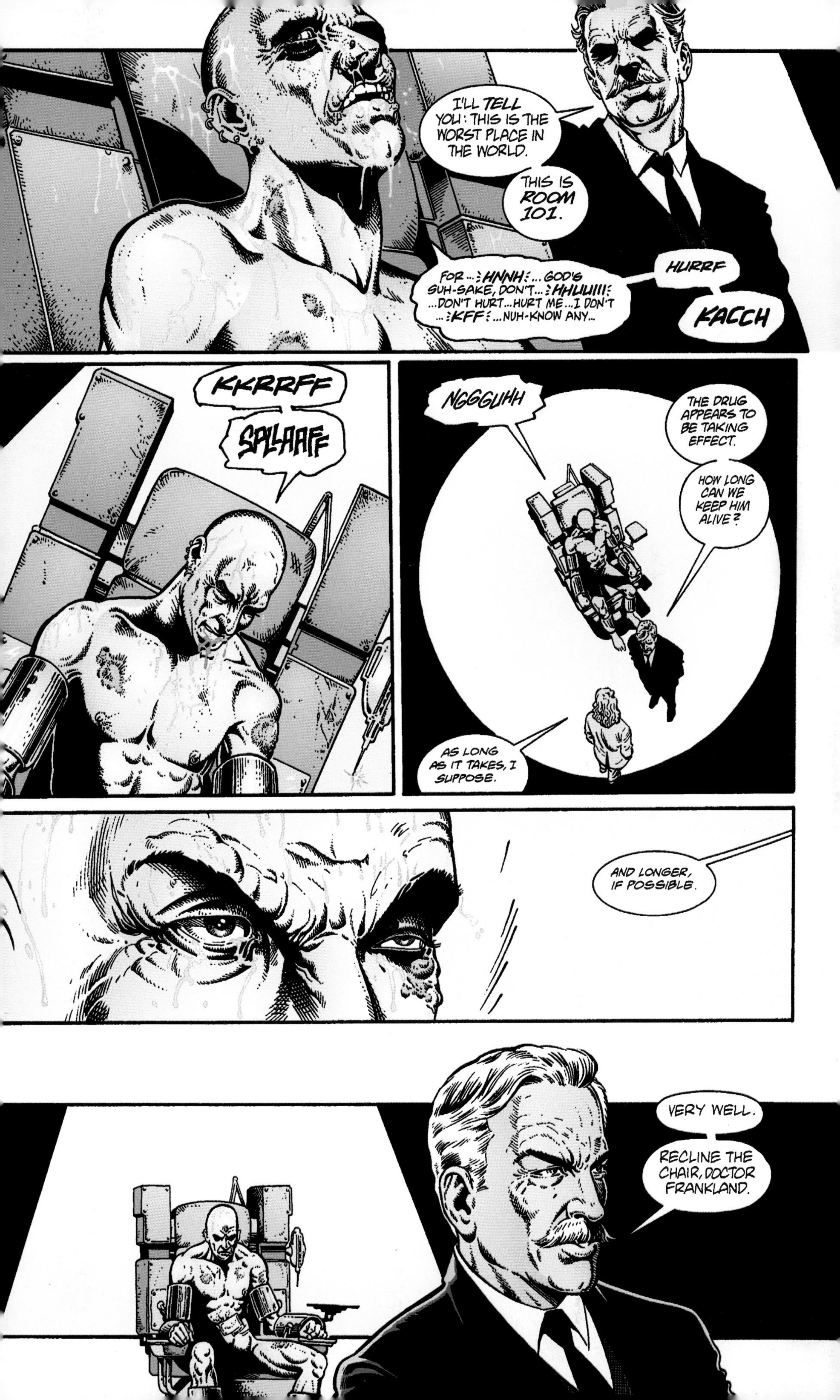
I'LL TELL YOU: THIS IS THE WORST PLACE IN THE WORLD.
THIS IS ROOM 101.
FOR... HNNH ...GOD'S SUH-SAKE, DON'T... HHUUH ...DON'T HURT...HURT ME...I DON'T ... KFF ...NUH-KNOW ANY...
HURRF
KACCH
KKRRFF
SPLLAAFF
NGGGUHH
THE DRUG APPEARS TO BE TAKING EFFECT.
HOW LONG CAN WE KEEP HIM ALIVE?
AS LONG AS IT TAKES, I SUPPOSE.
AND LONGER, IF POSSIBLE.
VERY WELL.
RECLINE THE CHAIR, DOCTOR FRANKLAND.

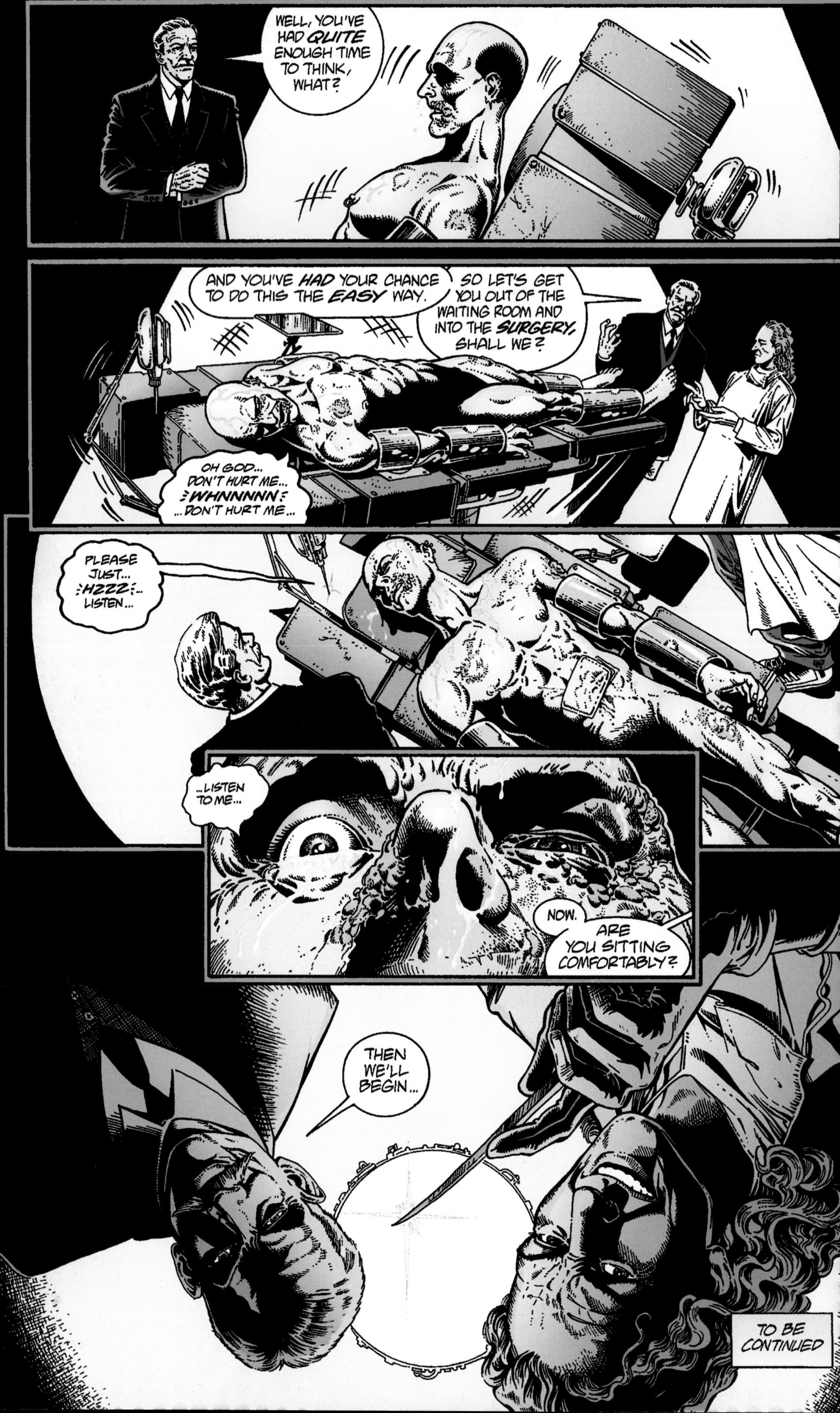
WELL, YOU'VE HAD QUITE ENOUGH TIME TO THINK, WHAT?
AND YOU'VE HAD YOUR CHANCE TO DO THIS THE EASY WAY.
SO LET'S GET YOU OUT OF THE WAITING ROOM AND INTO THE SURGERY, SHALL WE?
OH GOD... DON'T HURT ME... WHNNNNN ...DON'T HURT ME...
PLEASE JUST... HZZZ... LISTEN...
...LISTEN TO ME...
NOW.
ARE YOU SITTING COMFORTABLY?
THEN WE'LL BEGIN...
TO BE CONTINUED

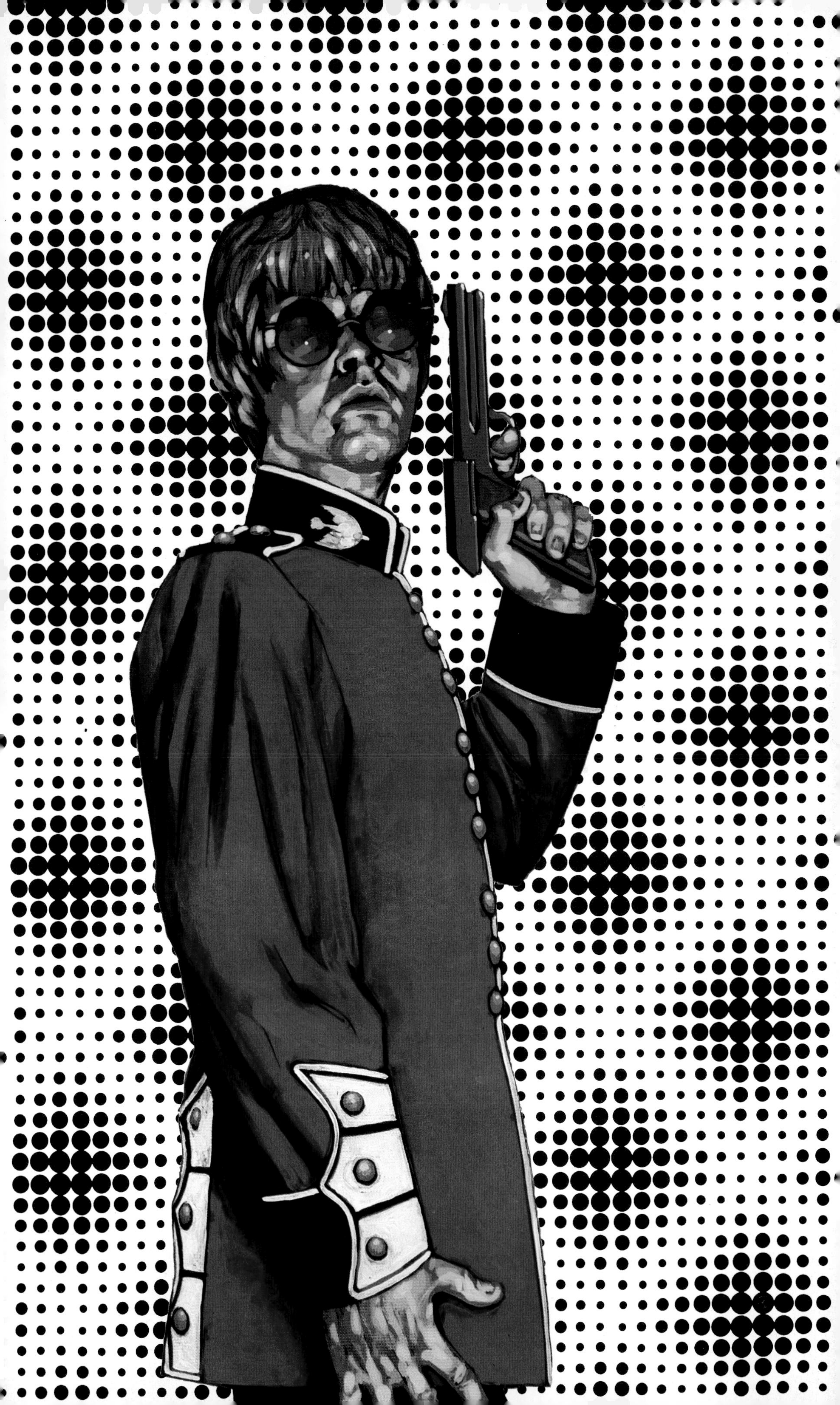

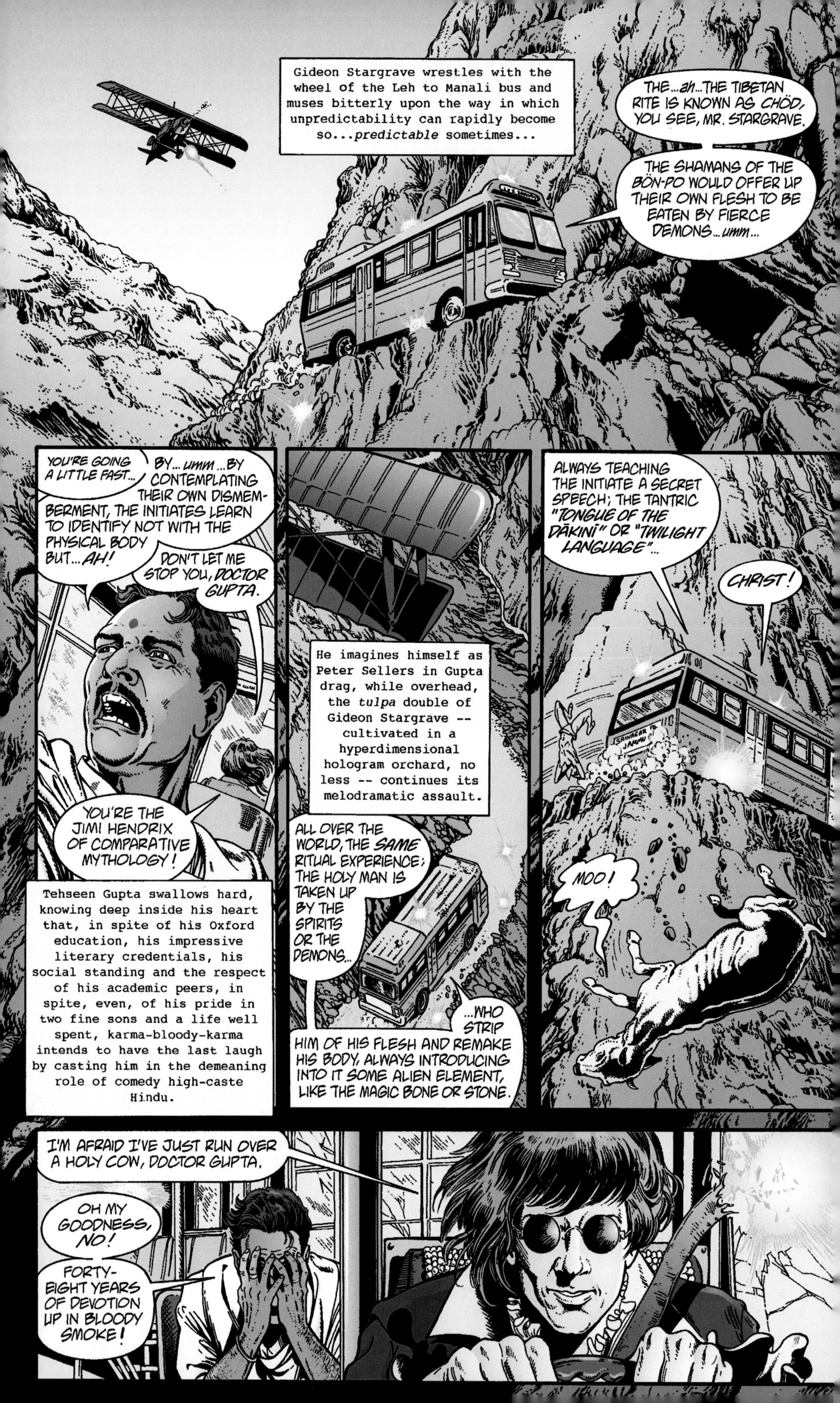

Gideon Stargrave wrestles with the wheel of the Leh to Manali bus and muses bitterly upon the way in which unpredictability can rapidly become so...*predictable* sometimes...
THE...*ah*...THE TIBETAN RITE IS KNOWN AS *CHÖD*, YOU SEE, MR. STARGRAVE.
THE SHAMANS OF THE BÖN-PO WOULD OFFER UP THEIR OWN FLESH TO BE EATEN BY FIERCE DEMONS...*umm*...
YOU'RE GOING A LITTLE FAST...
BY...*umm*...BY CONTEMPLATING THEIR OWN DISMEMBERMENT, THE INITIATES LEARN TO IDENTIFY NOT WITH THE PHYSICAL BODY BUT...*AH!*
DON'T LET ME STOP YOU, *DOCTOR GUPTA*.
YOU'RE THE JIMI HENDRIX OF COMPARATIVE MYTHOLOGY!
Tehseen Gupta swallows hard, knowing deep inside his heart that, in spite of his Oxford education, his impressive literary credentials, his social standing and the respect of his academic peers, in spite, even, of his pride in two fine sons and a life well spent, karma-bloody-karma intends to have the last laugh by casting him in the demeaning role of comedy high-caste Hindu.
He imagines himself as Peter Sellers in Gupta drag, while overhead, the *tulpa* double of Gideon Stargrave -- cultivated in a hyperdimensional hologram orchard, no less -- continues its melodramatic assault.
ALL OVER THE WORLD, THE *SAME* RITUAL EXPERIENCE; THE HOLY MAN IS TAKEN UP BY THE SPIRITS OR THE DEMONS...
...WHO STRIP HIM OF HIS FLESH AND REMAKE HIS BODY, ALWAYS INTRODUCING INTO IT SOME ALIEN ELEMENT, LIKE THE MAGIC BONE OR STONE.
ALWAYS TEACHING THE INITIATE A SECRET SPEECH; THE TANTRIC *"TONGUE OF THE DĀKINĪ"* OR *"TWILIGHT LANGUAGE"*...
CHRIST!
MOO!
I'M AFRAID I'VE JUST RUN OVER A HOLY COW, DOCTOR GUPTA.
OH MY GOODNESS, *NO!*
FORTY-EIGHT YEARS OF DEVOTION UP IN BLOODY SMOKE!

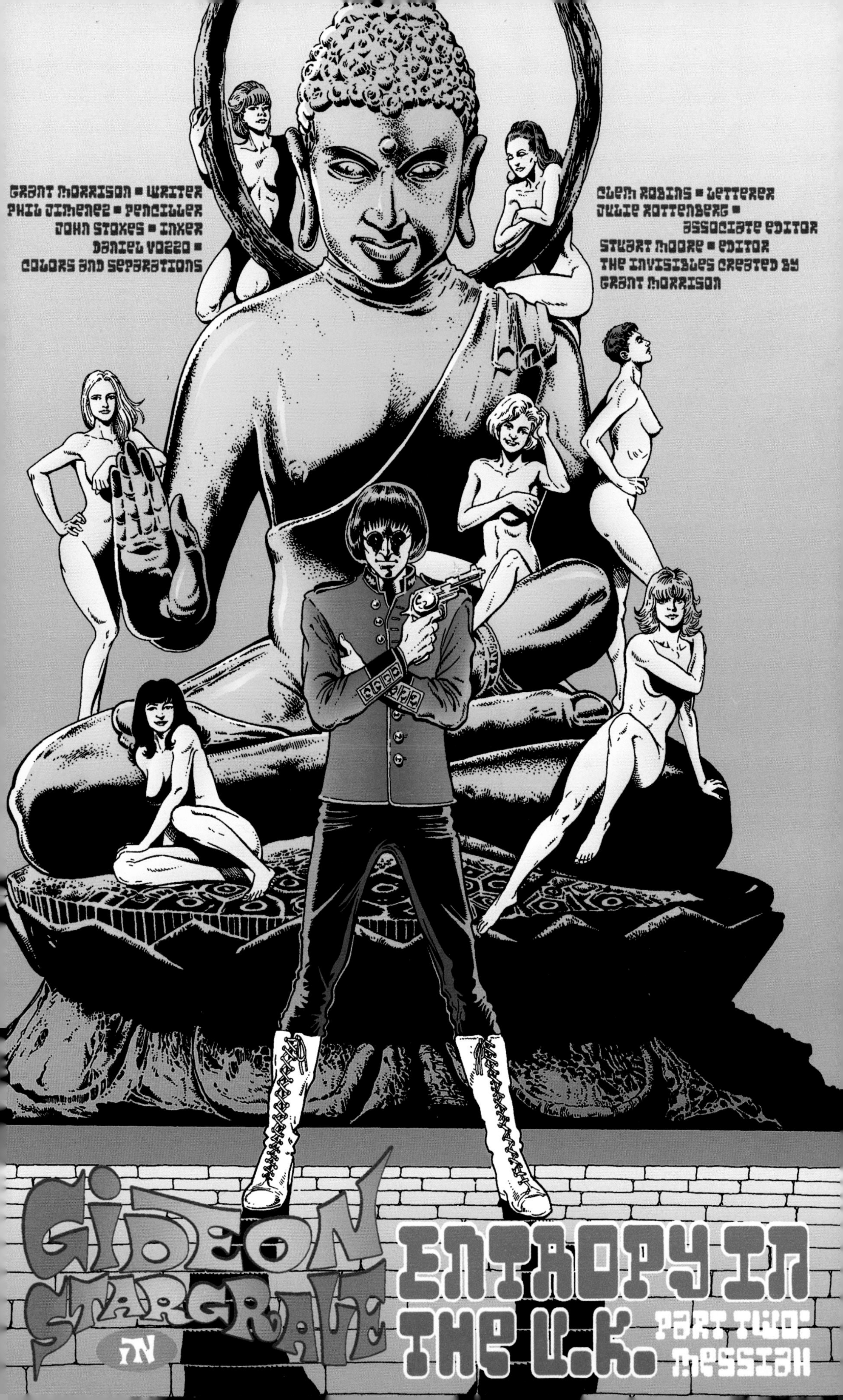

GRANT MORRISON = WRITER
PHIL JIMENEZ = PENCILLER
JOHN STOKES = INKER
DANIEL VOZZO = COLORS AND SEPARATIONS
CLEM ROBINS = LETTERER
JULIE ROTTENBERG = ASSOCIATE EDITOR
STUART MOORE = EDITOR
THE INVISIBLES CREATED BY GRANT MORRISON
GIDEON STARGRAVE IN
ENTROPY IN THE U.K.
PART TWO: MESSIAH

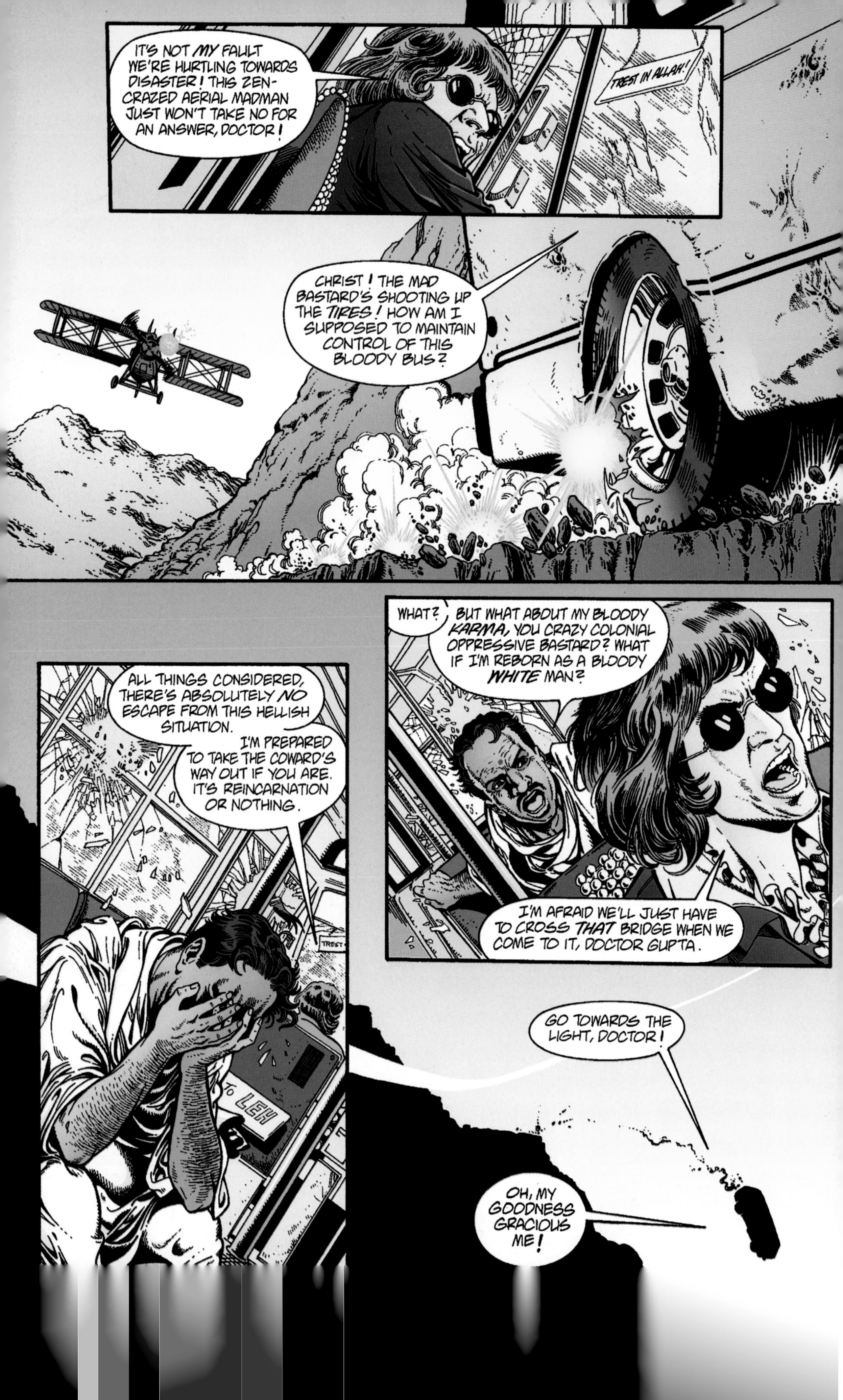
IT'S NOT MY FAULT WE'RE HURTLING TOWARDS DISASTER! THIS ZEN-CRAZED AERIAL MADMAN JUST WON'T TAKE NO FOR AN ANSWER, DOCTOR!
TREST IN ALLAH!
CHRIST! THE MAD BASTARD'S SHOOTING UP THE TIRES! HOW AM I SUPPOSED TO MAINTAIN CONTROL OF THIS BLOODY BUS?
ALL THINGS CONSIDERED, THERE'S ABSOLUTELY NO ESCAPE FROM THIS HELLISH SITUATION.
I'M PREPARED TO TAKE THE COWARD'S WAY OUT IF YOU ARE. IT'S REINCARNATION OR NOTHING.
TREST
TO LEH
WHAT?
BUT WHAT ABOUT MY BLOODY KARMA, YOU CRAZY COLONIAL OPPRESSIVE BASTARD? WHAT IF I'M REBORN AS A BLOODY WHITE MAN?
I'M AFRAID WE'LL JUST HAVE TO CROSS THAT BRIDGE WHEN WE COME TO IT, DOCTOR GUPTA.
GO TOWARDS THE LIGHT, DOCTOR!
OH, MY GOODNESS GRACIOUS ME!

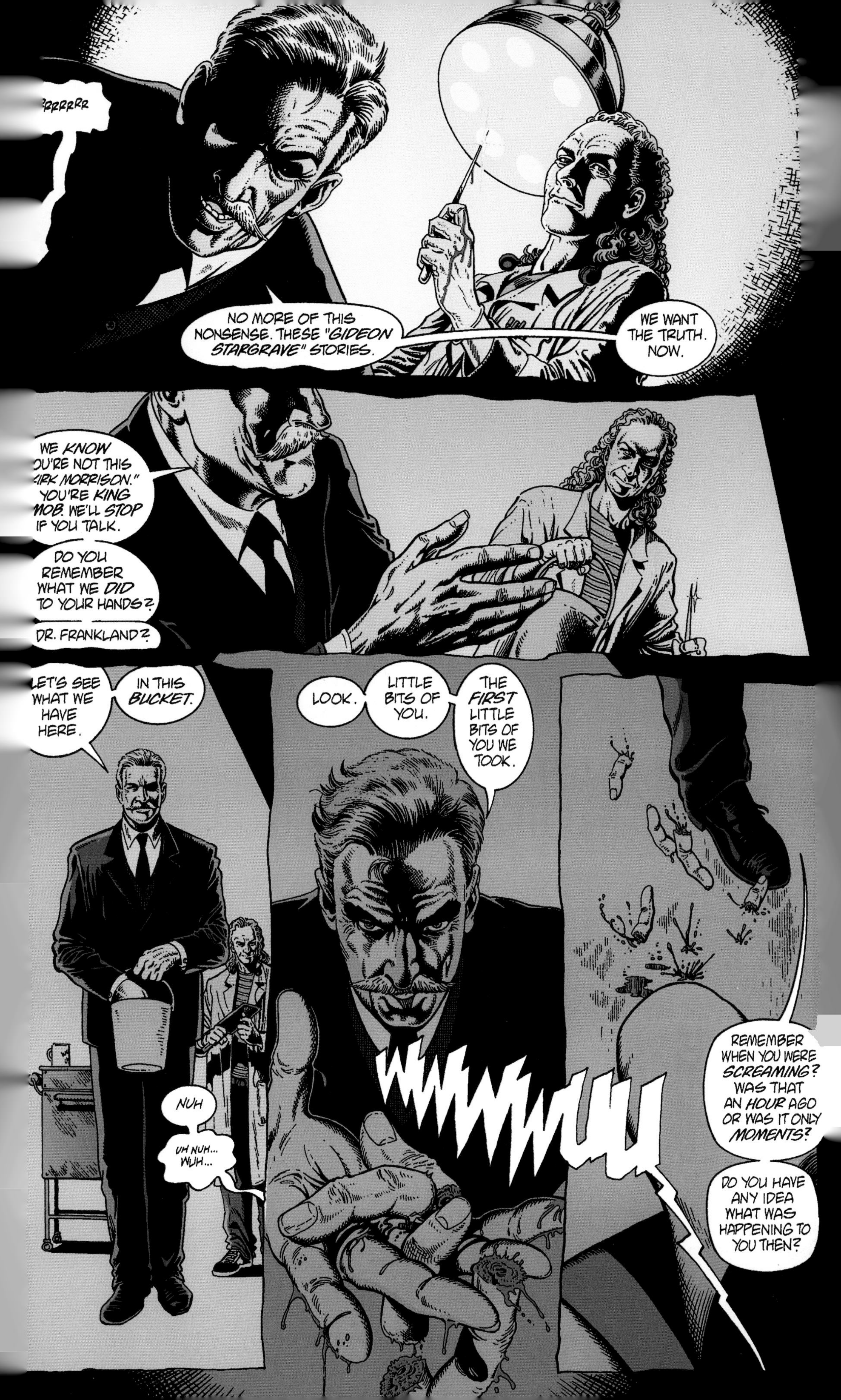

ERRRRRR
NO MORE OF THIS NONSENSE. THESE "GIDEON STARGRAVE" STORIES.
WE WANT THE TRUTH. NOW.
WE KNOW YOU'RE NOT THIS "KIRK MORRISON." YOU'RE KING MOB. WE'LL STOP IF YOU TALK.
DO YOU REMEMBER WHAT WE DID TO YOUR HANDS?
DR. FRANKLAND?
LET'S SEE WHAT WE HAVE HERE.
IN THIS BUCKET.
NUH
UH NUH... WUH...
LOOK.
LITTLE BITS OF YOU.
THE FIRST LITTLE BITS OF YOU WE TOOK.
WWWWUU
REMEMBER WHEN YOU WERE SCREAMING? WAS THAT AN HOUR AGO OR WAS IT ONLY MOMENTS?
DO YOU HAVE ANY IDEA WHAT WAS HAPPENING TO YOU THEN?

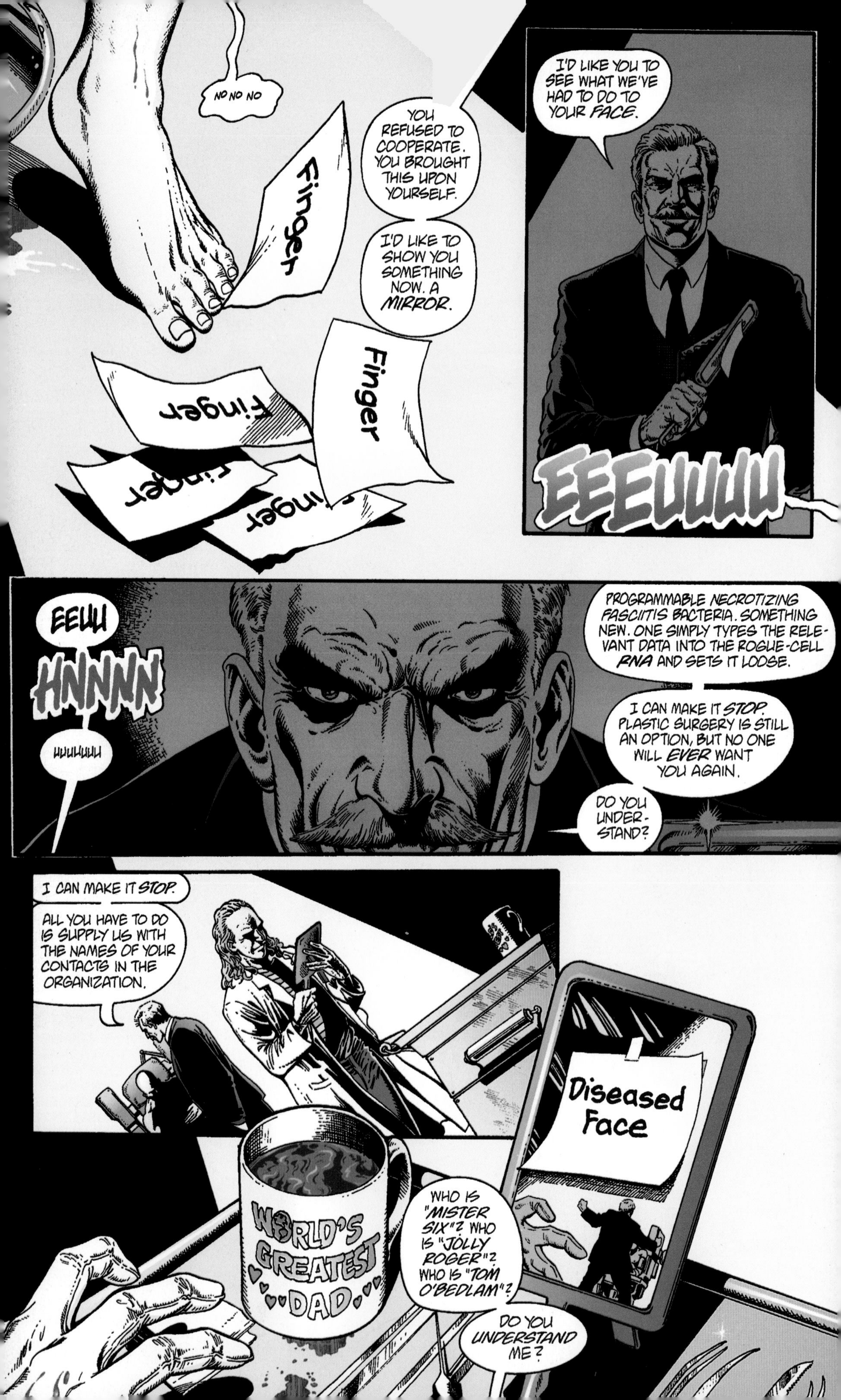

NO NO NO
YOU REFUSED TO COOPERATE. YOU BROUGHT THIS UPON YOURSELF.
I'D LIKE TO SHOW YOU SOMETHING NOW. A MIRROR.
Finger
Finger
Finger
Finger
inger
I'D LIKE YOU TO SEE WHAT WE'VE HAD TO DO TO YOUR FACE.
EEEUUUU
EEUU
HNNNN
UUUUUUU
PROGRAMMABLE NECROTIZING FASCIITIS BACTERIA. SOMETHING NEW. ONE SIMPLY TYPES THE RELEVANT DATA INTO THE ROGUE-CELL RNA AND SETS IT LOOSE.
I CAN MAKE IT STOP. PLASTIC SURGERY IS STILL AN OPTION, BUT NO ONE WILL EVER WANT YOU AGAIN.
DO YOU UNDERSTAND?
I CAN MAKE IT STOP.
ALL YOU HAVE TO DO IS SUPPLY US WITH THE NAMES OF YOUR CONTACTS IN THE ORGANIZATION.
Diseased Face
WORLD'S GREATEST DAD
WHO IS "MISTER SIX"? WHO IS "JOLLY ROGER"? WHO IS "TOM O'BEDLAM"?
DO YOU UNDERSTAND ME?

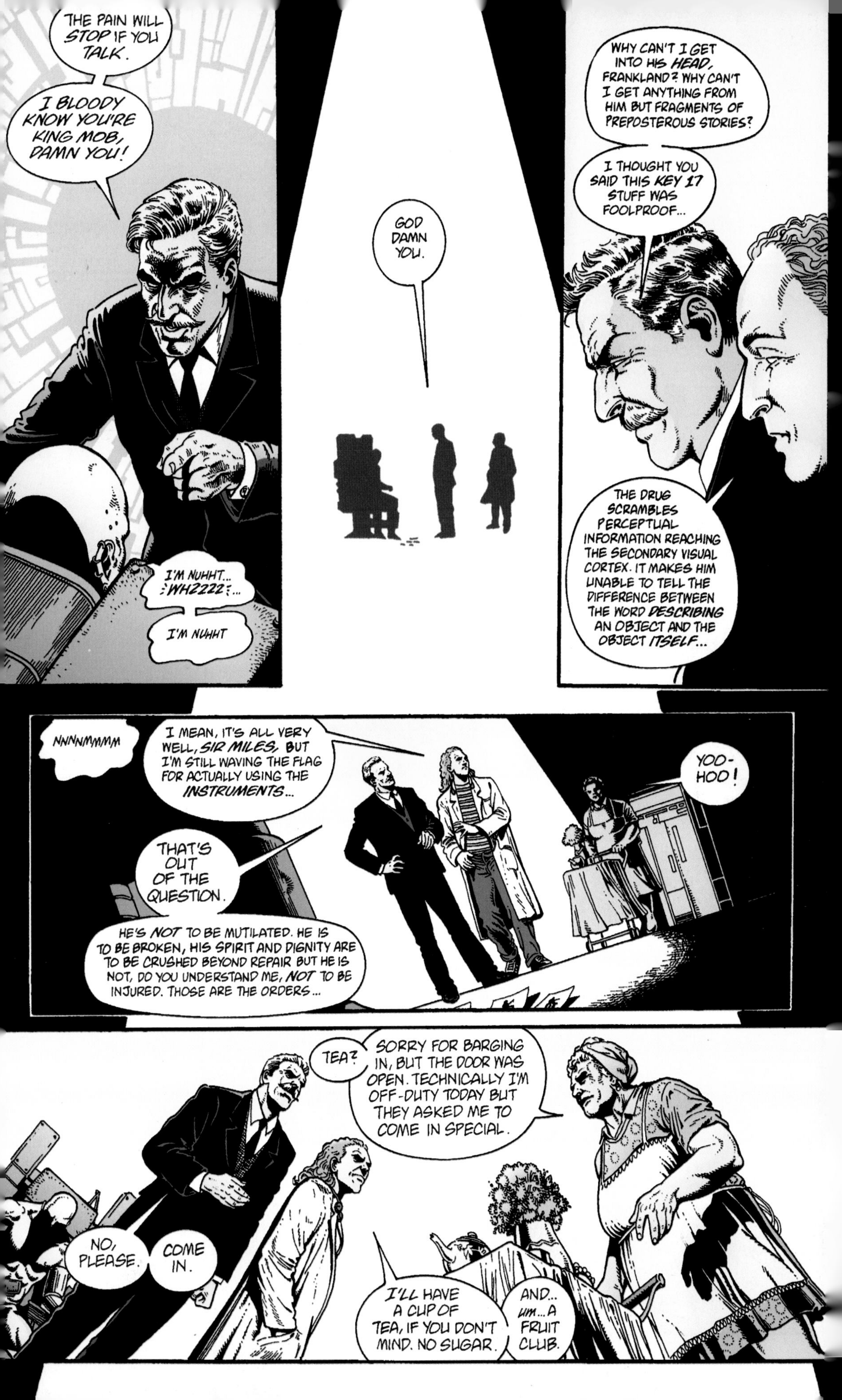
THE PAIN WILL STOP IF YOU TALK.
I BLOODY KNOW YOU'RE KING MOB, DAMN YOU!
I'M NUHHT... WHZZZZ... I'M NUHHT
GOD DAMN YOU.
WHY CAN'T I GET INTO HIS HEAD, FRANKLAND? WHY CAN'T I GET ANYTHING FROM HIM BUT FRAGMENTS OF PREPOSTEROUS STORIES?
I THOUGHT YOU SAID THIS KEY 17 STUFF WAS FOOLPROOF...
THE DRUG SCRAMBLES PERCEPTUAL INFORMATION REACHING THE SECONDARY VISUAL CORTEX. IT MAKES HIM UNABLE TO TELL THE DIFFERENCE BETWEEN THE WORD DESCRIBING AN OBJECT AND THE OBJECT ITSELF...
NNNNMMMM
I MEAN, IT'S ALL VERY WELL, SIR MILES, BUT I'M STILL WAVING THE FLAG FOR ACTUALLY USING THE INSTRUMENTS...
THAT'S OUT OF THE QUESTION.
HE'S NOT TO BE MUTILATED. HE IS TO BE BROKEN, HIS SPIRIT AND DIGNITY ARE TO BE CRUSHED BEYOND REPAIR BUT HE IS NOT, DO YOU UNDERSTAND ME, NOT TO BE INJURED. THOSE ARE THE ORDERS...
YOO-HOO!
TEA?
SORRY FOR BARGING IN, BUT THE DOOR WAS OPEN. TECHNICALLY I'M OFF-DUTY TODAY BUT THEY ASKED ME TO COME IN SPECIAL.
NO, PLEASE.
COME IN.
I'LL HAVE A CUP OF TEA, IF YOU DON'T MIND. NO SUGAR.
AND... UM... A FRUIT CLUB.

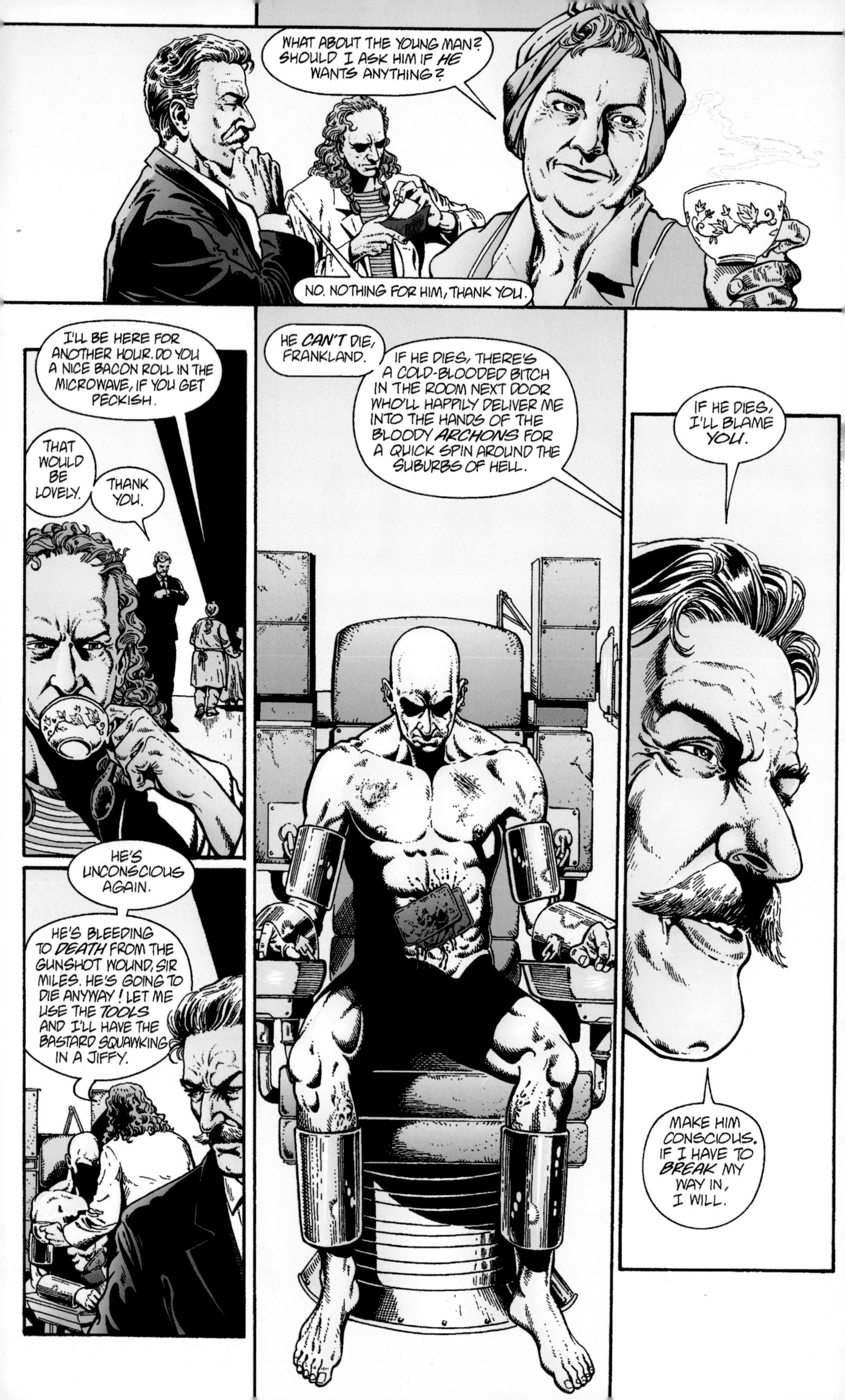
WHAT ABOUT THE YOUNG MAN? SHOULD I ASK HIM IF HE WANTS ANYTHING?
NO. NOTHING FOR HIM, THANK YOU.
I'LL BE HERE FOR ANOTHER HOUR. DO YOU A NICE BACON ROLL IN THE MICROWAVE, IF YOU GET PECKISH.
THAT WOULD BE LOVELY.
THANK YOU.
HE'S UNCONSCIOUS AGAIN.
HE'S BLEEDING TO DEATH FROM THE GUNSHOT WOUND, SIR MILES. HE'S GOING TO DIE ANYWAY! LET ME USE THE TOOLS AND I'LL HAVE THE BASTARD SQUAWKING IN A JIFFY.
HE CAN'T DIE, FRANKLAND.
IF HE DIES, THERE'S A COLD-BLOODED BITCH IN THE ROOM NEXT DOOR WHO'LL HAPPILY DELIVER ME INTO THE HANDS OF THE BLOODY ARCHONS FOR A QUICK SPIN AROUND THE SUBURBS OF HELL.
IF HE DIES, I'LL BLAME YOU.
MAKE HIM CONSCIOUS. IF I HAVE TO BREAK MY WAY IN, I WILL.

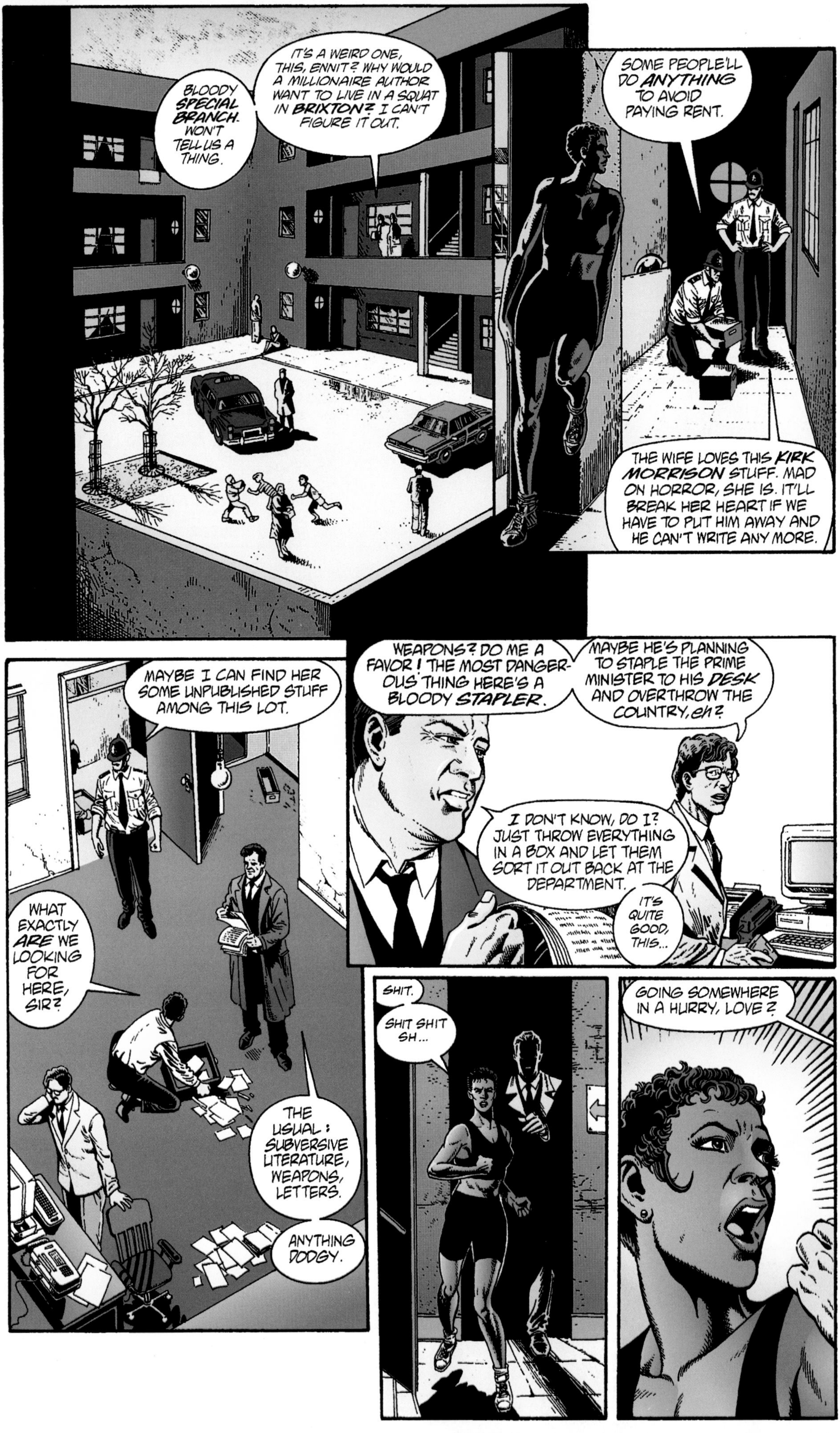
BLOODY SPECIAL BRANCH. WON'T TELL US A THING.
IT'S A WEIRD ONE, THIS, ENNIT? WHY WOULD A MILLIONAIRE AUTHOR WANT TO LIVE IN A SQUAT IN BRIXTON? I CAN'T FIGURE IT OUT.
SOME PEOPLE'LL DO ANYTHING TO AVOID PAYING RENT.
THE WIFE LOVES THIS KIRK MORRISON STUFF. MAD ON HORROR, SHE IS. IT'LL BREAK HER HEART IF WE HAVE TO PUT HIM AWAY AND HE CAN'T WRITE ANY MORE.
MAYBE I CAN FIND HER SOME UNPUBLISHED STUFF AMONG THIS LOT.
WHAT EXACTLY ARE WE LOOKING FOR HERE, SIR?
THE USUAL: SUBVERSIVE LITERATURE, WEAPONS, LETTERS.
ANYTHING DODGY.
WEAPONS? DO ME A FAVOR! THE MOST DANGEROUS THING HERE'S A BLOODY STAPLER.
MAYBE HE'S PLANNING TO STAPLE THE PRIME MINISTER TO HIS DESK AND OVERTHROW THE COUNTRY, eh?
I DON'T KNOW, DO I? JUST THROW EVERYTHING IN A BOX AND LET THEM SORT IT OUT BACK AT THE DEPARTMENT.
IT'S QUITE GOOD, THIS...
SHIT.
SHIT SHIT SH...
GOING SOMEWHERE IN A HURRY, LOVE?

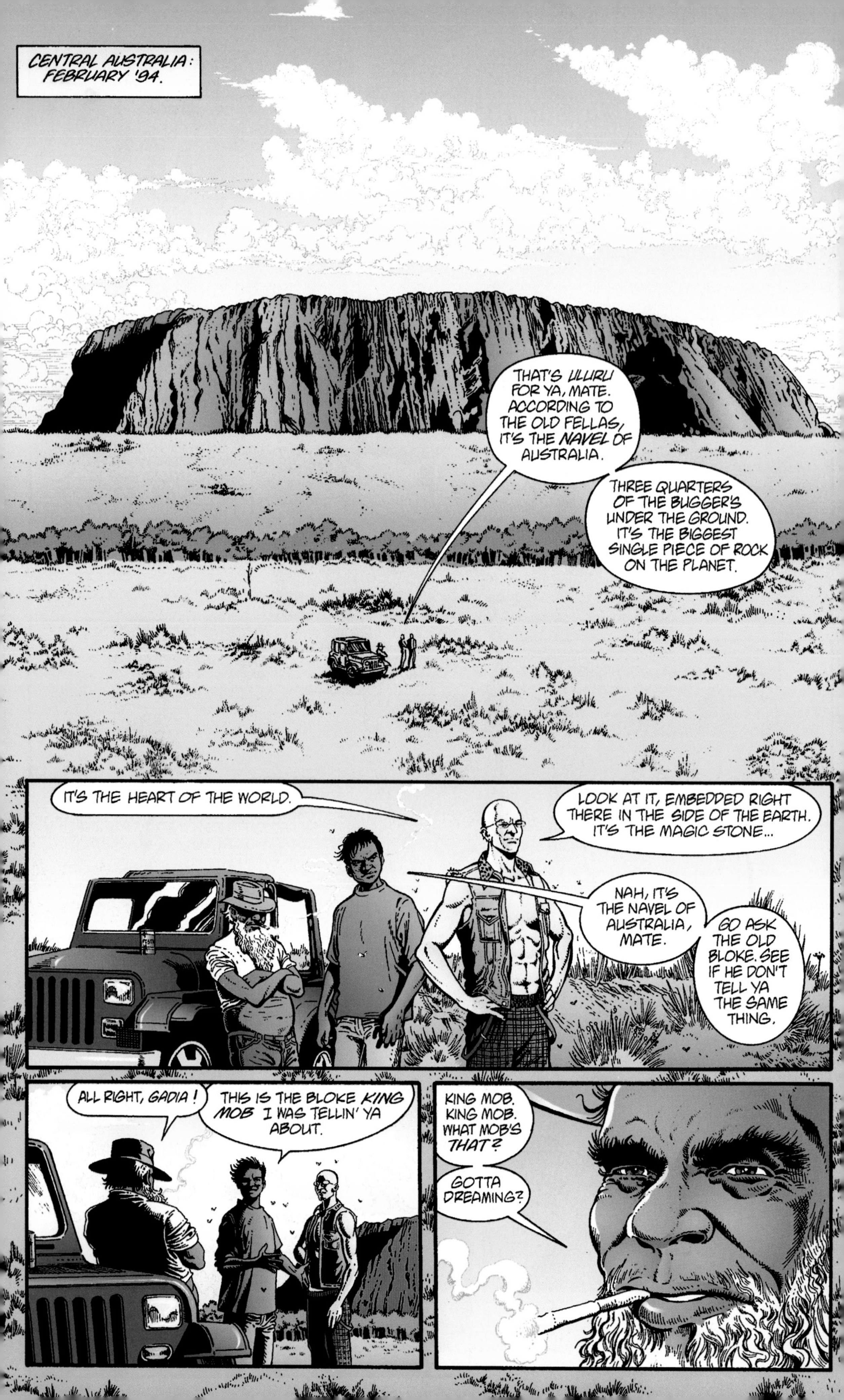
CENTRAL AUSTRALIA: FEBRUARY '94.
THAT'S ULURU FOR YA, MATE. ACCORDING TO THE OLD FELLAS, IT'S THE NAVEL OF AUSTRALIA.
THREE QUARTERS OF THE BUGGER'S UNDER THE GROUND. IT'S THE BIGGEST SINGLE PIECE OF ROCK ON THE PLANET.
IT'S THE HEART OF THE WORLD.
LOOK AT IT, EMBEDDED RIGHT THERE IN THE SIDE OF THE EARTH. IT'S THE MAGIC STONE...
NAH, IT'S THE NAVEL OF AUSTRALIA, MATE.
GO ASK THE OLD BLOKE. SEE IF HE DON'T TELL YA THE SAME THING.
ALL RIGHT, GADIA!
THIS IS THE BLOKE KING MOB I WAS TELLIN' YA ABOUT.
KING MOB. KING MOB. WHAT MOB'S THAT?
GOTTA DREAMING?

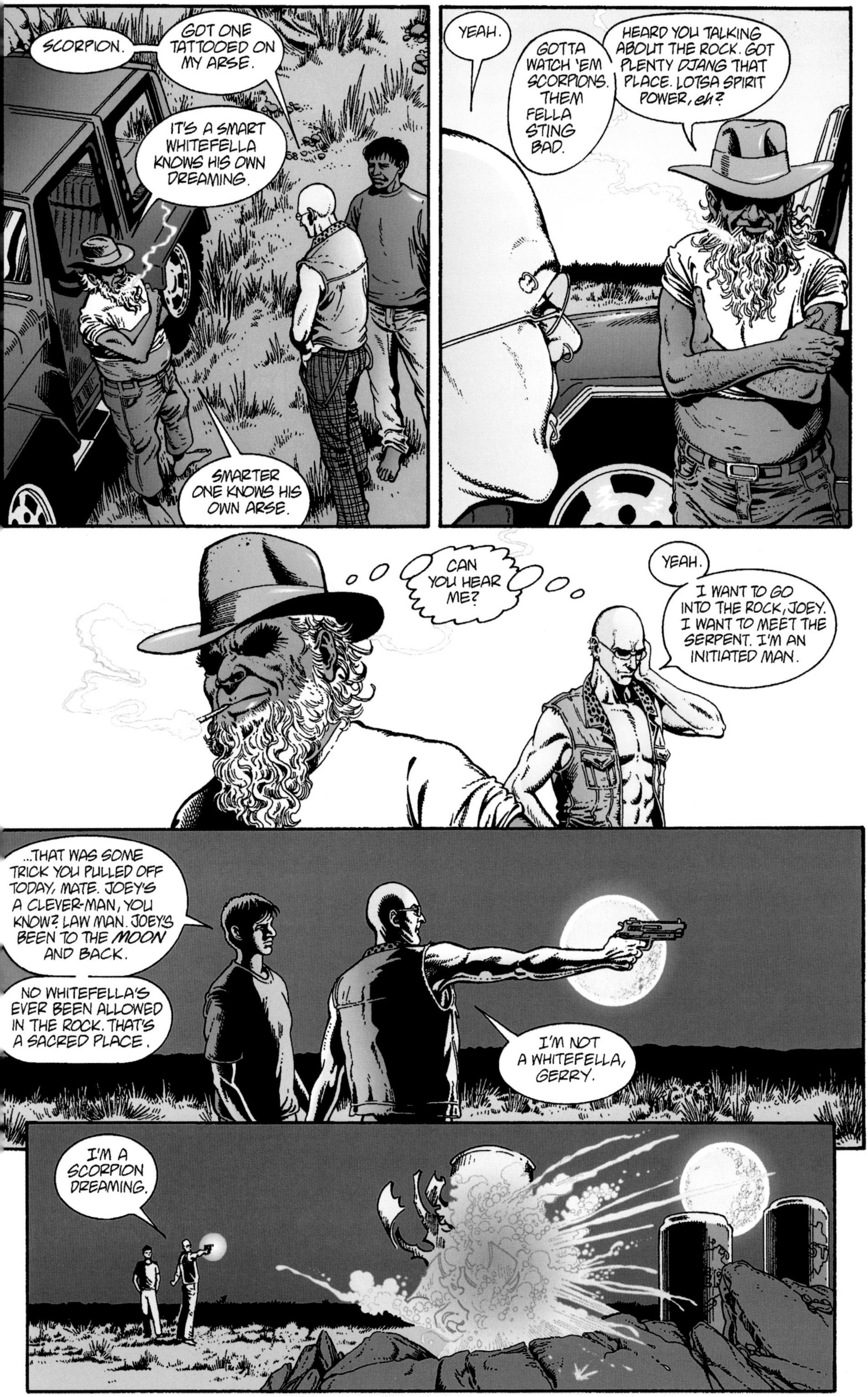
SCORPION.
GOT ONE TATTOOED ON MY ARSE.
IT'S A SMART WHITEFELLA KNOWS HIS OWN DREAMING.
SMARTER ONE KNOWS HIS OWN ARSE.
YEAH.
HEARD YOU TALKING ABOUT THE ROCK. GOT PLENTY DJANG THAT PLACE. LOTSA SPIRIT POWER, eh?
GOTTA WATCH 'EM SCORPIONS. THEM FELLA STING BAD.
CAN YOU HEAR ME?
YEAH.
I WANT TO GO INTO THE ROCK, JOEY. I WANT TO MEET THE SERPENT. I'M AN INITIATED MAN.
...THAT WAS SOME TRICK YOU PULLED OFF TODAY, MATE. JOEY'S A CLEVER-MAN, YOU KNOW? LAW MAN. JOEY'S BEEN TO THE MOON AND BACK.
NO WHITEFELLA'S EVER BEEN ALLOWED IN THE ROCK. THAT'S A SACRED PLACE.
I'M NOT A WHITEFELLA, GERRY.
I'M A SCORPION DREAMING.

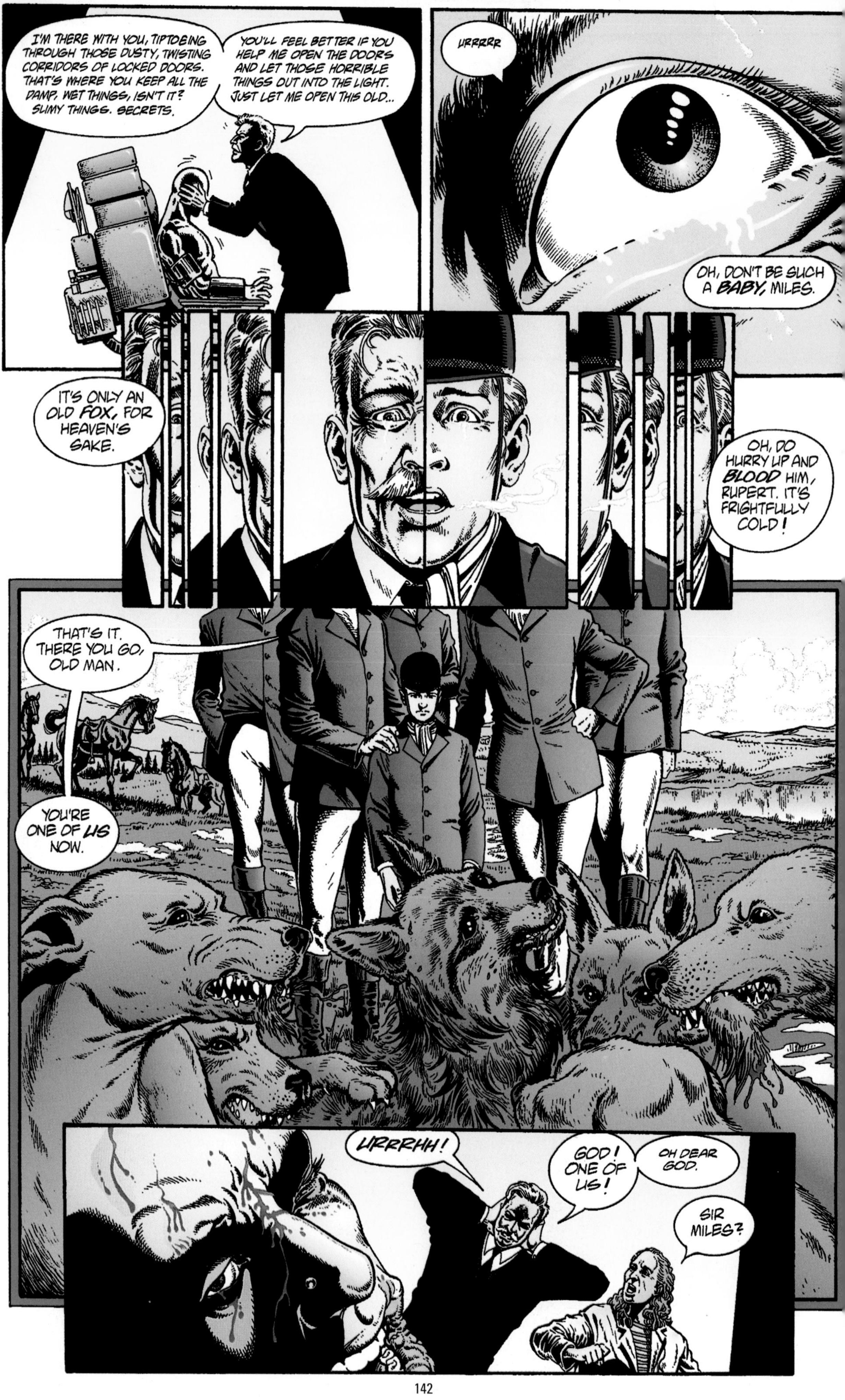
I'M THERE WITH YOU, TIPTOEING THROUGH THOSE DUSTY, TWISTING CORRIDORS OF LOCKED DOORS. THAT'S WHERE YOU KEEP ALL THE DAMP, WET THINGS, ISN'T IT? SLIMY THINGS. SECRETS.
YOU'LL FEEL BETTER IF YOU HELP ME OPEN THE DOORS AND LET THOSE HORRIBLE THINGS OUT INTO THE LIGHT. JUST LET ME OPEN THIS OLD...
URRRRR
OH, DON'T BE SUCH A BABY, MILES.
IT'S ONLY AN OLD FOX, FOR HEAVEN'S SAKE.
OH, DO HURRY UP AND BLOOD HIM, RUPERT. IT'S FRIGHTFULLY COLD!
THAT'S IT. THERE YOU GO, OLD MAN.
YOU'RE ONE OF US NOW.
URRRHH!
GOD! ONE OF US!
OH DEAR GOD.
SIR MILES?

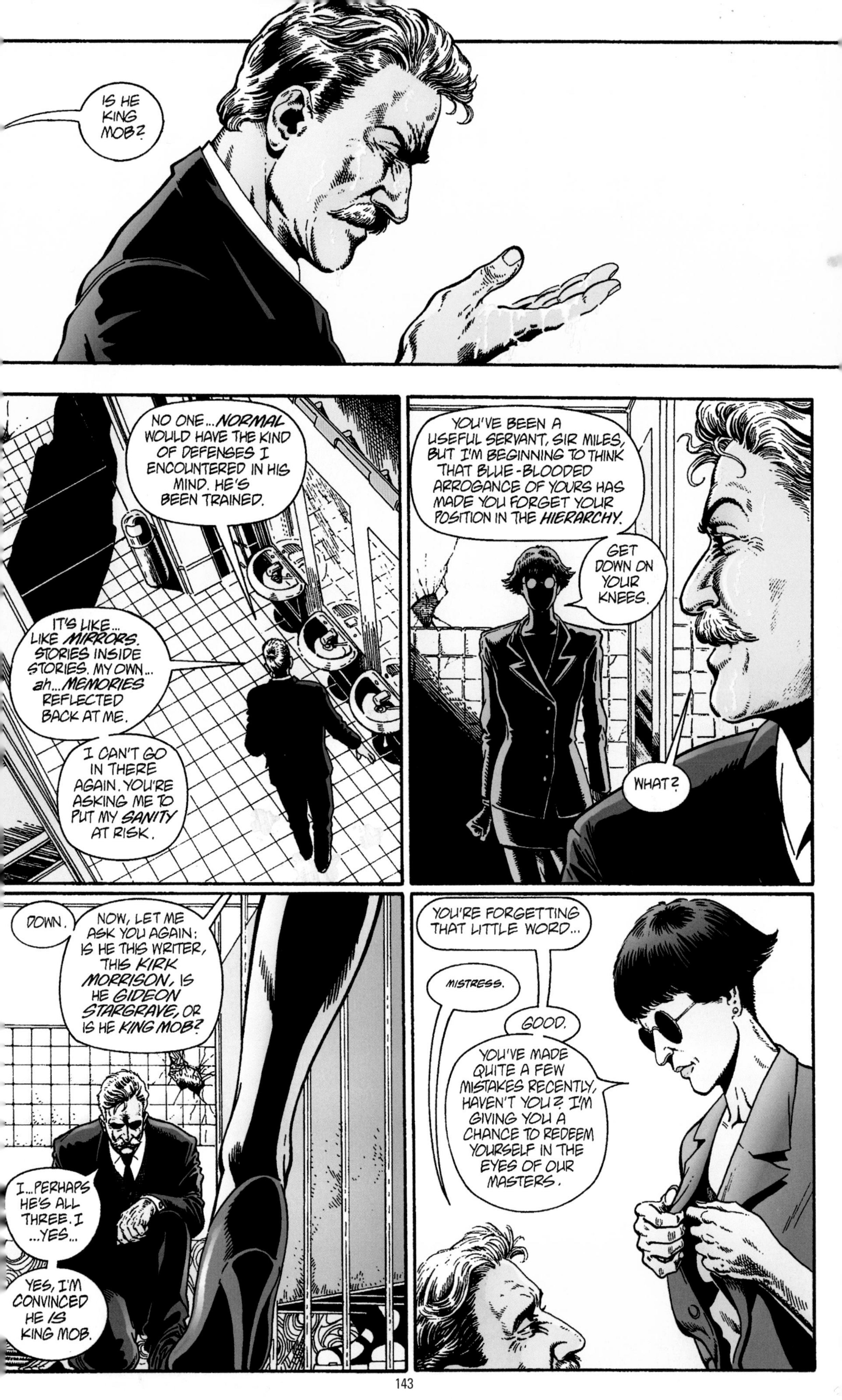
IS HE KING MOB?
NO ONE... NORMAL WOULD HAVE THE KIND OF DEFENSES I ENCOUNTERED IN HIS MIND. HE'S BEEN TRAINED.
IT'S LIKE... LIKE MIRRORS. STORIES INSIDE STORIES. MY OWN... ah... MEMORIES REFLECTED BACK AT ME.
I CAN'T GO IN THERE AGAIN. YOU'RE ASKING ME TO PUT MY SANITY AT RISK.
YOU'VE BEEN A USEFUL SERVANT, SIR MILES, BUT I'M BEGINNING TO THINK THAT BLUE-BLOODED ARROGANCE OF YOURS HAS MADE YOU FORGET YOUR POSITION IN THE HIERARCHY.
GET DOWN ON YOUR KNEES.
WHAT?
DOWN.
NOW, LET ME ASK YOU AGAIN: IS HE THIS WRITER, THIS KIRK MORRISON, IS HE GIDEON STARGRAVE, OR IS HE KING MOB?
I... PERHAPS HE'S ALL THREE. I ...YES...
YES, I'M CONVINCED HE IS KING MOB.
YOU'RE FORGETTING THAT LITTLE WORD...
MISTRESS.
GOOD.
YOU'VE MADE QUITE A FEW MISTAKES RECENTLY, HAVEN'T YOU? I'M GIVING YOU A CHANCE TO REDEEM YOURSELF IN THE EYES OF OUR MASTERS.

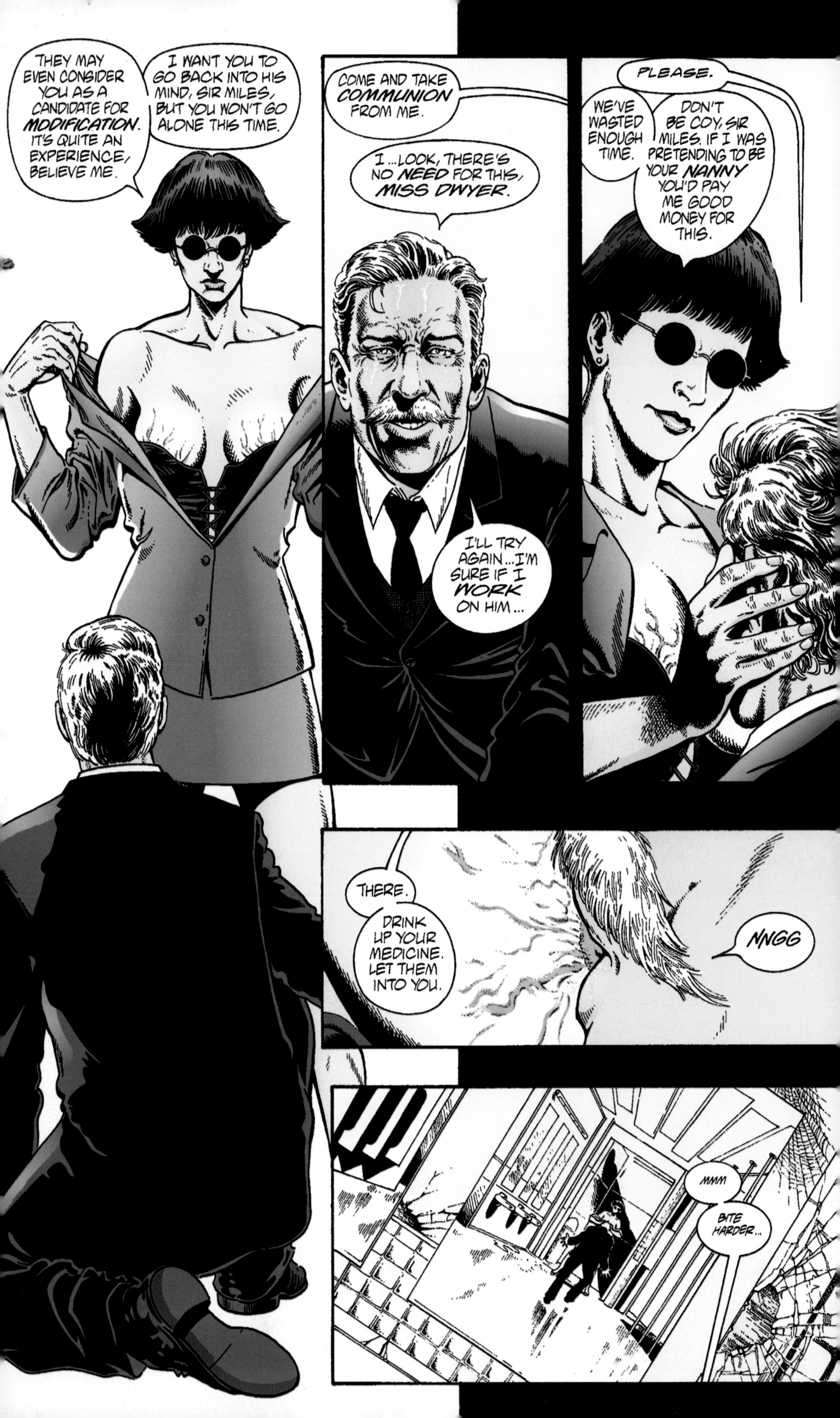
THEY MAY EVEN CONSIDER YOU AS A CANDIDATE FOR MODIFICATION. IT'S QUITE AN EXPERIENCE, BELIEVE ME.
I WANT YOU TO GO BACK INTO HIS MIND, SIR MILES, BUT YOU WON'T GO ALONE THIS TIME.
COME AND TAKE COMMUNION FROM ME.
I...LOOK, THERE'S NO NEED FOR THIS, MISS DWYER.
I'LL TRY AGAIN...I'M SURE IF I WORK ON HIM...
PLEASE.
WE'VE WASTED ENOUGH TIME.
DON'T BE COY, SIR MILES. IF I WAS PRETENDING TO BE YOUR NANNY YOU'D PAY ME GOOD MONEY FOR THIS.
THERE.
DRINK UP YOUR MEDICINE. LET THEM INTO YOU.
NNGG
MMM
BITE HARDER...

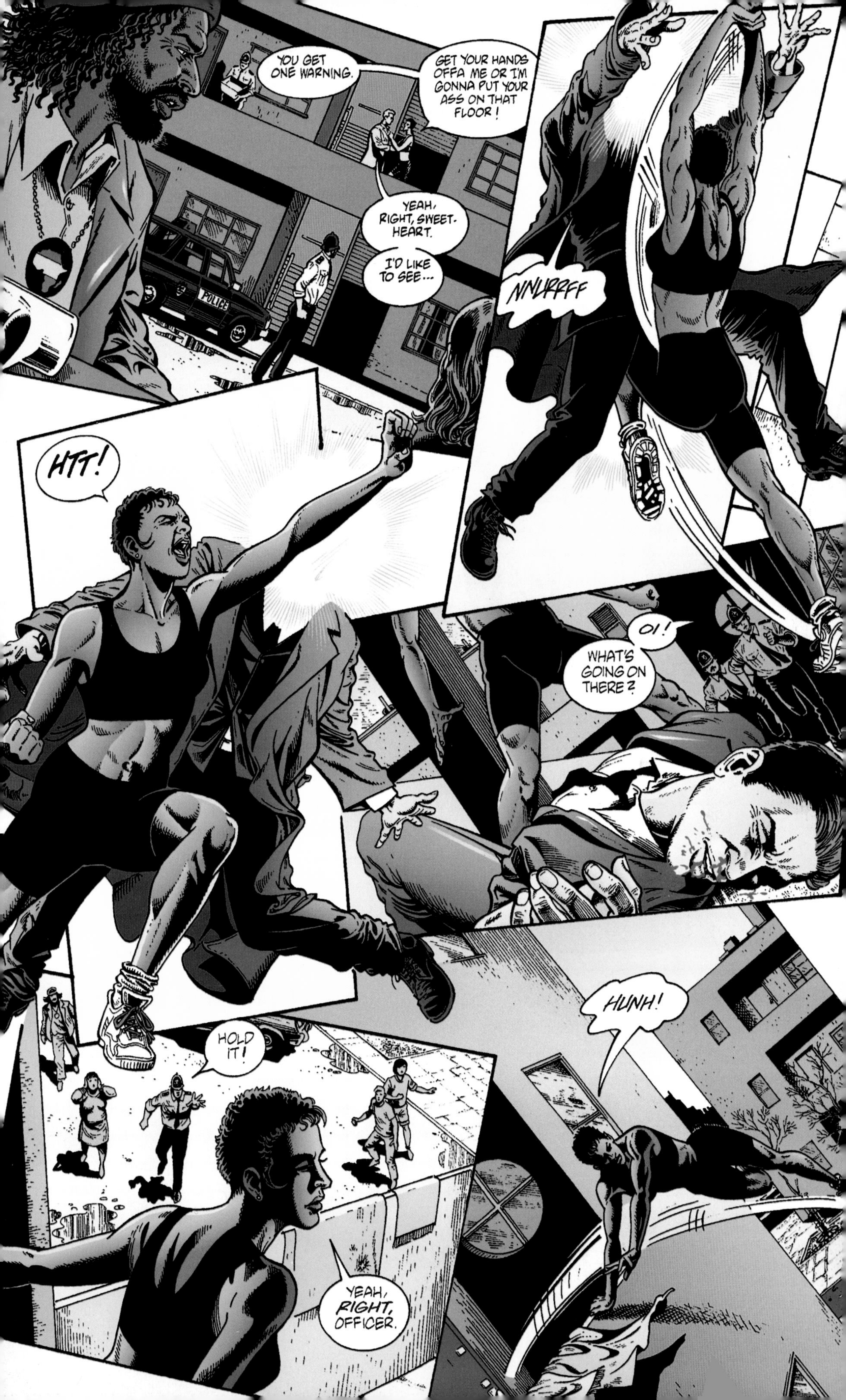
YOU GET ONE WARNING.
GET YOUR HANDS OFFA ME OR I'M GONNA PUT YOUR ASS ON THAT FLOOR!
YEAH, RIGHT, SWEET-HEART.
I'D LIKE TO SEE...
NNURRFF
HTT!
OI!
WHAT'S GOING ON THERE?
HOLD IT!
YEAH, RIGHT, OFFICER.
HUNH!

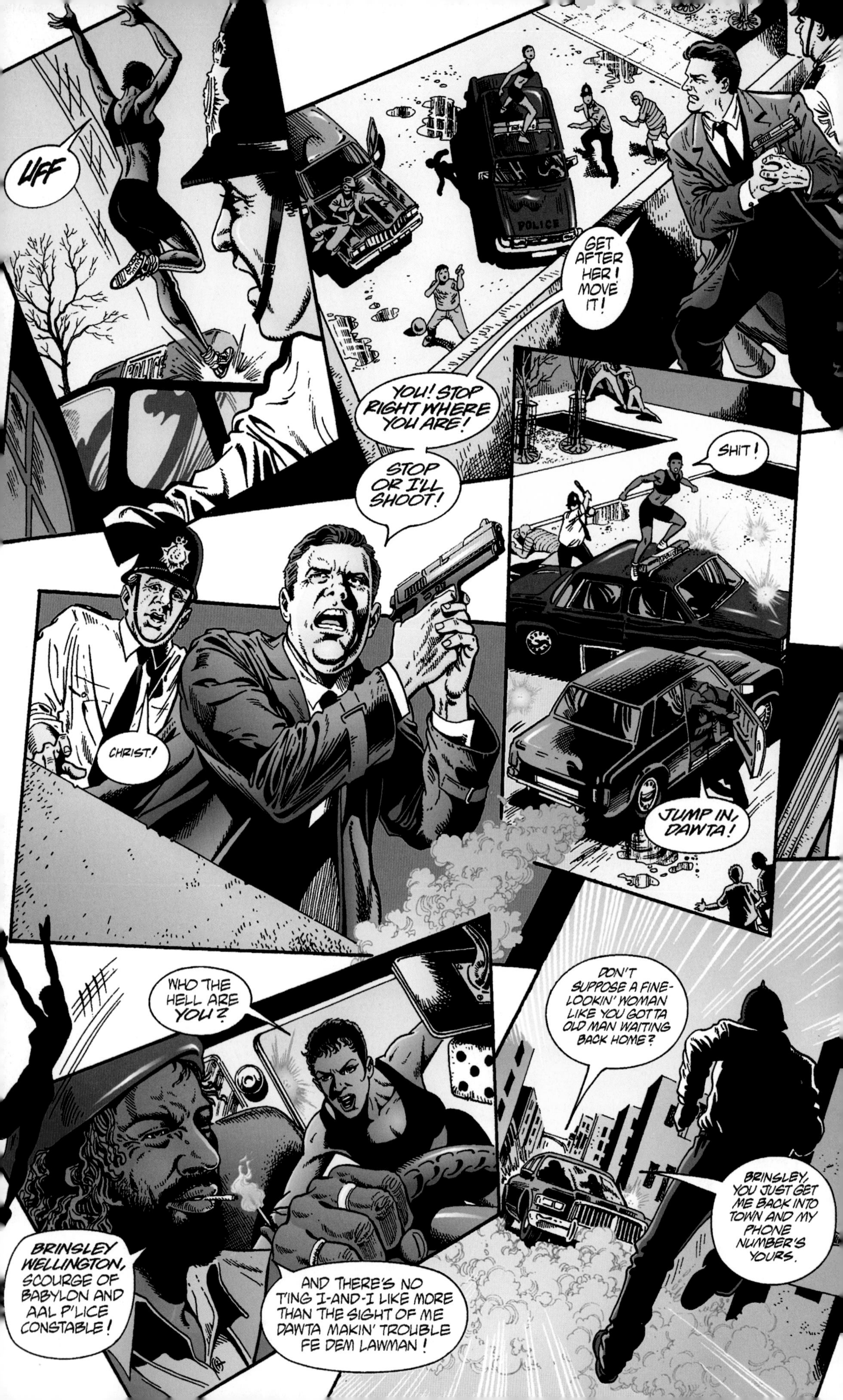
UFF
GET AFTER HER! MOVE IT!
YOU! STOP RIGHT WHERE YOU ARE!
STOP OR I'LL SHOOT!
SHIT!
CHRIST!
JUMP IN, DAWTA!
WHO THE HELL ARE YOU?
BRINSLEY WELLINGTON, SCOURGE OF BABYLON AND AAL P'LICE CONSTABLE!
AND THERE'S NO T'ING I-AND-I LIKE MORE THAN THE SIGHT OF ME DAWTA MAKIN' TROUBLE FE DEM LAWMAN!
DON'T SUPPOSE A FINE-LOOKIN' WOMAN LIKE YOU GOTTA OLD MAN WAITING BACK HOME?
BRINSLEY, YOU JUST GET ME BACK INTO TOWN AND MY PHONE NUMBER'S YOURS.

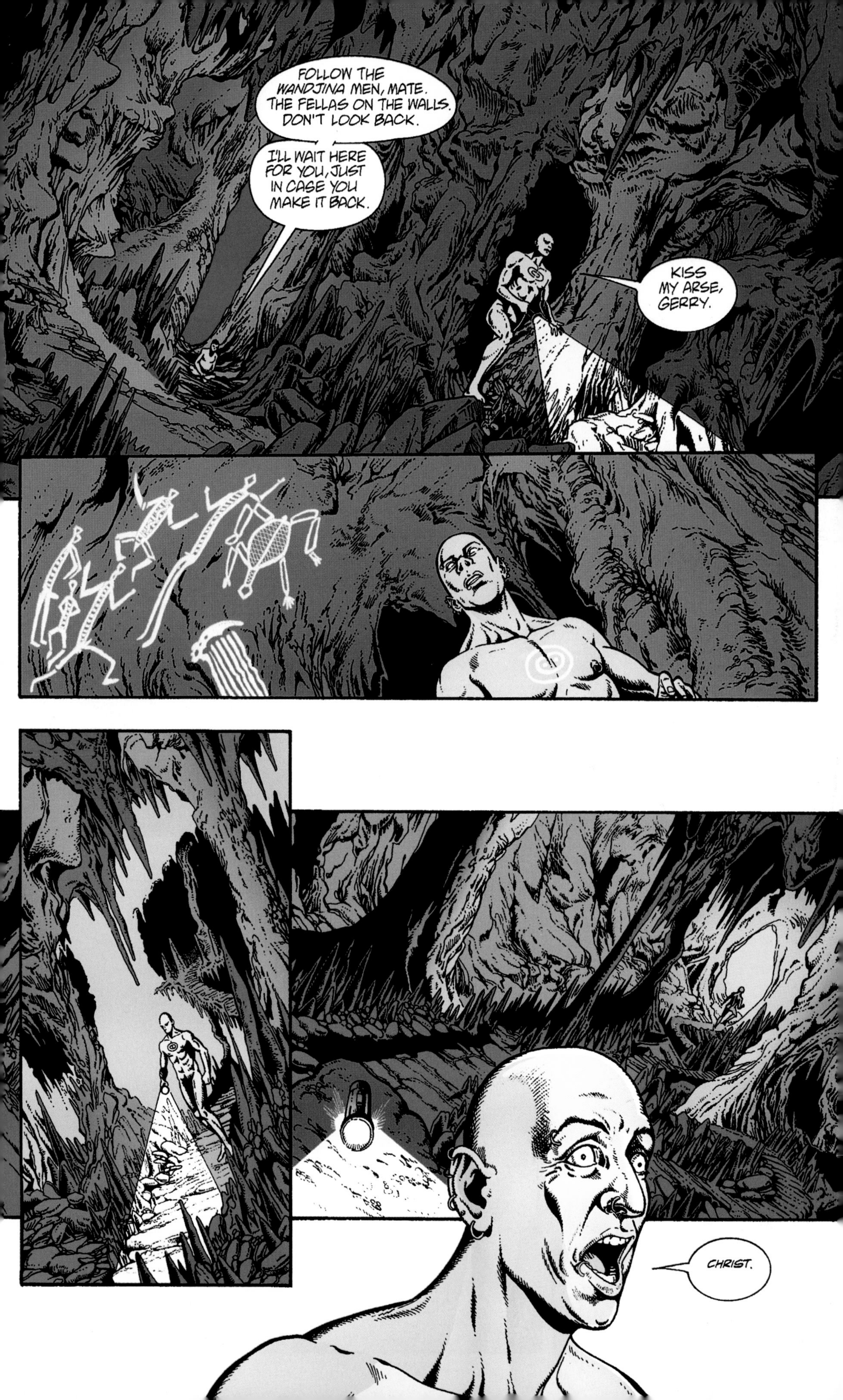
FOLLOW THE WANDJINA MEN, MATE. THE FELLAS ON THE WALLS. DON'T LOOK BACK.
I'LL WAIT HERE FOR YOU, JUST IN CASE YOU MAKE IT BACK.
KISS MY ARSE, GERRY.
CHRIST.

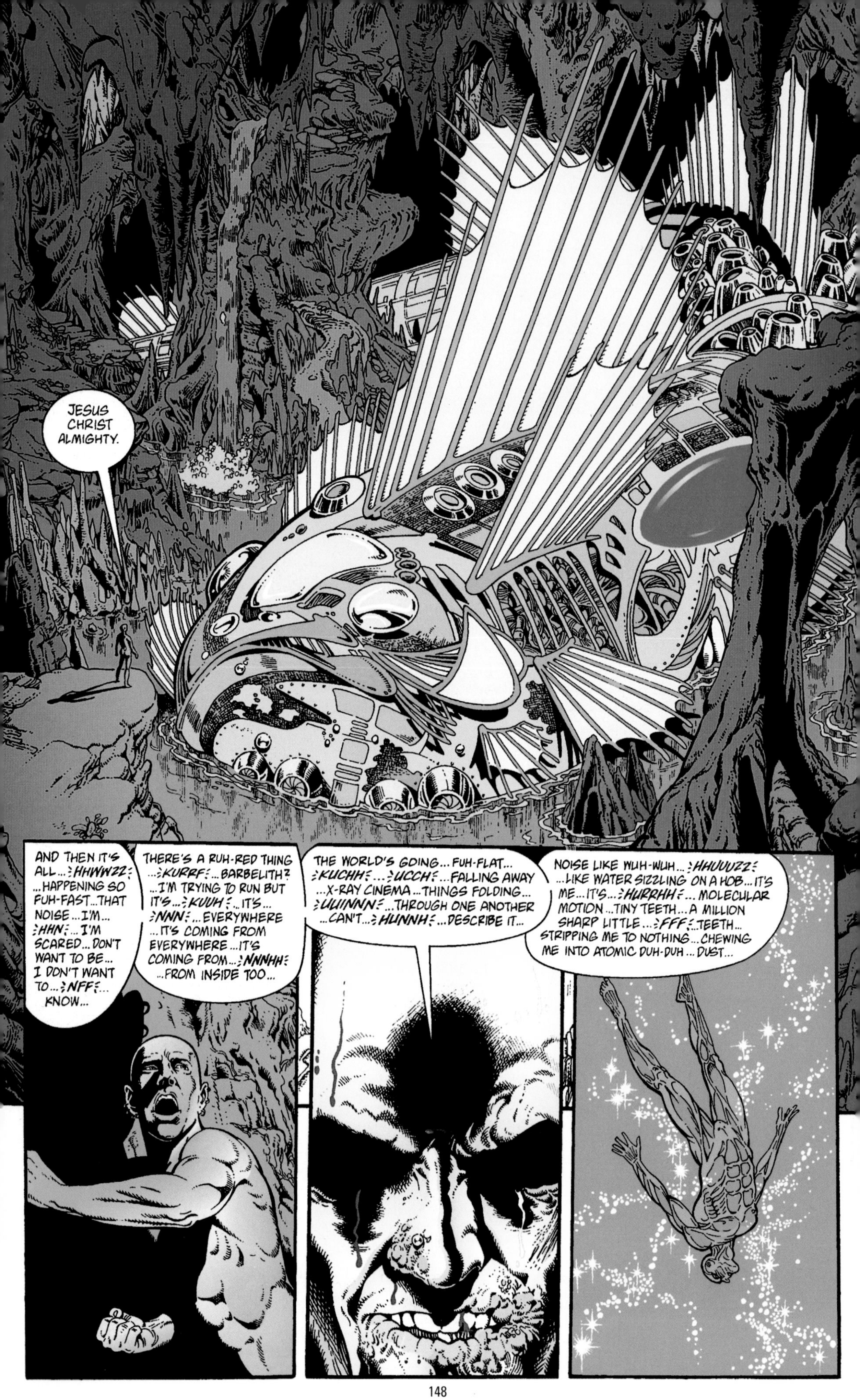
JESUS CHRIST ALMIGHTY.
AND THEN IT'S ALL... HHWWZZ ...HAPPENING SO FUH-FAST...THAT NOISE...I'M... HHN ...I'M SCARED...DON'T WANT TO BE... I DON'T WANT TO... NFF... KNOW...
THERE'S A RUH-RED THING ...KURRF...BARBELITH? ...I'M TRYING TO RUN BUT IT'S... KUUH ...IT'S... NNN ...EVERYWHERE ...IT'S COMING FROM EVERYWHERE...IT'S COMING FROM... NNNHH ...FROM INSIDE TOO...
THE WORLD'S GOING...FUH-FLAT... KUCHH... UCCH ...FALLING AWAY ...X-RAY CINEMA...THINGS FOLDING... UUINNN ...THROUGH ONE ANOTHER ...CAN'T... HUNNH ...DESCRIBE IT...
NOISE LIKE WUH-WUH... HHUUUZZ ...LIKE WATER SIZZLING ON A HOB...IT'S ME...IT'S... HURRHH ...MOLECULAR MOTION...TINY TEETH...A MILLION SHARP LITTLE... FFF ...TEETH... STRIPPING ME TO NOTHING...CHEWING ME INTO ATOMIC DUH-DUH...DUST...

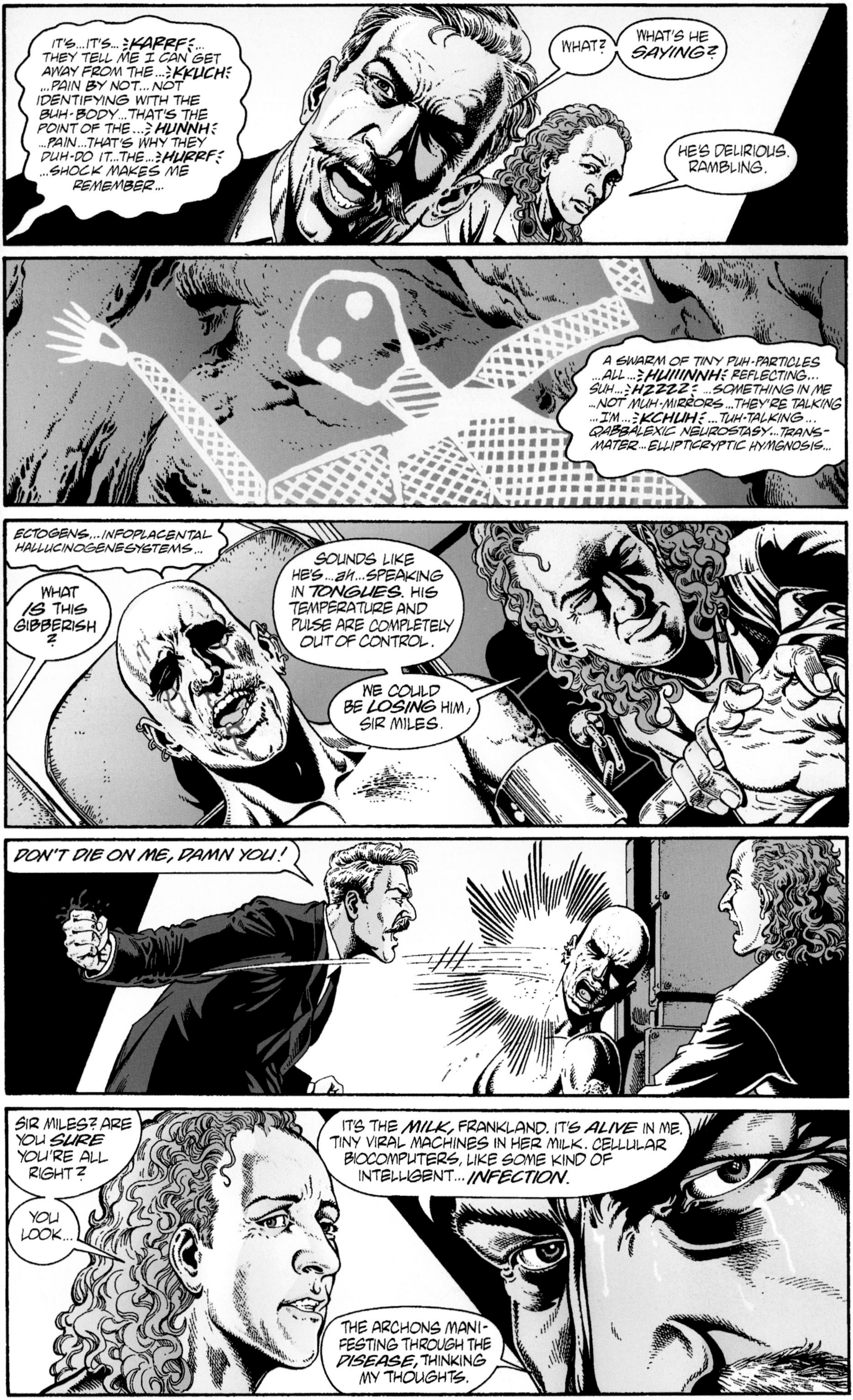
IT'S...IT'S... KARRF ... THEY TELL ME I CAN GET AWAY FROM THE... KKUCH ...PAIN BY NOT... NOT IDENTIFYING WITH THE BUH-BODY...THAT'S THE POINT OF THE... HUNNH ...PAIN...THAT'S WHY THEY DUH-DO IT...THE... HURRF ...SHOCK MAKES ME REMEMBER...
WHAT?
WHAT'S HE SAYING?
HE'S DELIRIOUS. RAMBLING.
A SWARM OF TINY PUH-PARTICLES ...ALL... HUIIINNH REFLECTING... SUH... HZZZZ ...SOMETHING IN ME ...NOT MUH-MIRRORS...THEY'RE TALKING ...I'M... KCHUH ...TUH-TALKING... QABBALEXIC NEUROSTASY...TRANS-MATER...ELLIPTICRYPTIC HYMGNOSIS...
ECTOGENS...INFOPLACENTAL HALLUCINOGENESYSTEMS...
WHAT IS THIS GIBBERISH?
SOUNDS LIKE HE'S...ah...SPEAKING IN TONGUES. HIS TEMPERATURE AND PULSE ARE COMPLETELY OUT OF CONTROL.
WE COULD BE LOSING HIM, SIR MILES.
DON'T DIE ON ME, DAMN YOU!
SIR MILES? ARE YOU SURE YOU'RE ALL RIGHT?
YOU LOOK...
IT'S THE MILK, FRANKLAND. IT'S ALIVE IN ME. TINY VIRAL MACHINES IN HER MILK. CELLULAR BIOCOMPUTERS, LIKE SOME KIND OF INTELLIGENT... INFECTION.
THE ARCHONS MANI-FESTING THROUGH THE DISEASE, THINKING MY THOUGHTS.

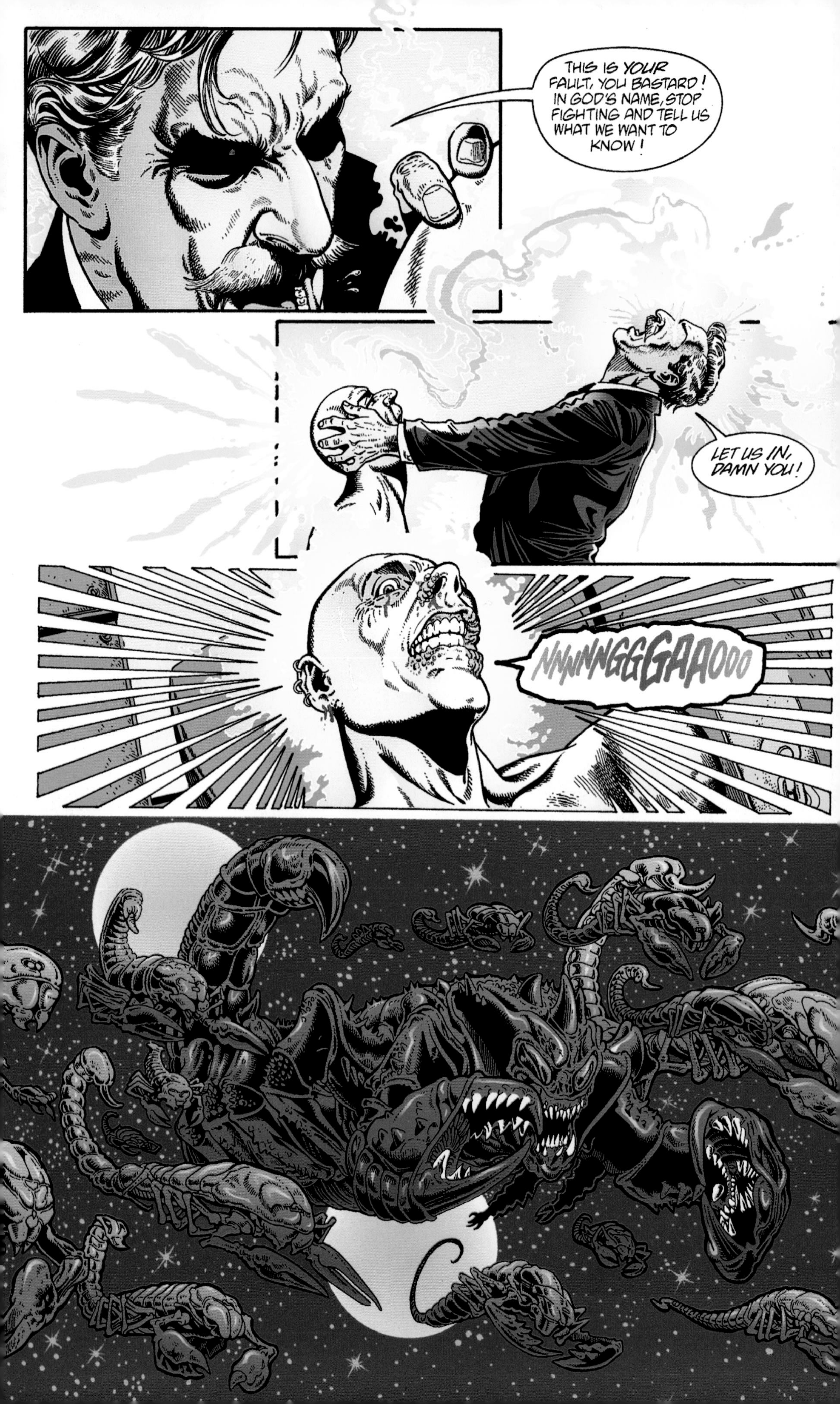
THIS IS YOUR FAULT, YOU BASTARD! IN GOD'S NAME, STOP FIGHTING AND TELL US WHAT WE WANT TO KNOW!
LET US IN, DAMN YOU!
NNNNNGGGAAOOO

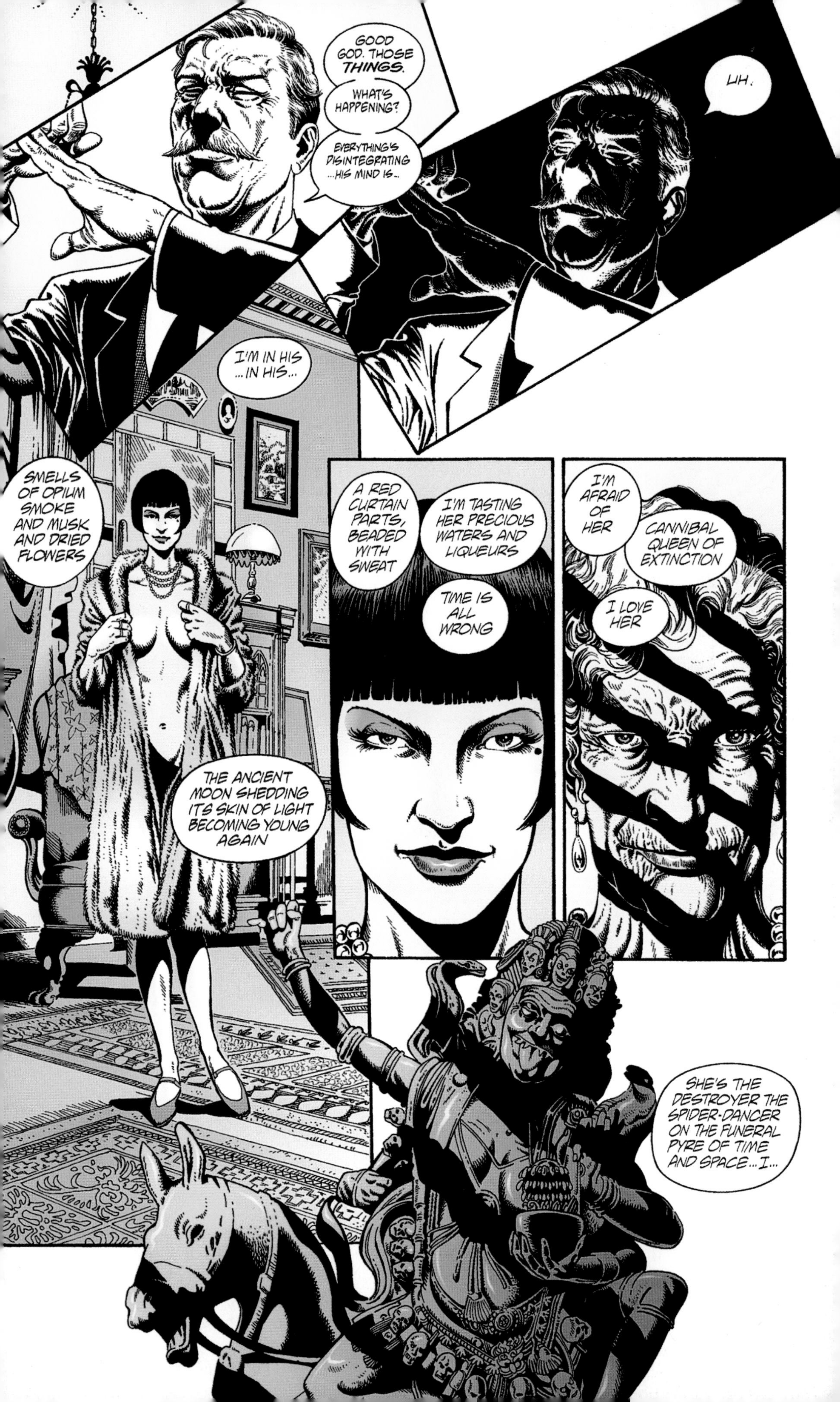
GOOD GOD. THOSE THINGS.
WHAT'S HAPPENING?
EVERYTHING'S DISINTEGRATING ...HIS MIND IS...
UH.
I'M IN HIS ...IN HIS...
SMELLS OF OPIUM SMOKE AND MUSK AND DRIED FLOWERS
THE ANCIENT MOON SHEDDING ITS SKIN OF LIGHT BECOMING YOUNG AGAIN
A RED CURTAIN PARTS, BEADED WITH SWEAT
I'M TASTING HER PRECIOUS WATERS AND LIQUEURS
TIME IS ALL WRONG
I'M AFRAID OF HER
CANNIBAL QUEEN OF EXTINCTION
I LOVE HER
SHE'S THE DESTROYER THE SPIDER-DANCER ON THE FUNERAL PYRE OF TIME AND SPACE... I...

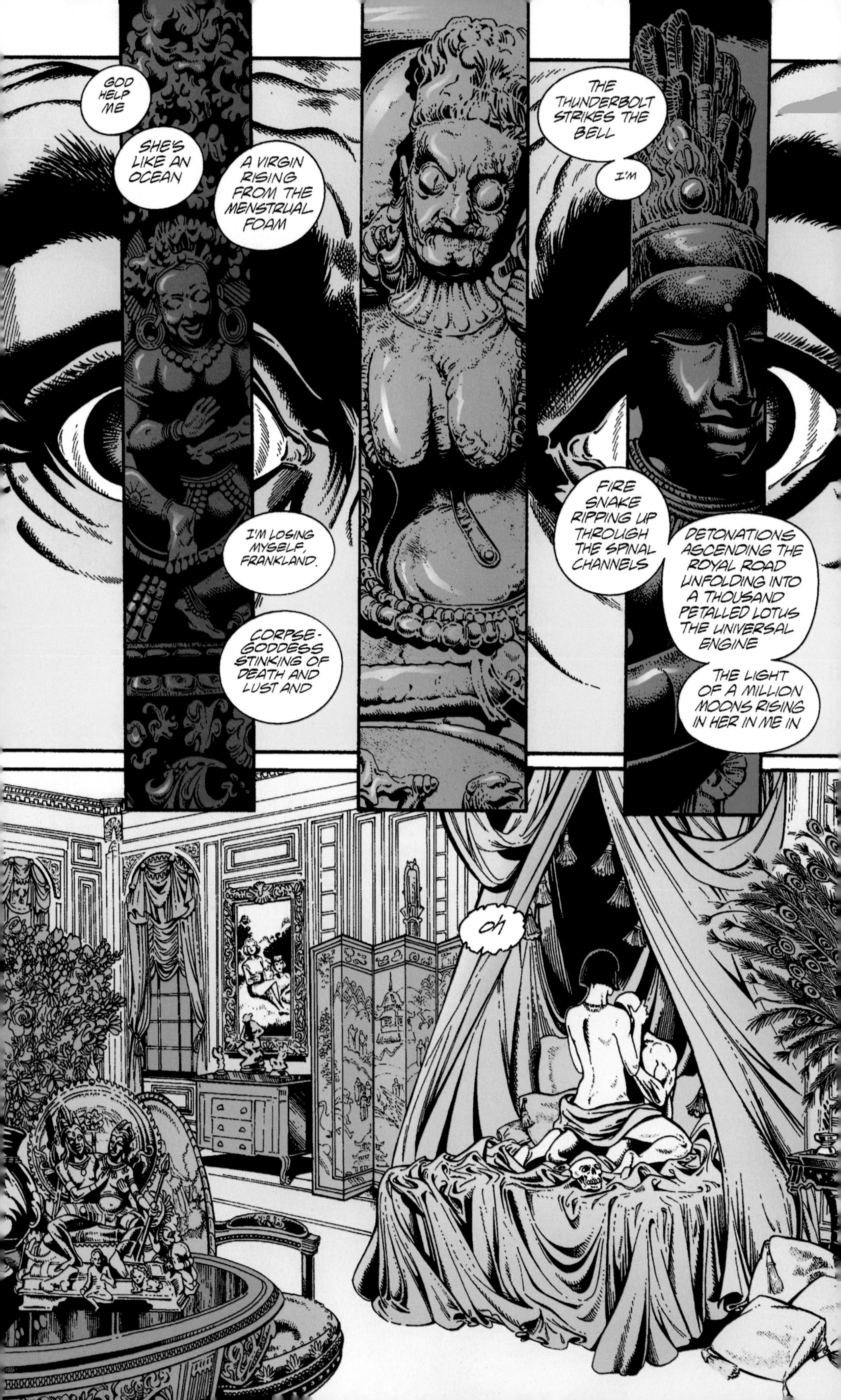
GOD HELP ME
SHE'S LIKE AN OCEAN
A VIRGIN RISING FROM THE MENSTRUAL FOAM
THE THUNDERBOLT STRIKES THE BELL
I'M
I'M LOSING MYSELF, FRANKLAND.
CORPSE-GODDESS STINKING OF DEATH AND LUST AND
FIRE SNAKE RIPPING UP THROUGH THE SPINAL CHANNELS
DETONATIONS ASCENDING THE ROYAL ROAD UNFOLDING INTO A THOUSAND PETALLED LOTUS THE UNIVERSAL ENGINE
THE LIGHT OF A MILLION MOONS RISING IN HER IN ME IN
oh

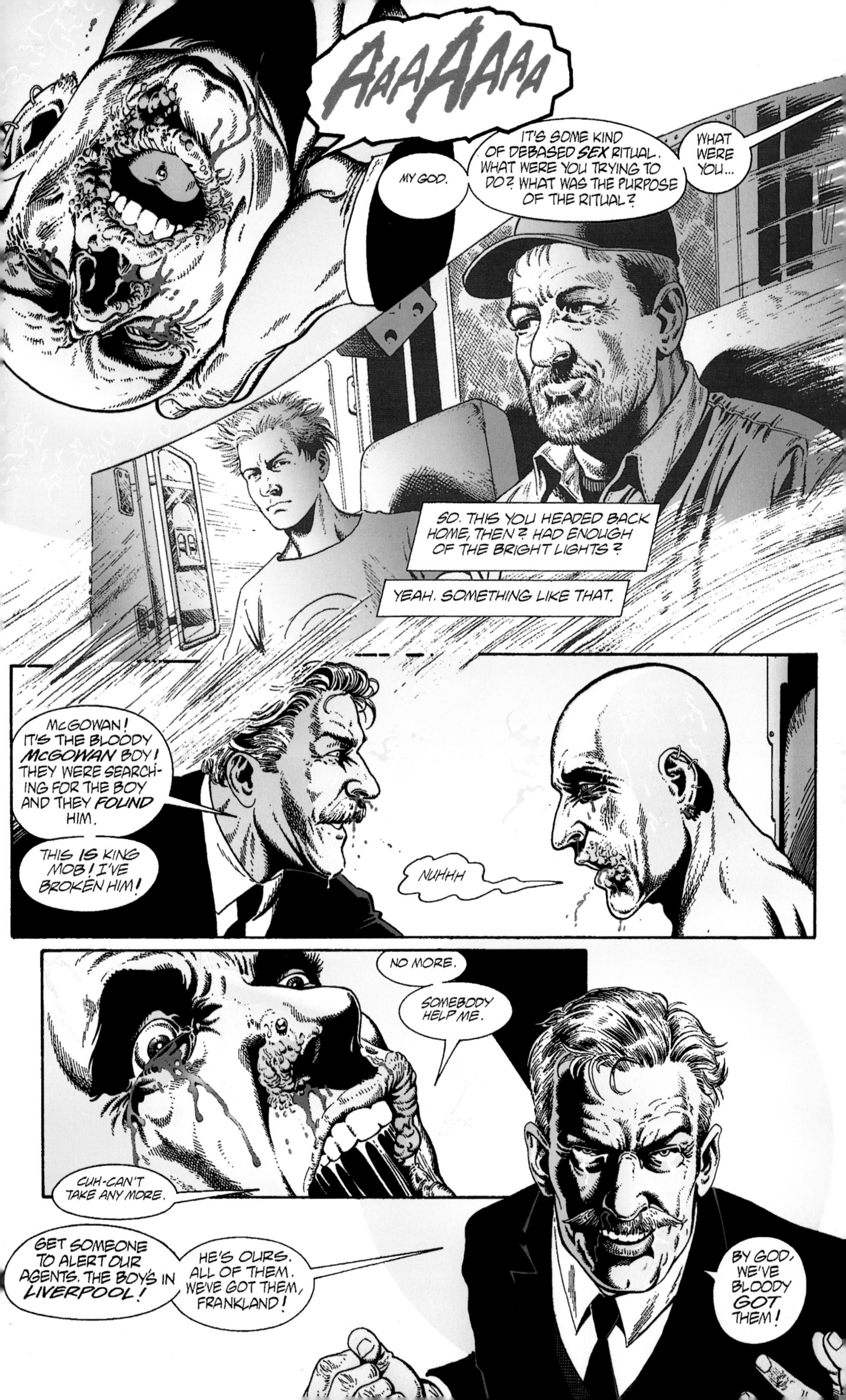
AAAAAAA
MY GOD.
IT'S SOME KIND OF DEBASED SEX RITUAL. WHAT WERE YOU TRYING TO DO? WHAT WAS THE PURPOSE OF THE RITUAL?
WHAT WERE YOU...
SO. THIS YOU HEADED BACK HOME, THEN? HAD ENOUGH OF THE BRIGHT LIGHTS?
YEAH. SOMETHING LIKE THAT.
McGOWAN! IT'S THE BLOODY McGOWAN BOY! THEY WERE SEARCHING FOR THE BOY AND THEY FOUND HIM.
THIS IS KING MOB! I'VE BROKEN HIM!
NUHHH
NO MORE.
SOMEBODY HELP ME.
CUH-CAN'T TAKE ANY MORE.
GET SOMEONE TO ALERT OUR AGENTS. THE BOY'S IN LIVERPOOL!
HE'S OURS. ALL OF THEM. WE'VE GOT THEM, FRANKLAND!
BY GOD, WE'VE BLOODY GOT THEM!

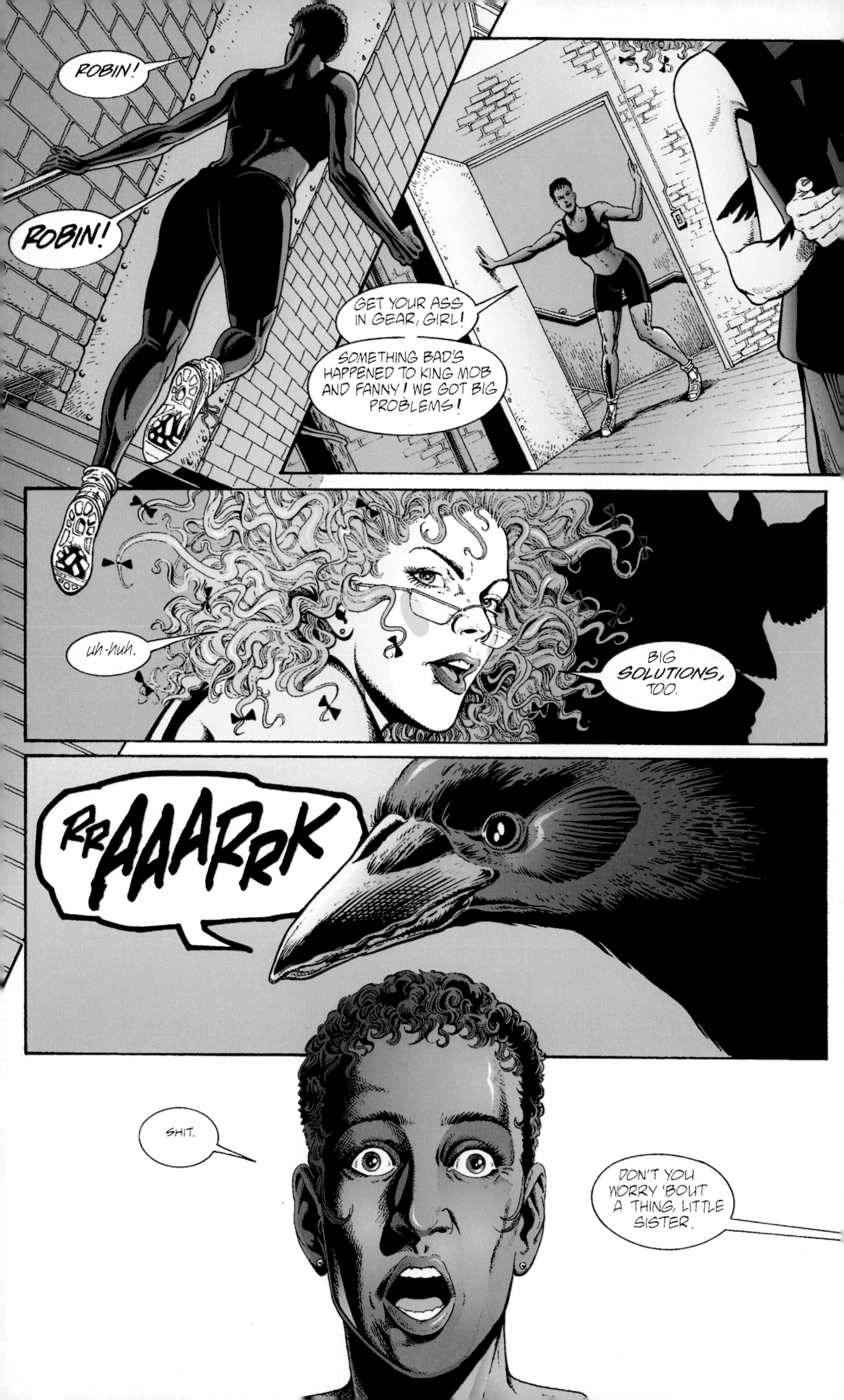
ROBIN!
ROBIN!
GET YOUR ASS IN GEAR, GIRL!
SOMETHING BAD'S HAPPENED TO KING MOB AND FANNY! WE GOT BIG PROBLEMS!
uh-huh.
BIG SOLUTIONS, TOO.
RRAAAARRRK
SHIT.
DON'T YOU WORRY 'BOUT A THING, LITTLE SISTER.

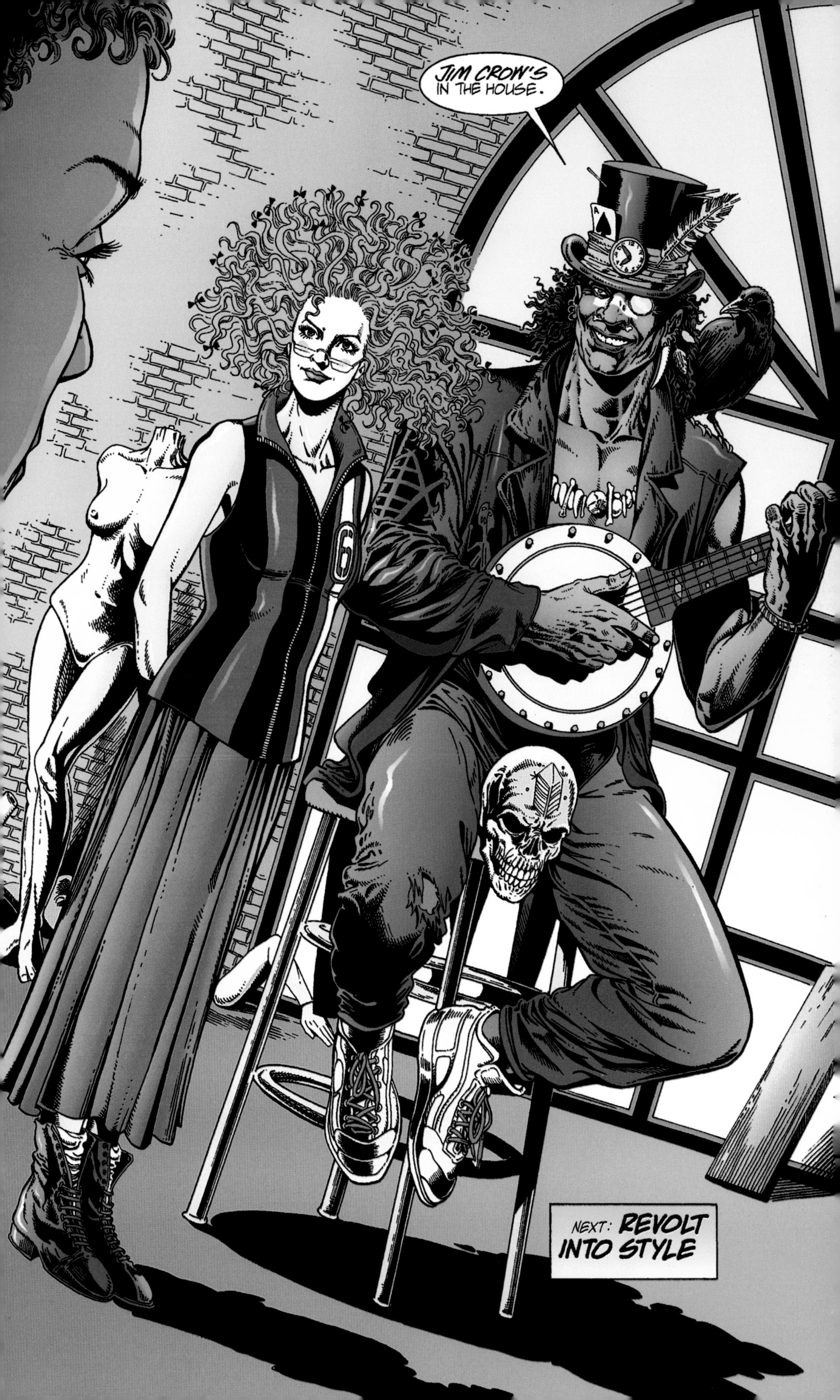

JIM CROW'S IN THE HOUSE.
NEXT: REVOLT INTO STYLE

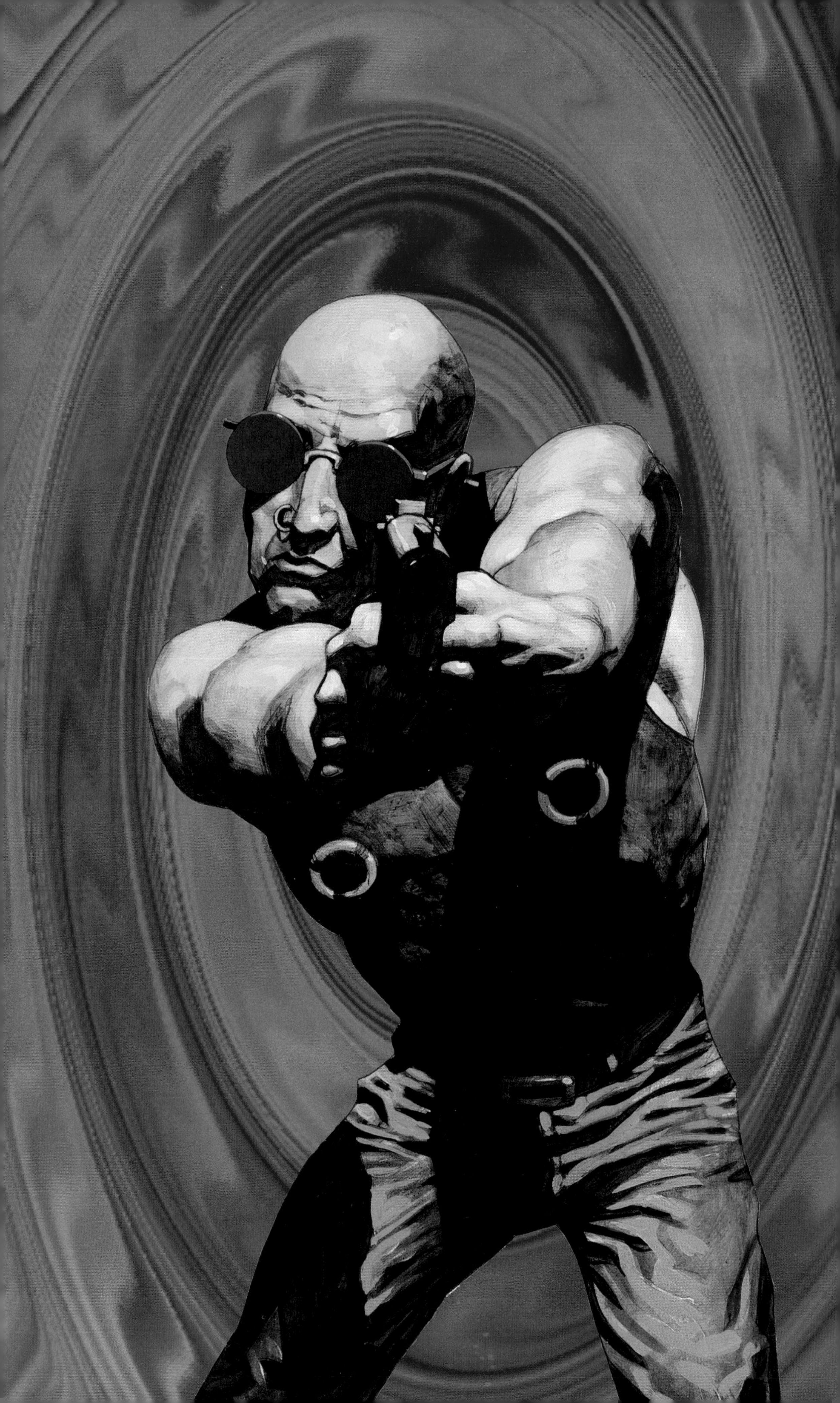

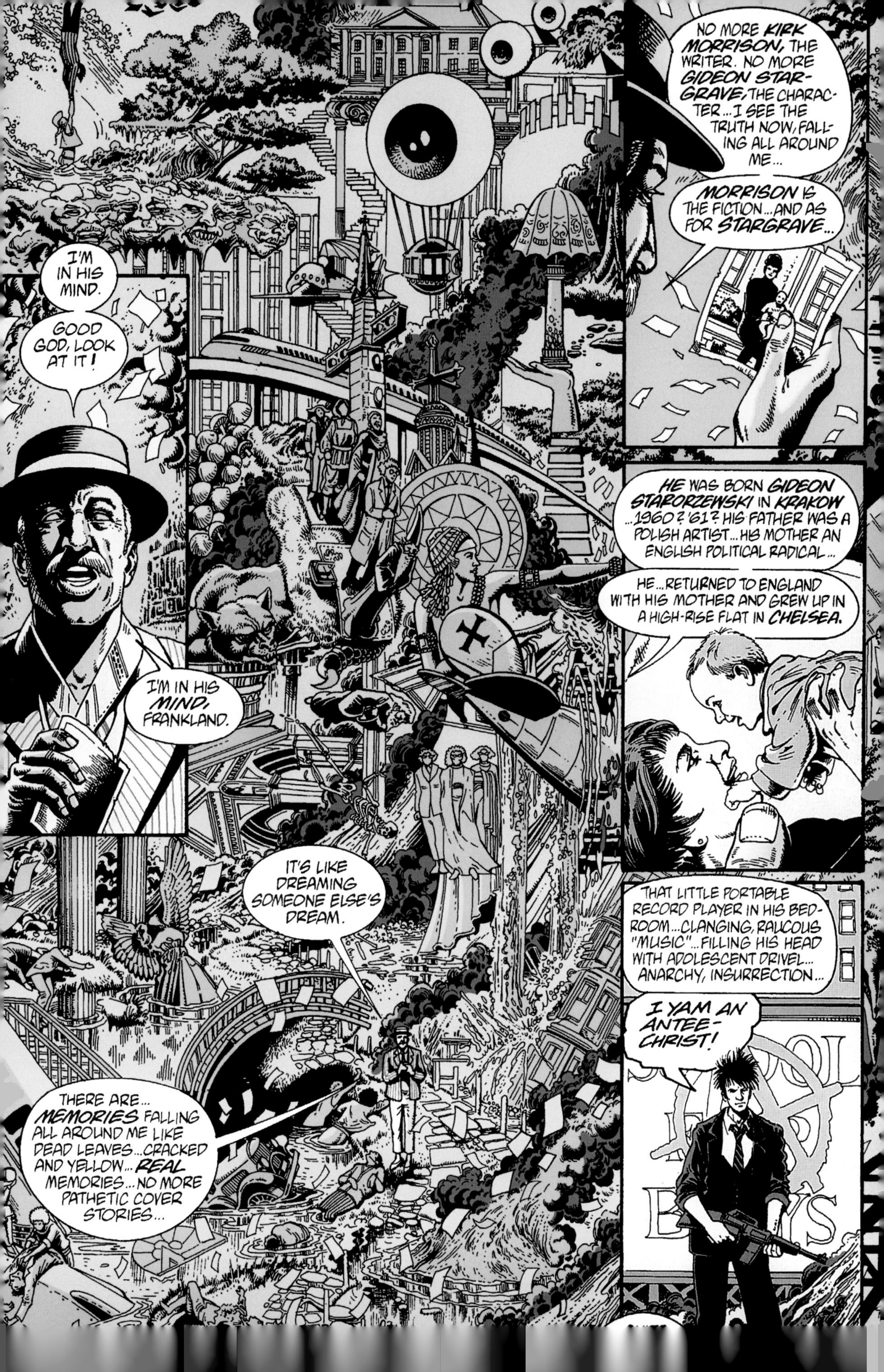

I'M IN HIS MIND.
GOOD GOD, LOOK AT IT!
I'M IN HIS MIND, FRANKLAND.
IT'S LIKE DREAMING SOMEONE ELSE'S DREAM.
THERE ARE... MEMORIES FALLING ALL AROUND ME LIKE DEAD LEAVES...CRACKED AND YELLOW...REAL MEMORIES...NO MORE PATHETIC COVER STORIES...
NO MORE KIRK MORRISON, THE WRITER. NO MORE GIDEON STARGRAVE, THE CHARACTER...I SEE THE TRUTH NOW, FALLING ALL AROUND ME...
MORRISON IS THE FICTION...AND AS FOR STARGRAVE...
HE WAS BORN GIDEON STARORZEWSKI IN KRAKOW ...1960? '61? HIS FATHER WAS A POLISH ARTIST...HIS MOTHER AN ENGLISH POLITICAL RADICAL...
HE...RETURNED TO ENGLAND WITH HIS MOTHER AND GREW UP IN A HIGH-RISE FLAT IN CHELSEA.
THAT LITTLE PORTABLE RECORD PLAYER IN HIS BEDROOM...CLANGING, RAUCOUS "MUSIC"...FILLING HIS HEAD WITH ADOLESCENT DRIVEL...ANARCHY, INSURRECTION...
I YAM AN ANTEE-CHRIST!

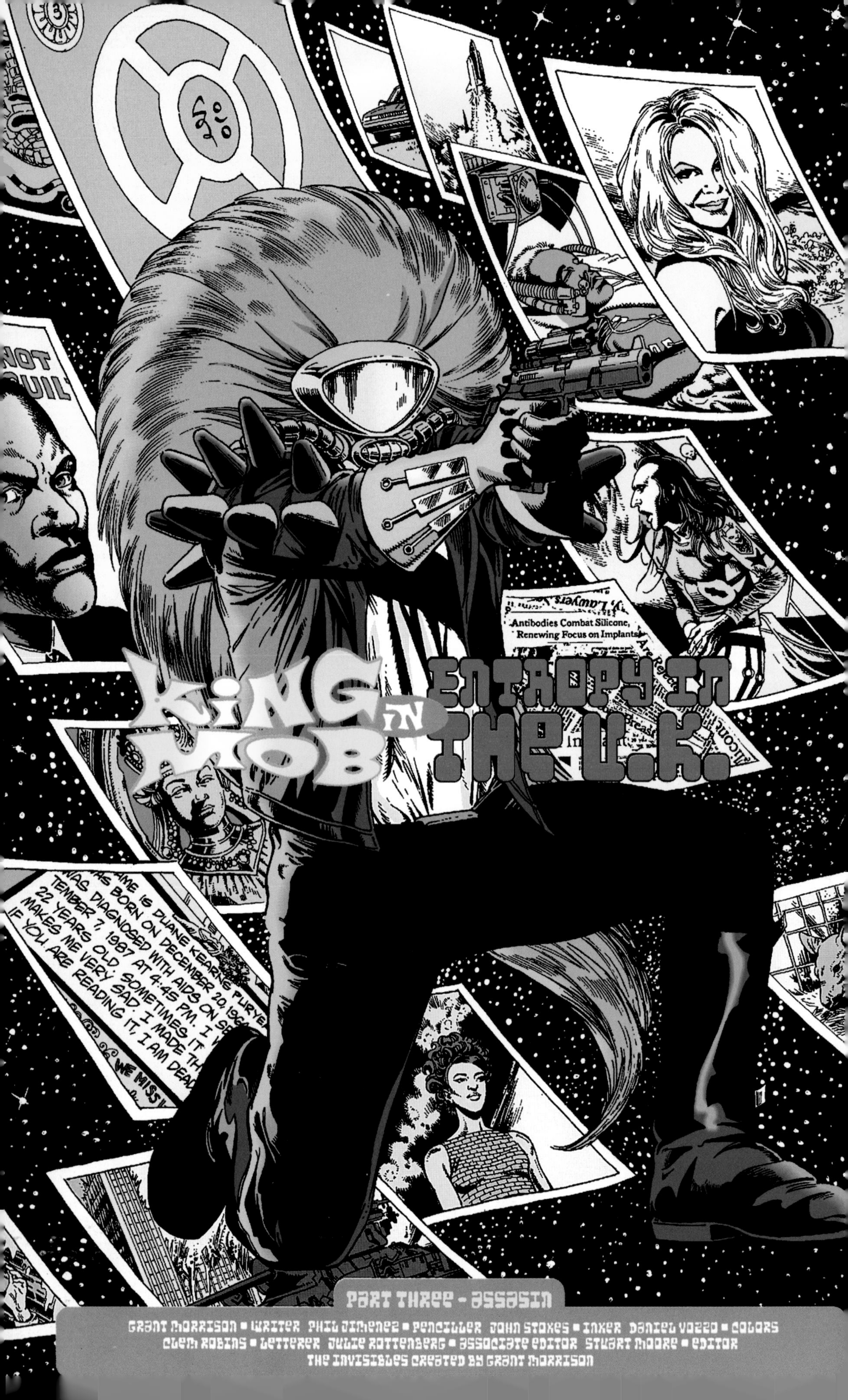
NOT
GUIL
Antibodies Combat Silicone,
Renewing Focus on Implants
KING IN MOB
ENTROPY IN THE U.K.
AME IS DUANE KEARNS PURYE
AS BORN ON DECEMBER 20, 196
WAS DIAGNOSED WITH AIDS ON SE
TEMBER 7, 1987 AT 4:45 PM. I W
22 YEARS OLD. SOMETIMES IT
MAKES ME VERY SAD. I MADE TH
IF YOU ARE READING IT, I AM DEAD
WE MISS
PART THREE - ASSASIN
GRANT MORRISON • WRITER PHIL JIMENEZ • PENCILLER JOHN STOKES • INKER DANIEL VOZZO • COLORS
CLEM ROBINS • LETTERER JULIE ROTTENBERG • ASSOCIATE EDITOR STUART MOORE • EDITOR
THE INVISIBLES CREATED BY GRANT MORRISON

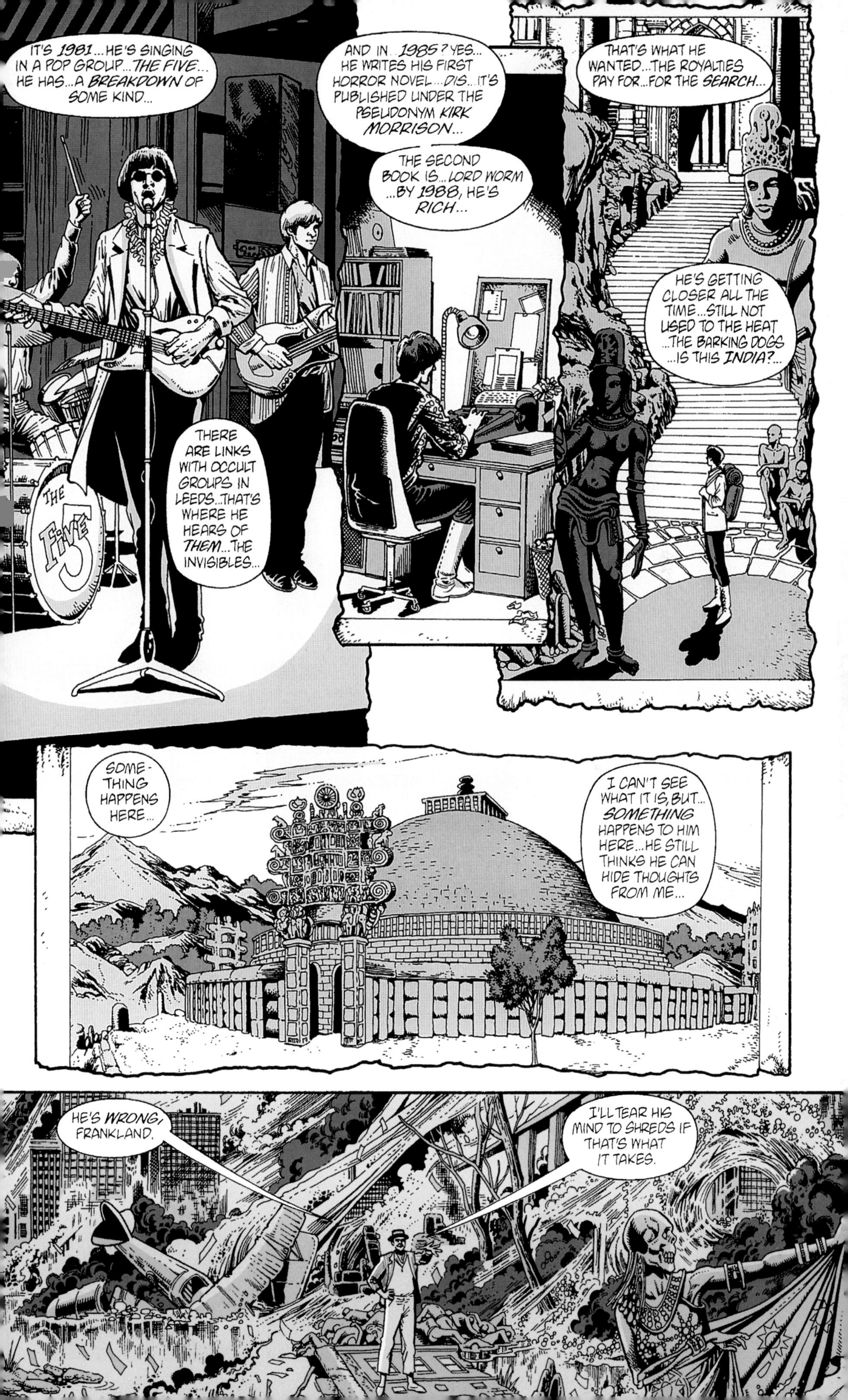
IT'S 1981 ... HE'S SINGING IN A POP GROUP... THE FIVE... HE HAS... A BREAKDOWN OF SOME KIND...
THERE ARE LINKS WITH OCCULT GROUPS IN LEEDS...THAT'S WHERE HE HEARS OF THEM... THE INVISIBLES...
THE FIVE
AND IN... 1985? YES... HE WRITES HIS FIRST HORROR NOVEL... DIS... IT'S PUBLISHED UNDER THE PSEUDONYM KIRK MORRISON...
THE SECOND BOOK IS... LORD WORM ...BY 1988, HE'S RICH...
THAT'S WHAT HE WANTED...THE ROYALTIES PAY FOR...FOR THE SEARCH...
HE'S GETTING CLOSER ALL THE TIME...STILL NOT USED TO THE HEAT ...THE BARKING DOGS ...IS THIS INDIA?...
SOME-THING HAPPENS HERE...
I CAN'T SEE WHAT IT IS, BUT... SOMETHING HAPPENS TO HIM HERE...HE STILL THINKS HE CAN HIDE THOUGHTS FROM ME...
HE'S WRONG, FRANKLAND.
I'LL TEAR HIS MIND TO SHREDS IF THAT'S WHAT IT TAKES.

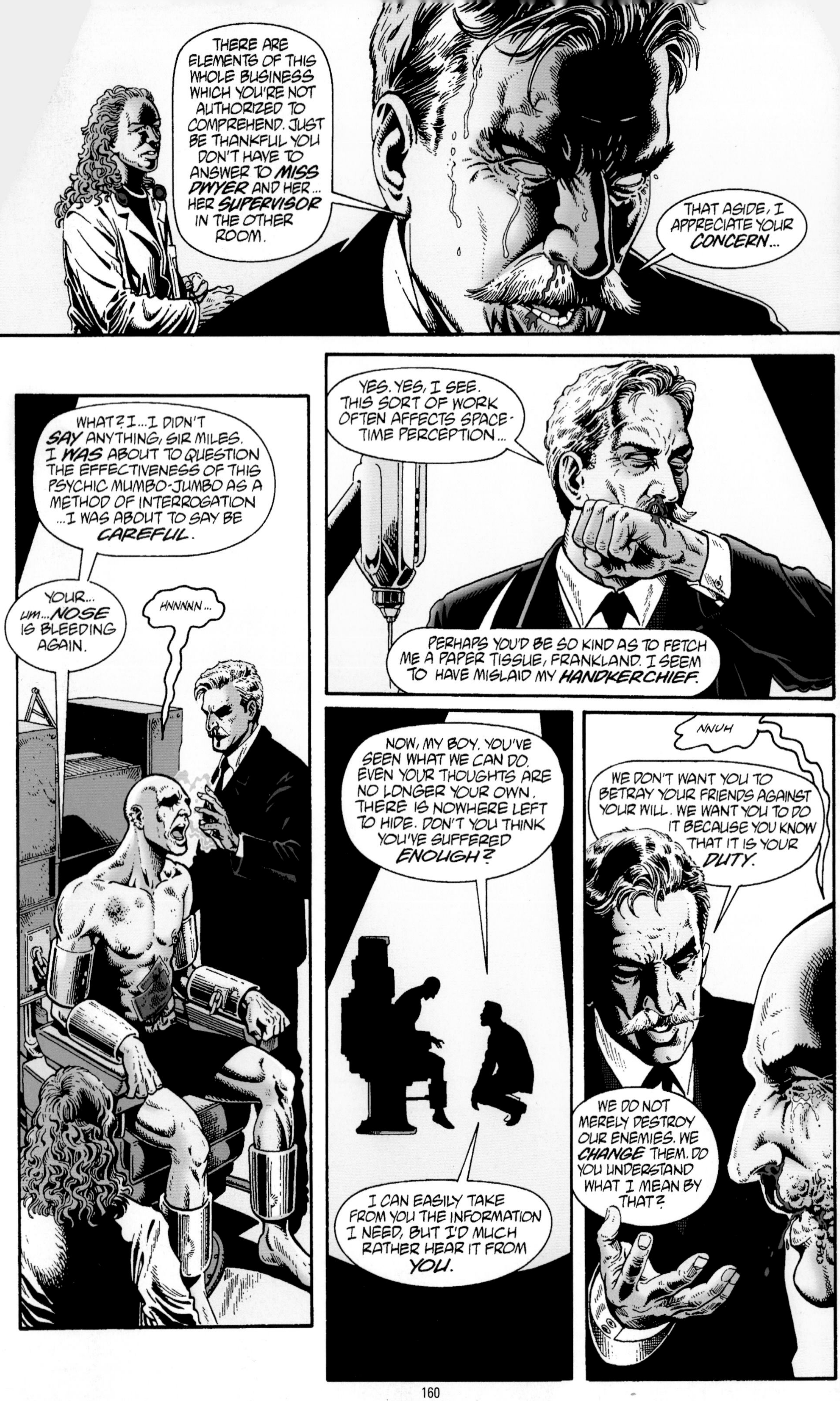
THERE ARE ELEMENTS OF THIS WHOLE BUSINESS WHICH YOU'RE NOT AUTHORIZED TO COMPREHEND. JUST BE THANKFUL YOU DON'T HAVE TO ANSWER TO MISS DWYER AND HER... HER SUPERVISOR IN THE OTHER ROOM.
THAT ASIDE, I APPRECIATE YOUR CONCERN...
WHAT? I...I DIDN'T SAY ANYTHING, SIR MILES. I WAS ABOUT TO QUESTION THE EFFECTIVENESS OF THIS PSYCHIC MUMBO-JUMBO AS A METHOD OF INTERROGATION ...I WAS ABOUT TO SAY BE CAREFUL.
YOUR... UM...NOSE IS BLEEDING AGAIN.
HNNNNN...
YES. YES, I SEE. THIS SORT OF WORK OFTEN AFFECTS SPACE-TIME PERCEPTION...
PERHAPS YOU'D BE SO KIND AS TO FETCH ME A PAPER TISSUE, FRANKLAND. I SEEM TO HAVE MISLAID MY HANDKERCHIEF.
NOW, MY BOY. YOU'VE SEEN WHAT WE CAN DO. EVEN YOUR THOUGHTS ARE NO LONGER YOUR OWN. THERE IS NOWHERE LEFT TO HIDE. DON'T YOU THINK YOU'VE SUFFERED ENOUGH?
I CAN EASILY TAKE FROM YOU THE INFORMATION I NEED, BUT I'D MUCH RATHER HEAR IT FROM YOU.
NNUH
WE DON'T WANT YOU TO BETRAY YOUR FRIENDS AGAINST YOUR WILL. WE WANT YOU TO DO IT BECAUSE YOU KNOW THAT IT IS YOUR DUTY.
WE DO NOT MERELY DESTROY OUR ENEMIES. WE CHANGE THEM. DO YOU UNDERSTAND WHAT I MEAN BY THAT?

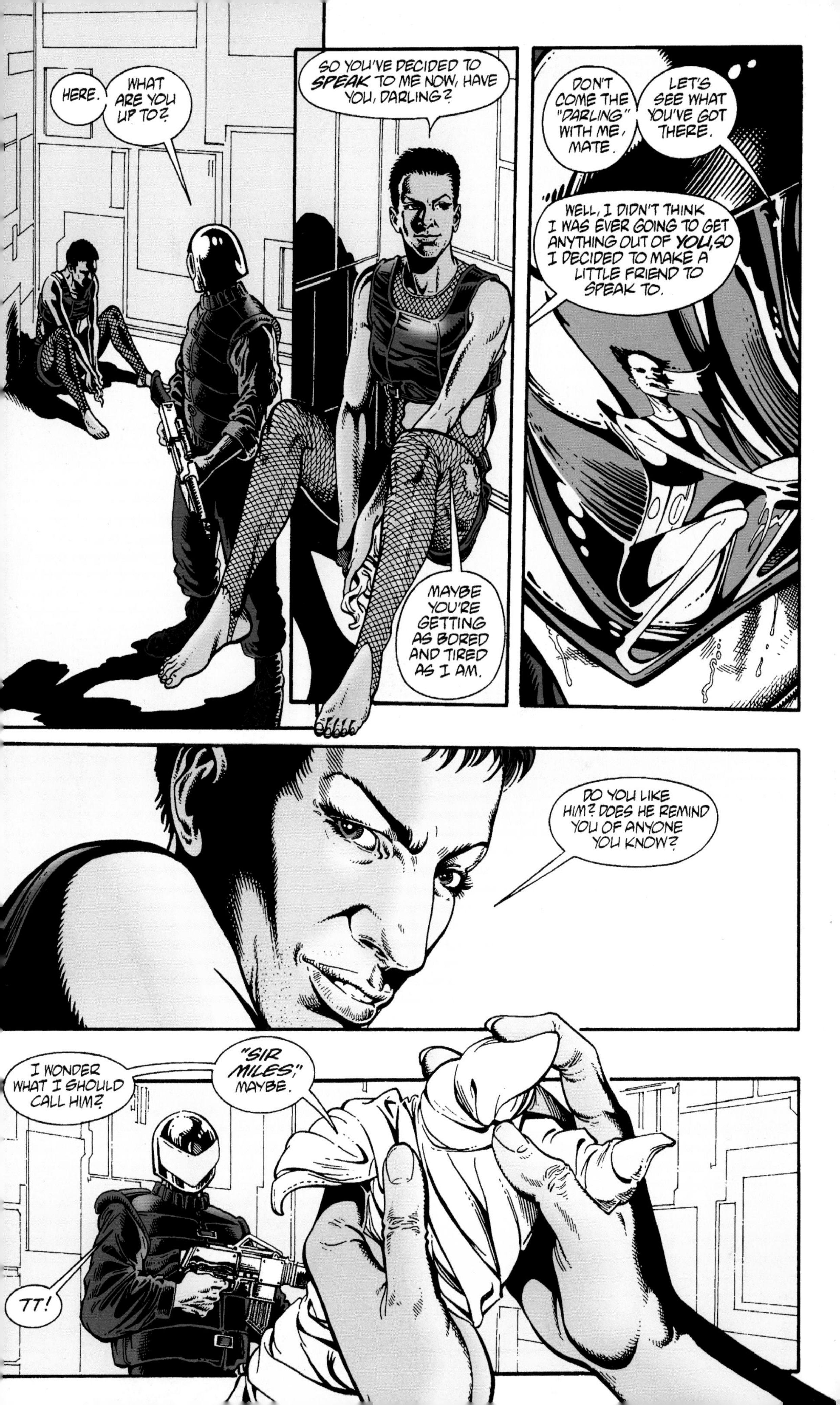
HERE.
WHAT ARE YOU UP TO?
SO YOU'VE DECIDED TO SPEAK TO ME NOW, HAVE YOU, DARLING?
MAYBE YOU'RE GETTING AS BORED AND TIRED AS I AM.
DON'T COME THE "DARLING" WITH ME, MATE.
LET'S SEE WHAT YOU'VE GOT THERE.
WELL, I DIDN'T THINK I WAS EVER GOING TO GET ANYTHING OUT OF YOU, SO I DECIDED TO MAKE A LITTLE FRIEND TO SPEAK TO.
DO YOU LIKE HIM? DOES HE REMIND YOU OF ANYONE YOU KNOW?
I WONDER WHAT I SHOULD CALL HIM?
"SIR MILES," MAYBE.
TT!

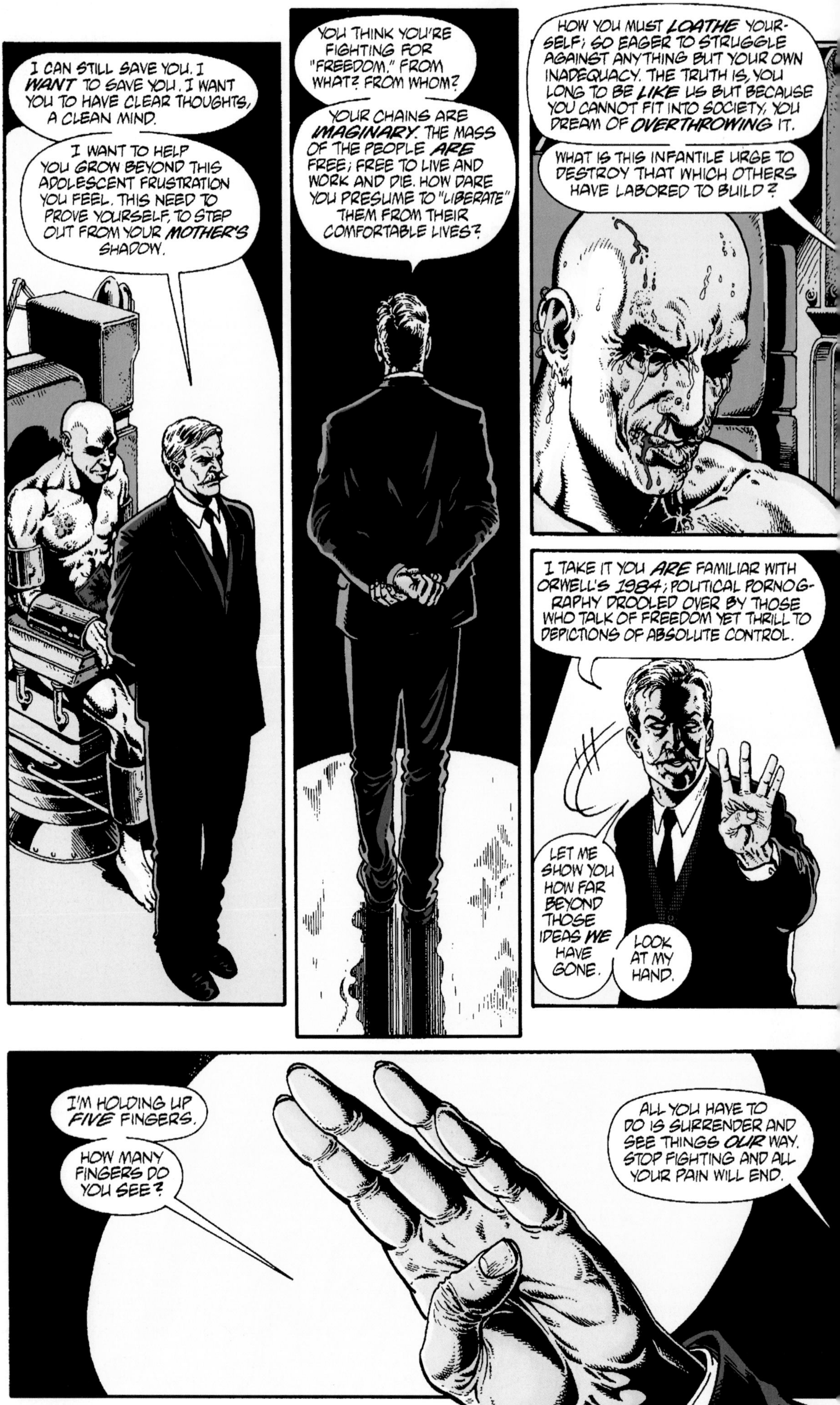
I CAN STILL SAVE YOU. I WANT TO SAVE YOU. I WANT YOU TO HAVE CLEAR THOUGHTS, A CLEAN MIND.
I WANT TO HELP YOU GROW BEYOND THIS ADOLESCENT FRUSTRATION YOU FEEL. THIS NEED TO PROVE YOURSELF, TO STEP OUT FROM YOUR MOTHER'S SHADOW.
YOU THINK YOU'RE FIGHTING FOR "FREEDOM." FROM WHAT? FROM WHOM?
YOUR CHAINS ARE IMAGINARY. THE MASS OF THE PEOPLE ARE FREE; FREE TO LIVE AND WORK AND DIE. HOW DARE YOU PRESUME TO "LIBERATE" THEM FROM THEIR COMFORTABLE LIVES?
HOW YOU MUST LOATHE YOURSELF; SO EAGER TO STRUGGLE AGAINST ANYTHING BUT YOUR OWN INADEQUACY. THE TRUTH IS, YOU LONG TO BE LIKE US BUT BECAUSE YOU CANNOT FIT INTO SOCIETY, YOU DREAM OF OVERTHROWING IT.
WHAT IS THIS INFANTILE URGE TO DESTROY THAT WHICH OTHERS HAVE LABORED TO BUILD?
I TAKE IT YOU ARE FAMILIAR WITH ORWELL'S 1984; POLITICAL PORNOGRAPHY DROOLED OVER BY THOSE WHO TALK OF FREEDOM YET THRILL TO DEPICTIONS OF ABSOLUTE CONTROL.
LET ME SHOW YOU HOW FAR BEYOND THOSE IDEAS WE HAVE GONE.
LOOK AT MY HAND.
I'M HOLDING UP FIVE FINGERS.
HOW MANY FINGERS DO YOU SEE?
ALL YOU HAVE TO DO IS SURRENDER AND SEE THINGS OUR WAY. STOP FIGHTING AND ALL YOUR PAIN WILL END.

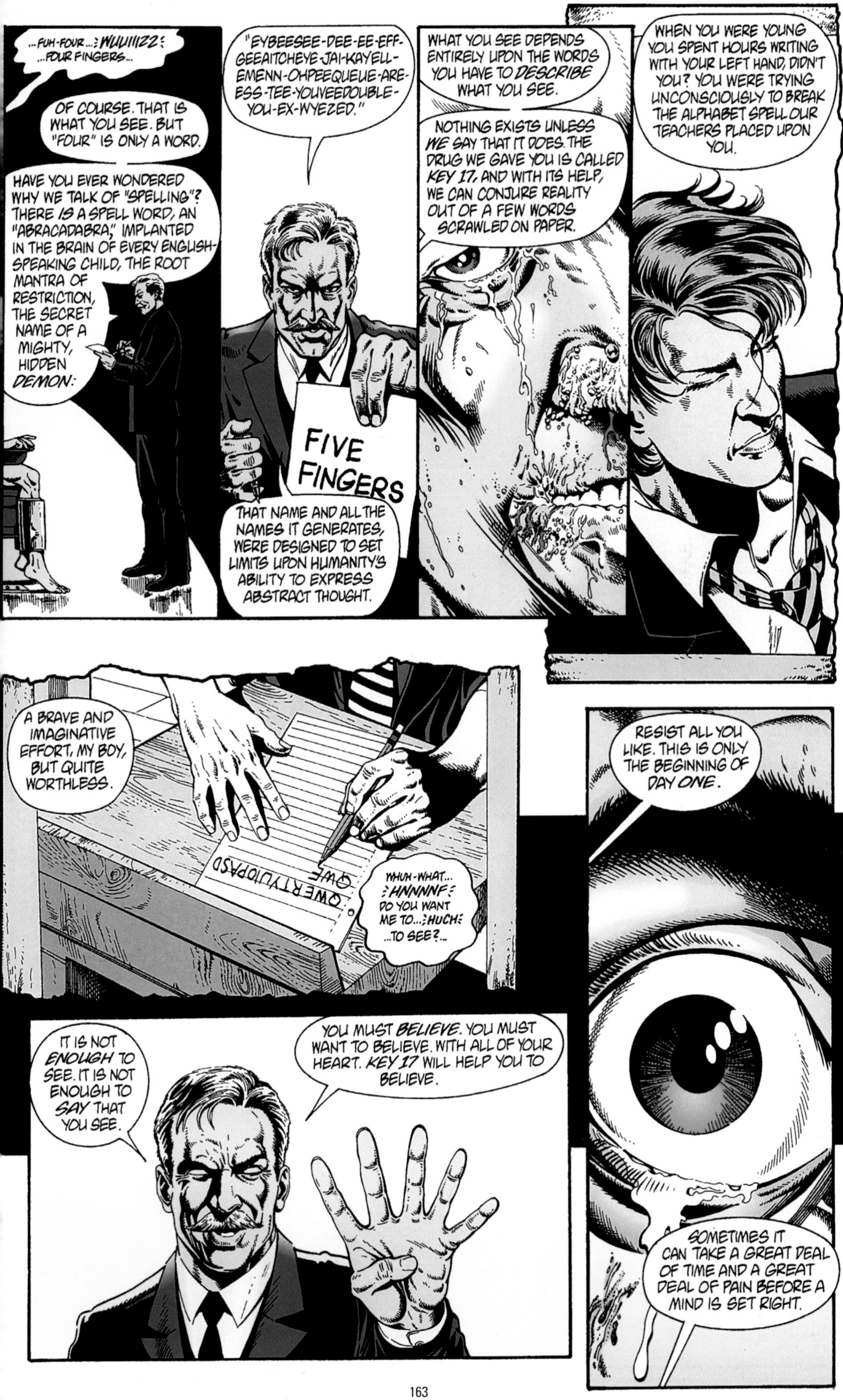
...FUH-FOUR...WUUIIIZZ ...FOUR FINGERS...
OF COURSE. THAT IS WHAT YOU SEE. BUT "FOUR" IS ONLY A WORD.
HAVE YOU EVER WONDERED WHY WE TALK OF "SPELLING"? THERE IS A SPELL WORD, AN "ABRACADABRA," IMPLANTED IN THE BRAIN OF EVERY ENGLISH-SPEAKING CHILD, THE ROOT MANTRA OF RESTRICTION, THE SECRET NAME OF A MIGHTY, HIDDEN DEMON:
"EYBEESEE-DEE-EE-EFF-GEEAITCHEYE-JAI-KAYELL-EMENN-OHPEEQUEUE-ARE-ESS-TEE-YOUVEEDOUBLE-YOU-EX-WYEZED."
FIVE FINGERS
THAT NAME AND ALL THE NAMES IT GENERATES, WERE DESIGNED TO SET LIMITS UPON HUMANITY'S ABILITY TO EXPRESS ABSTRACT THOUGHT.
WHAT YOU SEE DEPENDS ENTIRELY UPON THE WORDS YOU HAVE TO DESCRIBE WHAT YOU SEE.
NOTHING EXISTS UNLESS WE SAY THAT IT DOES. THE DRUG WE GAVE YOU IS CALLED KEY 17, AND WITH ITS HELP, WE CAN CONJURE REALITY OUT OF A FEW WORDS SCRAWLED ON PAPER.
WHEN YOU WERE YOUNG YOU SPENT HOURS WRITING WITH YOUR LEFT HAND, DIDN'T YOU? YOU WERE TRYING UNCONSCIOUSLY TO BREAK THE ALPHABET SPELL OUR TEACHERS PLACED UPON YOU.
A BRAVE AND IMAGINATIVE EFFORT, MY BOY, BUT QUITE WORTHLESS.
QWERTYUIOPASD
WHUH-WHAT... HNNNNF DO YOU WANT ME TO... HUCH ...TO SEE?...
RESIST ALL YOU LIKE. THIS IS ONLY THE BEGINNING OF DAY ONE.
IT IS NOT ENOUGH TO SEE. IT IS NOT ENOUGH TO SAY THAT YOU SEE.
YOU MUST BELIEVE. YOU MUST WANT TO BELIEVE. WITH ALL OF YOUR HEART. KEY 17 WILL HELP YOU TO BELIEVE.
SOMETIMES IT CAN TAKE A GREAT DEAL OF TIME AND A GREAT DEAL OF PAIN BEFORE A MIND IS SET RIGHT.

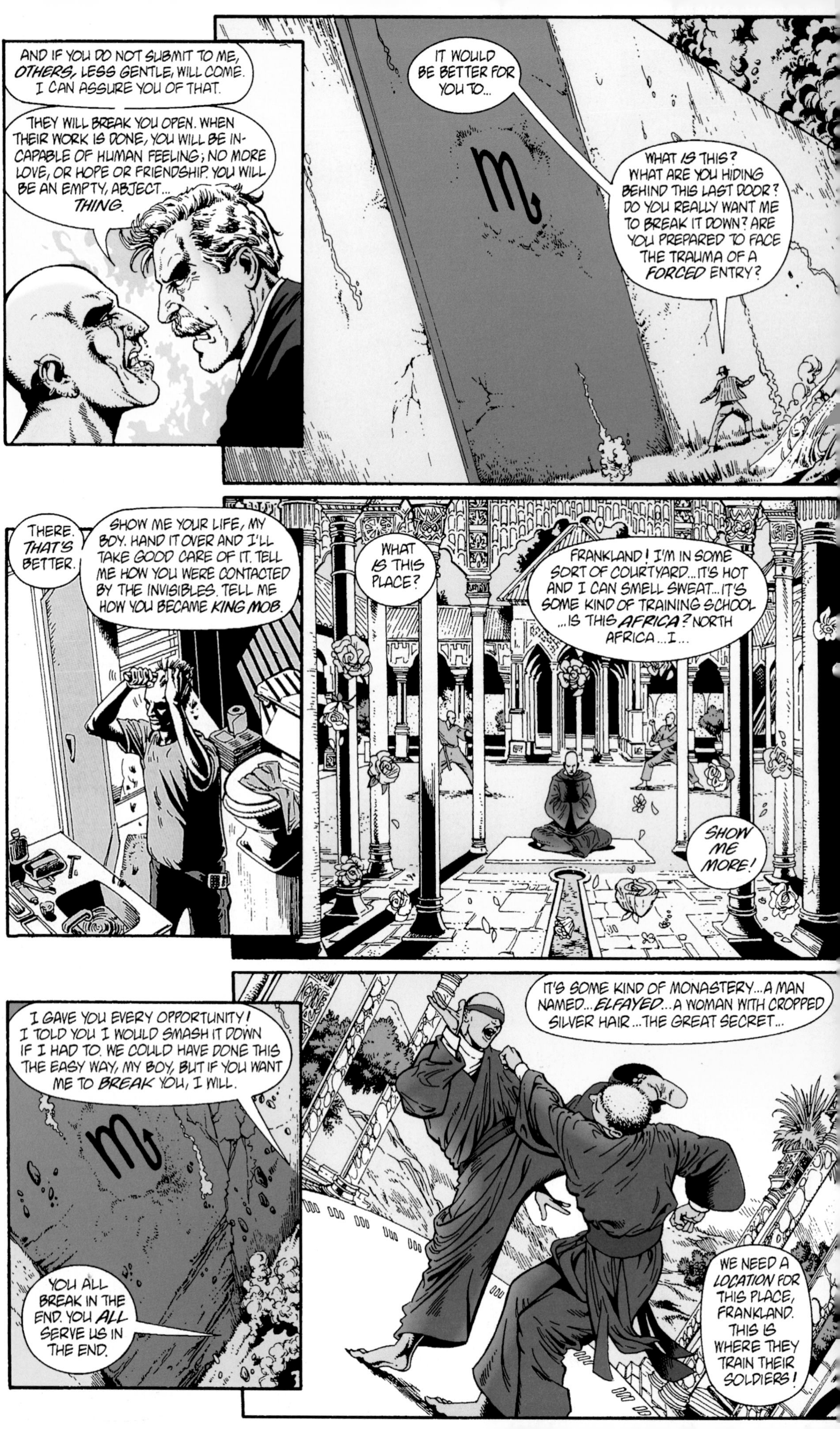
AND IF YOU DO NOT SUBMIT TO ME, OTHERS, LESS GENTLE, WILL COME. I CAN ASSURE YOU OF THAT.
THEY WILL BREAK YOU OPEN. WHEN THEIR WORK IS DONE, YOU WILL BE INCAPABLE OF HUMAN FEELING; NO MORE LOVE, OR HOPE OR FRIENDSHIP. YOU WILL BE AN EMPTY, ABJECT... THING.
IT WOULD BE BETTER FOR YOU TO...
WHAT IS THIS? WHAT ARE YOU HIDING BEHIND THIS LAST DOOR? DO YOU REALLY WANT ME TO BREAK IT DOWN? ARE YOU PREPARED TO FACE THE TRAUMA OF A FORCED ENTRY?
THERE. THAT'S BETTER.
SHOW ME YOUR LIFE, MY BOY. HAND IT OVER AND I'LL TAKE GOOD CARE OF IT. TELL ME HOW YOU WERE CONTACTED BY THE INVISIBLES. TELL ME HOW YOU BECAME KING MOB.
WHAT IS THIS PLACE?
FRANKLAND! I'M IN SOME SORT OF COURTYARD... IT'S HOT AND I CAN SMELL SWEAT... IT'S SOME KIND OF TRAINING SCHOOL ...IS THIS AFRICA? NORTH AFRICA... I...
SHOW ME MORE!
I GAVE YOU EVERY OPPORTUNITY! I TOLD YOU I WOULD SMASH IT DOWN IF I HAD TO. WE COULD HAVE DONE THIS THE EASY WAY, MY BOY, BUT IF YOU WANT ME TO BREAK YOU, I WILL.
YOU ALL BREAK IN THE END. YOU ALL SERVE US IN THE END.
IT'S SOME KIND OF MONASTERY... A MAN NAMED... ELFAYED... A WOMAN WITH CROPPED SILVER HAIR... THE GREAT SECRET...
WE NEED A LOCATION FOR THIS PLACE, FRANKLAND. THIS IS WHERE THEY TRAIN THEIR SOLDIERS!

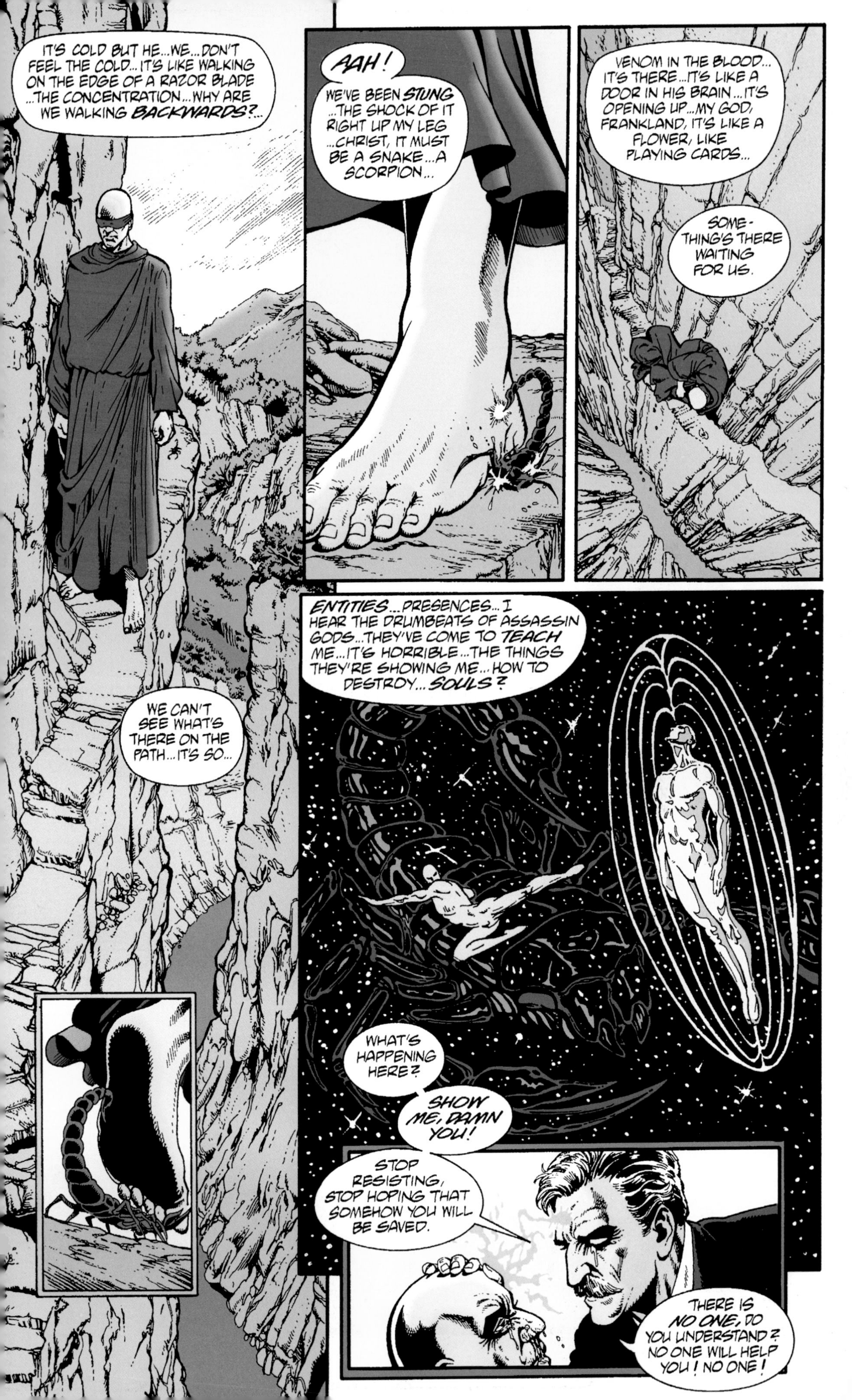
IT'S COLD BUT HE...WE...DON'T FEEL THE COLD... IT'S LIKE WALKING ON THE EDGE OF A RAZOR BLADE ...THE CONCENTRATION... WHY ARE WE WALKING BACKWARDS?...
AAH!
WE'VE BEEN STUNG ...THE SHOCK OF IT RIGHT UP MY LEG ...CHRIST, IT MUST BE A SNAKE...A SCORPION...
VENOM IN THE BLOOD... IT'S THERE...IT'S LIKE A DOOR IN HIS BRAIN...IT'S OPENING UP...MY GOD, FRANKLAND, IT'S LIKE A FLOWER, LIKE PLAYING CARDS...
SOME-THING'S THERE WAITING FOR US.
WE CAN'T SEE WHAT'S THERE ON THE PATH...IT'S SO...
ENTITIES...PRESENCES... I HEAR THE DRUMBEATS OF ASSASSIN GODS...THEY'VE COME TO TEACH ME...IT'S HORRIBLE...THE THINGS THEY'RE SHOWING ME... HOW TO DESTROY...SOULS?
WHAT'S HAPPENING HERE?
SHOW ME, DAMN YOU!
STOP RESISTING, STOP HOPING THAT SOMEHOW YOU WILL BE SAVED.
THERE IS NO ONE, DO YOU UNDERSTAND? NO ONE WILL HELP YOU! NO ONE!

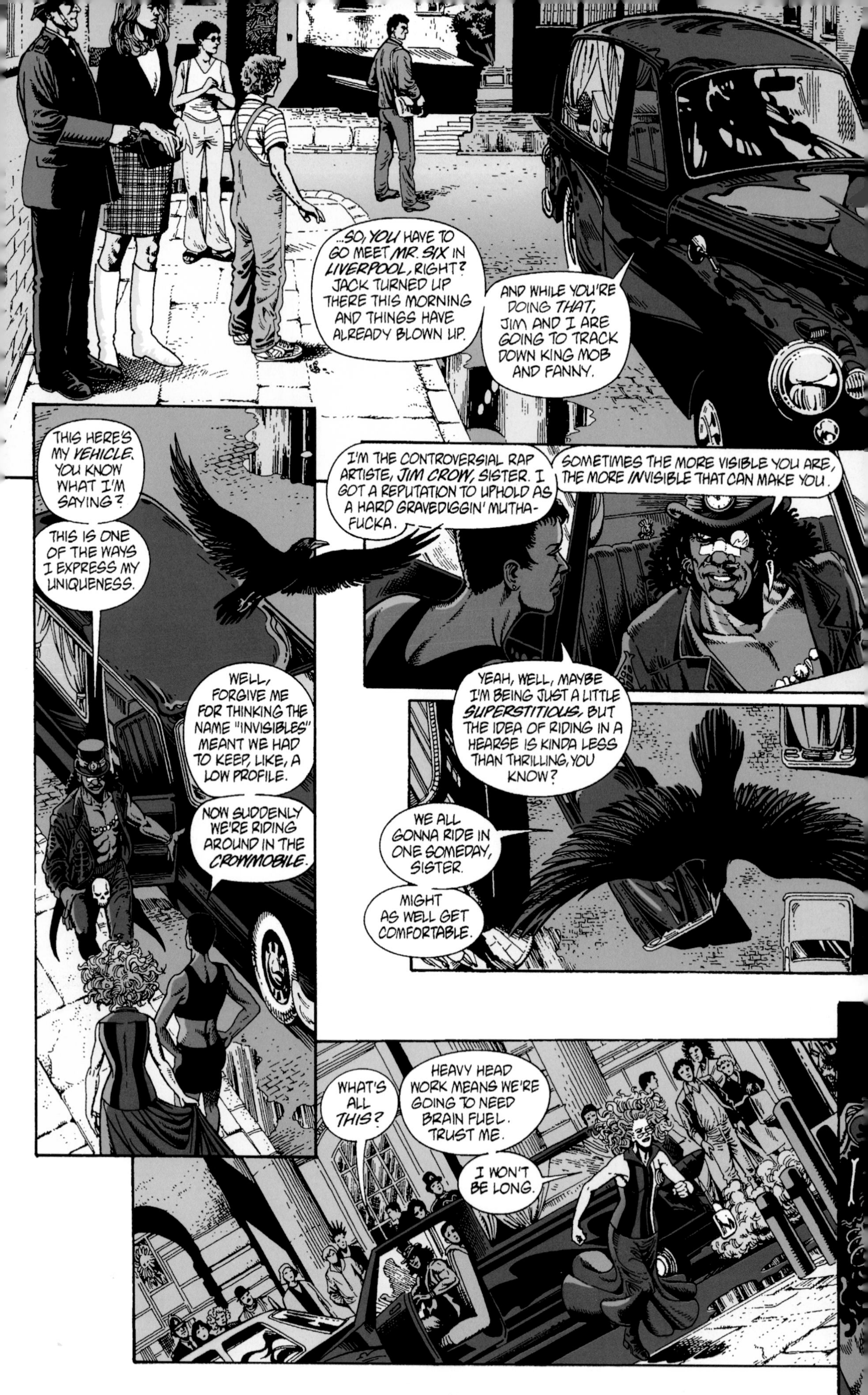
...SO, YOU HAVE TO GO MEET MR. SIX IN LIVERPOOL, RIGHT? JACK TURNED UP THERE THIS MORNING AND THINGS HAVE ALREADY BLOWN UP.
AND WHILE YOU'RE DOING THAT, JIM AND I ARE GOING TO TRACK DOWN KING MOB AND FANNY.
THIS HERE'S MY VEHICLE. YOU KNOW WHAT I'M SAYING?
THIS IS ONE OF THE WAYS I EXPRESS MY UNIQUENESS.
WELL, FORGIVE ME FOR THINKING THE NAME "INVISIBLES" MEANT WE HAD TO KEEP, LIKE, A LOW PROFILE.
NOW SUDDENLY WE'RE RIDING AROUND IN THE CROWMOBILE.
I'M THE CONTROVERSIAL RAP ARTISTE, JIM CROW, SISTER. I GOT A REPUTATION TO UPHOLD AS A HARD GRAVEDIGGIN' MUTHA-FUCKA.
SOMETIMES THE MORE VISIBLE YOU ARE, THE MORE INVISIBLE THAT CAN MAKE YOU.
YEAH, WELL, MAYBE I'M BEING JUST A LITTLE SUPERSTITIOUS, BUT THE IDEA OF RIDING IN A HEARSE IS KINDA LESS THAN THRILLING, YOU KNOW?
WE ALL GONNA RIDE IN ONE SOMEDAY, SISTER.
MIGHT AS WELL GET COMFORTABLE.
WHAT'S ALL THIS?
HEAVY HEAD WORK MEANS WE'RE GOING TO NEED BRAIN FUEL. TRUST ME.
I WON'T BE LONG.

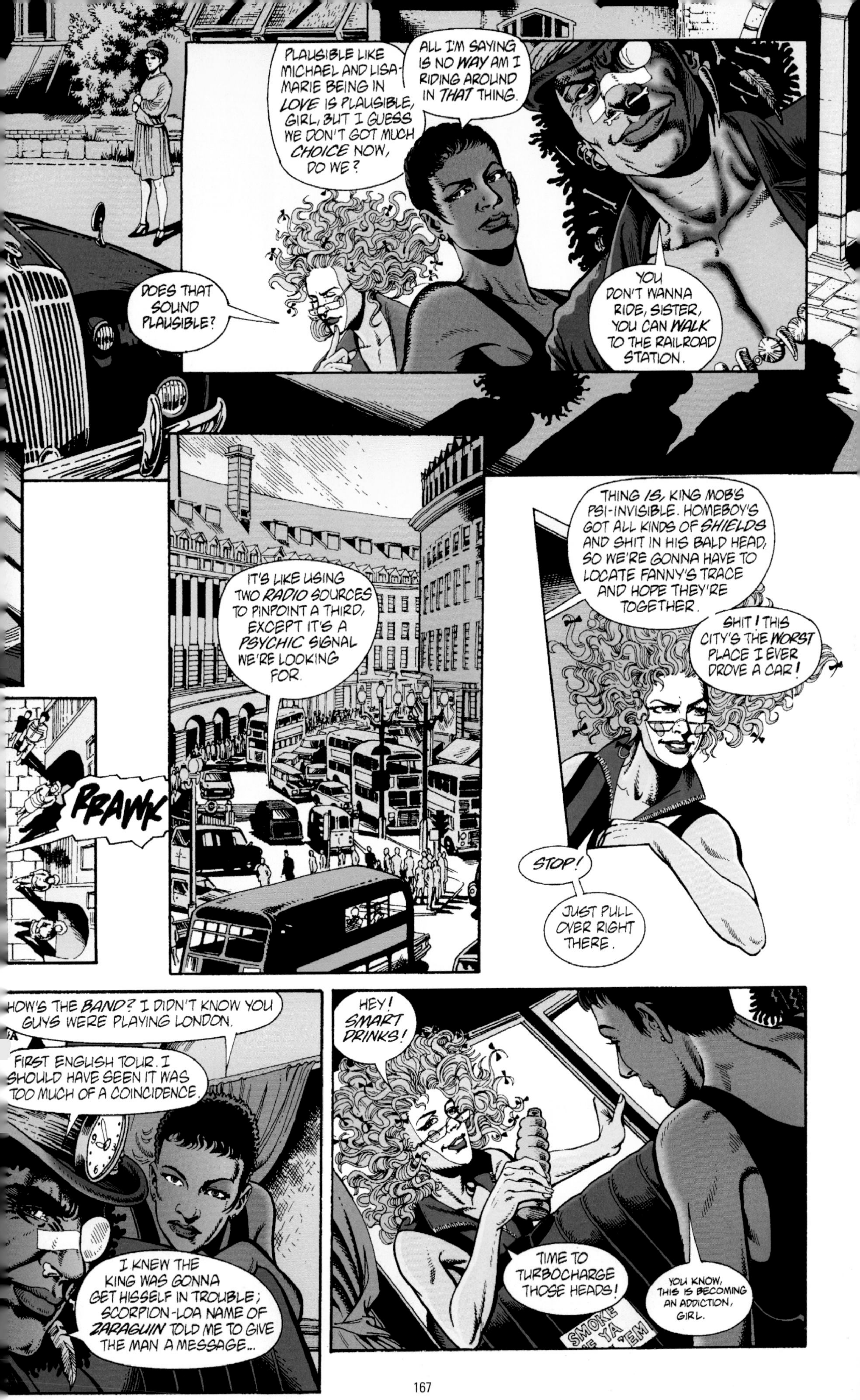
DOES THAT SOUND PLAUSIBLE?
PLAUSIBLE LIKE MICHAEL AND LISA-MARIE BEING IN LOVE IS PLAUSIBLE, GIRL, BUT I GUESS WE DON'T GOT MUCH CHOICE NOW, DO WE?
ALL I'M SAYING IS NO WAY AM I RIDING AROUND IN THAT THING.
YOU DON'T WANNA RIDE, SISTER, YOU CAN WALK TO THE RAILROAD STATION.
PRAWK
IT'S LIKE USING TWO RADIO SOURCES TO PINPOINT A THIRD, EXCEPT IT'S A PSYCHIC SIGNAL WE'RE LOOKING FOR.
THING IS, KING MOB'S PSI-INVISIBLE. HOMEBOY'S GOT ALL KINDS OF SHIELDS AND SHIT IN HIS BALD HEAD, SO WE'RE GONNA HAVE TO LOCATE FANNY'S TRACE AND HOPE THEY'RE TOGETHER.
SHIT! THIS CITY'S THE WORST PLACE I EVER DROVE A CAR!
STOP!
JUST PULL OVER RIGHT THERE.
HOW'S THE BAND? I DIDN'T KNOW YOU GUYS WERE PLAYING LONDON.
FIRST ENGLISH TOUR. I SHOULD HAVE SEEN IT WAS TOO MUCH OF A COINCIDENCE.
I KNEW THE KING WAS GONNA GET HISSELF IN TROUBLE; SCORPION-LOA NAME OF ZARAGUIN TOLD ME TO GIVE THE MAN A MESSAGE...
HEY! SMART DRINKS!
TIME TO TURBOCHARGE THOSE HEADS!
YOU KNOW, THIS IS BECOMING AN ADDICTION, GIRL.
SMOKE

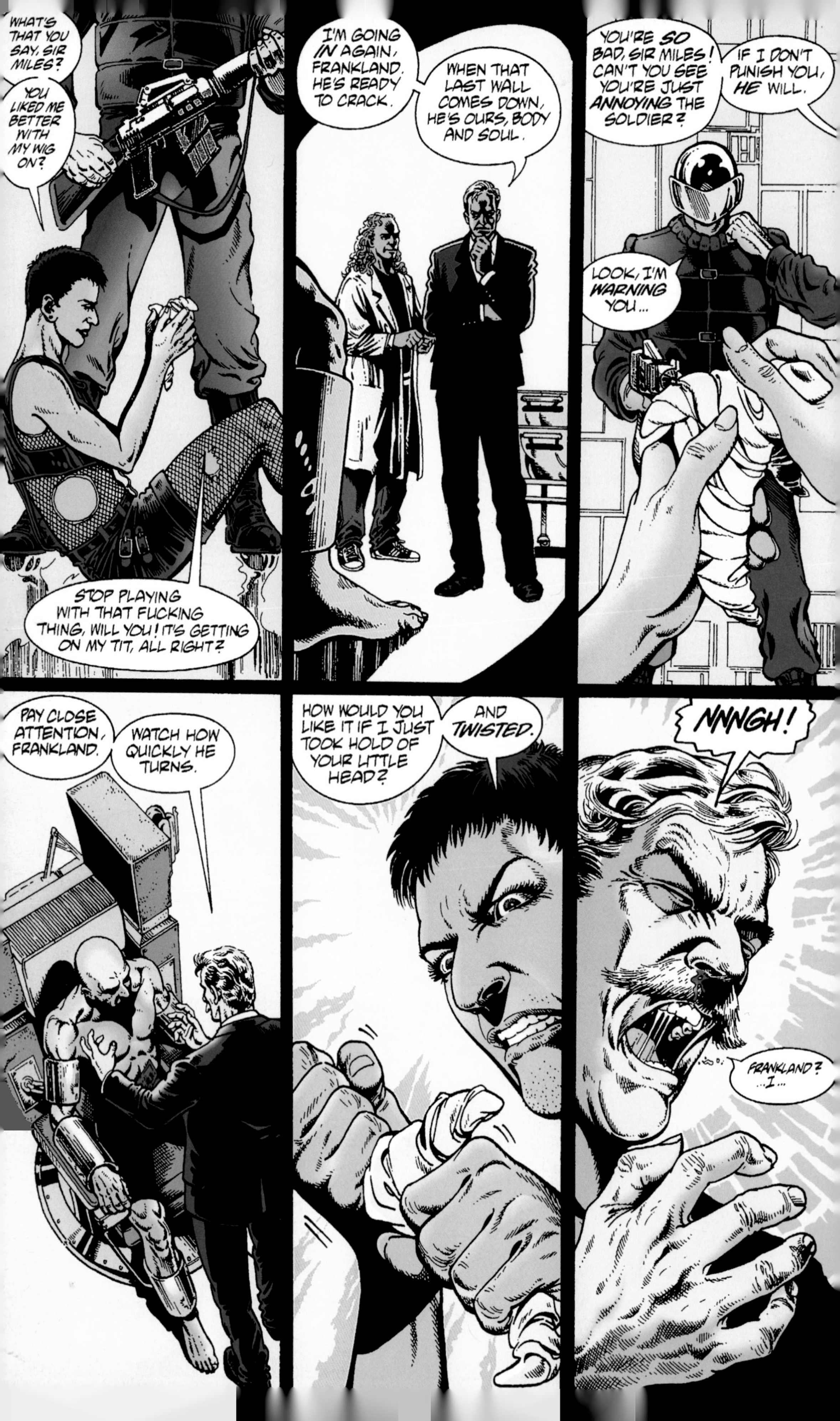
WHAT'S THAT YOU SAY, SIR MILES?
YOU LIKED ME BETTER WITH MY WIG ON?
STOP PLAYING WITH THAT FUCKING THING, WILL YOU! IT'S GETTING ON MY TIT, ALL RIGHT?
I'M GOING IN AGAIN, FRANKLAND. HE'S READY TO CRACK.
WHEN THAT LAST WALL COMES DOWN, HE'S OURS, BODY AND SOUL.
YOU'RE SO BAD, SIR MILES! CAN'T YOU SEE YOU'RE JUST ANNOYING THE SOLDIER?
IF I DON'T PUNISH YOU, HE WILL.
LOOK, I'M WARNING YOU...
PAY CLOSE ATTENTION, FRANKLAND.
WATCH HOW QUICKLY HE TURNS.
HOW WOULD YOU LIKE IT IF I JUST TOOK HOLD OF YOUR LITTLE HEAD?
AND TWISTED.
NNNGH!
FRANKLAND? ...I...

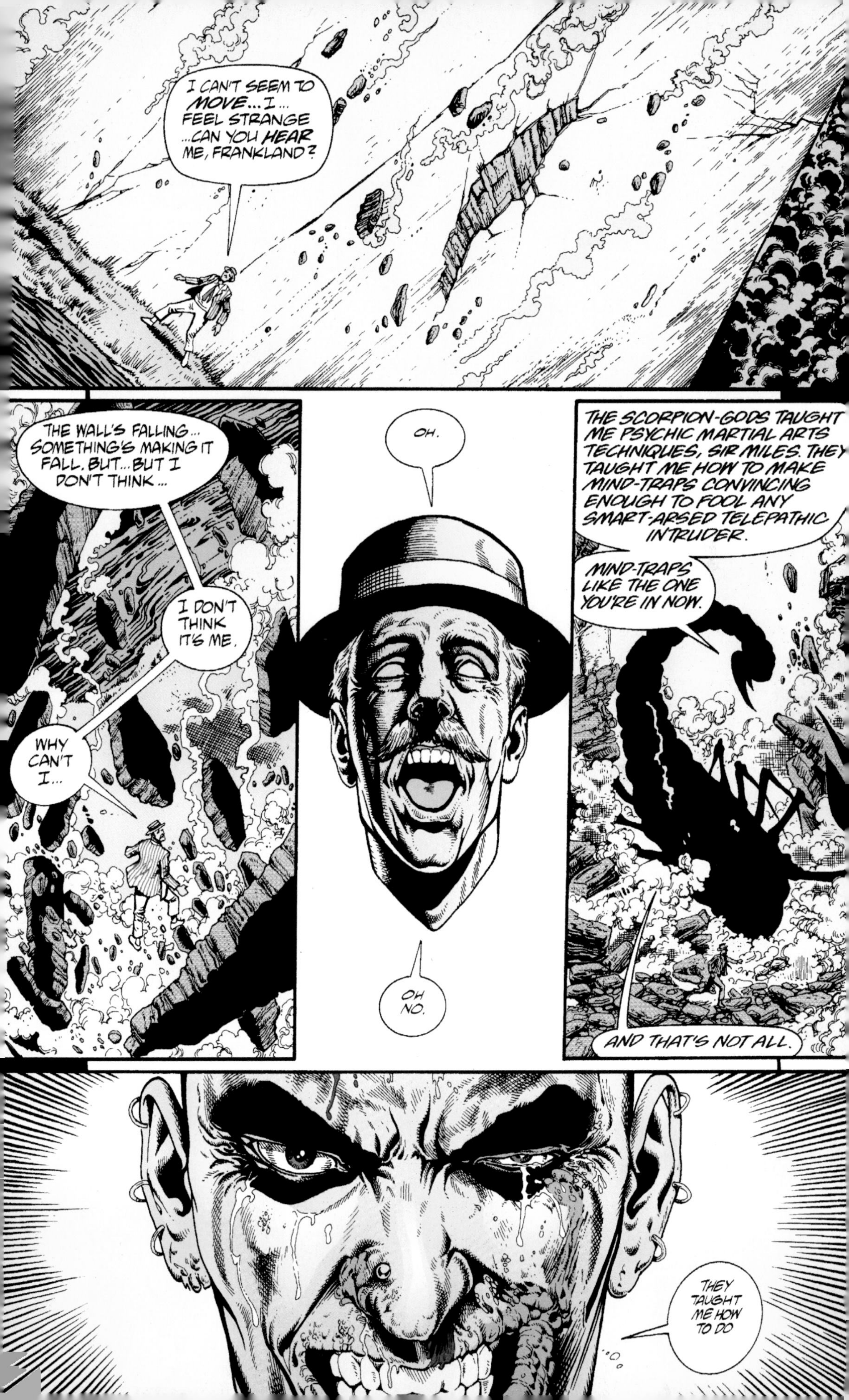
I CAN'T SEEM TO MOVE... I... FEEL STRANGE ...CAN YOU HEAR ME, FRANKLAND?
THE WALL'S FALLING... SOMETHING'S MAKING IT FALL. BUT... BUT I DON'T THINK...
I DON'T THINK IT'S ME.
WHY CAN'T I...
OH.
OH NO.
THE SCORPION-GODS TAUGHT ME PSYCHIC MARTIAL ARTS TECHNIQUES, SIR MILES. THEY TAUGHT ME HOW TO MAKE MIND-TRAPS CONVINCING ENOUGH TO FOOL ANY SMART-ARSED TELEPATHIC INTRUDER.
MIND-TRAPS LIKE THE ONE YOU'RE IN NOW.
AND THAT'S NOT ALL.
THEY TAUGHT ME HOW TO DO

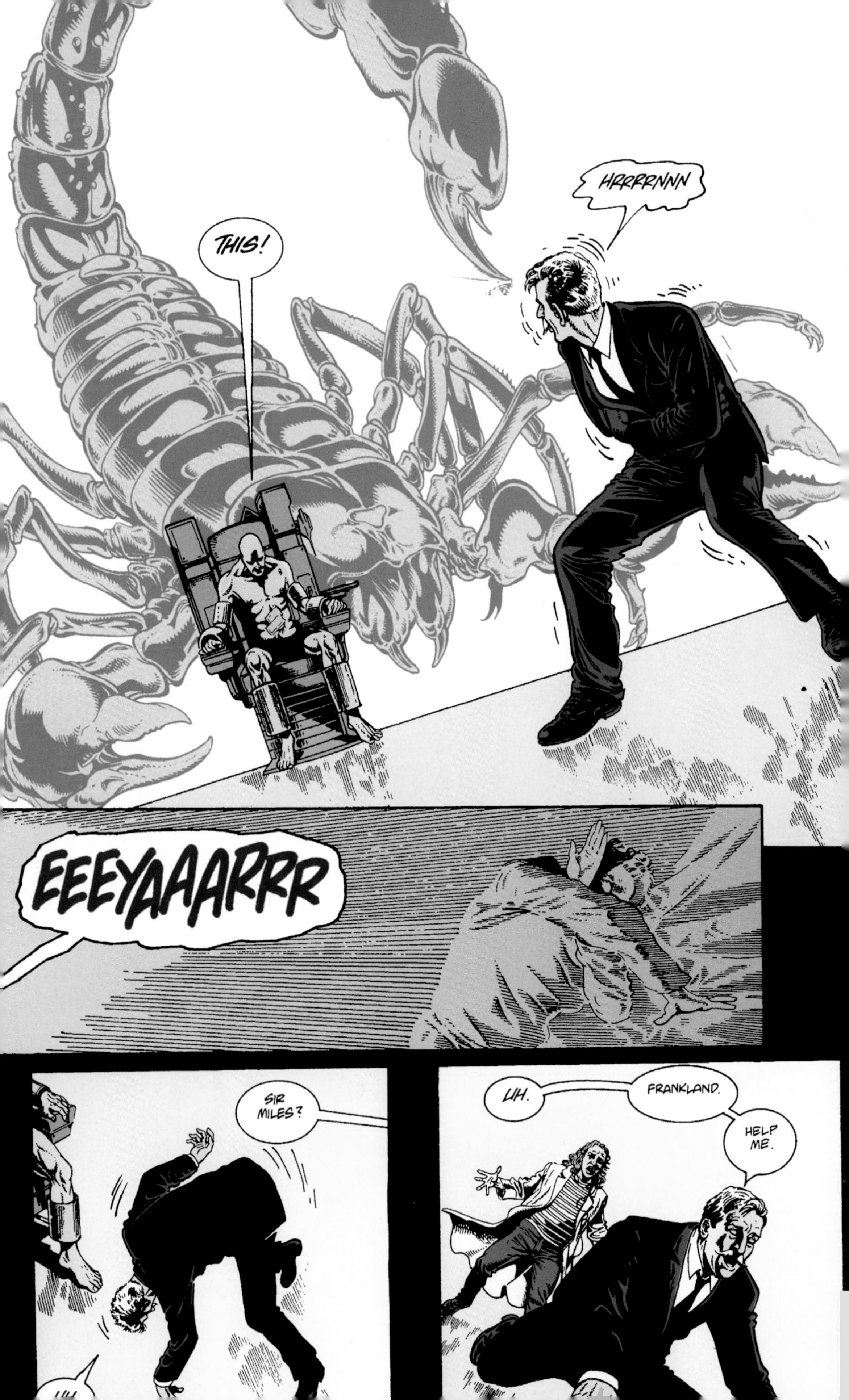
THIS!
HRRRRNNN
EEEYAAARRR
SIR MILES?
UH.
FRANKLAND.
HELP ME.

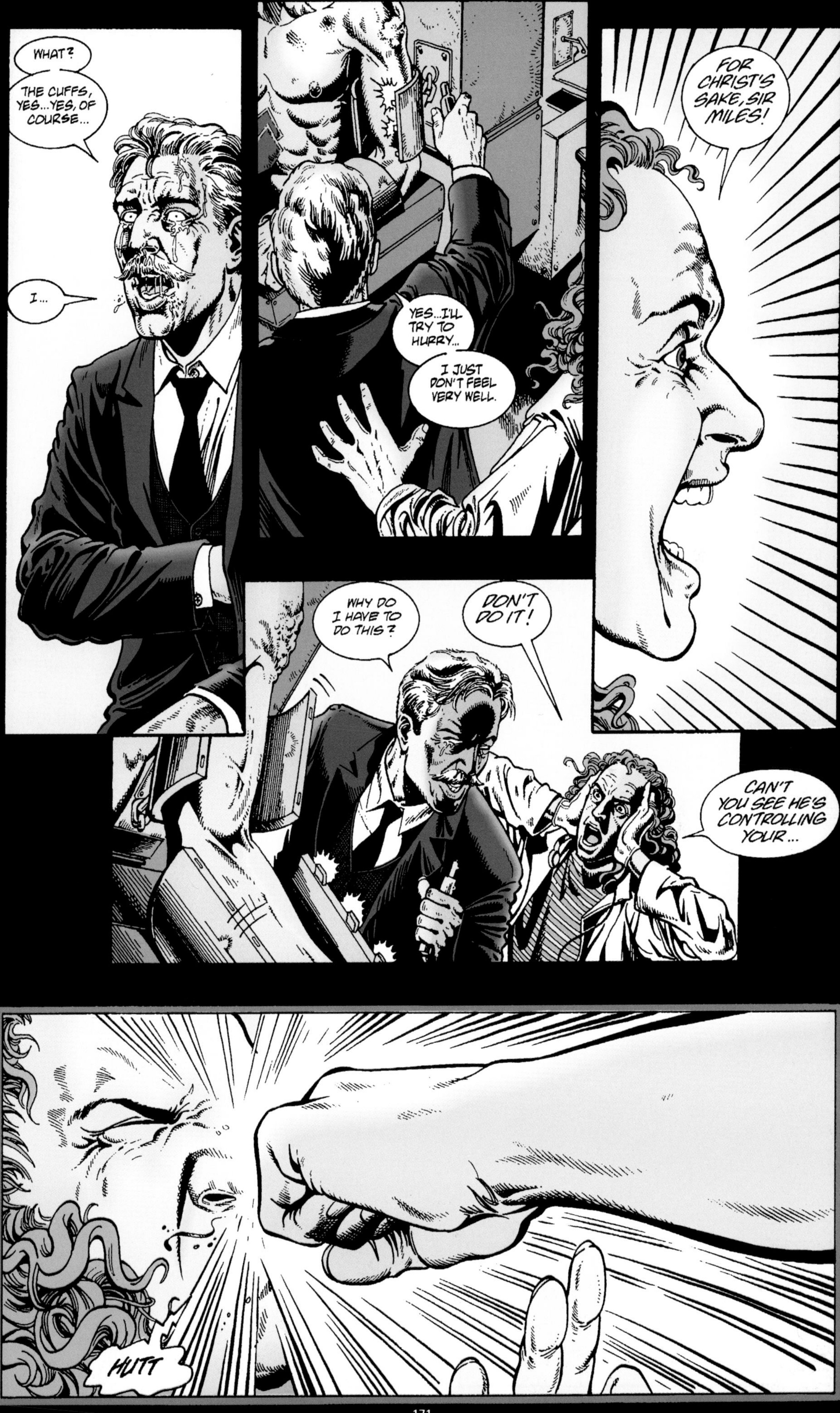
WHAT?
THE CUFFS, YES...YES, OF COURSE...
I...
YES...I'LL TRY TO HURRY...
I JUST DON'T FEEL VERY WELL.
FOR CHRIST'S SAKE, SIR MILES!
WHY DO I HAVE TO DO THIS?
DON'T DO IT!
CAN'T YOU SEE HE'S CONTROLLING YOUR...
HUTT

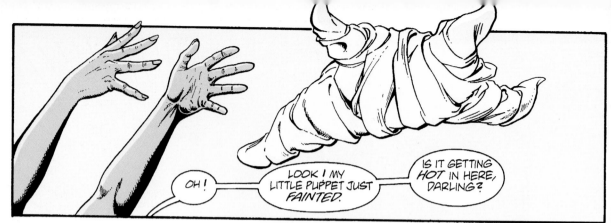

OH!

LOOK! MY LITTLE PUPPET JUST FAINTED.

IS IT GETTING *HOT* IN HERE, DARLING?

THIS IS THE KIND OF HEAT THAT BRINGS ON HEART ATTACKS.

CAN'T YOU *FEEL* IT?

I DON'T KNOW HOW YOU CAN *BREATHE* UNDER THAT HELMET.

IT MUST BE *SO* HARD TO BREATHE.

RIGHT!

JUST YOU STAY WHERE YOU ARE!

AND WHERE EXACTLY *IS* THAT, DARLING?

SHIT!

ARE YOU *HALLUCINATING?* IT'S THE *HEAT.* IT'S MAKING THE ROOM SPIN SO YOU CAN HARDLY KEEP YOUR BALANCE.

THAT CAN'T BE YOUR *HEART* I HEAR, CAN IT?

FUCK. OH, FUCK, WHAT'S HAPPENING? STOP IT.

MAKE IT STOP.

YOU WANT ME TO MAKE IT *STOP?*

ALL RIGHT.

UH.

172

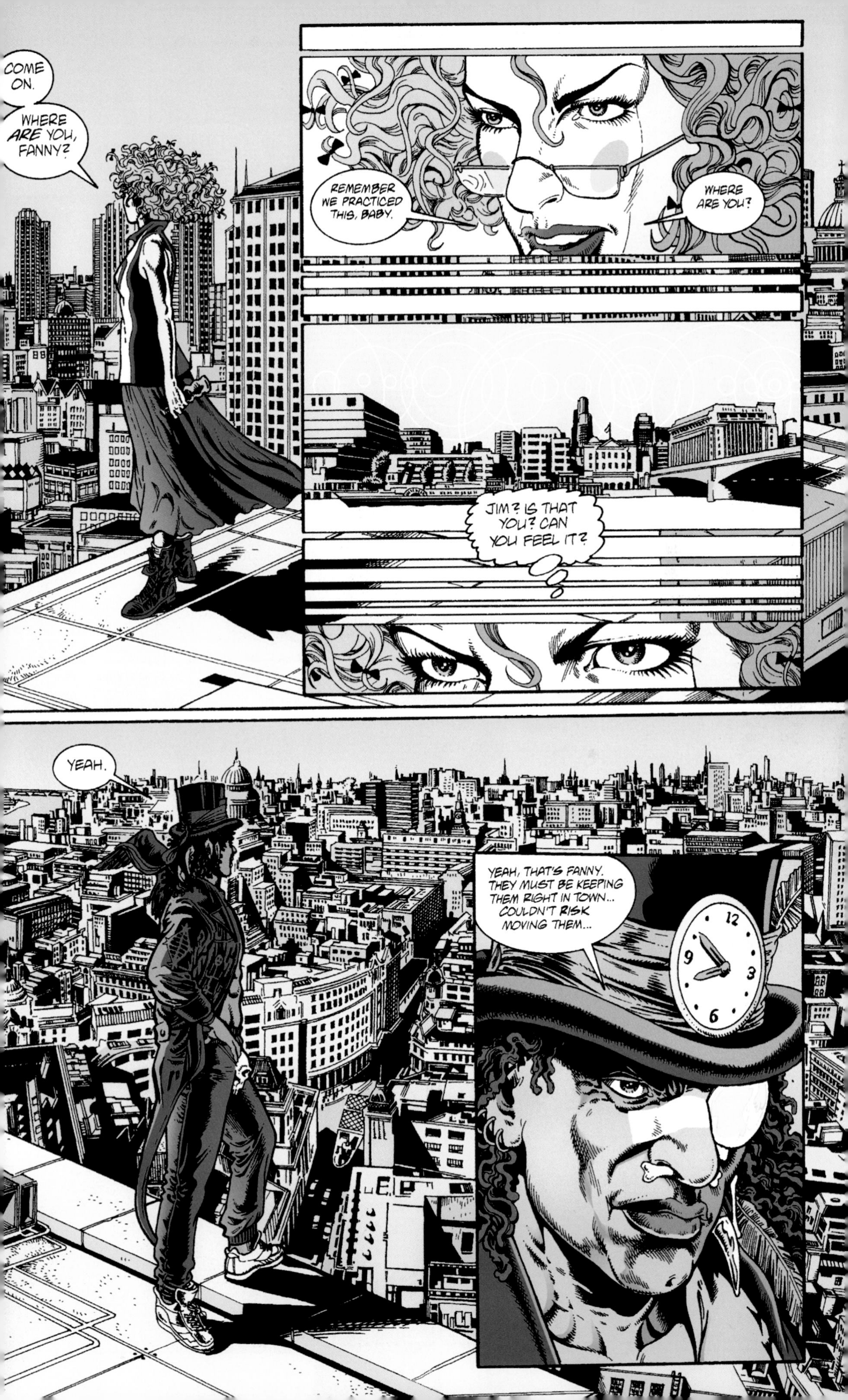
COME ON.
WHERE ARE YOU, FANNY?
REMEMBER WE PRACTICED THIS, BABY.
WHERE ARE YOU?
JIM? IS THAT YOU? CAN YOU FEEL IT?
YEAH.
YEAH, THAT'S FANNY. THEY MUST BE KEEPING THEM RIGHT IN TOWN... COULDN'T RISK MOVING THEM...

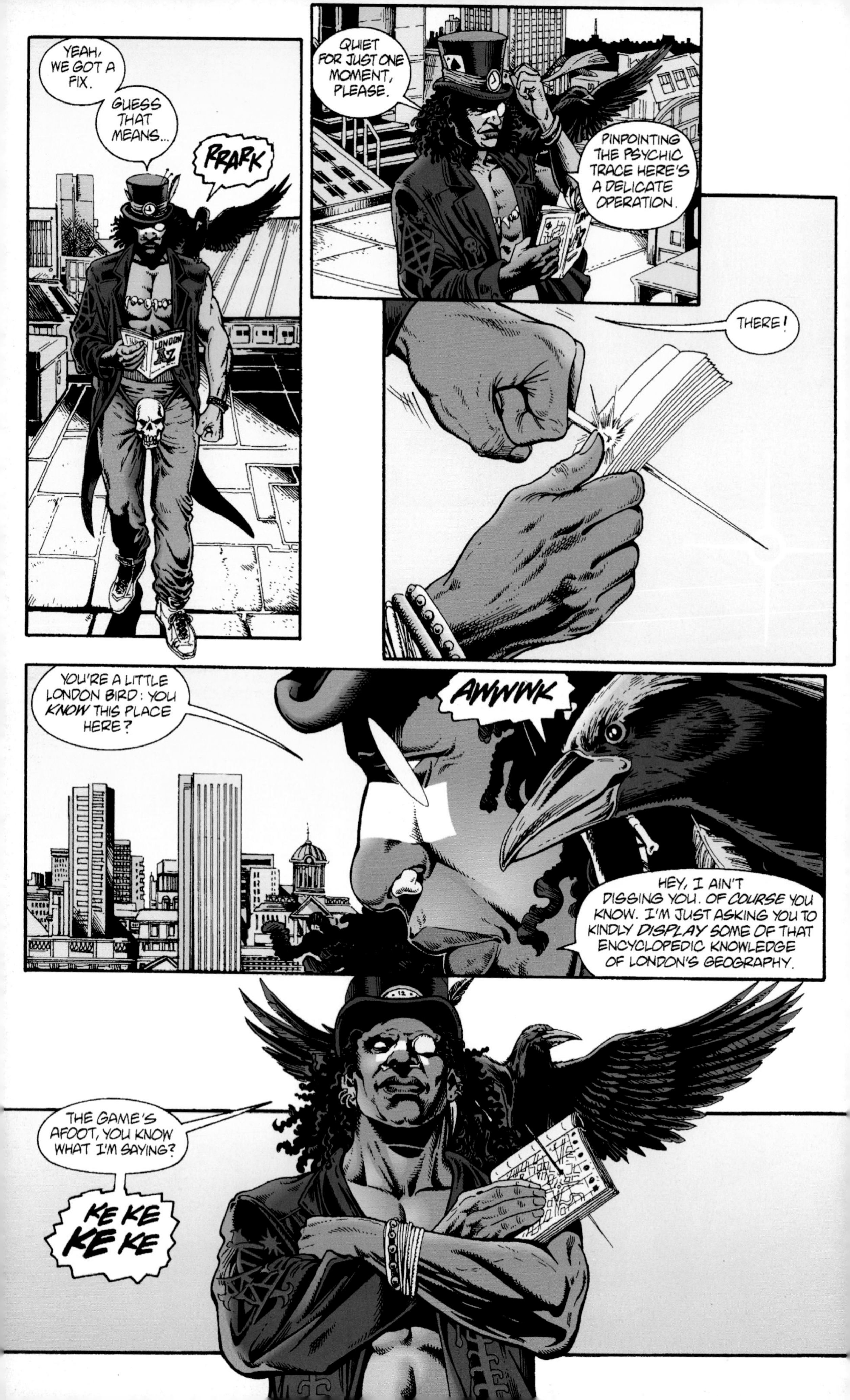
YEAH, WE GOT A FIX.
GUESS THAT MEANS...
RRARK
QUIET FOR JUST ONE MOMENT, PLEASE.
PINPOINTING THE PSYCHIC TRACE HERE'S A DELICATE OPERATION.
LONDON A-Z
THERE!
YOU'RE A LITTLE LONDON BIRD: YOU KNOW THIS PLACE HERE?
AWWWK
HEY, I AIN'T DISSING YOU. OF COURSE YOU KNOW. I'M JUST ASKING YOU TO KINDLY DISPLAY SOME OF THAT ENCYCLOPEDIC KNOWLEDGE OF LONDON'S GEOGRAPHY.
THE GAME'S AFOOT, YOU KNOW WHAT I'M SAYING?
KE KE KE KE

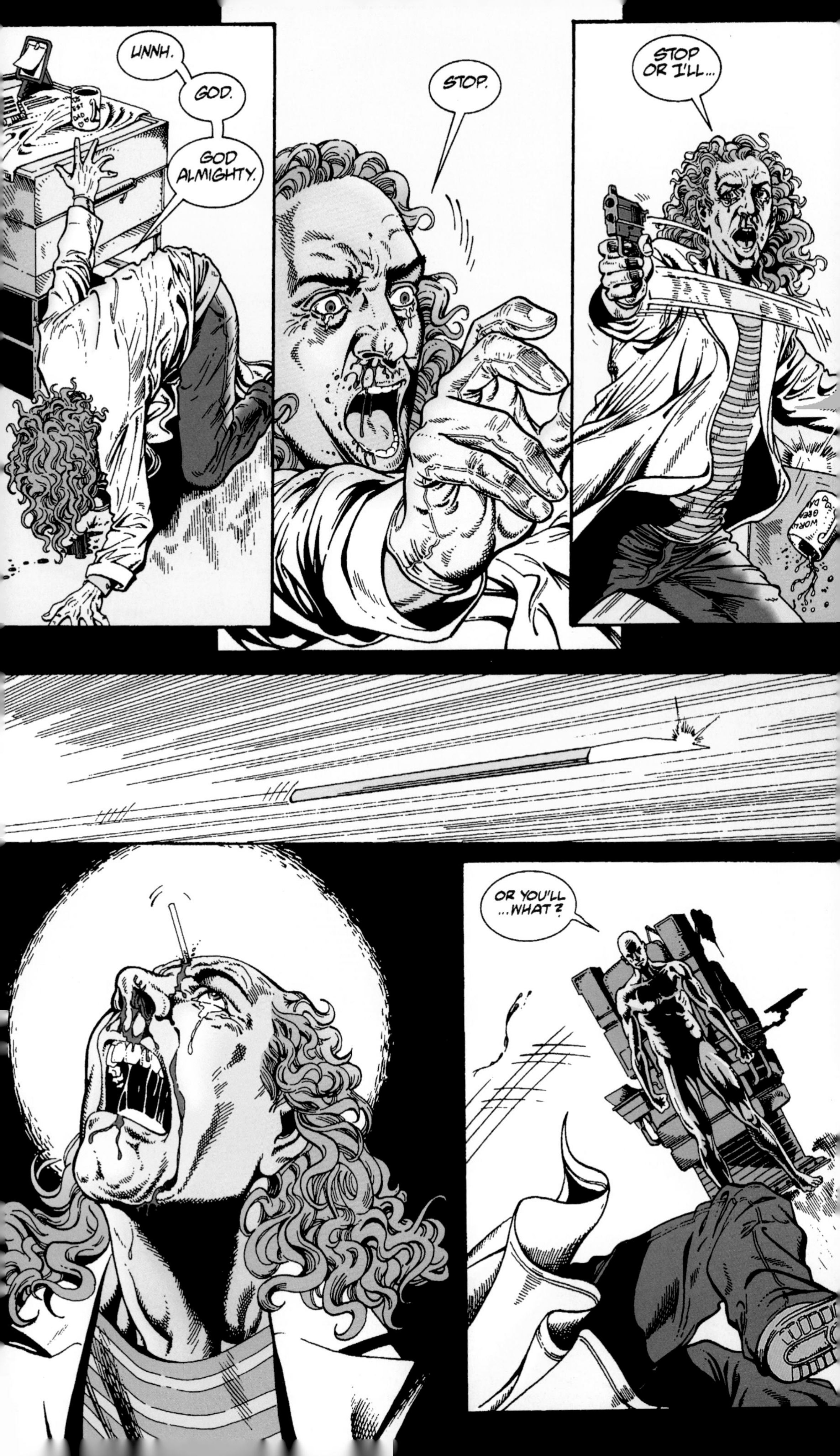
UNNH.
GOD.
GOD ALMIGHTY.
STOP.
STOP OR I'LL...
OR YOU'LL ...WHAT?

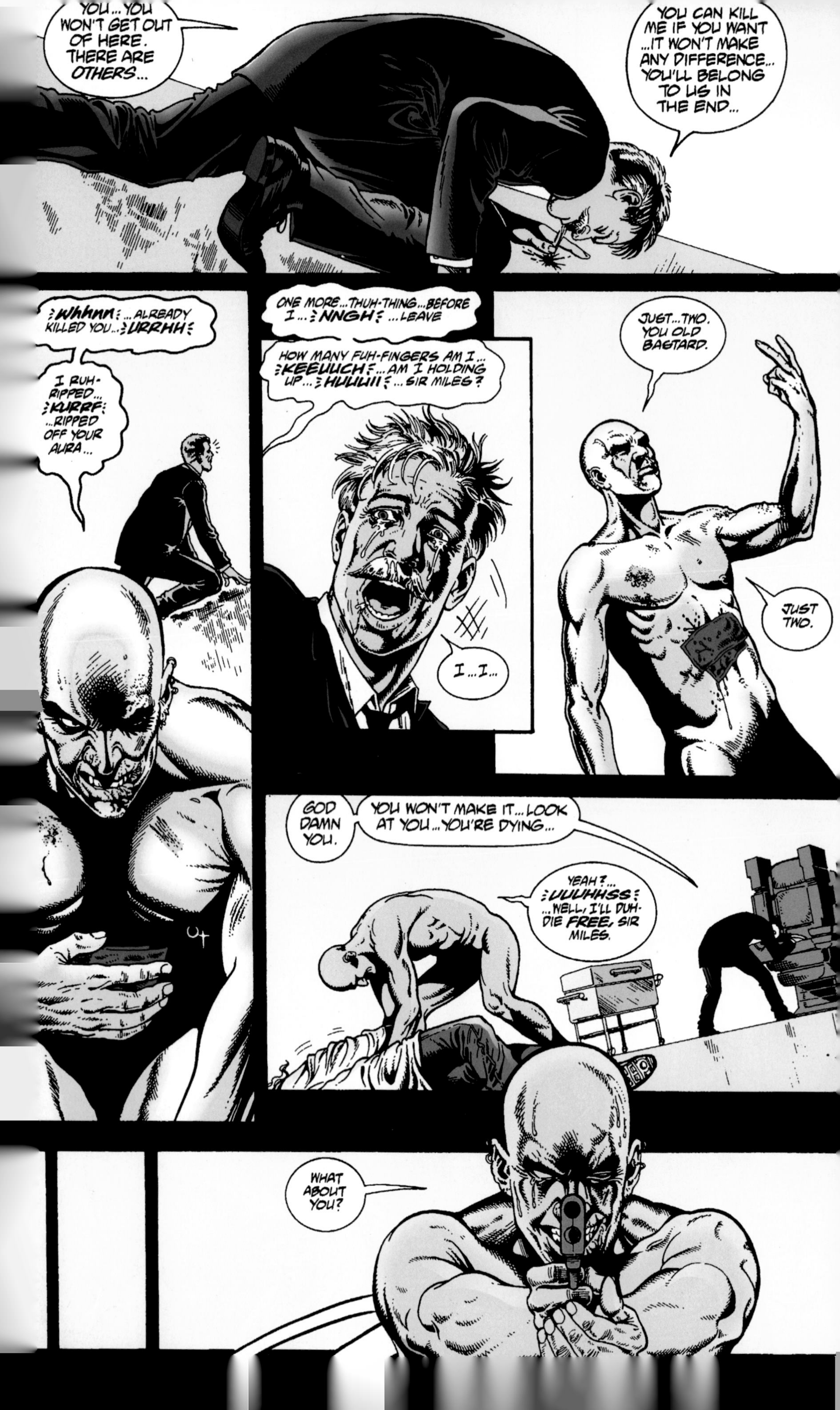

YOU... YOU WON'T GET OUT OF HERE. THERE ARE OTHERS...
YOU CAN KILL ME IF YOU WANT ...IT WON'T MAKE ANY DIFFERENCE... YOU'LL BELONG TO US IN THE END...
WHHNN ...ALREADY KILLED YOU... URRHH
I RUH-RIPPED... KURRF ...RIPPED OFF YOUR AURA...
ONE MORE...THUH-THING...BEFORE I... NNGH ...LEAVE
HOW MANY FUH-FINGERS AM I... KEEUUCH ...AM I HOLDING UP... HUUUII ...SIR MILES?
I...I...
JUST...TWO. YOU OLD BASTARD.
JUST TWO.
GOD DAMN YOU.
YOU WON'T MAKE IT... LOOK AT YOU... YOU'RE DYING...
YEAH?... UUUHHSS ...WELL, I'LL DUH-DIE FREE, SIR MILES.
WHAT ABOUT YOU?

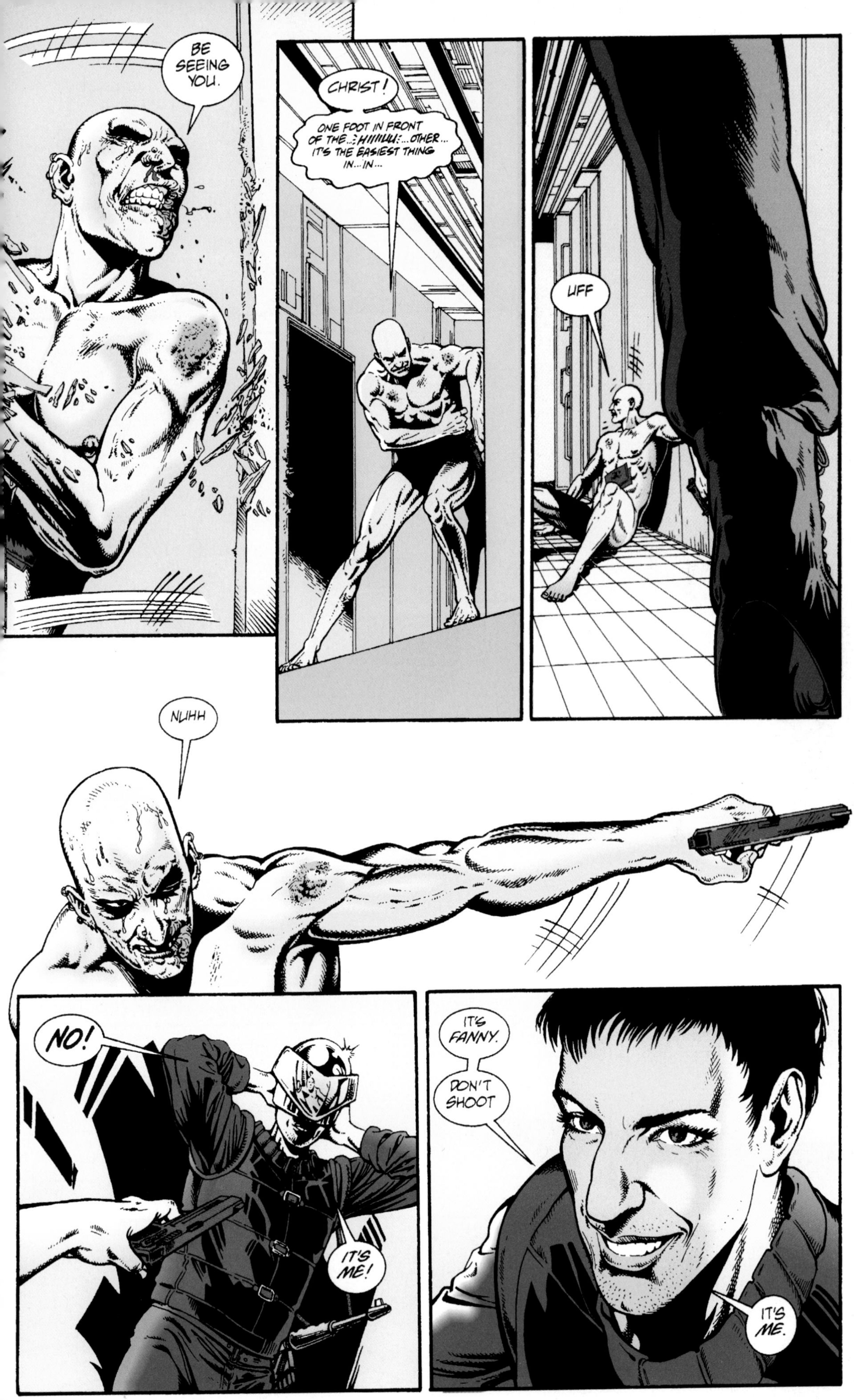
BE SEEING YOU.
CHRIST!
ONE FOOT IN FRONT OF THE... HIIIIUUU... OTHER... IT'S THE EASIEST THING IN... IN...
UFF
NUHH
NO!
IT'S ME!
IT'S FANNY.
DON'T SHOOT
IT'S ME.

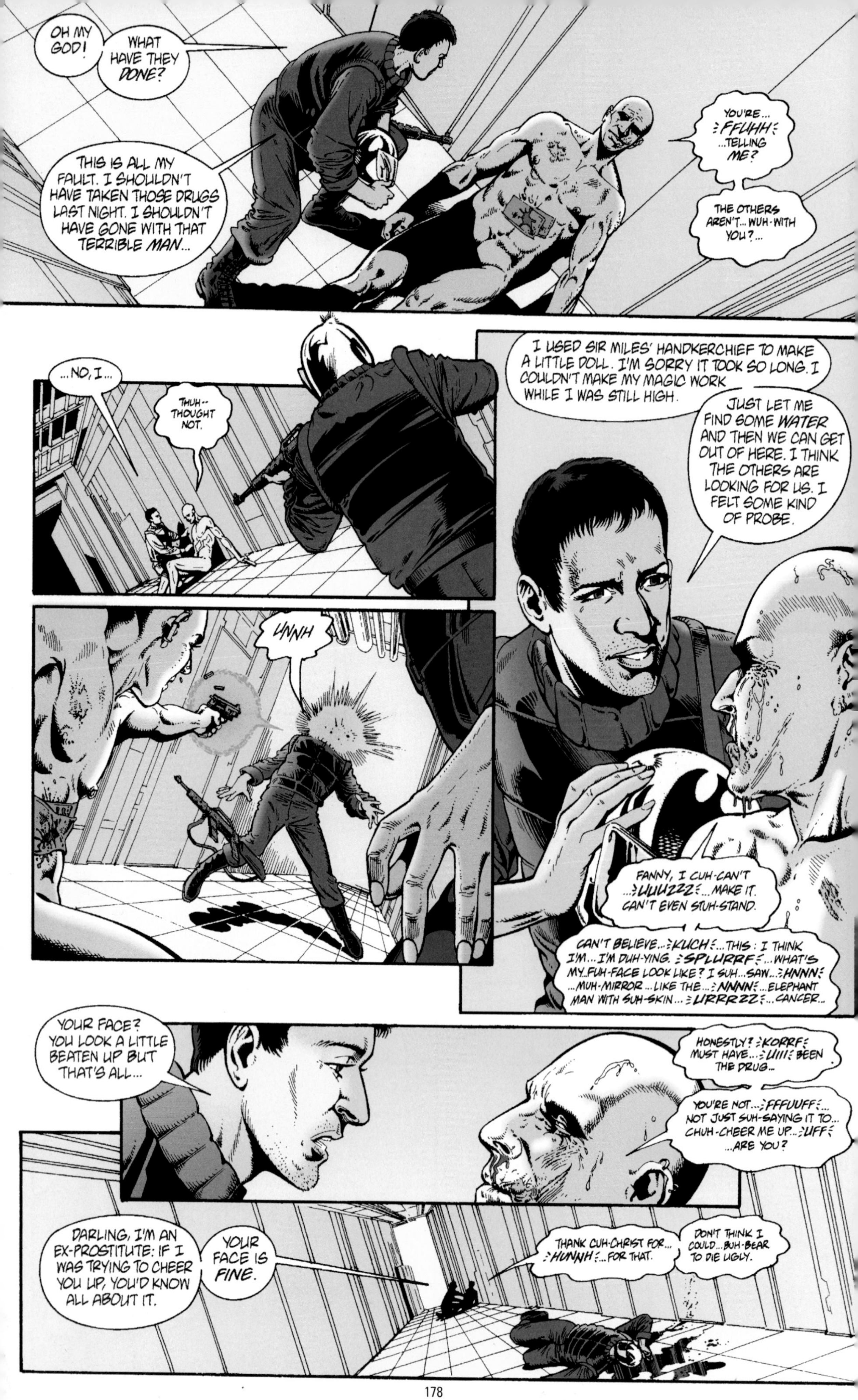

OH MY GOD!
WHAT HAVE THEY DONE?
THIS IS ALL MY FAULT. I SHOULDN'T HAVE TAKEN THOSE DRUGS LAST NIGHT. I SHOULDN'T HAVE GONE WITH THAT TERRIBLE MAN...
YOU'RE... FFUHH ...TELLING ME?
THE OTHERS AREN'T... WUH-WITH YOU?...
...NO, I...
THUH--THOUGHT NOT.
I USED SIR MILES' HANDKERCHIEF TO MAKE A LITTLE DOLL. I'M SORRY IT TOOK SO LONG. I COULDN'T MAKE MY MAGIC WORK WHILE I WAS STILL HIGH.
JUST LET ME FIND SOME WATER AND THEN WE CAN GET OUT OF HERE. I THINK THE OTHERS ARE LOOKING FOR US. I FELT SOME KIND OF PROBE.
UNNH
FANNY, I CUH-CAN'T ...UUUZZZ... MAKE IT. CAN'T EVEN STUH-STAND.
CAN'T BELIEVE... KUCH ...THIS: I THINK I'M... I'M DUH-YING. SPLURRF ...WHAT'S MY...FUH-FACE LOOK LIKE? I SUH... SAW... HNNN ...MUH-MIRROR ...LIKE THE... NNNN ...ELEPHANT MAN WITH SUH-SKIN... URRRZZ ...CANCER...
YOUR FACE? YOU LOOK A LITTLE BEATEN UP BUT THAT'S ALL...
HONESTLY? KORRF MUST HAVE... UIII BEEN THE DRUG...
YOU'RE NOT... FFFUUFF ...NOT JUST SUH-SAYING IT TO... CHUH-CHEER ME UP... UFF ...ARE YOU?
DARLING, I'M AN EX-PROSTITUTE: IF I WAS TRYING TO CHEER YOU UP, YOU'D KNOW ALL ABOUT IT.
YOUR FACE IS FINE.
THANK CUH-CHRIST FOR... HUNNH ...FOR THAT.
DON'T THINK I COULD... BUH-BEAR TO DIE UGLY.

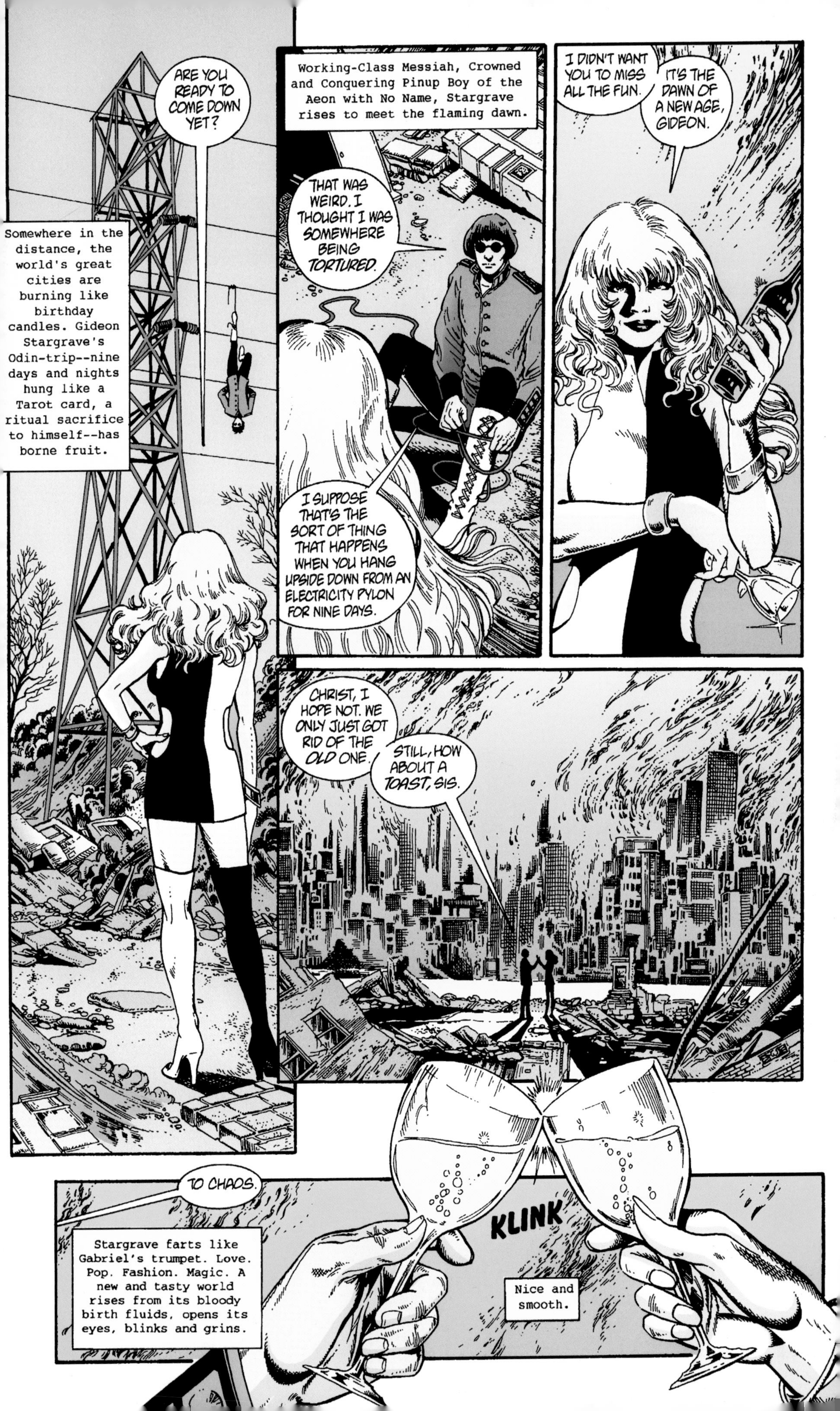
ARE YOU READY TO COME DOWN YET?
Somewhere in the distance, the world's great cities are burning like birthday candles. Gideon Stargrave's Odin-trip--nine days and nights hung like a Tarot card, a ritual sacrifice to himself--has borne fruit.
Working-Class Messiah, Crowned and Conquering Pinup Boy of the Aeon with No Name, Stargrave rises to meet the flaming dawn.
THAT WAS WEIRD. I THOUGHT I WAS SOMEWHERE BEING TORTURED.
I SUPPOSE THAT'S THE SORT OF THING THAT HAPPENS WHEN YOU HANG UPSIDE DOWN FROM AN ELECTRICITY PYLON FOR NINE DAYS.
I DIDN'T WANT YOU TO MISS ALL THE FUN.
IT'S THE DAWN OF A NEW AGE, GIDEON.
CHRIST, I HOPE NOT. WE ONLY JUST GOT RID OF THE OLD ONE.
STILL, HOW ABOUT A TOAST, SIS.
TO CHAOS.
Stargrave farts like Gabriel's trumpet. Love. Pop. Fashion. Magic. A new and tasty world rises from its bloody birth fluids, opens its eyes, blinks and grins.
KLINK
Nice and smooth.

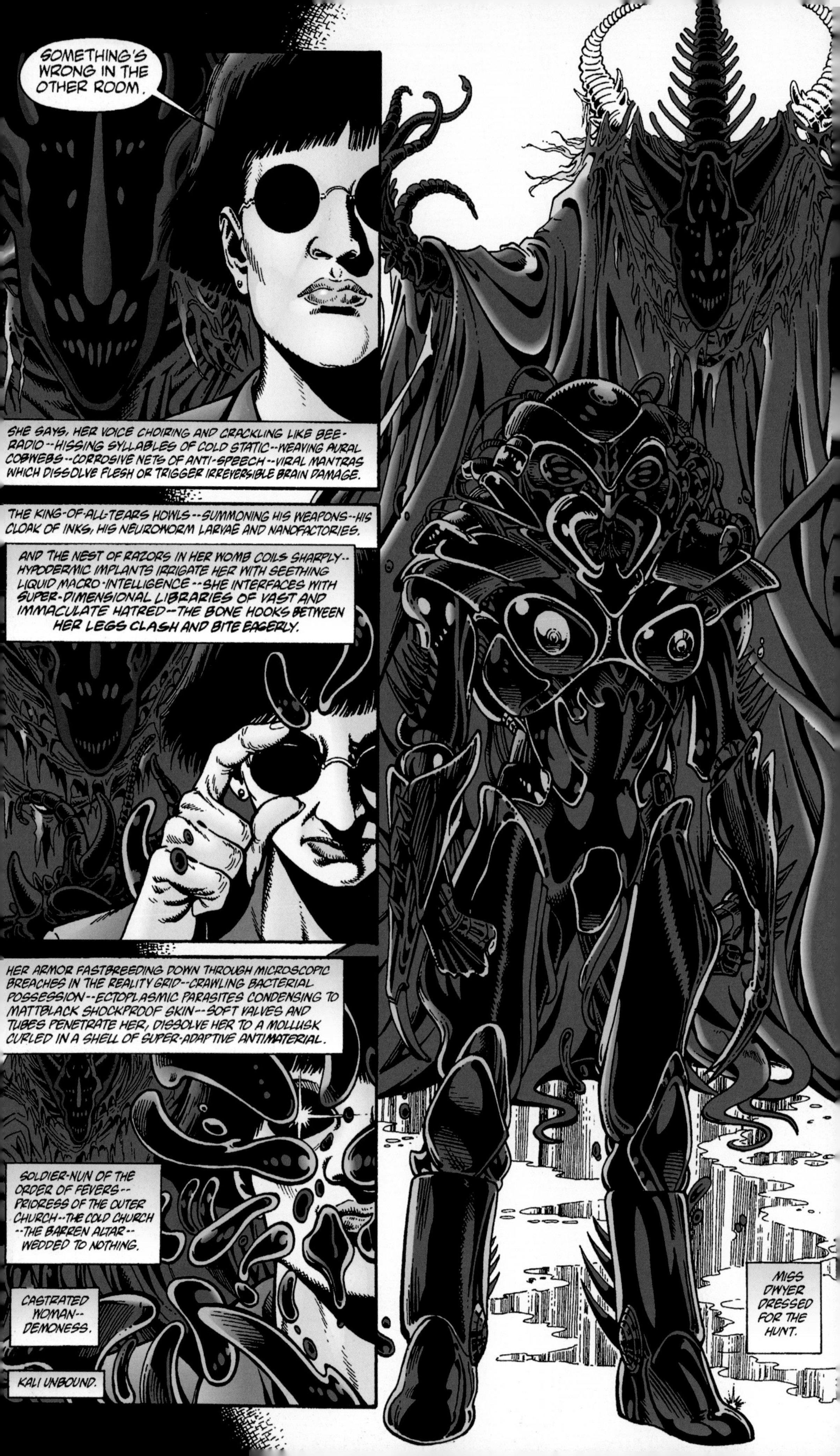
SOMETHING'S WRONG IN THE OTHER ROOM.
SHE SAYS, HER VOICE CHOIRING AND CRACKLING LIKE BEE-RADIO--HISSING SYLLABLES OF COLD STATIC--WEAVING AURAL COBWEBS--CORROSIVE NETS OF ANTI-SPEECH--VIRAL MANTRAS WHICH DISSOLVE FLESH OR TRIGGER IRREVERSIBLE BRAIN DAMAGE.
THE KING-OF-ALL-TEARS HOWLS--SUMMONING HIS WEAPONS--HIS CLOAK OF INKS, HIS NEUROWORM LARVAE AND NANOFACTORIES.
AND THE NEST OF RAZORS IN HER WOMB COILS SHARPLY--HYPODERMIC IMPLANTS IRRIGATE HER WITH SEETHING LIQUID MACRO-INTELLIGENCE--SHE INTERFACES WITH SUPER-DIMENSIONAL LIBRARIES OF VAST AND IMMACULATE HATRED--THE BONE HOOKS BETWEEN HER LEGS CLASH AND BITE EAGERLY.
HER ARMOR FASTBREEDING DOWN THROUGH MICROSCOPIC BREACHES IN THE REALITY GRID--CRAWLING BACTERIAL POSSESSION--ECTOPLASMIC PARASITES CONDENSING TO MATTBLACK SHOCKPROOF SKIN--SOFT VALVES AND TUBES PENETRATE HER, DISSOLVE HER TO A MOLLUSK CURLED IN A SHELL OF SUPER-ADAPTIVE ANTIMATERIAL.
SOLDIER-NUN OF THE ORDER OF FEVERS--PRIORESS OF THE OUTER CHURCH--THE COLD CHURCH--THE BARREN ALTAR--WEDDED TO NOTHING.
CASTRATED WOMAN--DEMONESS.
KALI UNBOUND.
MISS DWYER DRESSED FOR THE HUNT.

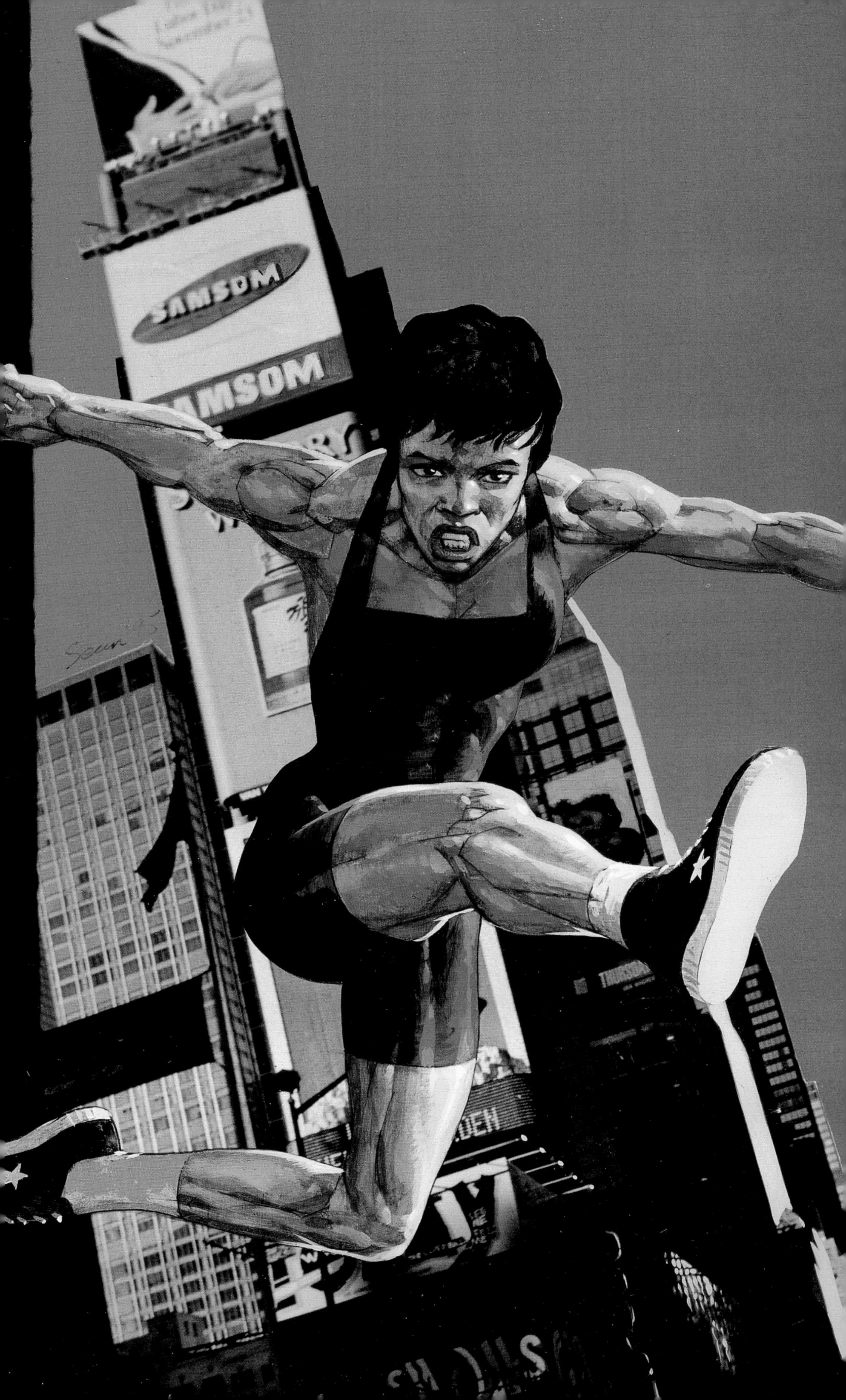
SAMSOM
AMSOM

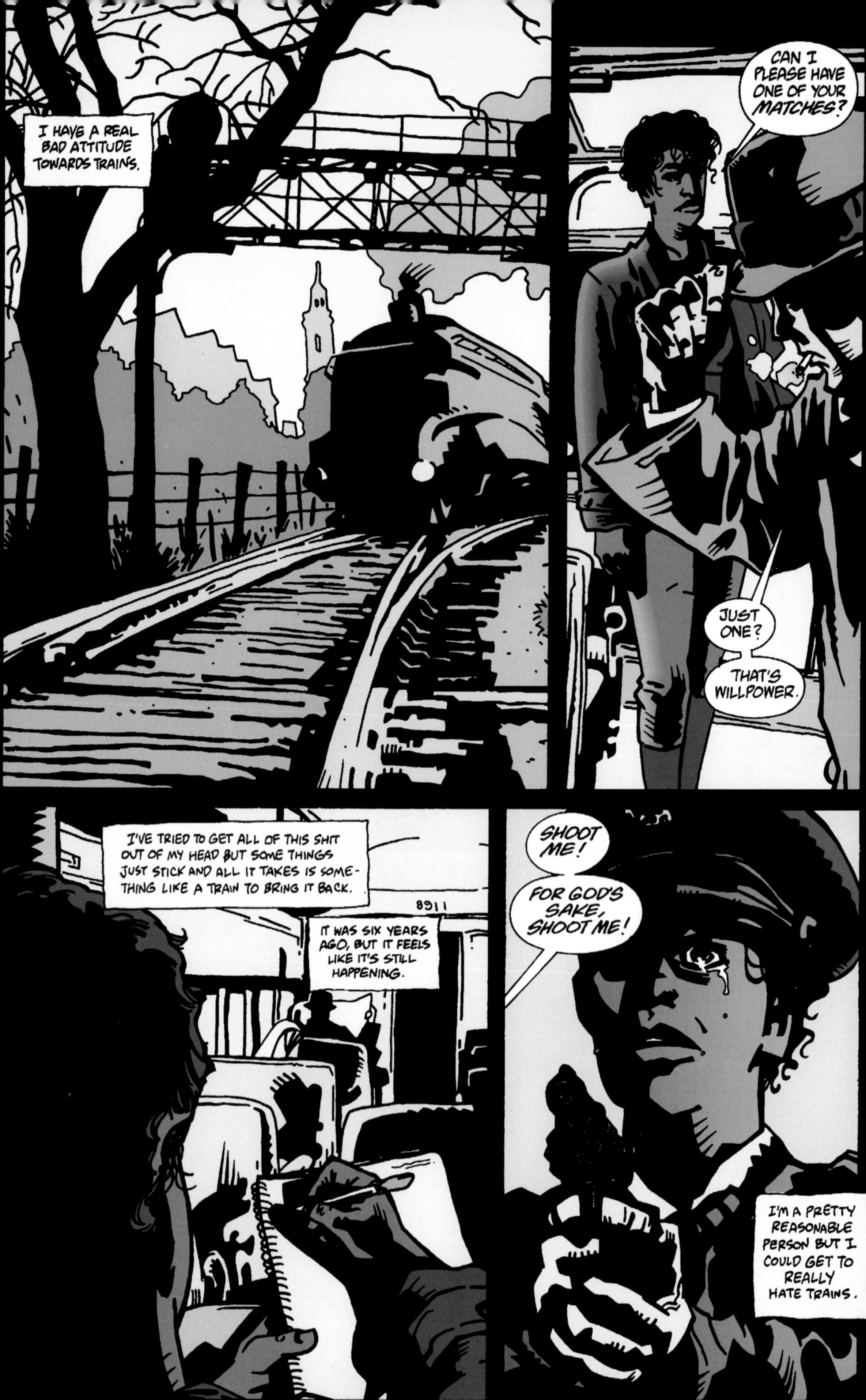
I HAVE A REAL BAD ATTITUDE TOWARDS TRAINS.
CAN I PLEASE HAVE ONE OF YOUR MATCHES?
JUST ONE?
THAT'S WILLPOWER.
I'VE TRIED TO GET ALL OF THIS SHIT OUT OF MY HEAD BUT SOME THINGS JUST STICK AND ALL IT TAKES IS SOME-THING LIKE A TRAIN TO BRING IT BACK.
8911
IT WAS SIX YEARS AGO, BUT IT FEELS LIKE IT'S STILL HAPPENING.
SHOOT ME!
FOR GOD'S SAKE, SHOOT ME!
I'M A PRETTY REASONABLE PERSON BUT I COULD GET TO REALLY HATE TRAINS.

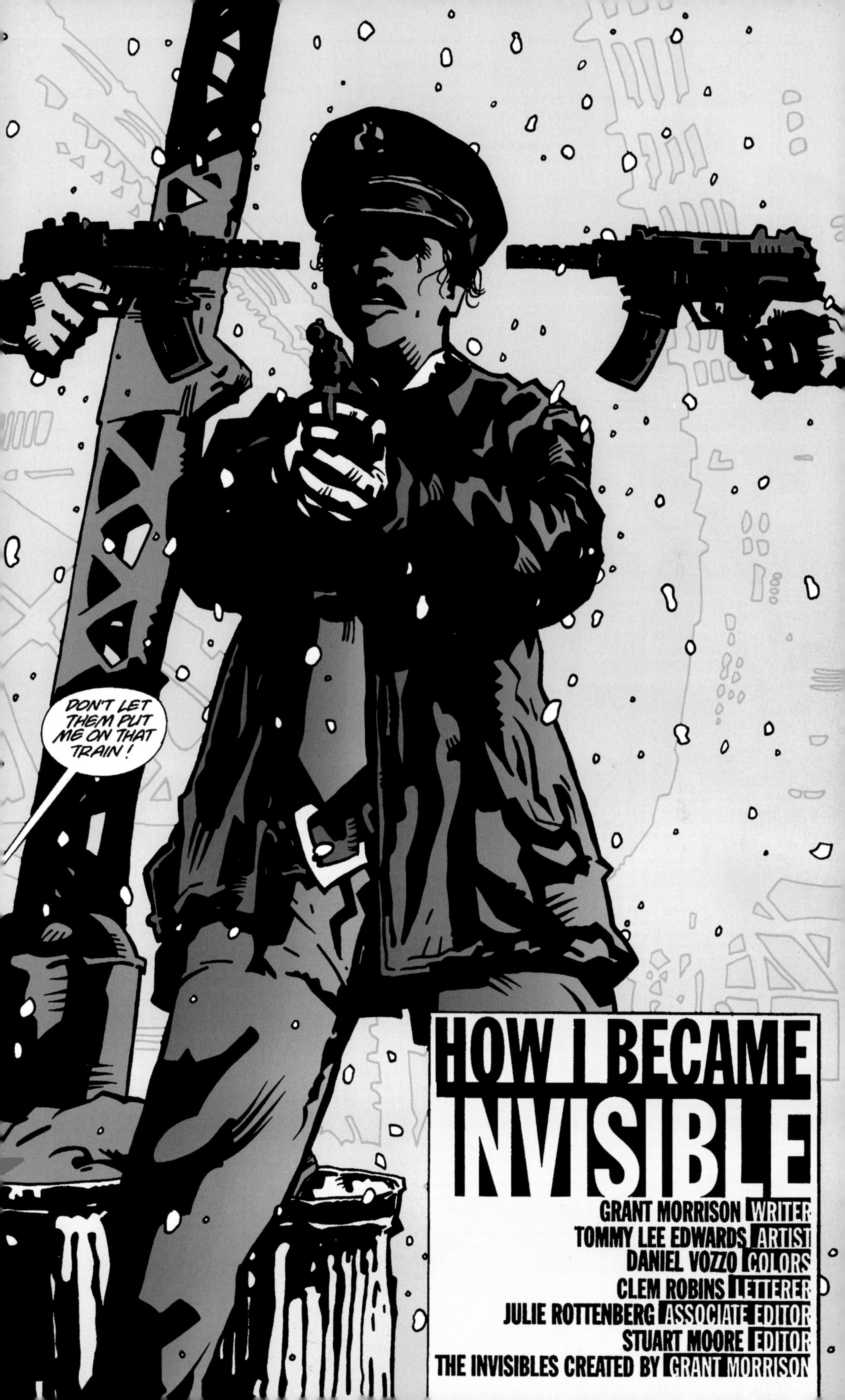

DON'T LET THEM PUT ME ON THAT TRAIN!
HOW I BECAME INVISIBLE
GRANT MORRISON WRITER
TOMMY LEE EDWARDS ARTIST
DANIEL VOZZO COLORS
CLEM ROBINS LETTERER
JULIE ROTTENBERG ASSOCIATE EDITOR
STUART MOORE EDITOR
THE INVISIBLES CREATED BY GRANT MORRISON

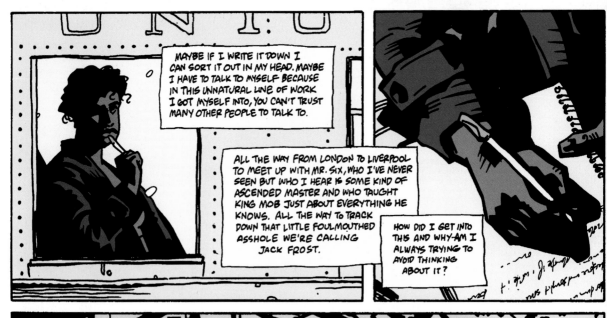

MAYBE IF I WRITE IT DOWN I CAN SORT IT OUT IN MY HEAD. MAYBE I HAVE TO TALK TO MYSELF BECAUSE IN THIS UNNATURAL LINE OF WORK I GOT MYSELF INTO, YOU CAN'T TRUST MANY OTHER PEOPLE TO TALK TO.

ALL THE WAY FROM LONDON TO LIVERPOOL TO MEET UP WITH MR. SIX, WHO I'VE NEVER SEEN BUT WHO I HEAR IS SOME KIND OF ASCENDED MASTER AND WHO TAUGHT KING MOB JUST ABOUT EVERYTHING HE KNOWS. ALL THE WAY TO TRACK DOWN THAT LITTLE FOULMOUTHED ASSHOLE WE'RE CALLING JACK FROST.

HOW DID I GET INTO THIS AND WHY AM I ALWAYS TRYING TO AVOID THINKING ABOUT IT?

MAYBE IF I WRITE IT DOWN THIS ONE TIME IT'LL PASS THE JOURNEY, AND STOP ME THINKING ABOUT THIS SHIT WE'RE GETTING NECK DEEP INTO.

AND IF I'M SO INSISTENT ABOUT CONFRONTING WHAT'S IN MY HEAD, THEN I SHOULD MAYBE STOP WRITING AROUND IT AND LOOK IT STRAIGHT IN THE EYE.

YEAH, MAYBE, GIRL. YOU DO THAT.

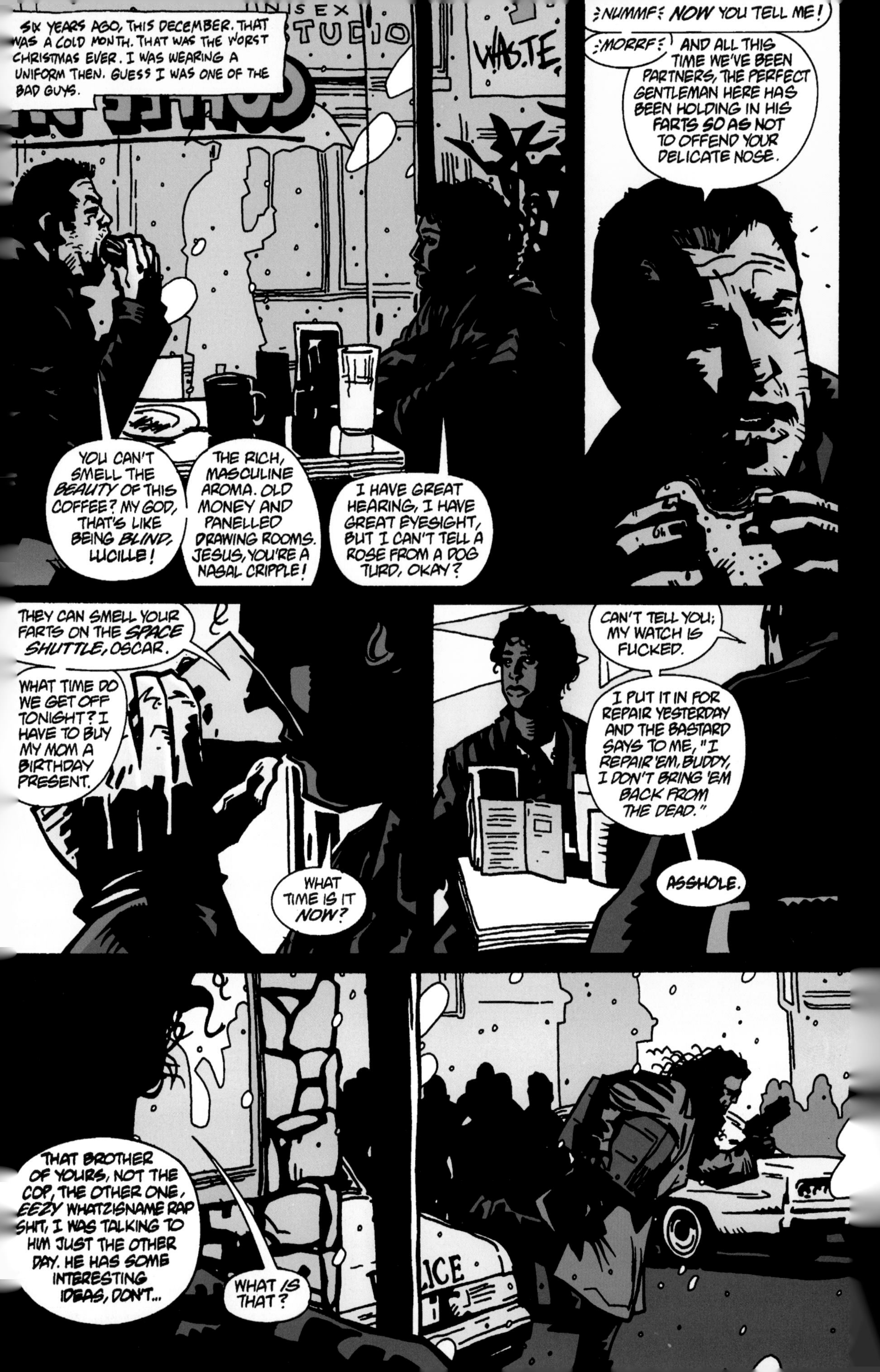
SIX YEARS AGO, THIS DECEMBER. THAT WAS A COLD MONTH. THAT WAS THE WORST CHRISTMAS EVER. I WAS WEARING A UNIFORM THEN. GUESS I WAS ONE OF THE BAD GUYS.
YOU CAN'T SMELL THE *BEAUTY* OF THIS COFFEE? MY GOD, THAT'S LIKE BEING *BLIND*, LUCILLE!
THE RICH, MASCULINE AROMA. OLD MONEY AND PANELLED DRAWING ROOMS. JESUS, YOU'RE A NASAL CRIPPLE!
I HAVE GREAT HEARING, I HAVE GREAT EYESIGHT, BUT I CAN'T TELL A ROSE FROM A DOG TURD, OKAY?
NUMMF *NOW* YOU TELL ME!
MORRF AND ALL THIS TIME WE'VE BEEN PARTNERS, THE PERFECT GENTLEMAN HERE HAS BEEN HOLDING IN HIS FARTS *SO* AS NOT TO OFFEND YOUR DELICATE NOSE.
THEY CAN SMELL YOUR FARTS ON THE *SPACE SHUTTLE*, OSCAR.
WHAT TIME DO WE GET OFF TONIGHT? I HAVE TO BUY MY MOM A BIRTHDAY PRESENT.
WHAT TIME IS IT *NOW*?
CAN'T TELL YOU; MY WATCH IS FUCKED.
I PUT IT IN FOR REPAIR YESTERDAY AND THE BASTARD SAYS TO ME, "I REPAIR 'EM, BUDDY, I DON'T BRING 'EM BACK FROM THE DEAD."
ASSHOLE.
THAT BROTHER OF YOURS, NOT THE COP, THE OTHER ONE, *EEZY* WHATZISNAME RAP SHIT, I WAS TALKING TO HIM JUST THE OTHER DAY. HE HAS SOME INTERESTING IDEAS, DON'T...
WHAT *IS* THAT?

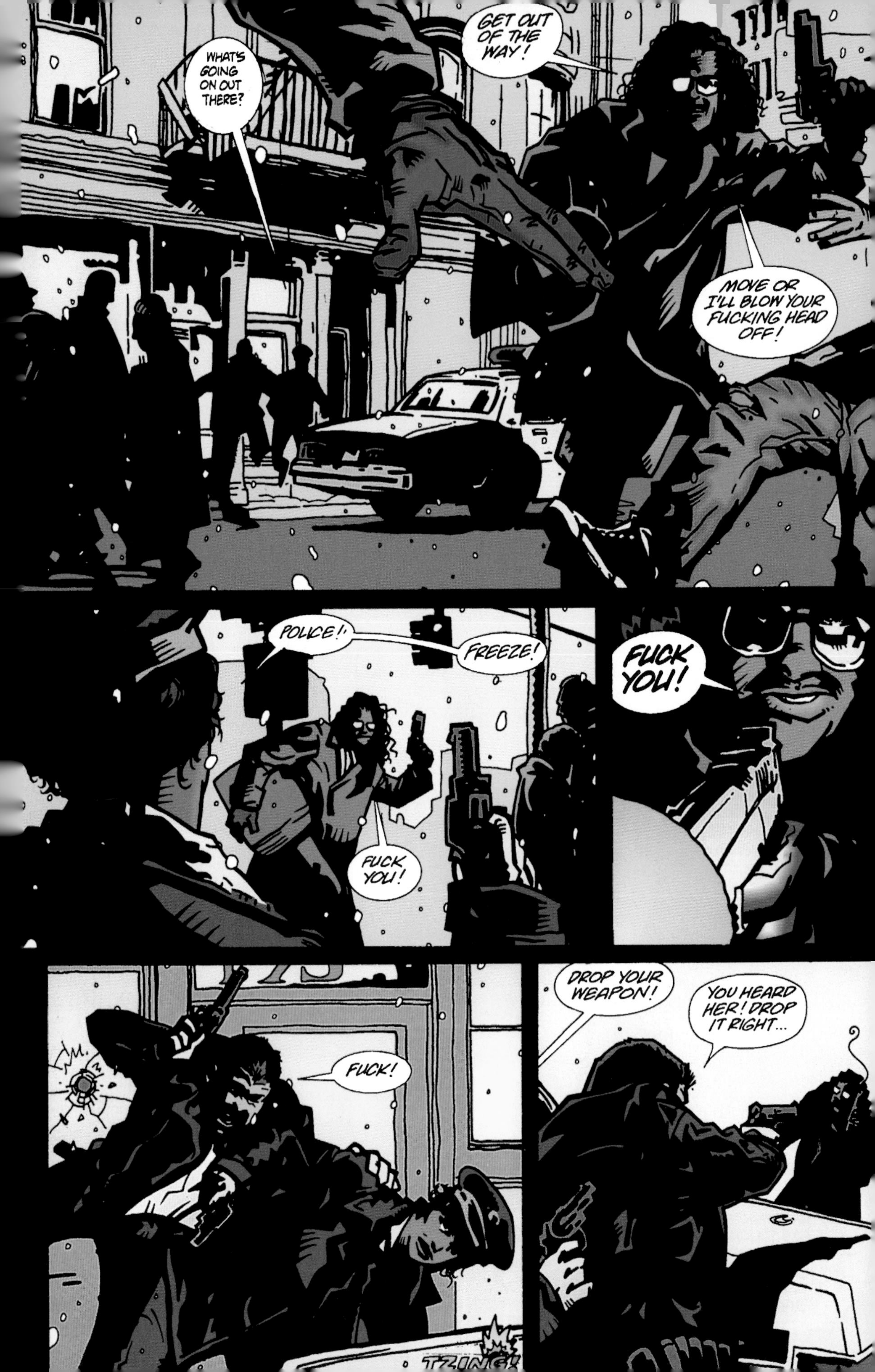
WHAT'S GOING ON OUT THERE?
GET OUT OF THE WAY!
MOVE OR I'LL BLOW YOUR FUCKING HEAD OFF!
POLICE!
FREEZE!
FUCK YOU!
FUCK YOU!
FUCK!
DROP YOUR WEAPON!
YOU HEARD HER! DROP IT RIGHT...

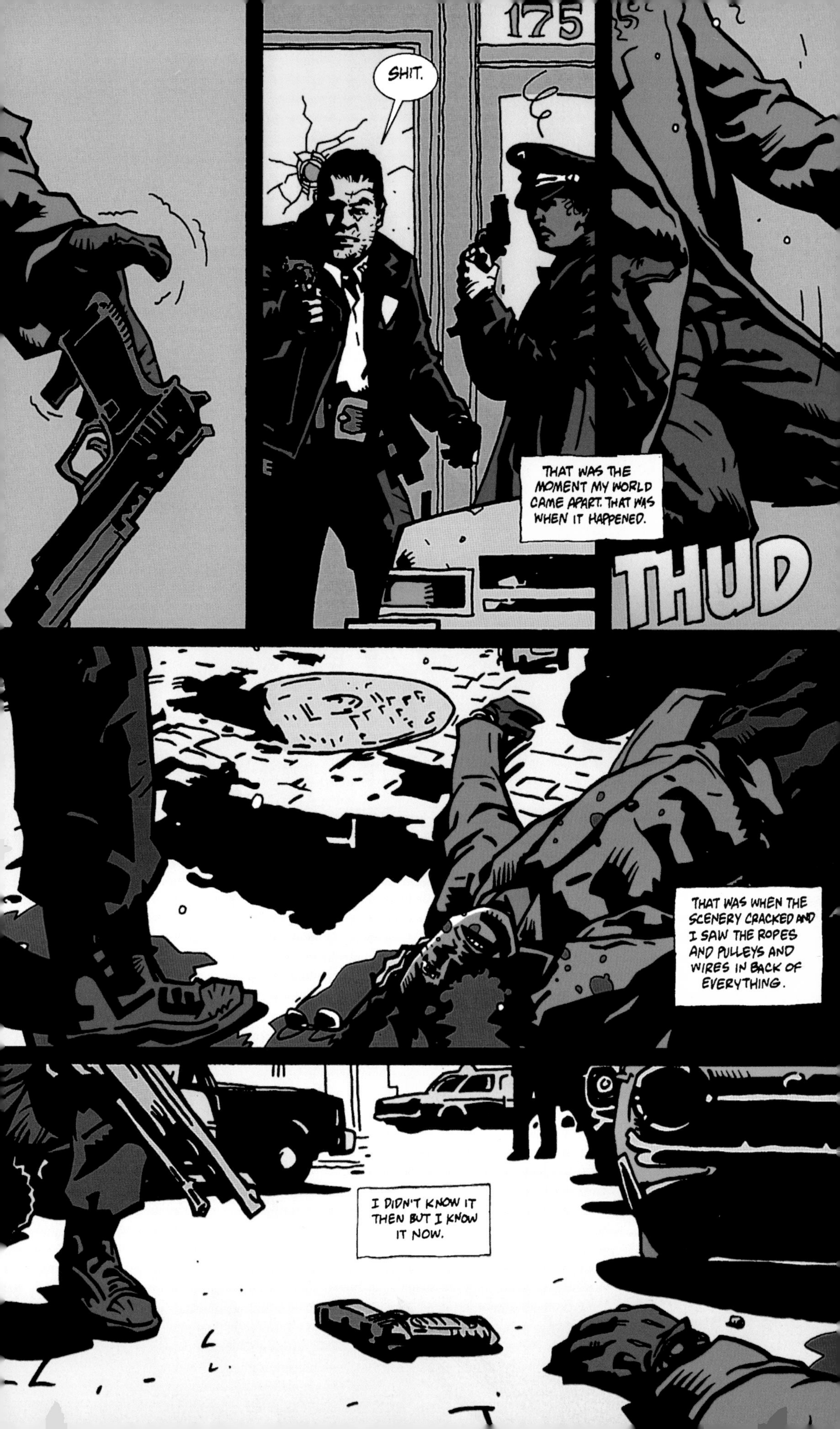
175
SHIT.
THAT WAS THE MOMENT MY WORLD CAME APART. THAT WAS WHEN IT HAPPENED.
THUD
THAT WAS WHEN THE SCENERY CRACKED AND I SAW THE ROPES AND PULLEYS AND WIRES IN BACK OF EVERYTHING.
I DIDN'T KNOW IT THEN BUT I KNOW IT NOW.

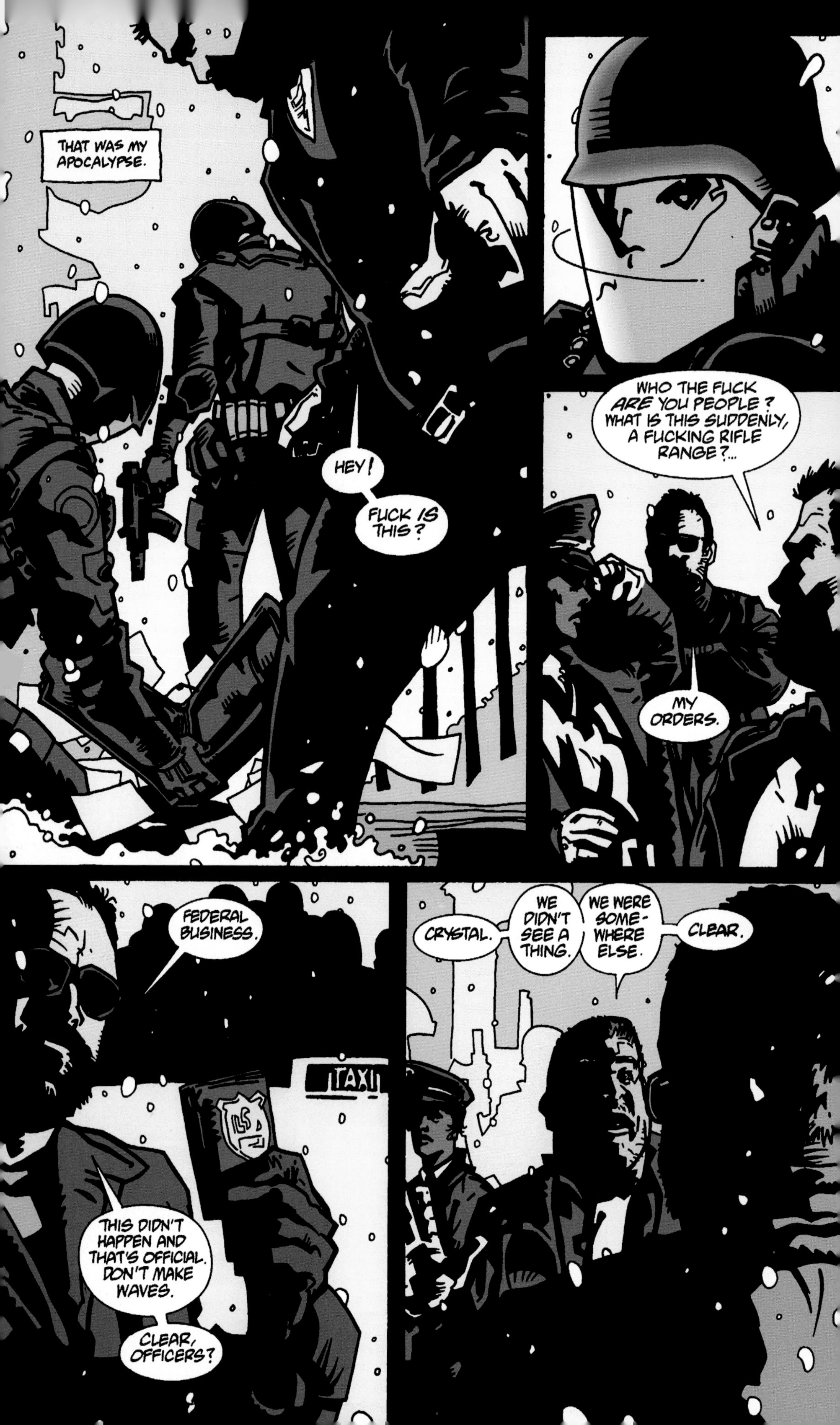
THAT WAS MY APOCALYPSE.
HEY!
FUCK IS THIS?
WHO THE FUCK ARE YOU PEOPLE? WHAT IS THIS SUDDENLY, A FUCKING RIFLE RANGE?...
MY ORDERS.
FEDERAL BUSINESS.
TAXI
THIS DIDN'T HAPPEN AND THAT'S OFFICIAL. DON'T MAKE WAVES.
CLEAR, OFFICERS?
CRYSTAL.
WE DIDN'T SEE A THING.
WE WERE SOME-WHERE ELSE.
CLEAR.

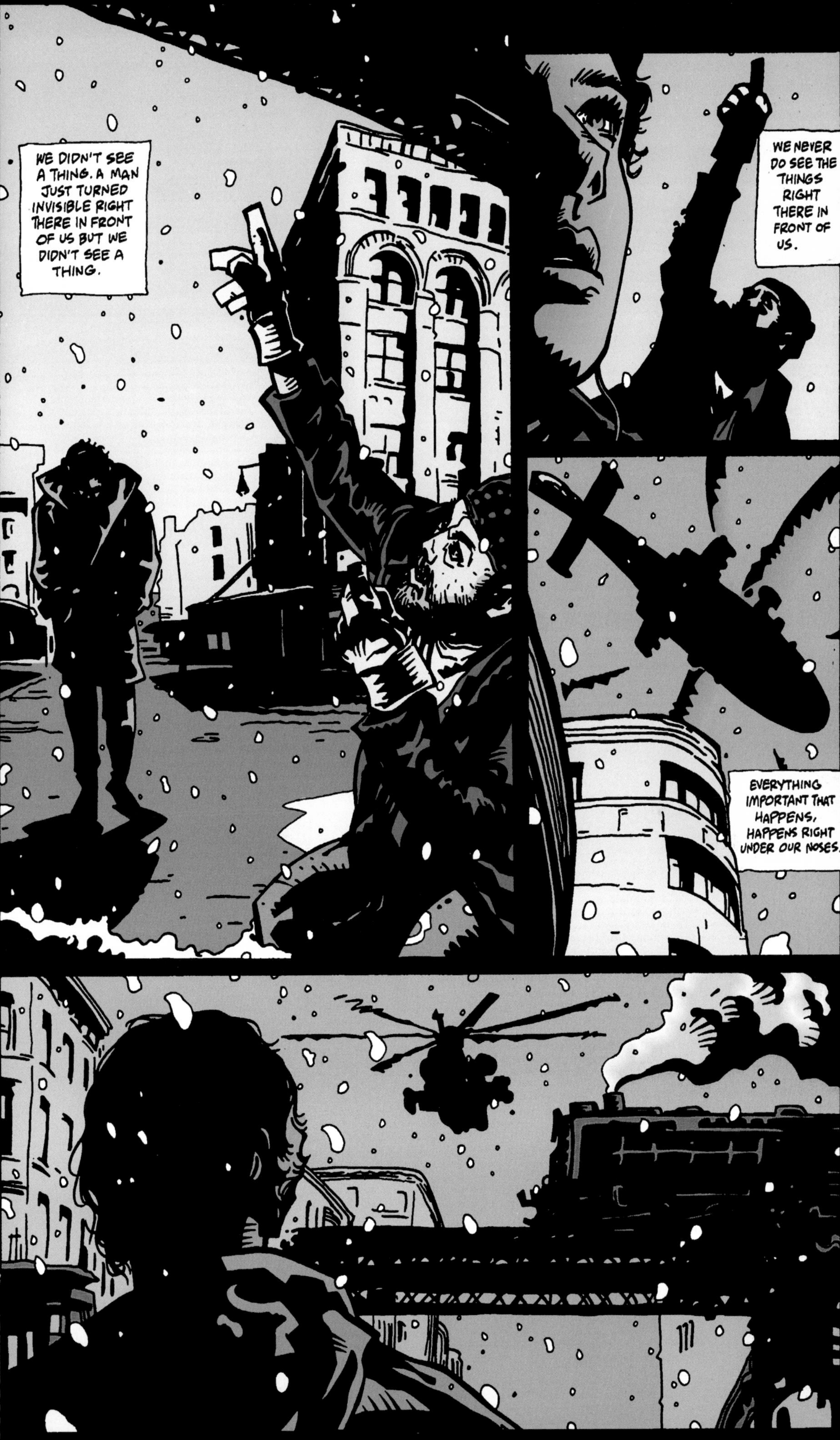
WE DIDN'T SEE A THING. A MAN JUST TURNED INVISIBLE RIGHT THERE IN FRONT OF US BUT WE DIDN'T SEE A THING.
WE NEVER DO SEE THE THINGS RIGHT THERE IN FRONT OF US.
EVERYTHING IMPORTANT THAT HAPPENS, HAPPENS RIGHT UNDER OUR NOSES.

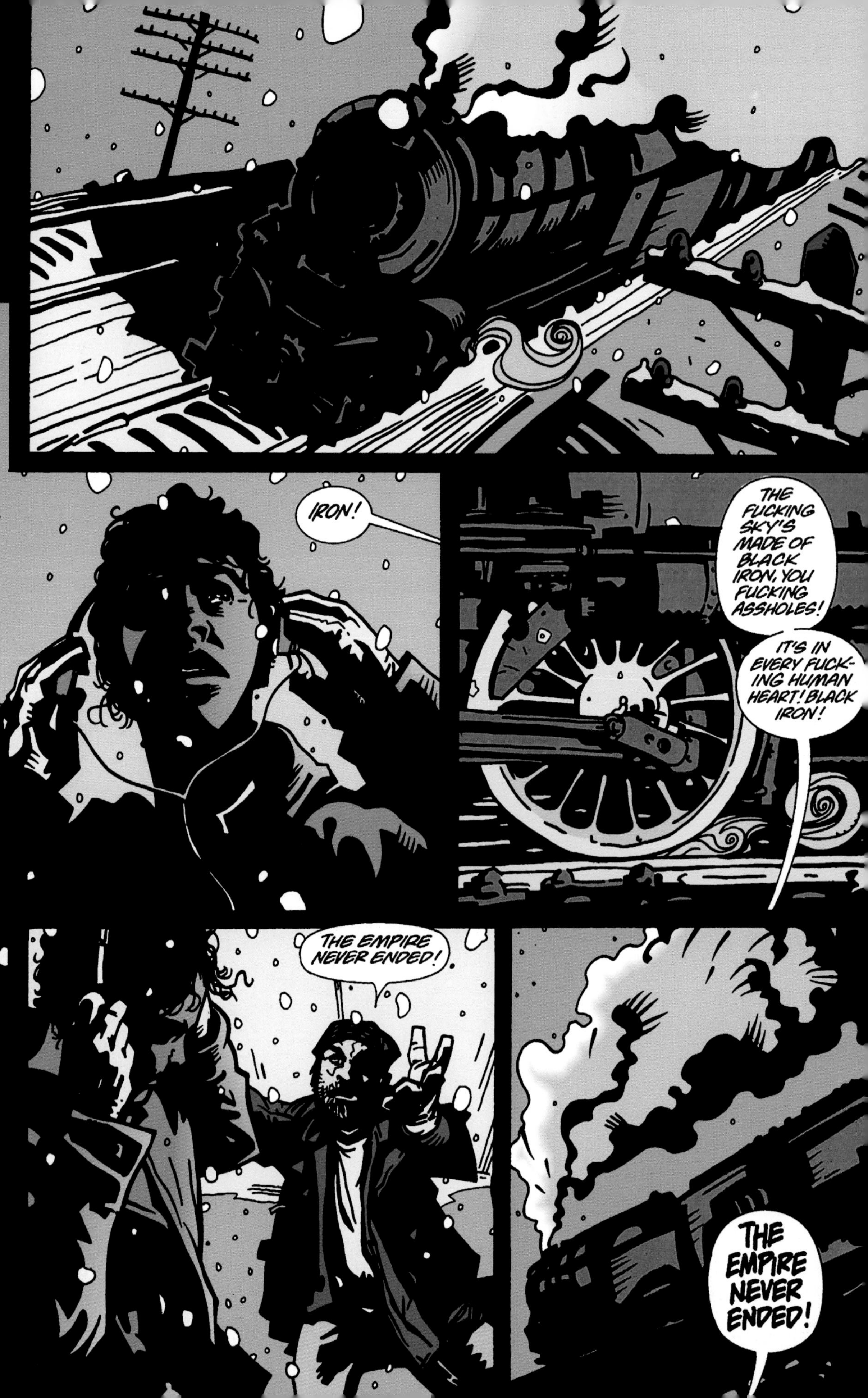
IRON!
THE FUCKING SKY'S MADE OF BLACK IRON, YOU FUCKING ASSHOLES!
IT'S IN EVERY FUCK-ING HUMAN HEART! BLACK IRON!
THE EMPIRE NEVER ENDED!
THE EMPIRE NEVER ENDED!

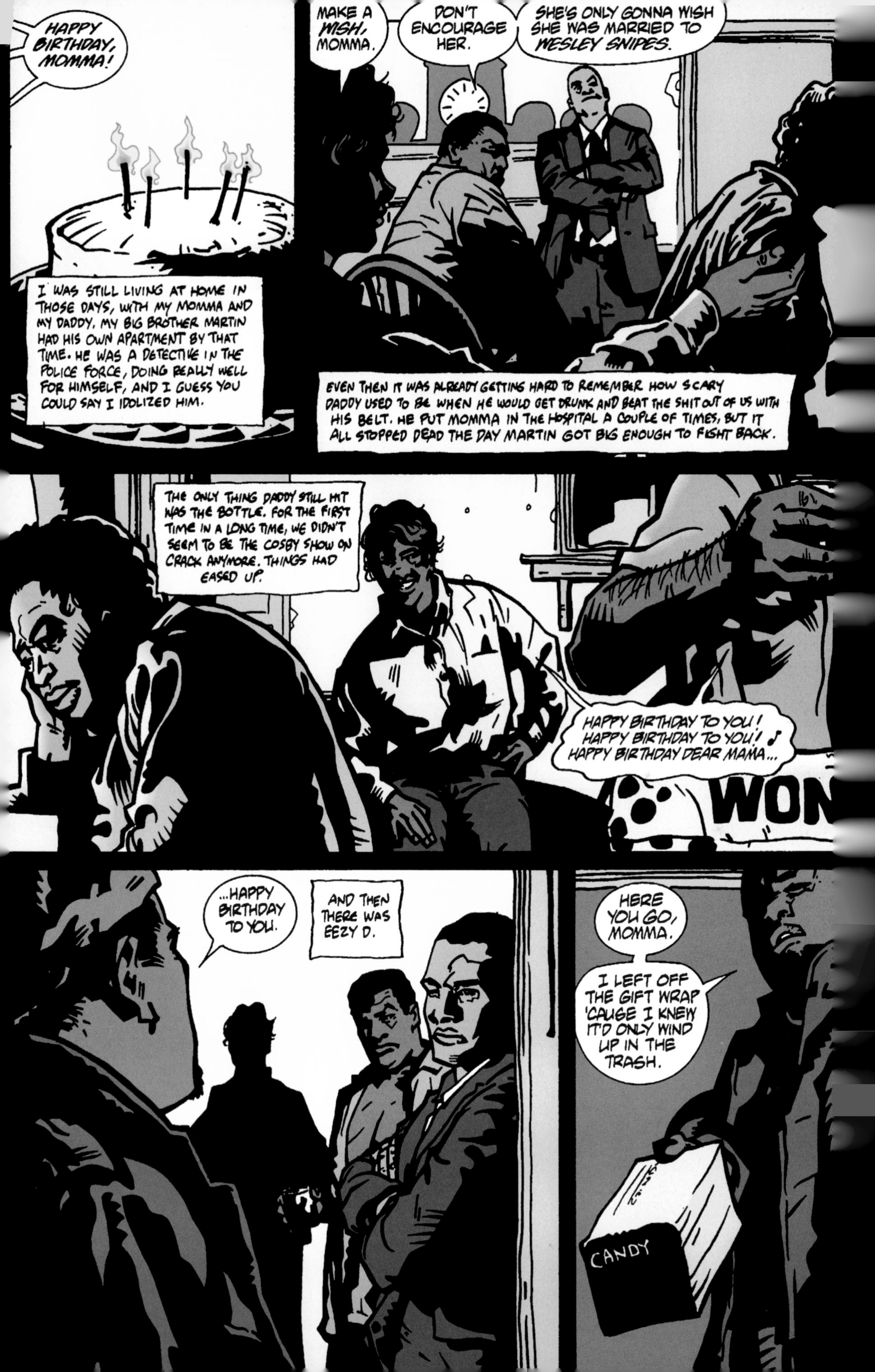
HAPPY BIRTHDAY, MOMMA!
I WAS STILL LIVING AT HOME IN THOSE DAYS, WITH MY MOMMA AND MY DADDY. MY BIG BROTHER MARTIN HAD HIS OWN APARTMENT BY THAT TIME. HE WAS A DETECTIVE IN THE POLICE FORCE, DOING REALLY WELL FOR HIMSELF, AND I GUESS YOU COULD SAY I IDOLIZED HIM.
MAKE A WISH, MOMMA.
DON'T ENCOURAGE HER.
SHE'S ONLY GONNA WISH SHE WAS MARRIED TO WESLEY SNIPES.
EVEN THEN IT WAS ALREADY GETTING HARD TO REMEMBER HOW SCARY DADDY USED TO BE WHEN HE WOULD GET DRUNK AND BEAT THE SHIT OUT OF US WITH HIS BELT. HE PUT MOMMA IN THE HOSPITAL A COUPLE OF TIMES, BUT IT ALL STOPPED DEAD THE DAY MARTIN GOT BIG ENOUGH TO FIGHT BACK.
THE ONLY THING DADDY STILL HIT WAS THE BOTTLE. FOR THE FIRST TIME IN A LONG TIME, WE DIDN'T SEEM TO BE THE COSBY SHOW ON CRACK ANYMORE. THINGS HAD EASED UP.
HAPPY BIRTHDAY TO YOU! HAPPY BIRTHDAY TO YOU! HAPPY BIRTHDAY DEAR MAMA...
WON
...HAPPY BIRTHDAY TO YOU.
AND THEN THERE WAS EEZY D.
HERE YOU GO, MOMMA.
I LEFT OFF THE GIFT WRAP 'CAUSE I KNEW IT'D ONLY WIND UP IN THE TRASH.
CANDY

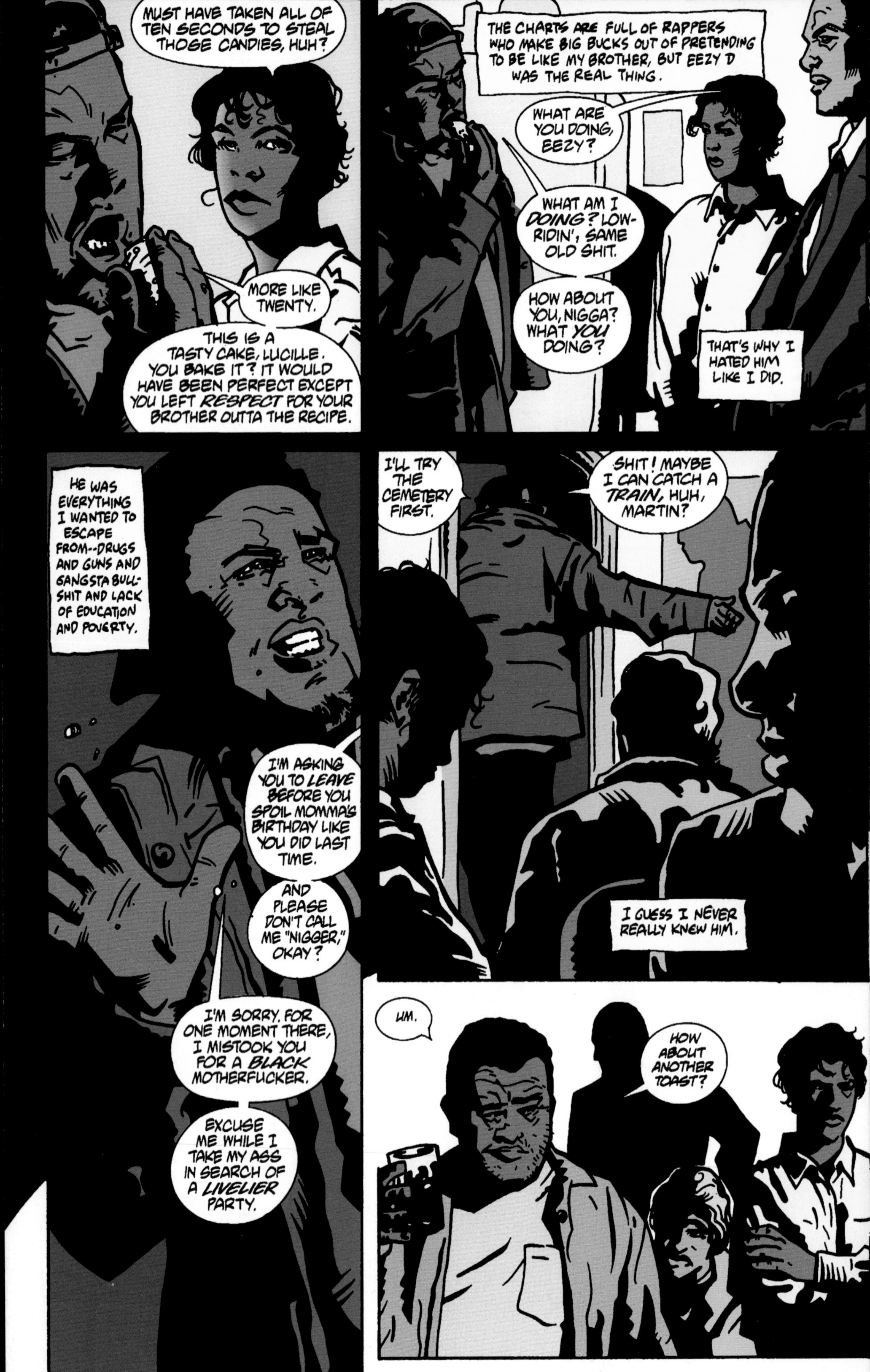
MUST HAVE TAKEN ALL OF TEN SECONDS TO STEAL THOSE CANDIES, HUH?
MORE LIKE TWENTY.
THIS IS A TASTY CAKE, LUCILLE. YOU BAKE IT? IT WOULD HAVE BEEN PERFECT EXCEPT YOU LEFT RESPECT FOR YOUR BROTHER OUTTA THE RECIPE.
THE CHARTS ARE FULL OF RAPPERS WHO MAKE BIG BUCKS OUT OF PRETENDING TO BE LIKE MY BROTHER, BUT EEZY D WAS THE REAL THING.
WHAT ARE YOU DOING, EEZY?
WHAT AM I DOING? LOW-RIDIN', SAME OLD SHIT.
HOW ABOUT YOU, NIGGA? WHAT YOU DOING?
THAT'S WHY I HATED HIM LIKE I DID.
HE WAS EVERYTHING I WANTED TO ESCAPE FROM--DRUGS AND GUNS AND GANGSTA BULL-SHIT AND LACK OF EDUCATION AND POVERTY.
I'M ASKING YOU TO LEAVE BEFORE YOU SPOIL MOMMA'S BIRTHDAY LIKE YOU DID LAST TIME.
AND PLEASE DON'T CALL ME "NIGGER," OKAY?
I'M SORRY. FOR ONE MOMENT THERE, I MISTOOK YOU FOR A BLACK MOTHERFUCKER.
EXCUSE ME WHILE I TAKE MY ASS IN SEARCH OF A LIVELIER PARTY.
I'LL TRY THE CEMETERY FIRST.
SHIT! MAYBE I CAN CATCH A TRAIN, HUH, MARTIN?
I GUESS I NEVER REALLY KNEW HIM.
UM.
HOW ABOUT ANOTHER TOAST?

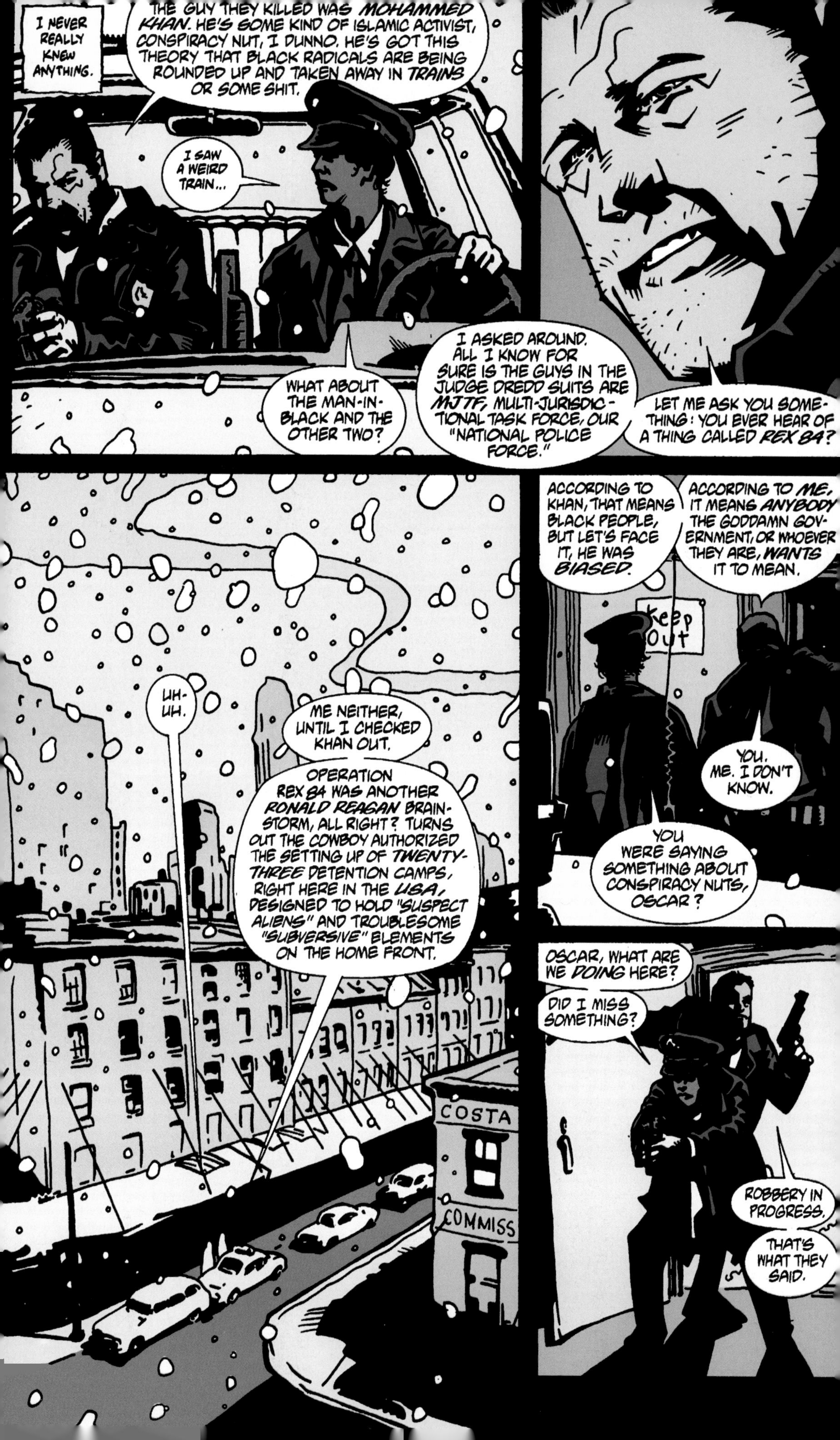

I NEVER REALLY KNEW ANYTHING.
THE GUY THEY KILLED WAS MOHAMMED KHAN. HE'S SOME KIND OF ISLAMIC ACTIVIST, CONSPIRACY NUT, I DUNNO. HE'S GOT THIS THEORY THAT BLACK RADICALS ARE BEING ROUNDED UP AND TAKEN AWAY IN TRAINS OR SOME SHIT.
I SAW A WEIRD TRAIN...
WHAT ABOUT THE MAN-IN-BLACK AND THE OTHER TWO?
I ASKED AROUND. ALL I KNOW FOR SURE IS THE GUYS IN THE JUDGE DREDD SUITS ARE MJTF, MULTI-JURISDICTIONAL TASK FORCE, OUR "NATIONAL POLICE FORCE."
LET ME ASK YOU SOMETHING: YOU EVER HEAR OF A THING CALLED REX 84?
UH-UH.
ME NEITHER, UNTIL I CHECKED KHAN OUT.
OPERATION REX 84 WAS ANOTHER RONALD REAGAN BRAINSTORM, ALL RIGHT? TURNS OUT THE COWBOY AUTHORIZED THE SETTING UP OF TWENTY-THREE DETENTION CAMPS, RIGHT HERE IN THE USA, DESIGNED TO HOLD "SUSPECT ALIENS" AND TROUBLESOME "SUBVERSIVE" ELEMENTS ON THE HOME FRONT.
COSTA
COMMISS
ACCORDING TO KHAN, THAT MEANS BLACK PEOPLE, BUT LET'S FACE IT, HE WAS BIASED.
ACCORDING TO ME, IT MEANS ANYBODY THE GODDAMN GOVERNMENT, OR WHOEVER THEY ARE, WANTS IT TO MEAN.
Keep Out
YOU. ME. I DON'T KNOW.
YOU WERE SAYING SOMETHING ABOUT CONSPIRACY NUTS, OSCAR?
OSCAR, WHAT ARE WE DOING HERE?
DID I MISS SOMETHING?
ROBBERY IN PROGRESS.
THAT'S WHAT THEY SAID.

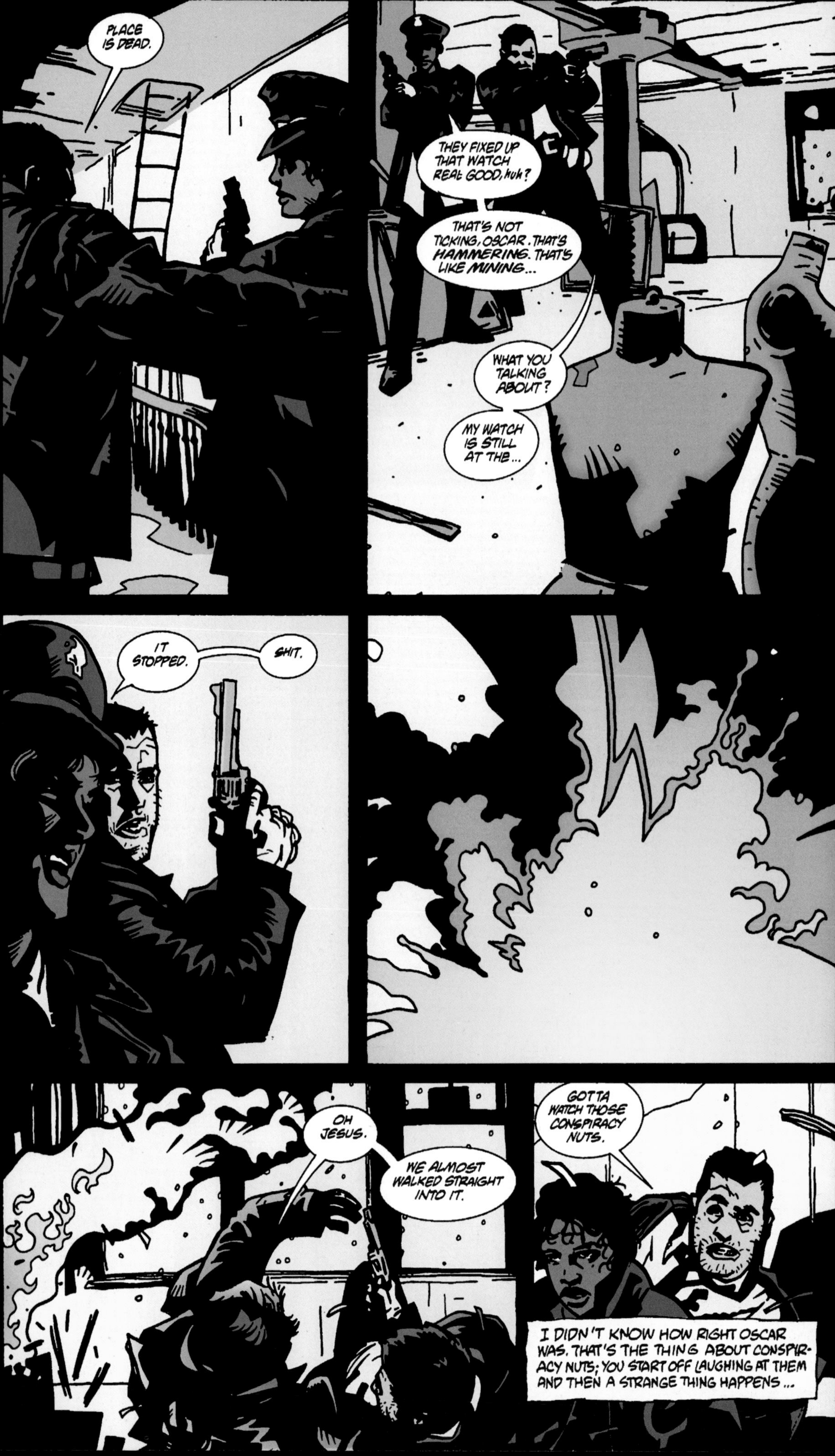
PLACE IS DEAD.
THEY FIXED UP THAT WATCH REAL GOOD, huh?
THAT'S NOT TICKING, OSCAR. THAT'S HAMMERING. THAT'S LIKE MINING...
WHAT YOU TALKING ABOUT?
MY WATCH IS STILL AT THE...
IT STOPPED.
SHIT.
OH JESUS.
WE ALMOST WALKED STRAIGHT INTO IT.
GOTTA WATCH THOSE CONSPIRACY NUTS.
I DIDN'T KNOW HOW RIGHT OSCAR WAS. THAT'S THE THING ABOUT CONSPIRACY NUTS; YOU START OFF LAUGHING AT THEM AND THEN A STRANGE THING HAPPENS...

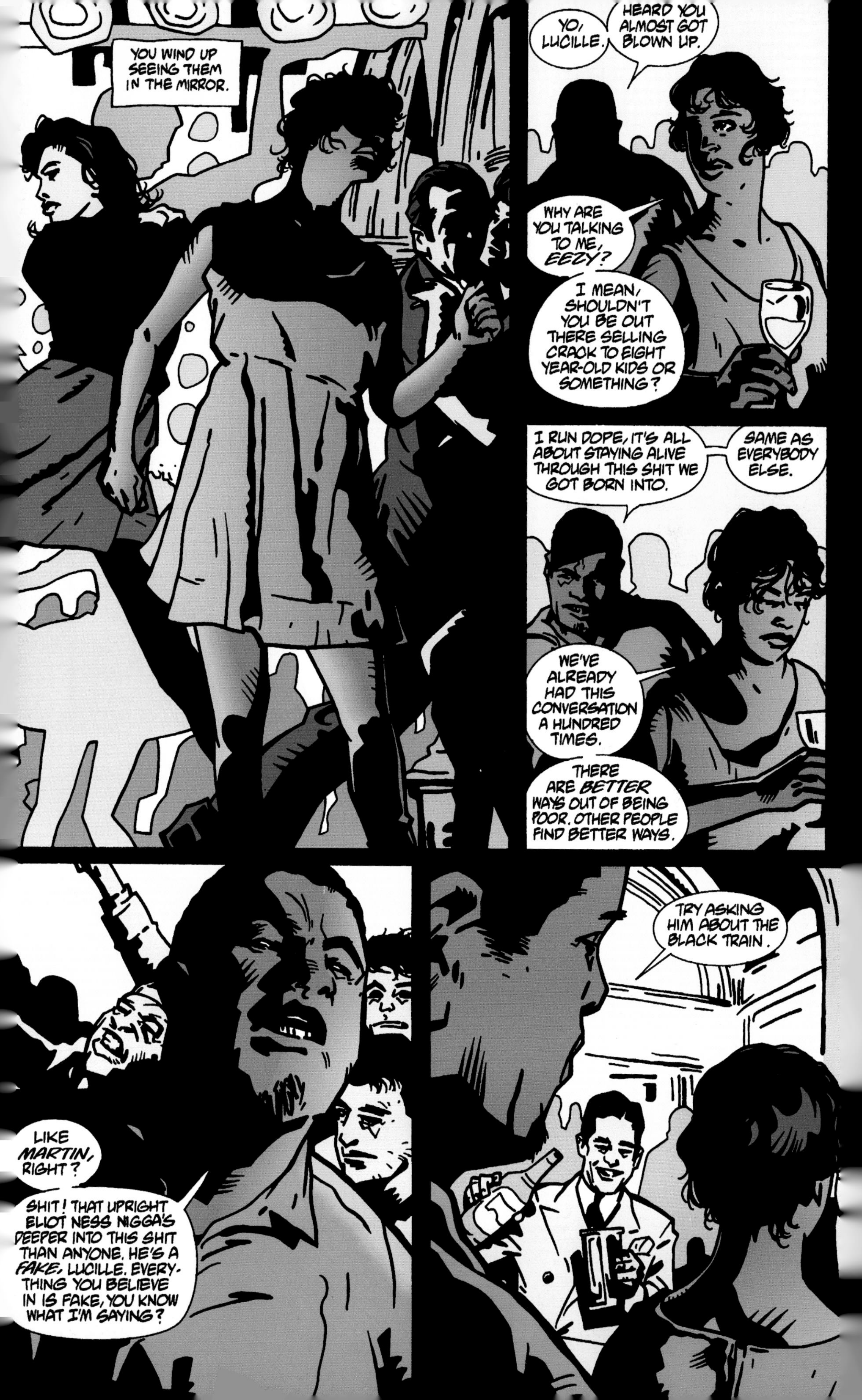
YOU WIND UP SEEING THEM IN THE MIRROR.
YO, LUCILLE.
HEARD YOU ALMOST GOT BLOWN UP.
WHY ARE YOU TALKING TO ME, EEZY?
I MEAN, SHOULDN'T YOU BE OUT THERE SELLING CRACK TO EIGHT YEAR-OLD KIDS OR SOMETHING?
I RUN DOPE, IT'S ALL ABOUT STAYING ALIVE THROUGH THIS SHIT WE GOT BORN INTO.
SAME AS EVERYBODY ELSE.
WE'VE ALREADY HAD THIS CONVERSATION A HUNDRED TIMES.
THERE ARE BETTER WAYS OUT OF BEING POOR. OTHER PEOPLE FIND BETTER WAYS.
LIKE MARTIN, RIGHT?
SHIT! THAT UPRIGHT ELIOT NESS NIGGA'S DEEPER INTO THIS SHIT THAN ANYONE. HE'S A FAKE, LUCILLE. EVERYTHING YOU BELIEVE IN IS FAKE, YOU KNOW WHAT I'M SAYING?
TRY ASKING HIM ABOUT THE BLACK TRAIN.

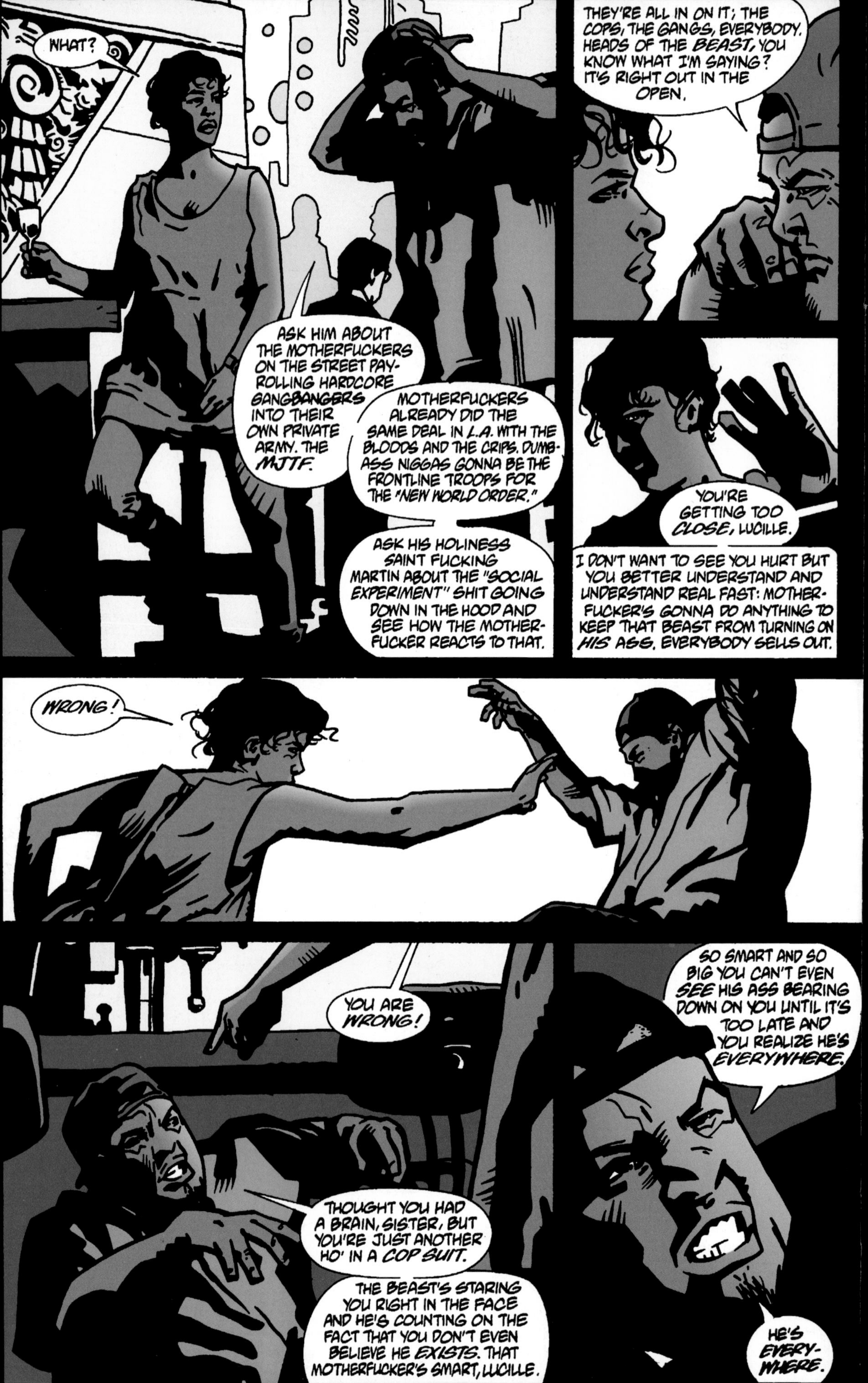
WHAT?
ASK HIM ABOUT THE MOTHERFUCKERS ON THE STREET PAY-ROLLING HARDCORE GANGBANGERS INTO THEIR OWN PRIVATE ARMY. THE MJTF.
MOTHERFUCKERS ALREADY DID THE SAME DEAL IN L.A. WITH THE BLOODS AND THE CRIPS. DUMB-ASS NIGGAS GONNA BE THE FRONTLINE TROOPS FOR THE "NEW WORLD ORDER."
ASK HIS HOLINESS SAINT FUCKING MARTIN ABOUT THE "SOCIAL EXPERIMENT" SHIT GOING DOWN IN THE HOOD AND SEE HOW THE MOTHER-FUCKER REACTS TO THAT.
THEY'RE ALL IN ON IT; THE COPS, THE GANGS, EVERYBODY. HEADS OF THE BEAST, YOU KNOW WHAT I'M SAYING? IT'S RIGHT OUT IN THE OPEN.
YOU'RE GETTING TOO CLOSE, LUCILLE.
I DON'T WANT TO SEE YOU HURT BUT YOU BETTER UNDERSTAND AND UNDERSTAND REAL FAST: MOTHER-FUCKER'S GONNA DO ANYTHING TO KEEP THAT BEAST FROM TURNING ON HIS ASS. EVERYBODY SELLS OUT.
WRONG!
YOU ARE WRONG!
THOUGHT YOU HAD A BRAIN, SISTER, BUT YOU'RE JUST ANOTHER HO' IN A COP SUIT.
THE BEAST'S STARING YOU RIGHT IN THE FACE AND HE'S COUNTING ON THE FACT THAT YOU DON'T EVEN BELIEVE HE EXISTS. THAT MOTHERFUCKER'S SMART, LUCILLE.
SO SMART AND SO BIG YOU CAN'T EVEN SEE HIS ASS BEARING DOWN ON YOU UNTIL IT'S TOO LATE AND YOU REALIZE HE'S EVERYWHERE.
HE'S EVERY-WHERE.

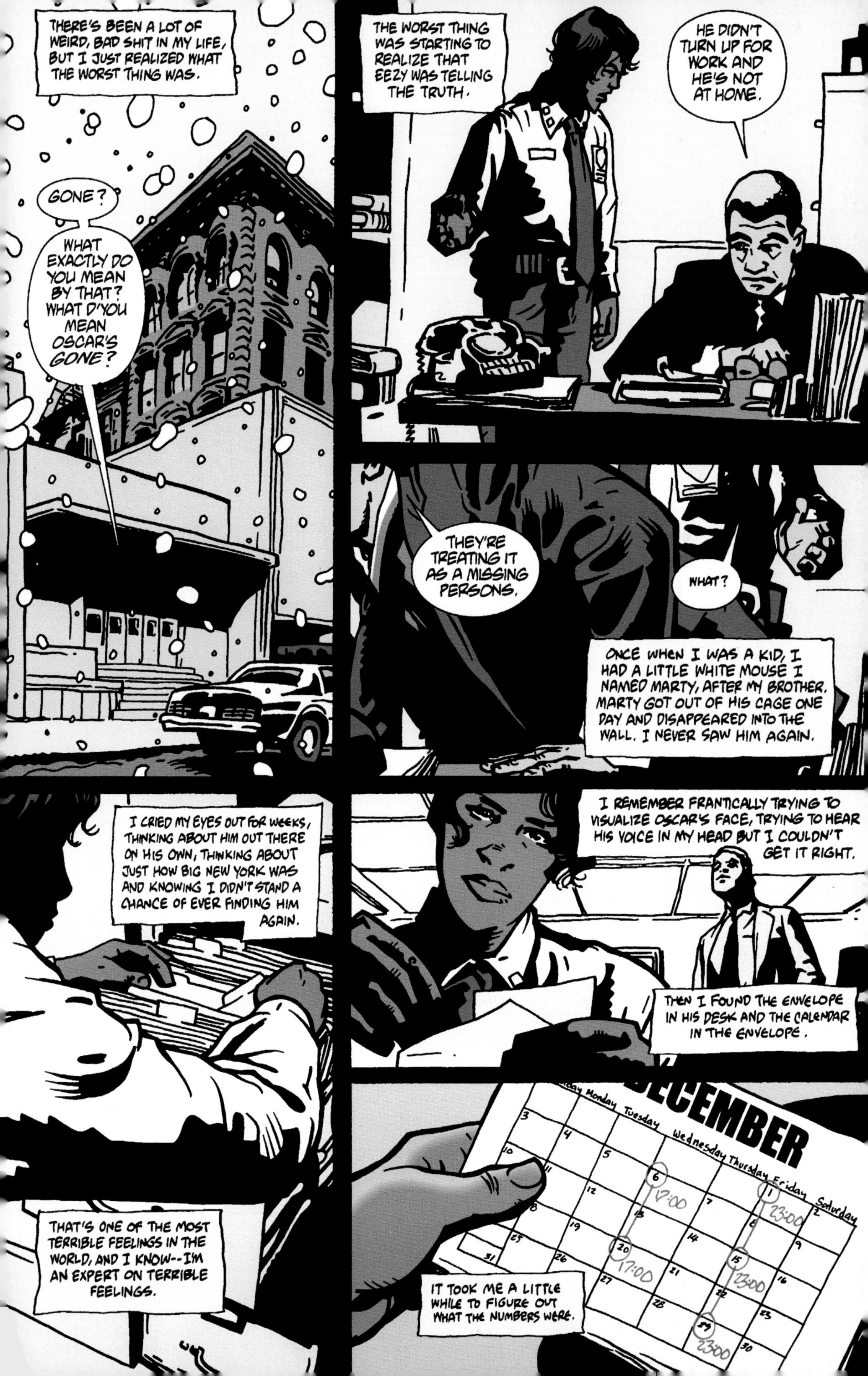
THERE'S BEEN A LOT OF WEIRD, BAD SHIT IN MY LIFE, BUT I JUST REALIZED WHAT THE WORST THING WAS.
GONE?
WHAT EXACTLY DO YOU MEAN BY THAT? WHAT D'YOU MEAN OSCAR'S GONE?
THE WORST THING WAS STARTING TO REALIZE THAT EEZY WAS TELLING THE TRUTH.
HE DIDN'T TURN UP FOR WORK AND HE'S NOT AT HOME.
THEY'RE TREATING IT AS A MISSING PERSONS.
WHAT?
ONCE WHEN I WAS A KID, I HAD A LITTLE WHITE MOUSE I NAMED MARTY, AFTER MY BROTHER. MARTY GOT OUT OF HIS CAGE ONE DAY AND DISAPPEARED INTO THE WALL. I NEVER SAW HIM AGAIN.
I CRIED MY EYES OUT FOR WEEKS, THINKING ABOUT HIM OUT THERE ON HIS OWN, THINKING ABOUT JUST HOW BIG NEW YORK WAS AND KNOWING I DIDN'T STAND A CHANCE OF EVER FINDING HIM AGAIN.
THAT'S ONE OF THE MOST TERRIBLE FEELINGS IN THE WORLD, AND I KNOW--I'M AN EXPERT ON TERRIBLE FEELINGS.
I REMEMBER FRANTICALLY TRYING TO VISUALIZE OSCAR'S FACE, TRYING TO HEAR HIS VOICE IN MY HEAD BUT I COULDN'T GET IT RIGHT.
THEN I FOUND THE ENVELOPE IN HIS DESK AND THE CALENDAR IN THE ENVELOPE.
DECEMBER
Monday Tuesday Wednesday Thursday Friday Saturday
17:00
23:00
IT TOOK ME A LITTLE WHILE TO FIGURE OUT WHAT THE NUMBERS WERE.

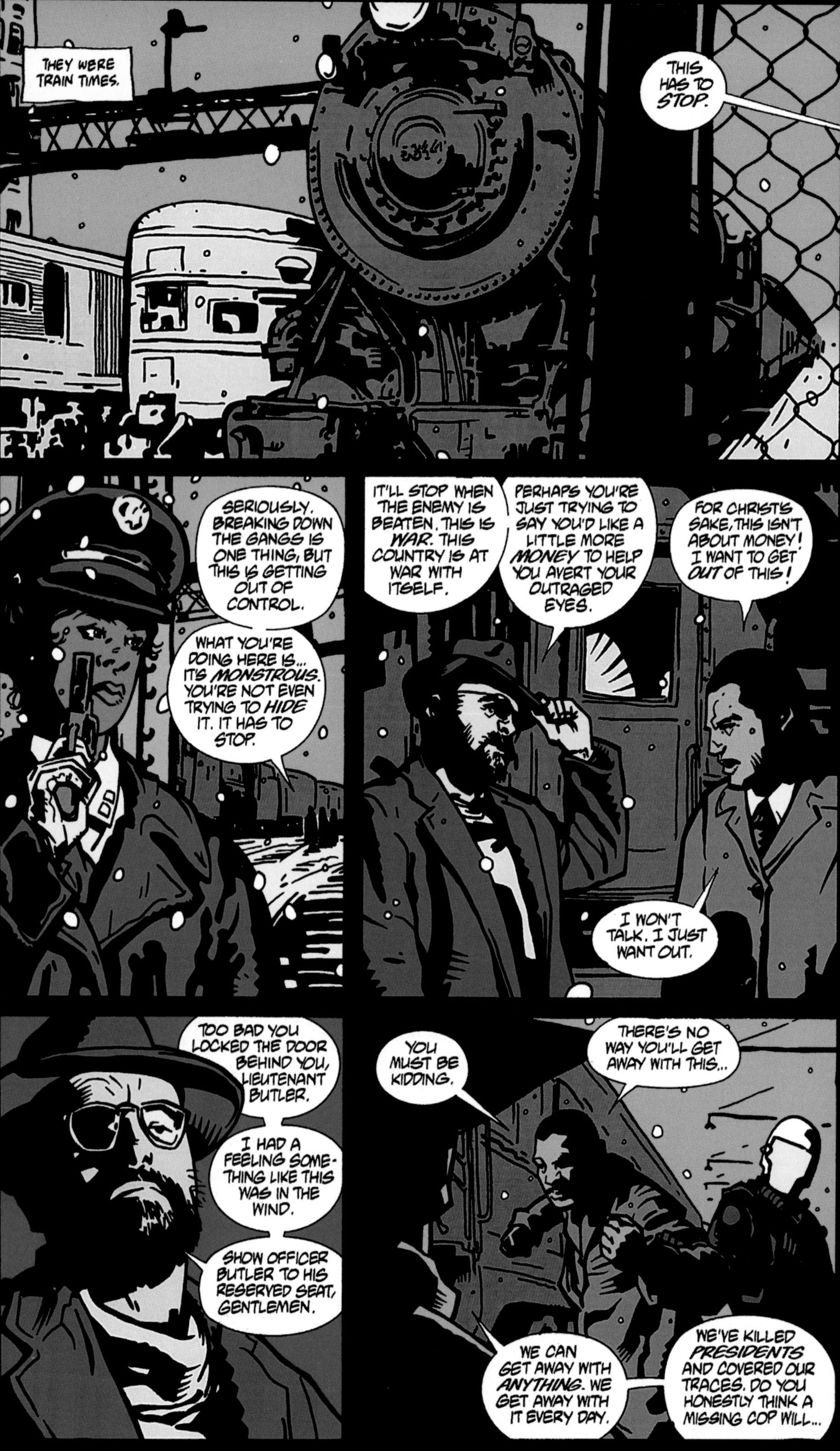
THEY WERE TRAIN TIMES.
THIS HAS TO STOP.
SERIOUSLY. BREAKING DOWN THE GANGS IS ONE THING, BUT THIS IS GETTING OUT OF CONTROL.
WHAT YOU'RE DOING HERE IS... IT'S MONSTROUS. YOU'RE NOT EVEN TRYING TO HIDE IT. IT HAS TO STOP.
IT'LL STOP WHEN THE ENEMY IS BEATEN. THIS IS WAR. THIS COUNTRY IS AT WAR WITH ITSELF.
PERHAPS YOU'RE JUST TRYING TO SAY YOU'D LIKE A LITTLE MORE MONEY TO HELP YOU AVERT YOUR OUTRAGED EYES.
FOR CHRIST'S SAKE, THIS ISN'T ABOUT MONEY! I WANT TO GET OUT OF THIS!
I WON'T TALK. I JUST WANT OUT.
TOO BAD YOU LOCKED THE DOOR BEHIND YOU, LIEUTENANT BUTLER.
I HAD A FEELING SOME-THING LIKE THIS WAS IN THE WIND.
SHOW OFFICER BUTLER TO HIS RESERVED SEAT, GENTLEMEN.
YOU MUST BE KIDDING.
THERE'S NO WAY YOU'LL GET AWAY WITH THIS...
WE CAN GET AWAY WITH ANYTHING. WE GET AWAY WITH IT EVERY DAY.
WE'VE KILLED PRESIDENTS AND COVERED OUR TRACES. DO YOU HONESTLY THINK A MISSING COP WILL...

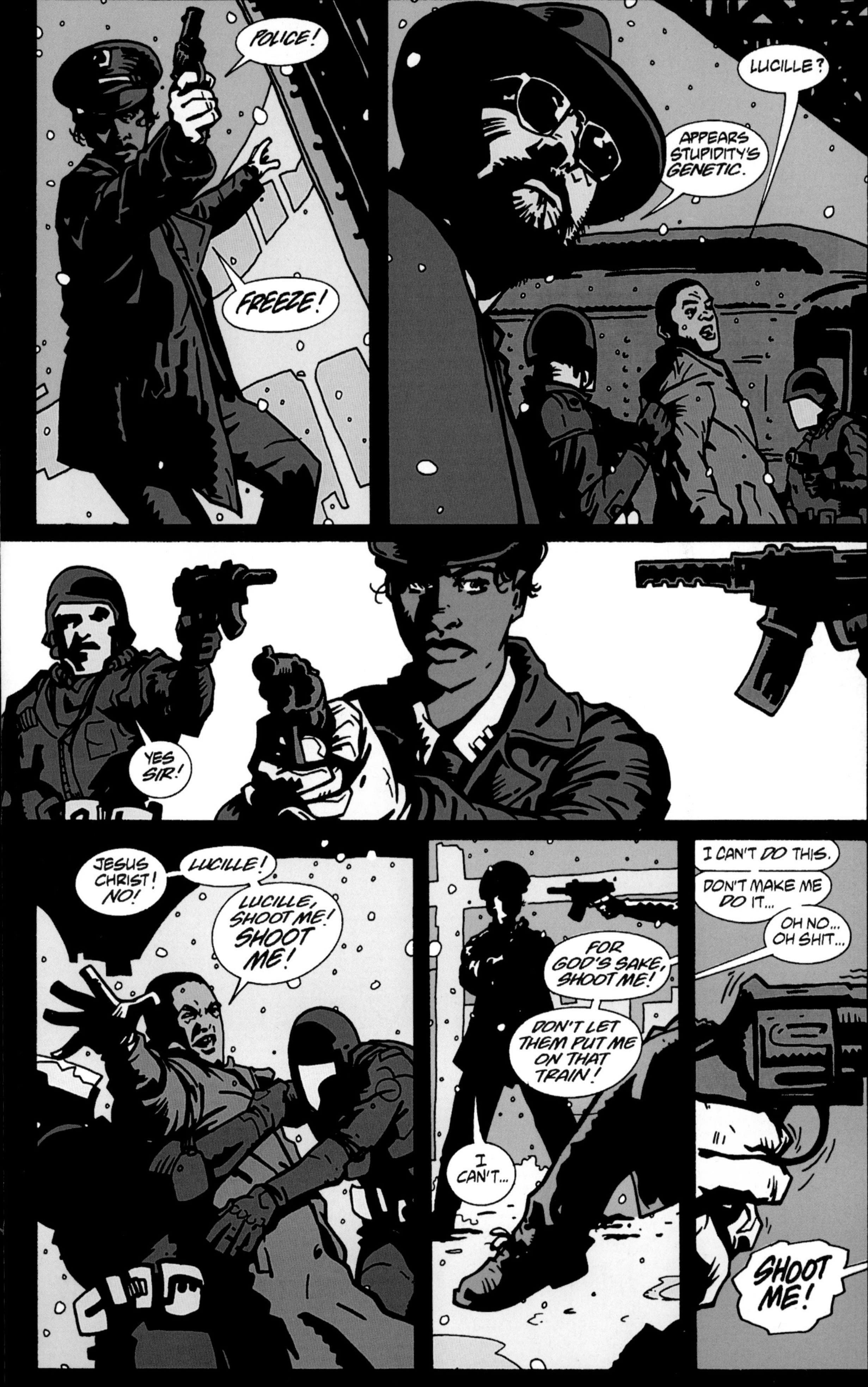
POLICE!
FREEZE!
LUCILLE?
APPEARS STUPIDITY'S GENETIC.
YES SIR!
JESUS CHRIST! NO!
LUCILLE!
LUCILLE, SHOOT ME! SHOOT ME!
FOR GOD'S SAKE, SHOOT ME!
DON'T LET THEM PUT ME ON THAT TRAIN!
I CAN'T...
I CAN'T DO THIS.
DON'T MAKE ME DO IT...
OH NO... OH SHIT...
SHOOT ME!

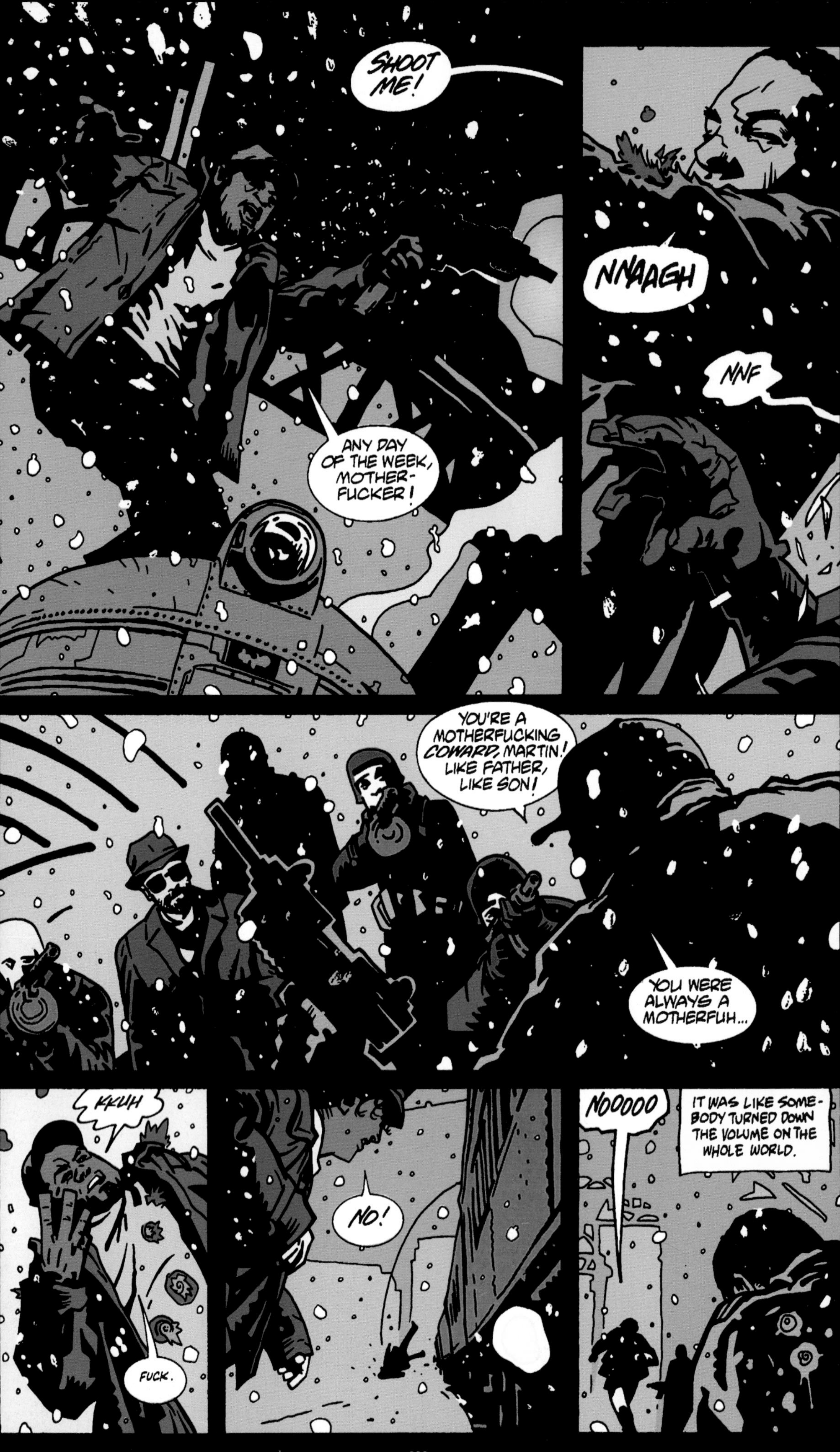
SHOOT ME!
ANY DAY OF THE WEEK, MOTHER-FUCKER!
NNAAGH
NNF
YOU'RE A MOTHERFUCKING COWARD, MARTIN! LIKE FATHER, LIKE SON!
YOU WERE ALWAYS A MOTHERFUH...
KKUH
FUCK.
NO!
NOOOOO
IT WAS LIKE SOMEBODY TURNED DOWN THE VOLUME ON THE WHOLE WORLD.

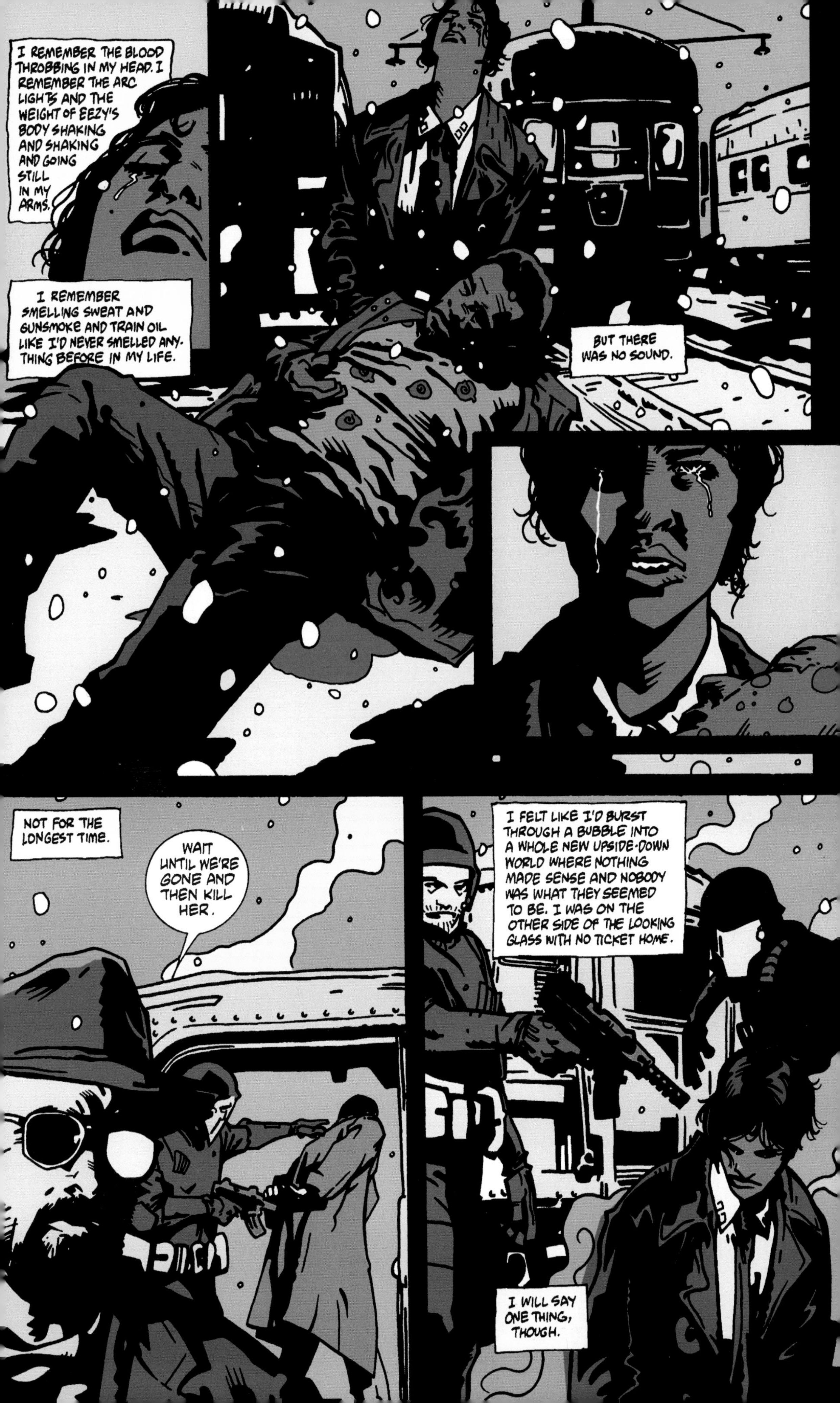
I REMEMBER THE BLOOD THROBBING IN MY HEAD. I REMEMBER THE ARC LIGHTS AND THE WEIGHT OF EEZY'S BODY SHAKING AND SHAKING AND GOING STILL IN MY ARMS.
I REMEMBER SMELLING SWEAT AND GUNSMOKE AND TRAIN OIL LIKE I'D NEVER SMELLED ANY-THING BEFORE IN MY LIFE.
BUT THERE WAS NO SOUND.
NOT FOR THE LONGEST TIME.
WAIT UNTIL WE'RE GONE AND THEN KILL HER.
I FELT LIKE I'D BURST THROUGH A BUBBLE INTO A WHOLE NEW UPSIDE-DOWN WORLD WHERE NOTHING MADE SENSE AND NOBODY WAS WHAT THEY SEEMED TO BE. I WAS ON THE OTHER SIDE OF THE LOOKING GLASS WITH NO TICKET HOME.
I WILL SAY ONE THING, THOUGH.

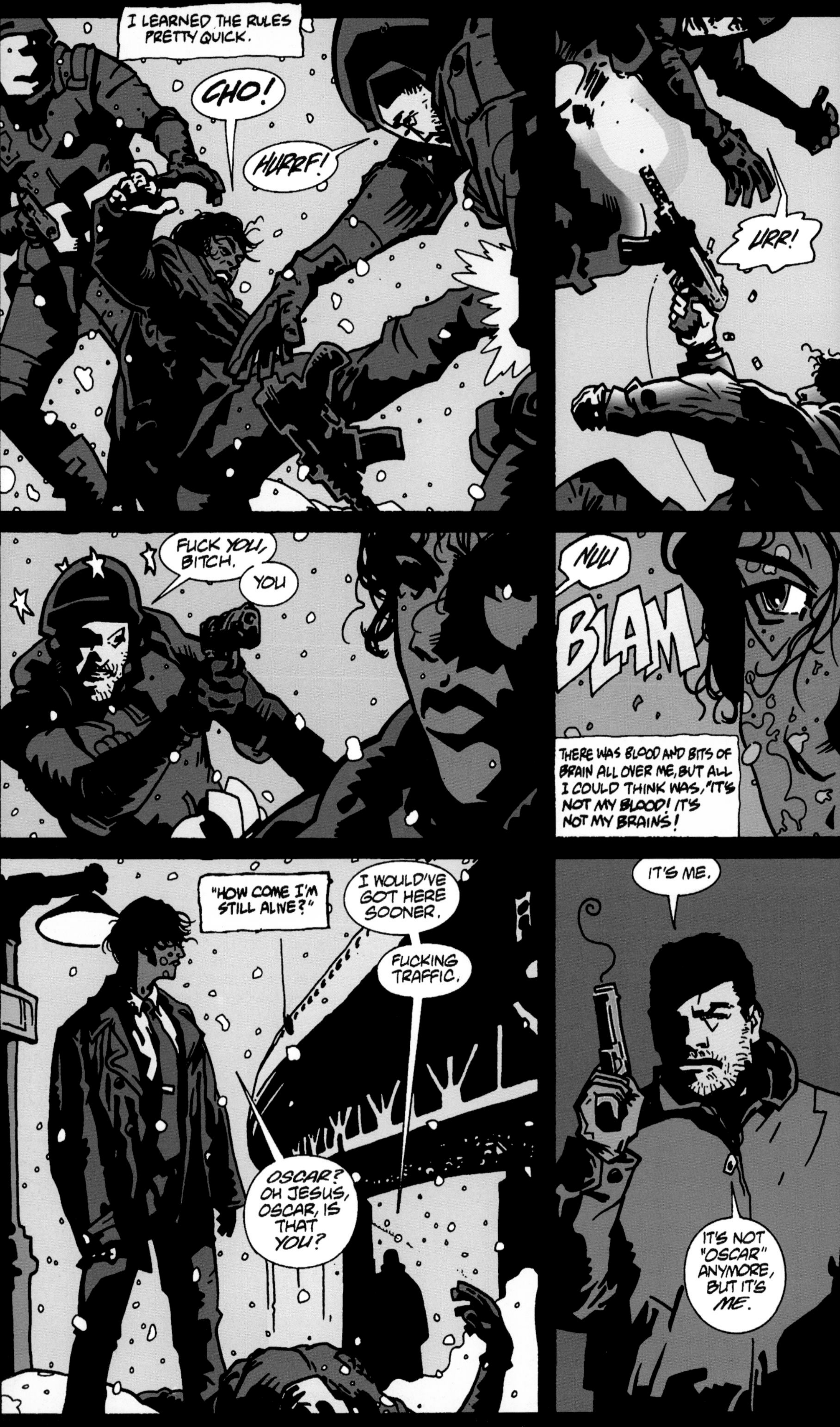
I LEARNED THE RULES PRETTY QUICK.
CHO!
HURRF!
URR!
FUCK YOU, BITCH.
YOU
NUU
BLAM
THERE WAS BLOOD AND BITS OF BRAIN ALL OVER ME, BUT ALL I COULD THINK WAS, "IT'S NOT MY BLOOD! IT'S NOT MY BRAINS!
"HOW COME I'M STILL ALIVE?"
I WOULD'VE GOT HERE SOONER.
FUCKING TRAFFIC.
OSCAR? OH JESUS, OSCAR, IS THAT YOU?
IT'S ME.
IT'S NOT "OSCAR" ANYMORE, BUT IT'S ME.

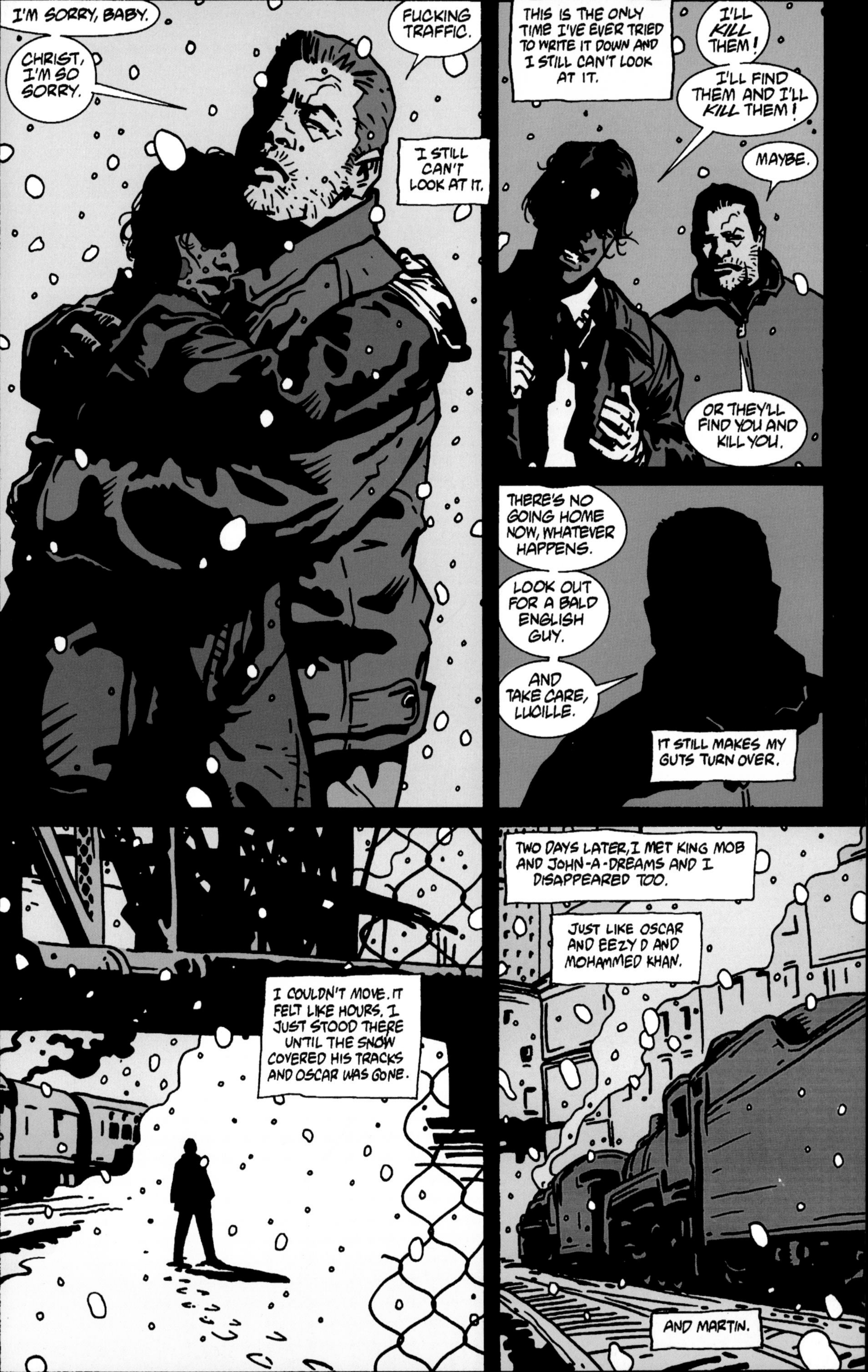
I'M SORRY, BABY.
CHRIST, I'M SO SORRY.
FUCKING TRAFFIC.
I STILL CAN'T LOOK AT IT.
THIS IS THE ONLY TIME I'VE EVER TRIED TO WRITE IT DOWN AND I STILL CAN'T LOOK AT IT.
I'LL KILL THEM!
I'LL FIND THEM AND I'LL KILL THEM!
MAYBE.
OR THEY'LL FIND YOU AND KILL YOU.
THERE'S NO GOING HOME NOW, WHATEVER HAPPENS.
LOOK OUT FOR A BALD ENGLISH GUY.
AND TAKE CARE, LUCILLE.
IT STILL MAKES MY GUTS TURN OVER.
I COULDN'T MOVE. IT FELT LIKE HOURS. I JUST STOOD THERE UNTIL THE SNOW COVERED HIS TRACKS AND OSCAR WAS GONE.
TWO DAYS LATER, I MET KING MOB AND JOHN-A-DREAMS AND I DISAPPEARED TOO.
JUST LIKE OSCAR AND EEZY D AND MOHAMMED KHAN.
AND MARTIN.

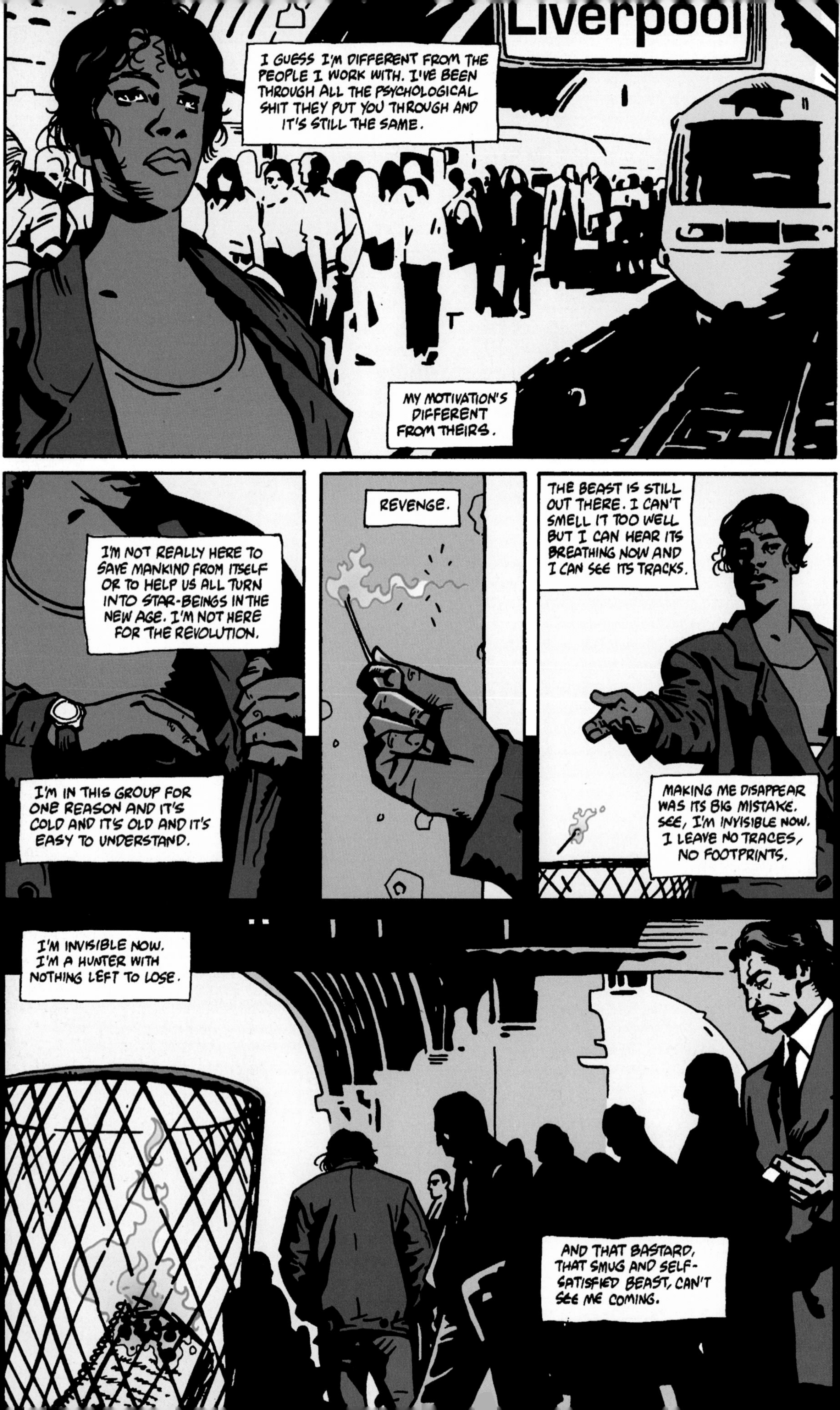
Liverpool
I GUESS I'M DIFFERENT FROM THE PEOPLE I WORK WITH. I'VE BEEN THROUGH ALL THE PSYCHOLOGICAL SHIT THEY PUT YOU THROUGH AND IT'S STILL THE SAME.
MY MOTIVATION'S DIFFERENT FROM THEIRS.
I'M NOT REALLY HERE TO SAVE MANKIND FROM ITSELF OR TO HELP US ALL TURN INTO STAR-BEINGS IN THE NEW AGE. I'M NOT HERE FOR THE REVOLUTION.
I'M IN THIS GROUP FOR ONE REASON AND IT'S COLD AND IT'S OLD AND IT'S EASY TO UNDERSTAND.
REVENGE.
THE BEAST IS STILL OUT THERE. I CAN'T SMELL IT TOO WELL BUT I CAN HEAR ITS BREATHING NOW AND I CAN SEE ITS TRACKS.
MAKING ME DISAPPEAR WAS ITS BIG MISTAKE. SEE, I'M INVISIBLE NOW. I LEAVE NO TRACES, NO FOOTPRINTS.
I'M INVISIBLE NOW. I'M A HUNTER WITH NOTHING LEFT TO LOSE.
AND THAT BASTARD, THAT SMUG AND SELF-SATISFIED BEAST, CAN'T SEE ME COMING.

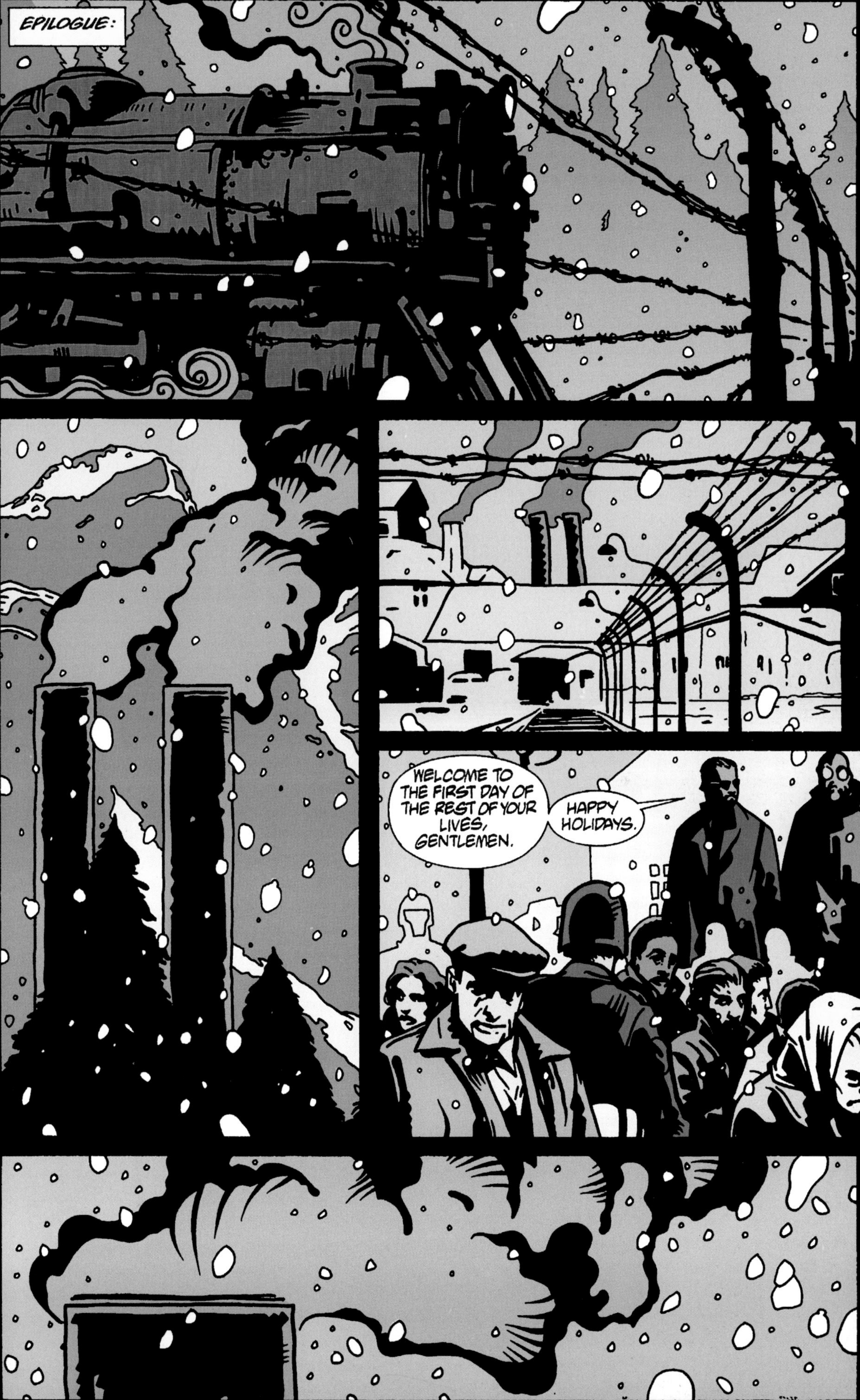
EPILOGUE:
WELCOME TO THE FIRST DAY OF THE REST OF YOUR LIVES, GENTLEMEN.
HAPPY HOLIDAYS.

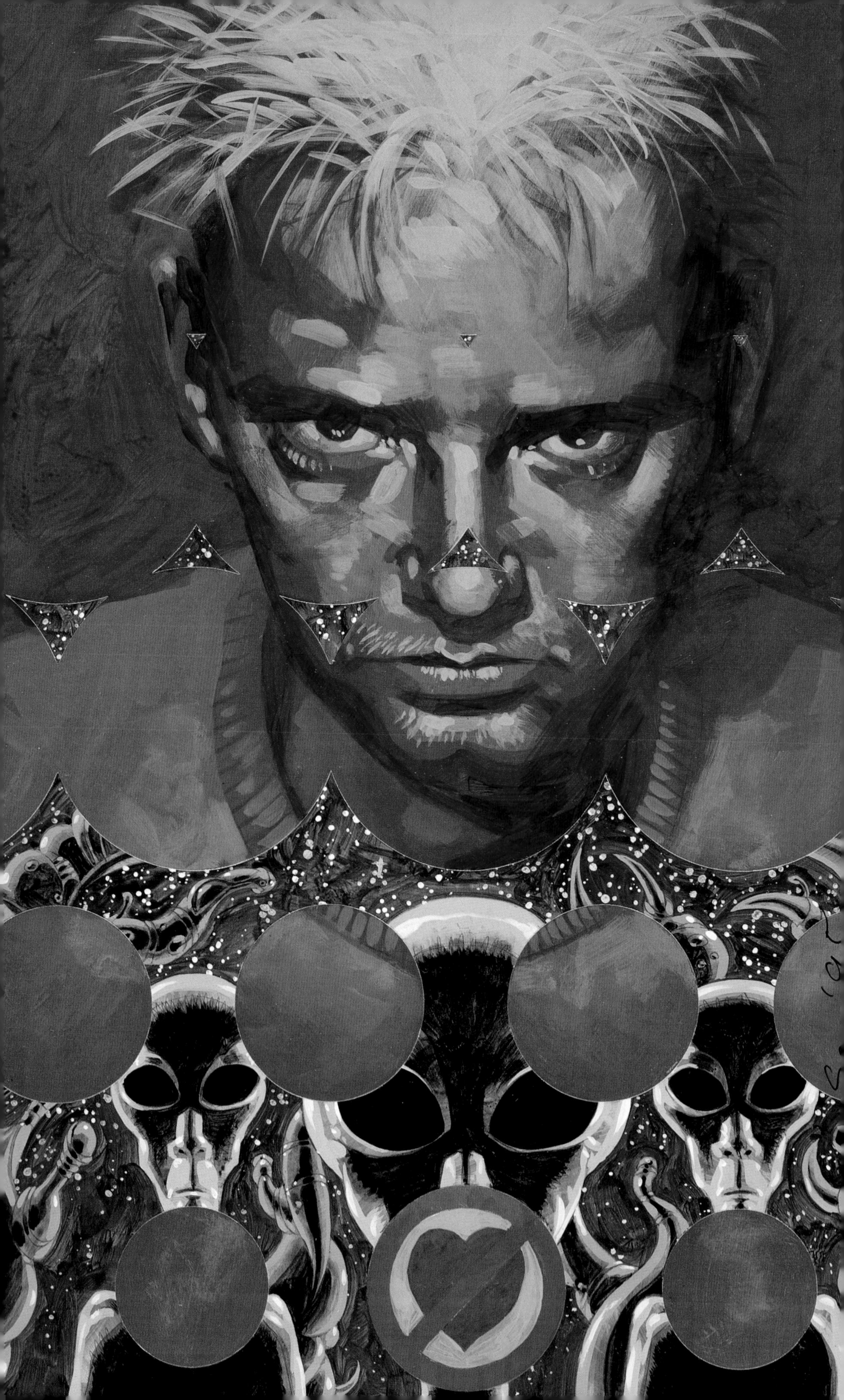

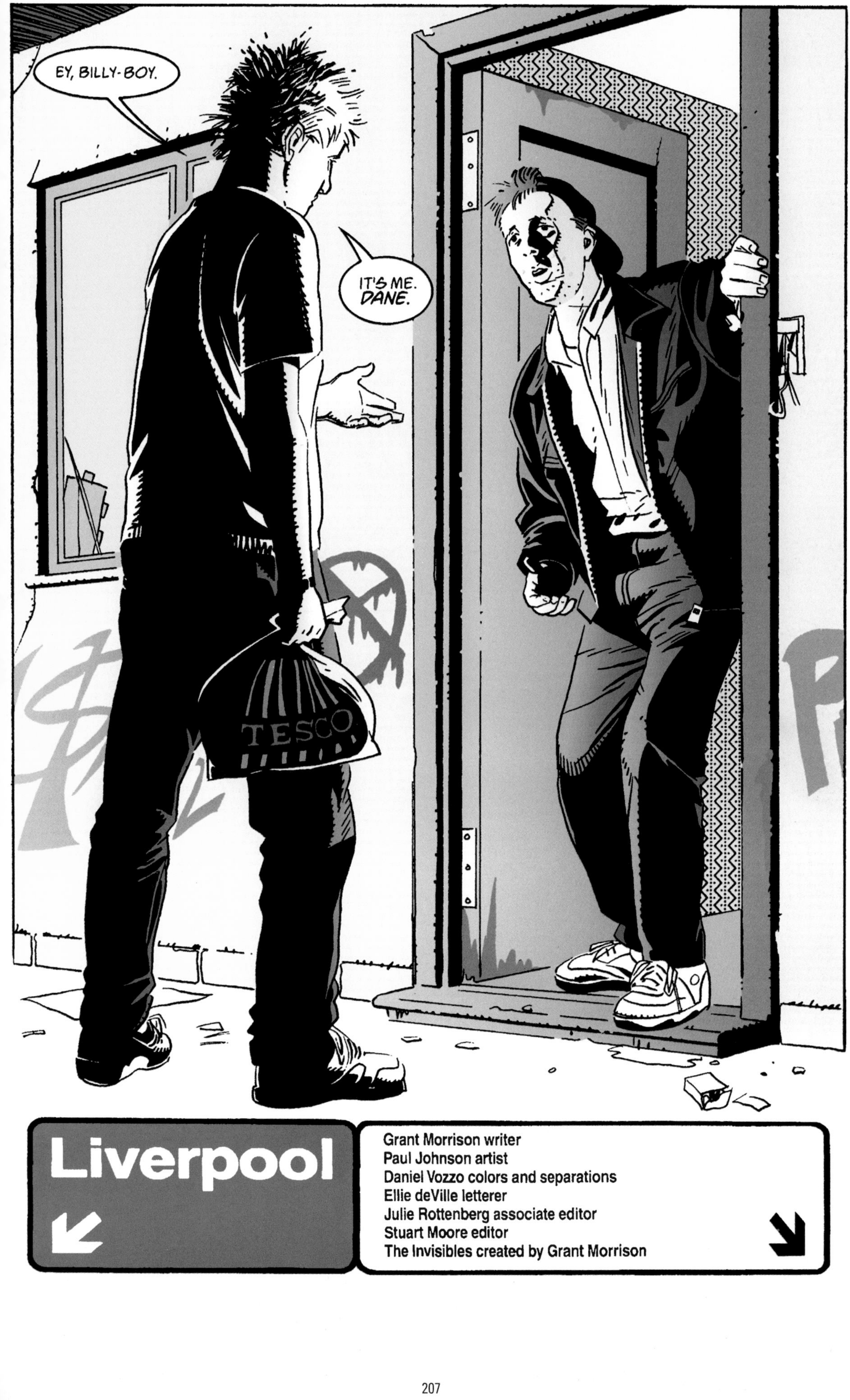
EY, BILLY-BOY.
IT'S ME. DANE.
TESCO

Liverpool

Grant Morrison writer
Paul Johnson artist
Daniel Vozzo colors and separations
Ellie deVille letterer
Julie Rottenberg associate editor
Stuart Moore editor
The Invisibles created by Grant Morrison

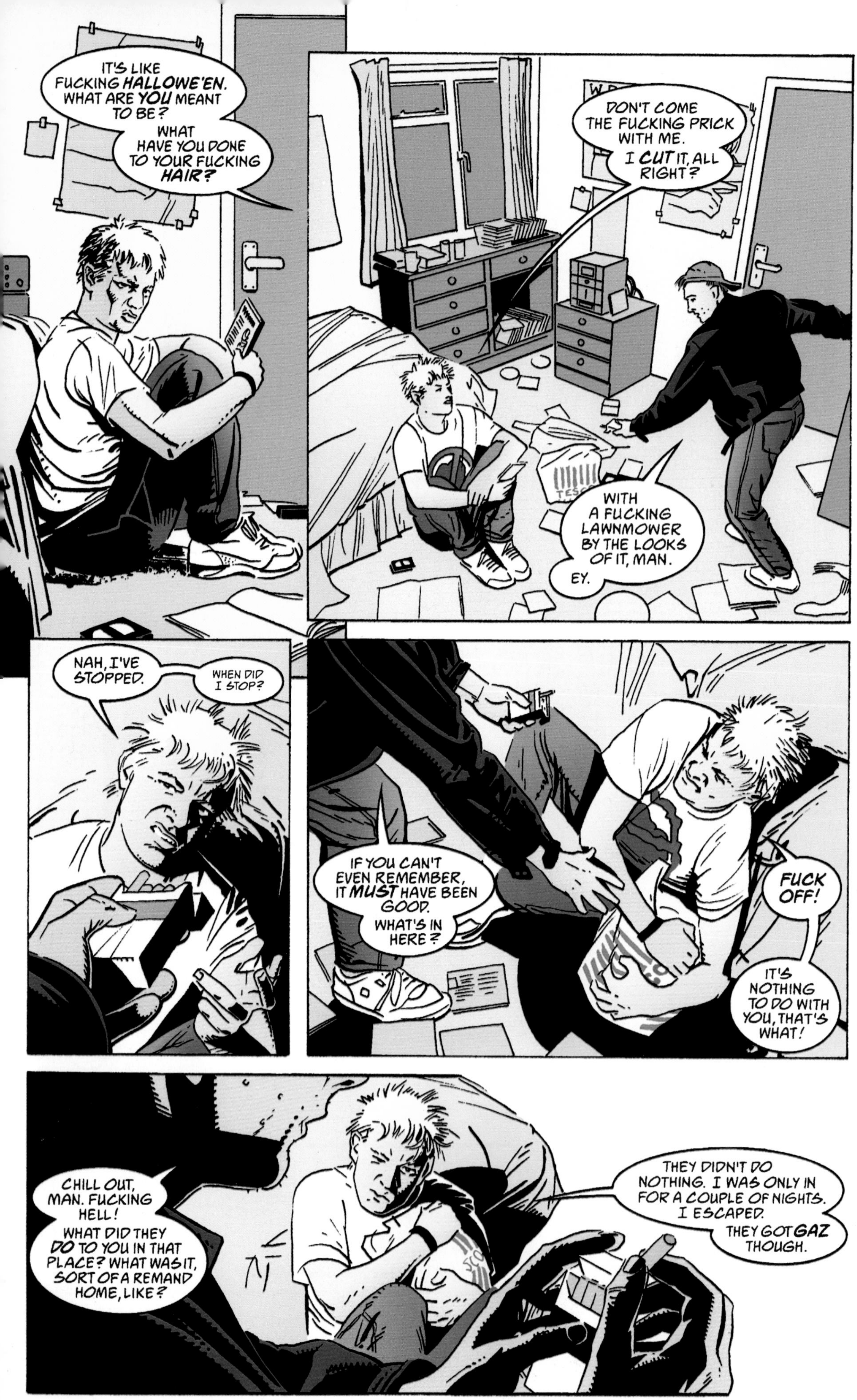
IT'S LIKE FUCKING HALLOWE'EN. WHAT ARE YOU MEANT TO BE?
WHAT HAVE YOU DONE TO YOUR FUCKING HAIR?
DON'T COME THE FUCKING PRICK WITH ME.
I CUT IT, ALL RIGHT?
WITH A FUCKING LAWNMOWER BY THE LOOKS OF IT, MAN.
EY.
NAH, I'VE STOPPED.
WHEN DID I STOP?
IF YOU CAN'T EVEN REMEMBER, IT MUST HAVE BEEN GOOD.
WHAT'S IN HERE?
FUCK OFF!
IT'S NOTHING TO DO WITH YOU, THAT'S WHAT!
CHILL OUT, MAN. FUCKING HELL!
WHAT DID THEY DO TO YOU IN THAT PLACE? WHAT WAS IT, SORT OF A REMAND HOME, LIKE?
THEY DIDN'T DO NOTHING. I WAS ONLY IN FOR A COUPLE OF NIGHTS. I ESCAPED.
THEY GOT GAZ THOUGH.

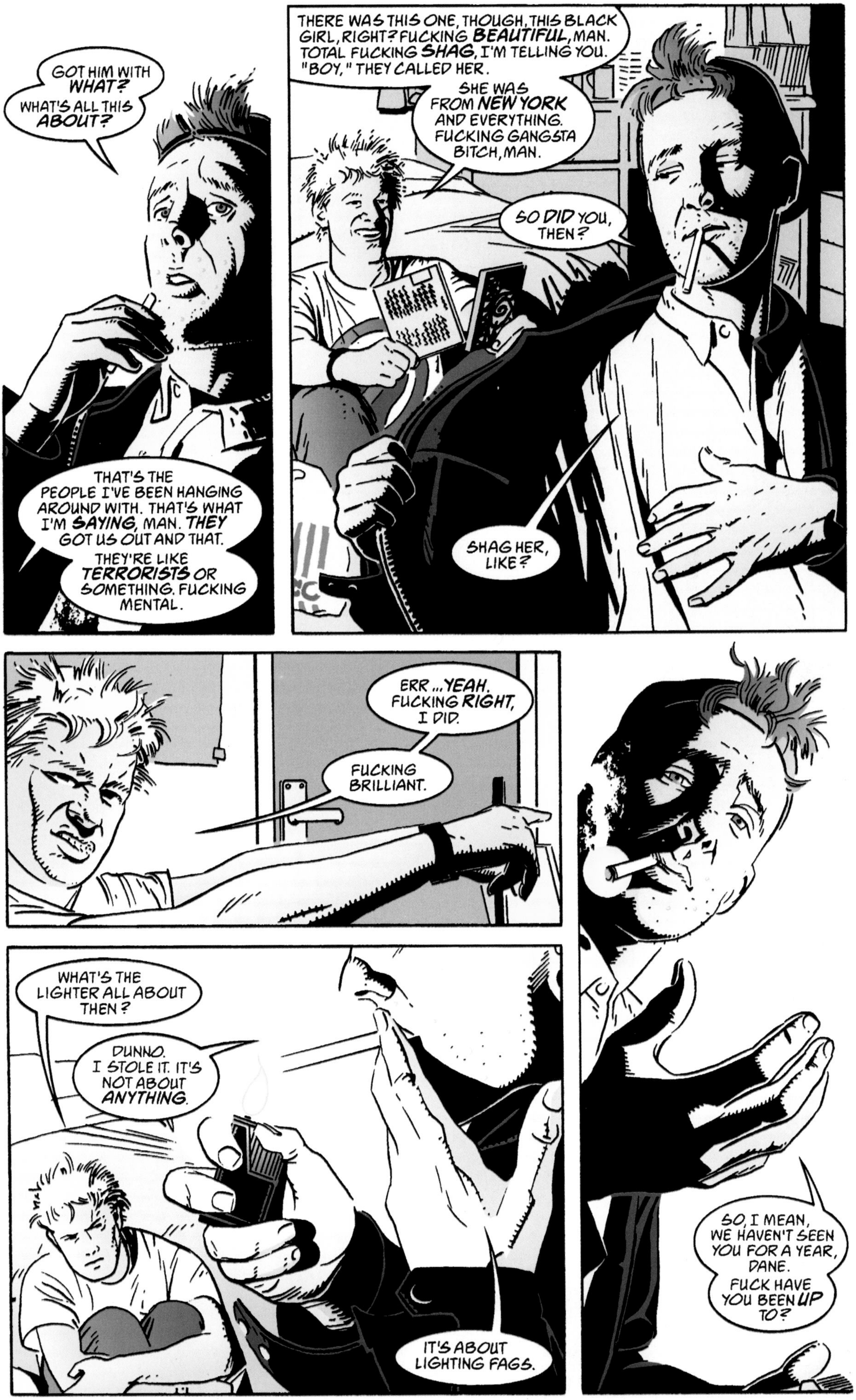
GOT HIM WITH WHAT? WHAT'S ALL THIS ABOUT?
THAT'S THE PEOPLE I'VE BEEN HANGING AROUND WITH. THAT'S WHAT I'M SAYING, MAN. THEY GOT US OUT AND THAT.
THEY'RE LIKE TERRORISTS OR SOMETHING. FUCKING MENTAL.
THERE WAS THIS ONE, THOUGH, THIS BLACK GIRL, RIGHT? FUCKING BEAUTIFUL, MAN. TOTAL FUCKING SHAG, I'M TELLING YOU. "BOY," THEY CALLED HER.
SHE WAS FROM NEW YORK AND EVERYTHING. FUCKING GANGSTA BITCH, MAN.
SO DID YOU, THEN?
SHAG HER, LIKE?
ERR ...YEAH. FUCKING RIGHT, I DID.
FUCKING BRILLIANT.
SO, I MEAN, WE HAVEN'T SEEN YOU FOR A YEAR, DANE.
FUCK HAVE YOU BEEN UP TO?
WHAT'S THE LIGHTER ALL ABOUT THEN?
DUNNO. I STOLE IT. IT'S NOT ABOUT ANYTHING.
IT'S ABOUT LIGHTING FAGS.

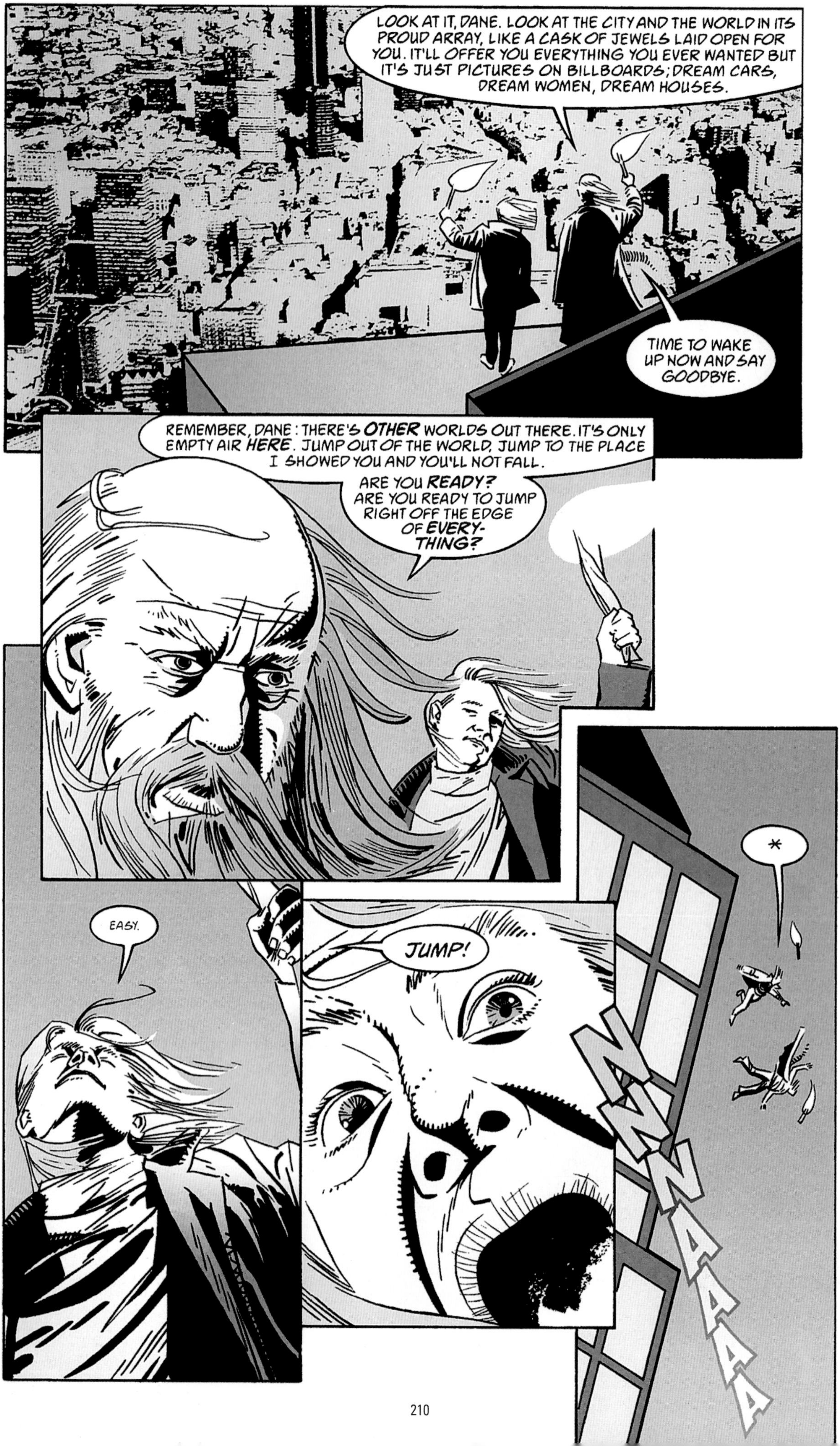
LOOK AT IT, DANE. LOOK AT THE CITY AND THE WORLD IN ITS PROUD ARRAY, LIKE A CASK OF JEWELS LAID OPEN FOR YOU. IT'LL OFFER YOU EVERYTHING YOU EVER WANTED BUT IT'S JUST PICTURES ON BILLBOARDS; DREAM CARS, DREAM WOMEN, DREAM HOUSES.
TIME TO WAKE UP NOW AND SAY GOODBYE.
REMEMBER, DANE: THERE'S OTHER WORLDS OUT THERE. IT'S ONLY EMPTY AIR HERE. JUMP OUT OF THE WORLD, JUMP TO THE PLACE I SHOWED YOU AND YOU'LL NOT FALL.
ARE YOU READY? ARE YOU READY TO JUMP RIGHT OFF THE EDGE OF EVERY-THING?
*
EASY.
JUMP!
NNNZAAAAA

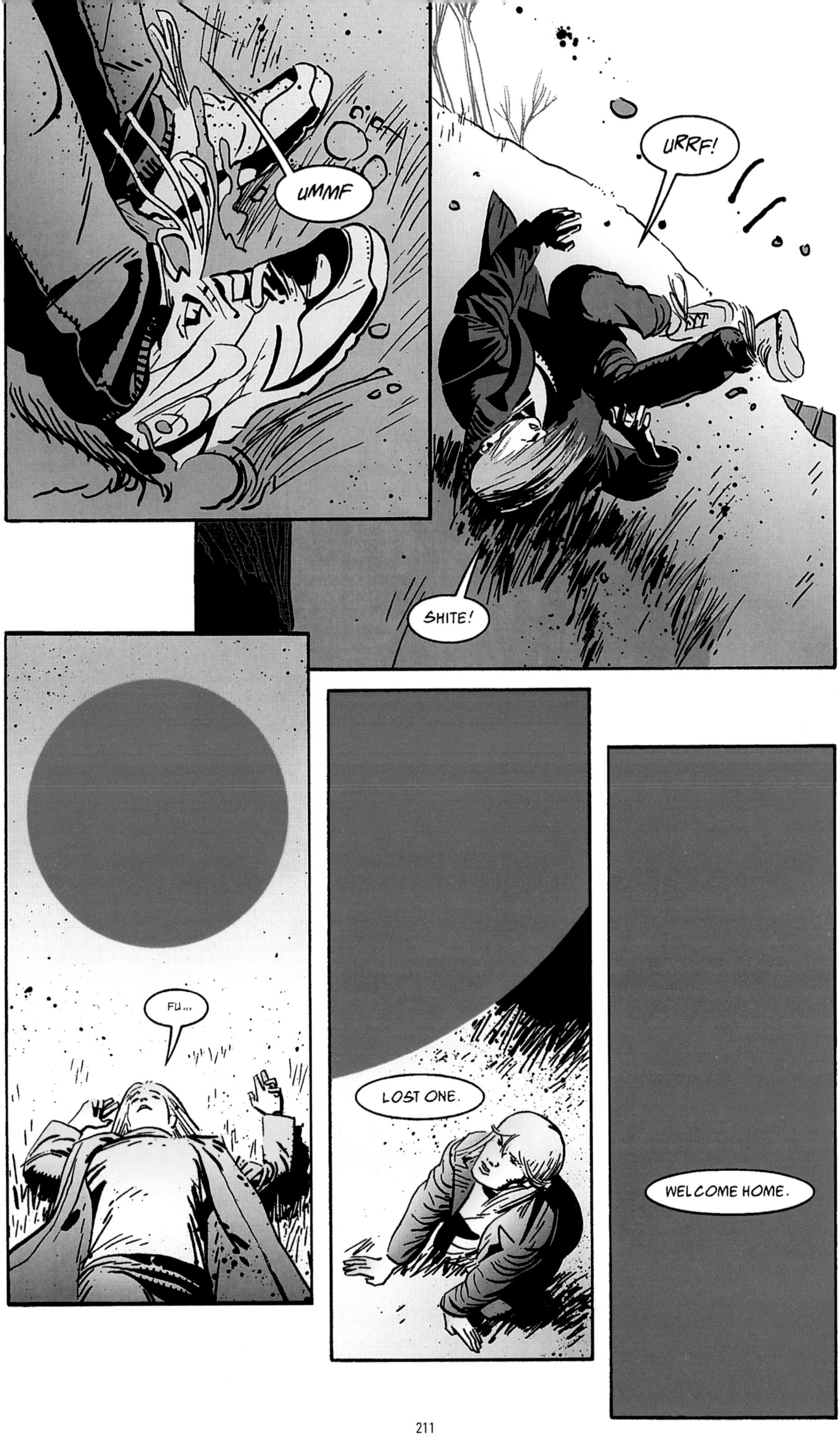
UMMF
URRF!
SHITE!
FU...
LOST ONE.
WELCOME HOME.

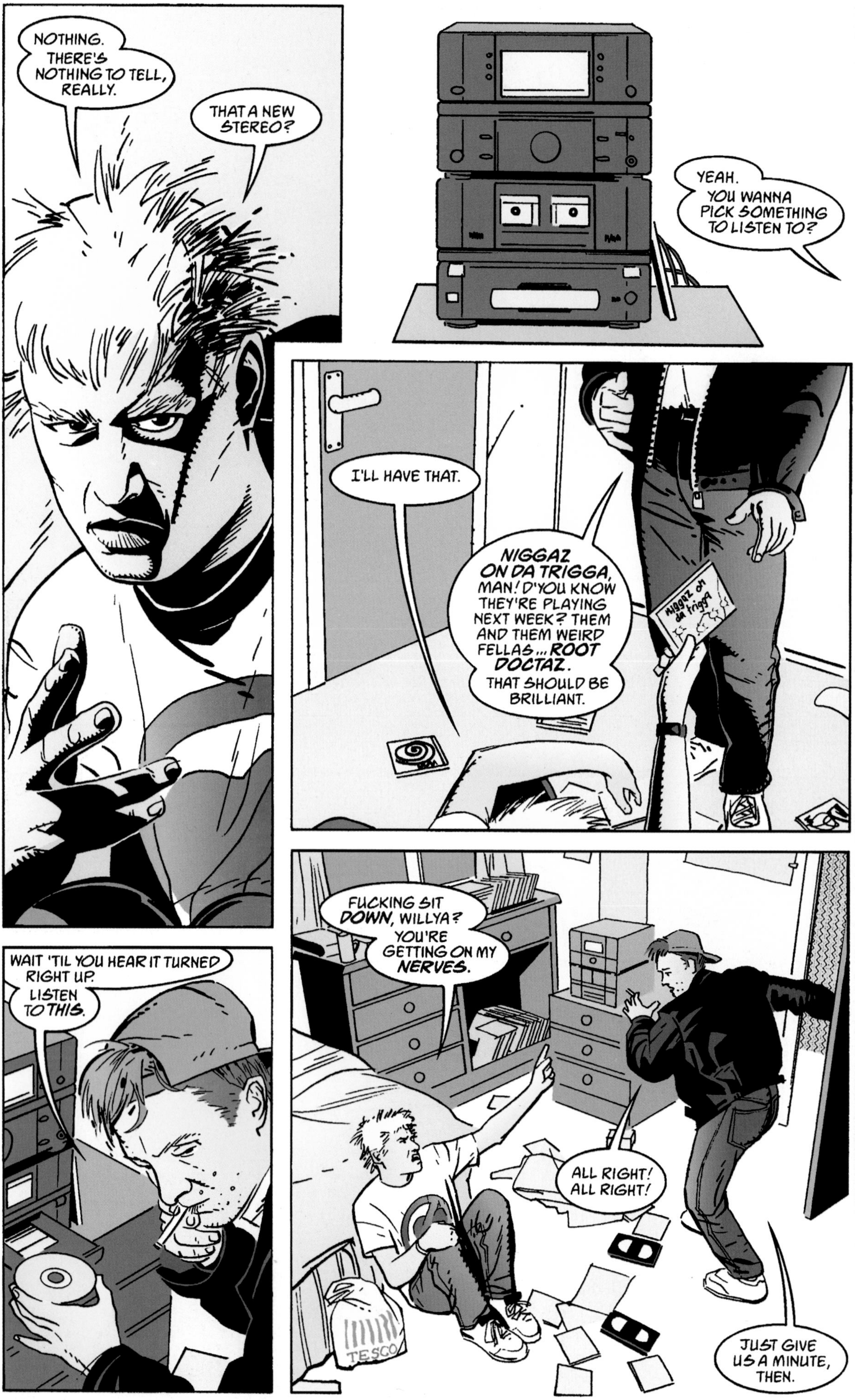
NOTHING. THERE'S NOTHING TO TELL, REALLY.
THAT A NEW STEREO?
YEAH. YOU WANNA PICK SOMETHING TO LISTEN TO?
I'LL HAVE THAT.
NIGGAZ ON DA TRIGGA, MAN! D'YOU KNOW THEY'RE PLAYING NEXT WEEK? THEM AND THEM WEIRD FELLAS... ROOT DOCTAZ. THAT SHOULD BE BRILLIANT.
niggaz on da trigga
WAIT 'TIL YOU HEAR IT TURNED RIGHT UP. LISTEN TO THIS.
FUCKING SIT DOWN, WILLYA? YOU'RE GETTING ON MY NERVES.
ALL RIGHT! ALL RIGHT!
JUST GIVE US A MINUTE, THEN.
TESCO

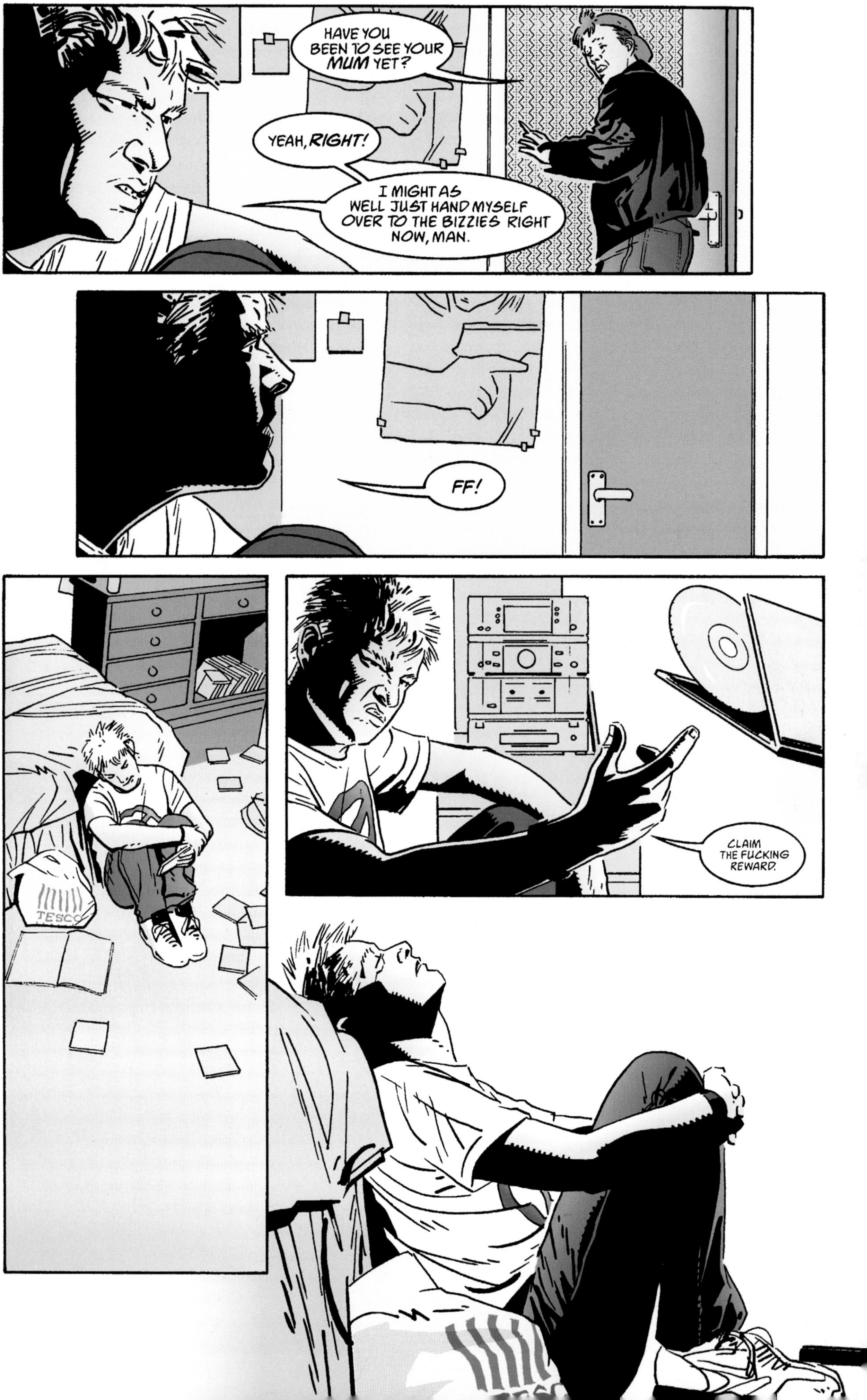
HAVE YOU BEEN TO SEE YOUR MUM YET?
YEAH, RIGHT!
I MIGHT AS WELL JUST HAND MYSELF OVER TO THE BIZZIES RIGHT NOW, MAN.
FF!
TESCO
CLAIM THE FUCKING REWARD.

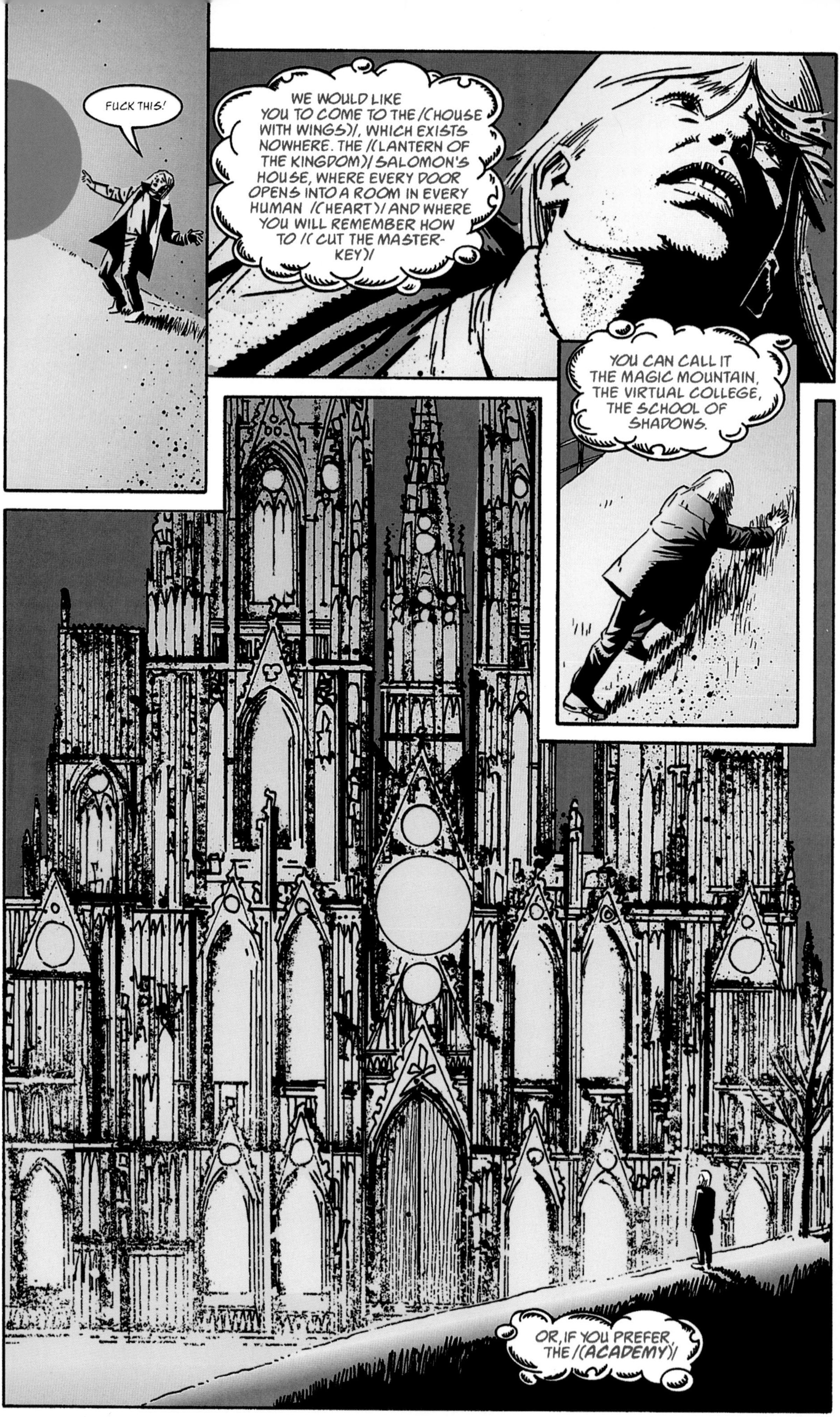
FUCK THIS!
WE WOULD LIKE YOU TO COME TO THE /(HOUSE WITH WINGS)/, WHICH EXISTS NOWHERE. THE /(LANTERN OF THE KINGDOM)/ SALOMON'S HOUSE, WHERE EVERY DOOR OPENS INTO A ROOM IN EVERY HUMAN /(HEART)/ AND WHERE YOU WILL REMEMBER HOW TO /(CUT THE MASTER-KEY)/
YOU CAN CALL IT THE MAGIC MOUNTAIN, THE VIRTUAL COLLEGE, THE SCHOOL OF SHADOWS.
OR, IF YOU PREFER, THE /(ACADEMY)/

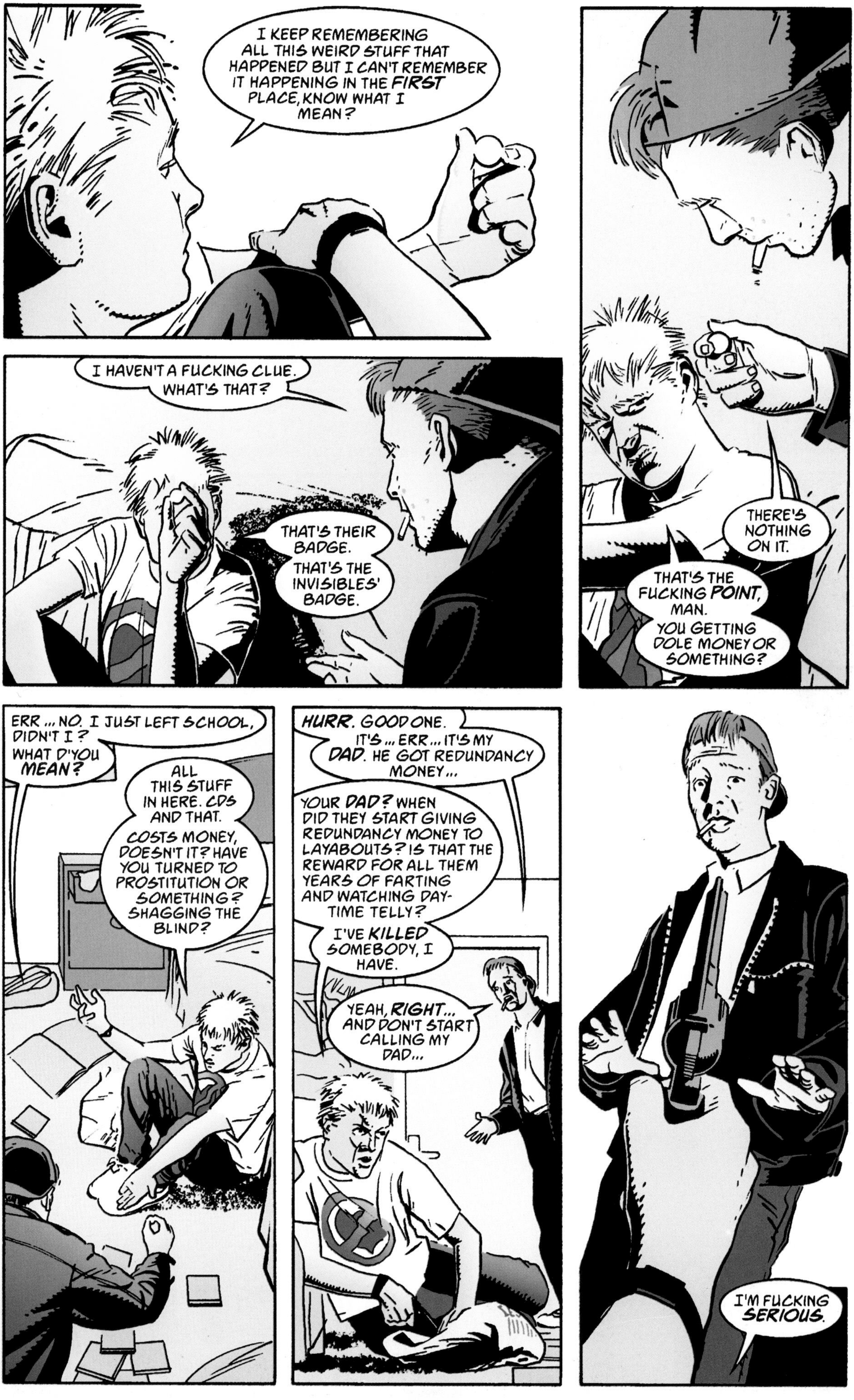

I KEEP REMEMBERING ALL THIS WEIRD STUFF THAT HAPPENED BUT I CAN'T REMEMBER IT HAPPENING IN THE FIRST PLACE, KNOW WHAT I MEAN?
I HAVEN'T A FUCKING CLUE. WHAT'S THAT?
THAT'S THEIR BADGE.
THAT'S THE INVISIBLES' BADGE.
THERE'S NOTHING ON IT.
THAT'S THE FUCKING POINT, MAN.
YOU GETTING DOLE MONEY OR SOMETHING?
ERR ... NO. I JUST LEFT SCHOOL, DIDN'T I?
WHAT D'YOU MEAN?
ALL THIS STUFF IN HERE. CDS AND THAT.
COSTS MONEY, DOESN'T IT? HAVE YOU TURNED TO PROSTITUTION OR SOMETHING? SHAGGING THE BLIND?
HURR. GOOD ONE.
IT'S ... ERR ... IT'S MY DAD. HE GOT REDUNDANCY MONEY...
YOUR DAD? WHEN DID THEY START GIVING REDUNDANCY MONEY TO LAYABOUTS? IS THAT THE REWARD FOR ALL THEM YEARS OF FARTING AND WATCHING DAY-TIME TELLY?
I'VE KILLED SOMEBODY, I HAVE.
YEAH, RIGHT... AND DON'T START CALLING MY DAD...
I'M FUCKING SERIOUS.

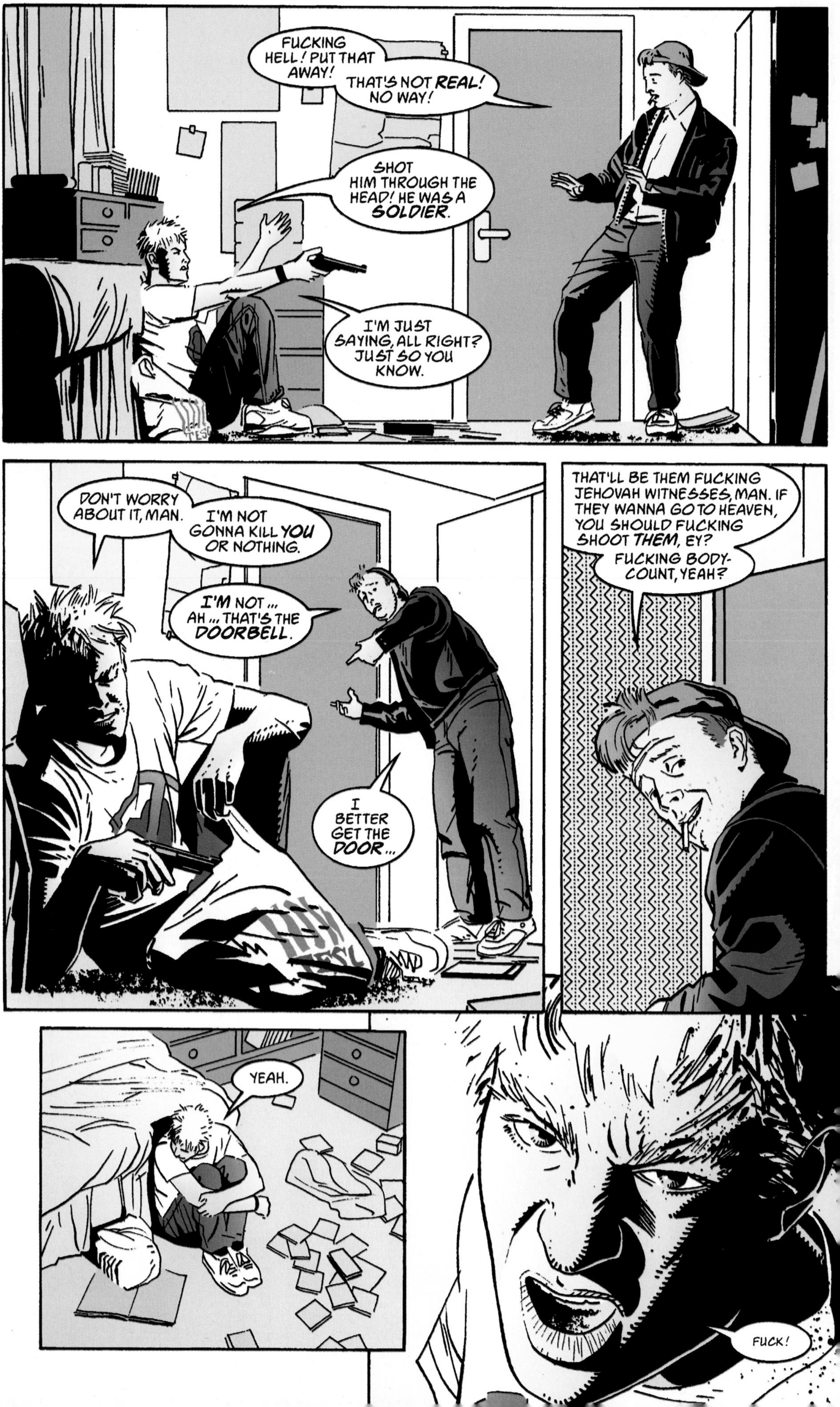

FUCKING HELL! PUT THAT AWAY!
THAT'S NOT REAL! NO WAY!
SHOT HIM THROUGH THE HEAD! HE WAS A SOLDIER.
I'M JUST SAYING, ALL RIGHT? JUST SO YOU KNOW.
DON'T WORRY ABOUT IT, MAN.
I'M NOT GONNA KILL YOU OR NOTHING.
I'M NOT ... AH ... THAT'S THE DOORBELL.
I BETTER GET THE DOOR...
THAT'LL BE THEM FUCKING JEHOVAH WITNESSES, MAN. IF THEY WANNA GO TO HEAVEN, YOU SHOULD FUCKING SHOOT THEM, EY?
FUCKING BODY-COUNT, YEAH?
YEAH.
FUCK!

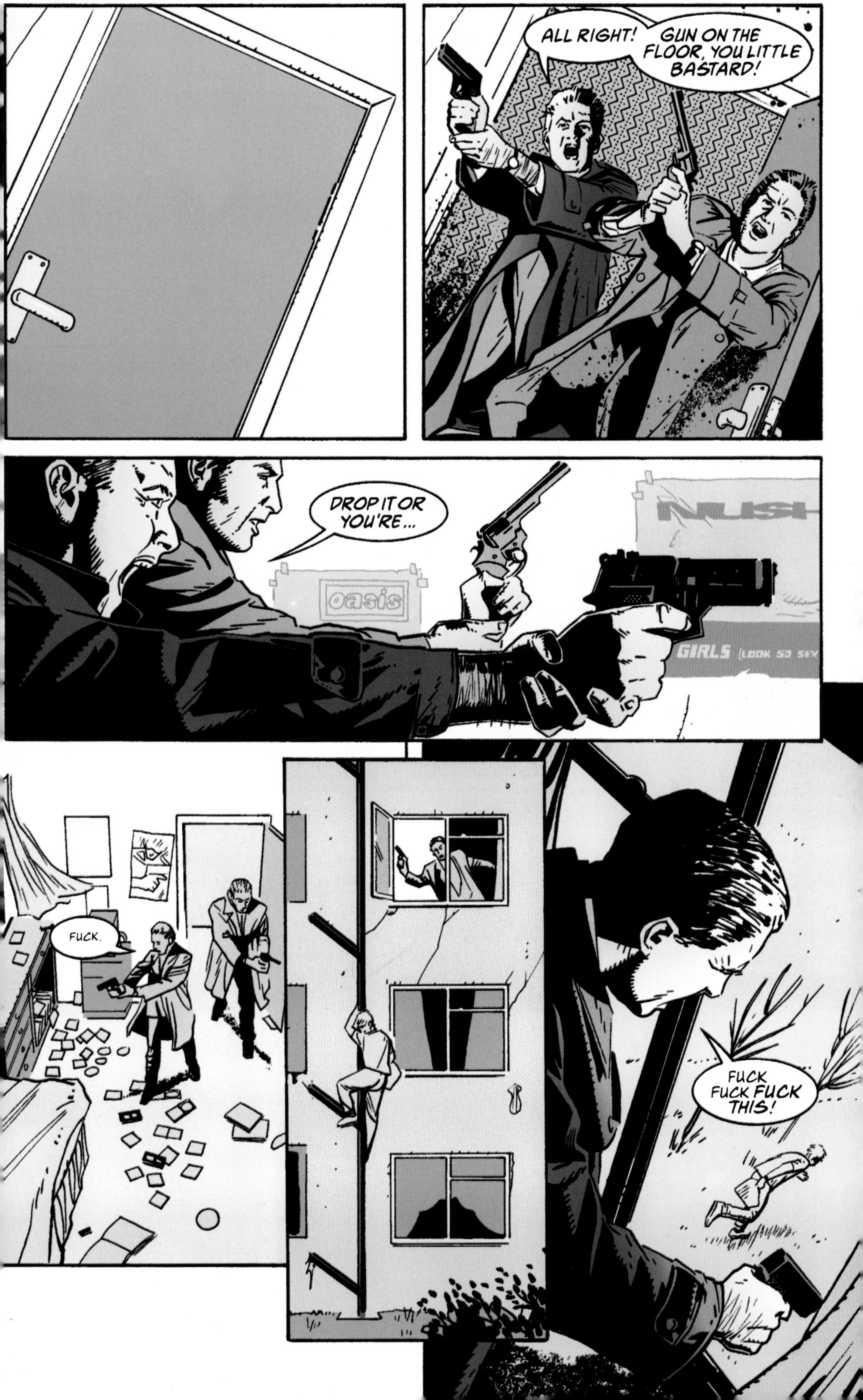
ALL RIGHT!
GUN ON THE FLOOR, YOU LITTLE BASTARD!
DROP IT OR YOU'RE...
oasis
GIRLS
FUCK.
FUCK FUCK FUCK THIS!

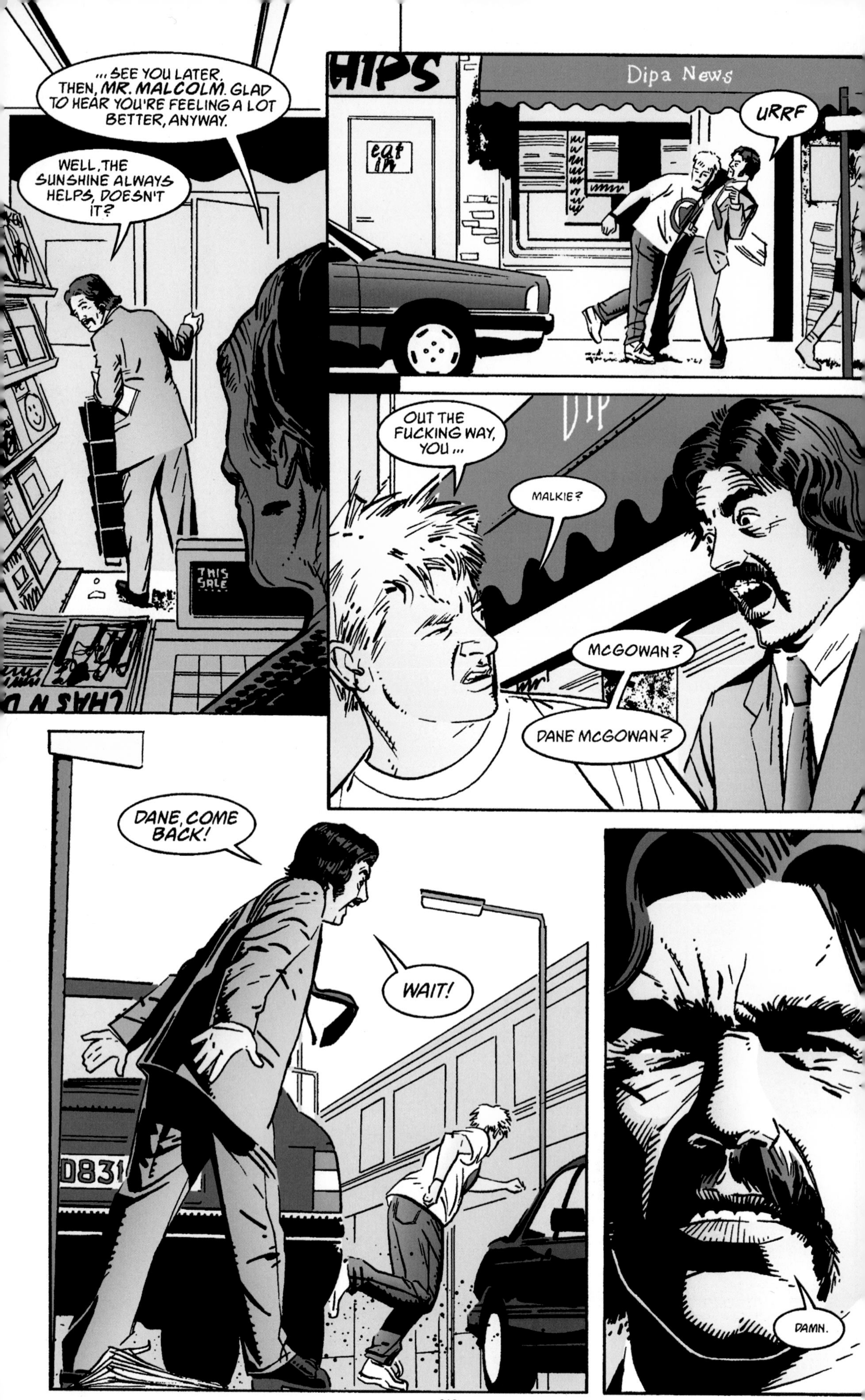
...SEE YOU LATER, THEN, MR. MALCOLM. GLAD TO HEAR YOU'RE FEELING A LOT BETTER, ANYWAY.
WELL, THE SUNSHINE ALWAYS HELPS, DOESN'T IT?
THIS SALE
HIPS
Dipa News
eat in
URRF
OUT THE FUCKING WAY, YOU...
MALKIE?
McGOWAN?
DANE McGOWAN?
DANE, COME BACK!
WAIT!
DAMN.

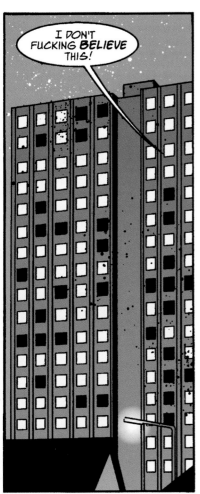

I DON'T FUCKING **BELIEVE** THIS!

WHO CUT YOUR HAIR ANYWAY? JACK THE RIPPER?

I CUT IT MYSELF. WHY'S EVERYBODY GOING ON ABOUT MY FUCKING **HAIR**? IT'S NOT FUCKING IMPORTANT!

LOOK AT ME, I'M **SHAKING.** I'M A BAG OF NERVES NOW. FIRST THEY TELL ME YOU'RE **DEAD**, THEN THEY TELL ME YOU GOT AWAY FROM THAT FIRE AND TO LET THEM KNOW IF YOU COME HOME AND NOW...

WHAT'S GOING **ON?** AND DON'T GIVE ME ANY MORE OF THIS **DOCTOR WHO** SHITE ABOUT SPACE ALIENS AND FUCKING TIME MACHINES AND FUCK KNOWS WHAT ELSE. I WANT THE **TRUTH.** NOW.

I'M **TELLING** YOU THE TRUTH, MAM.

I **KNOW** IT'S MAD. IT'S **ALL** MAD BUT IT'S **REAL.**

IT'S REAL. I KNOW ALL THE NAMES SOUND STUPID AND THAT, BUT THAT'S WHAT THEY DO SO NOBODY KNOWS WHO THEY ARE. I WAS "JACK FROST."

TEA.

DON'T WANT IT.

YOU DON'T KNOW THE THINGS I'VE SEEN ...YOU HAVEN'T ANY IDEA WHAT ...IT'S JUST ... YOU'RE ALL LIKE FUCKING COWS CHEWING GRASS IN A FIELD NEXT TO A FUCKING SLAUGHTER-HOUSE. YOU DON'T KNOW WHAT'S GOING ON ...

WHO DO YOU THINK YOU'RE CALLING A COW? YOU MIND YOUR FUCKING LANGUAGE!

ARE YOU ON DRUGS? I FUCKING KNEW IT!

I'M NOT ON ANYTHING. EVERYBODY'S AFTER ME. I CAN'T KEEP RUNNING AND RUNNING. I FEEL AS IF I'M GOING MAD WITH ALL THIS STUFF.

YOU JUST DON'T KNOW.

WHAT'S IN THE BAG?

STUFF. THAT OLD MAN GAVE IT TO ME. TOM. THE ONE I TOLD YOU ABOUT.

WORTH ANYTHING, IS IT?

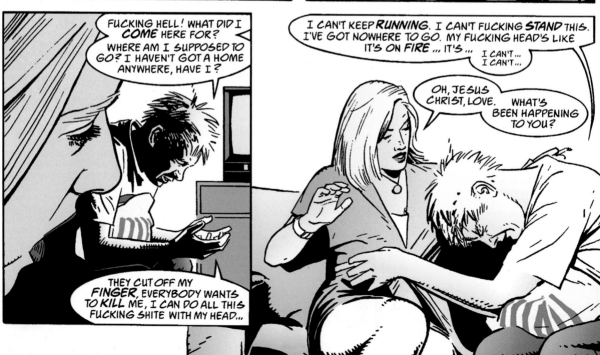

FUCKING HELL! WHAT DID I COME HERE FOR? WHERE AM I SUPPOSED TO GO? I HAVEN'T GOT A HOME ANYWHERE, HAVE I?

THEY CUT OFF MY FINGER, EVERYBODY WANTS TO KILL ME, I CAN DO ALL THIS FUCKING SHITE WITH MY HEAD...

I CAN'T KEEP RUNNING. I CAN'T FUCKING STAND THIS. I'VE GOT NOWHERE TO GO. MY FUCKING HEAD'S LIKE IT'S ON FIRE ... IT'S ... I CAN'T... I CAN'T...

OH, JESUS CHRIST, LOVE. WHAT'S BEEN HAPPENING TO YOU?

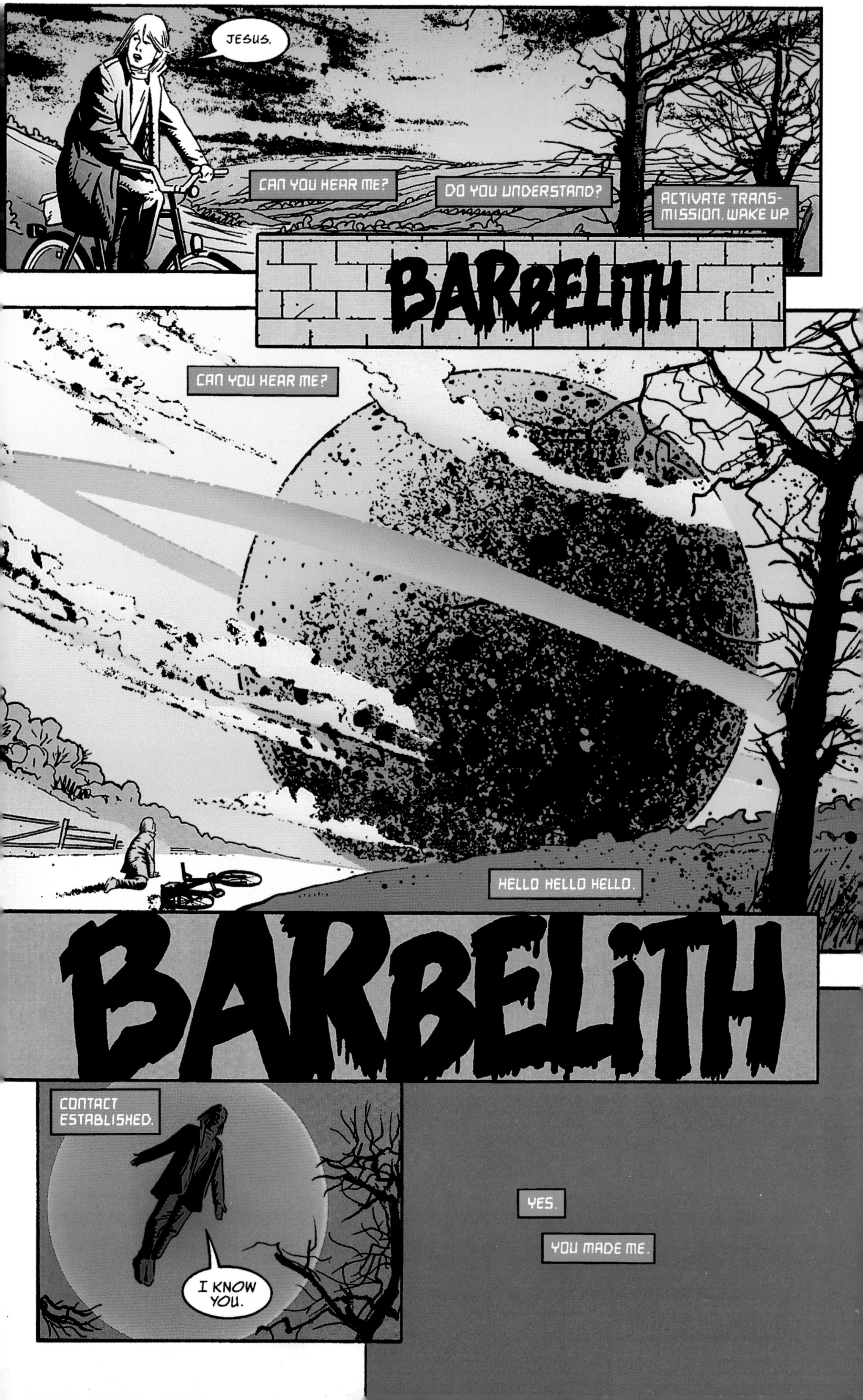
JESUS.
CAN YOU HEAR ME?
DO YOU UNDERSTAND?
ACTIVATE TRANS-MISSION. WAKE UP.
BARBELITH
CAN YOU HEAR ME?
HELLO HELLO HELLO.
BARBELITH
CONTACT ESTABLISHED.
I KNOW YOU.
YES.
YOU MADE ME.

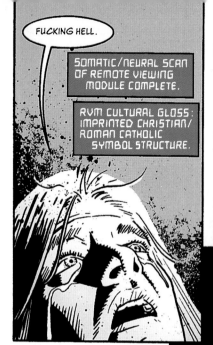

FUCKING HELL.

SOMATIC/NEURAL SCAN OF REMOTE VIEWING MODULE COMPLETE.

RVM CULTURAL GLOSS: IMPRINTED CHRISTIAN/ ROMAN CATHOLIC SYMBOL STRUCTURE.

ACTIVATE.

NNGGH! FUCKED UP! EVERYTHING'S FUCKED UP! IT'S ALL FUCKED AND IT'LL NEVER GET FIXED.

WAKE UP.

NNNNYAAAARRGH

I CAN'T GET THE FUCKING NAILS OUT.

I CAN'T DO IT. I CAN'T FUCKING DO IT.

WHY CAN'T I DO IT?

TRY TO REMEMBER.

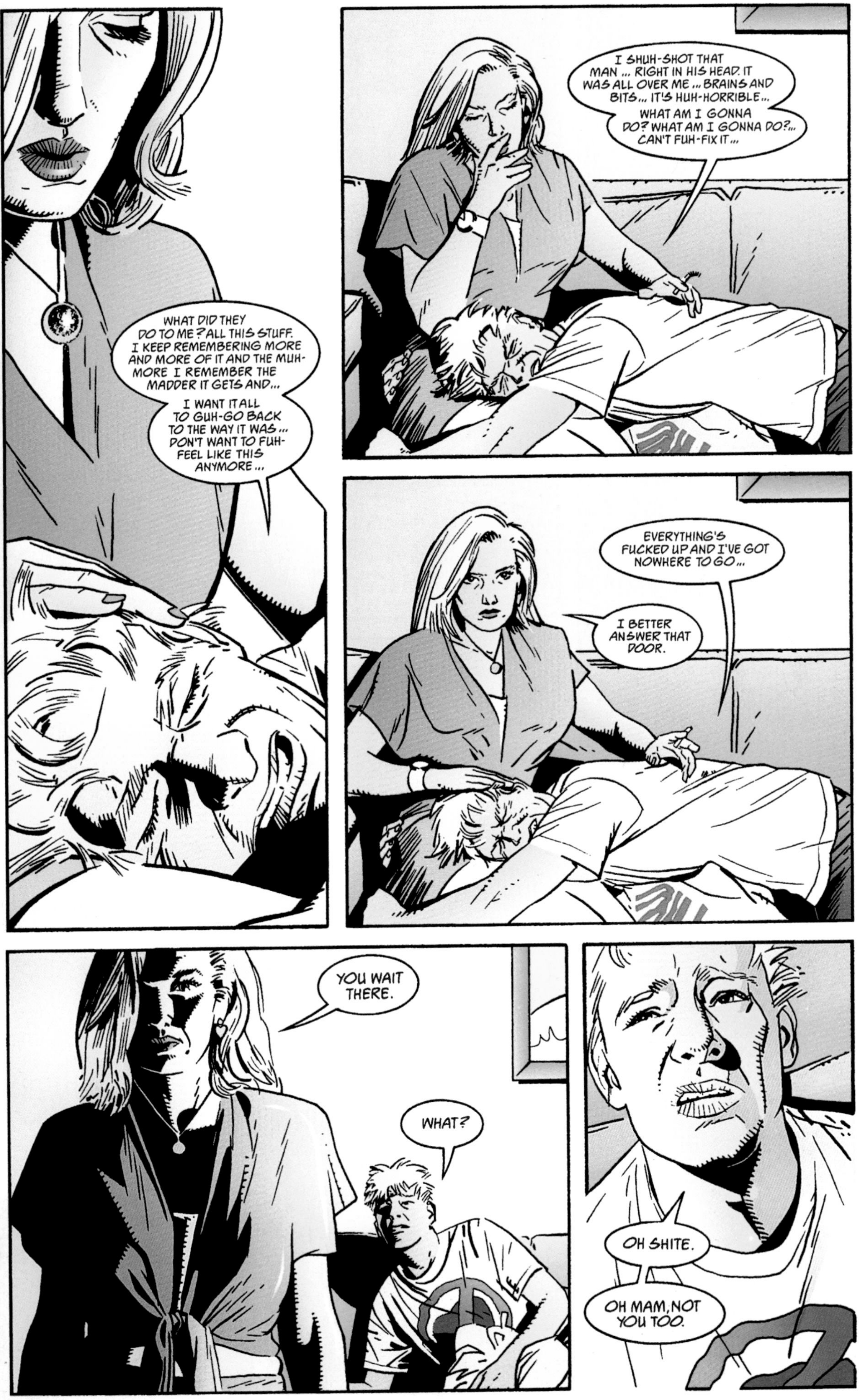
WHAT DID THEY DO TO ME? ALL THIS STUFF. I KEEP REMEMBERING MORE AND MORE OF IT AND THE MUH-MORE I REMEMBER THE MADDER IT GETS AND...
I WANT IT ALL TO GUH-GO BACK TO THE WAY IT WAS... DON'T WANT TO FUH-FEEL LIKE THIS ANYMORE...
I SHUH-SHOT THAT MAN... RIGHT IN HIS HEAD. IT WAS ALL OVER ME... BRAINS AND BITS... IT'S HUH-HORRIBLE...
WHAT AM I GONNA DO? WHAT AM I GONNA DO?... CAN'T FUH-FIX IT...
EVERYTHING'S FUCKED UP AND I'VE GOT NOWHERE TO GO...
I BETTER ANSWER THAT DOOR.
YOU WAIT THERE.
WHAT?
OH SHITE.
OH MAM, NOT YOU TOO.

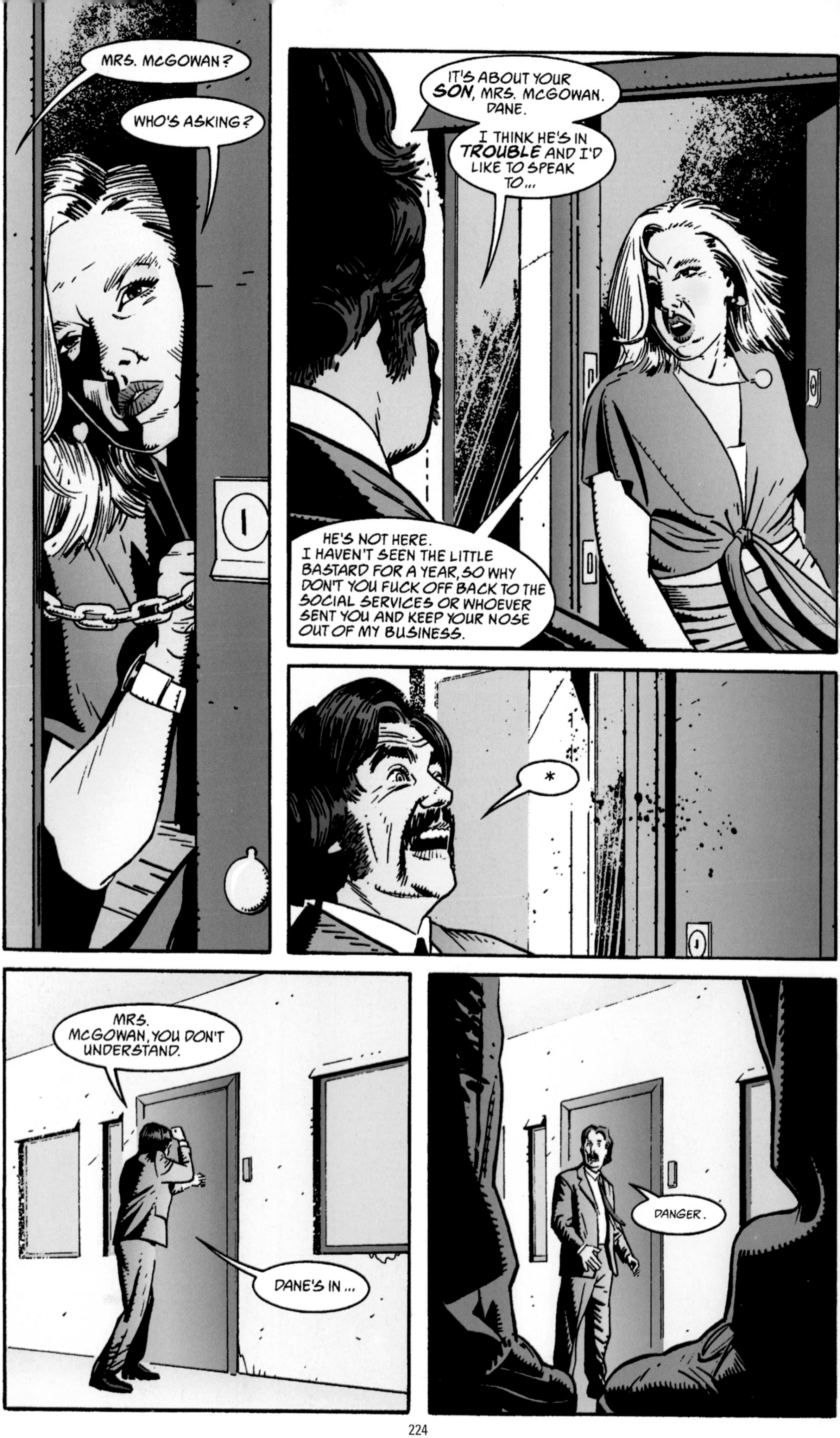
MRS. McGOWAN?
WHO'S ASKING?
IT'S ABOUT YOUR SON, MRS. McGOWAN. DANE.
I THINK HE'S IN TROUBLE AND I'D LIKE TO SPEAK TO...
HE'S NOT HERE. I HAVEN'T SEEN THE LITTLE BASTARD FOR A YEAR, SO WHY DON'T YOU FUCK OFF BACK TO THE SOCIAL SERVICES OR WHOEVER SENT YOU AND KEEP YOUR NOSE OUT OF MY BUSINESS.
*
MRS. McGOWAN, YOU DON'T UNDERSTAND.
DANE'S IN...
DANGER.

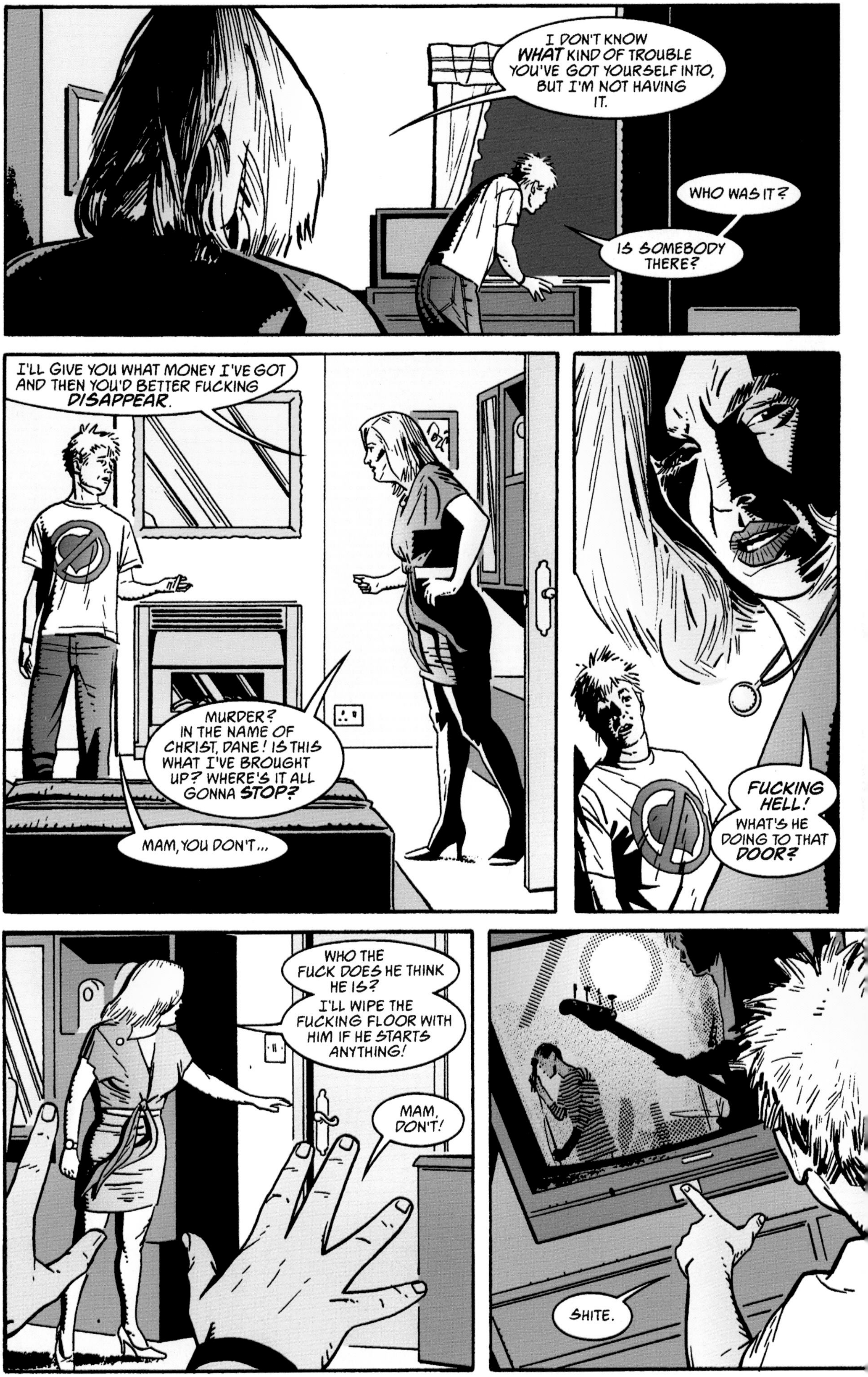
I DON'T KNOW WHAT KIND OF TROUBLE YOU'VE GOT YOURSELF INTO, BUT I'M NOT HAVING IT.
WHO WAS IT?
IS SOMEBODY THERE?
I'LL GIVE YOU WHAT MONEY I'VE GOT AND THEN YOU'D BETTER FUCKING DISAPPEAR.
MURDER? IN THE NAME OF CHRIST, DANE! IS THIS WHAT I'VE BROUGHT UP? WHERE'S IT ALL GONNA STOP?
MAM, YOU DON'T...
FUCKING HELL! WHAT'S HE DOING TO THAT DOOR?
WHO THE FUCK DOES HE THINK HE IS? I'LL WIPE THE FUCKING FLOOR WITH HIM IF HE STARTS ANYTHING!
MAM, DON'T!
SHITE.

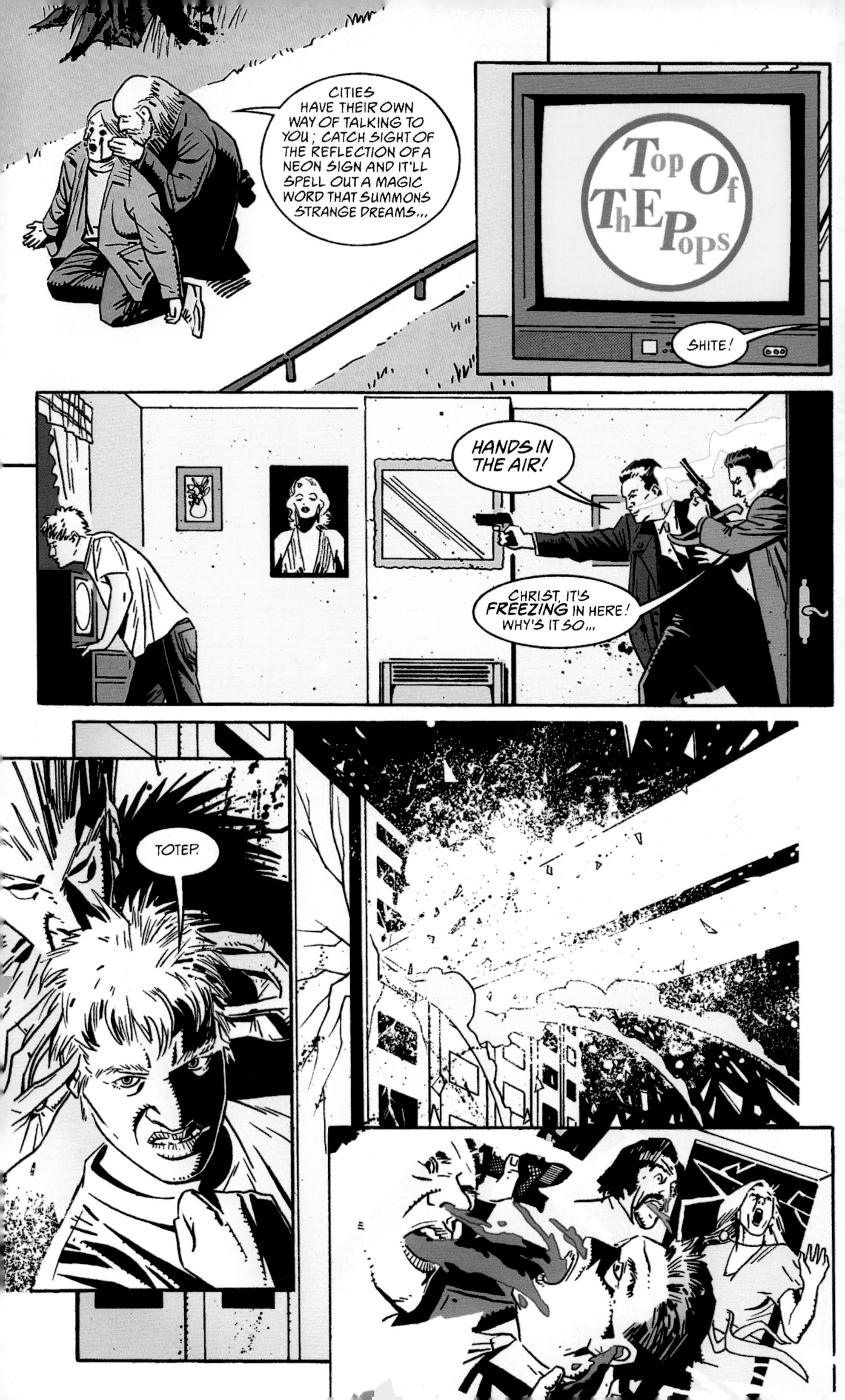
CITIES HAVE THEIR OWN WAY OF TALKING TO YOU; CATCH SIGHT OF THE REFLECTION OF A NEON SIGN AND IT'LL SPELL OUT A MAGIC WORD THAT SUMMONS STRANGE DREAMS...
Top Of ThE Pops
SHITE!
HANDS IN THE AIR!
CHRIST, IT'S FREEZING IN HERE! WHY'S IT SO...
TOTEP.

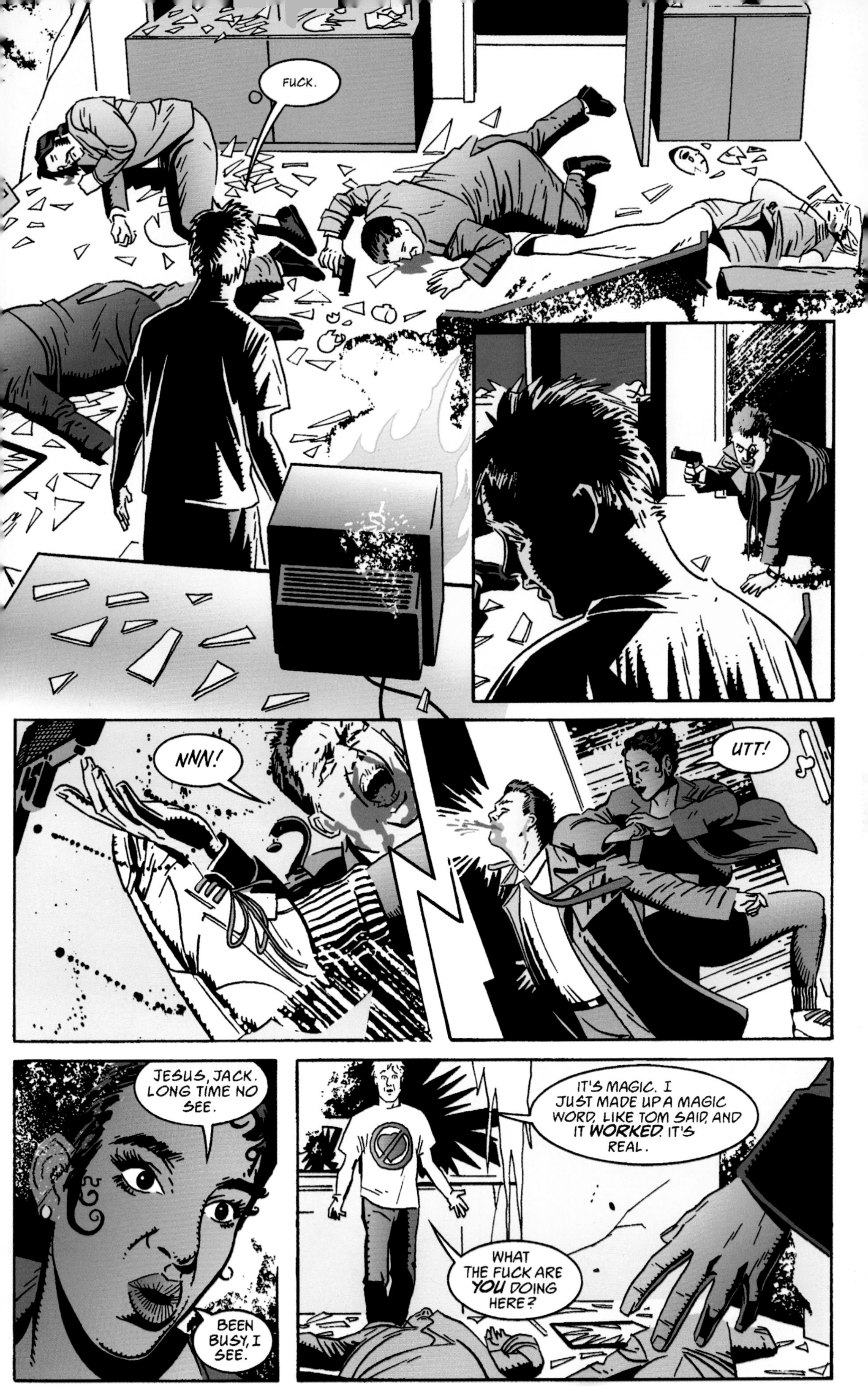
FUCK.
NNN!
UTT!
JESUS, JACK. LONG TIME NO SEE.
BEEN BUSY, I SEE.
IT'S MAGIC. I JUST MADE UP A MAGIC WORD, LIKE TOM SAID, AND IT **WORKED**. IT'S REAL.
WHAT THE FUCK ARE ***YOU*** DOING HERE?

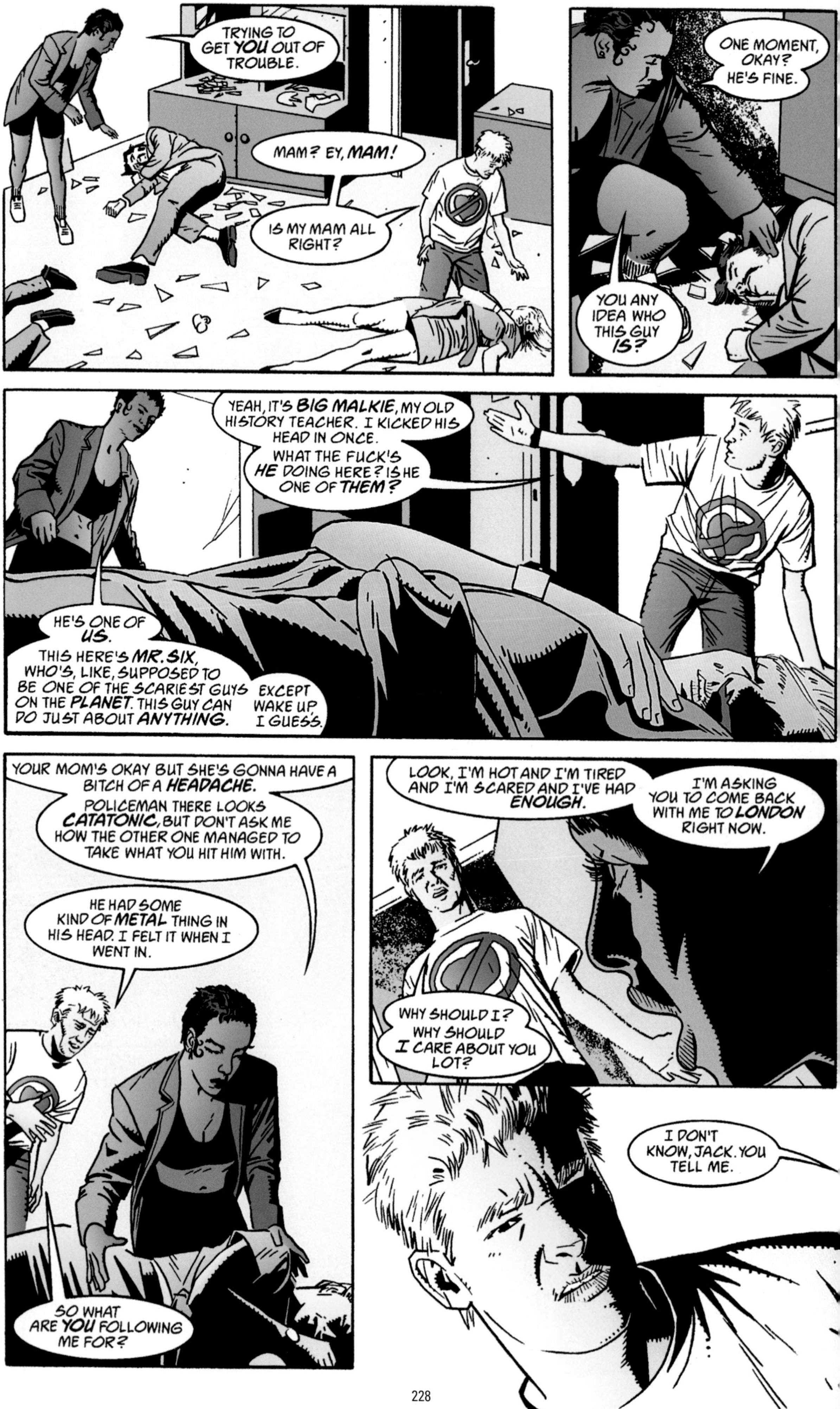
TRYING TO GET YOU OUT OF TROUBLE.
MAM? EY, MAM!
IS MY MAM ALL RIGHT?
ONE MOMENT, OKAY? HE'S FINE.
YOU ANY IDEA WHO THIS GUY IS?
YEAH, IT'S BIG MALKIE, MY OLD HISTORY TEACHER. I KICKED HIS HEAD IN ONCE.
WHAT THE FUCK'S HE DOING HERE? IS HE ONE OF THEM?
HE'S ONE OF US.
THIS HERE'S MR. SIX, WHO'S, LIKE, SUPPOSED TO BE ONE OF THE SCARIEST GUYS ON THE PLANET. THIS GUY CAN DO JUST ABOUT ANYTHING.
EXCEPT WAKE UP, I GUESS.
YOUR MOM'S OKAY BUT SHE'S GONNA HAVE A BITCH OF A HEADACHE.
POLICEMAN THERE LOOKS CATATONIC, BUT DON'T ASK ME HOW THE OTHER ONE MANAGED TO TAKE WHAT YOU HIT HIM WITH.
HE HAD SOME KIND OF METAL THING IN HIS HEAD. I FELT IT WHEN I WENT IN.
SO WHAT ARE YOU FOLLOWING ME FOR?
LOOK, I'M HOT AND I'M TIRED AND I'M SCARED AND I'VE HAD ENOUGH.
I'M ASKING YOU TO COME BACK WITH ME TO LONDON RIGHT NOW.
WHY SHOULD I? WHY SHOULD I CARE ABOUT YOU LOT?
I DON'T KNOW, JACK. YOU TELL ME.

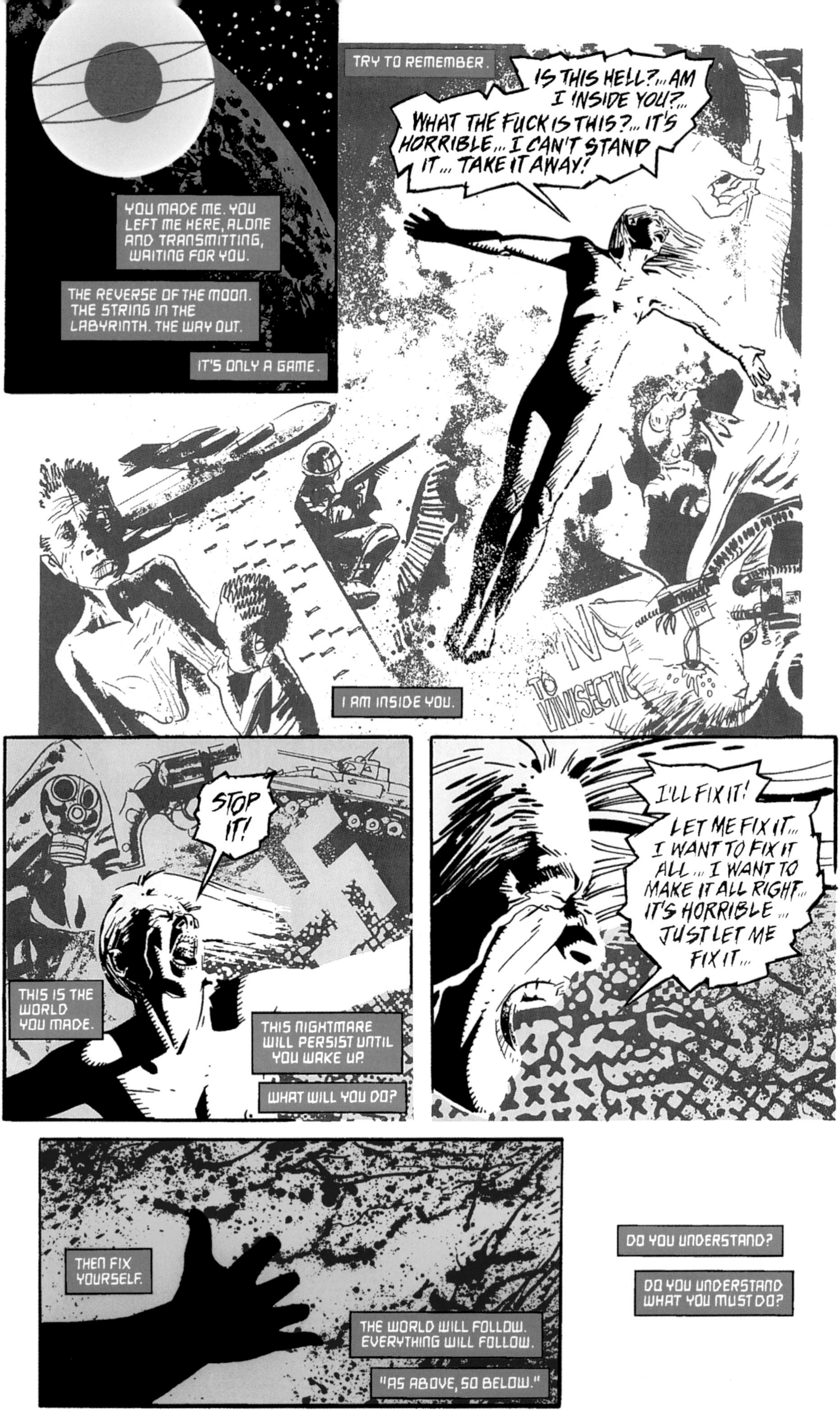
YOU MADE ME. YOU LEFT ME HERE, ALONE AND TRANSMITTING, WAITING FOR YOU.
THE REVERSE OF THE MOON. THE STRING IN THE LABYRINTH. THE WAY OUT.
IT'S ONLY A GAME.
TRY TO REMEMBER.
IS THIS HELL?... AM I INSIDE YOU?... WHAT THE FUCK IS THIS?... IT'S HORRIBLE... I CAN'T STAND IT... TAKE IT AWAY!
NO TO VIVISECTIO
I AM INSIDE YOU.
STOP IT!
THIS IS THE WORLD YOU MADE.
THIS NIGHTMARE WILL PERSIST UNTIL YOU WAKE UP.
WHAT WILL YOU DO?
I'LL FIX IT!
LET ME FIX IT... I WANT TO FIX IT ALL... I WANT TO MAKE IT ALL RIGHT... IT'S HORRIBLE... JUST LET ME FIX IT...
THEN FIX YOURSELF.
THE WORLD WILL FOLLOW. EVERYTHING WILL FOLLOW.
"AS ABOVE, SO BELOW."
DO YOU UNDERSTAND?
DO YOU UNDERSTAND WHAT YOU MUST DO?

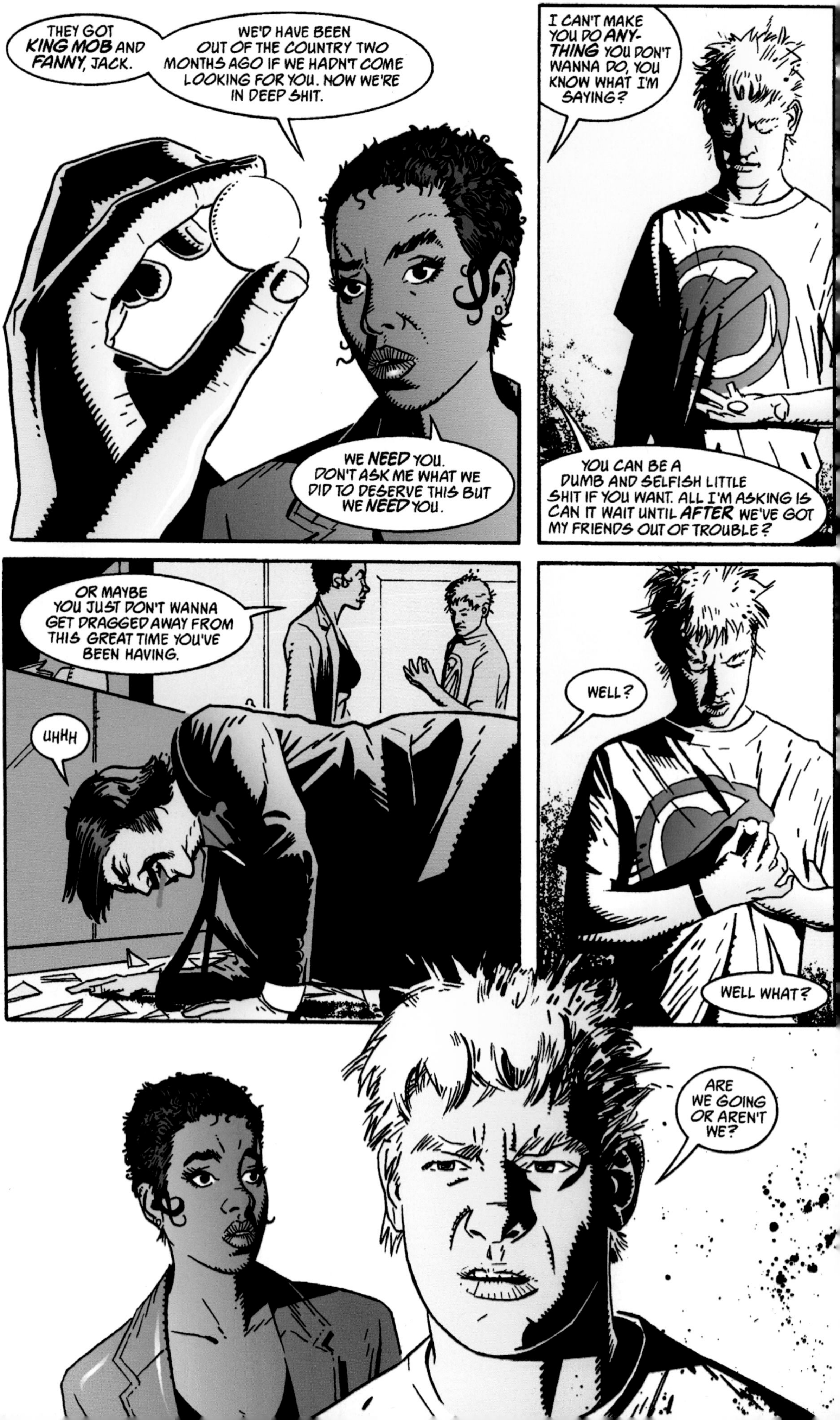
THEY GOT KING MOB AND FANNY, JACK.
WE'D HAVE BEEN OUT OF THE COUNTRY TWO MONTHS AGO IF WE HADN'T COME LOOKING FOR YOU. NOW WE'RE IN DEEP SHIT.
WE NEED YOU. DON'T ASK ME WHAT WE DID TO DESERVE THIS BUT WE NEED YOU.
I CAN'T MAKE YOU DO ANY-THING YOU DON'T WANNA DO, YOU KNOW WHAT I'M SAYING?
YOU CAN BE A DUMB AND SELFISH LITTLE SHIT IF YOU WANT. ALL I'M ASKING IS CAN IT WAIT UNTIL AFTER WE'VE GOT MY FRIENDS OUT OF TROUBLE?
OR MAYBE YOU JUST DON'T WANNA GET DRAGGED AWAY FROM THIS GREAT TIME YOU'VE BEEN HAVING.
UHHH
WELL?
WELL WHAT?
ARE WE GOING OR AREN'T WE?

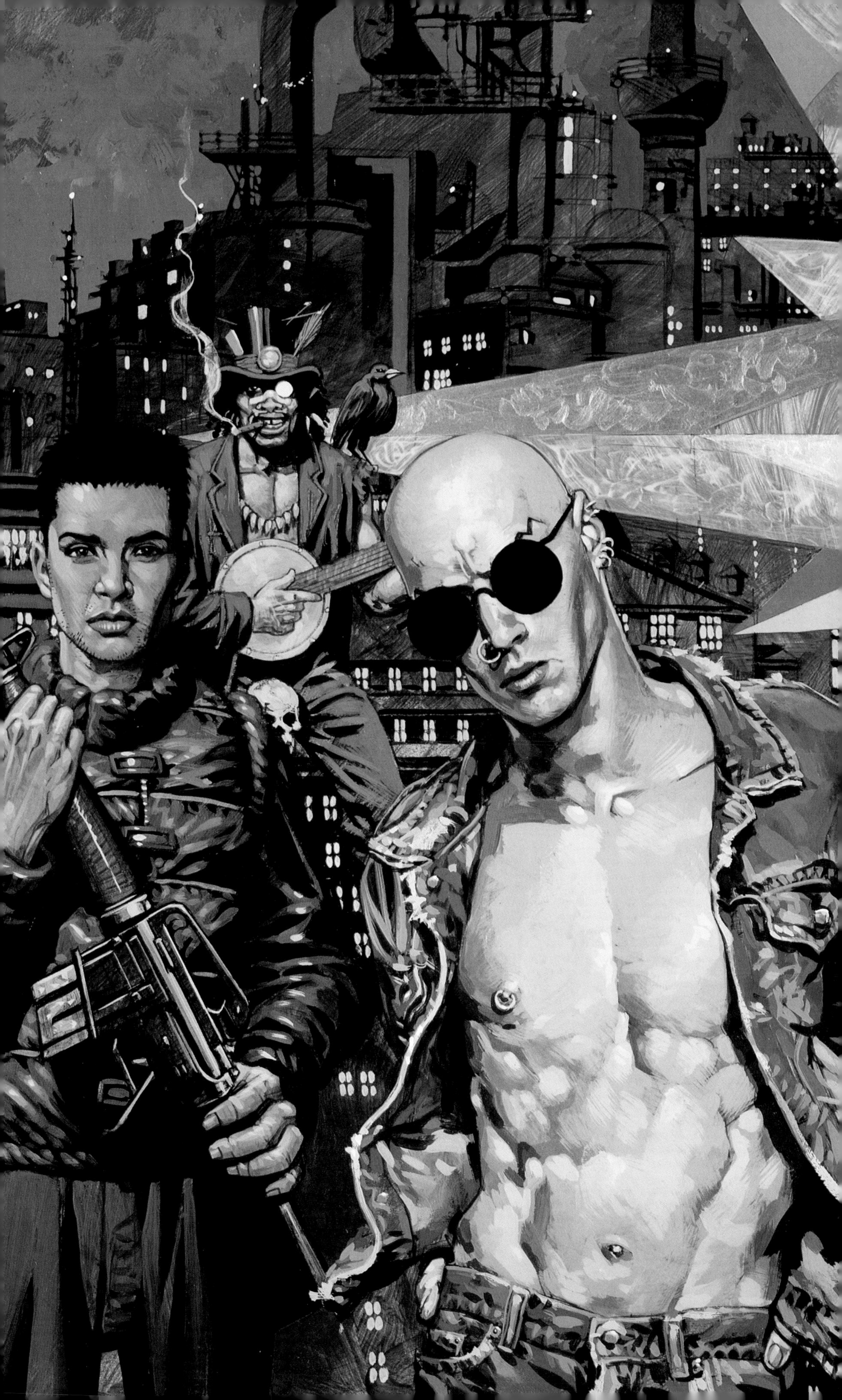

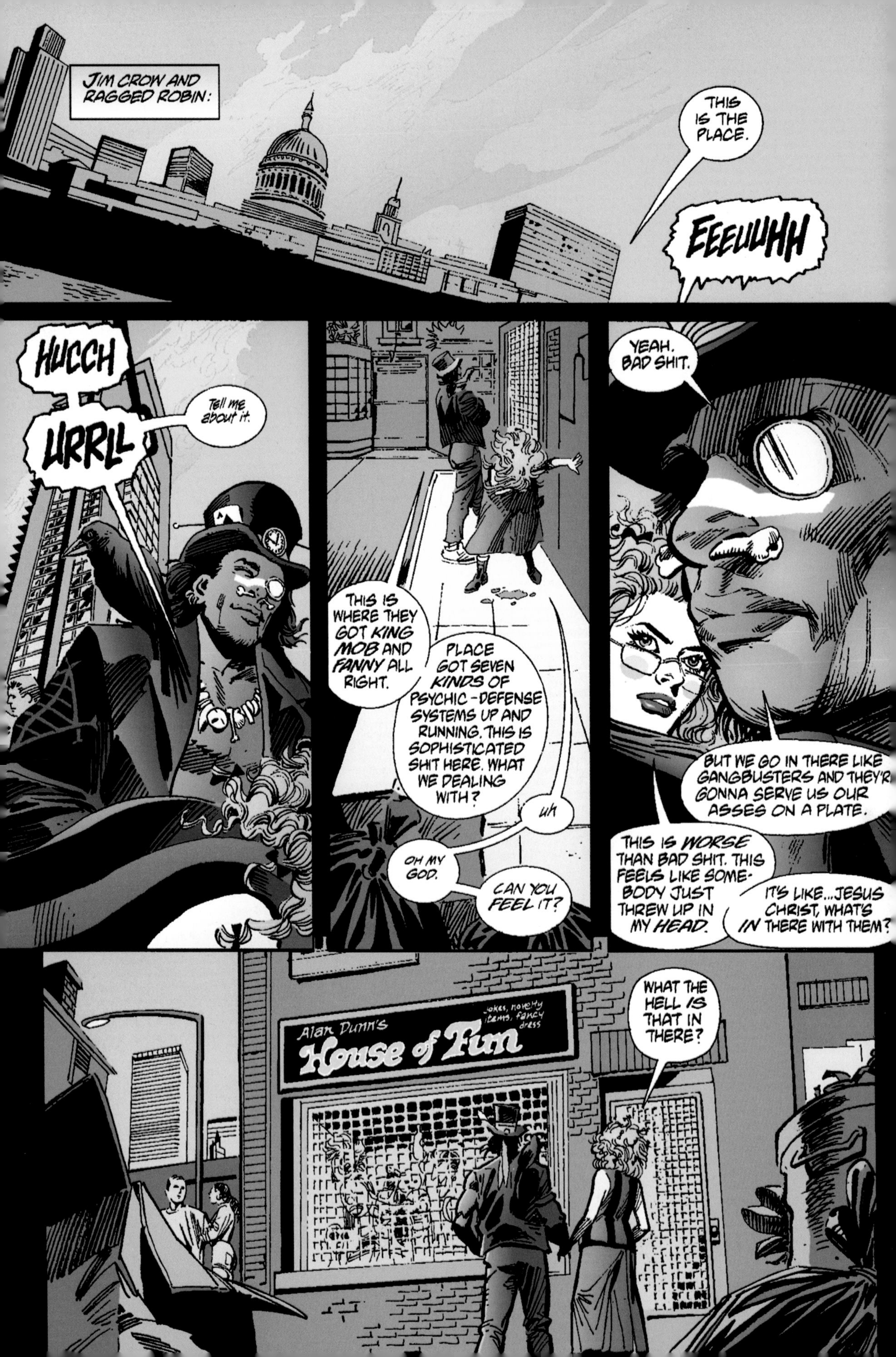
JIM CROW AND RAGGED ROBIN:
THIS IS THE PLACE.
EEEUUHH
HUCCH
URRLL
Tell me about it.
THIS IS WHERE THEY GOT KING MOB AND FANNY ALL RIGHT.
PLACE GOT SEVEN KINDS OF PSYCHIC-DEFENSE SYSTEMS UP AND RUNNING. THIS IS SOPHISTICATED SHIT HERE. WHAT WE DEALING WITH?
uh
OH MY GOD.
CAN YOU FEEL IT?
YEAH. BAD SHIT.
BUT WE GO IN THERE LIKE GANGBUSTERS AND THEY'R GONNA SERVE US OUR ASSES ON A PLATE.
THIS IS WORSE THAN BAD SHIT. THIS FEELS LIKE SOME-BODY JUST THREW UP IN MY HEAD.
IT'S LIKE...JESUS CHRIST, WHAT'S IN THERE WITH THEM?
Alan Dunn's House of Fun
jokes, novelty items, fancy dress
WHAT THE HELL IS THAT IN THERE?

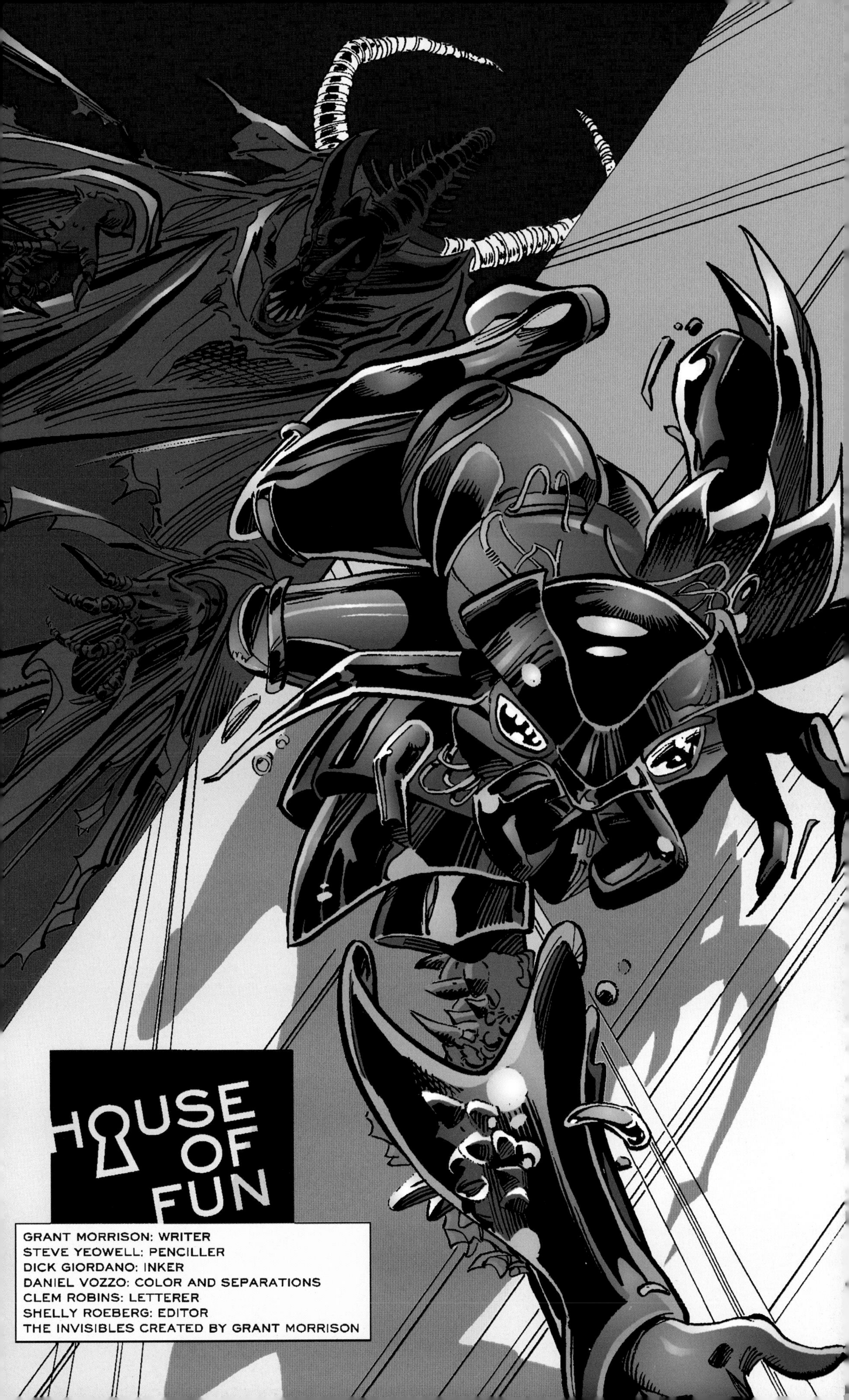
HOUSE OF FUN
GRANT MORRISON: WRITER
STEVE YEOWELL: PENCILLER
DICK GIORDANO: INKER
DANIEL VOZZO: COLOR AND SEPARATIONS
CLEM ROBINS: LETTERER
SHELLY ROEBERG: EDITOR
THE INVISIBLES CREATED BY GRANT MORRISON

MISS DWYER AND THE KING-OF-ALL TEARS:

THE WORLD-THAT-WAS FACETS--HONEYCOMBED BY HER COMPOUND EYES--SHE SCUTTLES THROUGH A JEWELLED MAZE OF APPALLING NEW COLORS, VAST PERFUMES AND GROTESQUE EMOTIONS--OPTIC LENSES MORPH TO ACCOMMODATE CHANGES IN THE LIGHT-STAINED GLASS VISION--MIGRAINE AGONY ON OVERDRIVE--EVERYTHING SEEMS SICKENING, ARTIFICIAL.

TRANSHUMAN, SHE SPINS ECTOPLASMIC LUMINOUS SNARES--SCENTS THE ENEMY AND DROOLS CARCINODELIC BUG-ACID-- THE FLOWERING NEURAL NETWORKS OF THE OUTER CHURCH SPASM AND BURST AND FLOOD HER WITH BOILING DATA--DEATH-PRAYERS AND OBSCENE ROSARIES.

HER REMADE PALATE CLICKERS AND WHIRS-- THE HYMNS OF HER ORDER SELF-REPLICATE THROUGH THE BUILDING, MAKING IT RESONATE LIKE A HIVE.

HER BRAIN OVERLOADS WITH FLOODLIT 4-D SCHEMATICS --FLAYED BODIES, LACERATED MINDS TORN ON THE LOOMS OF HELL--REHEARSING THE DEGRADATIONS AND THE TORMENTS SHE WILL VISIT UPON HER ENEMIES--DRUNK ON ATROCITY, MISS DWYER BUZZES JOYOUSLY AND DRIZZLES HALLUCINOGENIC POISON ACROSS THE WALLS AND CEILING.

AND AT HER SIDE THE KING-OF-ALL-TEARS--GOD OF THE ENDLESS IRON ROOM--MANIFESTING IN EARTH-PLANE MATTER--THE WARNING SIREN OF HIS VOICE RISING AND FALLING--ACTIVATING THE FOURTEEN CHAKRAS AND HYPER-CHAKRAS IN HIS SPINAL LATTICE--EACH LAMENTING OUTCRY CAREFULLY MODULATED TO PROGRAMME HIS NANOFACTORIES WITH DYNAMIC MOBILE BLUEPRINTS OF A MORE WELCOMING ENVIRONMENT.

THEY SWARM AND BREED, INFECTING THE SIMPLISTIC ATOMIC STRUCTURE OF THE LOCAL REALITY GRID.

CONTAGION TAKES, CONTAGION SPREADS, CONTAGION RAGES ALONG PRECISE PARAMETERS.

THE WORLD SICKENS AND BEGINS TO CHANGE.

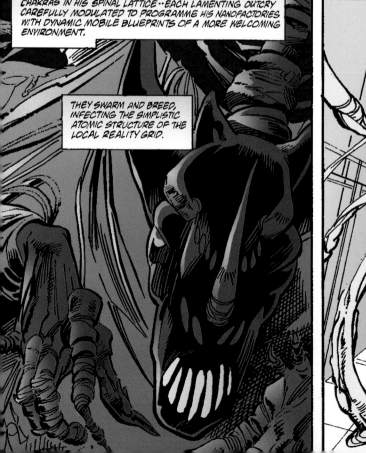

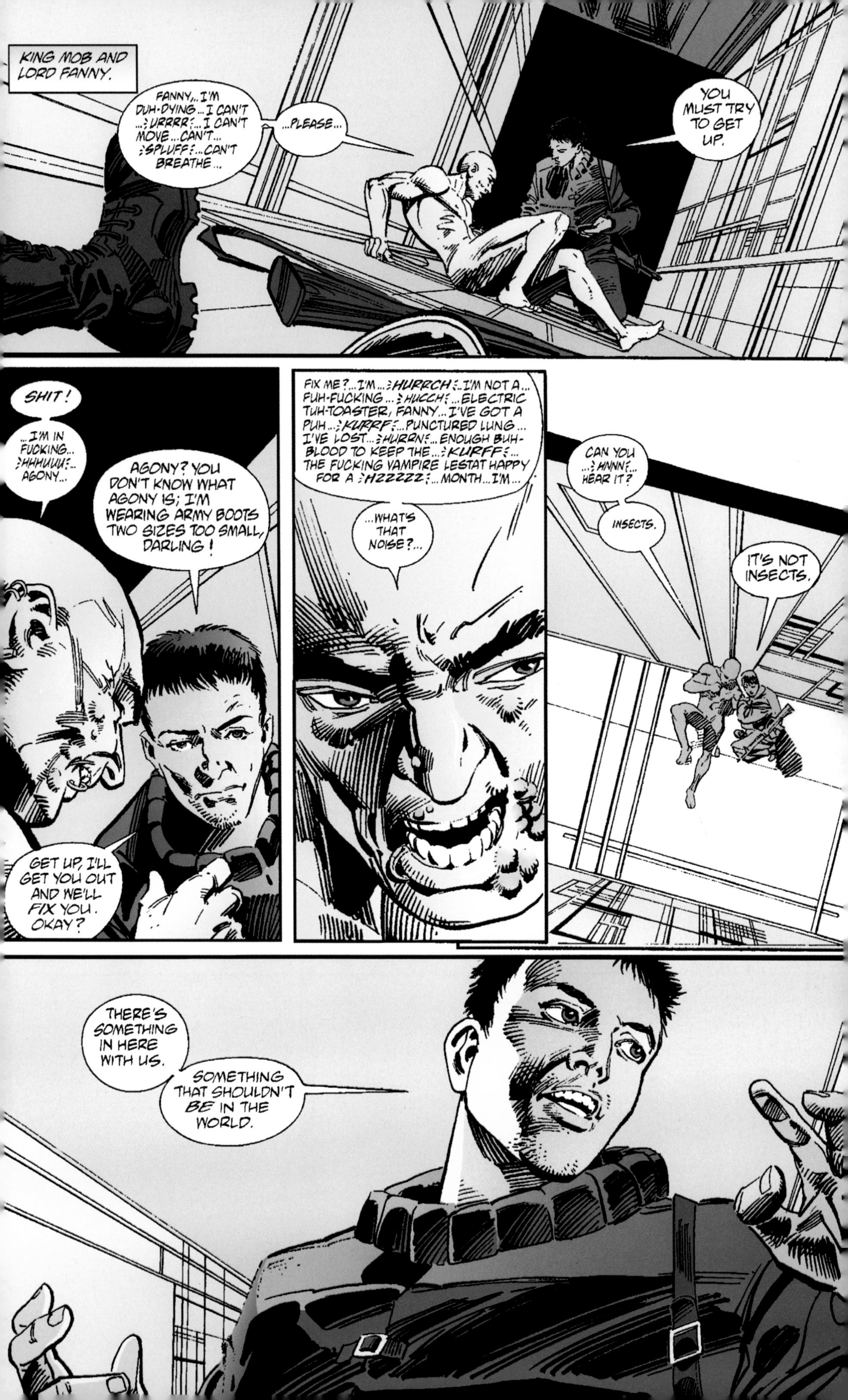
KING MOB AND LORD FANNY.
FANNY... I'M DUH-DYING... I CAN'T ...URRRR... I CAN'T MOVE... CAN'T... SPLUFF... CAN'T BREATHE...
...PLEASE...
YOU MUST TRY TO GET UP.
SHIT!
...I'M IN FUCKING... HHHUUU... AGONY...
AGONY? YOU DON'T KNOW WHAT AGONY IS; I'M WEARING ARMY BOOTS TWO SIZES TOO SMALL, DARLING!
GET UP, I'LL GET YOU OUT AND WE'LL FIX YOU. OKAY?
FIX ME?... I'M... HURRCH... I'M NOT A... FUH-FUCKING... HUCCH... ELECTRIC TUH-TOASTER, FANNY... I'VE GOT A PUH... KURRF... PUNCTURED LUNG... I'VE LOST... HURRN... ENOUGH BUH-BLOOD TO KEEP THE... KURFF... THE FUCKING VAMPIRE LESTAT HAPPY FOR A HZZZZZ... MONTH... I'M...
...WHAT'S THAT NOISE?...
CAN YOU ...HNNN... HEAR IT?
INSECTS.
IT'S NOT INSECTS.
THERE'S SOMETHING IN HERE WITH US.
SOMETHING THAT SHOULDN'T BE IN THE WORLD.

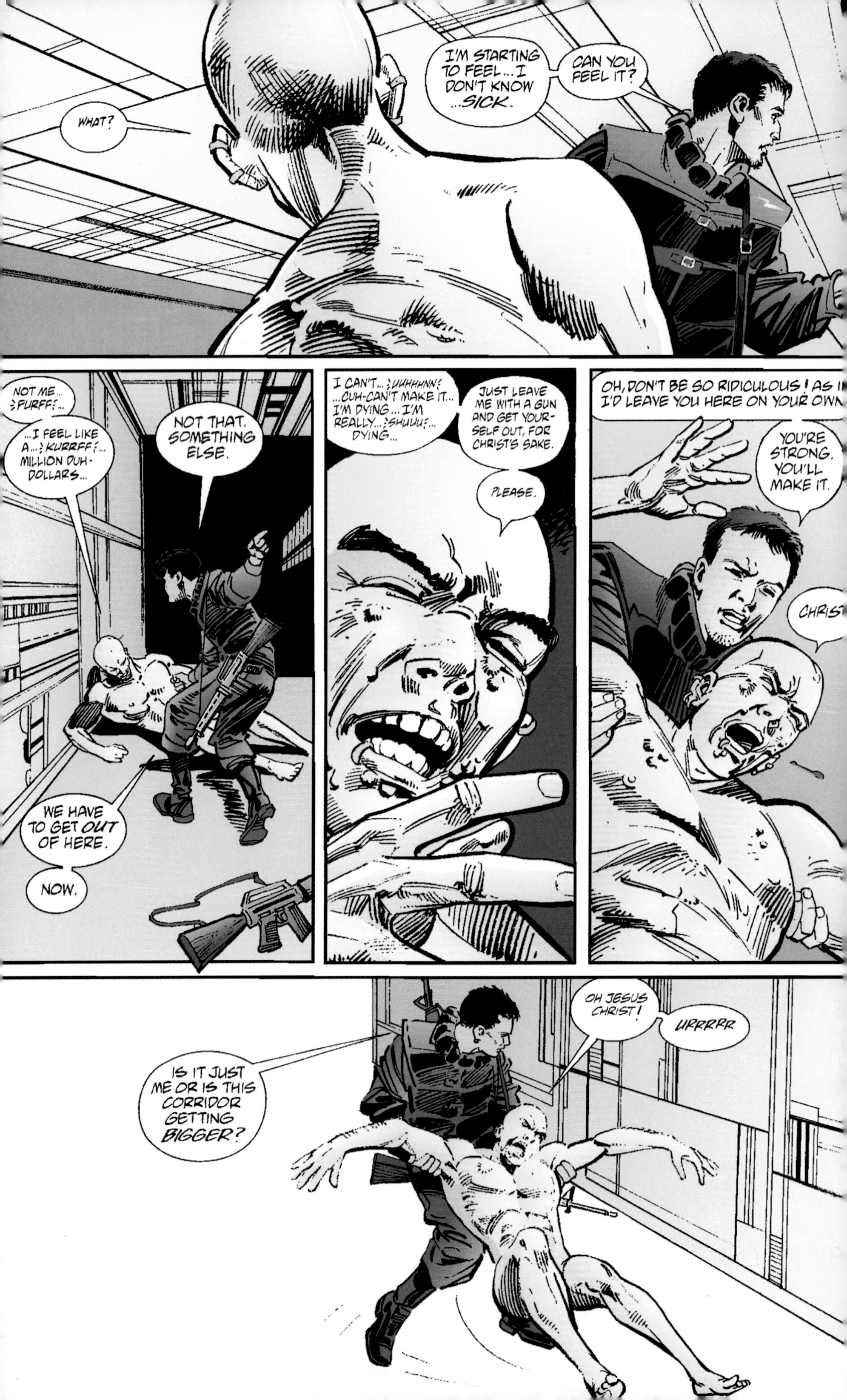
WHAT?
I'M STARTING TO FEEL... I DON'T KNOW ...SICK.
CAN YOU FEEL IT?
NOT ME... FURFF...
...I FEEL LIKE A... KURRFF... MILLION DUH-DOLLARS...
NOT THAT. SOMETHING ELSE.
WE HAVE TO GET OUT OF HERE.
NOW.
I CAN'T... UHHHHNN... ...CUH-CAN'T MAKE IT... I'M DYING... I'M REALLY... SHUUU... DYING...
JUST LEAVE ME WITH A GUN AND GET YOURSELF OUT, FOR CHRIST'S SAKE.
PLEASE.
OH, DON'T BE SO RIDICULOUS! AS I
I'D LEAVE YOU HERE ON YOUR OWN
YOU'RE STRONG. YOU'LL MAKE IT.
CHRIST
IS IT JUST ME OR IS THIS CORRIDOR GETTING BIGGER?
OH JESUS CHRIST!
URRRRR

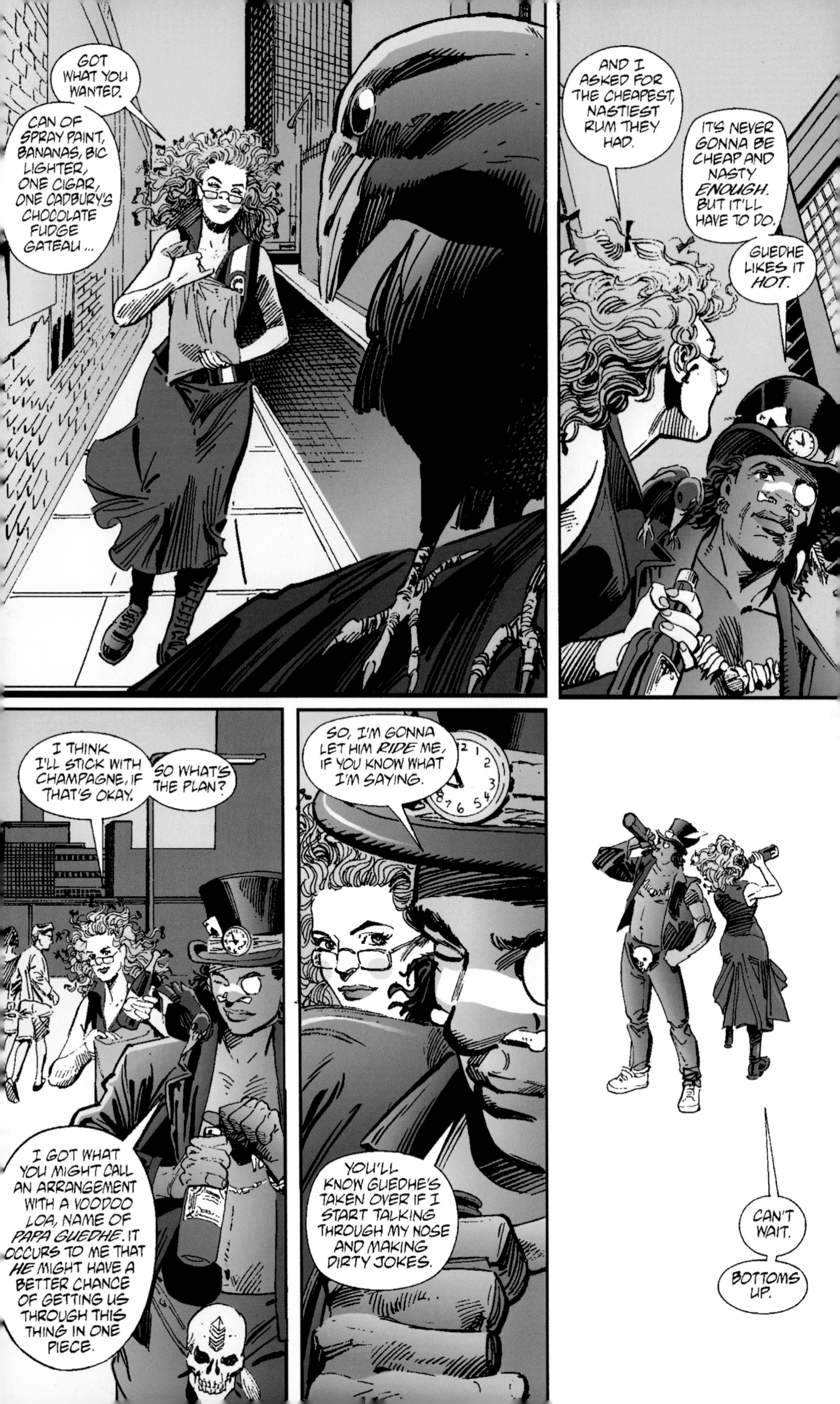
GOT WHAT YOU WANTED.
CAN OF SPRAY PAINT, BANANAS, BIC LIGHTER, ONE CIGAR, ONE CADBURY'S CHOCOLATE FUDGE GATEAU ...
AND I ASKED FOR THE CHEAPEST, NASTIEST RUM THEY HAD.
IT'S NEVER GONNA BE CHEAP AND NASTY *ENOUGH*. BUT IT'LL HAVE TO DO.
GUEDHE LIKES IT *HOT*.
I THINK I'LL STICK WITH CHAMPAGNE, IF THAT'S OKAY.
SO WHAT'S THE PLAN?
I GOT WHAT YOU MIGHT CALL AN ARRANGEMENT WITH A VOODOO LOA, NAME OF *PAPA GUEDHE*. IT OCCURS TO ME THAT *HE* MIGHT HAVE A BETTER CHANCE OF GETTING US THROUGH THIS THING IN ONE PIECE.
SO, I'M GONNA LET HIM *RIDE* ME, IF YOU KNOW WHAT I'M SAYING.
YOU'LL KNOW GUEDHE'S TAKEN OVER IF I START TALKING THROUGH MY NOSE AND MAKING DIRTY JOKES.
CAN'T WAIT.
BOTTOMS UP.

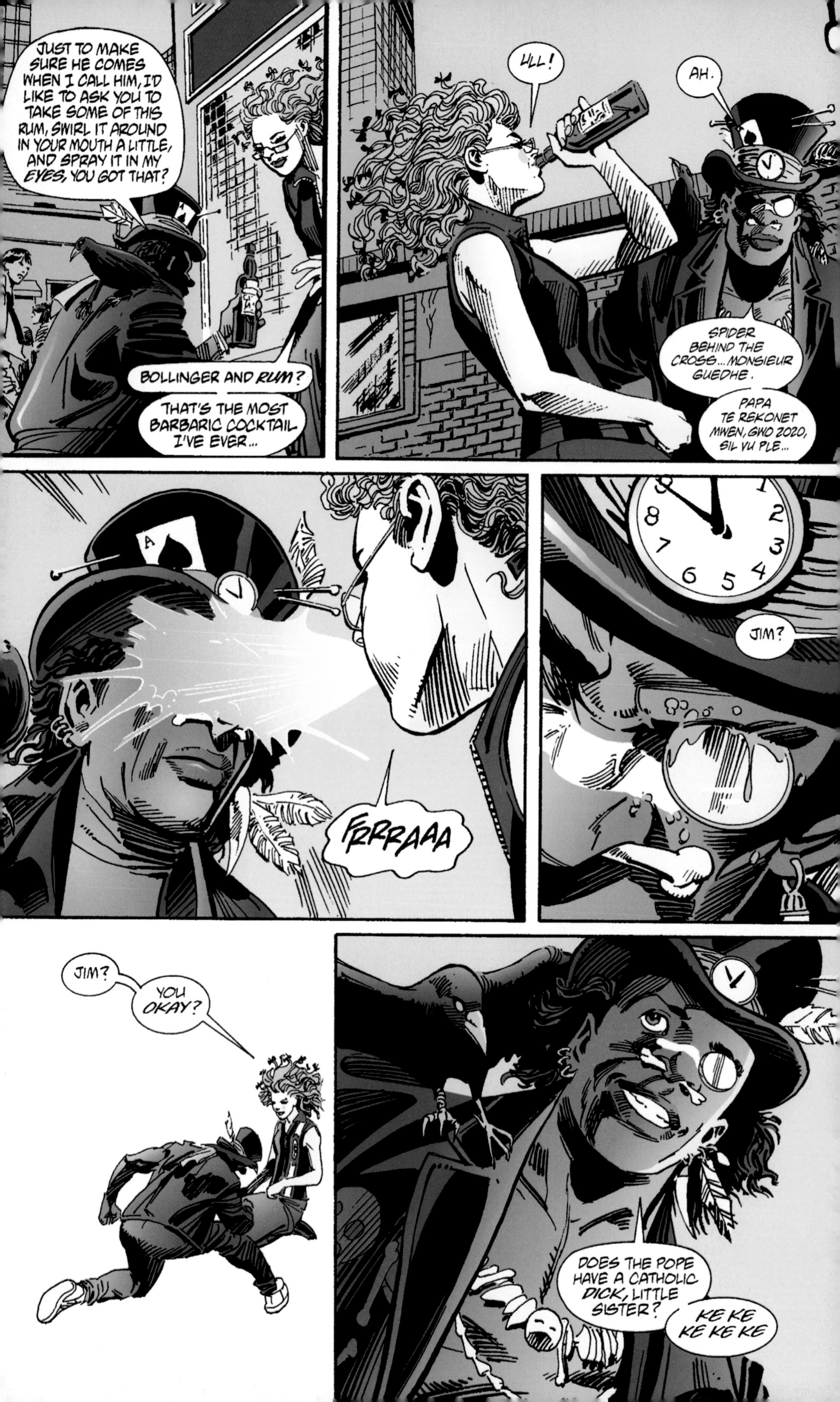
JUST TO MAKE SURE HE COMES WHEN I CALL HIM, I'D LIKE TO ASK YOU TO TAKE SOME OF THIS RUM, SWIRL IT AROUND IN YOUR MOUTH A LITTLE, AND SPRAY IT IN MY EYES, YOU GOT THAT?
BOLLINGER AND RUM?
THAT'S THE MOST BARBARIC COCKTAIL I'VE EVER...
ULL!
AH.
SPIDER BEHIND THE CROSS... MONSIEUR GUEDHE.
PAPA TE REKONET MWEN, GWO ZOZO, SIL VU PLE...
FRRRAAA
JIM?
JIM?
YOU OKAY?
DOES THE POPE HAVE A CATHOLIC DICK, LITTLE SISTER?
KE KE KE KE KE

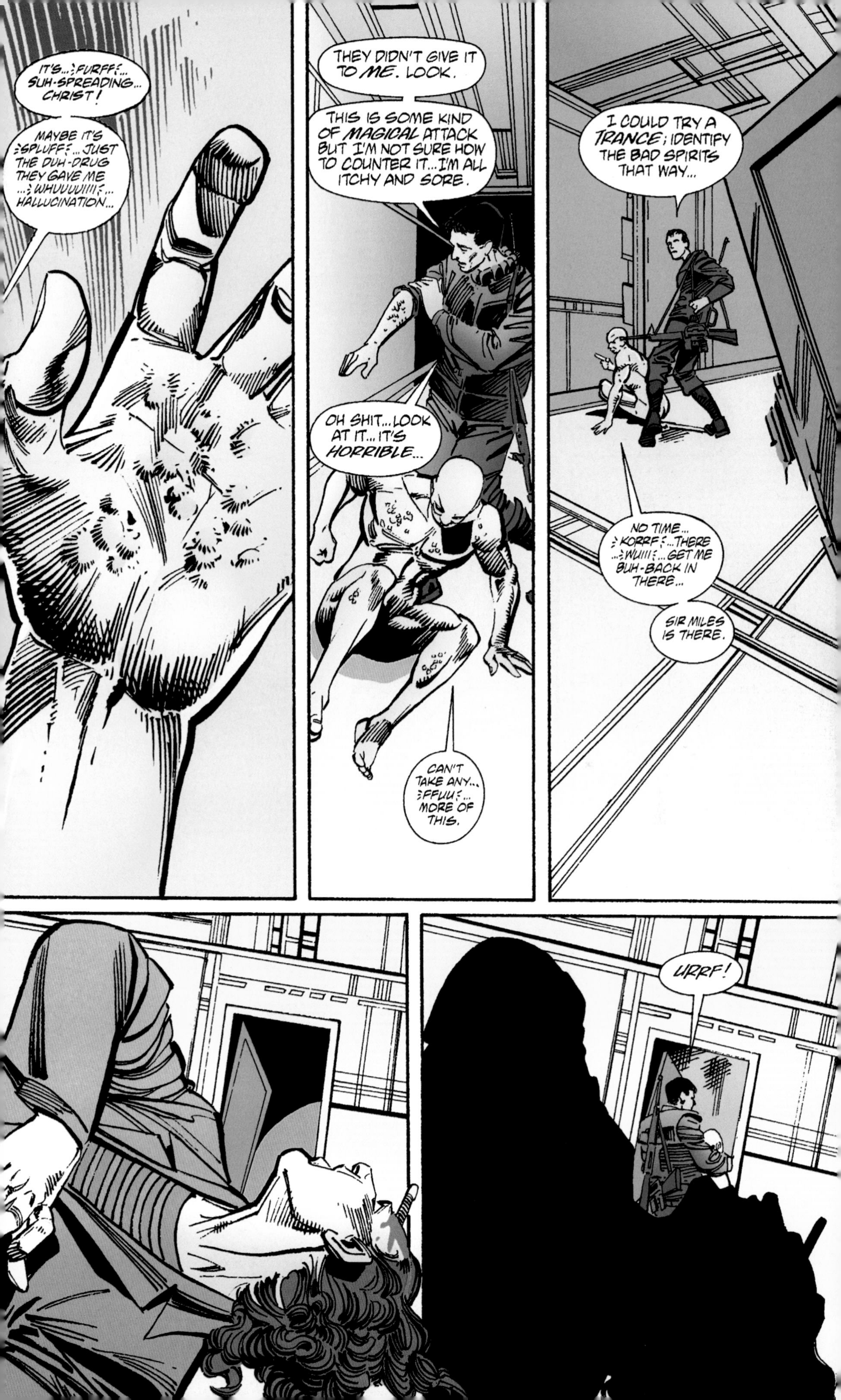
IT'S... FURFF... SUH-SPREADING... CHRIST!
MAYBE IT'S SPLUFF... JUST THE DUH-DRUG THEY GAVE ME ... WHUUUU... HALLUCINATION...
THEY DIDN'T GIVE IT TO ME. LOOK.
THIS IS SOME KIND OF MAGICAL ATTACK BUT I'M NOT SURE HOW TO COUNTER IT... I'M ALL ITCHY AND SORE.
OH SHIT... LOOK AT IT... IT'S HORRIBLE...
CAN'T TAKE ANY... FFUU... MORE OF THIS.
I COULD TRY A TRANCE; IDENTIFY THE BAD SPIRITS THAT WAY...
NO TIME... KORRF... THERE ... WUII... GET ME BUH-BACK IN THERE...
SIR MILES IS THERE.
URRF!

WHO'S THERE?

I DIDN'T...

STAY AWAY FROM ME!

CHUH· CHECK HIM... ⟨KKUUH⟩ ...OUT.

NOTHING. NO BLISTERS, NO SCABS, NO BOILS.

AND YET SOME· HOW HE'S STILL UNATTRACTIVE...

WHAT IS THIS SHUH-SHIT ON US? WHAT DID YOU... ⟨LUFF⟩ ...DO TO US?

UH!

IT'S NOT ME. IT'S THEM!

OH MY GOD. I THINK THIS IS A TUMOR.

IT'S THEM.

MISS DWYER AND THAT... THING. IT'S ONE OF THEM, ONE OF THE ARCHONS, THE KINGS OF THE EARTH.

I BELIEVE YOUR PEOPLE CALL THEM THE 'LOST ONES'.

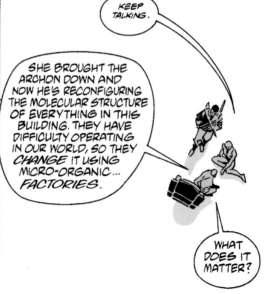

KEEP TALKING.

SHE BROUGHT THE ARCHON DOWN AND NOW HE'S RECONFIGURING THE MOLECULAR STRUCTURE OF EVERYTHING IN THIS BUILDING. THEY HAVE DIFFICULTY OPERATING IN OUR WORLD, SO THEY CHANGE IT USING MICRO-ORGANIC... FACTORIES.

WHAT DOES IT MATTER?

240

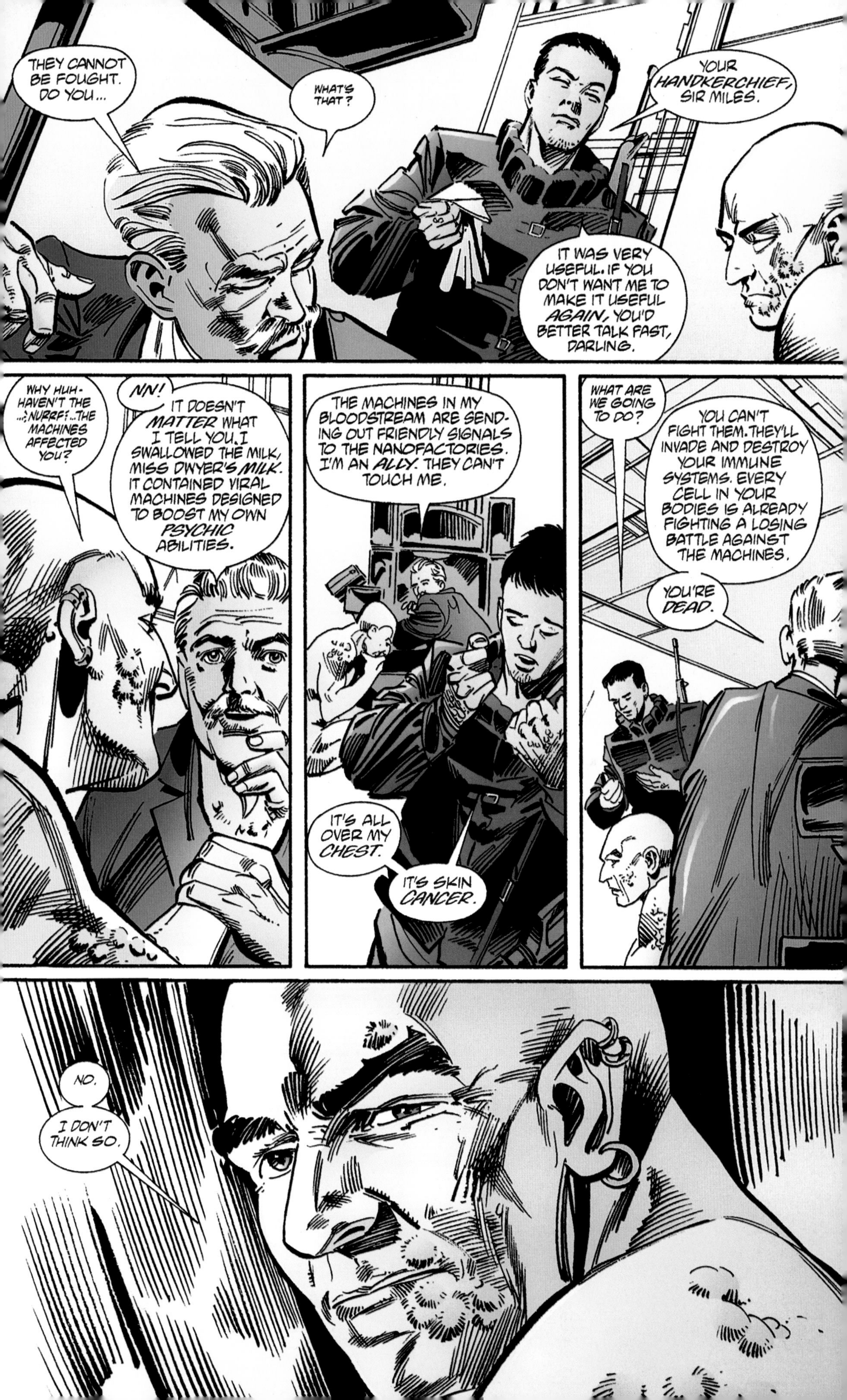
THEY CANNOT BE FOUGHT. DO YOU...
WHAT'S THAT?
YOUR HANDKERCHIEF, SIR MILES.
IT WAS VERY USEFUL. IF YOU DON'T WANT ME TO MAKE IT USEFUL AGAIN, YOU'D BETTER TALK FAST, DARLING.
WHY HUH-HAVEN'T THE ...NURRF!...THE MACHINES AFFECTED YOU?
NN!
IT DOESN'T MATTER WHAT I TELL YOU. I SWALLOWED THE MILK, MISS DWYER'S MILK. IT CONTAINED VIRAL MACHINES DESIGNED TO BOOST MY OWN PSYCHIC ABILITIES.
THE MACHINES IN MY BLOODSTREAM ARE SENDING OUT FRIENDLY SIGNALS TO THE NANOFACTORIES. I'M AN ALLY. THEY CAN'T TOUCH ME.
IT'S ALL OVER MY CHEST.
IT'S SKIN CANCER.
WHAT ARE WE GOING TO DO?
YOU CAN'T FIGHT THEM. THEY'LL INVADE AND DESTROY YOUR IMMUNE SYSTEMS. EVERY CELL IN YOUR BODIES IS ALREADY FIGHTING A LOSING BATTLE AGAINST THE MACHINES.
YOU'RE DEAD.
NO.
I DON'T THINK SO.

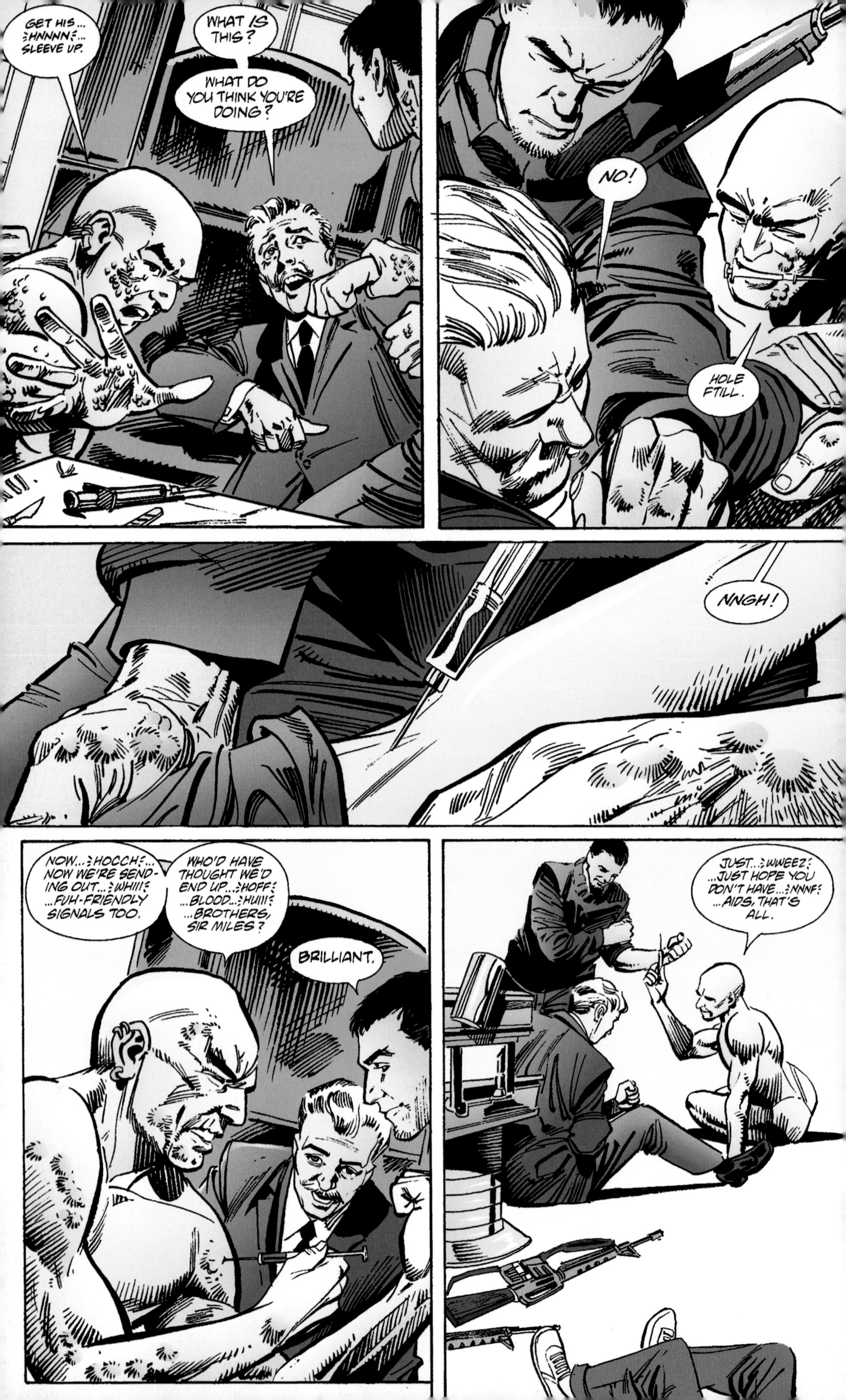
GET HIS... HNNNN!... SLEEVE UP.
WHAT IS THIS?
WHAT DO YOU THINK YOU'RE DOING?
NO!
HOLE FTILL.
NNGH!
NOW... HOCCH!... NOW WE'RE SENDING OUT... WHII!! ...FUH-FRIENDLY SIGNALS TOO.
WHO'D HAVE THOUGHT WE'D END UP... HOFF! ...BLOOD... HUII! ...BROTHERS, SIR MILES?
BRILLIANT.
JUST... WHEEZ! ...JUST HOPE YOU DON'T HAVE... NNNF! ...AIDS, THAT'S ALL.

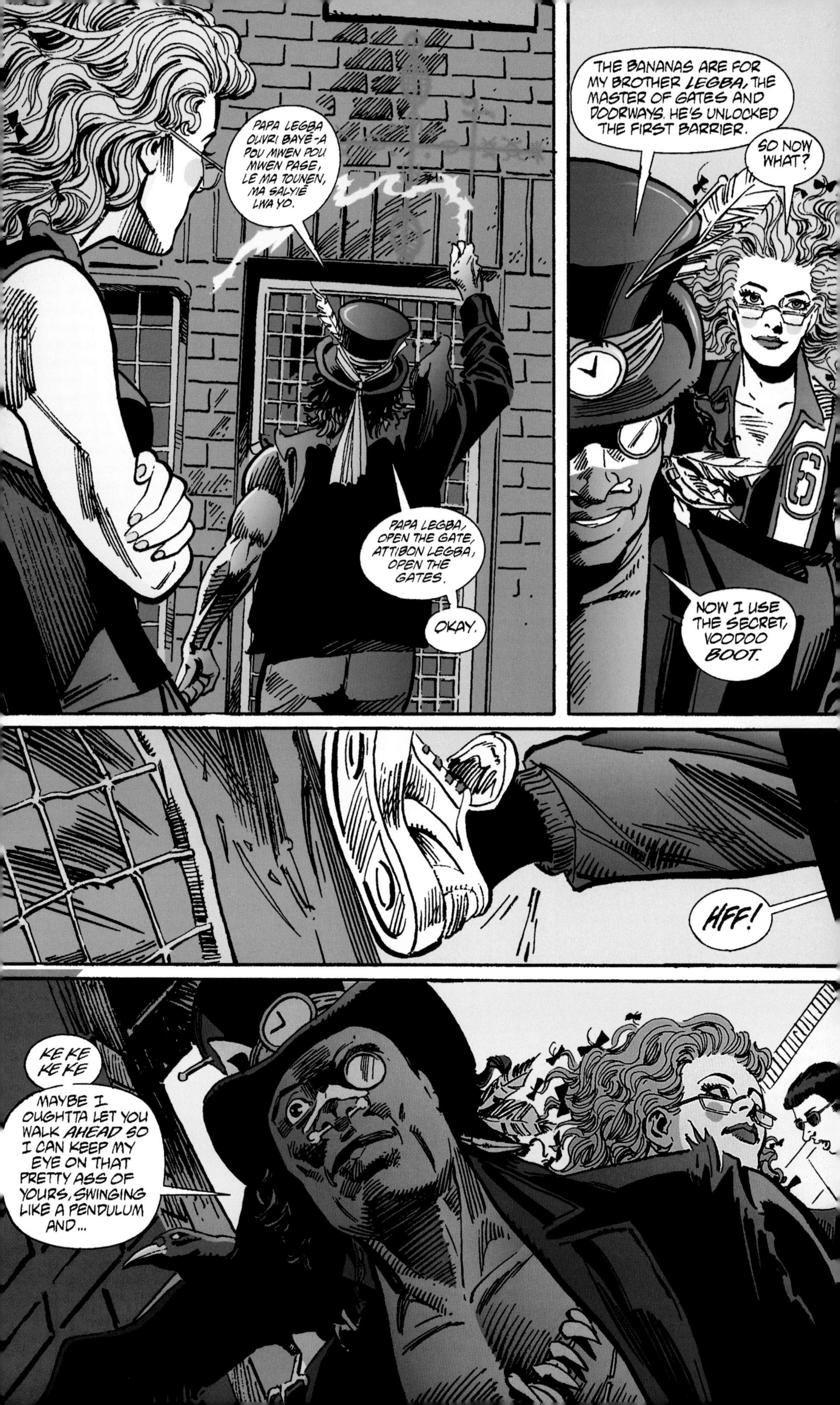

PAPA LEGBA OUVRI BAYÉ-A POU MWEN POU MWEN PASE, LE MA TOUNEN, MA SALYIÉ LWA YO.
PAPA LEGBA, OPEN THE GATE, ATTIBON LEGBA, OPEN THE GATES.
OKAY.
THE BANANAS ARE FOR MY BROTHER LEGBA, THE MASTER OF GATES AND DOORWAYS. HE'S UNLOCKED THE FIRST BARRIER.
SO NOW WHAT?
NOW I USE THE SECRET, VOODOO BOOT.
HFF!
KE KE KE KE
MAYBE I OUGHTTA LET YOU WALK AHEAD SO I CAN KEEP MY EYE ON THAT PRETTY ASS OF YOURS, SWINGING LIKE A PENDULUM AND...

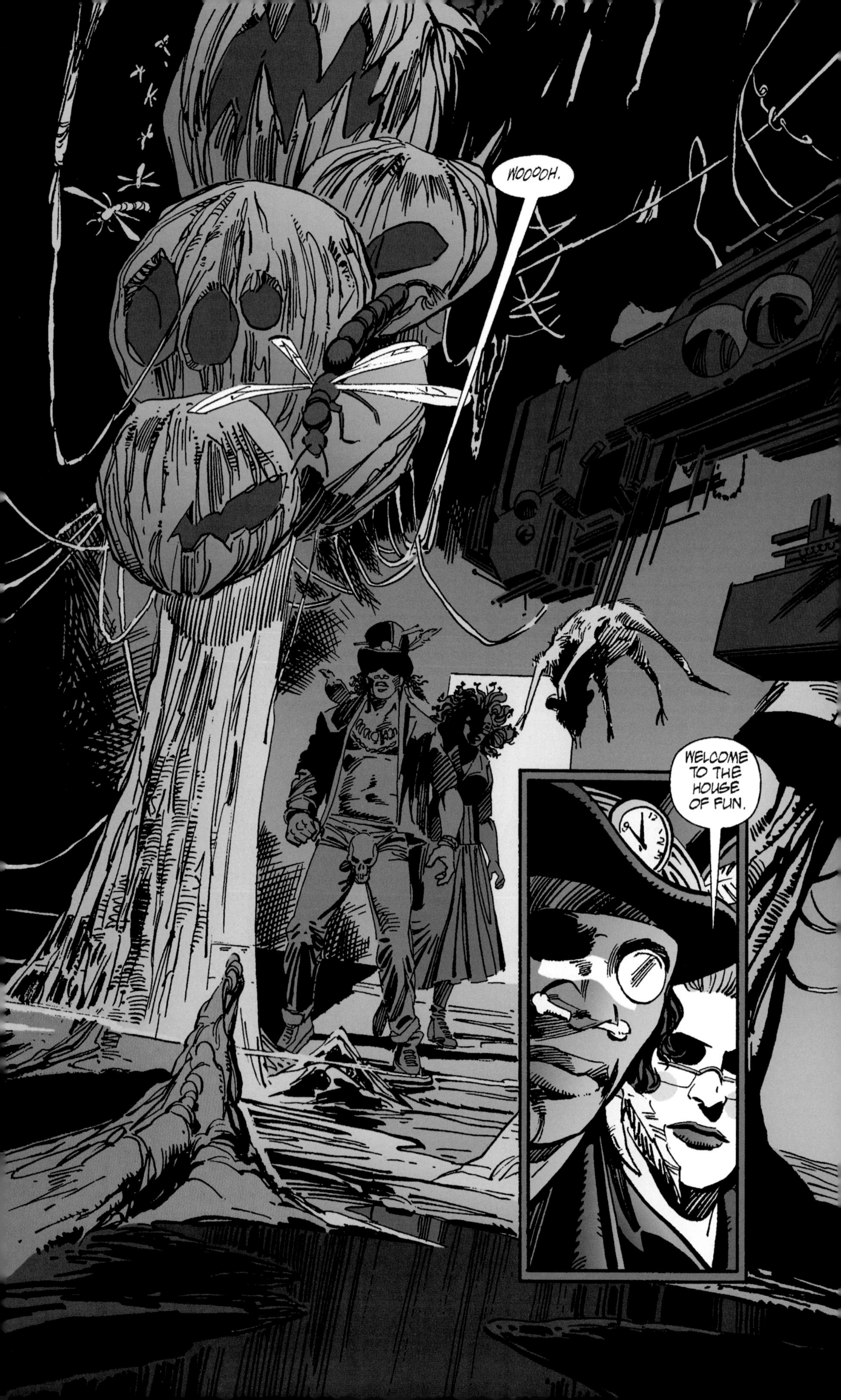
WOOOOH.
WELCOME TO THE HOUSE OF FUN.

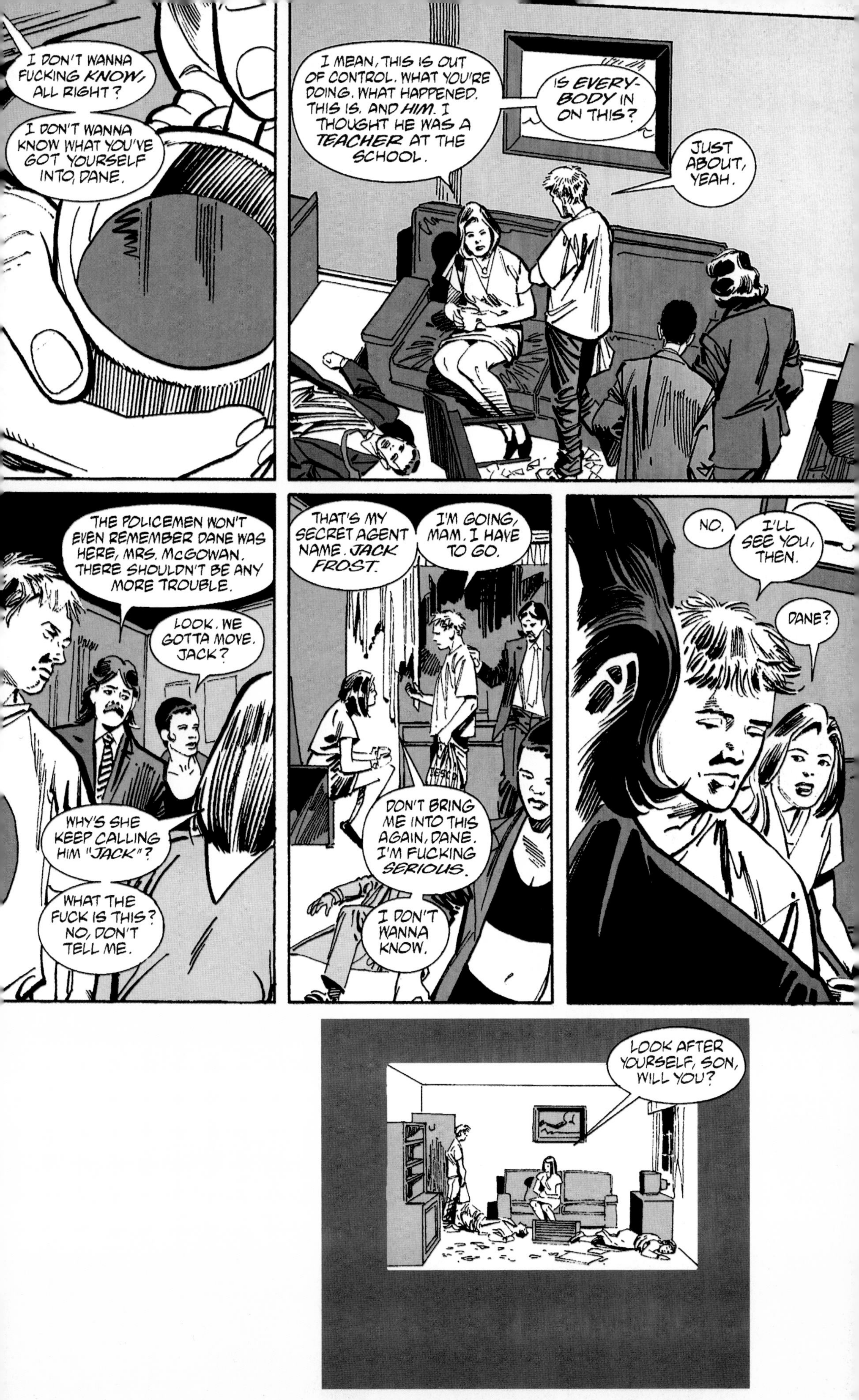
I DON'T WANNA FUCKING KNOW, ALL RIGHT?
I DON'T WANNA KNOW WHAT YOU'VE GOT YOURSELF INTO, DANE.
I MEAN, THIS IS OUT OF CONTROL. WHAT YOU'RE DOING. WHAT HAPPENED. THIS IS. AND HIM. I THOUGHT HE WAS A TEACHER AT THE SCHOOL.
IS EVERYBODY IN ON THIS?
JUST ABOUT, YEAH.
THE POLICEMEN WON'T EVEN REMEMBER DANE WAS HERE, MRS. McGOWAN. THERE SHOULDN'T BE ANY MORE TROUBLE.
LOOK. WE GOTTA MOVE. JACK?
WHY'S SHE KEEP CALLING HIM "JACK"?
WHAT THE FUCK IS THIS? NO, DON'T TELL ME.
THAT'S MY SECRET AGENT NAME. JACK FROST.
I'M GOING, MAM. I HAVE TO GO.
TESCO
DON'T BRING ME INTO THIS AGAIN, DANE. I'M FUCKING SERIOUS.
I DON'T WANNA KNOW.
NO.
I'LL SEE YOU, THEN.
DANE?
LOOK AFTER YOURSELF, SON, WILL YOU?

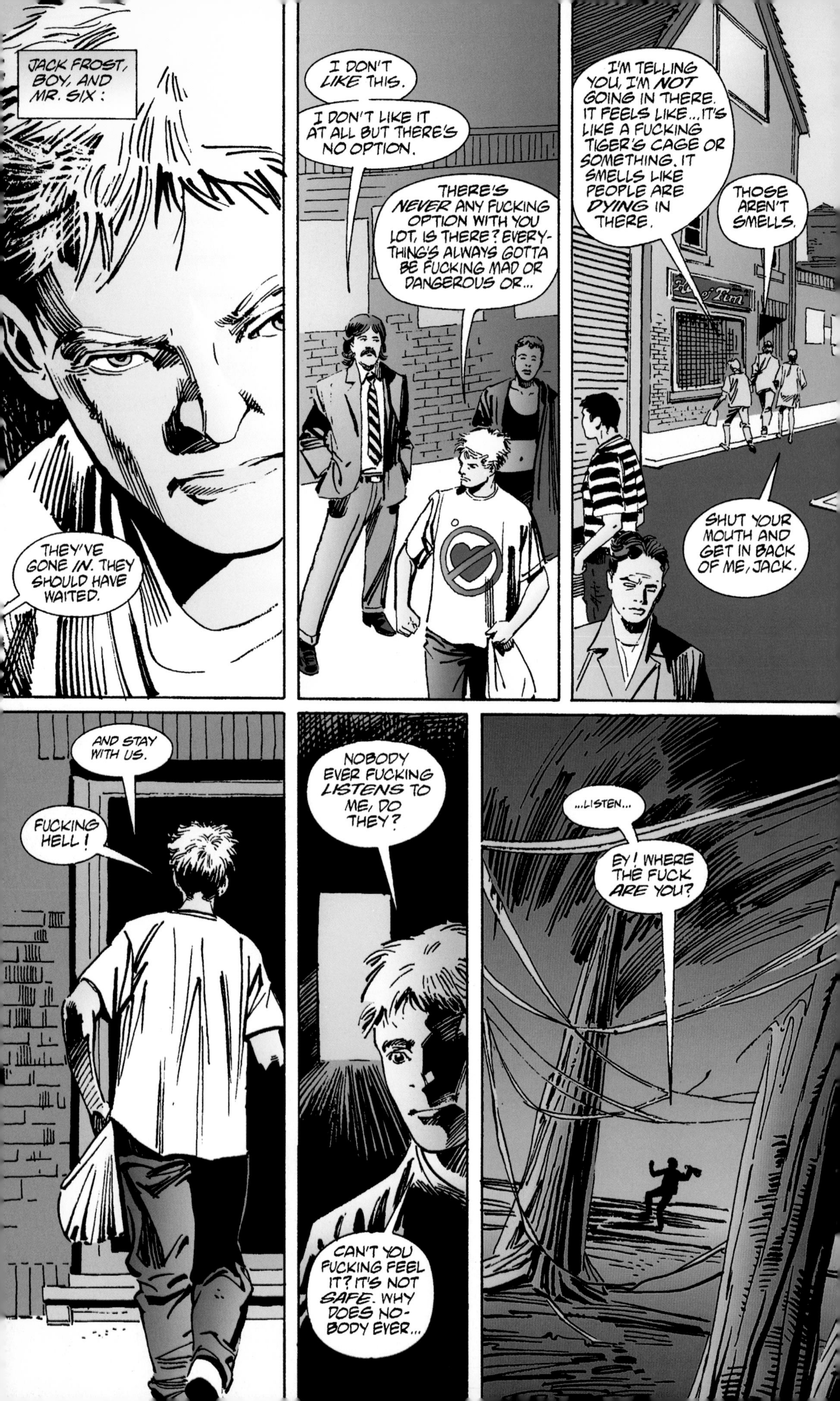
JACK FROST, BOY, AND MR. SIX:
THEY'VE GONE IN. THEY SHOULD HAVE WAITED.
I DON'T LIKE THIS.
I DON'T LIKE IT AT ALL BUT THERE'S NO OPTION.
THERE'S NEVER ANY FUCKING OPTION WITH YOU LOT, IS THERE? EVERYTHING'S ALWAYS GOTTA BE FUCKING MAD OR DANGEROUS OR...
I'M TELLING YOU, I'M NOT GOING IN THERE. IT FEELS LIKE... IT'S LIKE A FUCKING TIGER'S CAGE OR SOMETHING. IT SMELLS LIKE PEOPLE ARE DYING IN THERE.
THOSE AREN'T SMELLS.
SHUT YOUR MOUTH AND GET IN BACK OF ME, JACK.
AND STAY WITH US.
FUCKING HELL!
NOBODY EVER FUCKING LISTENS TO ME, DO THEY?
CAN'T YOU FUCKING FEEL IT? IT'S NOT SAFE. WHY DOES NOBODY EVER...
...LISTEN...
EY! WHERE THE FUCK ARE YOU?

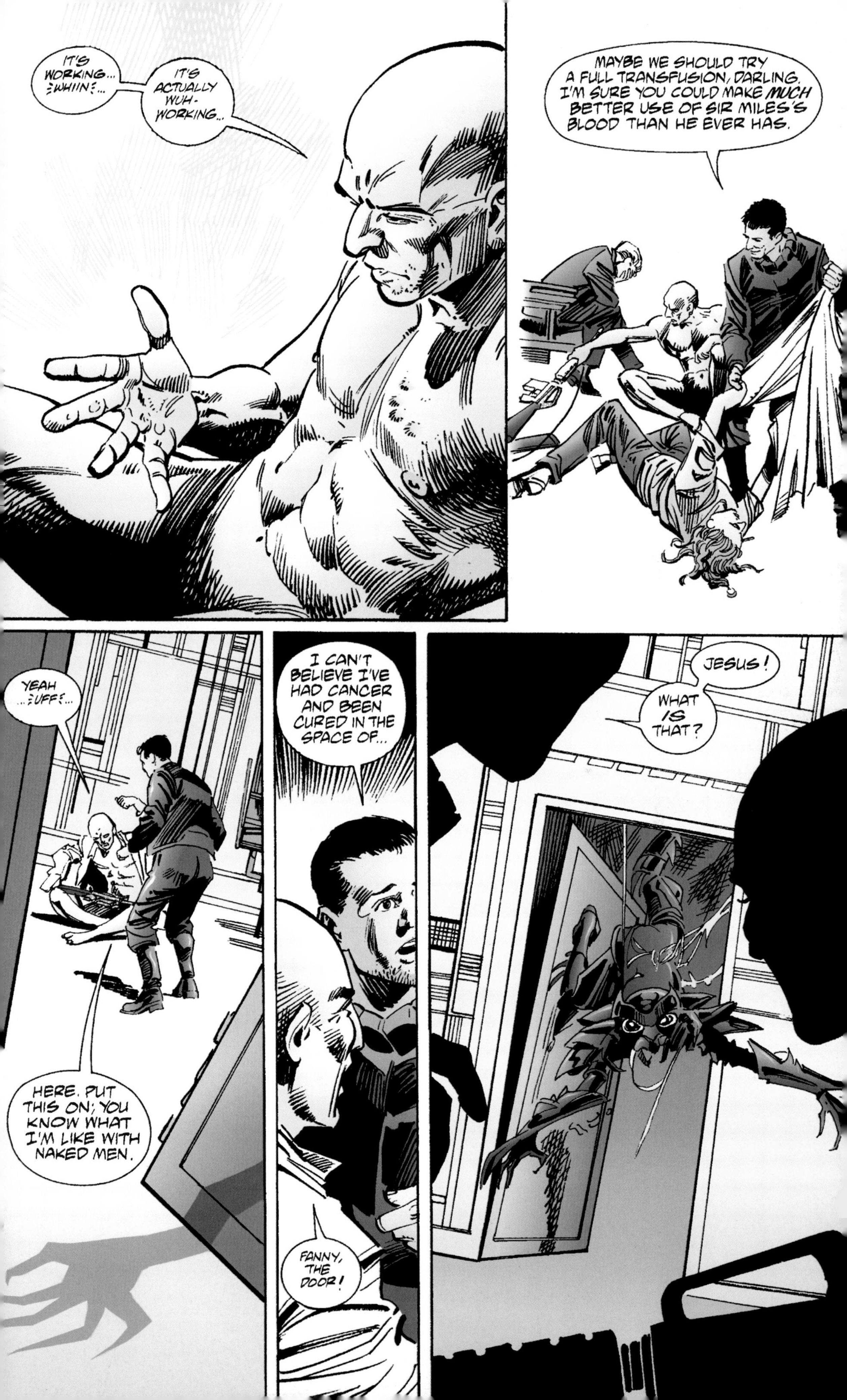
IT'S WORKING... WHIIN...
IT'S ACTUALLY WUH-WORKING...
MAYBE WE SHOULD TRY A FULL TRANSFUSION, DARLING. I'M SURE YOU COULD MAKE MUCH BETTER USE OF SIR MILES'S BLOOD THAN HE EVER HAS.
YEAH ...UFF...
HERE. PUT THIS ON; YOU KNOW WHAT I'M LIKE WITH NAKED MEN.
I CAN'T BELIEVE I'VE HAD CANCER AND BEEN CURED IN THE SPACE OF...
FANNY, THE DOOR!
JESUS!
WHAT IS THAT?

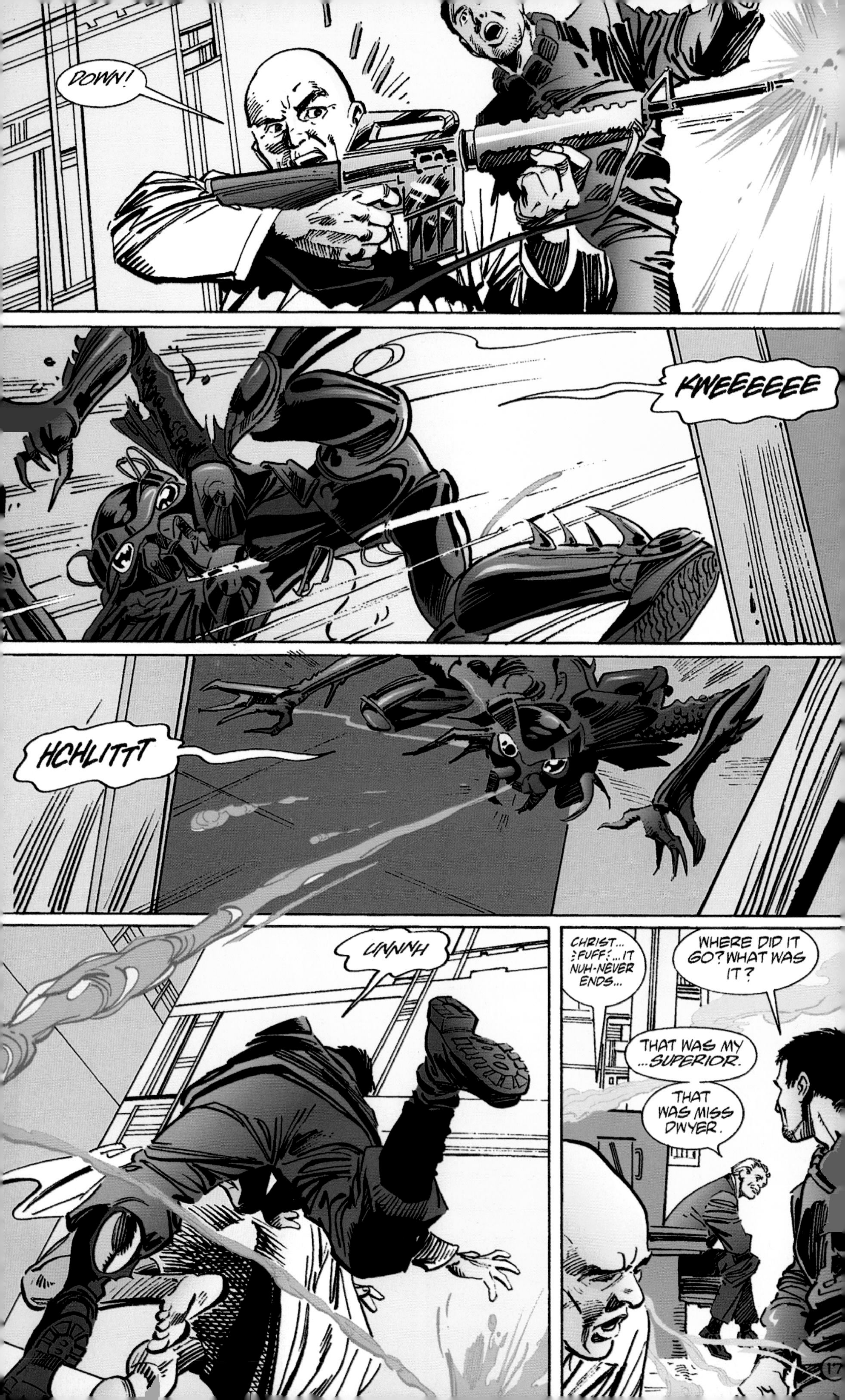
DOWN!
KWEEEEEE
HCHLITTT
UNNNH
CHRIST... FUFF... IT NUH-NEVER ENDS...
WHERE DID IT GO? WHAT WAS IT?
THAT WAS MY ...SUPERIOR.
THAT WAS MISS DWYER.

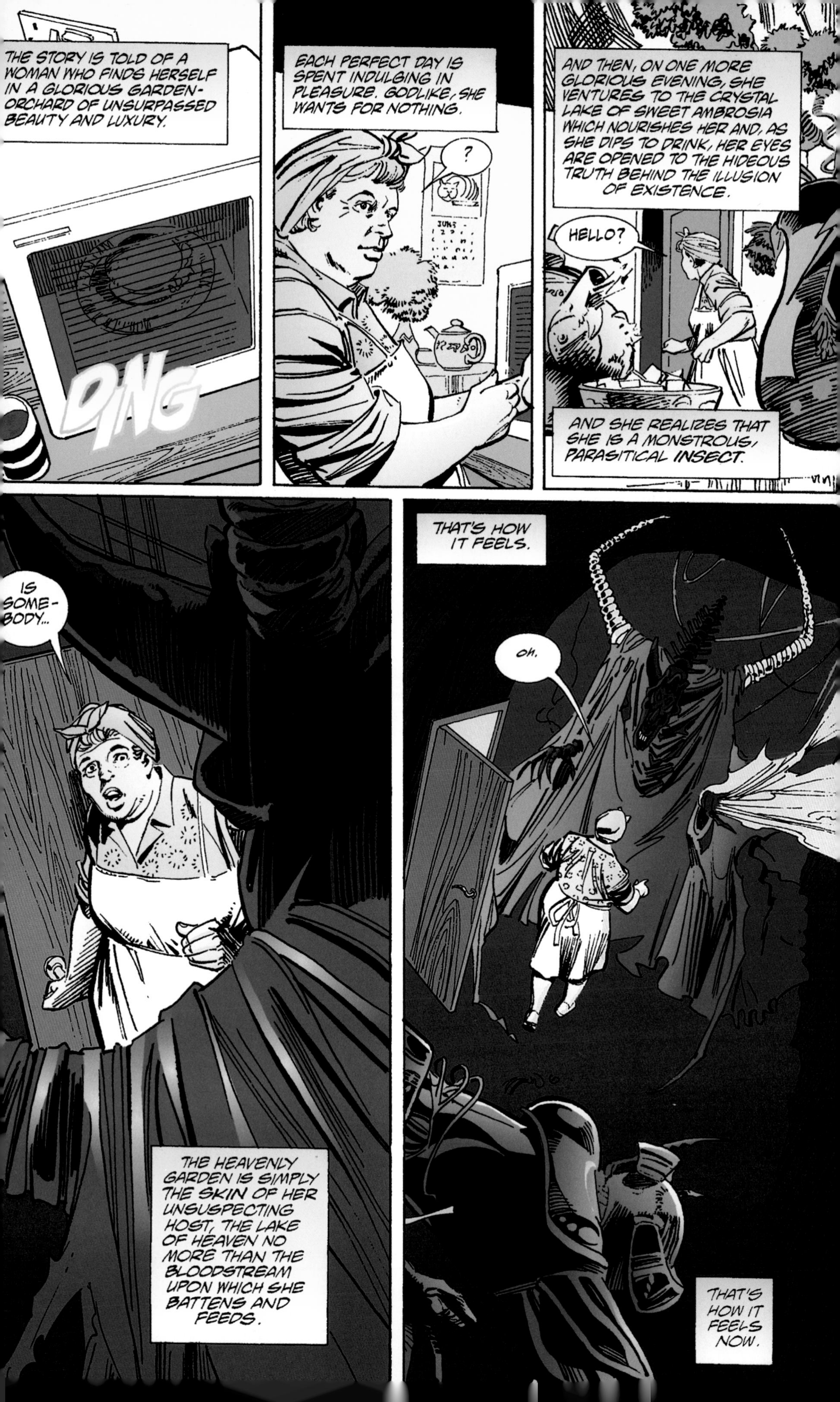
THE STORY IS TOLD OF A WOMAN WHO FINDS HERSELF IN A GLORIOUS GARDEN-ORCHARD OF UNSURPASSED BEAUTY AND LUXURY.
DING
EACH PERFECT DAY IS SPENT INDULGING IN PLEASURE. GODLIKE, SHE WANTS FOR NOTHING.
?
AND THEN, ON ONE MORE GLORIOUS EVENING, SHE VENTURES TO THE CRYSTAL LAKE OF SWEET AMBROSIA WHICH NOURISHES HER AND, AS SHE DIPS TO DRINK, HER EYES ARE OPENED TO THE HIDEOUS TRUTH BEHIND THE ILLUSION OF EXISTENCE.
HELLO?
AND SHE REALIZES THAT SHE IS A MONSTROUS, PARASITICAL INSECT.
IS SOME-BODY...
THE HEAVENLY GARDEN IS SIMPLY THE SKIN OF HER UNSUSPECTING HOST, THE LAKE OF HEAVEN NO MORE THAN THE BLOODSTREAM UPON WHICH SHE BATTENS AND FEEDS.
THAT'S HOW IT FEELS.
oh.
THAT'S HOW IT FEELS NOW.

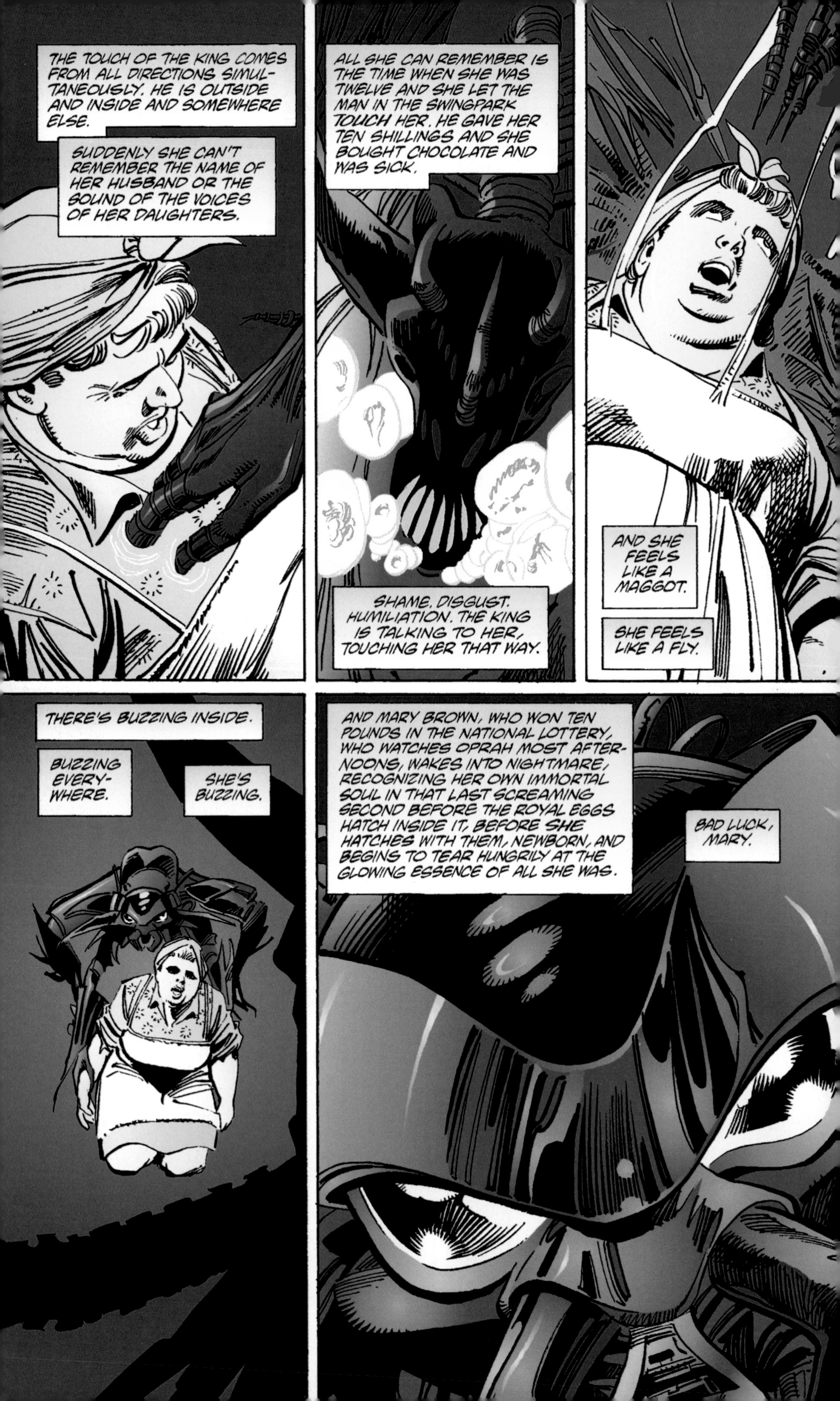
THE TOUCH OF THE KING COMES FROM ALL DIRECTIONS SIMULTANEOUSLY. HE IS OUTSIDE AND INSIDE AND SOMEWHERE ELSE.
SUDDENLY SHE CAN'T REMEMBER THE NAME OF HER HUSBAND OR THE SOUND OF THE VOICES OF HER DAUGHTERS.
ALL SHE CAN REMEMBER IS THE TIME WHEN SHE WAS TWELVE AND SHE LET THE MAN IN THE SWINGPARK TOUCH HER. HE GAVE HER TEN SHILLINGS AND SHE BOUGHT CHOCOLATE AND WAS SICK.
SHAME. DISGUST. HUMILIATION. THE KING IS TALKING TO HER, TOUCHING HER THAT WAY.
AND SHE FEELS LIKE A MAGGOT.
SHE FEELS LIKE A FLY.
THERE'S BUZZING INSIDE.
BUZZING EVERYWHERE.
SHE'S BUZZING.
AND MARY BROWN, WHO WON TEN POUNDS IN THE NATIONAL LOTTERY, WHO WATCHES OPRAH MOST AFTERNOONS, WAKES INTO NIGHTMARE, RECOGNIZING HER OWN IMMORTAL SOUL IN THAT LAST SCREAMING SECOND BEFORE THE ROYAL EGGS HATCH INSIDE IT, BEFORE SHE HATCHES WITH THEM, NEWBORN, AND BEGINS TO TEAR HUNGRILY AT THE GLOWING ESSENCE OF ALL SHE WAS.
BAD LUCK, MARY.

RRRAAWK

YOU SAID IT.

SOMEBODY JUST *DIED* IN HERE, DIED BAD.

I FEEL SICK AS A DOG, JIM.

I THINK ONE OF THE LOST ONES HAS MANIFESTED HERE; THIS IS ULTRADIMENSIONAL TECHNOLOGY.

WE'RE IN *TROUBLE.*

MAYBE.

AND MAYBE THEY MADE A BIG MISTAKE THINKING THIS SPOOKY DEATH FETISH SHIT WAS GONNA BOTHER *ME* THIS IS A HOME AWAY FROM HOME!

WOHH! THAT'S A NICE BIG SMILE YOU GOT THERE.

YOU EVER THOUGHT ABOUT *MODELLING?*

KE KE KE KE

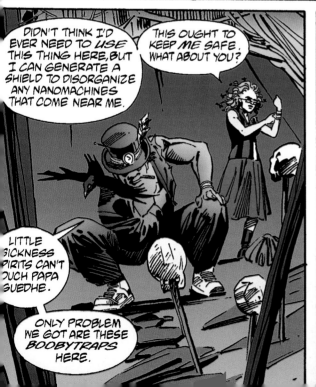

DIDN'T THINK I'D EVER NEED TO *USE* THIS THING HERE, BUT I CAN GENERATE A SHIELD TO DISORGANIZE ANY NANOMACHINES THAT COME NEAR ME.

THIS OUGHT TO KEEP *ME* SAFE. WHAT ABOUT YOU?

LITTLE SICKNESS SPIRITS CAN'T TOUCH PAPA GUEDHE.

ONLY PROBLEM WE GOT ARE THESE *BOOBYTRAPS* HERE.

FORTUNATELY I GOT MY *SKELETON KEY* WITH ME.

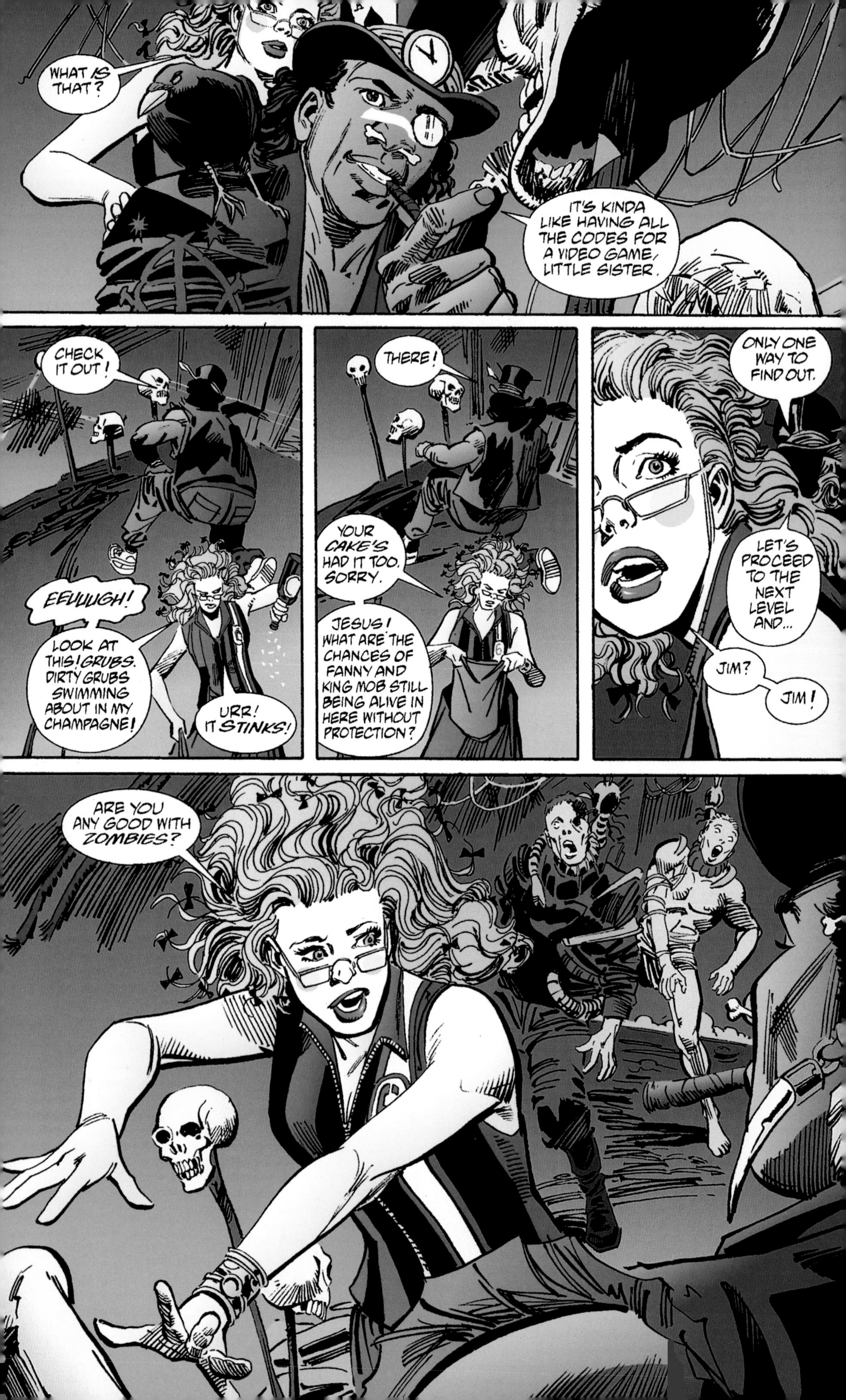
WHAT IS THAT?
IT'S KINDA LIKE HAVING ALL THE CODES FOR A VIDEO GAME, LITTLE SISTER.
CHECK IT OUT!
EEUUUGH!
LOOK AT THIS! GRUBS. DIRTY GRUBS SWIMMING ABOUT IN MY CHAMPAGNE!
URR! IT STINKS!
THERE!
YOUR CAKE'S HAD IT TOO. SORRY.
JESUS! WHAT ARE THE CHANCES OF FANNY AND KING MOB STILL BEING ALIVE IN HERE WITHOUT PROTECTION?
ONLY ONE WAY TO FIND OUT.
LET'S PROCEED TO THE NEXT LEVEL AND...
JIM?
JIM!
ARE YOU ANY GOOD WITH ZOMBIES?

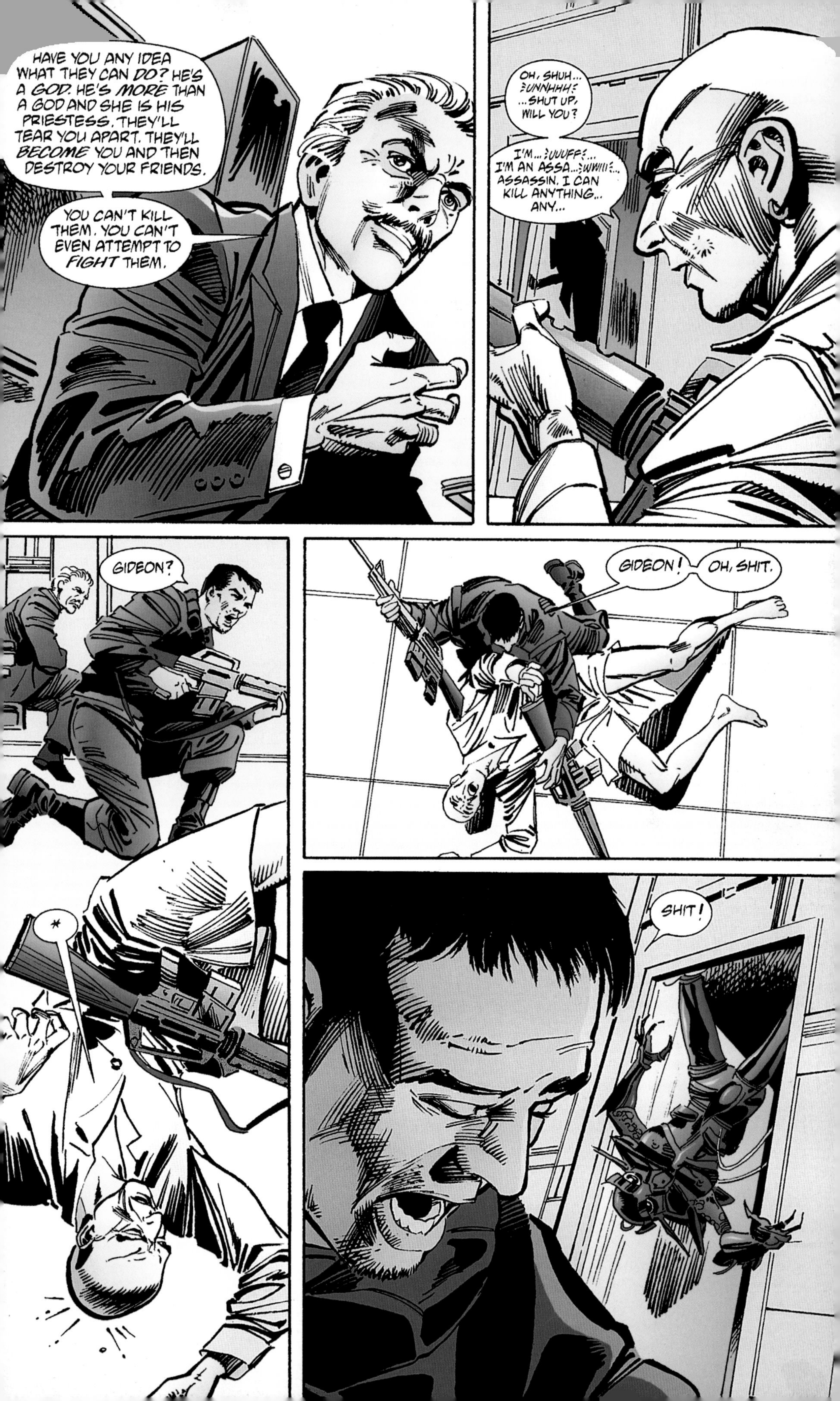
HAVE YOU ANY IDEA WHAT THEY CAN DO? HE'S A GOD. HE'S MORE THAN A GOD AND SHE IS HIS PRIESTESS. THEY'LL TEAR YOU APART. THEY'LL BECOME YOU AND THEN DESTROY YOUR FRIENDS.
YOU CAN'T KILL THEM. YOU CAN'T EVEN ATTEMPT TO FIGHT THEM.
OH, SHUH... UNNHHH ...SHUT UP, WILL YOU?
I'M... UUUFF... I'M AN ASSA... WWIII... ASSASSIN. I CAN KILL ANYTHING... ANY...
GIDEON?
GIDEON!
OH, SHIT.
*
SHIT!

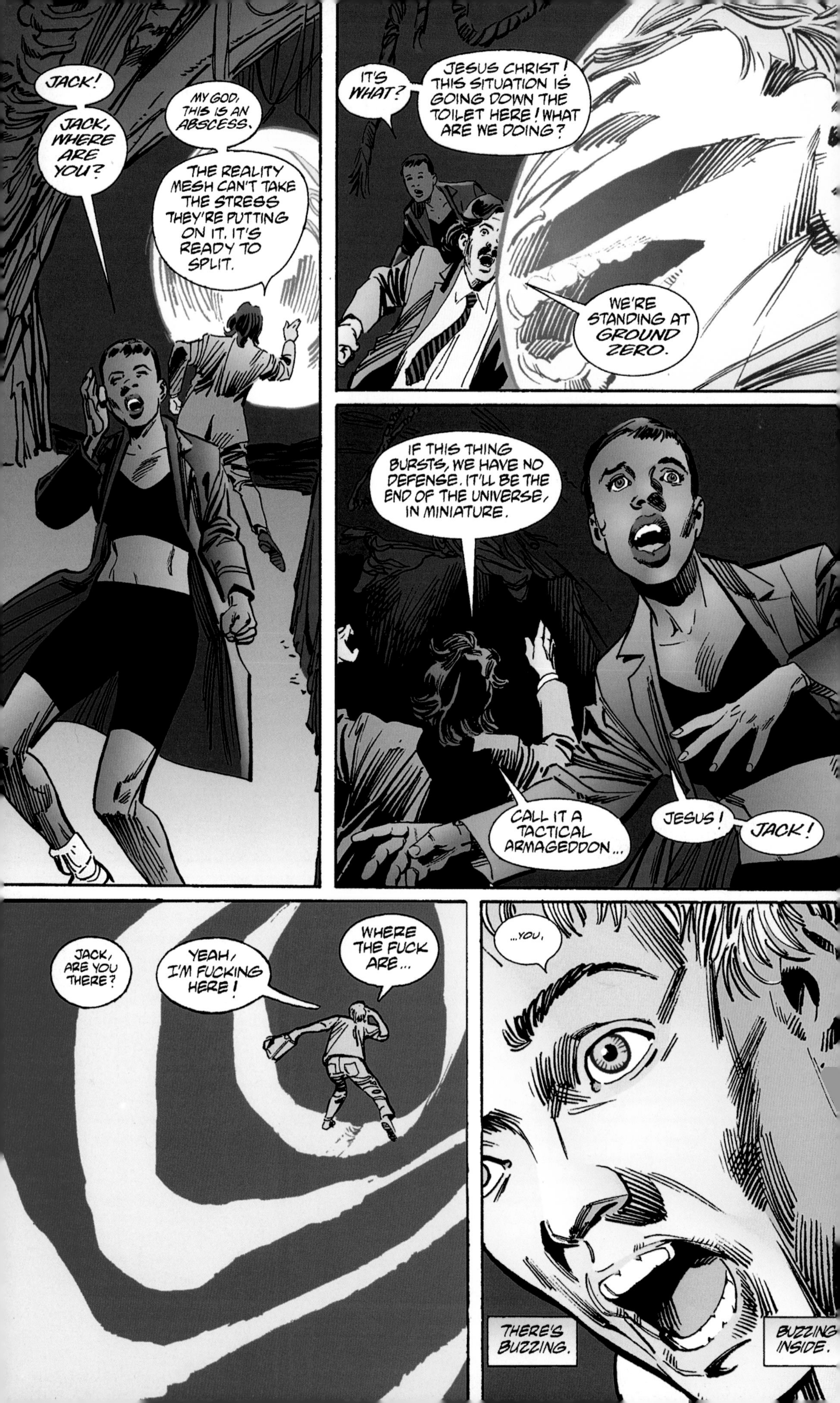

JACK!
JACK, WHERE ARE YOU?
MY GOD, THIS IS AN ABSCESS.
THE REALITY MESH CAN'T TAKE THE STRESS THEY'RE PUTTING ON IT. IT'S READY TO SPLIT.
IT'S WHAT?
JESUS CHRIST! THIS SITUATION IS GOING DOWN THE TOILET HERE! WHAT ARE WE DOING?
WE'RE STANDING AT GROUND ZERO.
IF THIS THING BURSTS, WE HAVE NO DEFENSE. IT'LL BE THE END OF THE UNIVERSE, IN MINIATURE.
CALL IT A TACTICAL ARMAGEDDON...
JESUS!
JACK!
JACK, ARE YOU THERE?
YEAH, I'M FUCKING HERE!
WHERE THE FUCK ARE...
...YOU,
THERE'S BUZZING.
BUZZING INSIDE.

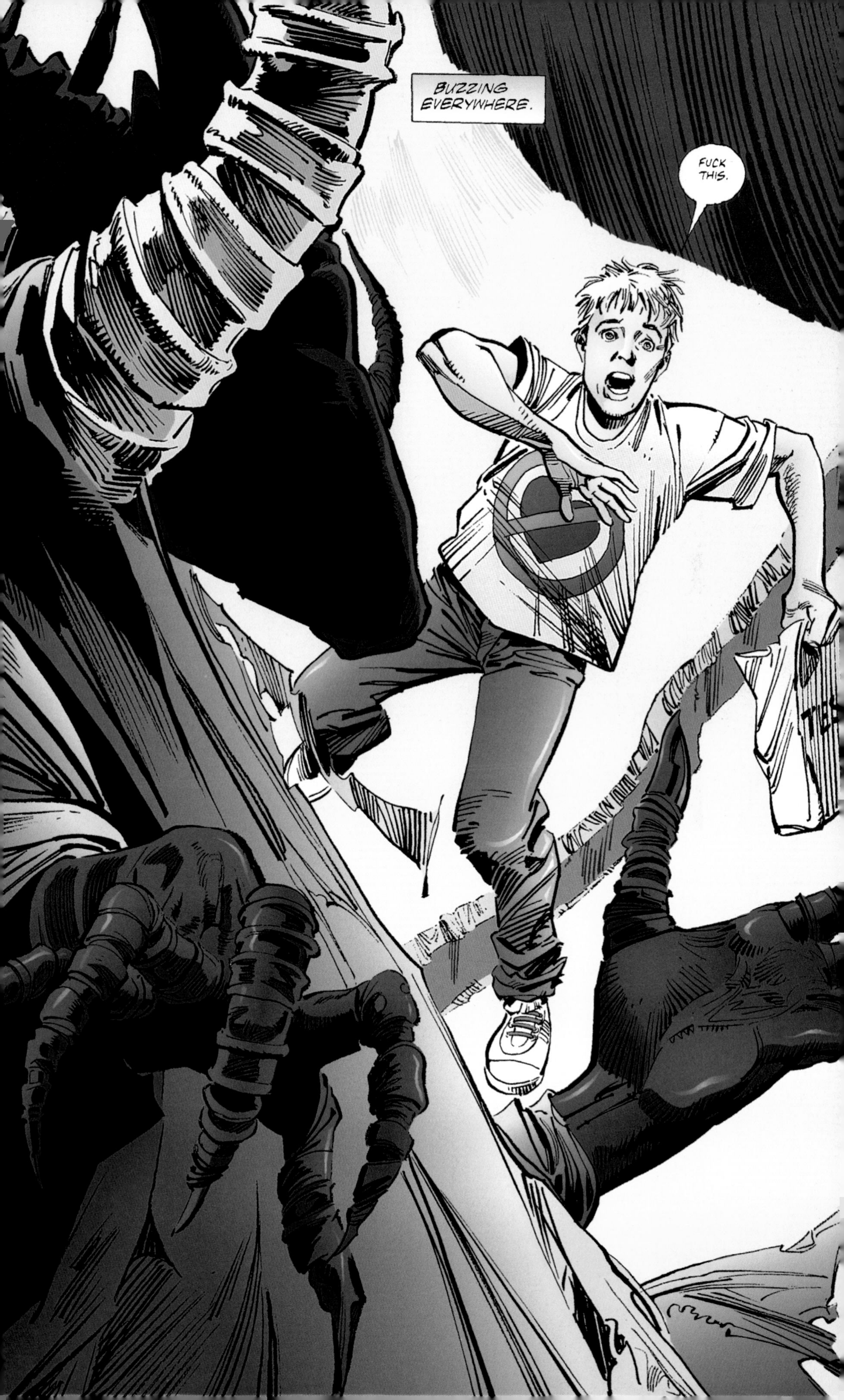
BUZZING EVERYWHERE.
FUCK THIS.

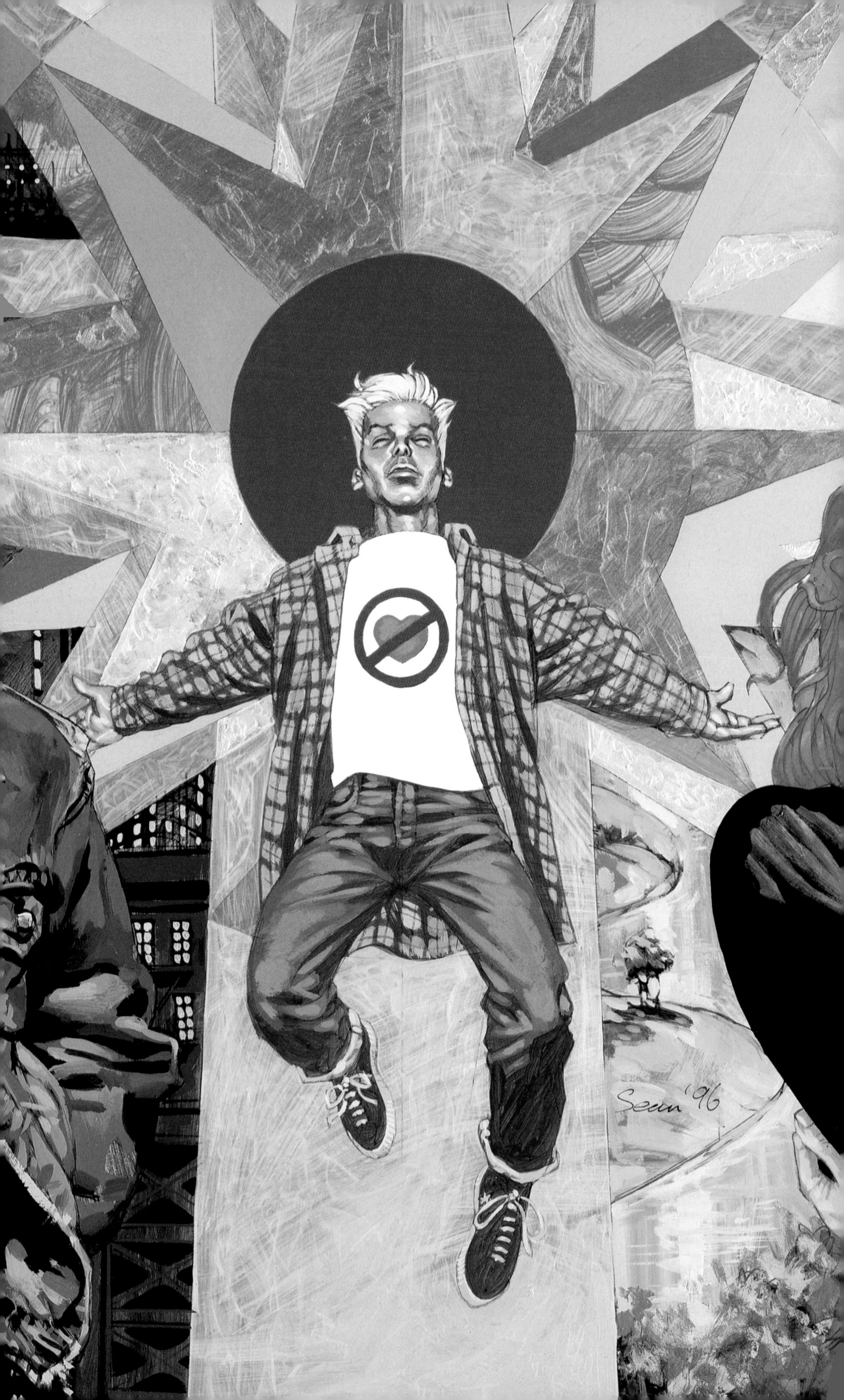
Sean '96

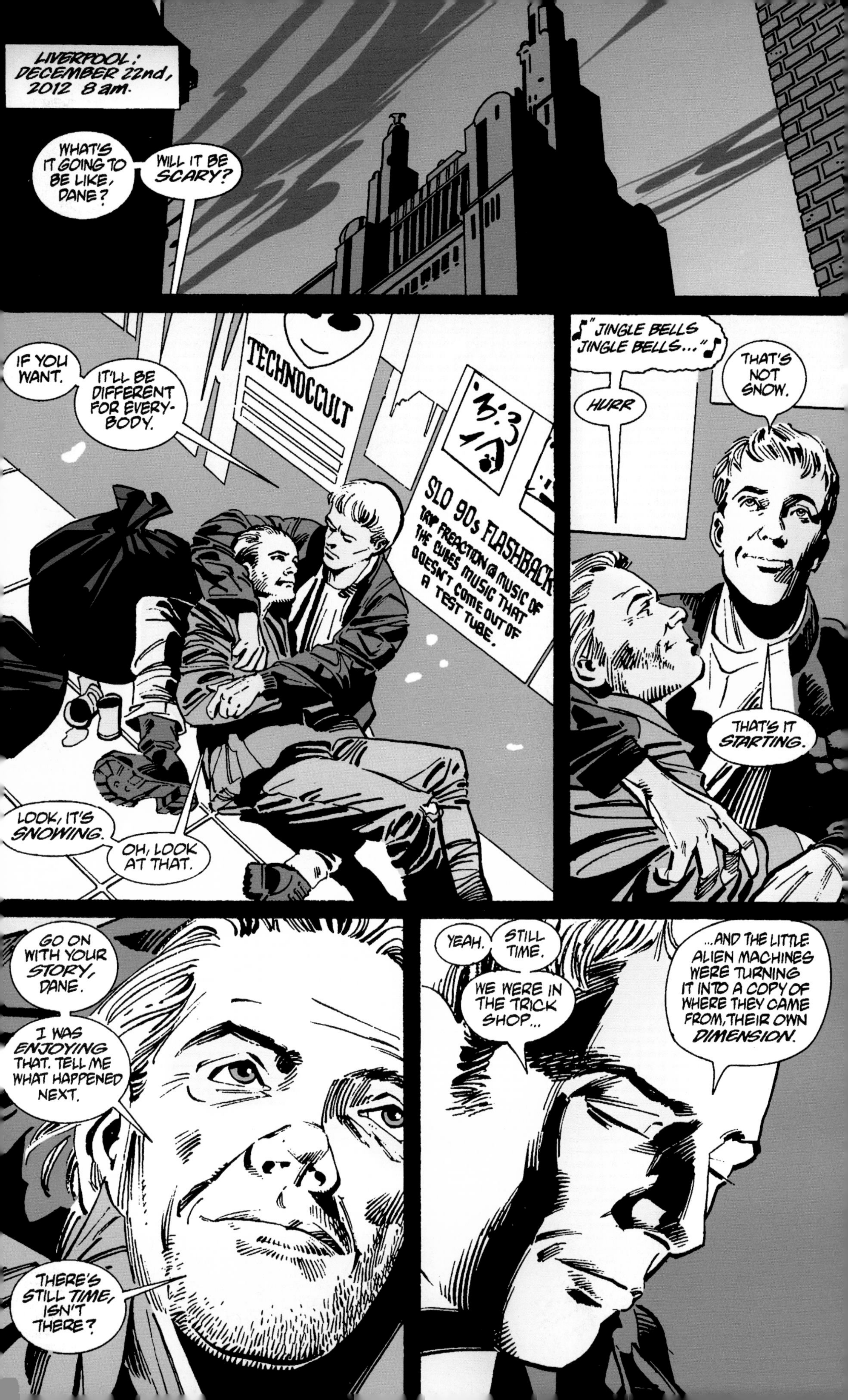
LIVERPOOL: DECEMBER 22nd, 2012 8 am.
WHAT'S IT GOING TO BE LIKE, DANE?
WILL IT BE SCARY?
IF YOU WANT.
IT'LL BE DIFFERENT FOR EVERY-BODY.
TECHNOCCULT
SLO 90s FLASHBACK TRIP FREACTION @ MUSIC OF THE CUBES MUSIC THAT DOESN'T COME OUT OF A TEST TUBE.
LOOK, IT'S SNOWING.
OH, LOOK AT THAT.
"JINGLE BELLS JINGLE BELLS..."
HURR
THAT'S NOT SNOW.
THAT'S IT STARTING.
GO ON WITH YOUR STORY, DANE.
I WAS ENJOYING THAT. TELL ME WHAT HAPPENED NEXT.
THERE'S STILL TIME, ISN'T THERE?
YEAH.
STILL TIME.
WE WERE IN THE TRICK SHOP...
...AND THE LITTLE ALIEN MACHINES WERE TURNING IT INTO A COPY OF WHERE THEY CAME FROM, THEIR OWN DIMENSION.

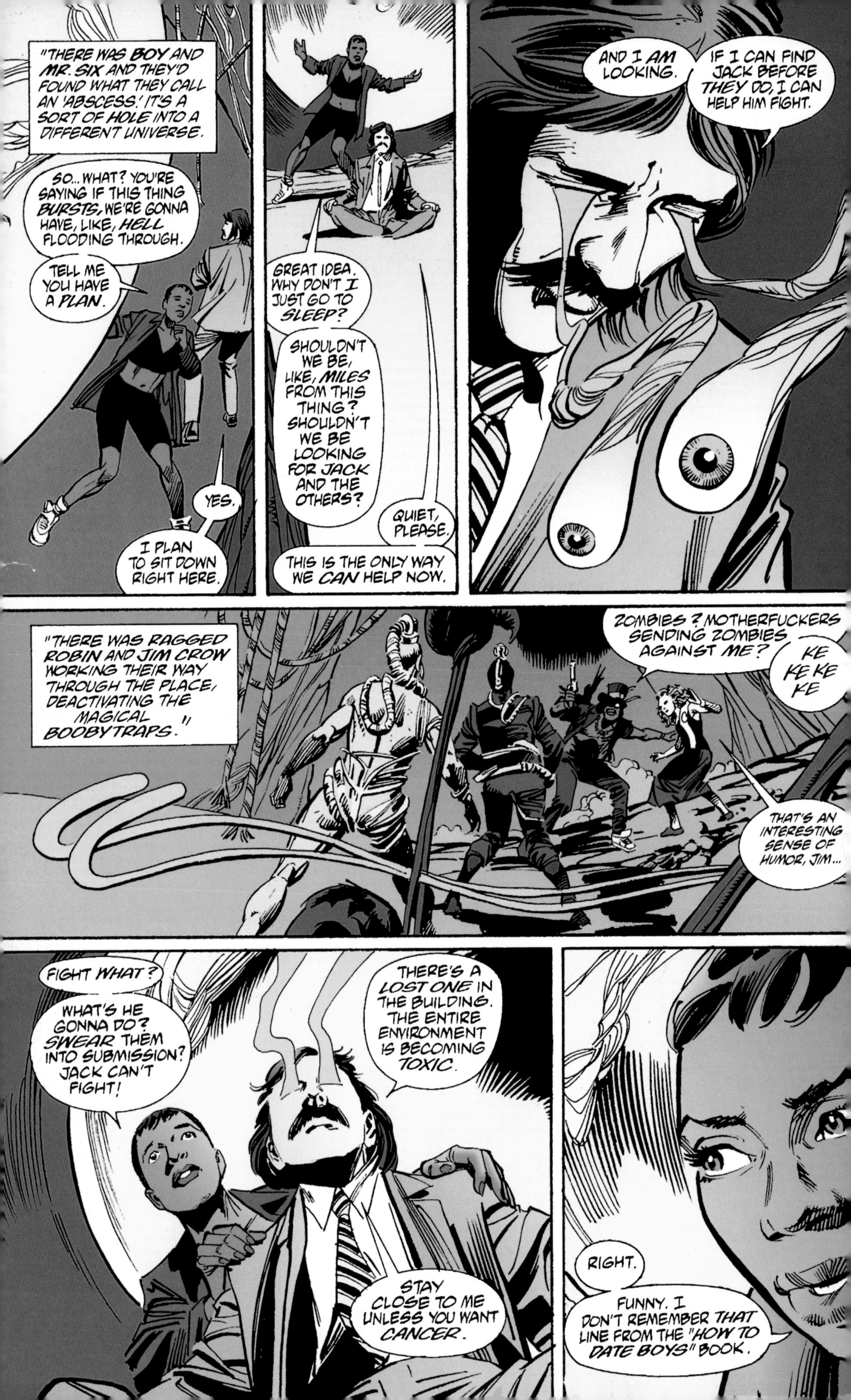
"THERE WAS BOY AND MR. SIX AND THEY'D FOUND WHAT THEY CALL AN 'ABSCESS.' IT'S A SORT OF HOLE INTO A DIFFERENT UNIVERSE.
SO... WHAT? YOU'RE SAYING IF THIS THING BURSTS, WE'RE GONNA HAVE, LIKE, HELL FLOODING THROUGH.
TELL ME YOU HAVE A PLAN.
YES.
I PLAN TO SIT DOWN RIGHT HERE.
GREAT IDEA. WHY DON'T I JUST GO TO SLEEP?
SHOULDN'T WE BE, LIKE, MILES FROM THIS THING? SHOULDN'T WE BE LOOKING FOR JACK AND THE OTHERS?
QUIET, PLEASE.
THIS IS THE ONLY WAY WE CAN HELP NOW.
AND I AM LOOKING.
IF I CAN FIND JACK BEFORE THEY DO, I CAN HELP HIM FIGHT.
"THERE WAS RAGGED ROBIN AND JIM CROW WORKING THEIR WAY THROUGH THE PLACE, DEACTIVATING THE MAGICAL BOOBYTRAPS."
ZOMBIES? MOTHERFUCKERS SENDING ZOMBIES AGAINST ME?
KE KE KE KE
THAT'S AN INTERESTING SENSE OF HUMOR, JIM...
FIGHT WHAT?
WHAT'S HE GONNA DO? SWEAR THEM INTO SUBMISSION? JACK CAN'T FIGHT!
THERE'S A LOST ONE IN THE BUILDING. THE ENTIRE ENVIRONMENT IS BECOMING TOXIC.
STAY CLOSE TO ME UNLESS YOU WANT CANCER.
RIGHT.
FUNNY. I DON'T REMEMBER THAT LINE FROM THE "HOW TO DATE BOYS" BOOK.

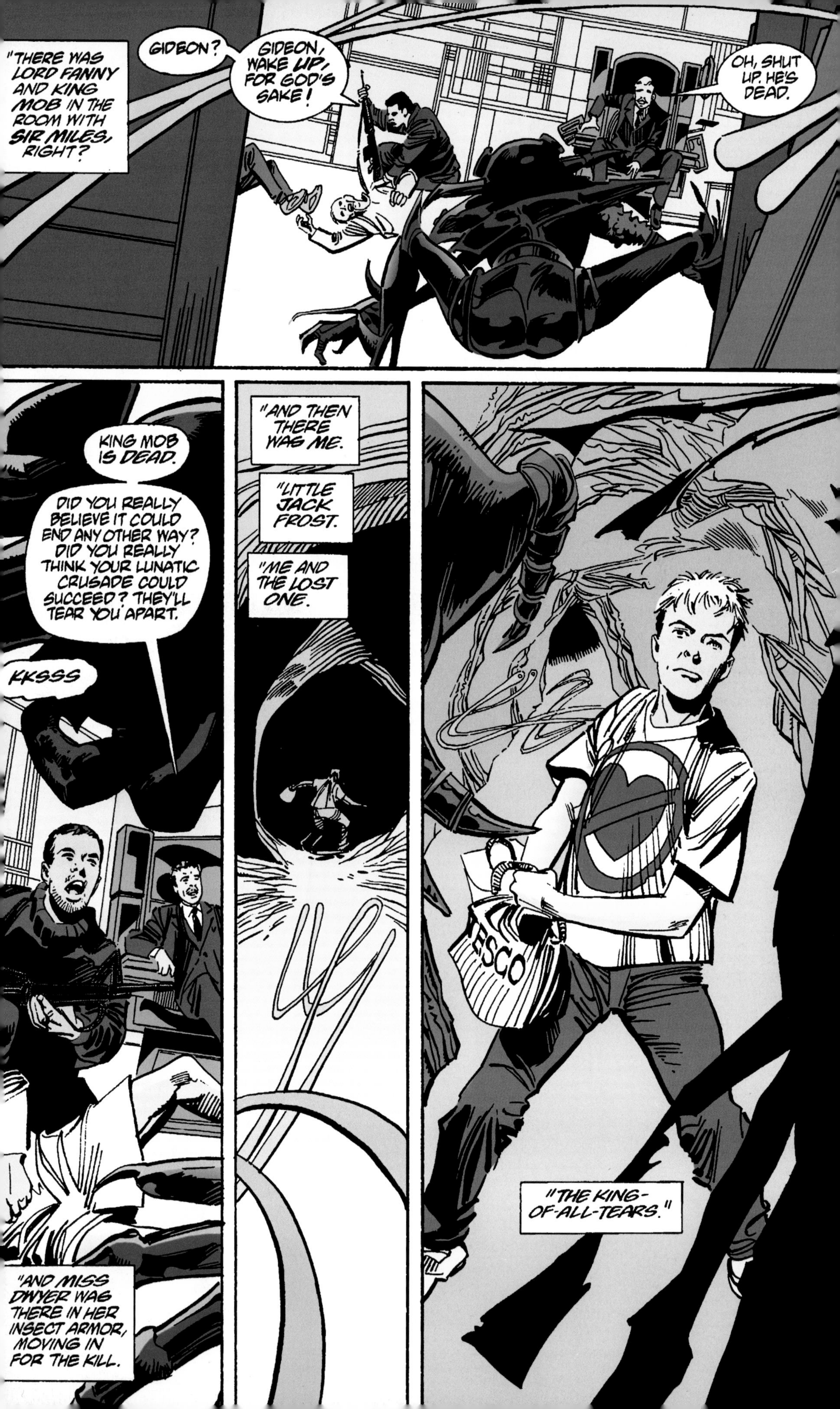

"THERE WAS LORD FANNY AND KING MOB IN THE ROOM WITH SIR MILES, RIGHT?
GIDEON?
GIDEON, WAKE UP, FOR GOD'S SAKE!
OH, SHUT UP. HE'S DEAD.
KING MOB IS DEAD.
DID YOU REALLY BELIEVE IT COULD END ANY OTHER WAY? DID YOU REALLY THINK YOUR LUNATIC CRUSADE COULD SUCCEED? THEY'LL TEAR YOU APART.
KKSSS
"AND MISS DWYER WAS THERE IN HER INSECT ARMOR, MOVING IN FOR THE KILL.
"AND THEN THERE WAS ME.
"LITTLE JACK FROST.
"ME AND THE LOST ONE.
TESCO
"THE KING-OF-ALL-TEARS."

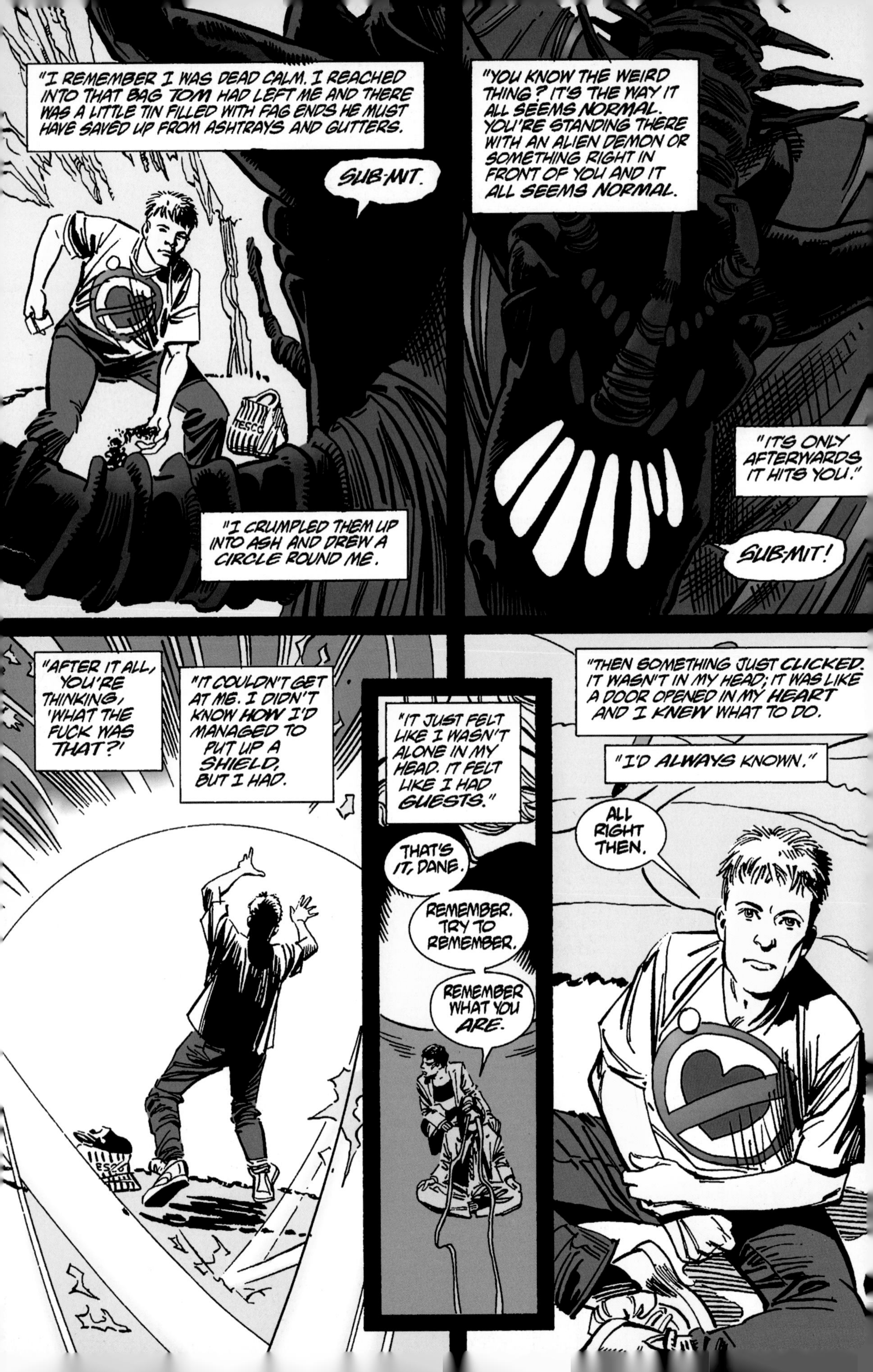
"I REMEMBER I WAS DEAD CALM. I REACHED INTO THAT BAG TOM HAD LEFT ME AND THERE WAS A LITTLE TIN FILLED WITH FAG ENDS HE MUST HAVE SAVED UP FROM ASHTRAYS AND GUTTERS.
SUB-MIT.
"I CRUMPLED THEM UP INTO ASH AND DREW A CIRCLE ROUND ME.
TESCO
"YOU KNOW THE WEIRD THING? IT'S THE WAY IT ALL SEEMS NORMAL. YOU'RE STANDING THERE WITH AN ALIEN DEMON OR SOMETHING RIGHT IN FRONT OF YOU AND IT ALL SEEMS NORMAL.
"IT'S ONLY AFTERWARDS IT HITS YOU."
SUB-MIT!
"AFTER IT ALL, YOU'RE THINKING, 'WHAT THE FUCK WAS THAT?'
"IT COULDN'T GET AT ME. I DIDN'T KNOW HOW I'D MANAGED TO PUT UP A SHIELD, BUT I HAD.
"IT JUST FELT LIKE I WASN'T ALONE IN MY HEAD. IT FELT LIKE I HAD GUESTS."
THAT'S IT, DANE.
REMEMBER. TRY TO REMEMBER.
REMEMBER WHAT YOU ARE.
"THEN SOMETHING JUST CLICKED. IT WASN'T IN MY HEAD; IT WAS LIKE A DOOR OPENED IN MY HEART AND I KNEW WHAT TO DO.
"I'D ALWAYS KNOWN."
ALL RIGHT THEN.

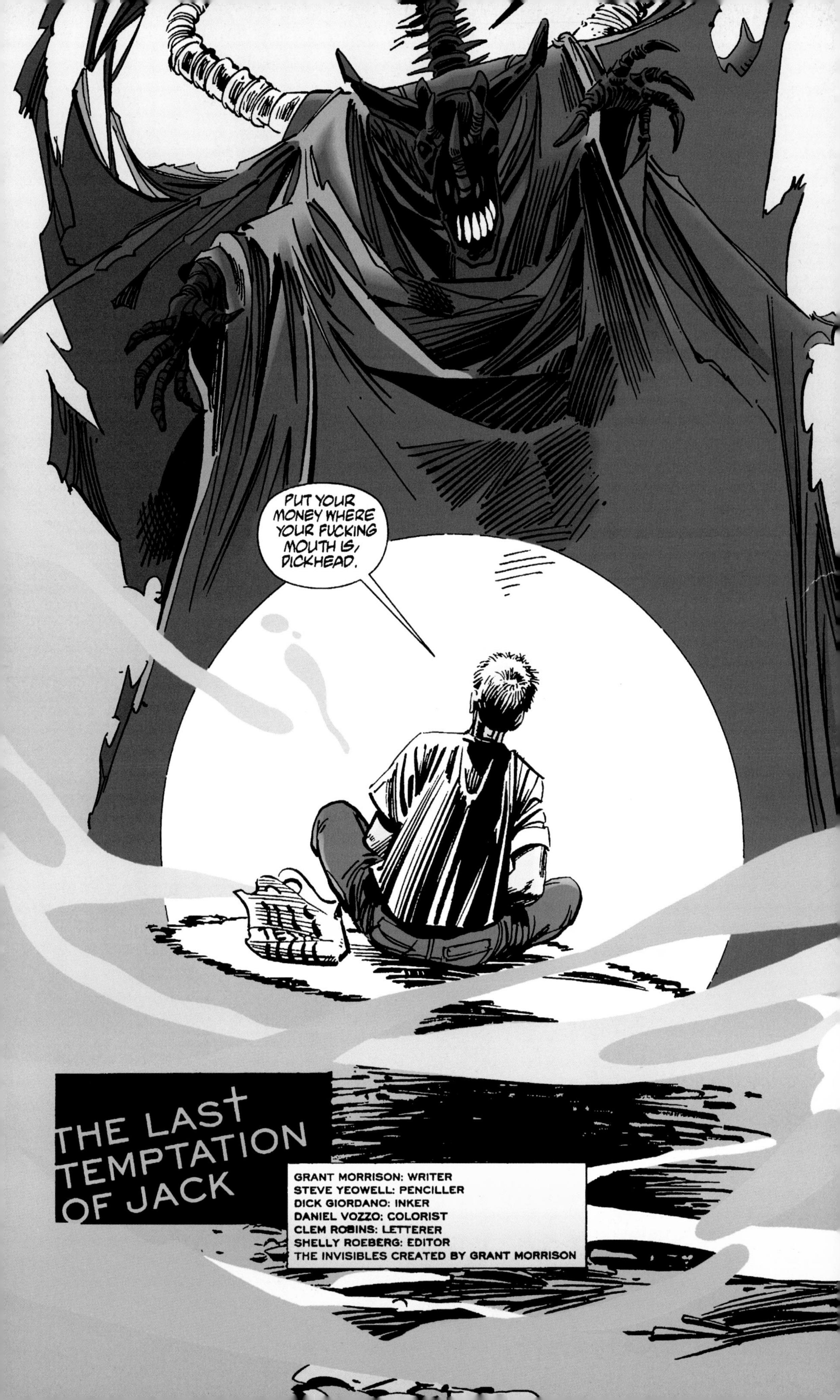
PUT YOUR MONEY WHERE YOUR FUCKING MOUTH IS, DICKHEAD.
THE LAST TEMPTATION OF JACK
GRANT MORRISON: WRITER
STEVE YEOWELL: PENCILLER
DICK GIORDANO: INKER
DANIEL VOZZO: COLORIST
CLEM ROBINS: LETTERER
SHELLY ROEBERG: EDITOR
THE INVISIBLES CREATED BY GRANT MORRISON

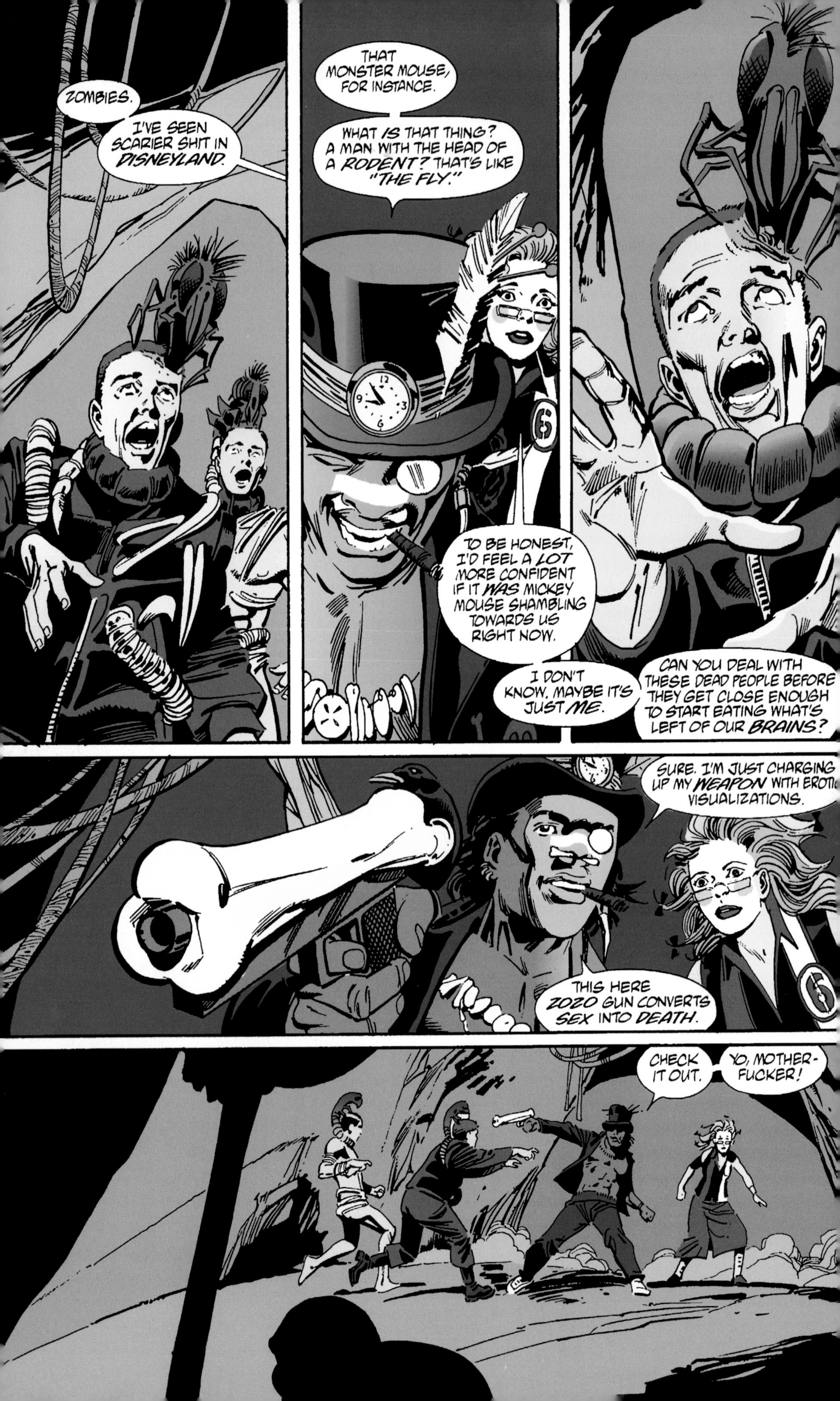
ZOMBIES.
I'VE SEEN SCARIER SHIT IN DISNEYLAND.
THAT MONSTER MOUSE, FOR INSTANCE.
WHAT IS THAT THING? A MAN WITH THE HEAD OF A RODENT? THAT'S LIKE "THE FLY."
TO BE HONEST, I'D FEEL A LOT MORE CONFIDENT IF IT WAS MICKEY MOUSE SHAMBLING TOWARDS US RIGHT NOW.
I DON'T KNOW. MAYBE IT'S JUST ME.
CAN YOU DEAL WITH THESE DEAD PEOPLE BEFORE THEY GET CLOSE ENOUGH TO START EATING WHAT'S LEFT OF OUR BRAINS?
SURE. I'M JUST CHARGING UP MY WEAPON WITH EROTI VISUALIZATIONS.
THIS HERE ZOZO GUN CONVERTS SEX INTO DEATH.
CHECK IT OUT.
YO, MOTHER-FUCKER!

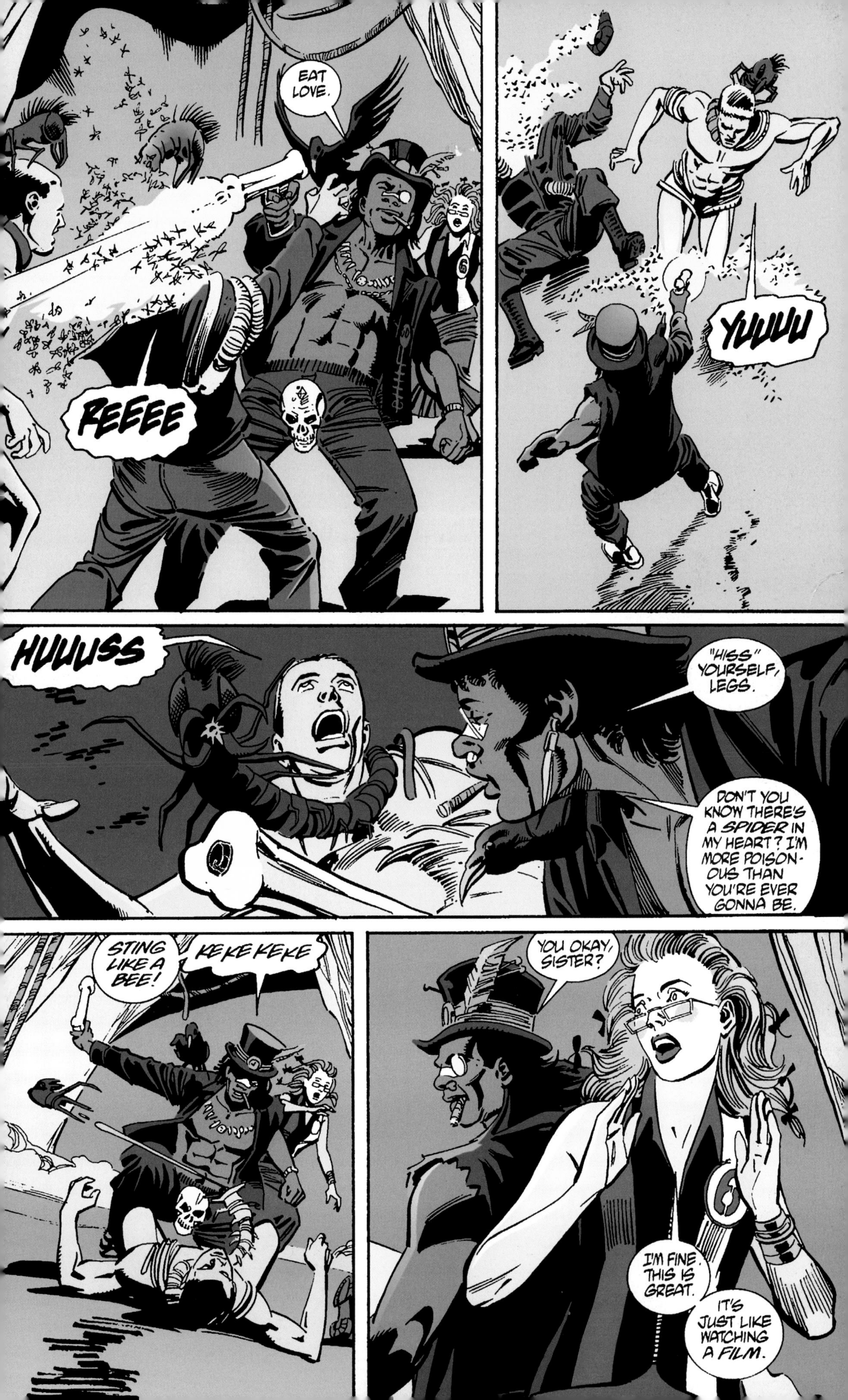
EAT LOVE.
REEEE
YUUUU
HUUUSS
"HISS" YOURSELF, LEGS.
DON'T YOU KNOW THERE'S A SPIDER IN MY HEART? I'M MORE POISON-OUS THAN YOU'RE EVER GONNA BE.
STING LIKE A BEE!
KEKEKEKE
YOU OKAY, SISTER?
I'M FINE. THIS IS GREAT.
IT'S JUST LIKE WATCHING A FILM.

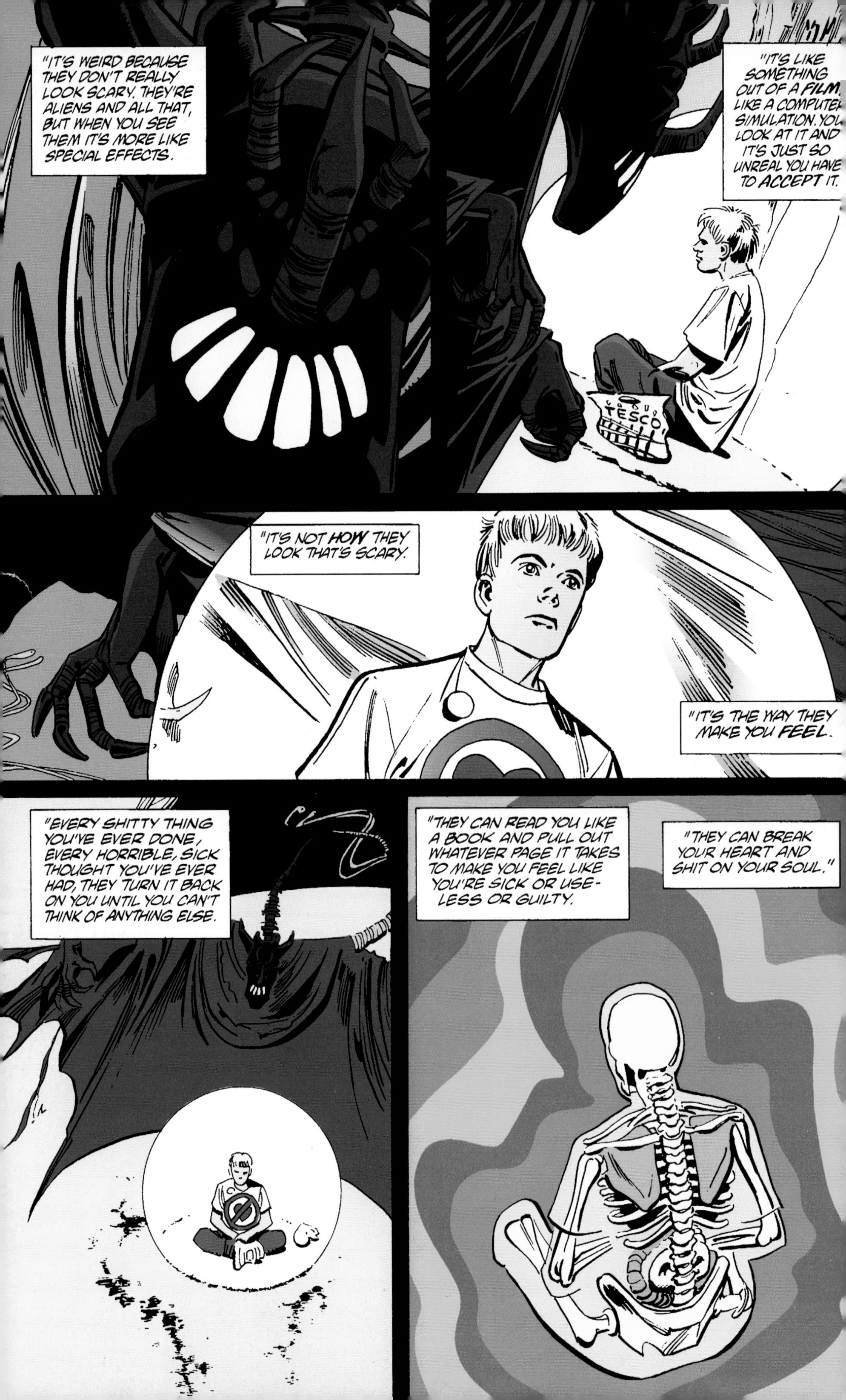
"IT'S WEIRD BECAUSE THEY DON'T REALLY LOOK SCARY. THEY'RE ALIENS AND ALL THAT, BUT WHEN YOU SEE THEM IT'S MORE LIKE SPECIAL EFFECTS.
"IT'S LIKE SOMETHING OUT OF A FILM. LIKE A COMPUTER SIMULATION. YOU LOOK AT IT AND IT'S JUST SO UNREAL YOU HAVE TO ACCEPT IT.
TESCO
"IT'S NOT HOW THEY LOOK THAT'S SCARY.
"IT'S THE WAY THEY MAKE YOU FEEL.
"EVERY SHITTY THING YOU'VE EVER DONE, EVERY HORRIBLE, SICK THOUGHT YOU'VE EVER HAD, THEY TURN IT BACK ON YOU UNTIL YOU CAN'T THINK OF ANYTHING ELSE.
"THEY CAN READ YOU LIKE A BOOK AND PULL OUT WHATEVER PAGE IT TAKES TO MAKE YOU FEEL LIKE YOU'RE SICK OR USE-LESS OR GUILTY.
"THEY CAN BREAK YOUR HEART AND SHIT ON YOUR SOUL."

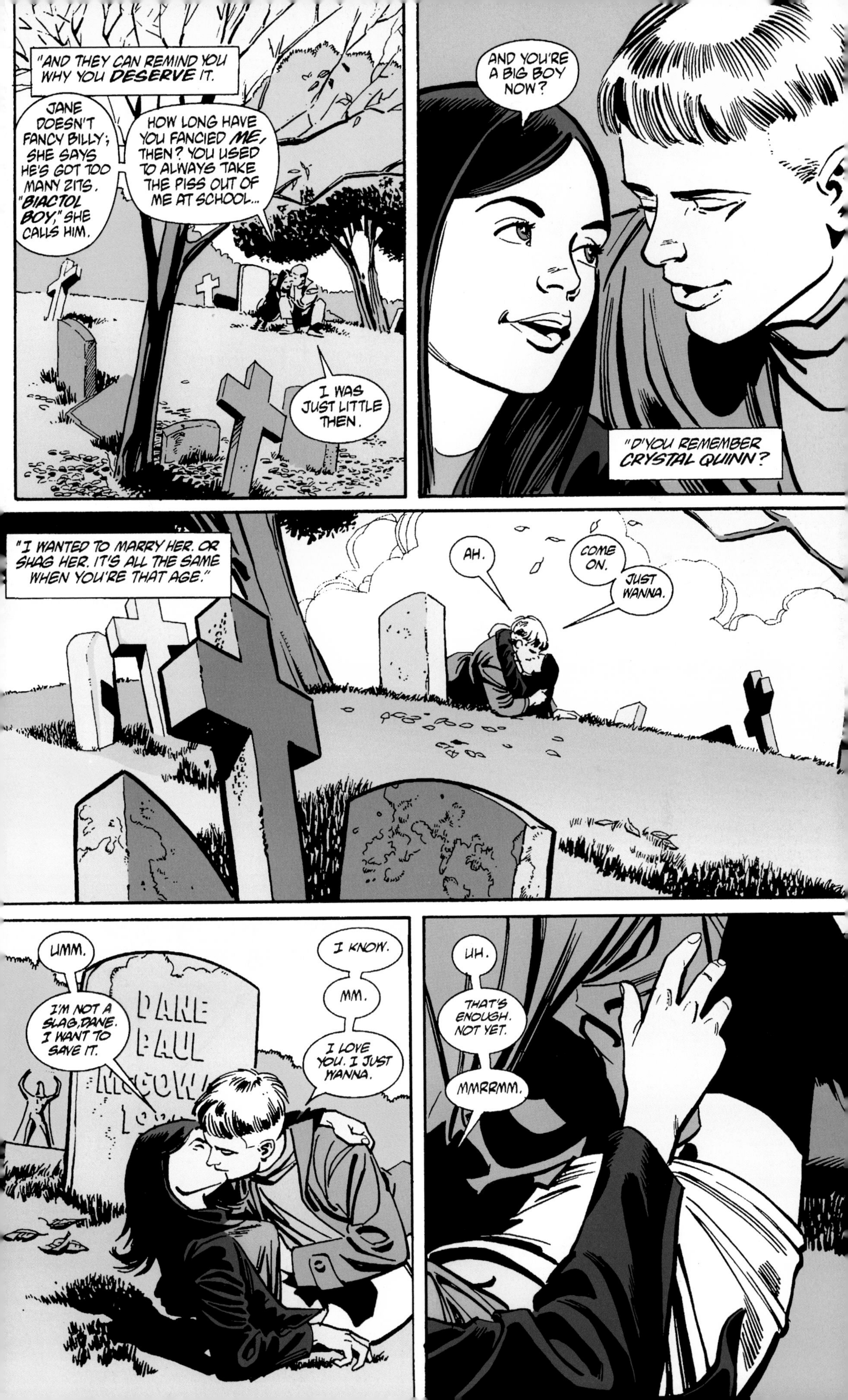

"AND THEY CAN REMIND YOU WHY YOU DESERVE IT.
JANE DOESN'T FANCY BILLY; SHE SAYS HE'S GOT TOO MANY ZITS. "BIACTOL BOY," SHE CALLS HIM.
HOW LONG HAVE YOU FANCIED ME, THEN? YOU USED TO ALWAYS TAKE THE PISS OUT OF ME AT SCHOOL...
I WAS JUST LITTLE THEN.
AND YOU'RE A BIG BOY NOW?
"D'YOU REMEMBER CRYSTAL QUINN?
"I WANTED TO MARRY HER. OR SHAG HER. IT'S ALL THE SAME WHEN YOU'RE THAT AGE."
AH.
COME ON.
JUST WANNA.
UMM.
I'M NOT A SLAG, DANE. I WANT TO SAVE IT.
I KNOW.
MM.
I LOVE YOU. I JUST WANNA.
DANE PAUL
UH.
THAT'S ENOUGH. NOT YET.
MMRRMM.

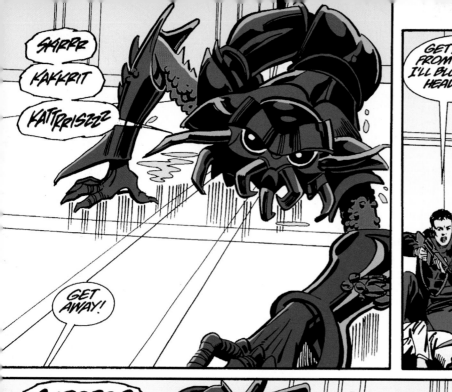

SKRRR
KAKKRIT
KATTRRISZZ

GET AWAY!

GET AWAY FROM ME OR I'LL BLOW YOUR HEAD OFF!

THE ARMOR'S IMPENETRABLE, YOU PATHETIC BLOODY WRETCH.

IT'S ALIVE! IT ABSORBS THE KINETIC ENERGY OF YOUR BULLETS AND FEEDS IT STRAIGHT BACK INTO ITS POWER SOURCE. YOU...

SHREEEE

NNNAAA

BITCH!

SHE'S JUST PLAYING WITH YOU.

ADRENAL GLANDS TASTE BETTER WHEN THEY'RE AROUSED.

SKWWIRRR
KRIIII

10

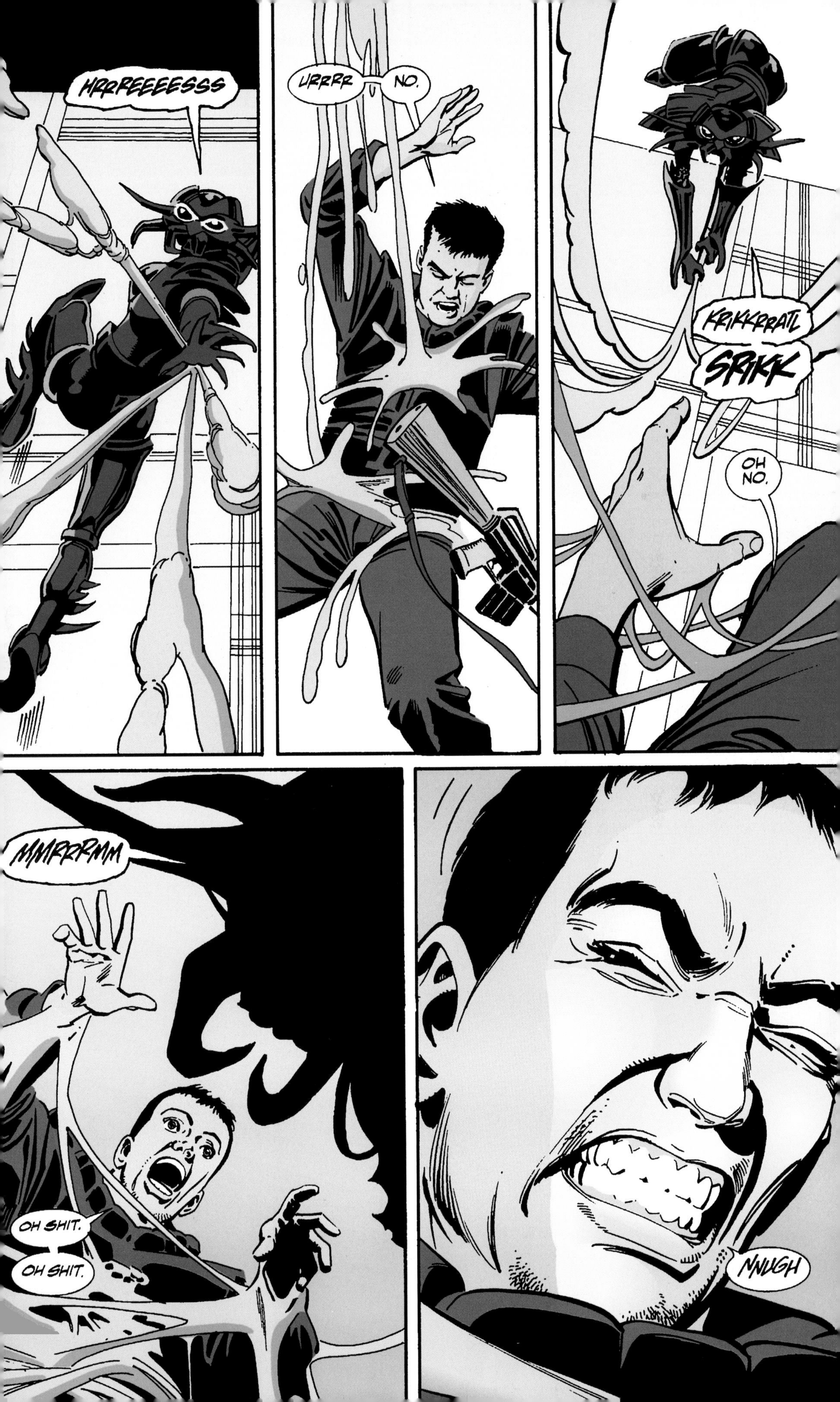
HRRREEEEESSS
URRRR
NO.
KRIKKRRATL
SRIKK
OH NO.
MMRRRMM
OH SHIT.
OH SHIT.
NNUGH

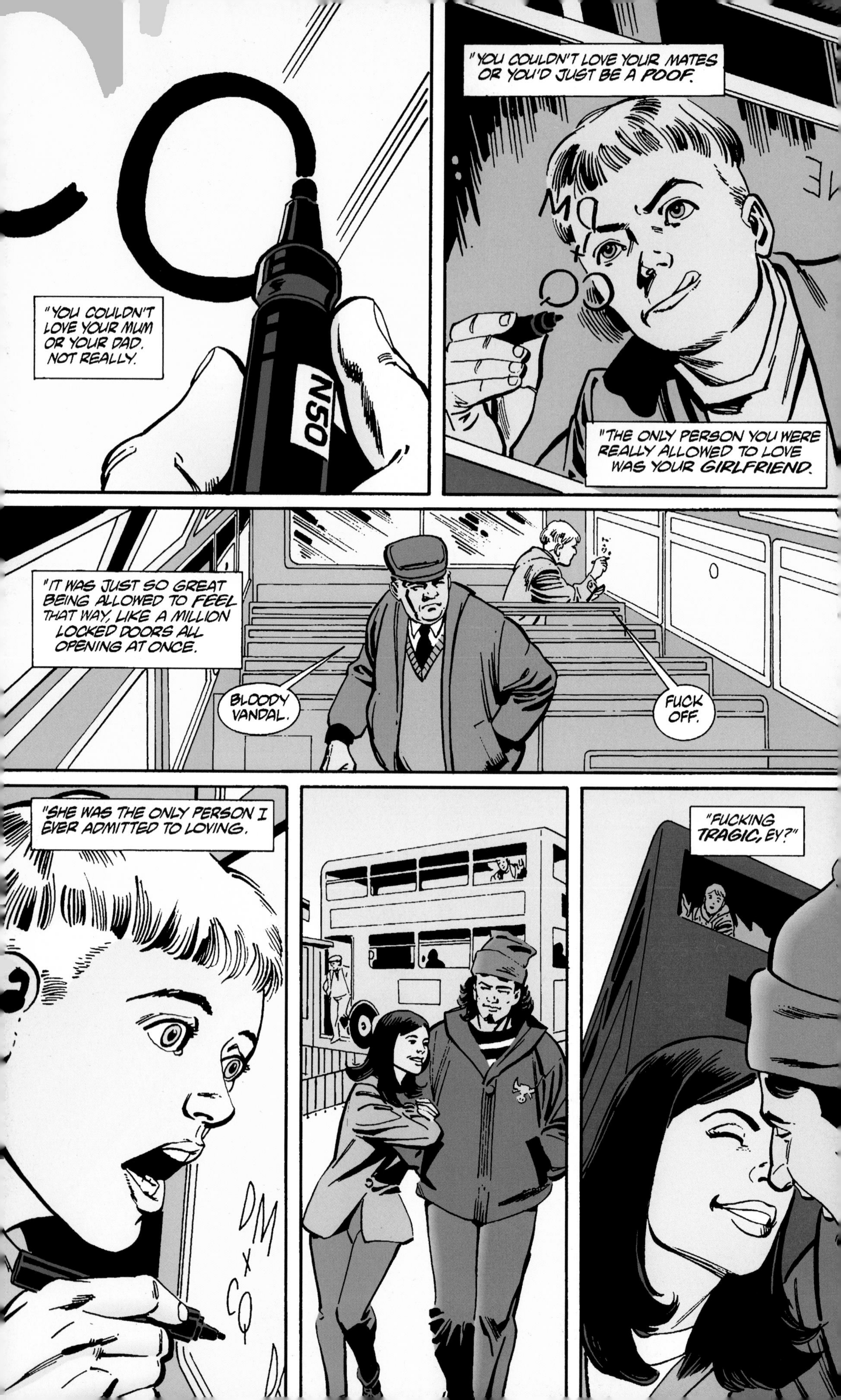

"YOU COULDN'T LOVE YOUR MUM OR YOUR DAD. NOT REALLY.
N50
"YOU COULDN'T LOVE YOUR MATES OR YOU'D JUST BE A POOF.
"THE ONLY PERSON YOU WERE REALLY ALLOWED TO LOVE WAS YOUR GIRLFRIEND.
"IT WAS JUST SO GREAT BEING ALLOWED TO FEEL THAT WAY, LIKE A MILLION LOCKED DOORS ALL OPENING AT ONCE.
BLOODY VANDAL.
FUCK OFF.
"SHE WAS THE ONLY PERSON I EVER ADMITTED TO LOVING.
"FUCKING TRAGIC, EY?"

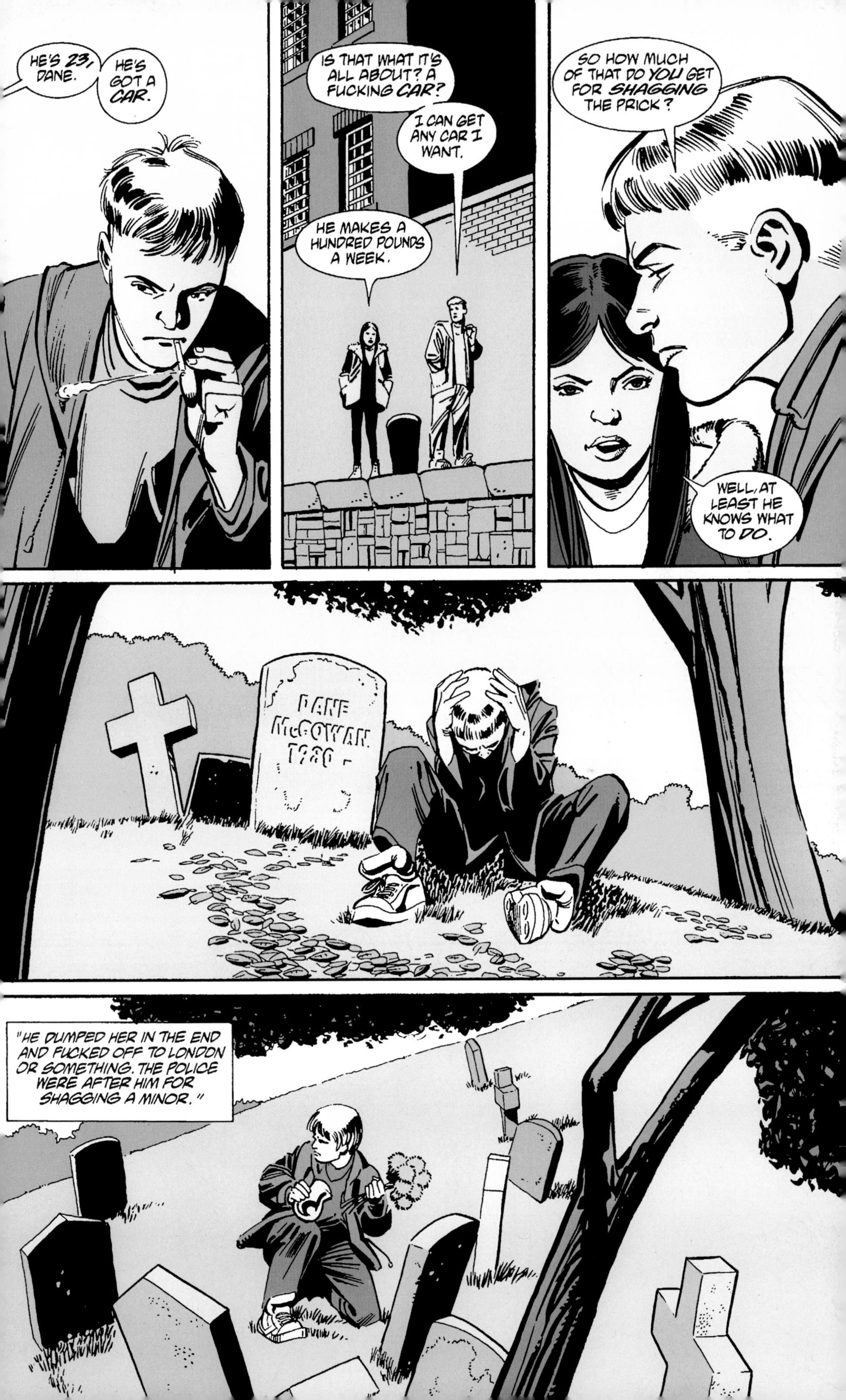
HE'S 23, DANE.
HE'S GOT A CAR.
IS THAT WHAT IT'S ALL ABOUT? A FUCKING CAR?
I CAN GET ANY CAR I WANT.
HE MAKES A HUNDRED POUNDS A WEEK.
SO HOW MUCH OF THAT DO YOU GET FOR SHAGGING THE PRICK?
WELL, AT LEAST HE KNOWS WHAT TO DO.
DANE McGOWAN 1980 -
"HE DUMPED HER IN THE END AND FUCKED OFF TO LONDON OR SOMETHING. THE POLICE WERE AFTER HIM FOR SHAGGING A MINOR."

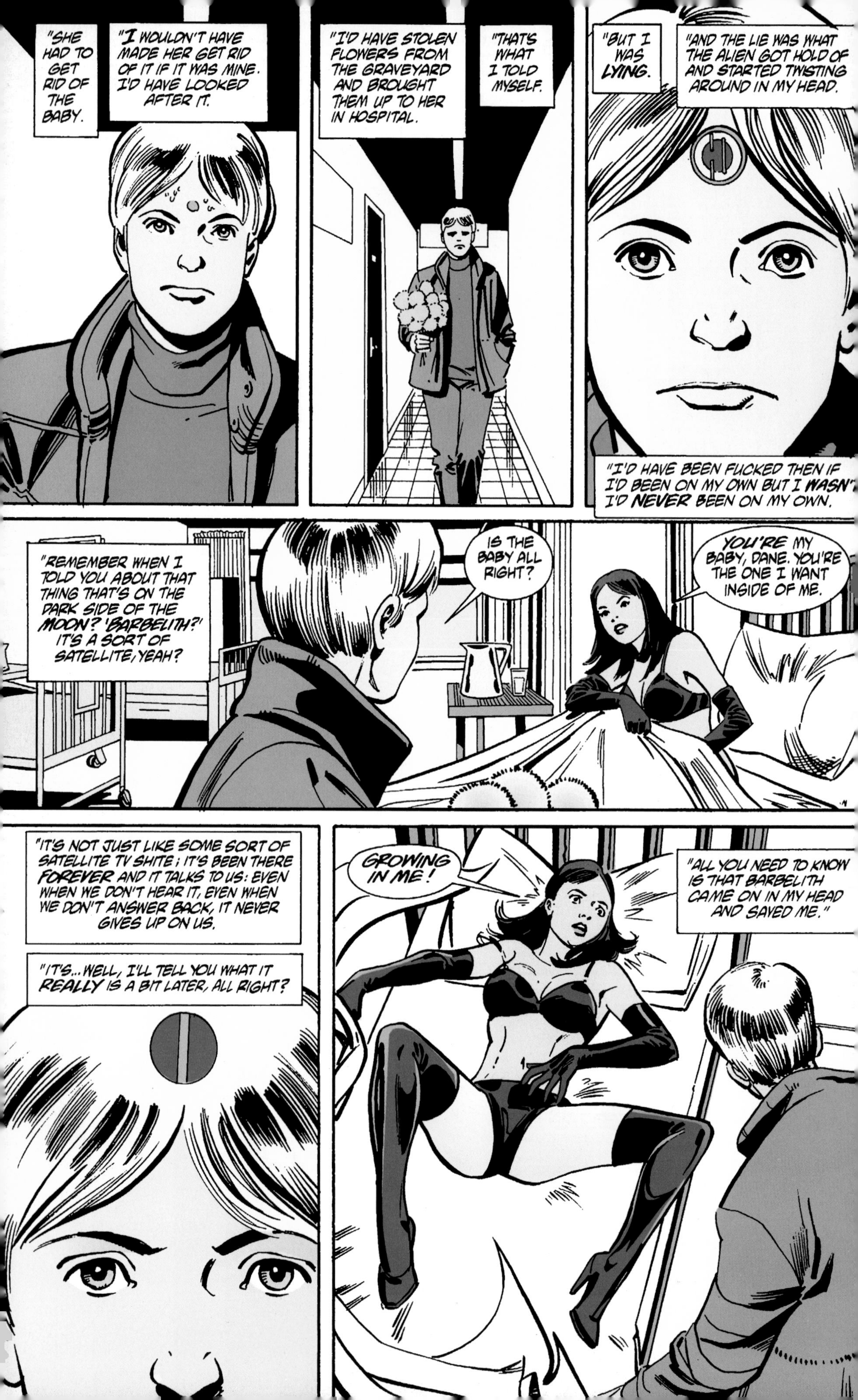
"SHE HAD TO GET RID OF THE BABY.
"I WOULDN'T HAVE MADE HER GET RID OF IT IF IT WAS MINE. I'D HAVE LOOKED AFTER IT.
"I'D HAVE STOLEN FLOWERS FROM THE GRAVEYARD AND BROUGHT THEM UP TO HER IN HOSPITAL.
"THAT'S WHAT I TOLD MYSELF.
"BUT I WAS LYING.
"AND THE LIE WAS WHAT THE ALIEN GOT HOLD OF AND STARTED TWISTING AROUND IN MY HEAD.
"I'D HAVE BEEN FUCKED THEN IF I'D BEEN ON MY OWN BUT I WASN'T. I'D NEVER BEEN ON MY OWN.
"REMEMBER WHEN I TOLD YOU ABOUT THAT THING THAT'S ON THE DARK SIDE OF THE MOON? 'BARBELITH?' IT'S A SORT OF SATELLITE, YEAH?
IS THE BABY ALL RIGHT?
YOU'RE MY BABY, DANE. YOU'RE THE ONE I WANT INSIDE OF ME.
"IT'S NOT JUST LIKE SOME SORT OF SATELLITE TV SHITE; IT'S BEEN THERE FOREVER AND IT TALKS TO US: EVEN WHEN WE DON'T HEAR IT, EVEN WHEN WE DON'T ANSWER BACK, IT NEVER GIVES UP ON US.
"IT'S... WELL, I'LL TELL YOU WHAT IT REALLY IS A BIT LATER, ALL RIGHT?
GROWING IN ME!
"ALL YOU NEED TO KNOW IS THAT BARBELITH CAME ON IN MY HEAD AND SAVED ME."

HOLD YUR HAND OUT, YU NAW-TY BOY!

I SAW YU! I SAW YU!

"JUST LIKE I'D TOLD IT TO DO WHEN I *MADE* IT.

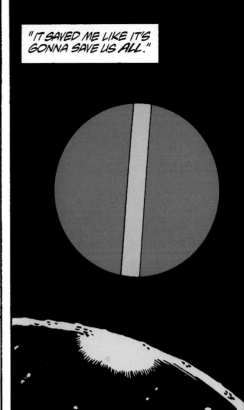

"IT SAVED ME LIKE IT'S GONNA SAVE US ALL."

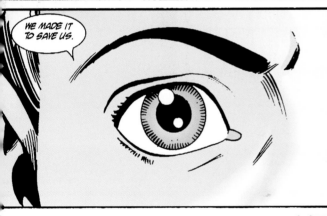

WE MADE IT TO SAVE US.

HE'S HALLUCINATING, DOCTOR.

THINK HE'S A BIT SCARED.

WHY WON'T HE JUST LET *GO*, FOR CHRIST'S SAKE?

STOP FIGHTING.

LET GO.

MR. McGOWAN?

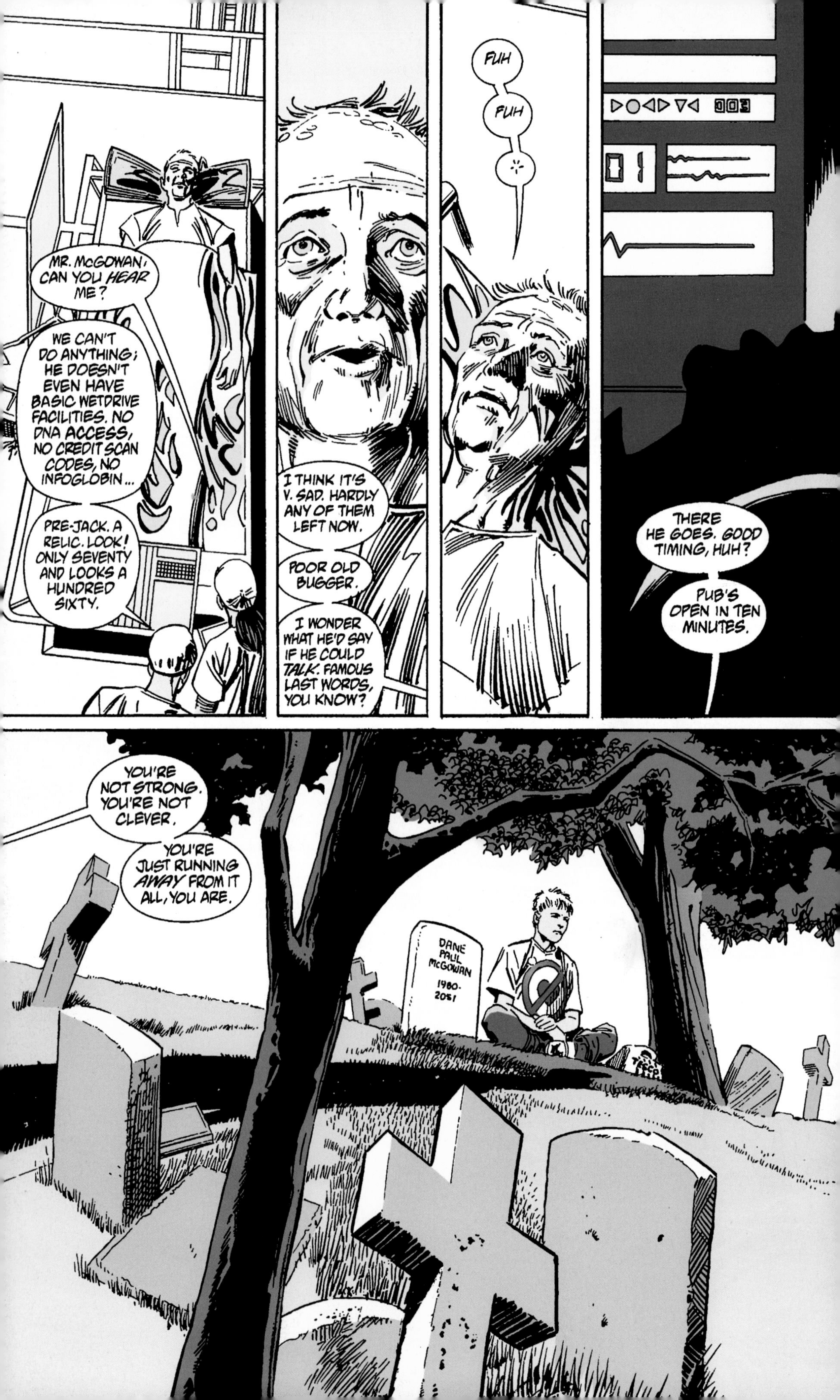
MR. McGOWAN, CAN YOU HEAR ME?
WE CAN'T DO ANYTHING; HE DOESN'T EVEN HAVE BASIC WETDRIVE FACILITIES. NO DNA ACCESS, NO CREDIT SCAN CODES, NO INFOGLOBIN...
PRE-JACK. A RELIC. LOOK! ONLY SEVENTY AND LOOKS A HUNDRED SIXTY.
I THINK IT'S V. SAD. HARDLY ANY OF THEM LEFT NOW.
POOR OLD BUGGER.
I WONDER WHAT HE'D SAY IF HE COULD TALK. FAMOUS LAST WORDS, YOU KNOW?
FUH
FUH
003
THERE HE GOES. GOOD TIMING, HUH?
PUB'S OPEN IN TEN MINUTES.
YOU'RE NOT STRONG. YOU'RE NOT CLEVER.
YOU'RE JUST RUNNING AWAY FROM IT ALL, YOU ARE.
DANE PAUL McGOWAN 1980-2051

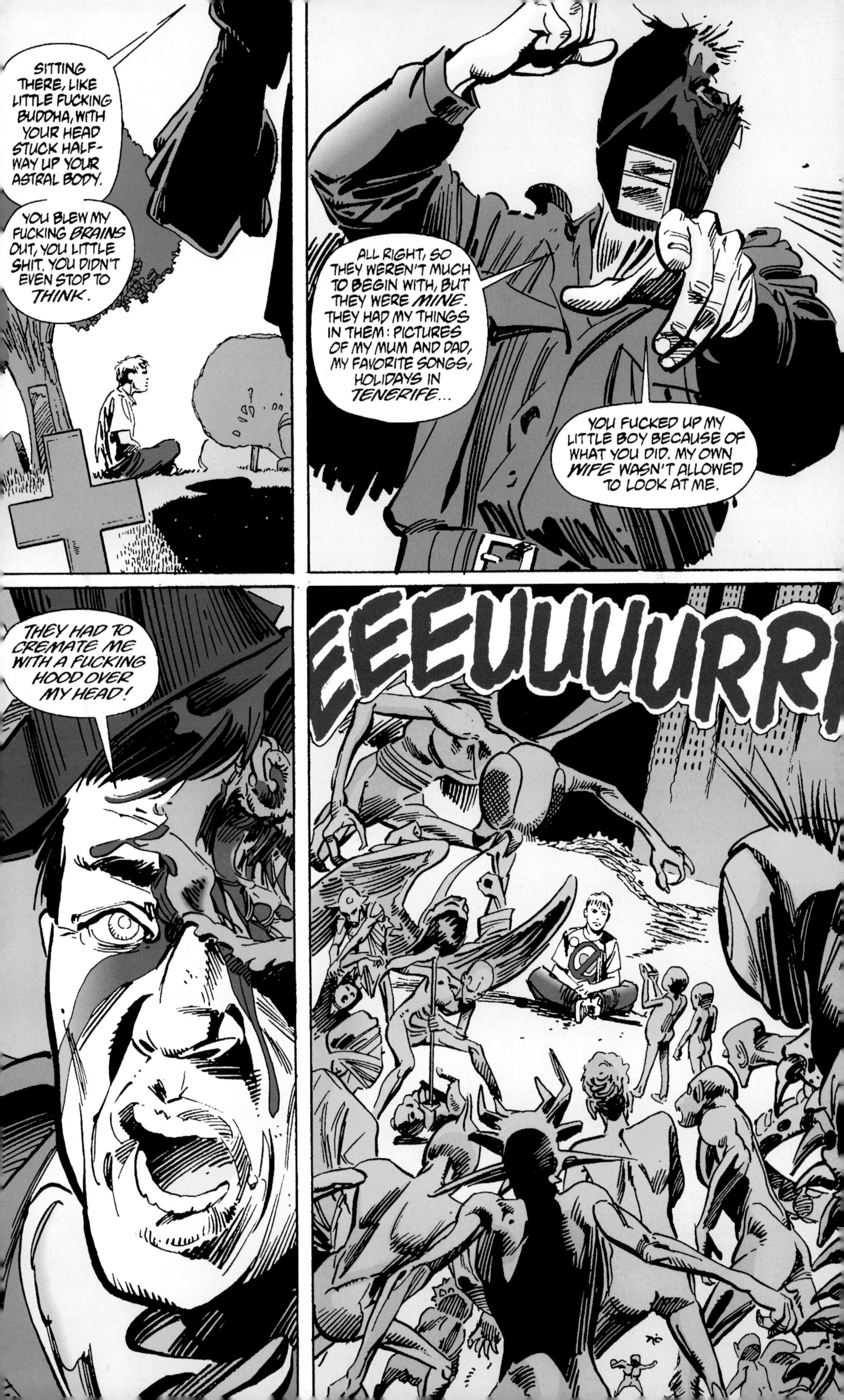
SITTING THERE, LIKE LITTLE FUCKING BUDDHA, WITH YOUR HEAD STUCK HALF-WAY UP YOUR ASTRAL BODY.
YOU BLEW MY FUCKING BRAINS OUT, YOU LITTLE SHIT. YOU DIDN'T EVEN STOP TO THINK.
ALL RIGHT, SO THEY WEREN'T MUCH TO BEGIN WITH, BUT THEY WERE MINE. THEY HAD MY THINGS IN THEM: PICTURES OF MY MUM AND DAD, MY FAVORITE SONGS, HOLIDAYS IN TENERIFE...
YOU FUCKED UP MY LITTLE BOY BECAUSE OF WHAT YOU DID. MY OWN WIFE WASN'T ALLOWED TO LOOK AT ME.
THEY HAD TO CREMATE ME WITH A FUCKING HOOD OVER MY HEAD!
EEEUUUURR

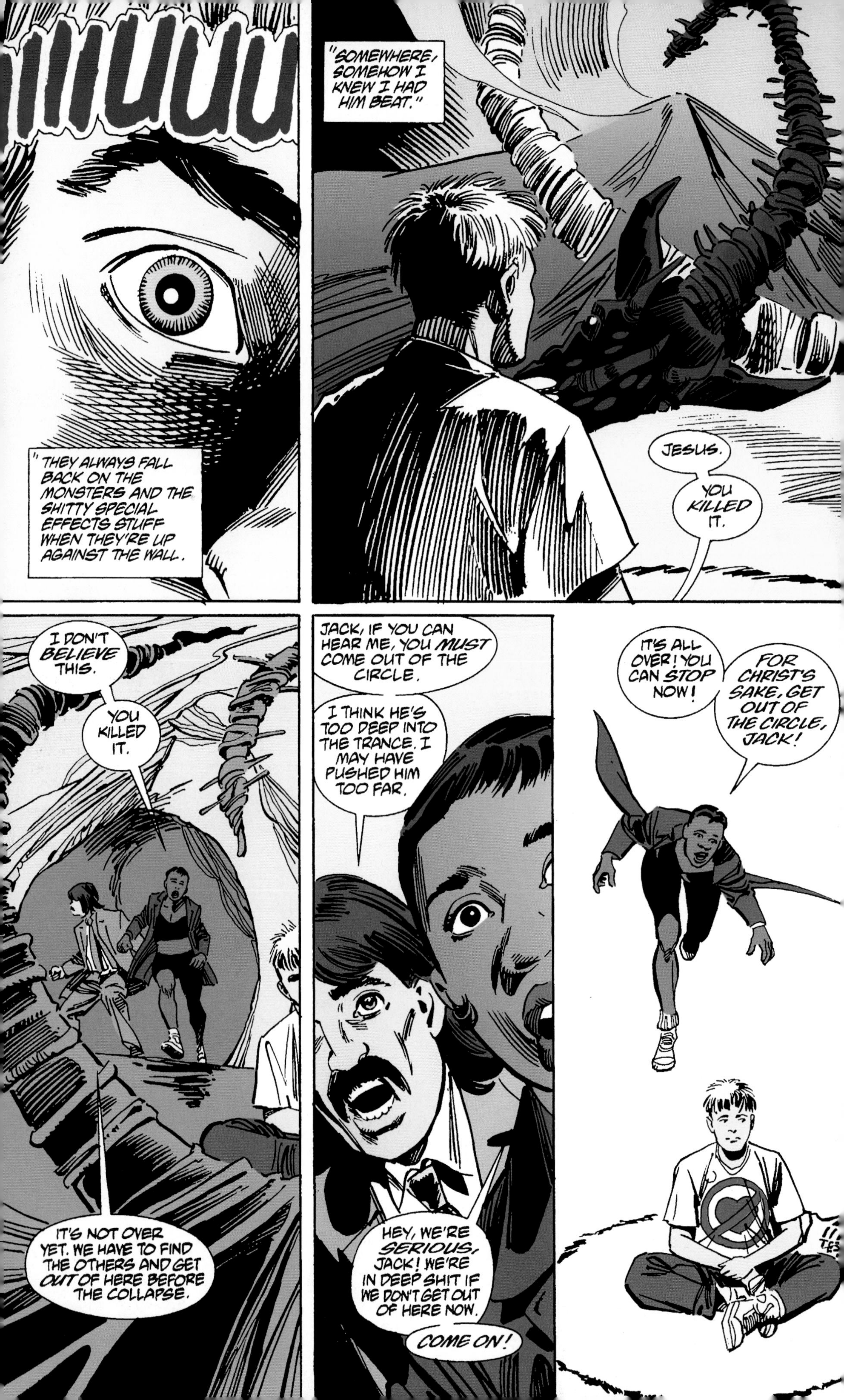
UUUUU
"THEY ALWAYS FALL BACK ON THE MONSTERS AND THE SHITTY SPECIAL EFFECTS STUFF WHEN THEY'RE UP AGAINST THE WALL.
"SOMEWHERE, SOMEHOW I KNEW I HAD HIM BEAT."
JESUS.
YOU KILLED IT.
I DON'T BELIEVE THIS.
YOU KILLED IT.
IT'S NOT OVER YET. WE HAVE TO FIND THE OTHERS AND GET OUT OF HERE BEFORE THE COLLAPSE.
JACK, IF YOU CAN HEAR ME, YOU MUST COME OUT OF THE CIRCLE.
I THINK HE'S TOO DEEP INTO THE TRANCE. I MAY HAVE PUSHED HIM TOO FAR.
HEY, WE'RE SERIOUS, JACK! WE'RE IN DEEP SHIT IF WE DON'T GET OUT OF HERE NOW.
COME ON!
IT'S ALL OVER! YOU CAN STOP NOW!
FOR CHRIST'S SAKE, GET OUT OF THE CIRCLE, JACK!

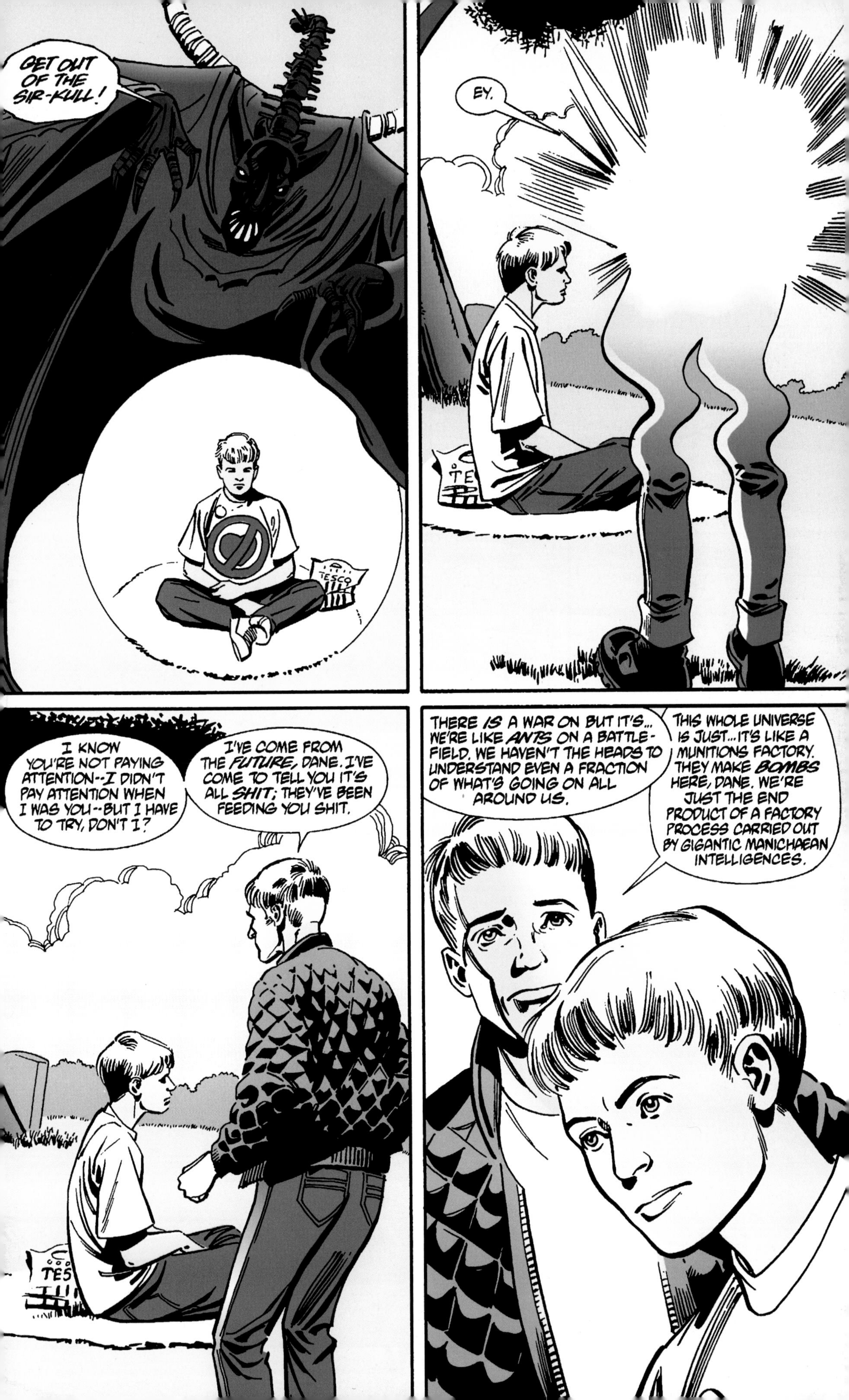
GET OUT OF THE SIR-KULL!
EY.
I KNOW YOU'RE NOT PAYING ATTENTION--I DIDN'T PAY ATTENTION WHEN I WAS YOU--BUT I HAVE TO TRY, DON'T I?
I'VE COME FROM THE FUTURE, DANE. I'VE COME TO TELL YOU IT'S ALL SHIT; THEY'VE BEEN FEEDING YOU SHIT.
THERE IS A WAR ON BUT IT'S... WE'RE LIKE ANTS ON A BATTLE-FIELD. WE HAVEN'T THE HEADS TO UNDERSTAND EVEN A FRACTION OF WHAT'S GOING ON ALL AROUND US.
THIS WHOLE UNIVERSE IS JUST... IT'S LIKE A MUNITIONS FACTORY. THEY MAKE BOMBS HERE, DANE. WE'RE JUST THE END PRODUCT OF A FACTORY PROCESS CARRIED OUT BY GIGANTIC MANICHAEAN INTELLIGENCES.

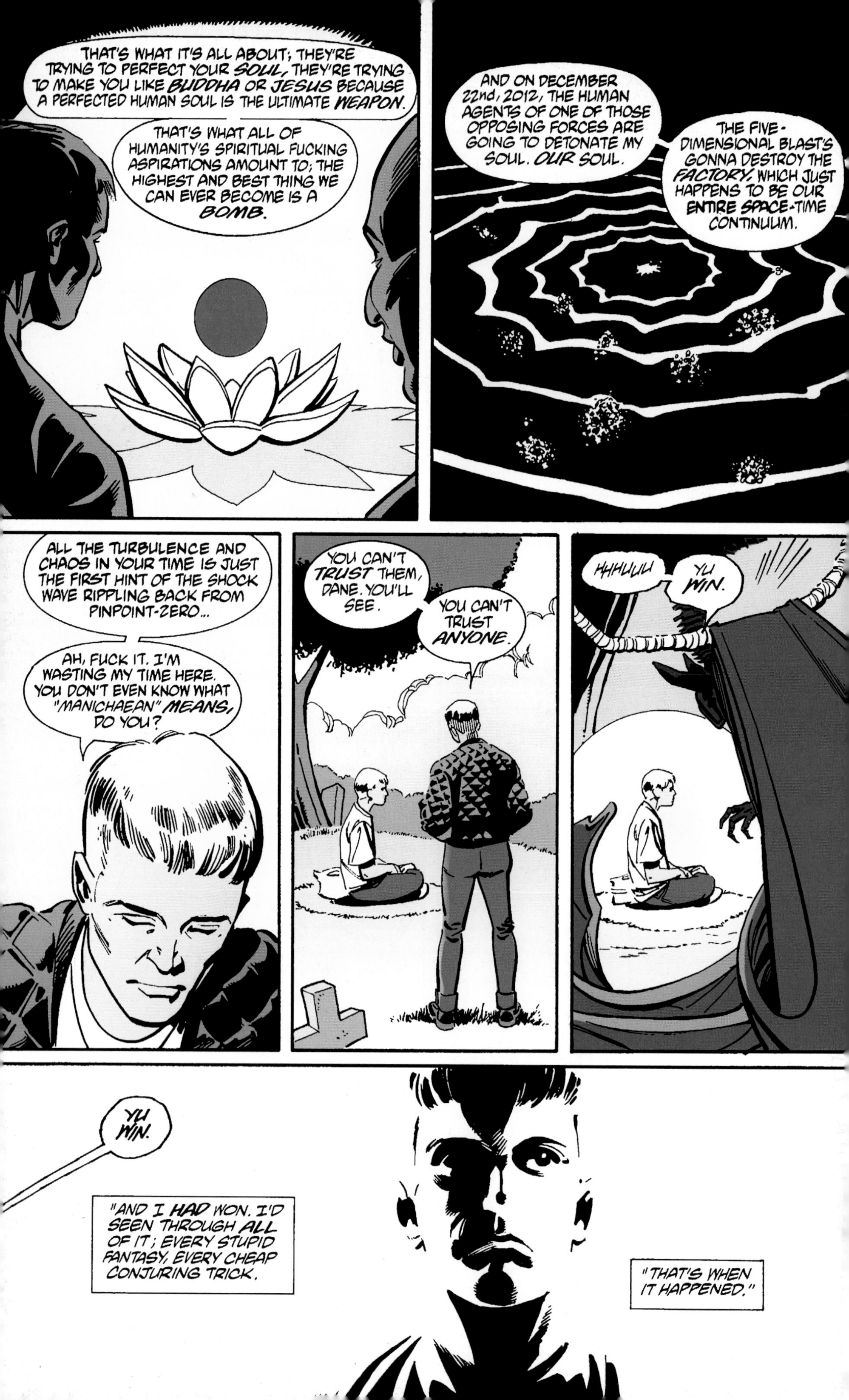
THAT'S WHAT IT'S ALL ABOUT; THEY'RE TRYING TO PERFECT YOUR SOUL, THEY'RE TRYING TO MAKE YOU LIKE BUDDHA OR JESUS BECAUSE A PERFECTED HUMAN SOUL IS THE ULTIMATE WEAPON.
THAT'S WHAT ALL OF HUMANITY'S SPIRITUAL FUCKING ASPIRATIONS AMOUNT TO; THE HIGHEST AND BEST THING WE CAN EVER BECOME IS A BOMB.
AND ON DECEMBER 22nd, 2012, THE HUMAN AGENTS OF ONE OF THOSE OPPOSING FORCES ARE GOING TO DETONATE MY SOUL. OUR SOUL.
THE FIVE-DIMENSIONAL BLAST'S GONNA DESTROY THE FACTORY, WHICH JUST HAPPENS TO BE OUR ENTIRE SPACE-TIME CONTINUUM.
ALL THE TURBULENCE AND CHAOS IN YOUR TIME IS JUST THE FIRST HINT OF THE SHOCK WAVE RIPPLING BACK FROM PINPOINT-ZERO...
AH, FUCK IT. I'M WASTING MY TIME HERE. YOU DON'T EVEN KNOW WHAT "MANICHAEAN" MEANS, DO YOU?
YOU CAN'T TRUST THEM, DANE. YOU'LL SEE.
YOU CAN'T TRUST ANYONE.
HHHUUU
YU WIN.
YU WIN.
"AND I HAD WON. I'D SEEN THROUGH ALL OF IT; EVERY STUPID FANTASY, EVERY CHEAP CONJURING TRICK.
"THAT'S WHEN IT HAPPENED."

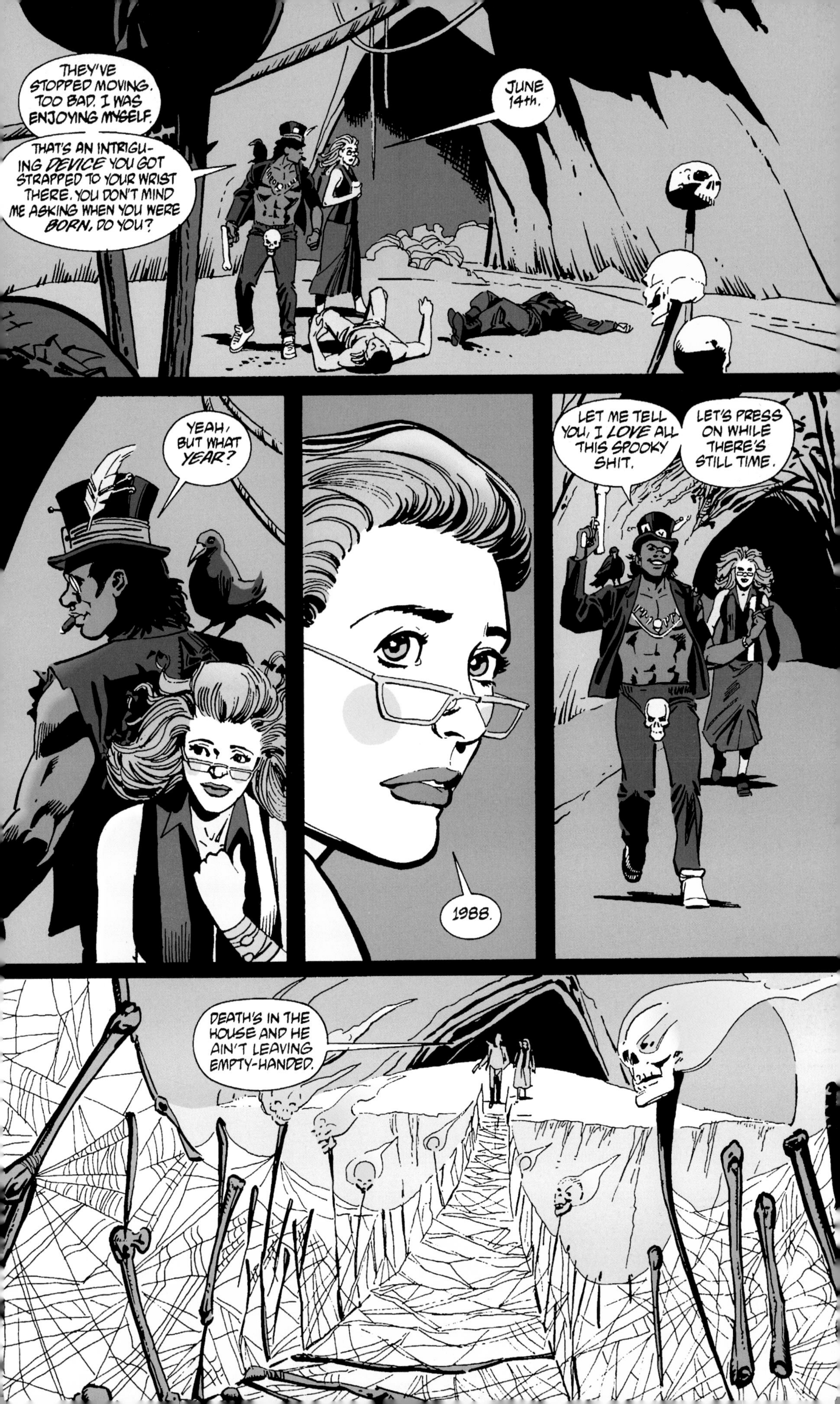
THEY'VE STOPPED MOVING. TOO BAD. I WAS ENJOYING MYSELF.
JUNE 14th.
THAT'S AN INTRIGU-ING DEVICE YOU GOT STRAPPED TO YOUR WRIST THERE. YOU DON'T MIND ME ASKING WHEN YOU WERE BORN, DO YOU?
YEAH, BUT WHAT YEAR?
1988.
LET ME TELL YOU, I LOVE ALL THIS SPOOKY SHIT.
LET'S PRESS ON WHILE THERE'S STILL TIME.
DEATH'S IN THE HOUSE AND HE AIN'T LEAVING EMPTY-HANDED.

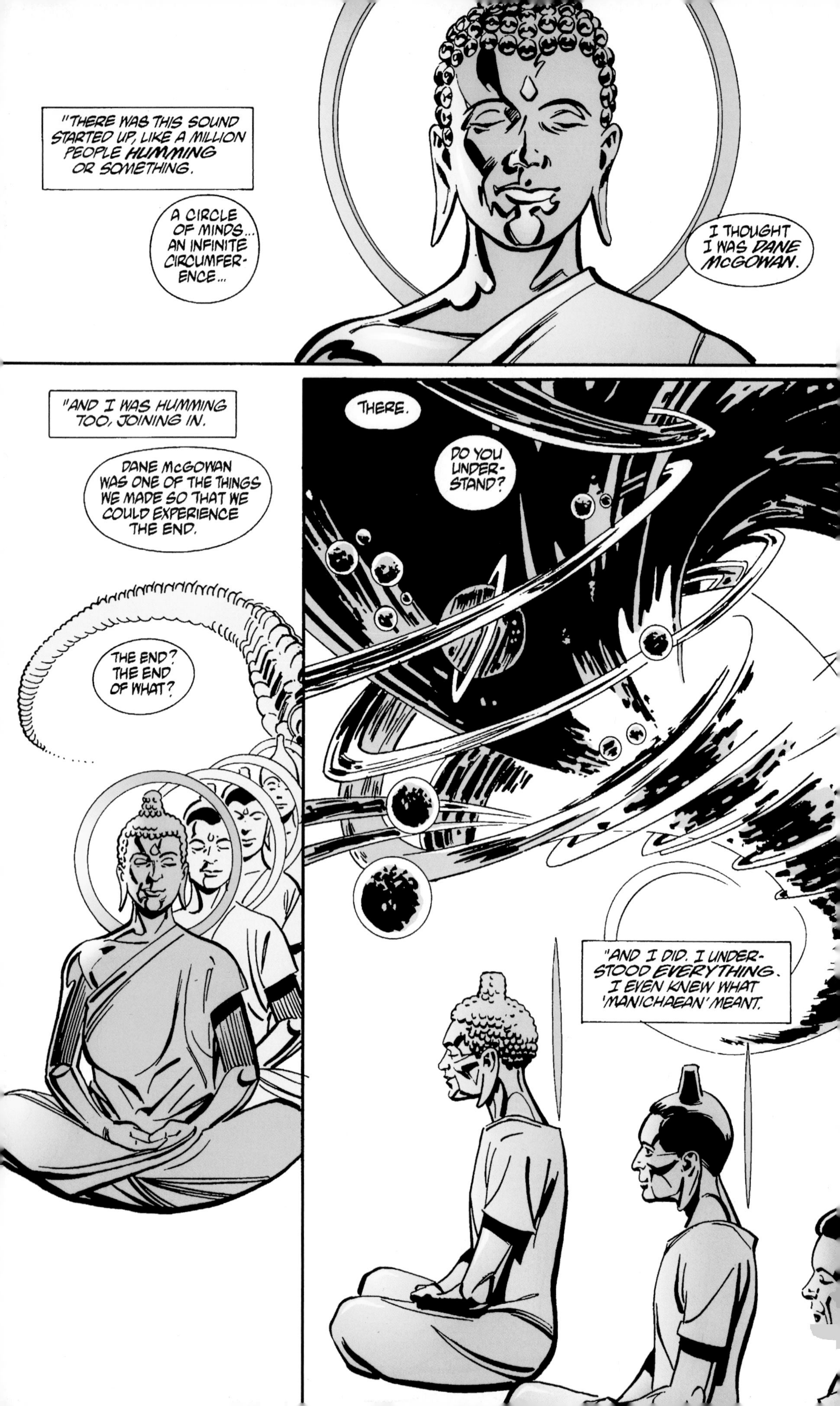
"THERE WAS THIS SOUND STARTED UP, LIKE A MILLION PEOPLE HUMMING OR SOMETHING.
A CIRCLE OF MINDS... AN INFINITE CIRCUMFERENCE...
I THOUGHT I WAS DANE McGOWAN.
"AND I WAS HUMMING TOO, JOINING IN.
DANE McGOWAN WAS ONE OF THE THINGS WE MADE SO THAT WE COULD EXPERIENCE THE END.
THE END? THE END OF WHAT?
THERE.
DO YOU UNDERSTAND?
"AND I DID. I UNDERSTOOD EVERYTHING. I EVEN KNEW WHAT 'MANICHAEAN' MEANT.

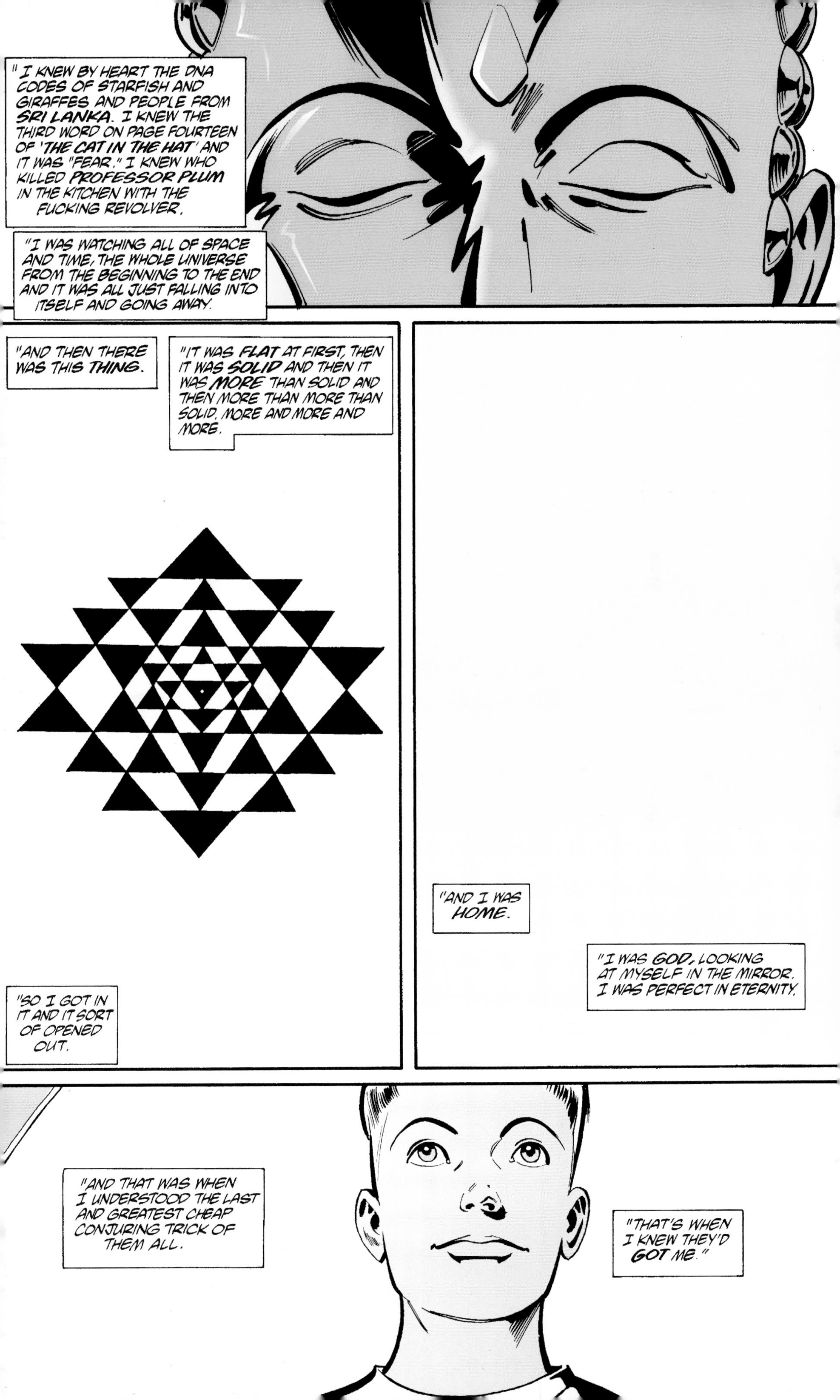
"I KNEW BY HEART THE DNA CODES OF STARFISH AND GIRAFFES AND PEOPLE FROM SRI LANKA. I KNEW THE THIRD WORD ON PAGE FOURTEEN OF 'THE CAT IN THE HAT' AND IT WAS "FEAR." I KNEW WHO KILLED PROFESSOR PLUM IN THE KITCHEN WITH THE FUCKING REVOLVER.
"I WAS WATCHING ALL OF SPACE AND TIME, THE WHOLE UNIVERSE FROM THE BEGINNING TO THE END AND IT WAS ALL JUST FALLING INTO ITSELF AND GOING AWAY.
"AND THEN THERE WAS THIS THING.
"IT WAS FLAT AT FIRST, THEN IT WAS SOLID AND THEN IT WAS MORE THAN SOLID AND THEN MORE THAN MORE THAN SOLID. MORE AND MORE AND MORE.
"SO I GOT IN IT AND IT SORT OF OPENED OUT.
"AND I WAS HOME.
"I WAS GOD, LOOKING AT MYSELF IN THE MIRROR. I WAS PERFECT IN ETERNITY.
"AND THAT WAS WHEN I UNDERSTOOD THE LAST AND GREATEST CHEAP CONJURING TRICK OF THEM ALL.
"THAT'S WHEN I KNEW THEY'D GOT ME."

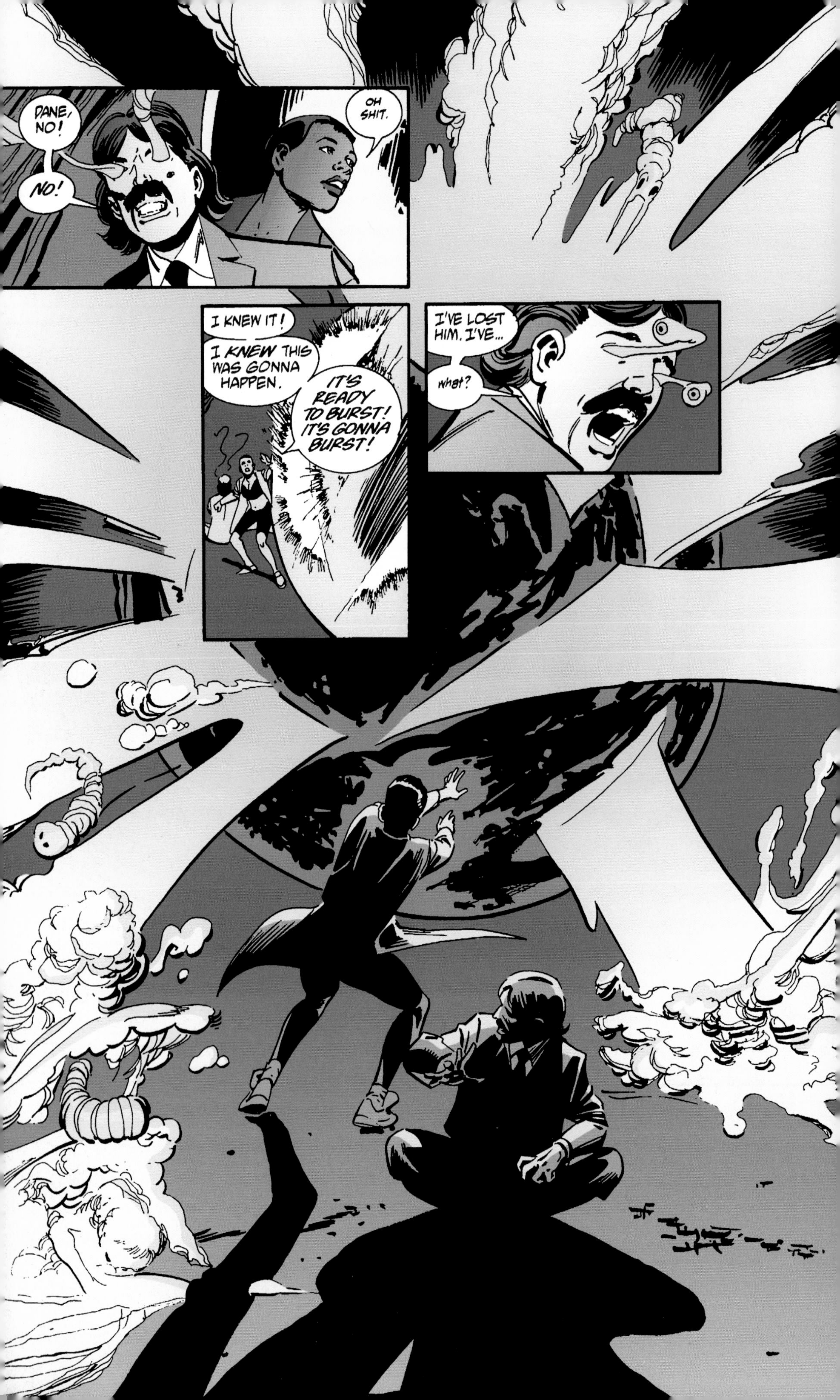

DANE, NO!
NO!
OH SHIT.
I KNEW IT!
I KNEW THIS WAS GONNA HAPPEN.
IT'S READY TO BURST! IT'S GONNA BURST!
I'VE LOST HIM. I'VE...
what?

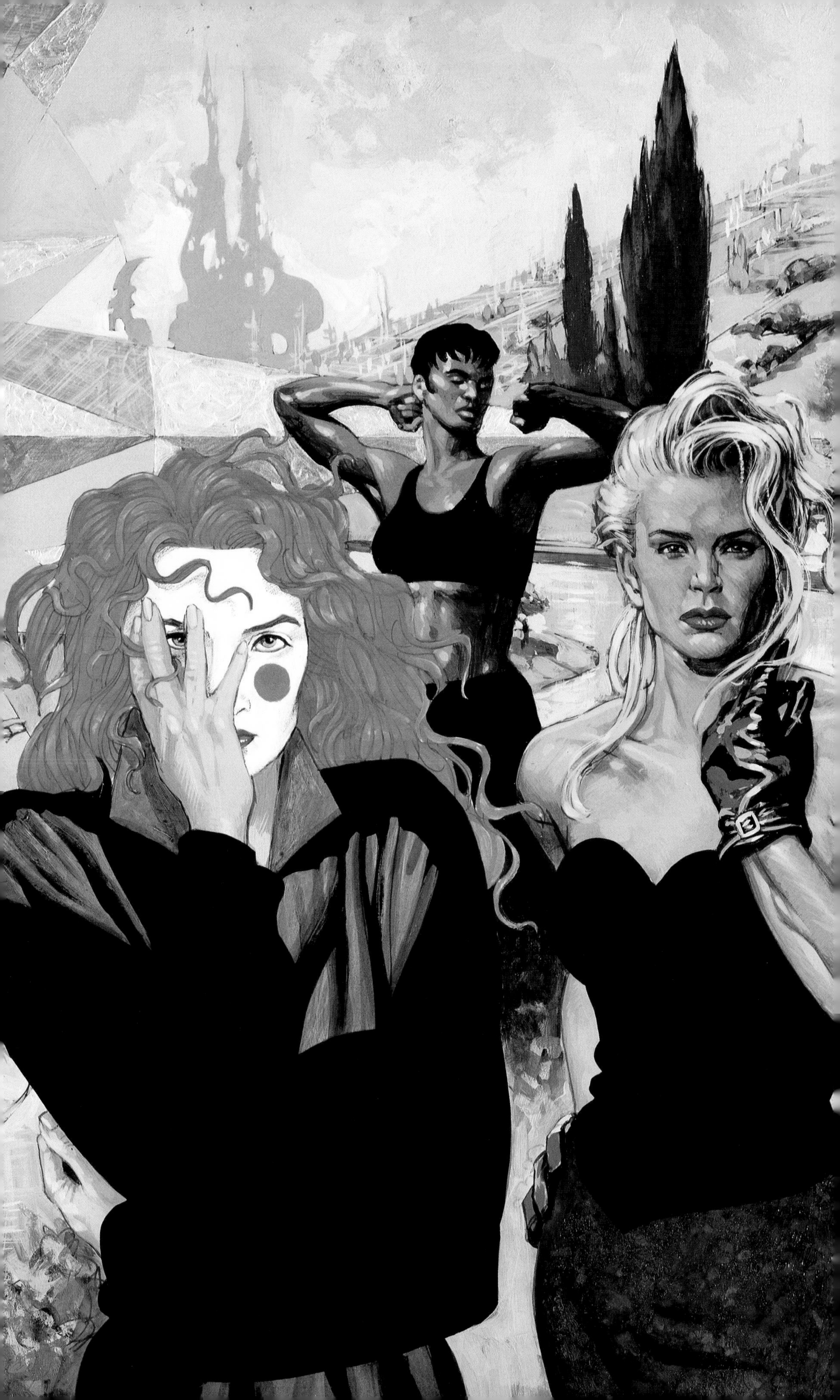

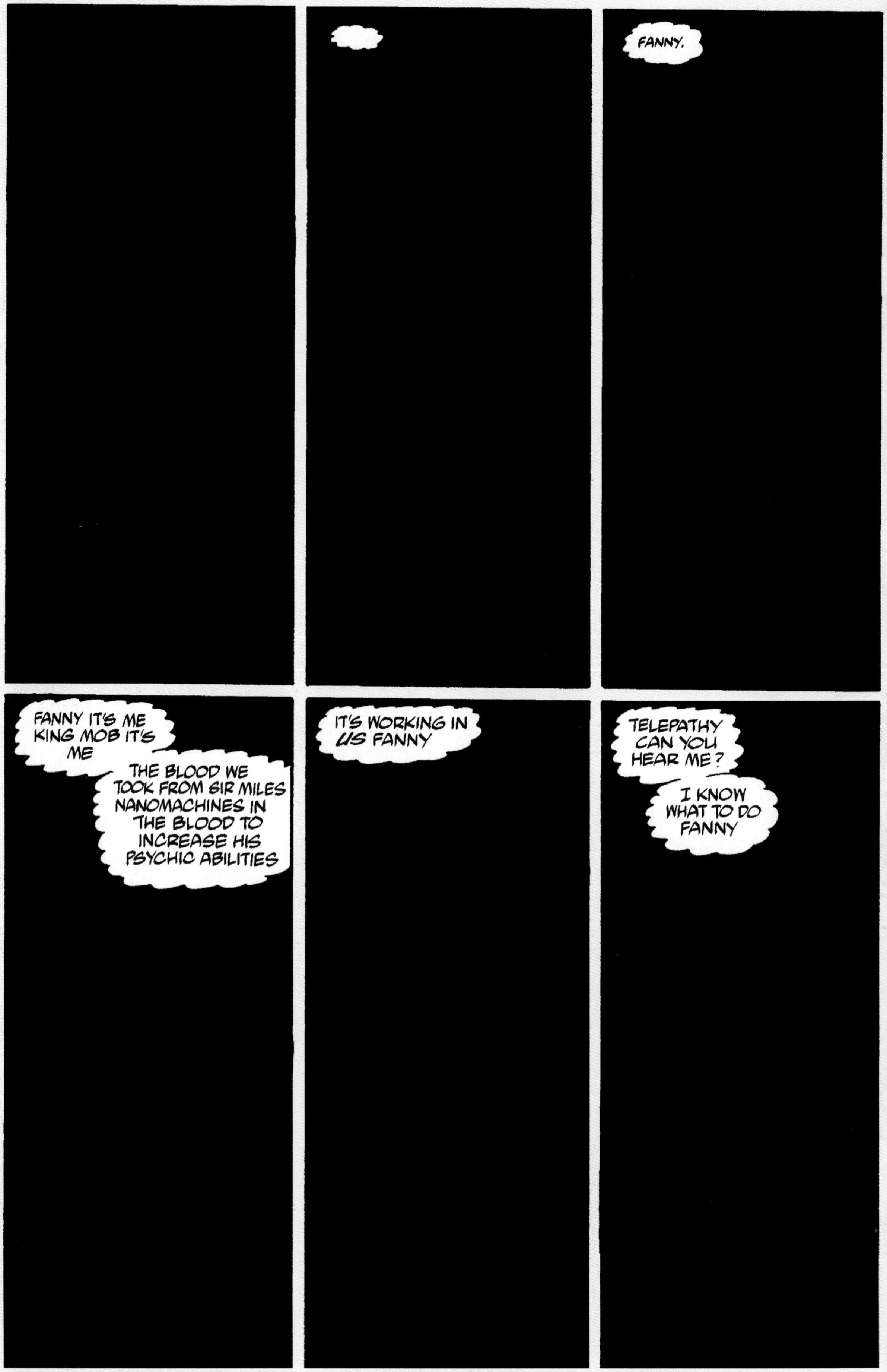
FANNY.
FANNY IT'S ME KING MOB IT'S ME
THE BLOOD WE TOOK FROM SIR MILES NANOMACHINES IN THE BLOOD TO INCREASE HIS PSYCHIC ABILITIES
IT'S WORKING IN US FANNY
TELEPATHY CAN YOU HEAR ME?
I KNOW WHAT TO DO FANNY

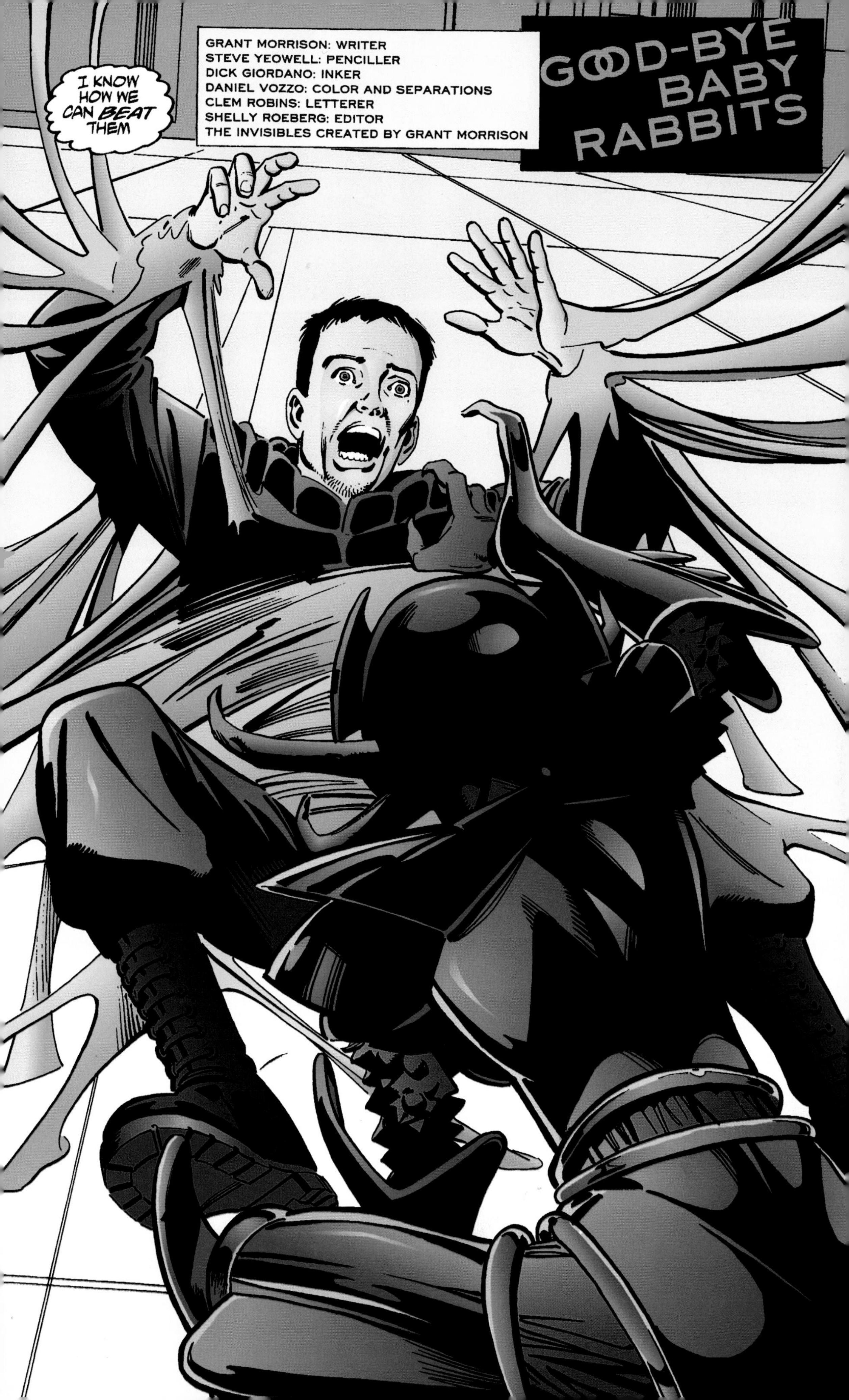
GOOD-BYE BABY RABBITS
GRANT MORRISON: WRITER
STEVE YEOWELL: PENCILLER
DICK GIORDANO: INKER
DANIEL VOZZO: COLOR AND SEPARATIONS
CLEM ROBINS: LETTERER
SHELLY ROEBERG: EDITOR
THE INVISIBLES CREATED BY GRANT MORRISON
I KNOW HOW WE CAN BEAT THEM

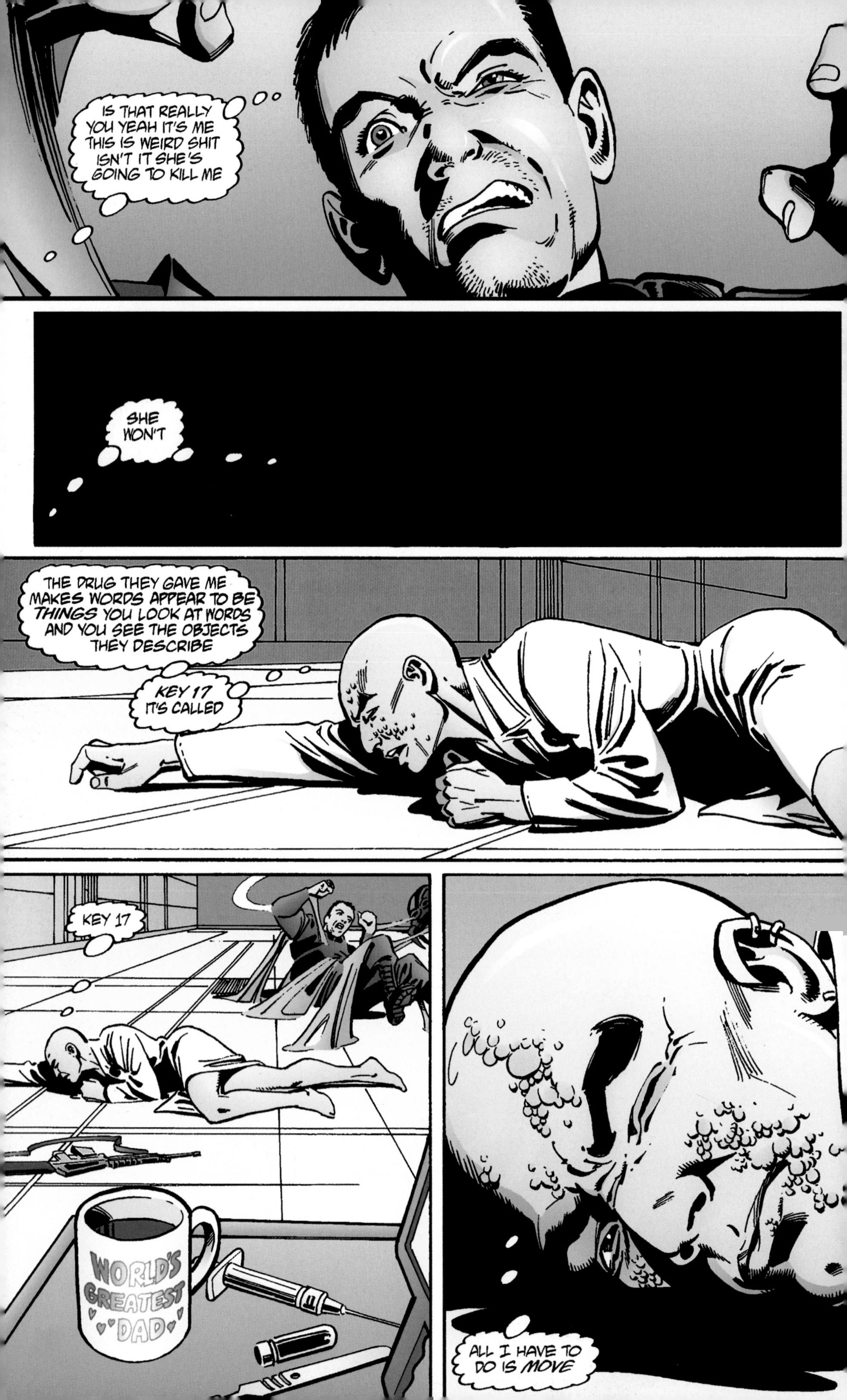
IS THAT REALLY YOU YEAH IT'S ME THIS IS WEIRD SHIT ISN'T IT SHE'S GOING TO KILL ME
SHE WON'T
THE DRUG THEY GAVE ME MAKES WORDS APPEAR TO BE *THINGS* YOU LOOK AT WORDS AND YOU SEE THE OBJECTS THEY DESCRIBE
KEY 17 IT'S CALLED
KEY 17
WORLD'S GREATEST DAD
ALL I HAVE TO DO IS *MOVE*

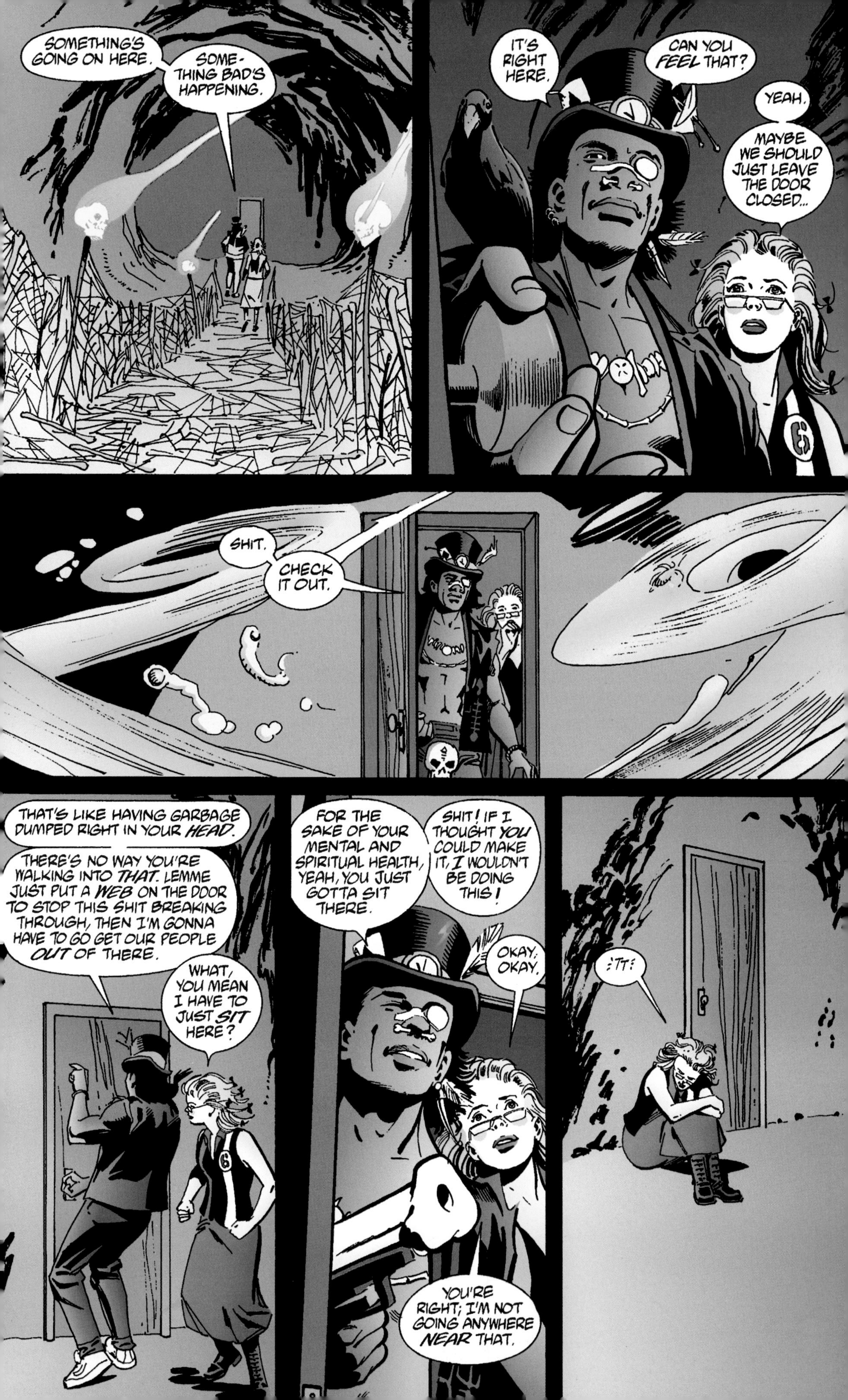
SOMETHING'S GOING ON HERE.
SOME-THING BAD'S HAPPENING.
IT'S RIGHT HERE.
CAN YOU FEEL THAT?
YEAH.
MAYBE WE SHOULD JUST LEAVE THE DOOR CLOSED...
SHIT.
CHECK IT OUT.
THAT'S LIKE HAVING GARBAGE DUMPED RIGHT IN YOUR HEAD.
THERE'S NO WAY YOU'RE WALKING INTO THAT. LEMME JUST PUT A WEB ON THE DOOR TO STOP THIS SHIT BREAKING THROUGH, THEN I'M GONNA HAVE TO GO GET OUR PEOPLE OUT OF THERE.
WHAT, YOU MEAN I HAVE TO JUST SIT HERE?
FOR THE SAKE OF YOUR MENTAL AND SPIRITUAL HEALTH, YEAH, YOU JUST GOTTA SIT THERE.
SHIT! IF I THOUGHT YOU COULD MAKE IT, I WOULDN'T BE DOING THIS!
OKAY; OKAY.
YOU'RE RIGHT; I'M NOT GOING ANYWHERE NEAR THAT.
:TT:

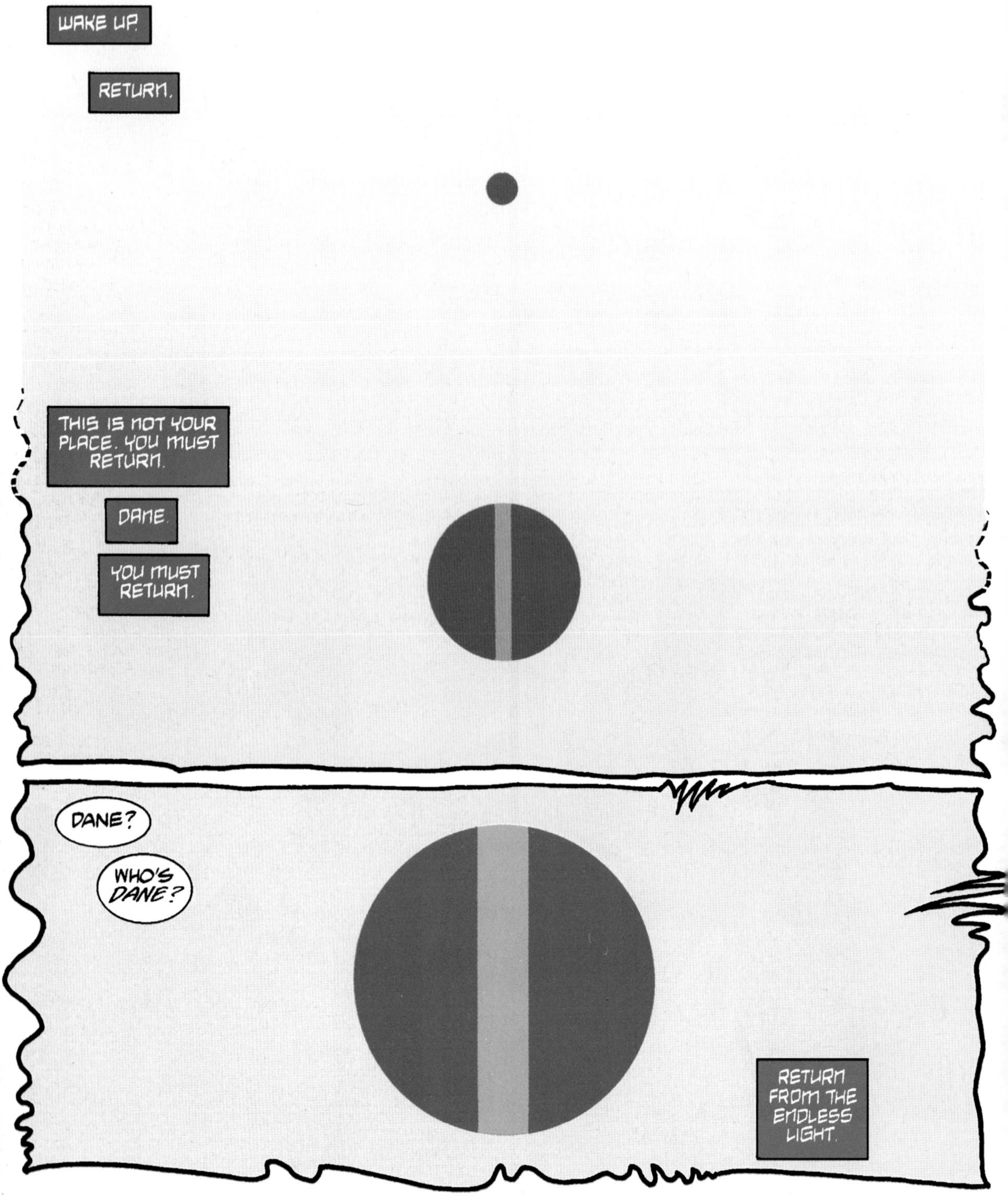
WAKE UP.
RETURN.
THIS IS NOT YOUR PLACE. YOU MUST RETURN.
DANE.
YOU MUST RETURN.
DANE?
WHO'S DANE?
RETURN FROM THE ENDLESS LIGHT.

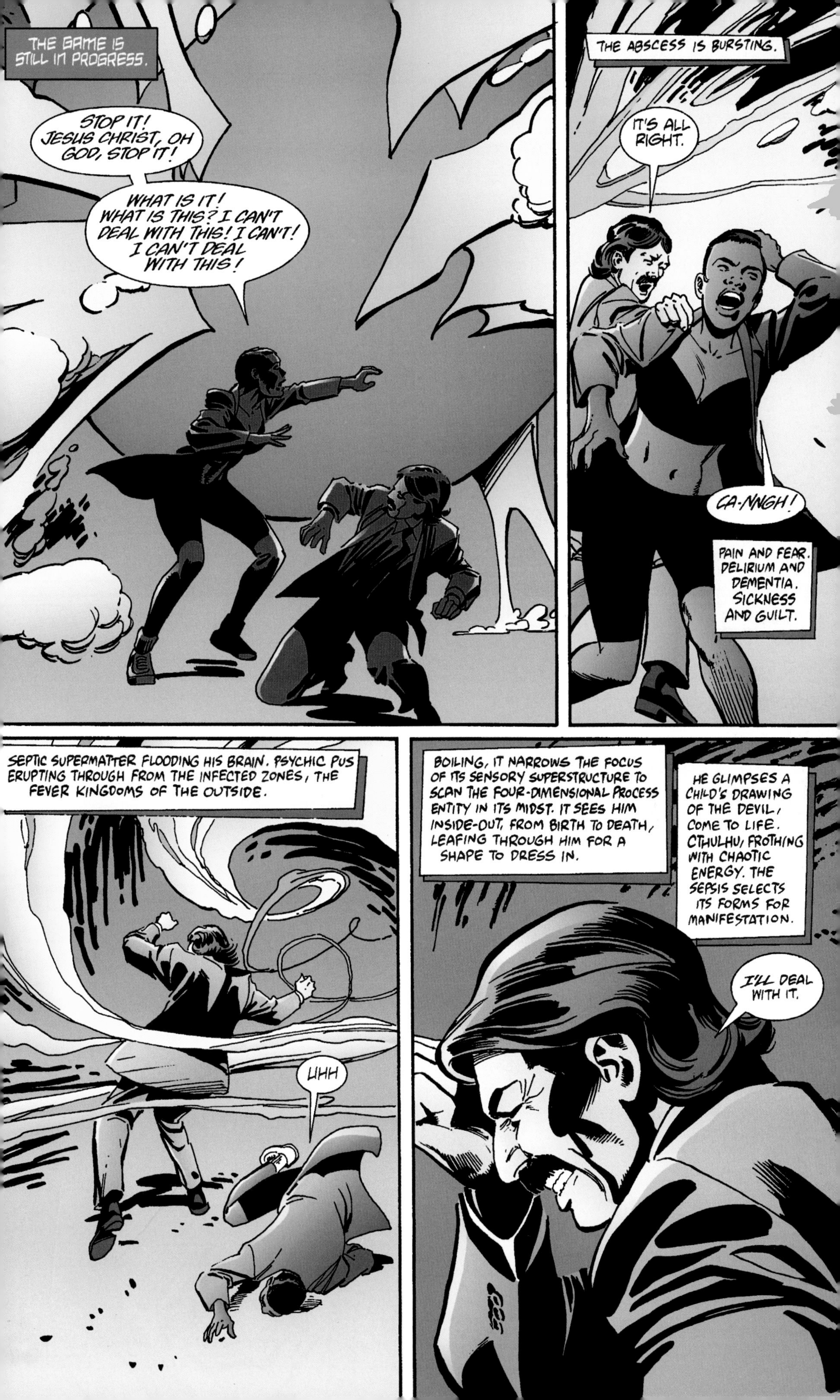
THE GAME IS STILL IN PROGRESS.
STOP IT! JESUS CHRIST, OH GOD, STOP IT!
WHAT IS IT! WHAT IS THIS? I CAN'T DEAL WITH THIS! I CAN'T! I CAN'T DEAL WITH THIS!
THE ABSCESS IS BURSTING.
IT'S ALL RIGHT.
CA-NNGH!
PAIN AND FEAR. DELIRIUM AND DEMENTIA. SICKNESS AND GUILT.
SEPTIC SUPERMATTER FLOODING HIS BRAIN. PSYCHIC PUS ERUPTING THROUGH FROM THE INFECTED ZONES, THE FEVER KINGDOMS OF THE OUTSIDE.
UHH
BOILING, IT NARROWS THE FOCUS OF ITS SENSORY SUPERSTRUCTURE TO SCAN THE FOUR-DIMENSIONAL PROCESS ENTITY IN ITS MIDST. IT SEES HIM INSIDE-OUT, FROM BIRTH TO DEATH, LEAFING THROUGH HIM FOR A SHAPE TO DRESS IN.
HE GLIMPSES A CHILD'S DRAWING OF THE DEVIL, COME TO LIFE. CTHULHU, FROTHING WITH CHAOTIC ENERGY. THE SEPSIS SELECTS ITS FORMS FOR MANIFESTATION.
I'LL DEAL WITH IT.

ONORTHOCRASI, MOTHER WITHOUT BOUNDARIES, WHO NOURISHES EFEMEMPHI, THE ANGEL OF PLEASURE AND IOCHO, ANGEL OF GREED AND NENETOPHNI, ANGEL OF PAIN AND LASTLY BLAOMEN, ANGEL OF FEAR. THESE AND THEIR THREE HUNDRED AND SIXTY ABORTIONS:

THE BROTHERHOOD OF THE SCOURGE IN RUBBER HOODS, EYES AND LIPS STAPLED SHUT, DUKES OF THE FIRST TRENCH.

A SACRIFICE.

A SACRIFICE MIGHT SEAL THE ABSCESS, HE'S THINKING, AS THE THOUGHTS SCREAM AND TEAR ONE ANOTHER APART. A DREADFUL CROWN IS SET IN PLACE, CRACKING OPEN HIS HEAD.

THE HORRORS MULTIPLY WITH MATHEMATICAL PRECISION..

THE IMBECILE POPE ON ITS JEWELLED COMMODE, VOIDING SHIT AND GOLD COINS, MUMBLING IDIOT PHRASES, JINGLES, POINT-LESS STATISTICS.

A SACRIFICE.

TOWERING BEHIND HIM, ONE OF NINE CORRUPT BUDDHAS --OBESE AND SENILE, HIS BRAIN ROTTED LIKE A TOOTH BY THE SWEET, UNENDING BLISS OF FALSE ENLIGHTENMENT, THE BUDDHA MASTURBATES LIKE A MONKEY IN A CAGE.

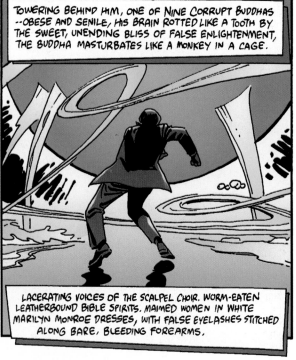

LACERATING VOICES OF THE SCALPEL CHOIR. WORM-EATEN LEATHERBOUND BIBLE SPIRITS, MAIMED WOMEN IN WHITE MARILYN MONROE DRESSES, WITH FALSE EYELASHES STITCHED ALONG BARE, BLEEDING FOREARMS.

IT NEEDS A SACRIFICE. THE ONLY THING HE HAS TO GIVE.

THE BANAL HORROR MOVIE HOST GATHERS TO SHRILL AND GIBBER. IT ALMOST SOUNDS LIKE WORDS, IF YOU LISTEN HARD ENOUGH. ONE WORD.

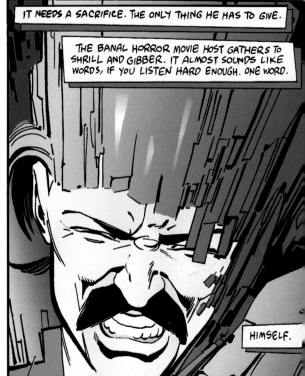

HIMSELF.

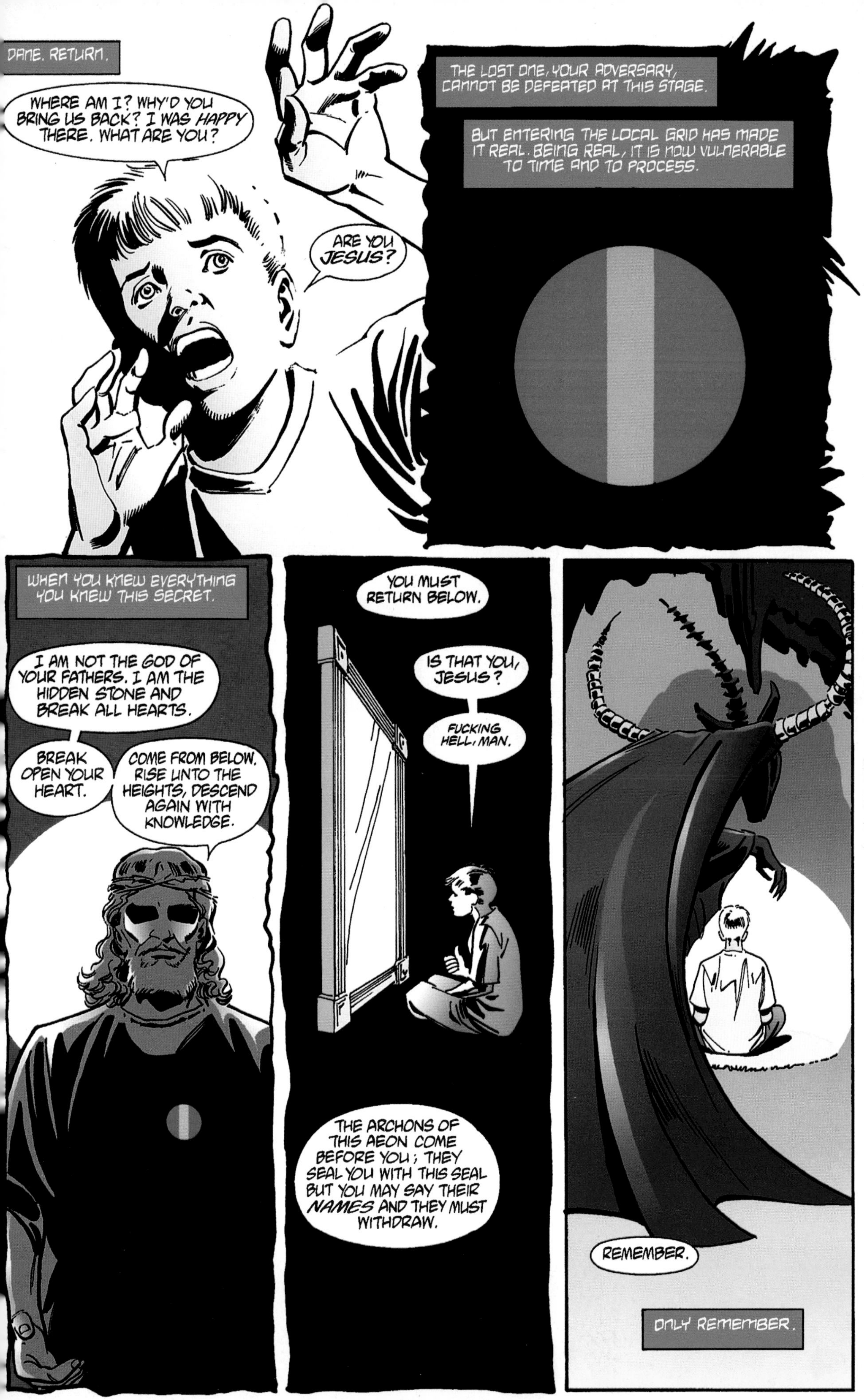

DANE. RETURN.
WHERE AM I? WHY'D YOU BRING US BACK? I WAS *HAPPY* THERE. WHAT ARE YOU?
ARE YOU *JESUS?*
THE LOST ONE, YOUR ADVERSARY, CANNOT BE DEFEATED AT THIS STAGE.
BUT ENTERING THE LOCAL GRID HAS MADE IT REAL. BEING REAL, IT IS NOW VULNERABLE TO TIME AND TO PROCESS.
WHEN YOU KNEW EVERYTHING YOU KNEW THIS SECRET.
I AM NOT THE GOD OF YOUR FATHERS. I AM THE HIDDEN STONE AND BREAK ALL HEARTS.
BREAK OPEN YOUR HEART.
COME FROM BELOW. RISE UNTO THE HEIGHTS, DESCEND AGAIN WITH KNOWLEDGE.
YOU MUST RETURN BELOW.
IS THAT YOU, JESUS?
FUCKING HELL, MAN.
THE ARCHONS OF THIS AEON COME BEFORE YOU; THEY SEAL YOU WITH THIS SEAL BUT YOU MAY SAY THEIR *NAMES* AND THEY MUST WITHDRAW.
REMEMBER.
ONLY REMEMBER.

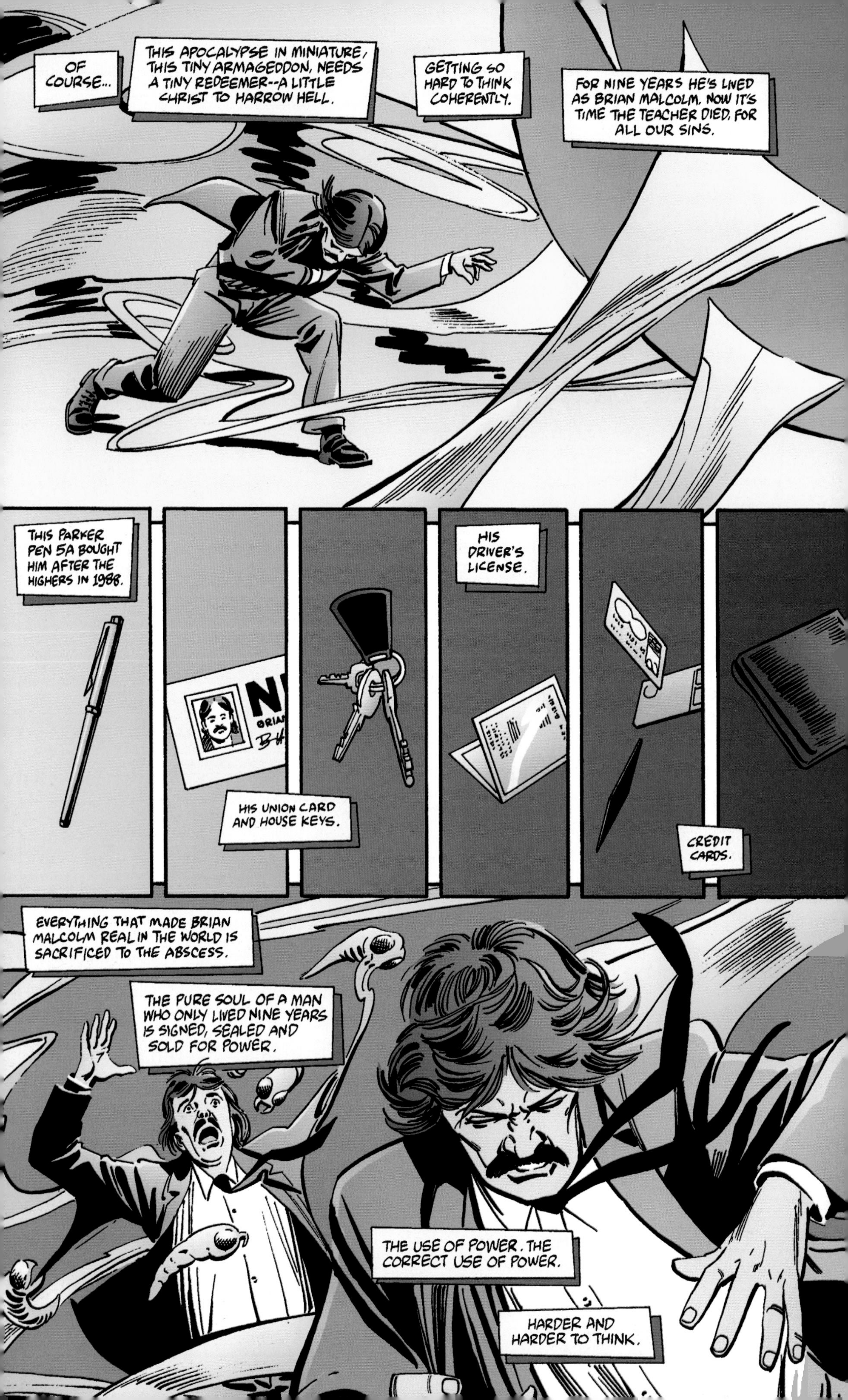
OF COURSE...
THIS APOCALYPSE IN MINIATURE, THIS TINY ARMAGEDDON, NEEDS A TINY REDEEMER--A LITTLE CHRIST TO HARROW HELL.
GETTING SO HARD TO THINK COHERENTLY.
FOR NINE YEARS HE'S LIVED AS BRIAN MALCOLM. NOW IT'S TIME THE TEACHER DIED, FOR ALL OUR SINS.
THIS PARKER PEN 5A BOUGHT HIM AFTER THE HIGHERS IN 1988.
HIS UNION CARD AND HOUSE KEYS.
HIS DRIVER'S LICENSE.
CREDIT CARDS.
EVERYTHING THAT MADE BRIAN MALCOLM REAL IN THE WORLD IS SACRIFICED TO THE ABSCESS.
THE PURE SOUL OF A MAN WHO ONLY LIVED NINE YEARS IS SIGNED, SEALED AND SOLD FOR POWER.
THE USE OF POWER. THE CORRECT USE OF POWER.
HARDER AND HARDER TO THINK.

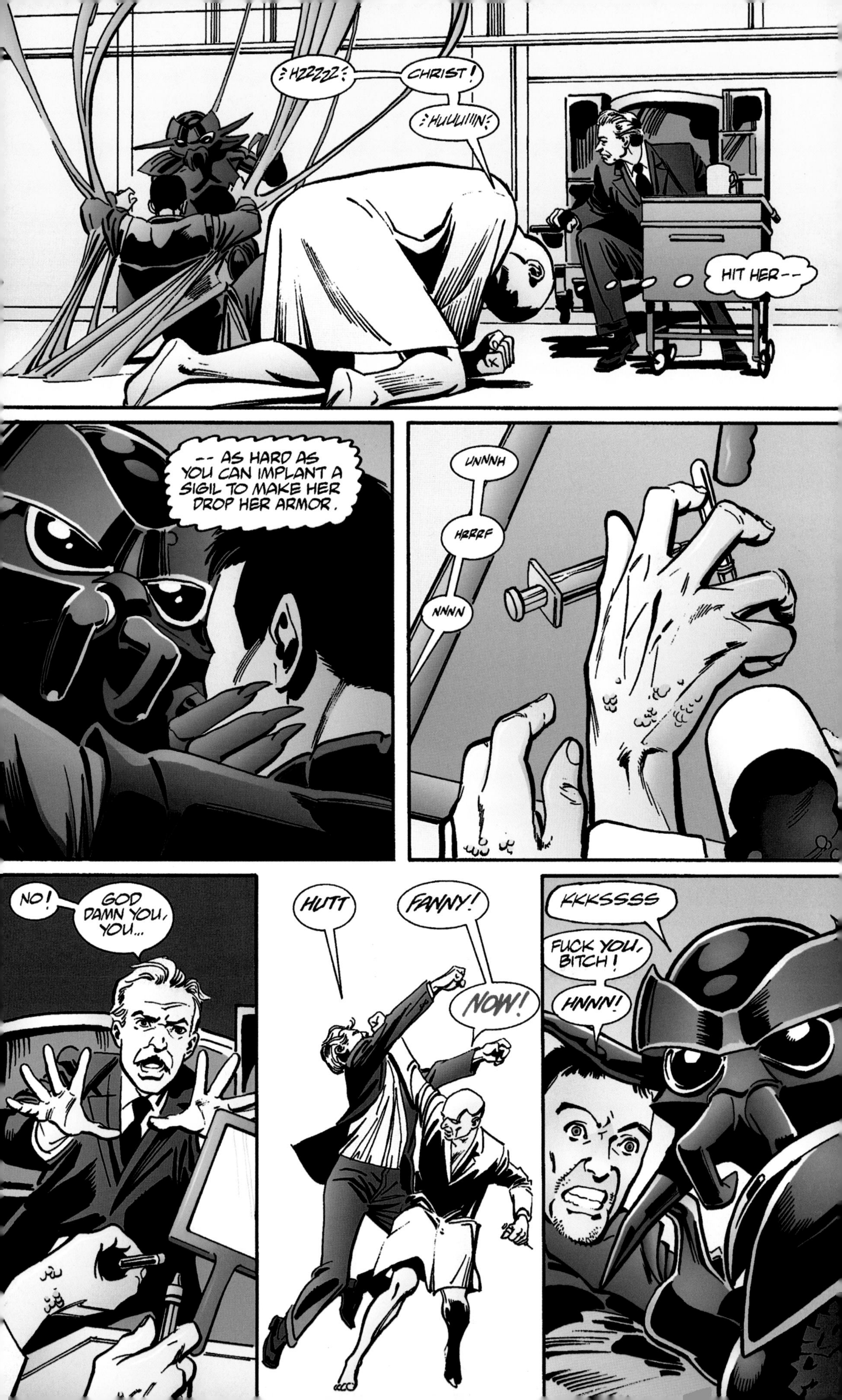
HZZZZZ
CHRIST!
HUUUUIIN
HIT HER--
-- AS HARD AS YOU CAN IMPLANT A SIGIL TO MAKE HER DROP HER ARMOR.
UNNNH
HRRRF
NNNN
NO!
GOD DAMN YOU, YOU...
HUTT
FANNY!
NOW!
KKKSSSS
FUCK YOU, BITCH!
HNNN!

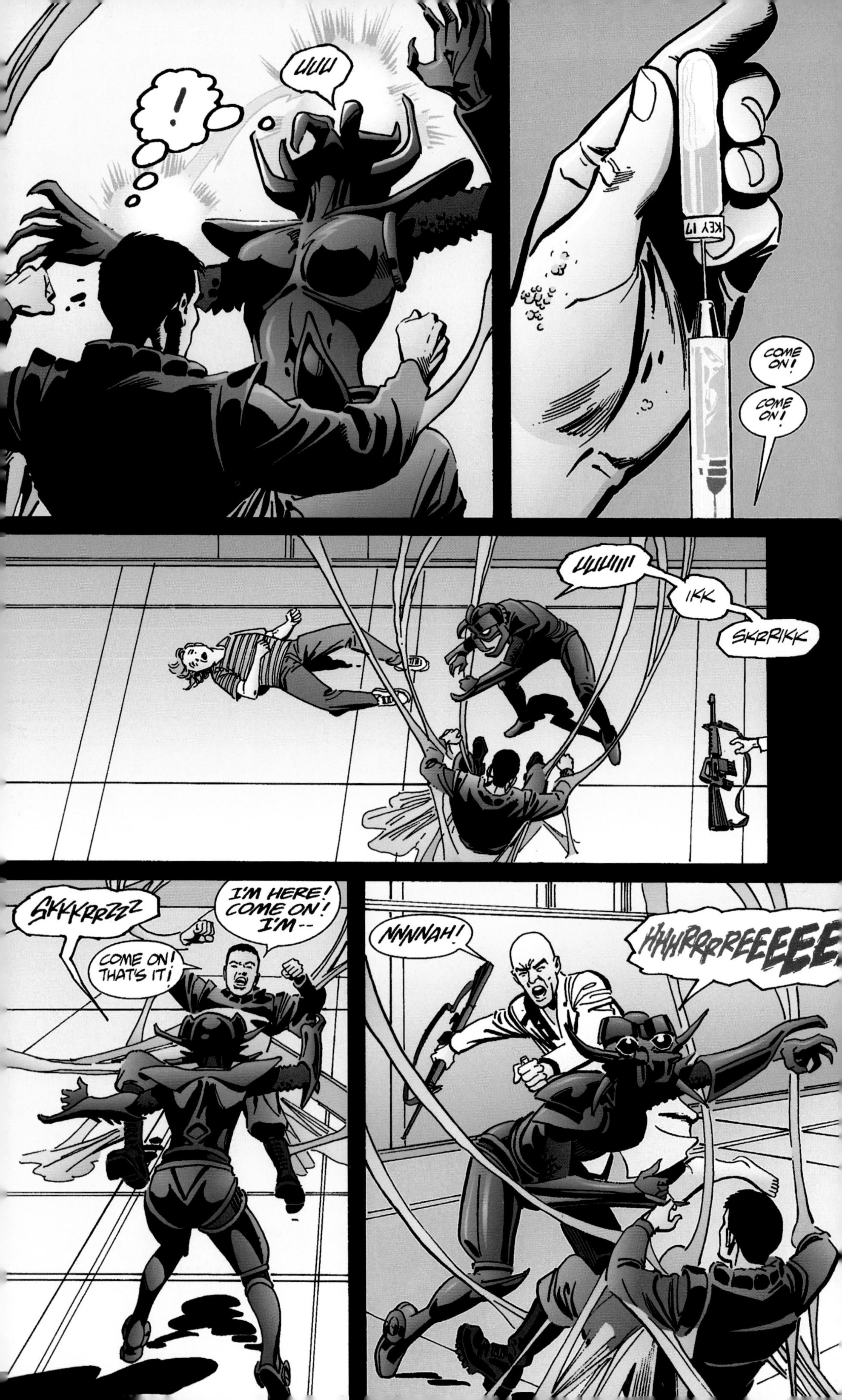
!
UUU
KEY 17
COME ON!
COME ON!
UUUIIII
IKK
SKRRIKK
SKKKRRZZZ
I'M HERE! COME ON! I'M--
COME ON! THAT'S IT!
NNNNAH!
HHHRRRREEEEEE

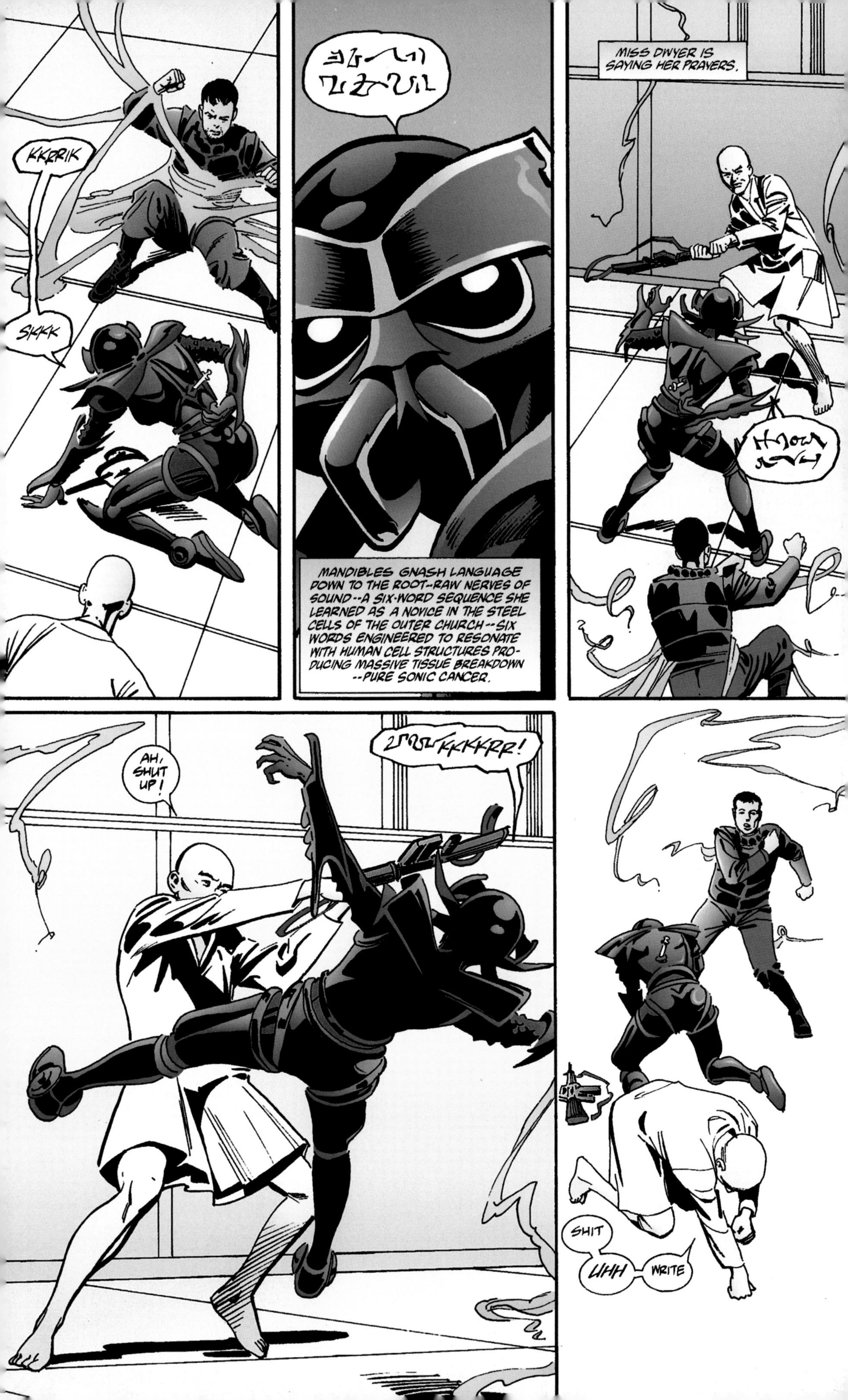
KKRRIK
SKKK
MANDIBLES GNASH LANGUAGE DOWN TO THE ROOT--RAW NERVES OF SOUND--A SIX-WORD SEQUENCE SHE LEARNED AS A NOVICE IN THE STEEL CELLS OF THE OUTER CHURCH--SIX WORDS ENGINEERED TO RESONATE WITH HUMAN CELL STRUCTURES PRODUCING MASSIVE TISSUE BREAKDOWN --PURE SONIC CANCER.
MISS DWYER IS SAYING HER PRAYERS.
AH, SHUT UP!
KKKKRR!
SHIT
UHH
WRITE

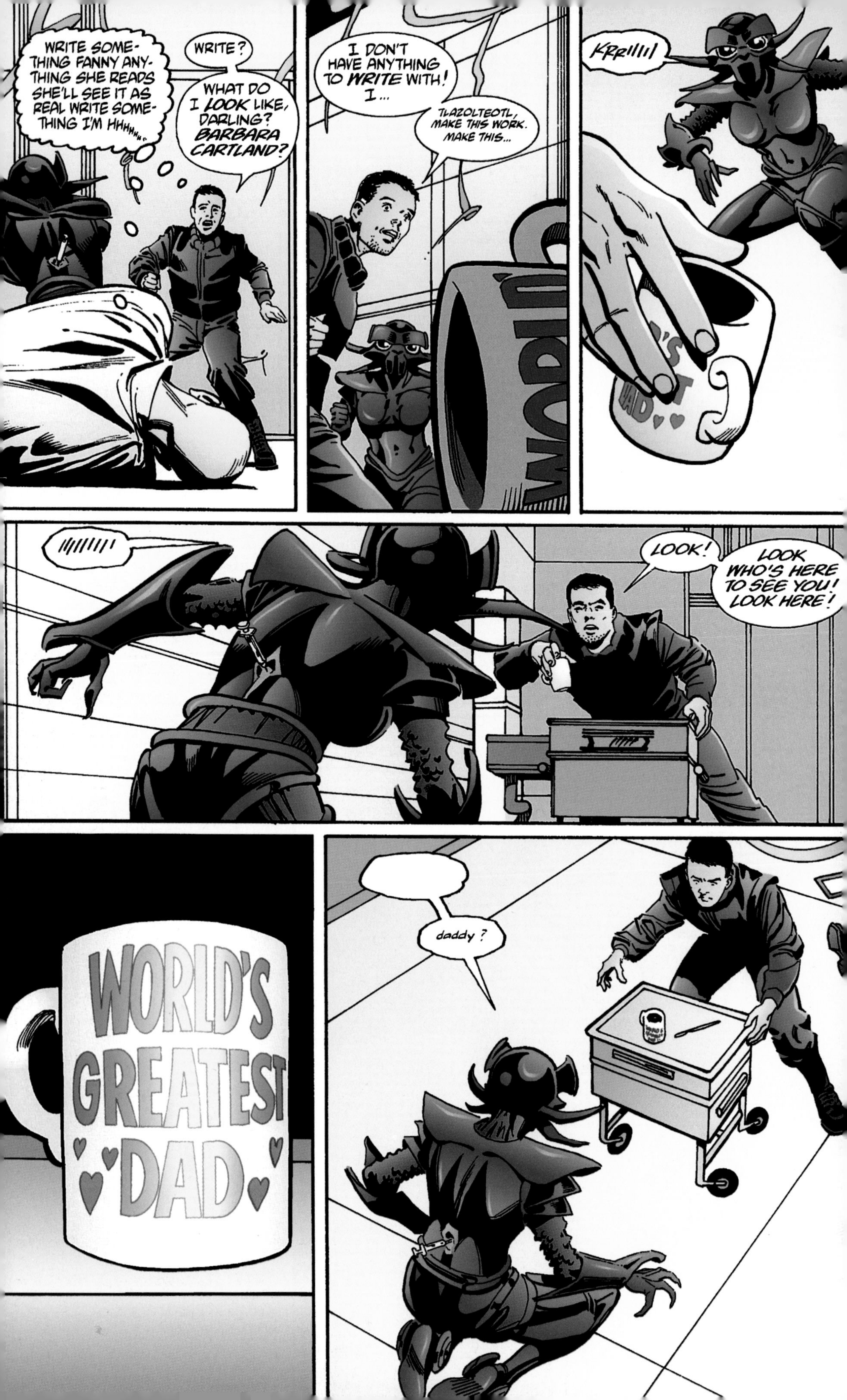
WRITE SOME-THING FANNY ANY-THING SHE READS SHE'LL SEE IT AS REAL WRITE SOME-THING I'M HHHHHH...
WRITE?
WHAT DO I LOOK LIKE, DARLING? BARBARA CARTLAND?
I DON'T HAVE ANYTHING TO WRITE WITH! I...
TLAZOLTEOTL, MAKE THIS WORK. MAKE THIS...
WORLD
KRR!!!!!
'S GREAT DAD
!!!!!!!!
LOOK!
LOOK WHO'S HERE TO SEE YOU! LOOK HERE!
WORLD'S GREATEST DAD
daddy?

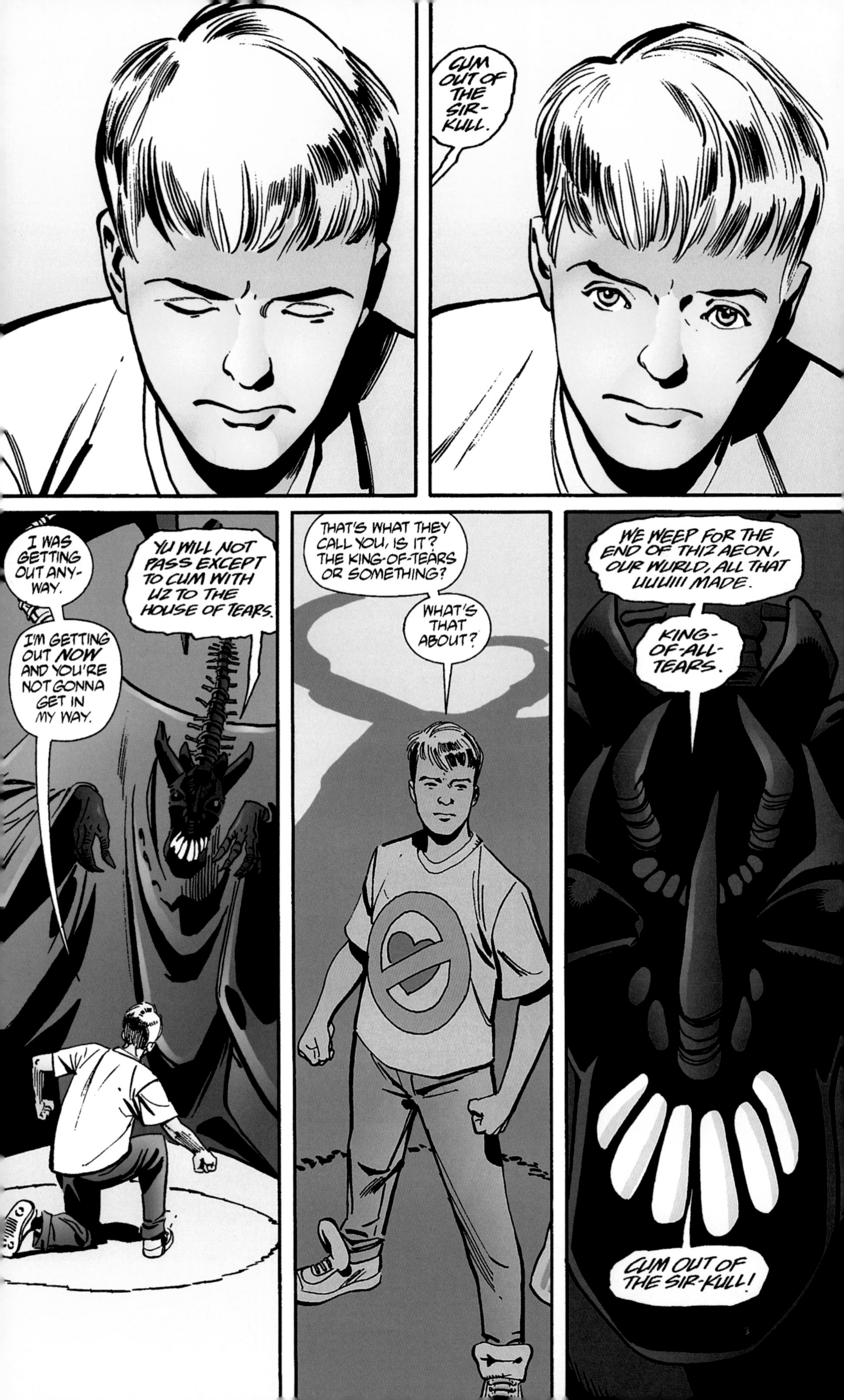
CUM OUT OF THE SIR-KULL.
I WAS GETTING OUT ANY-WAY.
YU WILL NOT PASS EXCEPT TO CUM WITH UZ TO THE HOUSE OF TEARS.
I'M GETTING OUT NOW AND YOU'RE NOT GONNA GET IN MY WAY.
THAT'S WHAT THEY CALL YOU, IS IT? THE KING-OF-TEARS OR SOMETHING?
WHAT'S THAT ABOUT?
WE WEEP FOR THE END OF THIZ AEON, OUR WURLD, ALL THAT UUUIII MADE.
KING-OF-ALL-TEARS.
CUM OUT OF THE SIR-KULL!

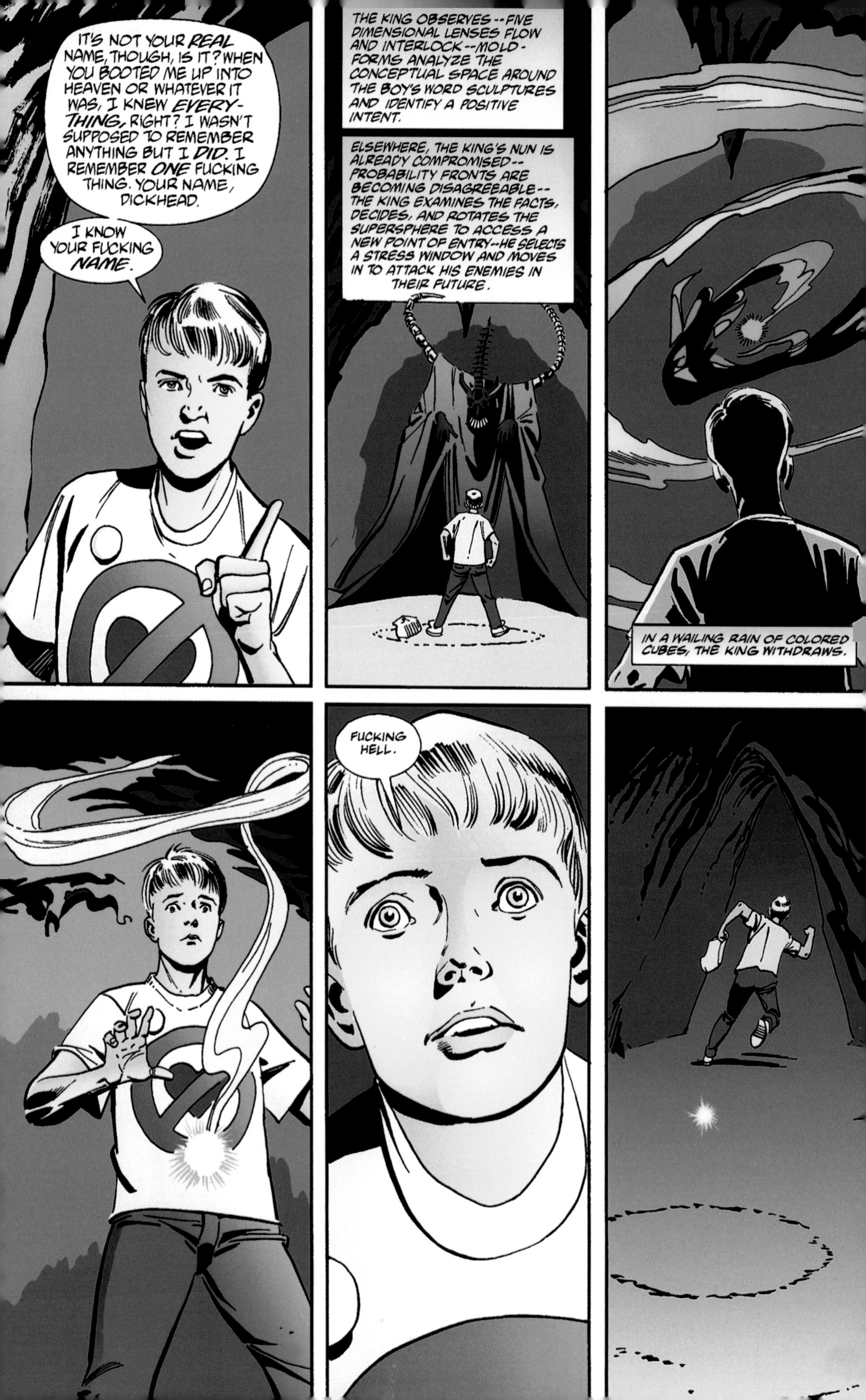
IT'S NOT YOUR REAL NAME, THOUGH, IS IT? WHEN YOU BOOTED ME UP INTO HEAVEN OR WHATEVER IT WAS, I KNEW EVERY-THING, RIGHT? I WASN'T SUPPOSED TO REMEMBER ANYTHING BUT I DID. I REMEMBER ONE FUCKING THING. YOUR NAME, DICKHEAD.
I KNOW YOUR FUCKING NAME.
THE KING OBSERVES--FIVE DIMENSIONAL LENSES FLOW AND INTERLOCK--MOLD-FORMS ANALYZE THE CONCEPTUAL SPACE AROUND THE BOY'S WORD SCULPTURES AND IDENTIFY A POSITIVE INTENT.
ELSEWHERE, THE KING'S NUN IS ALREADY COMPROMISED--PROBABILITY FRONTS ARE BECOMING DISAGREEABLE--THE KING EXAMINES THE FACTS, DECIDES, AND ROTATES THE SUPERSPHERE TO ACCESS A NEW POINT OF ENTRY--HE SELECTS A STRESS WINDOW AND MOVES IN TO ATTACK HIS ENEMIES IN THEIR FUTURE.
IN A WAILING RAIN OF COLORED CUBES, THE KING WITHDRAWS.
FUCKING HELL.

AND RAGGED ROBIN EXAMINES THE KEY TO THE STRUCTURE AND MEANING OF THE UNIVERSE IN THE FORM OF A MIRACULOUS PHOTOGRAPH.

WHILE BRIAN MALCOLM, ANTIBIOTIC, CLEANSES THE WOUND IN THE WALL OF THE WORLD BY THE POWER OF HIS SACRED DEATH.

RIGHT ON CUE, REALITY'S OWN PREPROGRAMMED IMMUNE SYSTEMS KICK IN, DRAWING ON THE POWER OF THE SACRIFICE TO SCOUR AWAY THE INFECTION WHICH THREATENS THE INTEGRITY OF THE LOCAL AGREED RULES.

THE WOUND BEGINS TO SEAL, PUCKERING INTO HIGHER DIMENSIONAL SPACES FOLDING BACK-WARDS, MATHEMATICAL.

(THE PURGING OF THESE DOOR-WAYS OFTEN RESULTS IN A CHARACTERISTIC SCAR ON REALITY--AN ANOMALY, A HAUNTING, A COLD SPOT, AN OBJECT THAT CANNOT BE SEEN CLEARLY OR HANDLED.)

AND THE SICKNESS LEAVES THROUGH THE SOLES OF HIS FEET LIKE SULPHUR AND TREACLE AND...

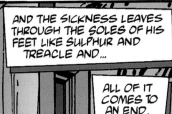

ALL OF IT COMES TO AN END.

WHICH LEAVES, APART FROM WHO HE'S GOING TO BE, NOW THAT BRIAN MALCOLM'S DEAD, ONLY ONE QUESTION.

WHO IS TELLING THIS, AND TO WHOM?

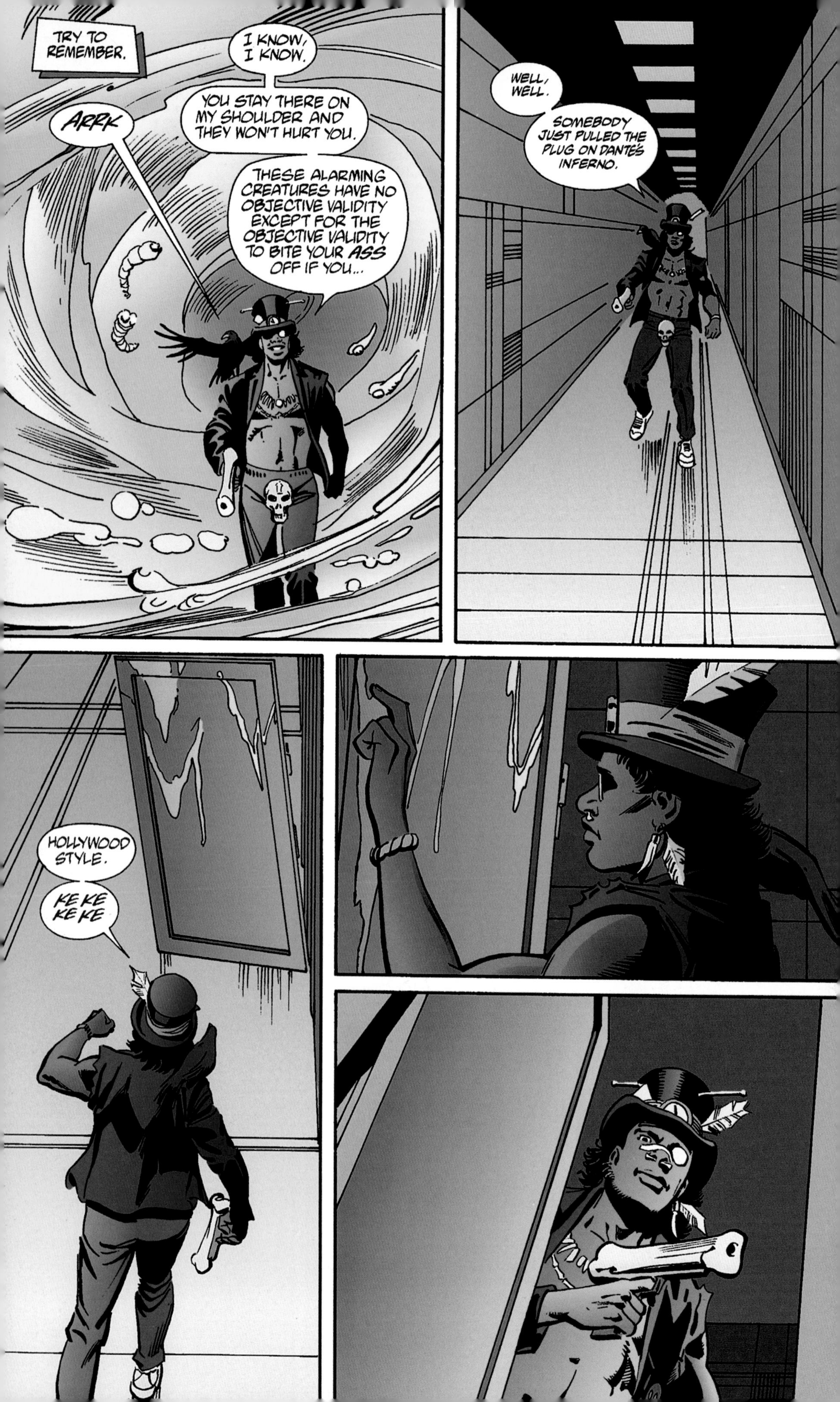
TRY TO REMEMBER.
I KNOW, I KNOW.
ARRK
YOU STAY THERE ON MY SHOULDER AND THEY WON'T HURT YOU.
THESE ALARMING CREATURES HAVE NO OBJECTIVE VALIDITY EXCEPT FOR THE OBJECTIVE VALIDITY TO BITE YOUR ASS OFF IF YOU...
WELL, WELL.
SOMEBODY JUST PULLED THE PLUG ON DANTE'S INFERNO.
HOLLYWOOD STYLE.
KE KE KE KE

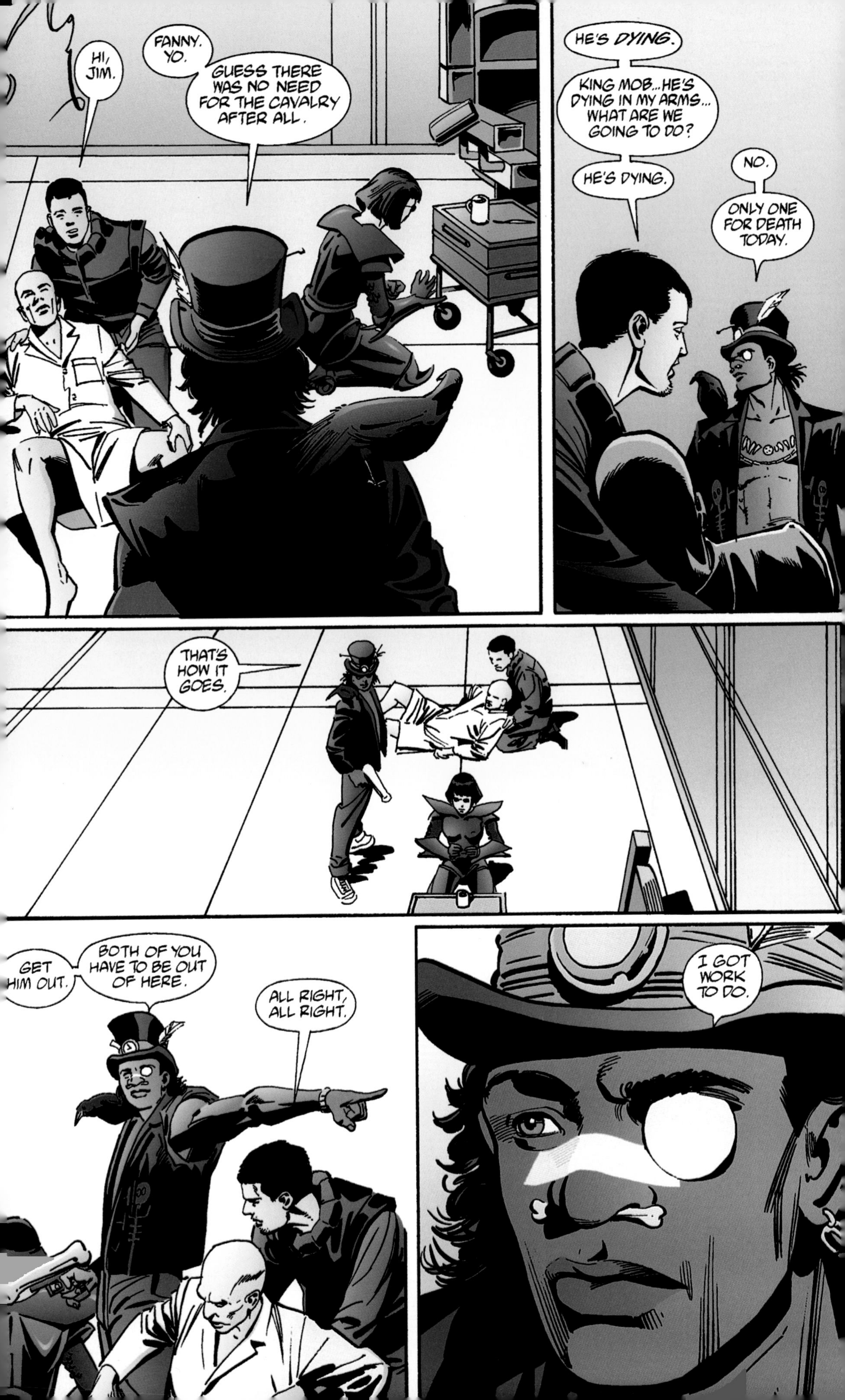
HI, JIM.
FANNY. YO.
GUESS THERE WAS NO NEED FOR THE CAVALRY AFTER ALL.
HE'S *DYING*.
KING MOB...HE'S DYING IN MY ARMS... WHAT ARE WE GOING TO DO?
HE'S DYING.
NO.
ONLY ONE FOR DEATH TODAY.
THAT'S HOW IT GOES.
GET HIM OUT.
BOTH OF YOU HAVE TO BE OUT OF HERE.
ALL RIGHT, ALL RIGHT.
I GOT WORK TO DO.

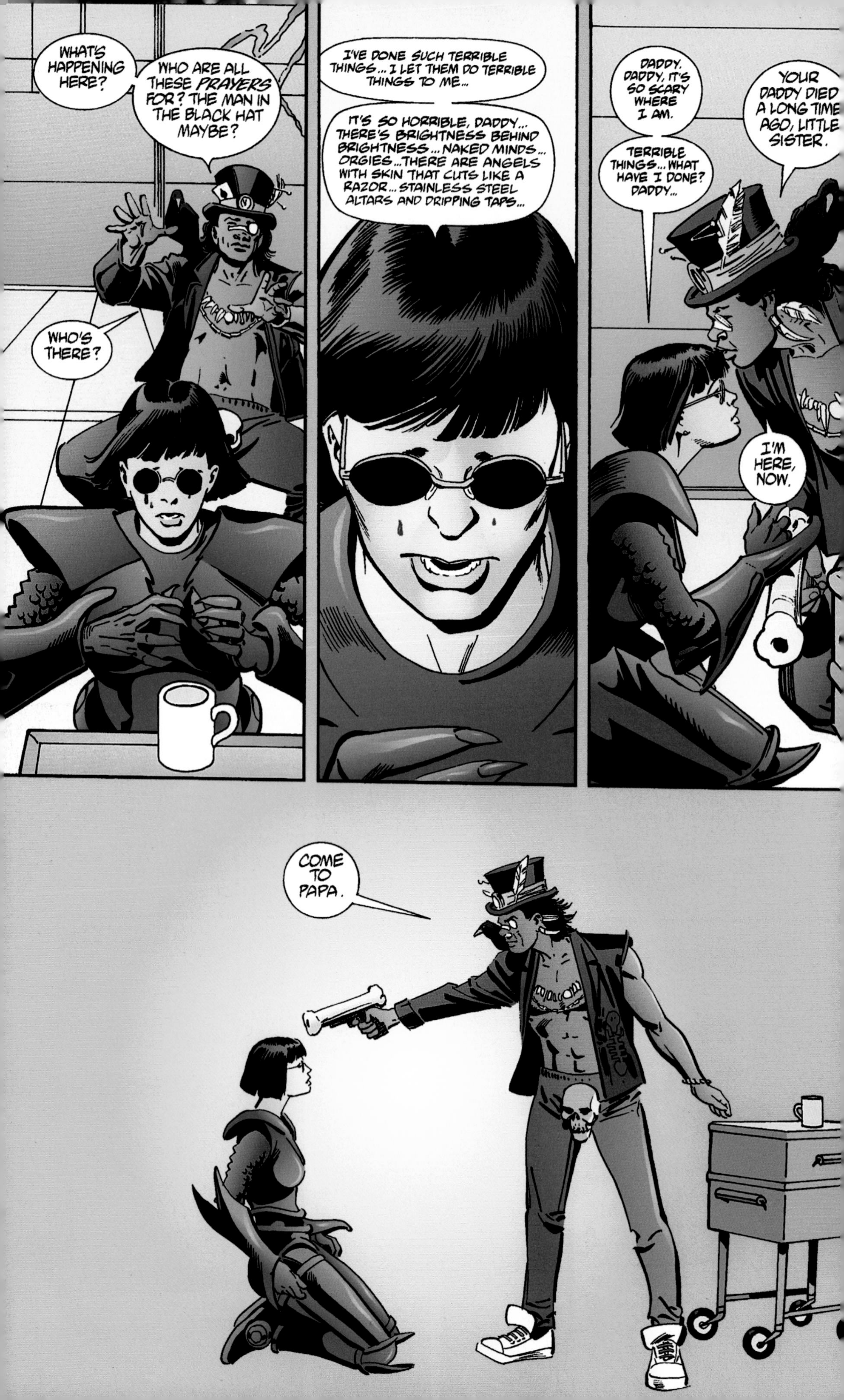
WHAT'S HAPPENING HERE?
WHO ARE ALL THESE *PRAYERS* FOR? THE MAN IN THE BLACK HAT MAYBE?
WHO'S THERE?
I'VE DONE SUCH TERRIBLE THINGS... I LET THEM DO TERRIBLE THINGS TO ME...
IT'S SO HORRIBLE, DADDY... THERE'S BRIGHTNESS BEHIND BRIGHTNESS... NAKED MINDS... ORGIES...THERE ARE ANGELS WITH SKIN THAT CUTS LIKE A RAZOR... STAINLESS STEEL ALTARS AND DRIPPING TAPS...
DADDY. DADDY, IT'S SO SCARY WHERE I AM.
TERRIBLE THINGS... WHAT HAVE I DONE? DADDY...
YOUR DADDY DIED A LONG TIME AGO, LITTLE SISTER.
I'M HERE, NOW.
COME TO PAPA.

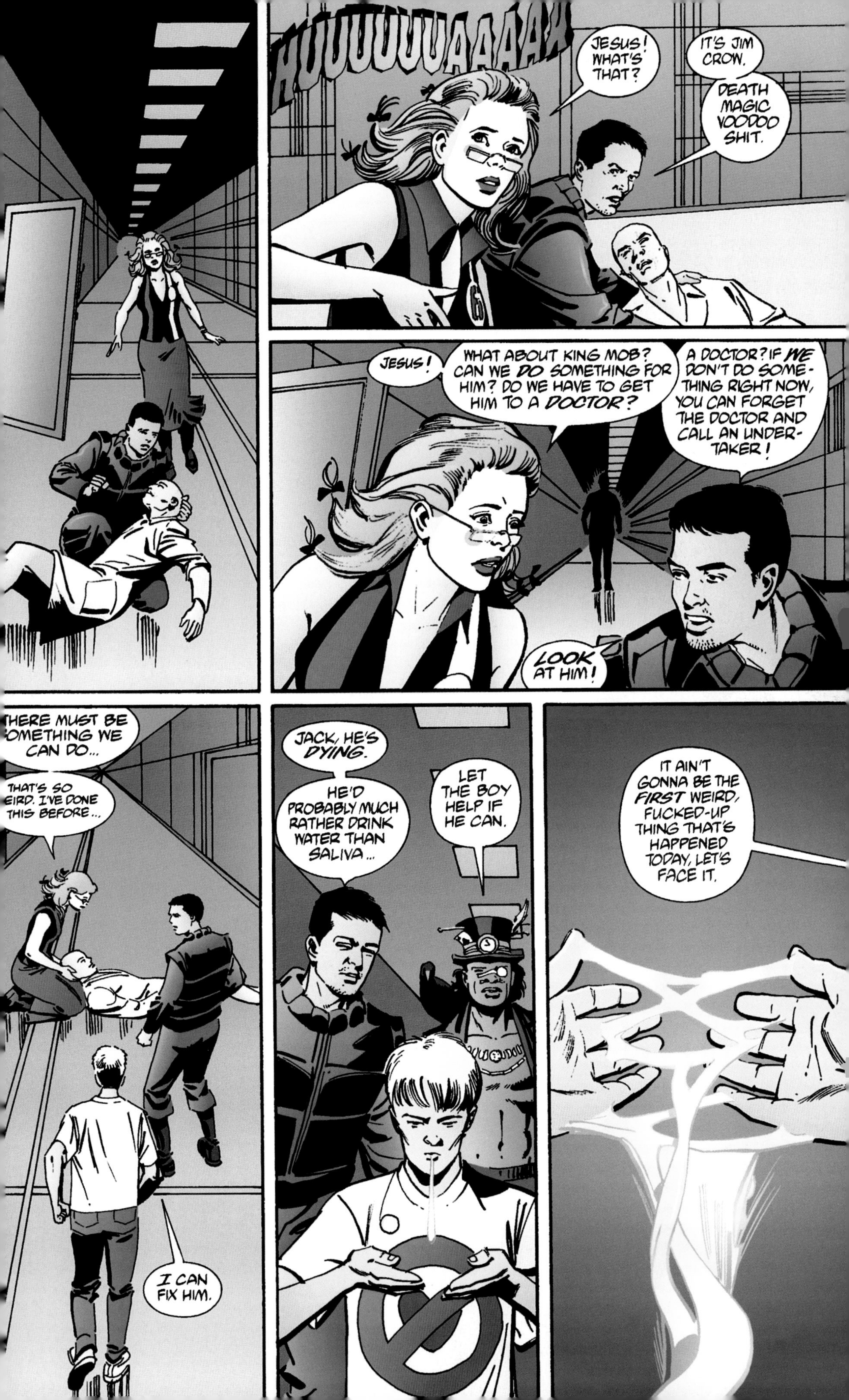
HUUUUUUAAAAH
JESUS! WHAT'S THAT?
IT'S JIM CROW.
DEATH MAGIC VOODOO SHIT.
JESUS!
WHAT ABOUT KING MOB? CAN WE DO SOMETHING FOR HIM? DO WE HAVE TO GET HIM TO A DOCTOR?
A DOCTOR? IF WE DON'T DO SOME-THING RIGHT NOW, YOU CAN FORGET THE DOCTOR AND CALL AN UNDER-TAKER!
LOOK AT HIM!
THERE MUST BE SOMETHING WE CAN DO...
THAT'S SO EIRD. I'VE DONE THIS BEFORE...
I CAN FIX HIM.
JACK, HE'S DYING.
HE'D PROBABLY MUCH RATHER DRINK WATER THAN SALIVA...
LET THE BOY HELP IF HE CAN.
IT AIN'T GONNA BE THE FIRST WEIRD, FUCKED-UP THING THAT'S HAPPENED TODAY, LET'S FACE IT.

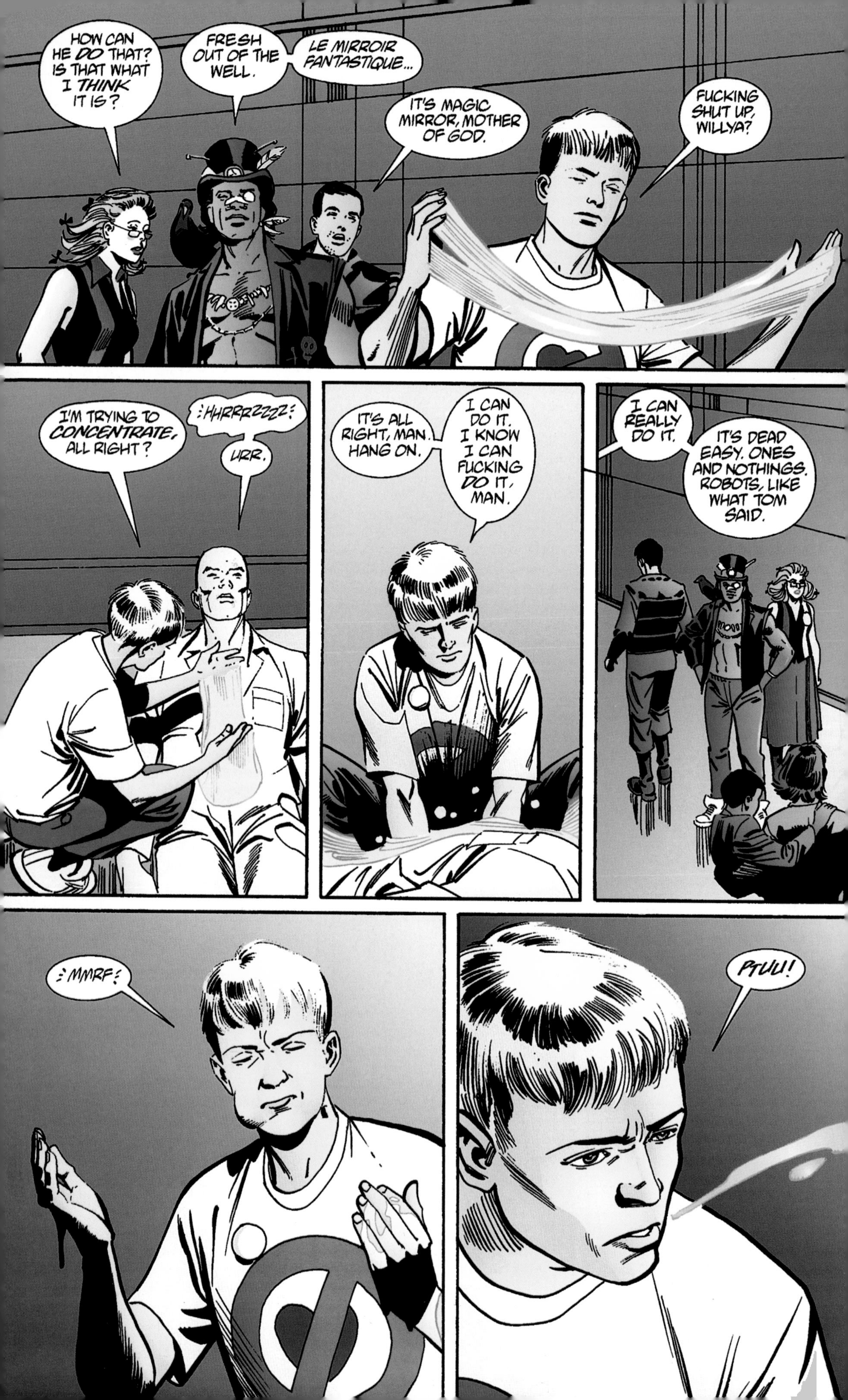
HOW CAN HE DO THAT? IS THAT WHAT I THINK IT IS?
FRESH OUT OF THE WELL.
LE MIRROIR FANTASTIQUE...
IT'S MAGIC MIRROR, MOTHER OF GOD.
FUCKING SHUT UP, WILLYA?
I'M TRYING TO CONCENTRATE, ALL RIGHT?
HHRRRZZZZZ
URR.
IT'S ALL RIGHT, MAN. HANG ON.
I CAN DO IT. I KNOW I CAN FUCKING DO IT, MAN.
I CAN REALLY DO IT.
IT'S DEAD EASY. ONES AND NOTHINGS. ROBOTS, LIKE WHAT TOM SAID.
MMRF
PTUU!

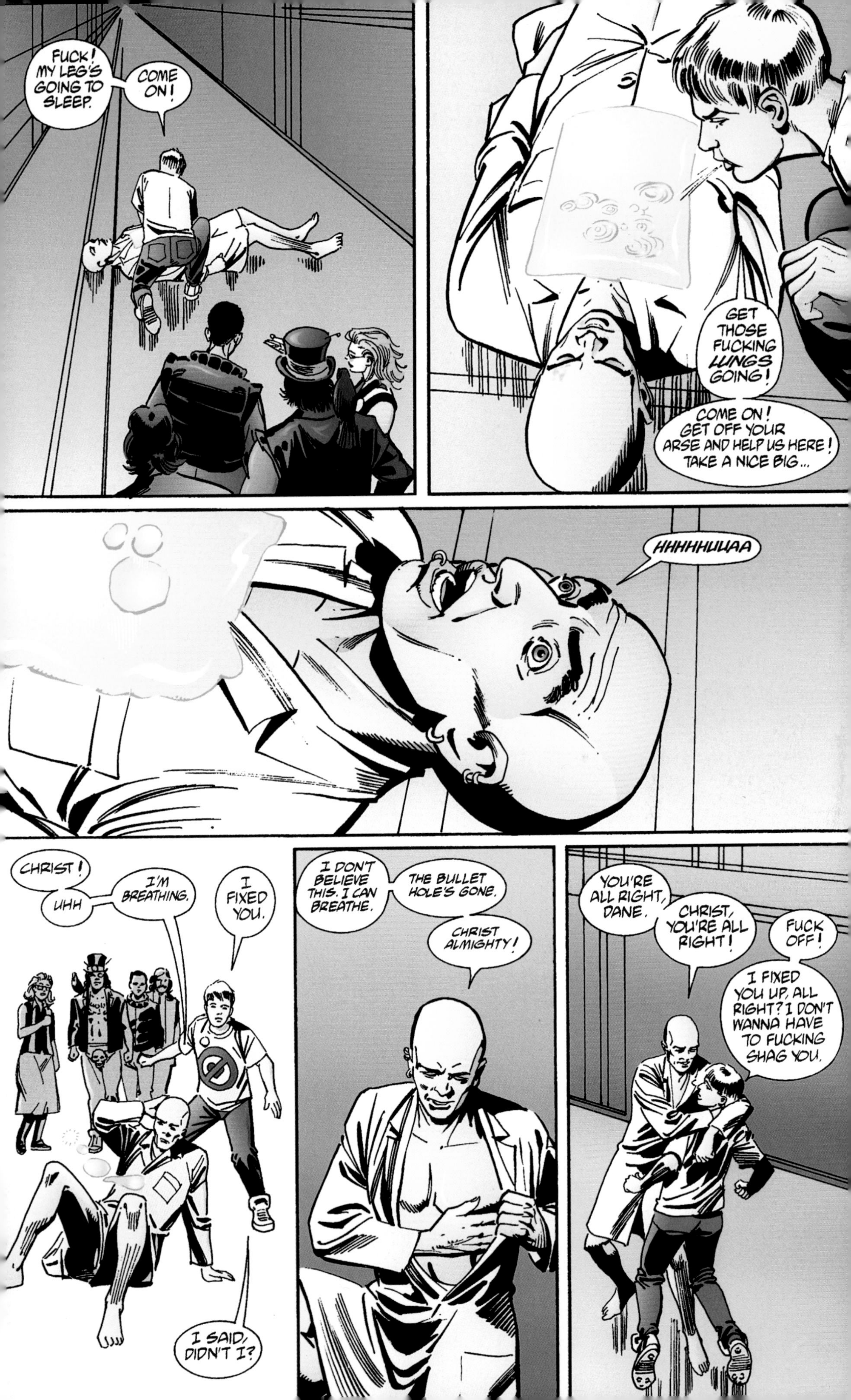
FUCK! MY LEG'S GOING TO SLEEP.
COME ON!
GET THOSE FUCKING LUNGS GOING!
COME ON! GET OFF YOUR ARSE AND HELP US HERE! TAKE A NICE BIG...
HHHHHUUAA
CHRIST!
UHH
I'M BREATHING.
I FIXED YOU.
I SAID, DIDN'T I?
I DON'T BELIEVE THIS. I CAN BREATHE.
THE BULLET HOLE'S GONE.
CHRIST ALMIGHTY!
YOU'RE ALL RIGHT, DANE.
CHRIST, YOU'RE ALL RIGHT!
FUCK OFF!
I FIXED YOU UP, ALL RIGHT? I DON'T WANNA HAVE TO FUCKING SHAG YOU.

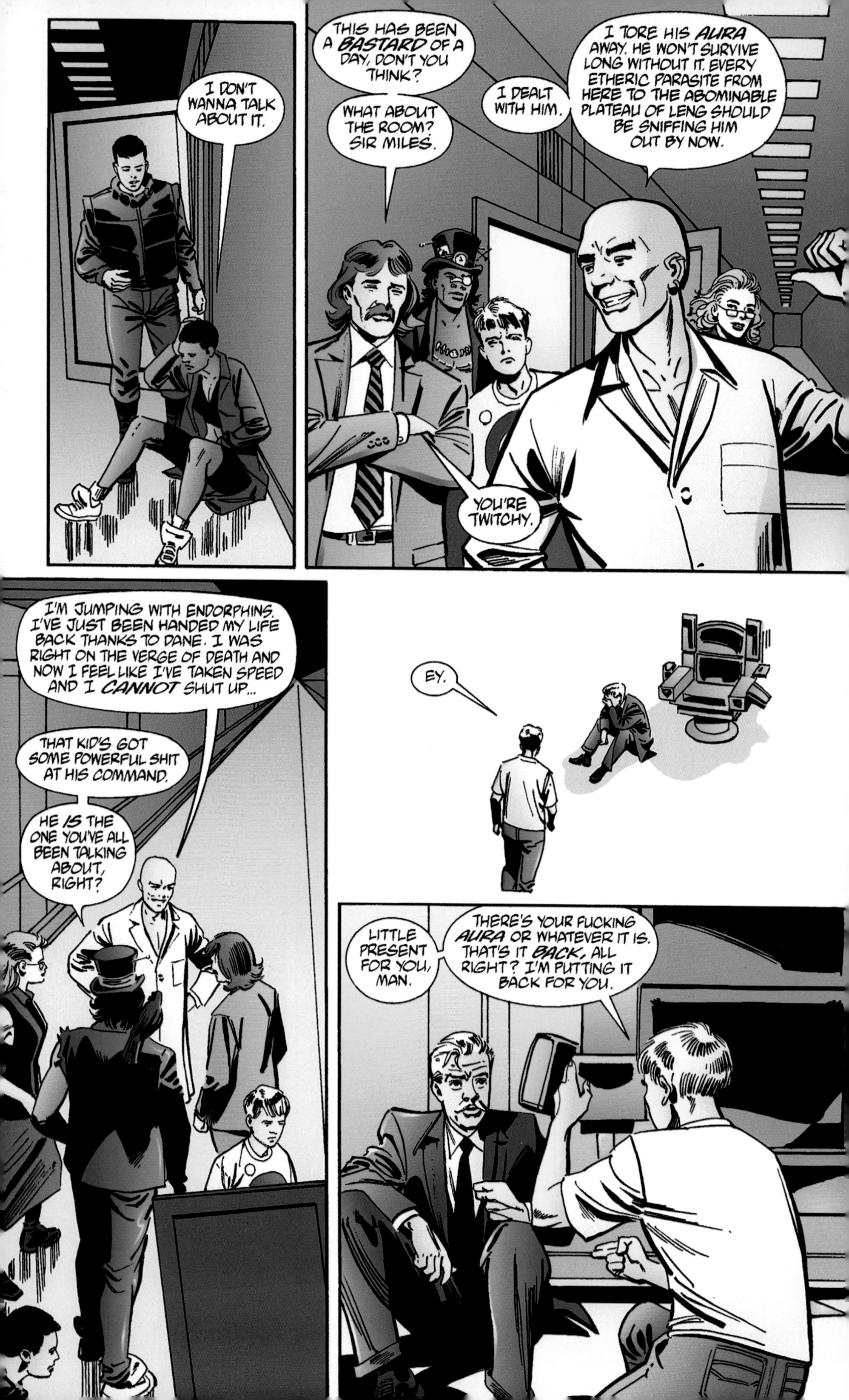
I DON'T WANNA TALK ABOUT IT.
THIS HAS BEEN A BASTARD OF A DAY, DON'T YOU THINK?
WHAT ABOUT THE ROOM? SIR MILES.
I DEALT WITH HIM.
I TORE HIS AURA AWAY. HE WON'T SURVIVE LONG WITHOUT IT. EVERY ETHERIC PARASITE FROM HERE TO THE ABOMINABLE PLATEAU OF LENG SHOULD BE SNIFFING HIM OUT BY NOW.
YOU'RE TWITCHY.
I'M JUMPING WITH ENDORPHINS. I'VE JUST BEEN HANDED MY LIFE BACK THANKS TO DANE. I WAS RIGHT ON THE VERGE OF DEATH AND NOW I FEEL LIKE I'VE TAKEN SPEED AND I CANNOT SHUT UP...
THAT KID'S GOT SOME POWERFUL SHIT AT HIS COMMAND.
HE IS THE ONE YOU'VE ALL BEEN TALKING ABOUT, RIGHT?
EY.
LITTLE PRESENT FOR YOU, MAN.
THERE'S YOUR FUCKING AURA OR WHATEVER IT IS. THAT'S IT BACK, ALL RIGHT? I'M PUTTING IT BACK FOR YOU.

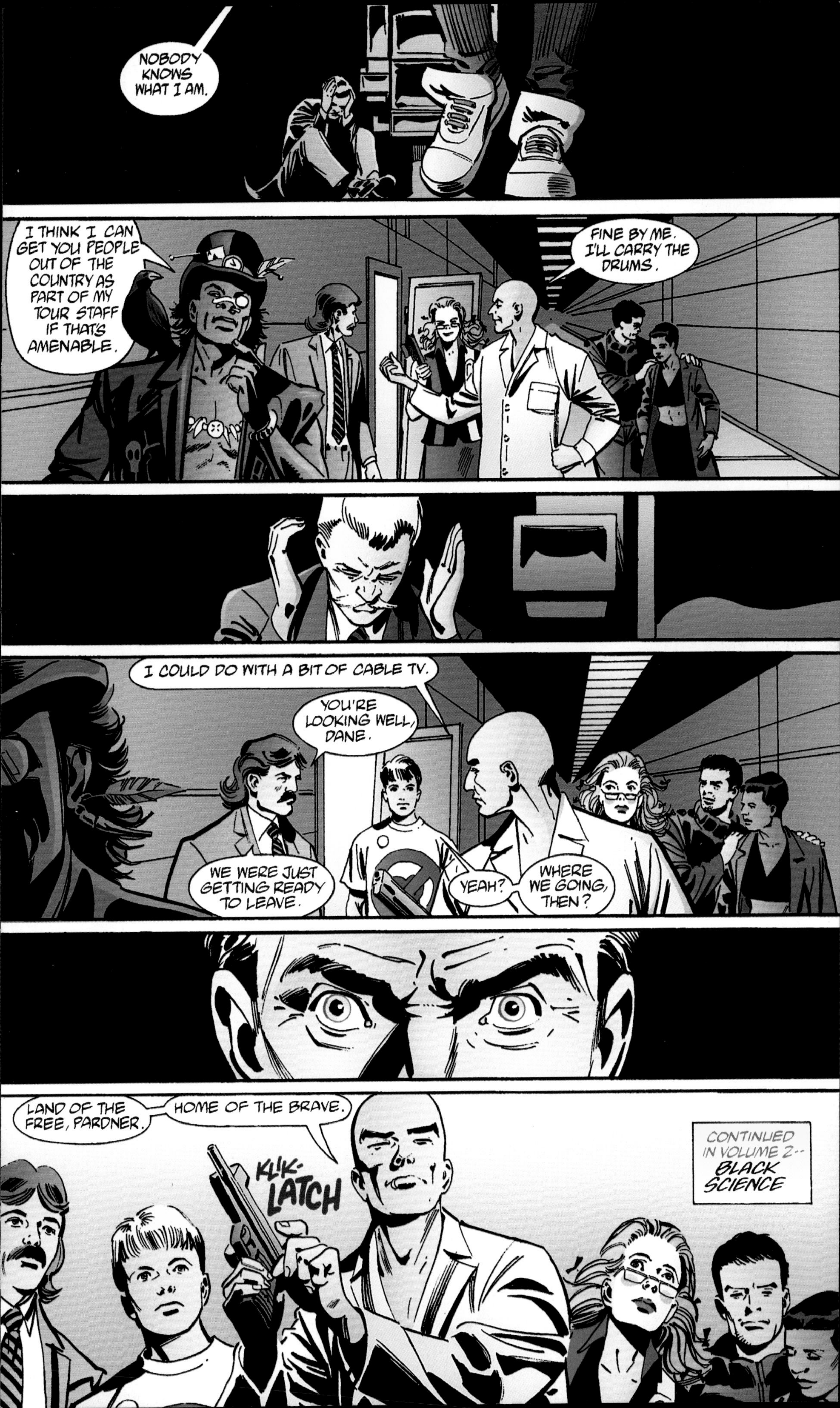

NOBODY KNOWS WHAT I AM.
I THINK I CAN GET YOU PEOPLE OUT OF THE COUNTRY AS PART OF MY TOUR STAFF IF THAT'S AMENABLE.
FINE BY ME. I'LL CARRY THE DRUMS.
I COULD DO WITH A BIT OF CABLE TV.
YOU'RE LOOKING WELL, DANE.
WE WERE JUST GETTING READY TO LEAVE.
YEAH?
WHERE WE GOING, THEN?
LAND OF THE FREE, PARDNER.
HOME OF THE BRAVE.
KLIK-LATCH
CONTINUED IN VOLUME 2-- BLACK SCIENCE

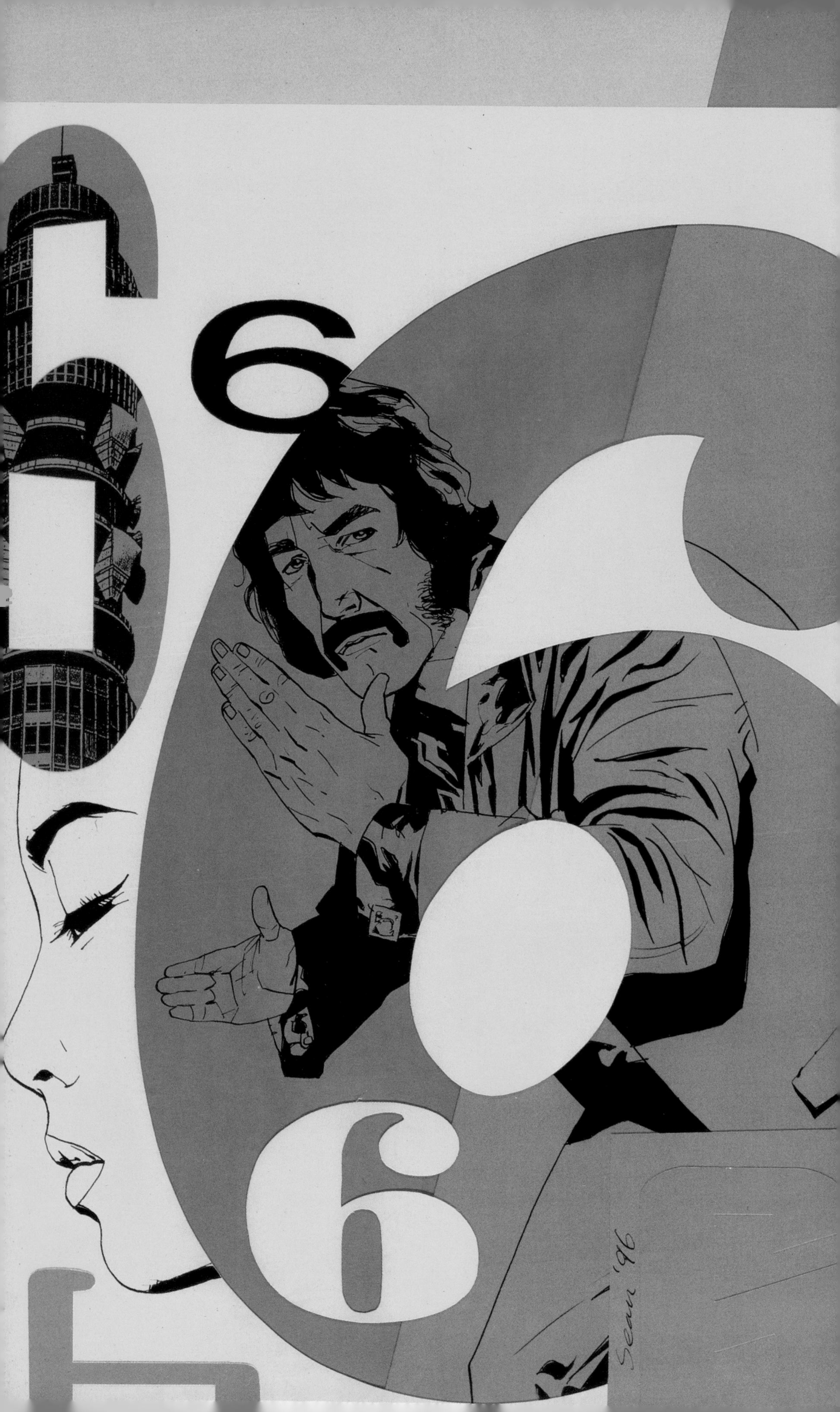
Sean '96

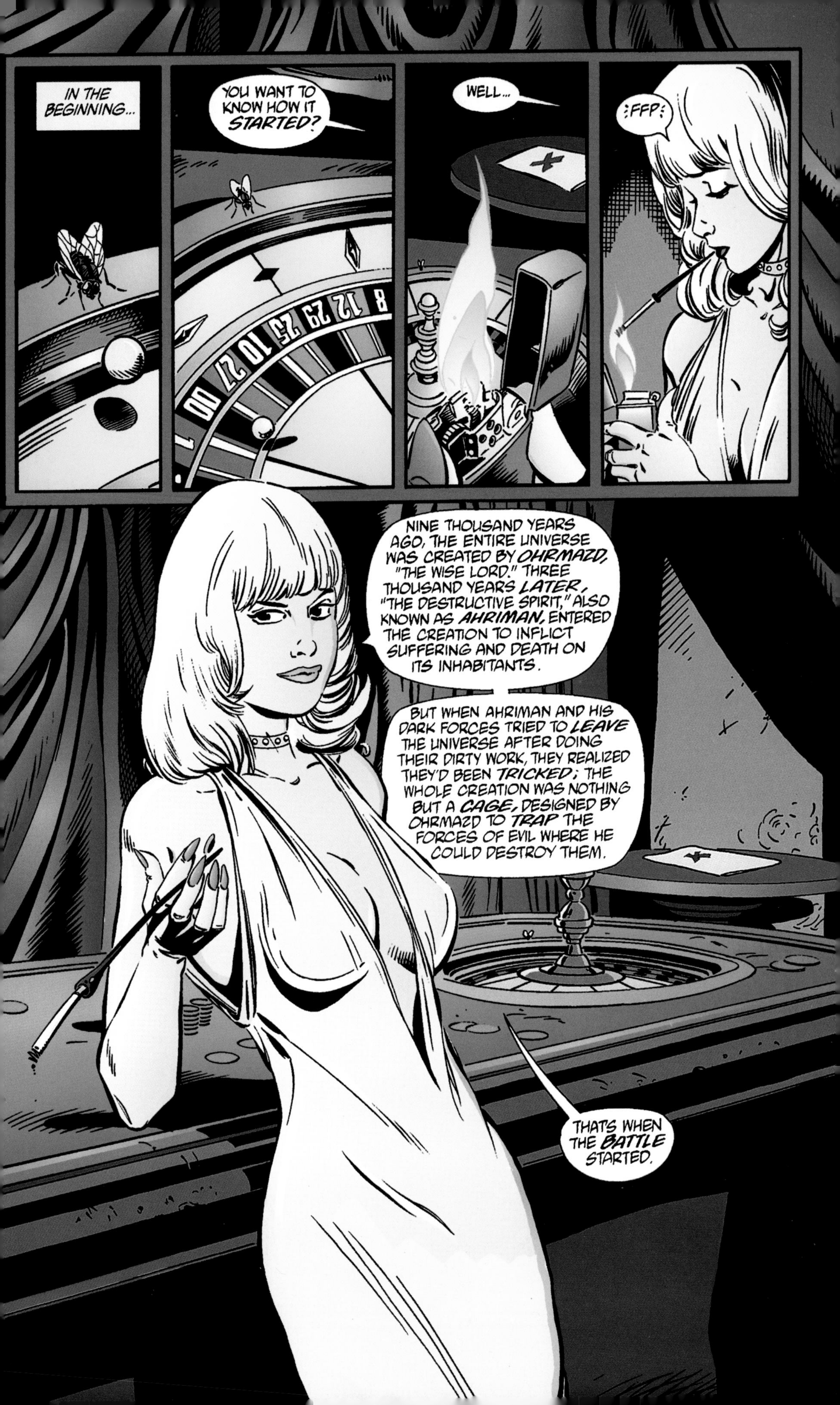

IN THE BEGINNING...
YOU WANT TO KNOW HOW IT STARTED?
WELL...
FFP
NINE THOUSAND YEARS AGO, THE ENTIRE UNIVERSE WAS CREATED BY OHRMAZD, "THE WISE LORD." THREE THOUSAND YEARS LATER, "THE DESTRUCTIVE SPIRIT," ALSO KNOWN AS AHRIMAN, ENTERED THE CREATION TO INFLICT SUFFERING AND DEATH ON ITS INHABITANTS.
BUT WHEN AHRIMAN AND HIS DARK FORCES TRIED TO LEAVE THE UNIVERSE AFTER DOING THEIR DIRTY WORK, THEY REALIZED THEY'D BEEN TRICKED; THE WHOLE CREATION WAS NOTHING BUT A CAGE, DESIGNED BY OHRMAZD TO TRAP THE FORCES OF EVIL WHERE HE COULD DESTROY THEM.
THAT'S WHEN THE BATTLE STARTED.

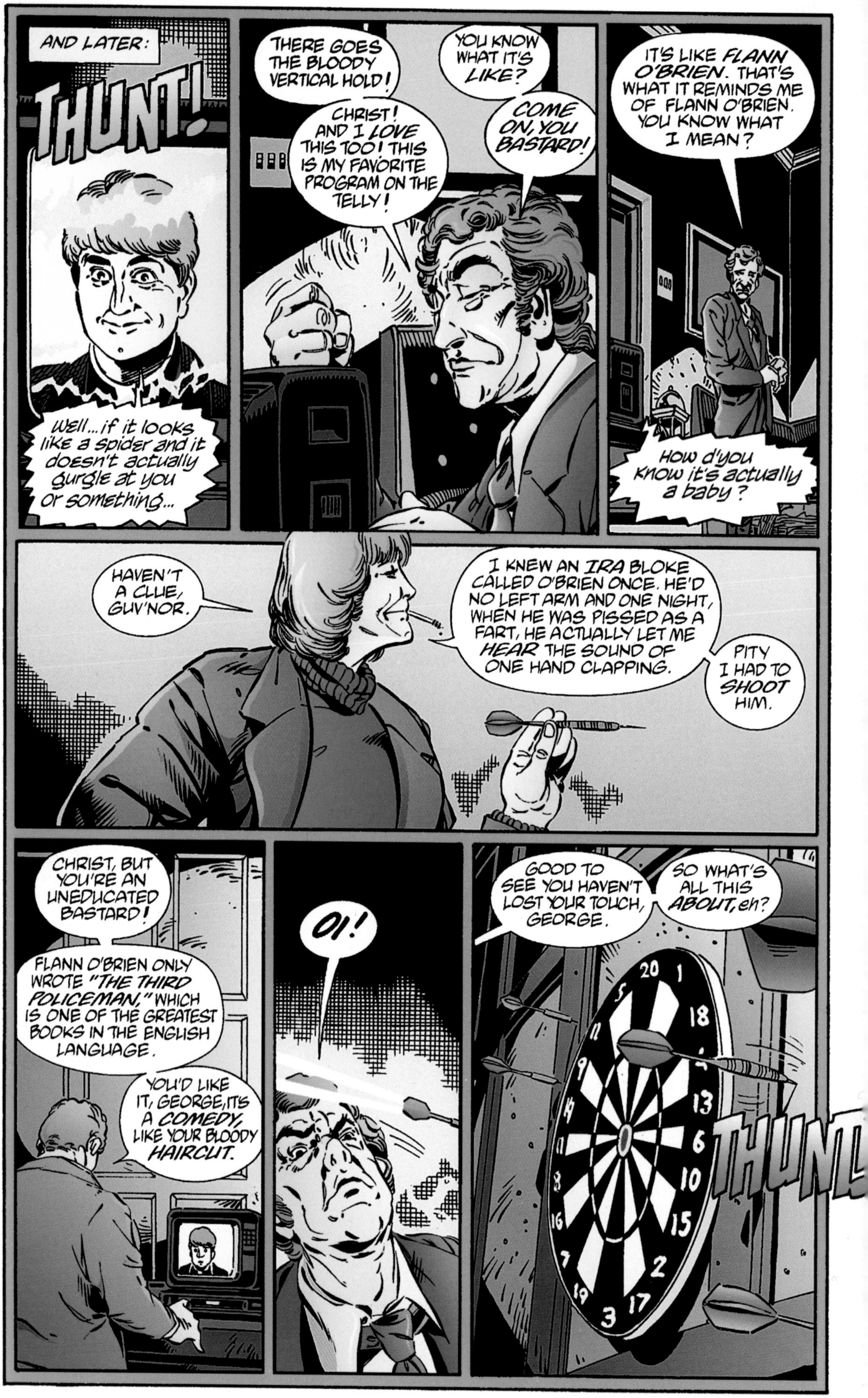
AND LATER:
THUNT!
Well... if it looks like a spider and it doesn't actually gurgle at you or something...
THERE GOES THE BLOODY VERTICAL HOLD!
CHRIST! AND I LOVE THIS TOO! THIS IS MY FAVORITE PROGRAM ON THE TELLY!
YOU KNOW WHAT IT'S LIKE?
COME ON, YOU BASTARD!
IT'S LIKE FLANN O'BRIEN. THAT'S WHAT IT REMINDS ME OF FLANN O'BRIEN. YOU KNOW WHAT I MEAN?
How d'you know it's actually a baby?
HAVEN'T A CLUE, GUV'NOR.
I KNEW AN IRA BLOKE CALLED O'BRIEN ONCE. HE'D NO LEFT ARM AND ONE NIGHT, WHEN HE WAS PISSED AS A FART, HE ACTUALLY LET ME HEAR THE SOUND OF ONE HAND CLAPPING.
PITY I HAD TO SHOOT HIM.
CHRIST, BUT YOU'RE AN UNEDUCATED BASTARD!
FLANN O'BRIEN ONLY WROTE "THE THIRD POLICEMAN," WHICH IS ONE OF THE GREATEST BOOKS IN THE ENGLISH LANGUAGE.
YOU'D LIKE IT, GEORGE, IT'S A COMEDY, LIKE YOUR BLOODY HAIRCUT.
OI!
GOOD TO SEE YOU HAVEN'T LOST YOUR TOUCH, GEORGE.
SO WHAT'S ALL THIS ABOUT, eh?

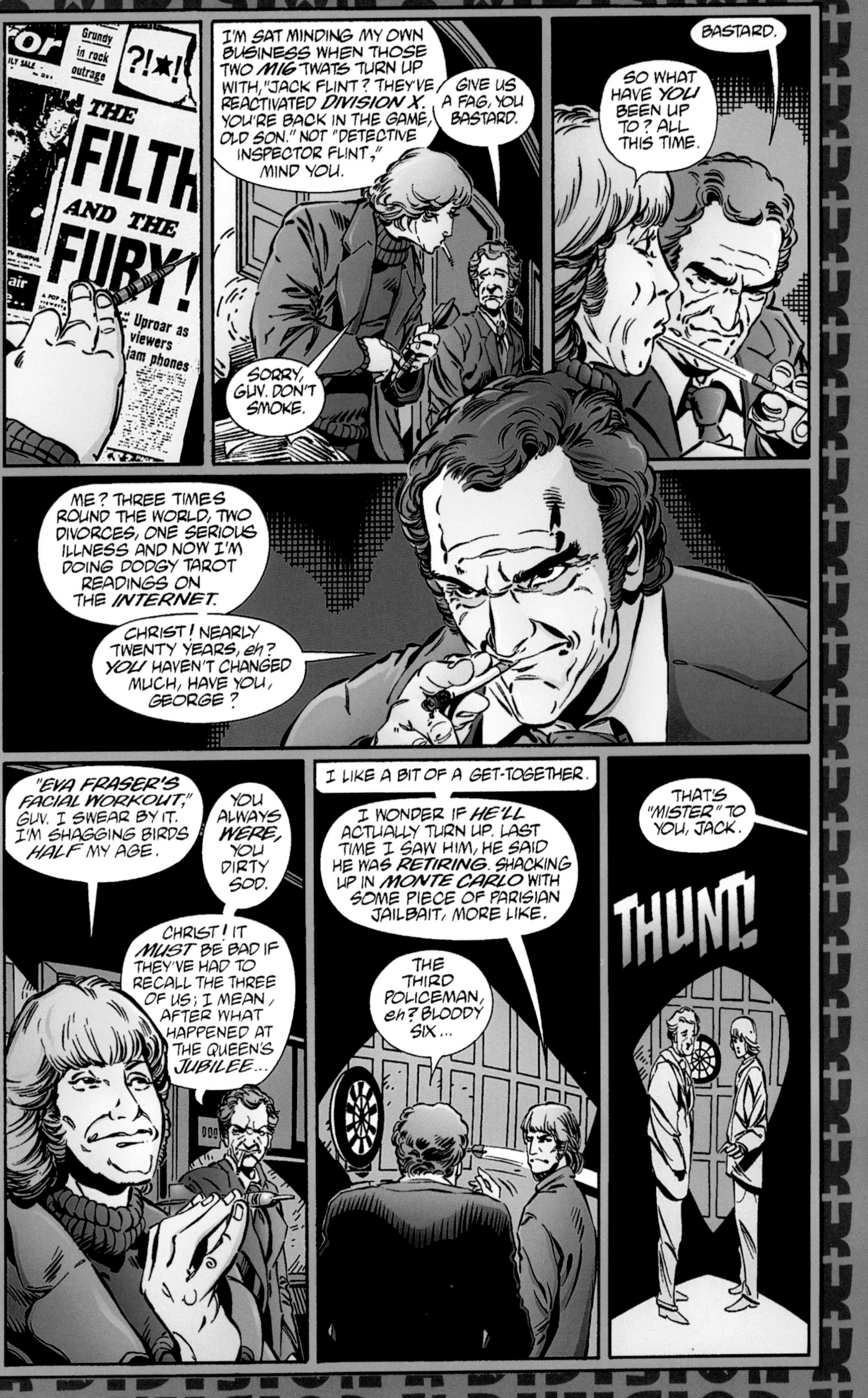
Grundy in rock outrage
?!★!
THE FILTH AND THE FURY!
Uproar as viewers jam phones
I'M SAT MINDING MY OWN BUSINESS WHEN THOSE TWO MI6 TWATS TURN UP WITH, "JACK FLINT? THEY'VE REACTIVATED DIVISION X. YOU'RE BACK IN THE GAME, OLD SON." NOT "DETECTIVE INSPECTOR FLINT," MIND YOU.
GIVE US A FAG, YOU BASTARD.
SORRY, GUV. DON'T SMOKE.
BASTARD.
SO WHAT HAVE YOU BEEN UP TO? ALL THIS TIME.
ME? THREE TIMES ROUND THE WORLD, TWO DIVORCES, ONE SERIOUS ILLNESS AND NOW I'M DOING DODGY TAROT READINGS ON THE INTERNET.
CHRIST! NEARLY TWENTY YEARS, eh? YOU HAVEN'T CHANGED MUCH, HAVE YOU, GEORGE?
"EVA FRASER'S FACIAL WORKOUT," GUV. I SWEAR BY IT. I'M SHAGGING BIRDS HALF MY AGE.
YOU ALWAYS WERE, YOU DIRTY SOD.
CHRIST! IT MUST BE BAD IF THEY'VE HAD TO RECALL THE THREE OF US; I MEAN, AFTER WHAT HAPPENED AT THE QUEEN'S JUBILEE...
I LIKE A BIT OF A GET-TOGETHER.
I WONDER IF HE'LL ACTUALLY TURN UP. LAST TIME I SAW HIM, HE SAID HE WAS RETIRING. SHACKING UP IN MONTE CARLO WITH SOME PIECE OF PARISIAN JAILBAIT, MORE LIKE.
THE THIRD POLICEMAN, eh? BLOODY SIX...
THAT'S "MISTER" TO YOU, JACK.
THUNT!
DIVISION X

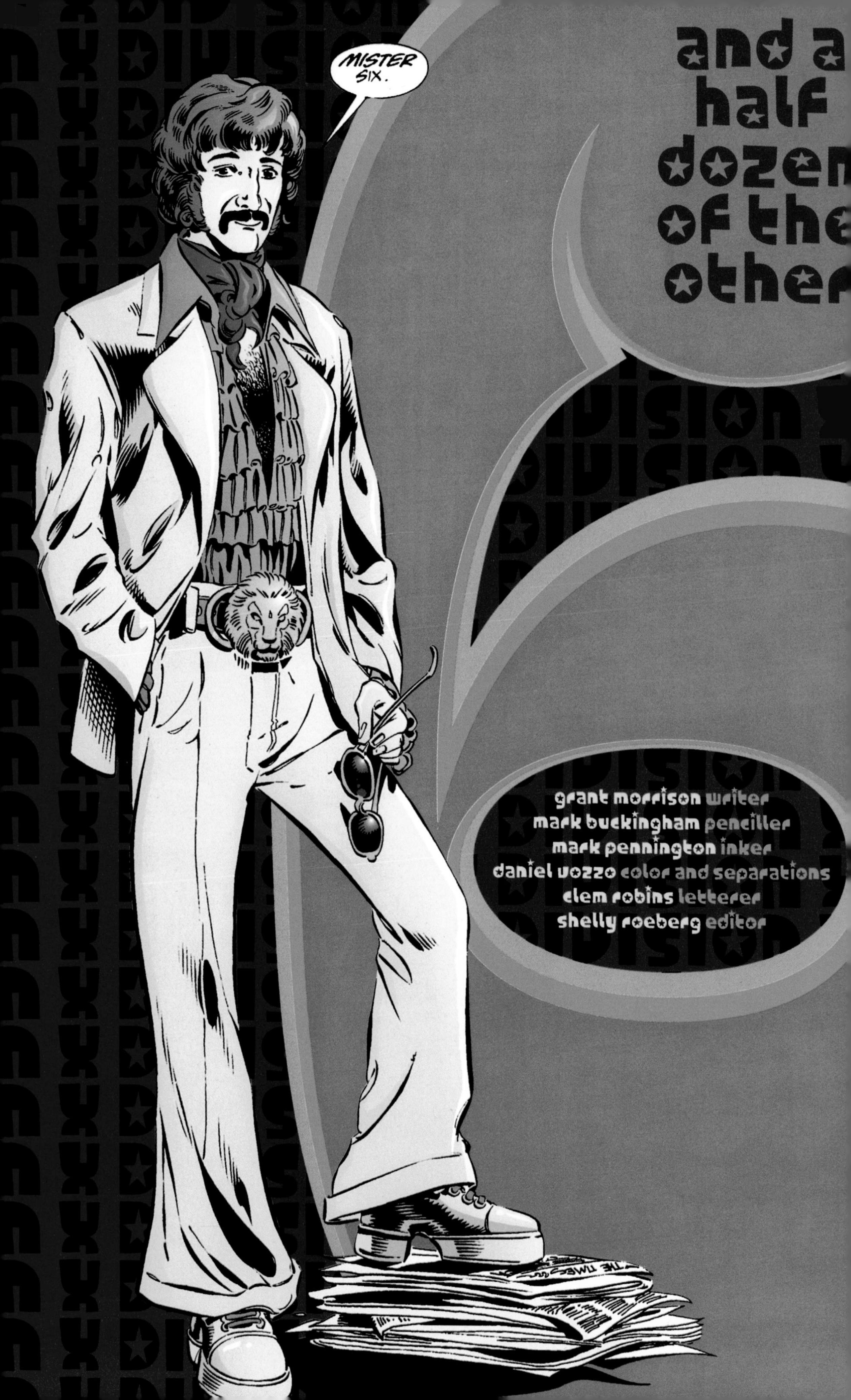
MISTER SIX.
and a half dozen of the other
grant morrison writer
mark buckingham penciller
mark pennington inker
daniel vozzo color and separations
clem robins letterer
shelly roeberg editor

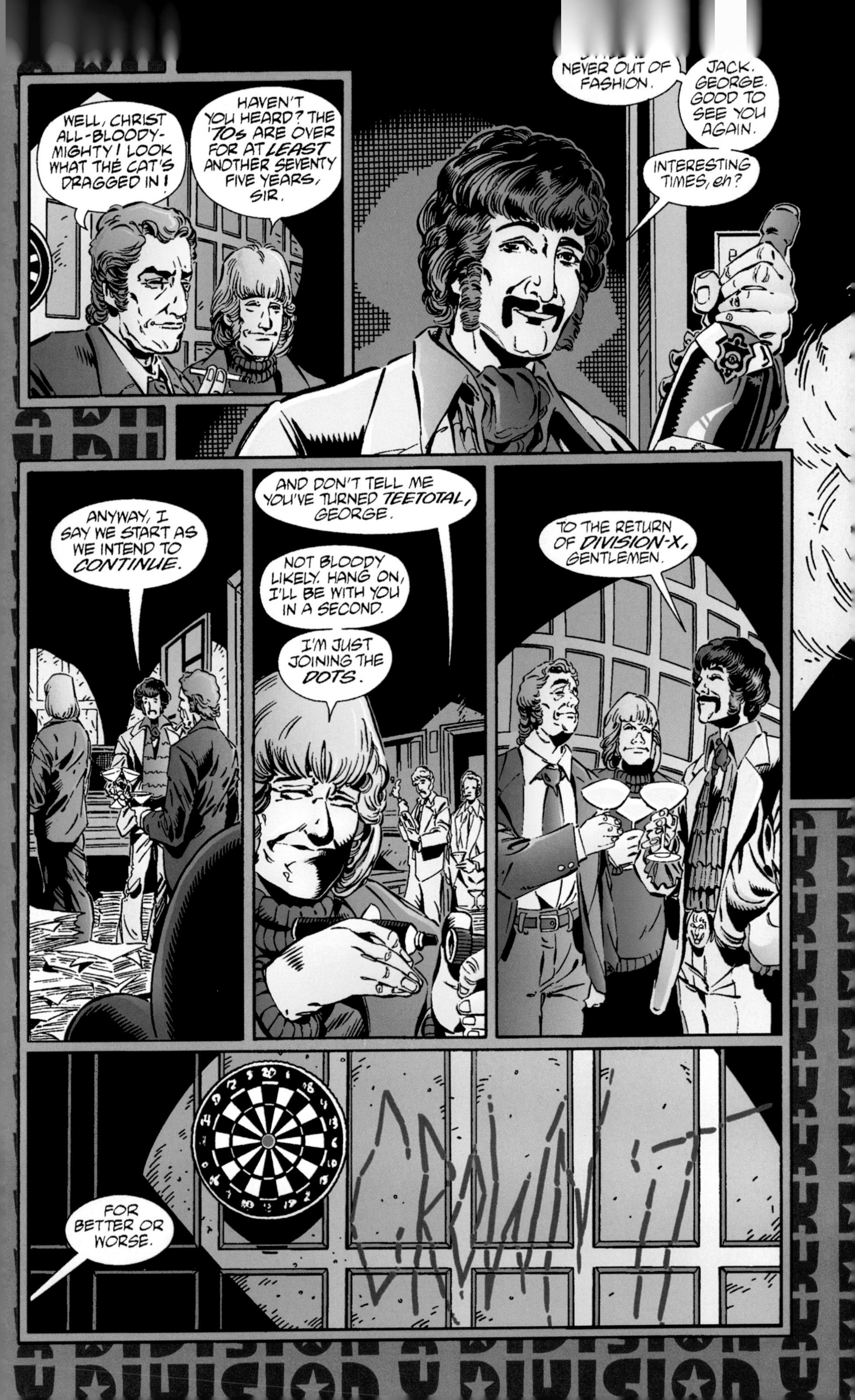

WELL, CHRIST ALL-BLOODY-MIGHTY! LOOK WHAT THE CAT'S DRAGGED IN!
HAVEN'T YOU HEARD? THE '70s ARE OVER FOR AT LEAST ANOTHER SEVENTY FIVE YEARS, SIR.
NEVER OUT OF FASHION.
JACK. GEORGE. GOOD TO SEE YOU AGAIN.
INTERESTING TIMES, eh?
ANYWAY, I SAY WE START AS WE INTEND TO CONTINUE.
AND DON'T TELL ME YOU'VE TURNED TEETOTAL, GEORGE.
NOT BLOODY LIKELY. HANG ON, I'LL BE WITH YOU IN A SECOND.
I'M JUST JOINING THE DOTS.
TO THE RETURN OF DIVISION-X, GENTLEMEN.
FOR BETTER OR WORSE.

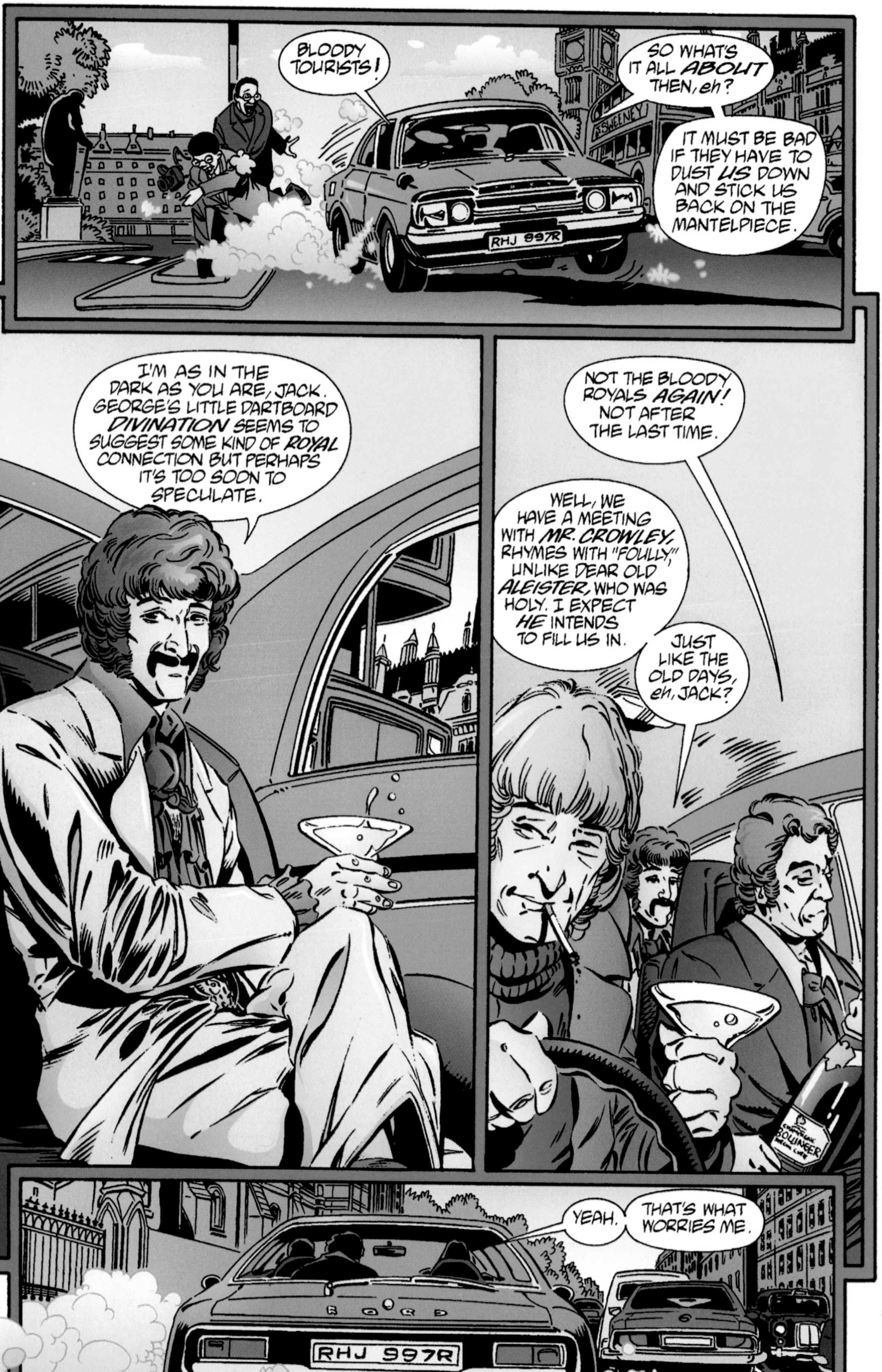
BLOODY TOURISTS!
SO WHAT'S IT ALL ABOUT THEN, eh?
IT MUST BE BAD IF THEY HAVE TO DUST US DOWN AND STICK US BACK ON THE MANTELPIECE.
RHJ 997R
I'M AS IN THE DARK AS YOU ARE, JACK. GEORGE'S LITTLE DARTBOARD DIVINATION SEEMS TO SUGGEST SOME KIND OF ROYAL CONNECTION BUT PERHAPS IT'S TOO SOON TO SPECULATE.
NOT THE BLOODY ROYALS AGAIN! NOT AFTER THE LAST TIME.
WELL, WE HAVE A MEETING WITH MR. CROWLEY, RHYMES WITH "FOULLY," UNLIKE DEAR OLD ALEISTER, WHO WAS HOLY. I EXPECT HE INTENDS TO FILL US IN.
JUST LIKE THE OLD DAYS, eh, JACK?
BOLLINGER
YEAH.
THAT'S WHAT WORRIES ME.
FORD
RHJ 997R

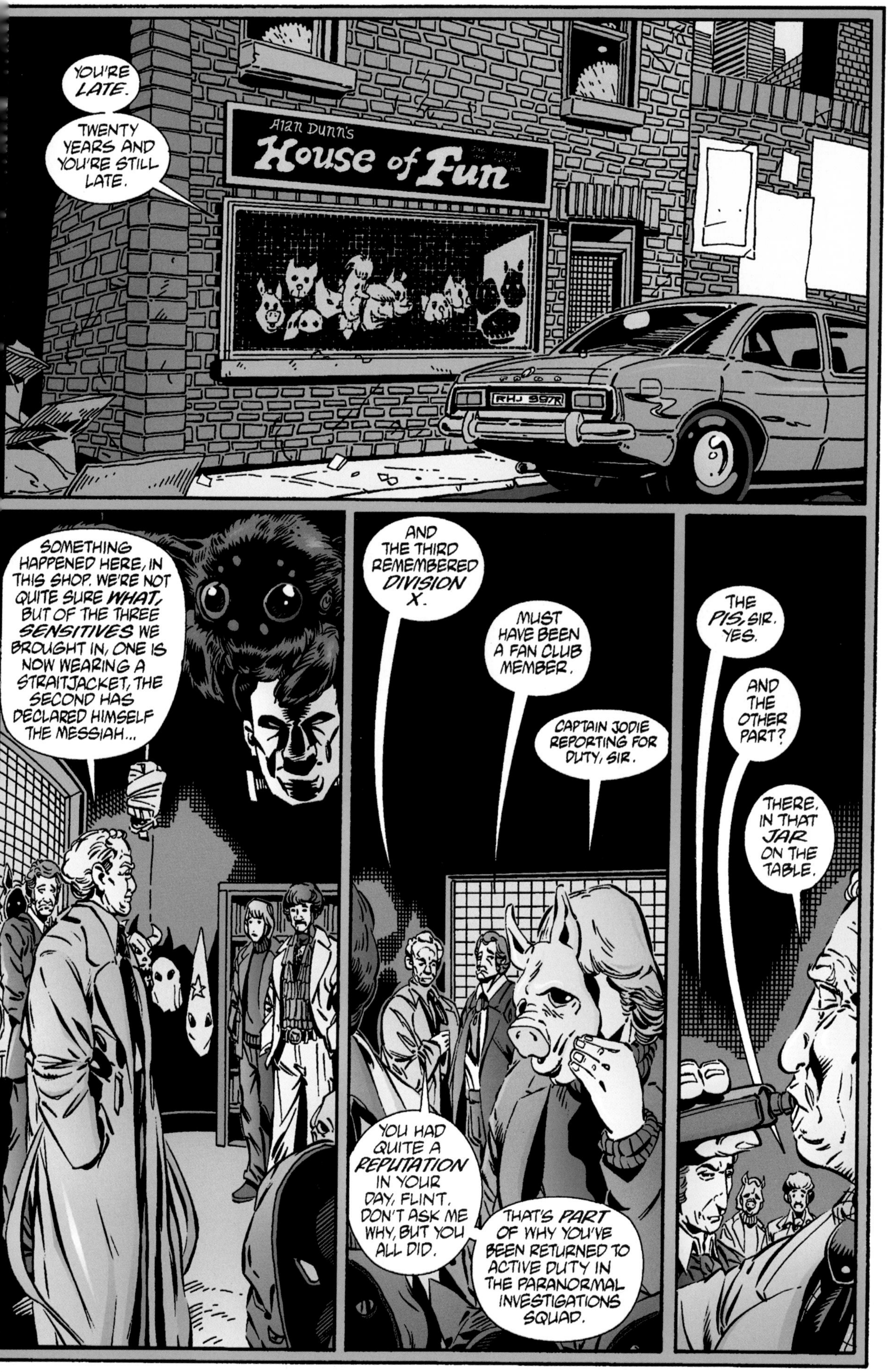
YOU'RE LATE.
TWENTY YEARS AND YOU'RE STILL LATE.
Alan Dunn's House of Fun
RHJ 997R
SOMETHING HAPPENED HERE, IN THIS SHOP. WE'RE NOT QUITE SURE WHAT, BUT OF THE THREE SENSITIVES WE BROUGHT IN, ONE IS NOW WEARING A STRAITJACKET, THE SECOND HAS DECLARED HIMSELF THE MESSIAH...
AND THE THIRD REMEMBERED DIVISION X.
MUST HAVE BEEN A FAN CLUB MEMBER.
CAPTAIN JODIE REPORTING FOR DUTY, SIR.
YOU HAD QUITE A REPUTATION IN YOUR DAY, FLINT. DON'T ASK ME WHY, BUT YOU ALL DID.
THAT'S PART OF WHY YOU'VE BEEN RETURNED TO ACTIVE DUTY IN THE PARANORMAL INVESTIGATIONS SQUAD.
THE PIS, SIR. YES.
AND THE OTHER PART?
THERE. IN THAT JAR ON THE TABLE.

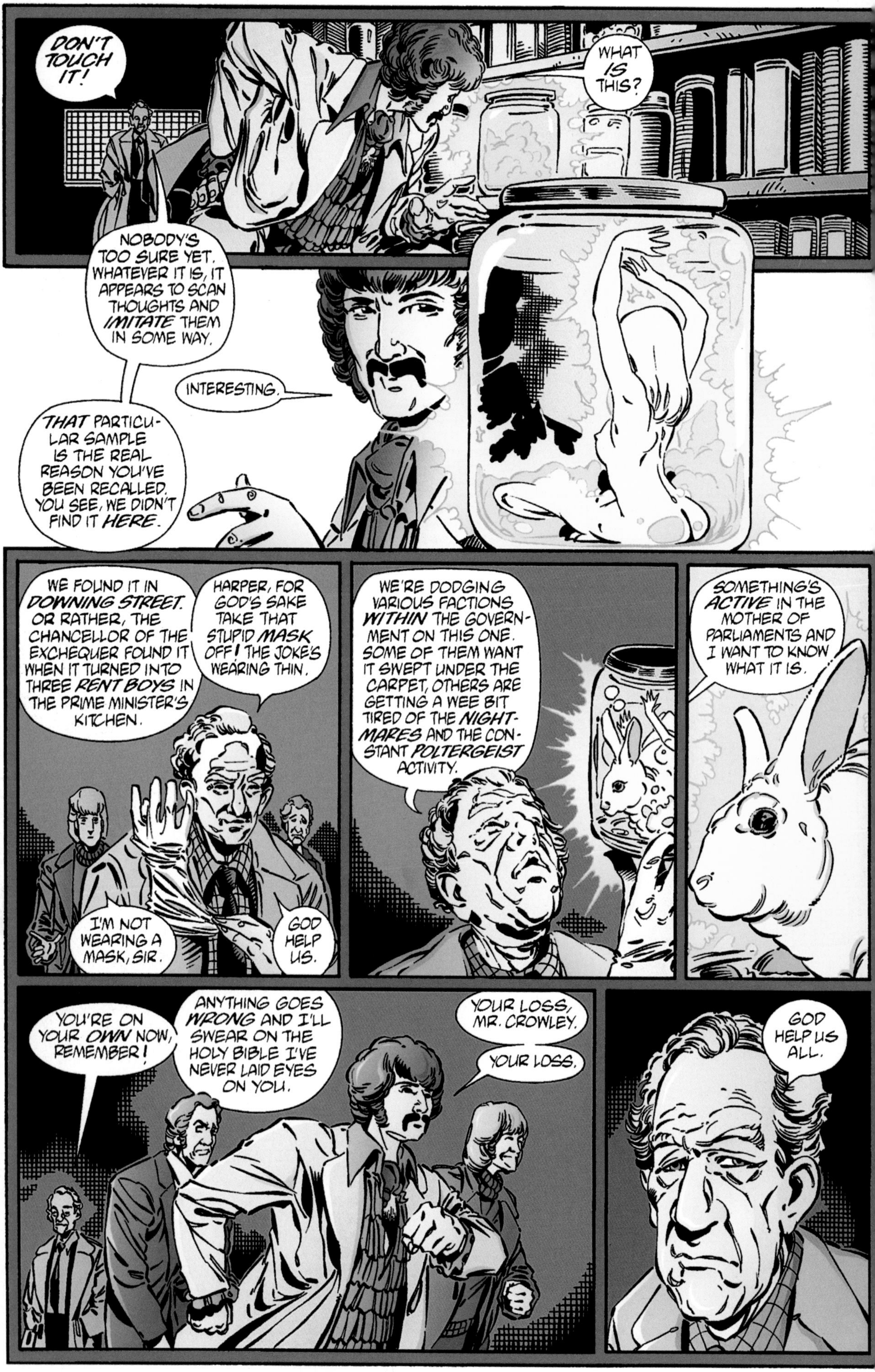

DON'T TOUCH IT!
WHAT IS THIS?
NOBODY'S TOO SURE YET. WHATEVER IT IS, IT APPEARS TO SCAN THOUGHTS AND IMITATE THEM IN SOME WAY.
INTERESTING.
THAT PARTICULAR SAMPLE IS THE REAL REASON YOU'VE BEEN RECALLED. YOU SEE, WE DIDN'T FIND IT HERE.
WE FOUND IT IN DOWNING STREET. OR RATHER, THE CHANCELLOR OF THE EXCHEQUER FOUND IT WHEN IT TURNED INTO THREE RENT BOYS IN THE PRIME MINISTER'S KITCHEN.
HARPER, FOR GOD'S SAKE TAKE THAT STUPID MASK OFF! THE JOKE'S WEARING THIN.
I'M NOT WEARING A MASK, SIR.
GOD HELP US.
WE'RE DODGING VARIOUS FACTIONS WITHIN THE GOVERNMENT ON THIS ONE. SOME OF THEM WANT IT SWEPT UNDER THE CARPET, OTHERS ARE GETTING A WEE BIT TIRED OF THE NIGHTMARES AND THE CONSTANT POLTERGEIST ACTIVITY.
SOMETHING'S ACTIVE IN THE MOTHER OF PARLIAMENTS AND I WANT TO KNOW WHAT IT IS.
YOU'RE ON YOUR OWN NOW, REMEMBER!
ANYTHING GOES WRONG AND I'LL SWEAR ON THE HOLY BIBLE I'VE NEVER LAID EYES ON YOU.
YOUR LOSS, MR. CROWLEY.
YOUR LOSS.
GOD HELP US ALL.

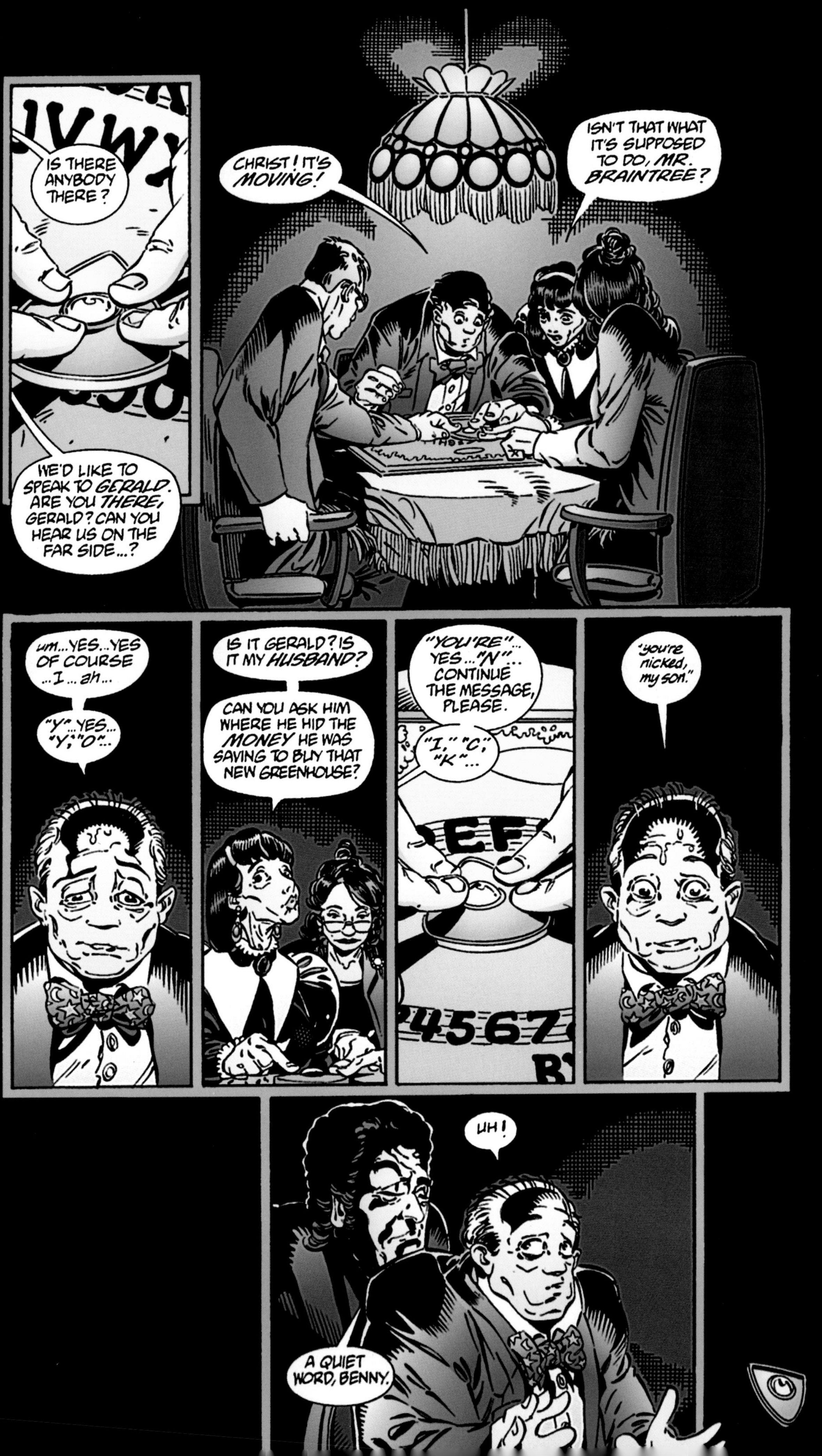
IS THERE ANYBODY THERE?
WE'D LIKE TO SPEAK TO GERALD. ARE YOU THERE, GERALD? CAN YOU HEAR US ON THE FAR SIDE...?
CHRIST! IT'S MOVING!
ISN'T THAT WHAT IT'S SUPPOSED TO DO, MR. BRAINTREE?
UM...YES...YES OF COURSE ...I ... AH...
"Y"...YES... "Y," "O"...
IS IT GERALD? IS IT MY HUSBAND?
CAN YOU ASK HIM WHERE HE HID THE MONEY HE WAS SAVING TO BUY THAT NEW GREENHOUSE?
"YOU'RE"... YES ..."N"... CONTINUE THE MESSAGE, PLEASE.
"I," "C," "K"...
"you're nicked, my son."
UH!
A QUIET WORD, BENNY.

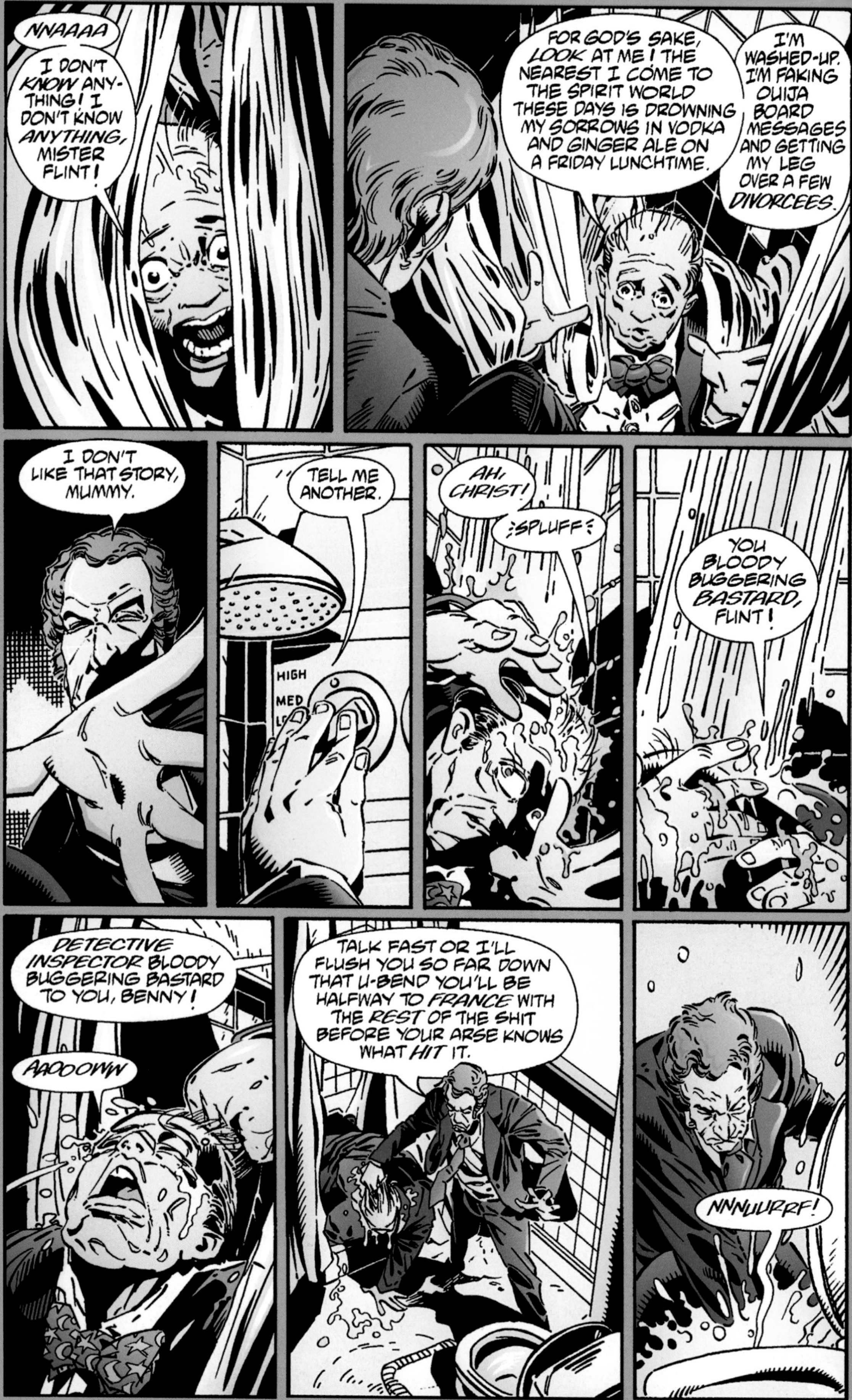
NNAAAA
I DON'T KNOW ANYTHING! I DON'T KNOW ANYTHING, MISTER FLINT!
FOR GOD'S SAKE, LOOK AT ME! THE NEAREST I COME TO THE SPIRIT WORLD THESE DAYS IS DROWNING MY SORROWS IN VODKA AND GINGER ALE ON A FRIDAY LUNCHTIME.
I'M WASHED-UP. I'M FAKING OUIJA BOARD MESSAGES AND GETTING MY LEG OVER A FEW DIVORCEES.
I DON'T LIKE THAT STORY, MUMMY.
TELL ME ANOTHER.
HIGH
MED
AH, CHRIST!
SPLUFF
YOU BLOODY BUGGERING BASTARD, FLINT!
DETECTIVE INSPECTOR BLOODY BUGGERING BASTARD TO YOU, BENNY!
AAOOOWW
TALK FAST OR I'LL FLUSH YOU SO FAR DOWN THAT U-BEND YOU'LL BE HALFWAY TO FRANCE WITH THE REST OF THE SHIT BEFORE YOUR ARSE KNOWS WHAT HIT IT.
NNNUURRF!

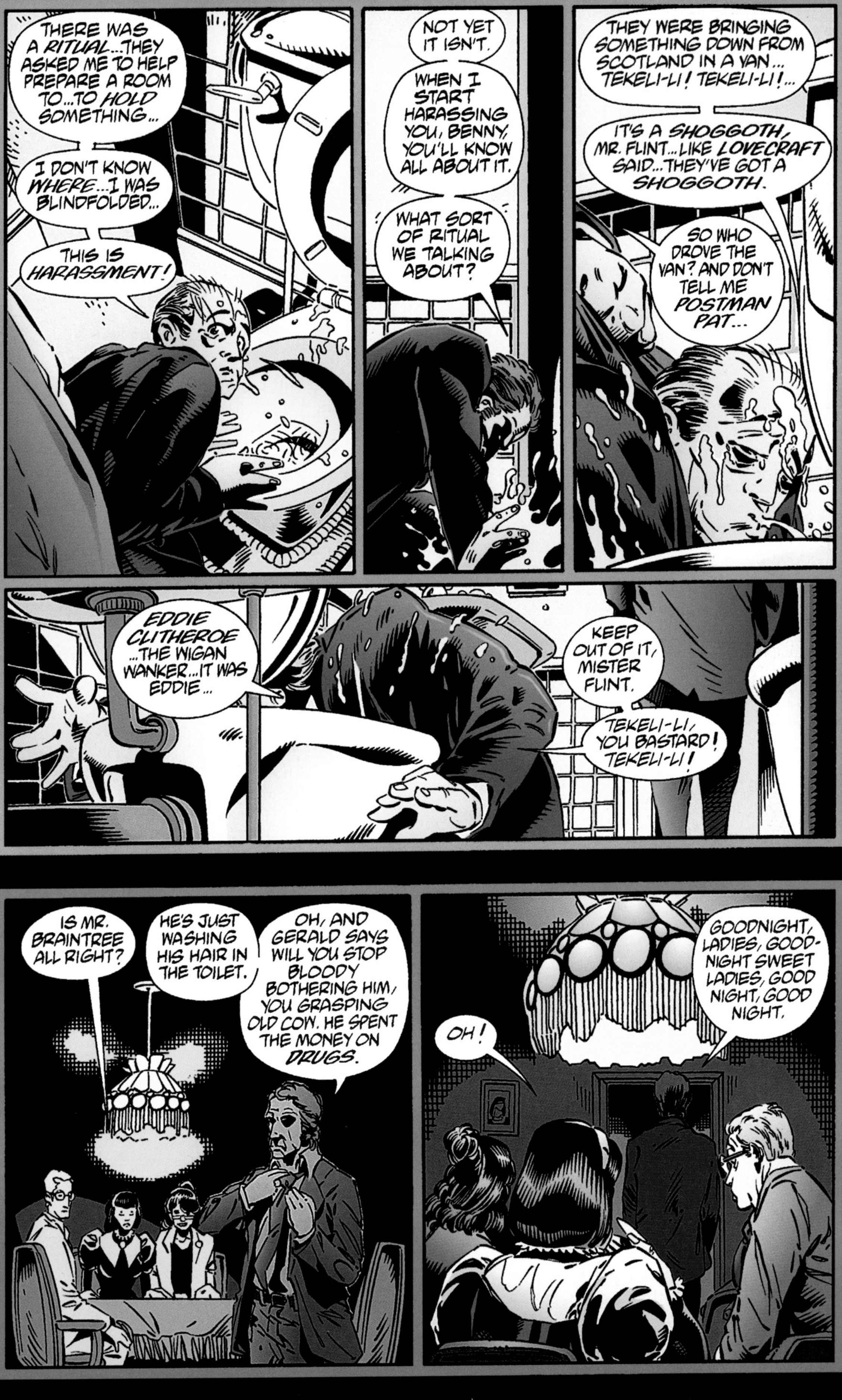
THERE WAS A RITUAL...THEY ASKED ME TO HELP PREPARE A ROOM TO...TO HOLD SOMETHING...
I DON'T KNOW WHERE...I WAS BLINDFOLDED...
THIS IS HARASSMENT!
NOT YET IT ISN'T.
WHEN I START HARASSING YOU, BENNY, YOU'LL KNOW ALL ABOUT IT.
WHAT SORT OF RITUAL WE TALKING ABOUT?
THEY WERE BRINGING SOMETHING DOWN FROM SCOTLAND IN A VAN... TEKELI-LI! TEKELI-LI!...
IT'S A SHOGGOTH, MR. FLINT...LIKE LOVECRAFT SAID...THEY'VE GOT A SHOGGOTH.
SO WHO DROVE THE VAN? AND DON'T TELL ME POSTMAN PAT...
EDDIE CLITHEROE ...THE WIGAN WANKER...IT WAS EDDIE...
KEEP OUT OF IT, MISTER FLINT.
TEKELI-LI, YOU BASTARD! TEKELI-LI!
IS MR. BRAINTREE ALL RIGHT?
HE'S JUST WASHING HIS HAIR IN THE TOILET.
OH, AND GERALD SAYS WILL YOU STOP BLOODY BOTHERING HIM, YOU GRASPING OLD COW. HE SPENT THE MONEY ON DRUGS.
OH!
GOODNIGHT, LADIES, GOOD-NIGHT SWEET LADIES, GOOD NIGHT, GOOD NIGHT.

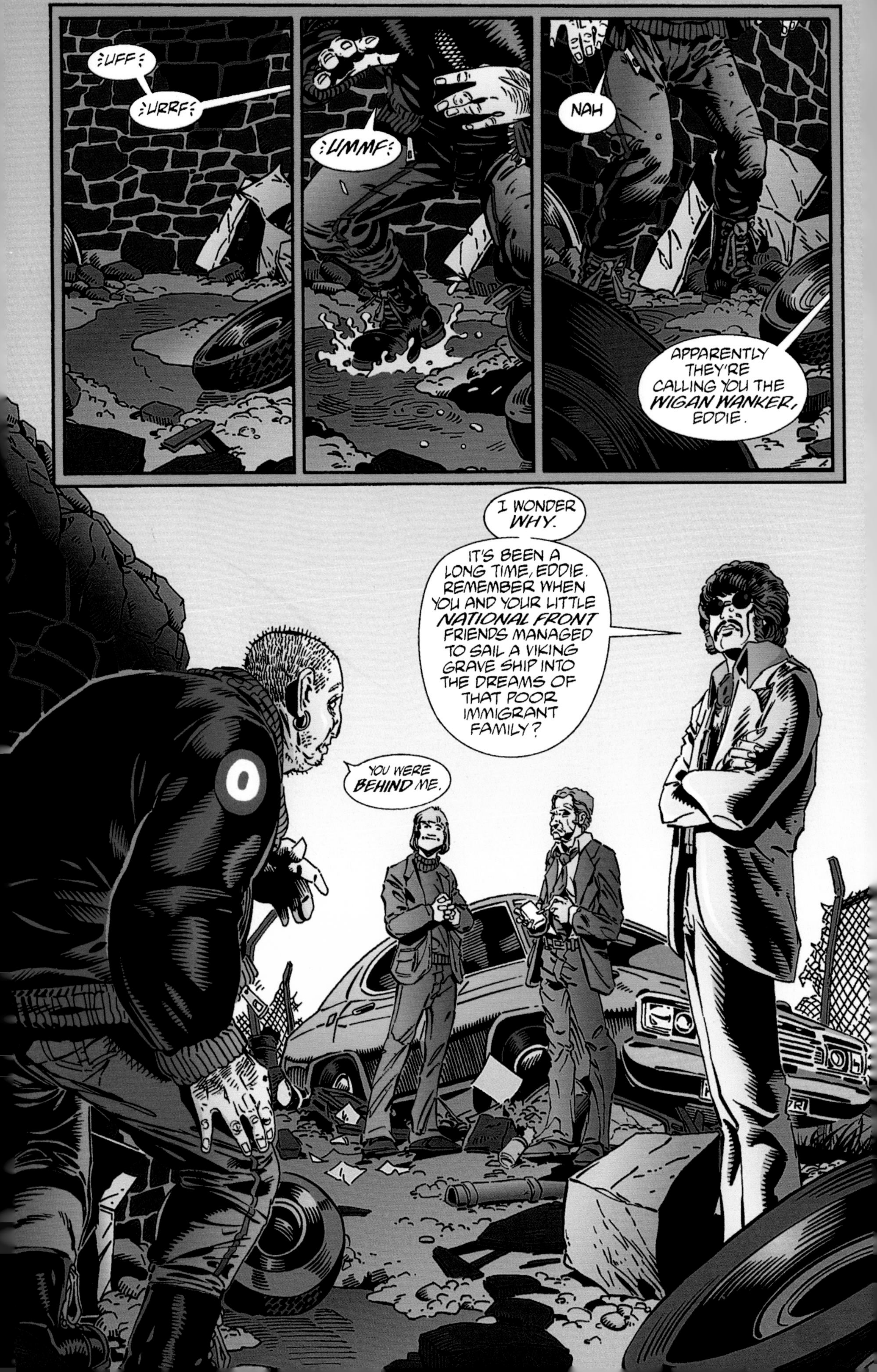
UFF
URRF
UMMF
NAH
APPARENTLY THEY'RE CALLING YOU THE WIGAN WANKER, EDDIE.
I WONDER WHY.
IT'S BEEN A LONG TIME, EDDIE. REMEMBER WHEN YOU AND YOUR LITTLE NATIONAL FRONT FRIENDS MANAGED TO SAIL A VIKING GRAVE SHIP INTO THE DREAMS OF THAT POOR IMMIGRANT FAMILY?
YOU WERE BEHIND ME.

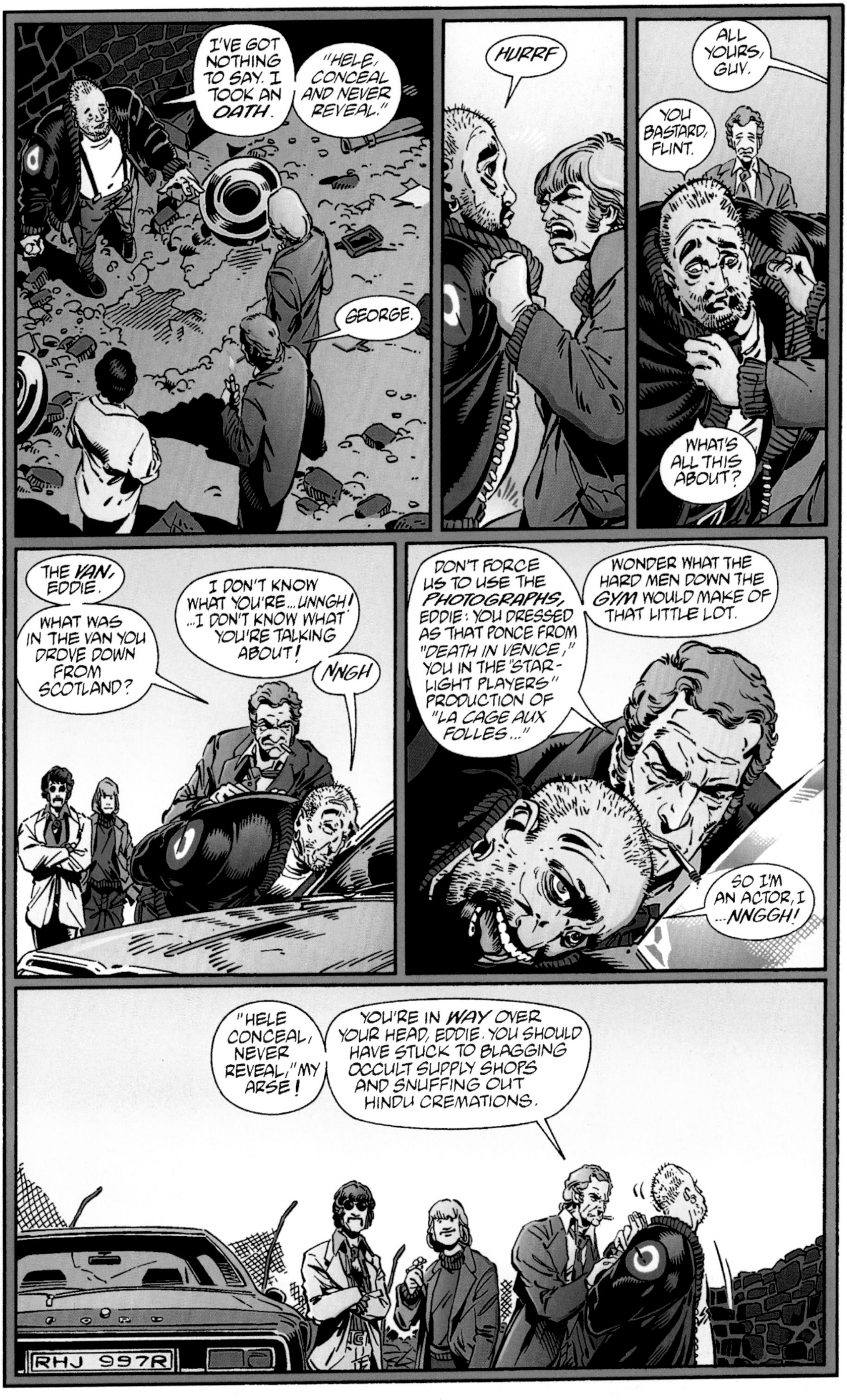
I'VE GOT NOTHING TO SAY. I TOOK AN OATH.
"HELE, CONCEAL AND NEVER REVEAL."
GEORGE.
HURRF
ALL YOURS, GUV.
YOU BASTARD, FLINT.
WHAT'S ALL THIS ABOUT?
THE VAN, EDDIE.
WHAT WAS IN THE VAN YOU DROVE DOWN FROM SCOTLAND?
I DON'T KNOW WHAT YOU'RE... UNNGH! ...I DON'T KNOW WHAT YOU'RE TALKING ABOUT!
NNGH
DON'T FORCE US TO USE THE PHOTOGRAPHS, EDDIE: YOU DRESSED AS THAT PONCE FROM "DEATH IN VENICE," YOU IN THE "STARLIGHT PLAYERS" PRODUCTION OF "LA CAGE AUX FOLLES..."
WONDER WHAT THE HARD MEN DOWN THE GYM WOULD MAKE OF THAT LITTLE LOT.
SO I'M AN ACTOR, I ...NNGGH!
"HELE CONCEAL, NEVER REVEAL," MY ARSE!
YOU'RE IN WAY OVER YOUR HEAD, EDDIE. YOU SHOULD HAVE STUCK TO BLAGGING OCCULT SUPPLY SHOPS AND SNUFFING OUT HINDU CREMATIONS.
RHJ 997R

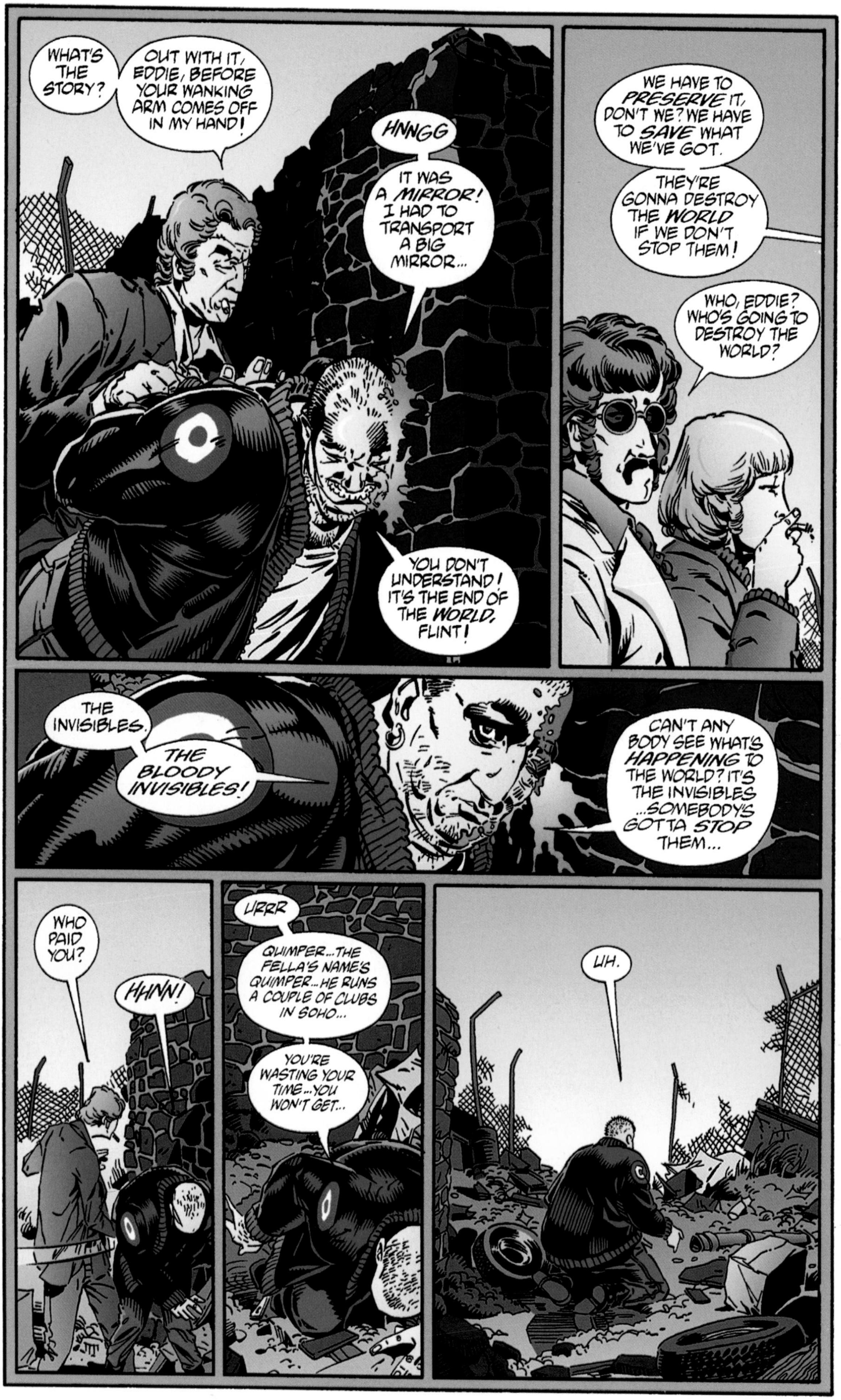
WHAT'S THE STORY?
OUT WITH IT, EDDIE, BEFORE YOUR WANKING ARM COMES OFF IN MY HAND!
HNNGG
IT WAS A MIRROR! I HAD TO TRANSPORT A BIG MIRROR...
YOU DON'T UNDERSTAND! IT'S THE END OF THE WORLD, FLINT!
WE HAVE TO PRESERVE IT, DON'T WE? WE HAVE TO SAVE WHAT WE'VE GOT.
THEY'RE GONNA DESTROY THE WORLD IF WE DON'T STOP THEM!
WHO, EDDIE? WHO'S GOING TO DESTROY THE WORLD?
THE INVISIBLES.
THE BLOODY INVISIBLES!
CAN'T ANY BODY SEE WHAT'S HAPPENING TO THE WORLD? IT'S THE INVISIBLES ...SOMEBODY'S GOTTA STOP THEM...
WHO PAID YOU?
HHNN!
URRR
QUIMPER...THE FELLA'S NAME'S QUIMPER...HE RUNS A COUPLE OF CLUBS IN SOHO...
YOU'RE WASTING YOUR TIME...YOU WON'T GET...
UH.

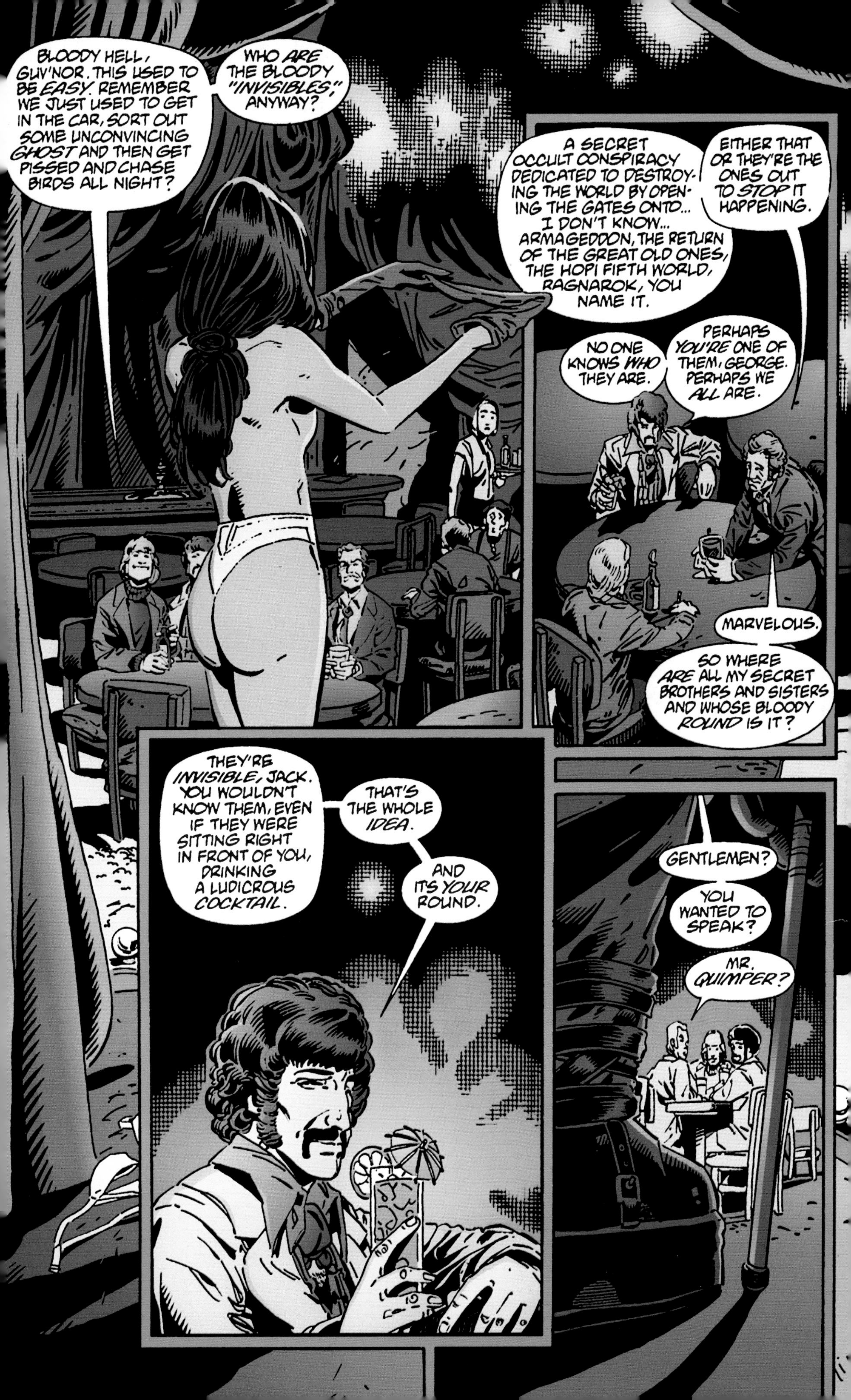
BLOODY HELL, GUV'NOR. THIS USED TO BE EASY. REMEMBER WE JUST USED TO GET IN THE CAR, SORT OUT SOME UNCONVINCING GHOST AND THEN GET PISSED AND CHASE BIRDS ALL NIGHT?
WHO ARE THE BLOODY "INVISIBLES," ANYWAY?
A SECRET OCCULT CONSPIRACY DEDICATED TO DESTROYING THE WORLD BY OPENING THE GATES ONTO... I DON'T KNOW... ARMAGEDDON, THE RETURN OF THE GREAT OLD ONES, THE HOPI FIFTH WORLD, RAGNAROK, YOU NAME IT.
EITHER THAT OR THEY'RE THE ONES OUT TO STOP IT HAPPENING.
NO ONE KNOWS WHO THEY ARE.
PERHAPS YOU'RE ONE OF THEM, GEORGE. PERHAPS WE ALL ARE.
MARVELOUS.
SO WHERE ARE ALL MY SECRET BROTHERS AND SISTERS AND WHOSE BLOODY ROUND IS IT?
THEY'RE INVISIBLE, JACK. YOU WOULDN'T KNOW THEM, EVEN IF THEY WERE SITTING RIGHT IN FRONT OF YOU, DRINKING A LUDICROUS COCKTAIL.
THAT'S THE WHOLE IDEA.
AND IT'S YOUR ROUND.
GENTLEMEN?
YOU WANTED TO SPEAK?
MR. QUIMPER?

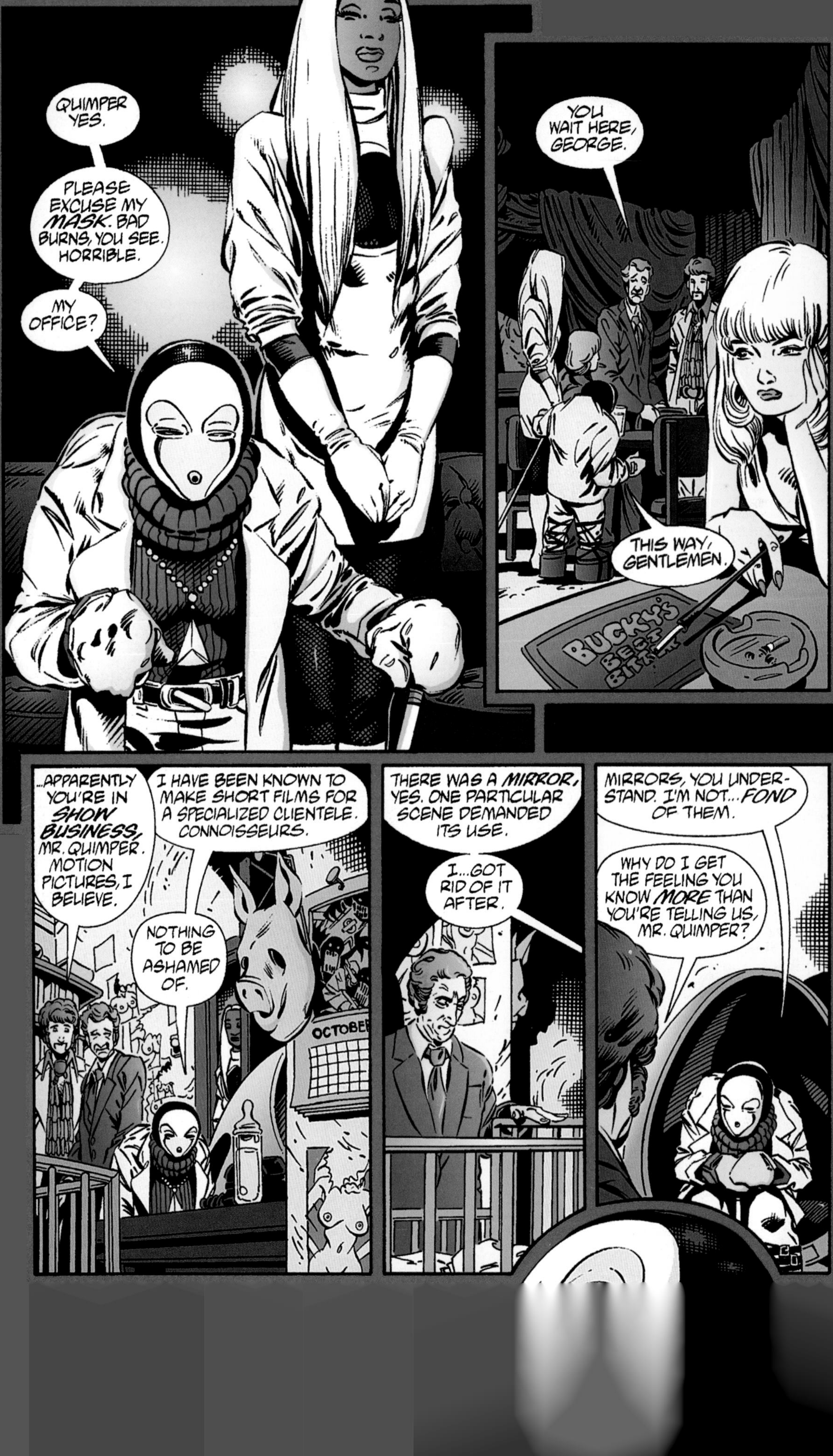
QUIMPER YES.
PLEASE EXCUSE MY MASK. BAD BURNS, YOU SEE. HORRIBLE.
MY OFFICE?
YOU WAIT HERE, GEORGE.
THIS WAY, GENTLEMEN.
BUCKY'S
...APPARENTLY YOU'RE IN SHOW BUSINESS, MR. QUIMPER. MOTION PICTURES, I BELIEVE.
I HAVE BEEN KNOWN TO MAKE SHORT FILMS FOR A SPECIALIZED CLIENTELE. CONNOISSEURS.
NOTHING TO BE ASHAMED OF.
OCTOBE
THERE WAS A MIRROR, YES. ONE PARTICULAR SCENE DEMANDED ITS USE.
I...GOT RID OF IT AFTER.
MIRRORS, YOU UNDER-STAND. I'M NOT... FOND OF THEM.
WHY DO I GET THE FEELING YOU KNOW MORE THAN YOU'RE TELLING US, MR. QUIMPER?

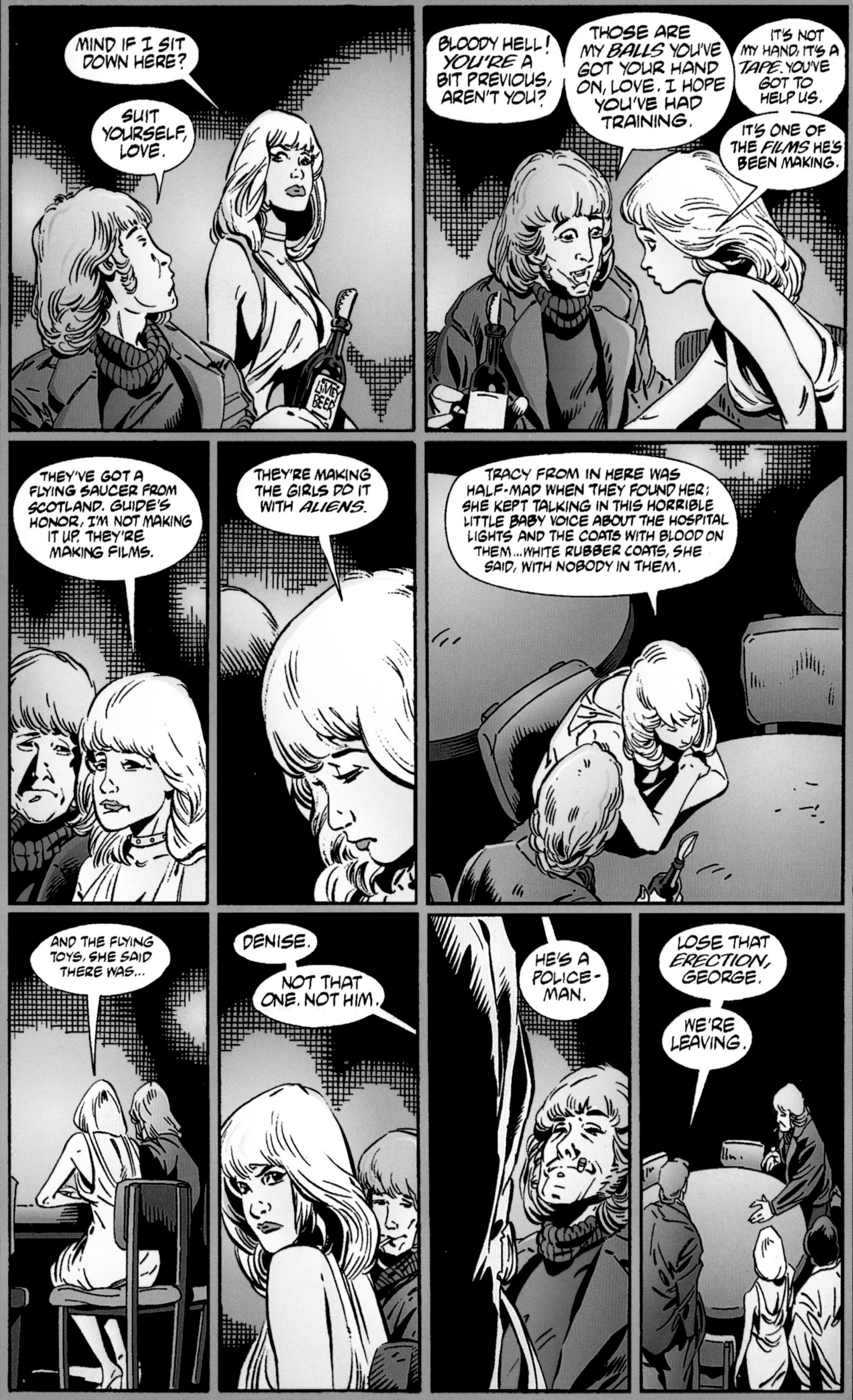
MIND IF I SIT DOWN HERE?
SUIT YOURSELF, LOVE.
BLOODY HELL! YOU'RE A BIT PREVIOUS, AREN'T YOU?
THOSE ARE MY BALLS YOU'VE GOT YOUR HAND ON, LOVE. I HOPE YOU'VE HAD TRAINING.
IT'S NOT MY HAND, IT'S A TAPE. YOU'VE GOT TO HELP US.
IT'S ONE OF THE FILMS HE'S BEEN MAKING.
THEY'VE GOT A FLYING SAUCER FROM SCOTLAND. GUIDE'S HONOR, I'M NOT MAKING IT UP. THEY'RE MAKING FILMS.
THEY'RE MAKING THE GIRLS DO IT WITH ALIENS.
TRACY FROM IN HERE WAS HALF-MAD WHEN THEY FOUND HER; SHE KEPT TALKING IN THIS HORRIBLE LITTLE BABY VOICE ABOUT THE HOSPITAL LIGHTS AND THE COATS WITH BLOOD ON THEM... WHITE RUBBER COATS, SHE SAID, WITH NOBODY IN THEM.
AND THE FLYING TOYS, SHE SAID THERE WAS...
DENISE.
NOT THAT ONE. NOT HIM.
HE'S A POLICE-MAN.
LOSE THAT ERECTION, GEORGE.
WE'RE LEAVING.

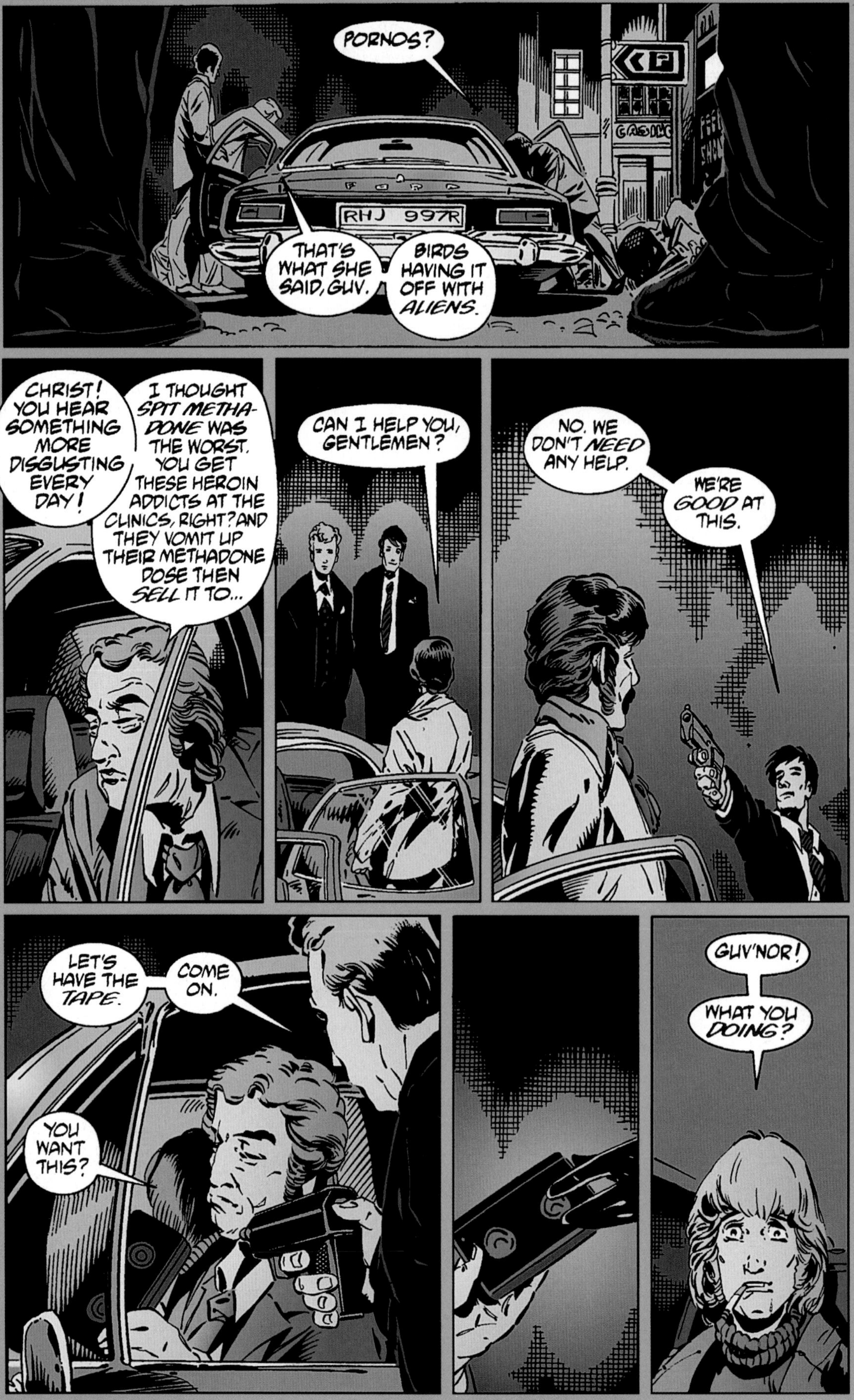
PORNOS?
THAT'S WHAT SHE SAID, GUV.
BIRDS HAVING IT OFF WITH ALIENS.
RHJ 997R
CASINO
CHRIST! YOU HEAR SOMETHING MORE DISGUSTING EVERY DAY!
I THOUGHT SPIT METHADONE WAS THE WORST. YOU GET THESE HEROIN ADDICTS AT THE CLINICS, RIGHT? AND THEY VOMIT UP THEIR METHADONE DOSE THEN SELL IT TO...
CAN I HELP YOU, GENTLEMEN?
NO. WE DON'T NEED ANY HELP.
WE'RE GOOD AT THIS.
LET'S HAVE THE TAPE.
COME ON.
YOU WANT THIS?
GUV'NOR!
WHAT YOU DOING?

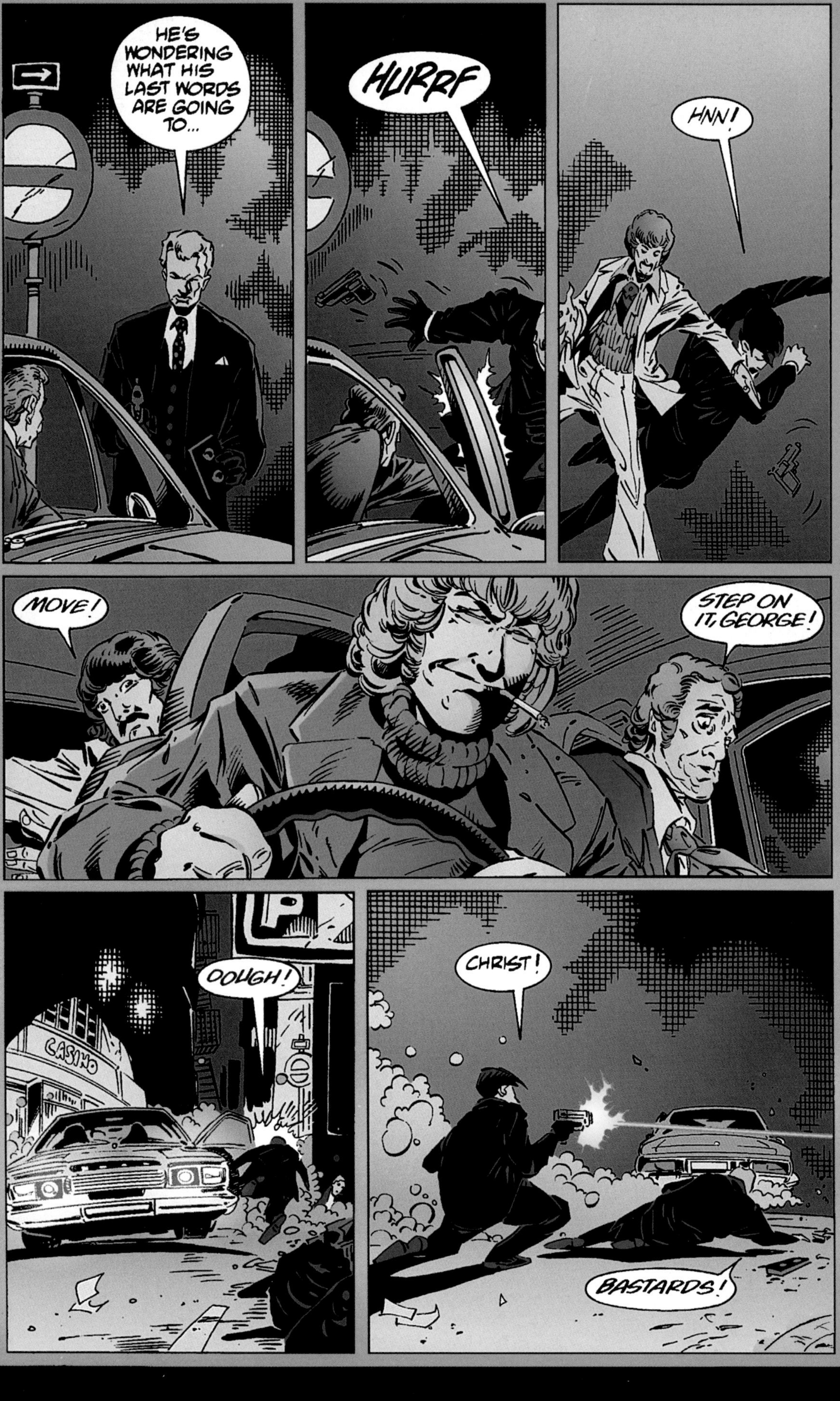
HE'S WONDERING WHAT HIS LAST WORDS ARE GOING TO...
HURRF
HNN!
MOVE!
STEP ON IT, GEORGE!
CASINO
OOUGH!
CHRIST!
BASTARDS!

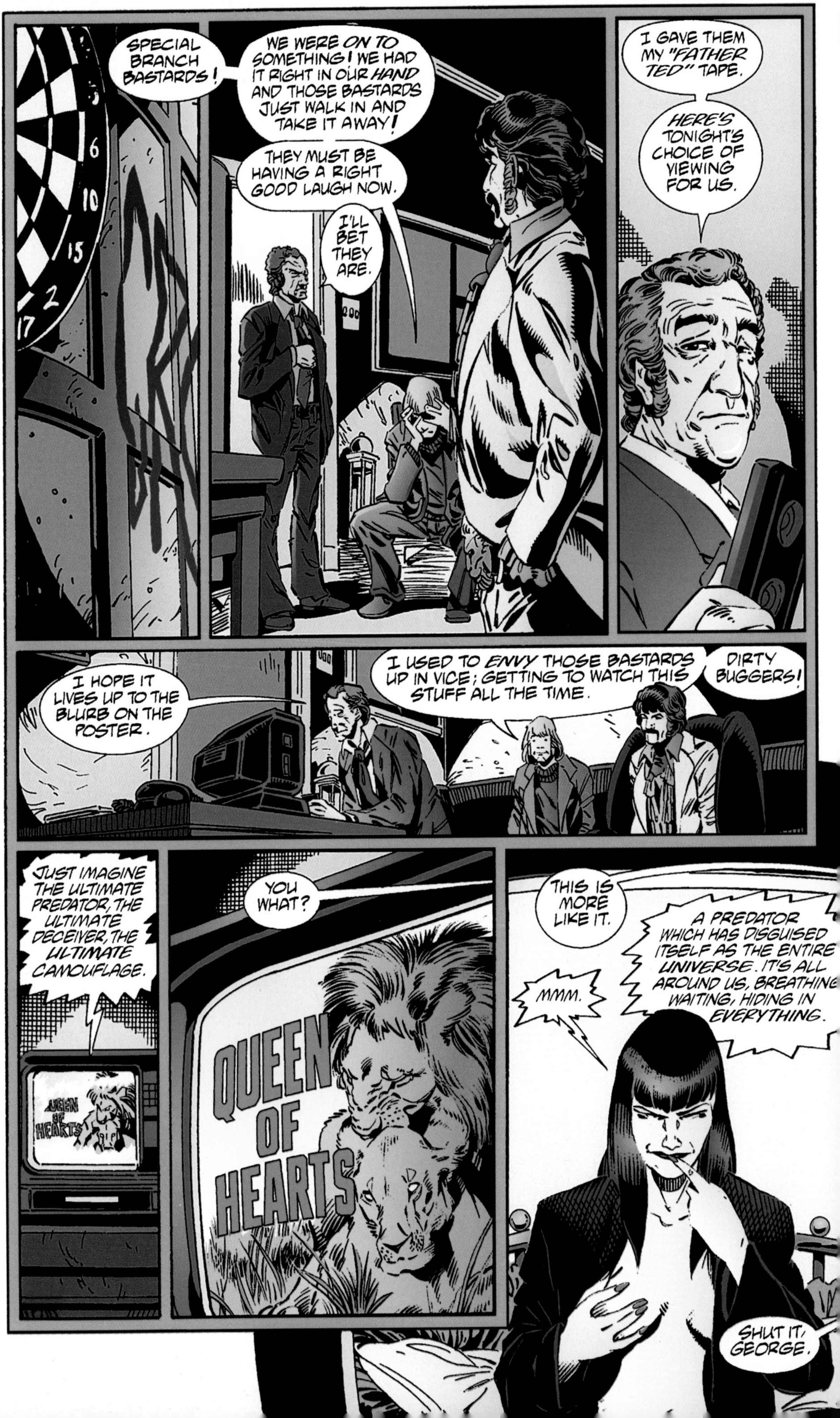
SPECIAL BRANCH BASTARDS!
WE WERE ON TO SOMETHING! WE HAD IT RIGHT IN OUR HAND AND THOSE BASTARDS JUST WALK IN AND TAKE IT AWAY!
THEY MUST BE HAVING A RIGHT GOOD LAUGH NOW.
I'LL BET THEY ARE.
I GAVE THEM MY "FATHER TED" TAPE.
HERE'S TONIGHT'S CHOICE OF VIEWING FOR US.
I HOPE IT LIVES UP TO THE BLURB ON THE POSTER.
I USED TO ENVY THOSE BASTARDS UP IN VICE; GETTING TO WATCH THIS STUFF ALL THE TIME.
DIRTY BUGGERS!
JUST IMAGINE THE ULTIMATE PREDATOR, THE ULTIMATE DECEIVER, THE ULTIMATE CAMOUFLAGE.
QUEEN OF HEARTS
YOU WHAT?
QUEEN OF HEARTS
THIS IS MORE LIKE IT.
A PREDATOR WHICH HAS DISGUISED ITSELF AS THE ENTIRE UNIVERSE. IT'S ALL AROUND US, BREATHING, WAITING, HIDING IN EVERYTHING.
MMM.
SHUT IT, GEORGE.

IMAGINE THE MOMENT WHEN IT STRIKES. IMAGINE THE DREAD AND THE TERROR OF THAT MOMENT WHEN IT DROPS ITS DISGUISE.

THAT MOMENT WHEN ALL THAT WE SEE AND KNOW BEGINS TO CHANGE AND THE BEAST IS REVEALED IN ITS AWFUL NAKEDNESS.

IT'S A BIT WEIRD, THIS, BUT IT'S ALL RIGHT SO FAR.

LOOK! THEY'VE GOT THAT BIRD DONE UP TO LOOK LIKE PRINCESS DI!

BRIDE OF THE BEAST!

SEE THE FIVE SUNS IN HIS MIRROR!

YOUR HUSBAND IS HERE TO MAKE YOU HIS PRINCESS!

EEEEEIIIIII

FREEZE THE FRAME!

MY GOD.

LOOK.

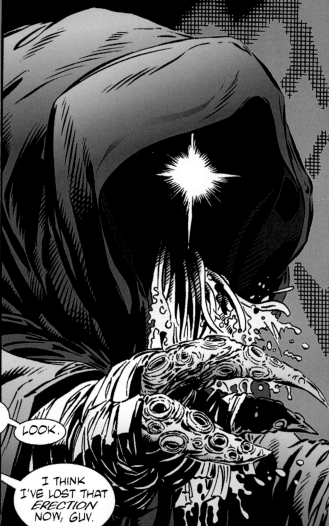

I THINK I'VE LOST THAT ERECTION NOW, GUV.

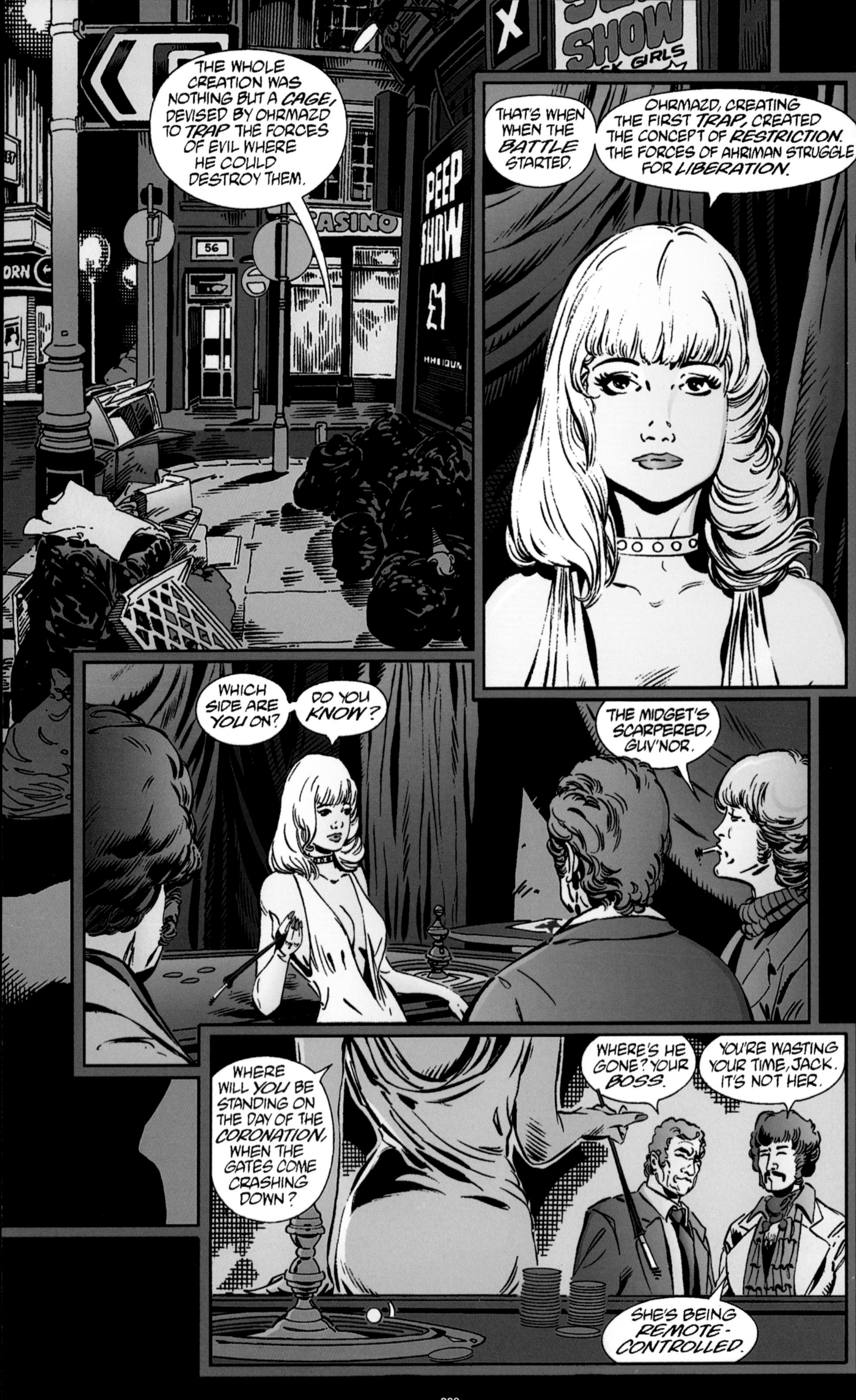
SHOW
GIRLS
PEEP SHOW £1
CASINO
56
THE WHOLE CREATION WAS NOTHING BUT A CAGE, DEVISED BY OHRMAZD TO TRAP THE FORCES OF EVIL WHERE HE COULD DESTROY THEM.
THAT'S WHEN WHEN THE BATTLE STARTED.
OHRMAZD, CREATING THE FIRST TRAP, CREATED THE CONCEPT OF RESTRICTION. THE FORCES OF AHRIMAN STRUGGLE FOR LIBERATION.
WHICH SIDE ARE YOU ON?
DO YOU KNOW?
THE MIDGET'S SCARPERED, GUV'NOR.
WHERE WILL YOU BE STANDING ON THE DAY OF THE CORONATION, WHEN THE GATES COME CRASHING DOWN?
WHERE'S HE GONE? YOUR BOSS.
YOU'RE WASTING YOUR TIME, JACK. IT'S NOT HER.
SHE'S BEING REMOTE-CONTROLLED.

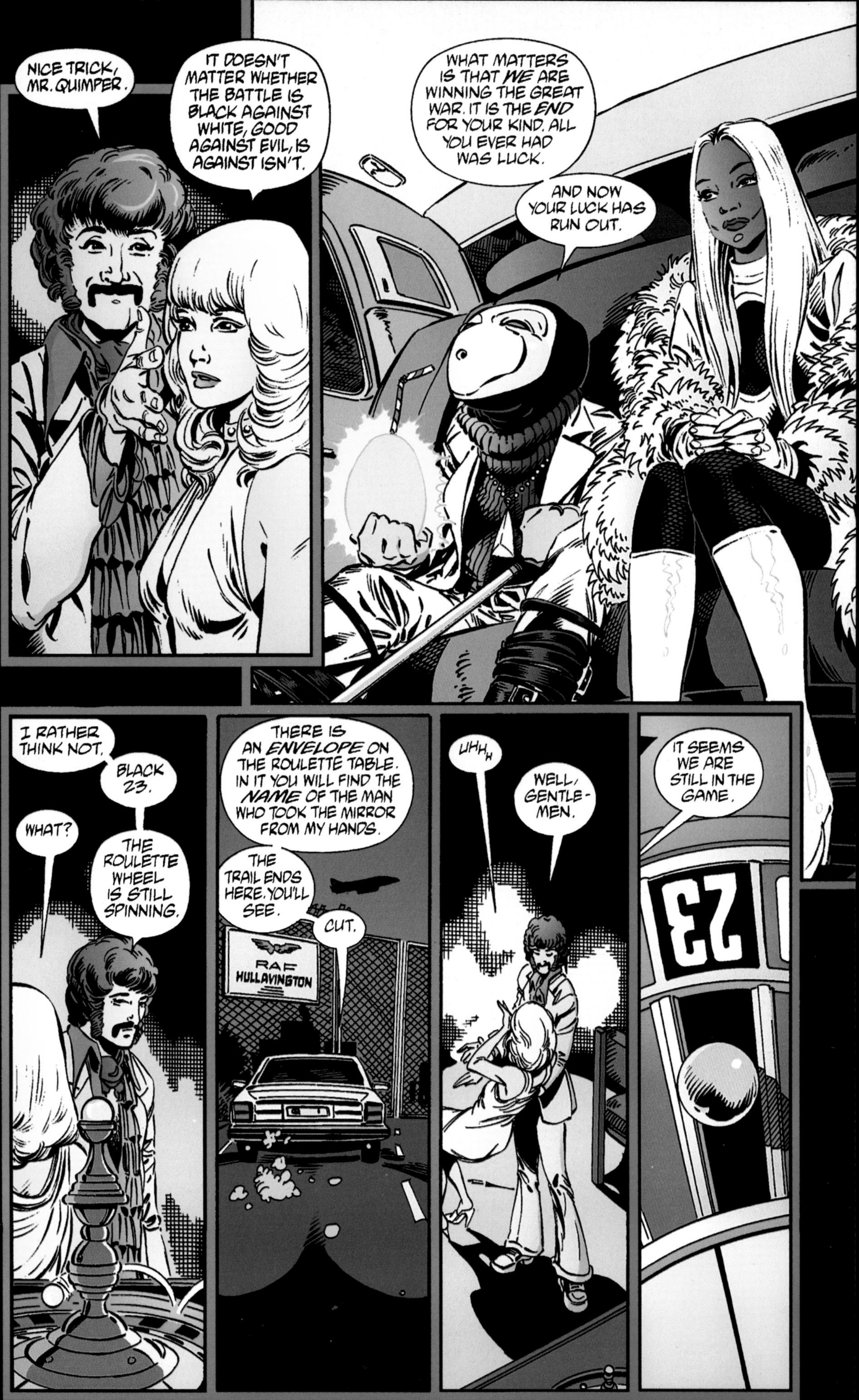

NICE TRICK, MR. QUIMPER.
IT DOESN'T MATTER WHETHER THE BATTLE IS BLACK AGAINST WHITE, GOOD AGAINST EVIL, IS AGAINST ISN'T.
WHAT MATTERS IS THAT *WE* ARE WINNING THE GREAT WAR. IT IS THE *END* FOR YOUR KIND. ALL YOU EVER HAD WAS LUCK.
AND NOW YOUR LUCK HAS RUN OUT.
I RATHER THINK NOT.
BLACK 23.
WHAT?
THE ROULETTE WHEEL IS STILL SPINNING.
THERE IS AN *ENVELOPE* ON THE ROULETTE TABLE. IN IT YOU WILL FIND THE *NAME* OF THE MAN WHO TOOK THE MIRROR FROM MY HANDS.
THE TRAIL ENDS HERE. YOU'LL SEE.
CUT.
RAF HULLAVINGTON
UHHH
WELL, GENTLEMEN.
IT SEEMS WE ARE STILL IN THE GAME.
23

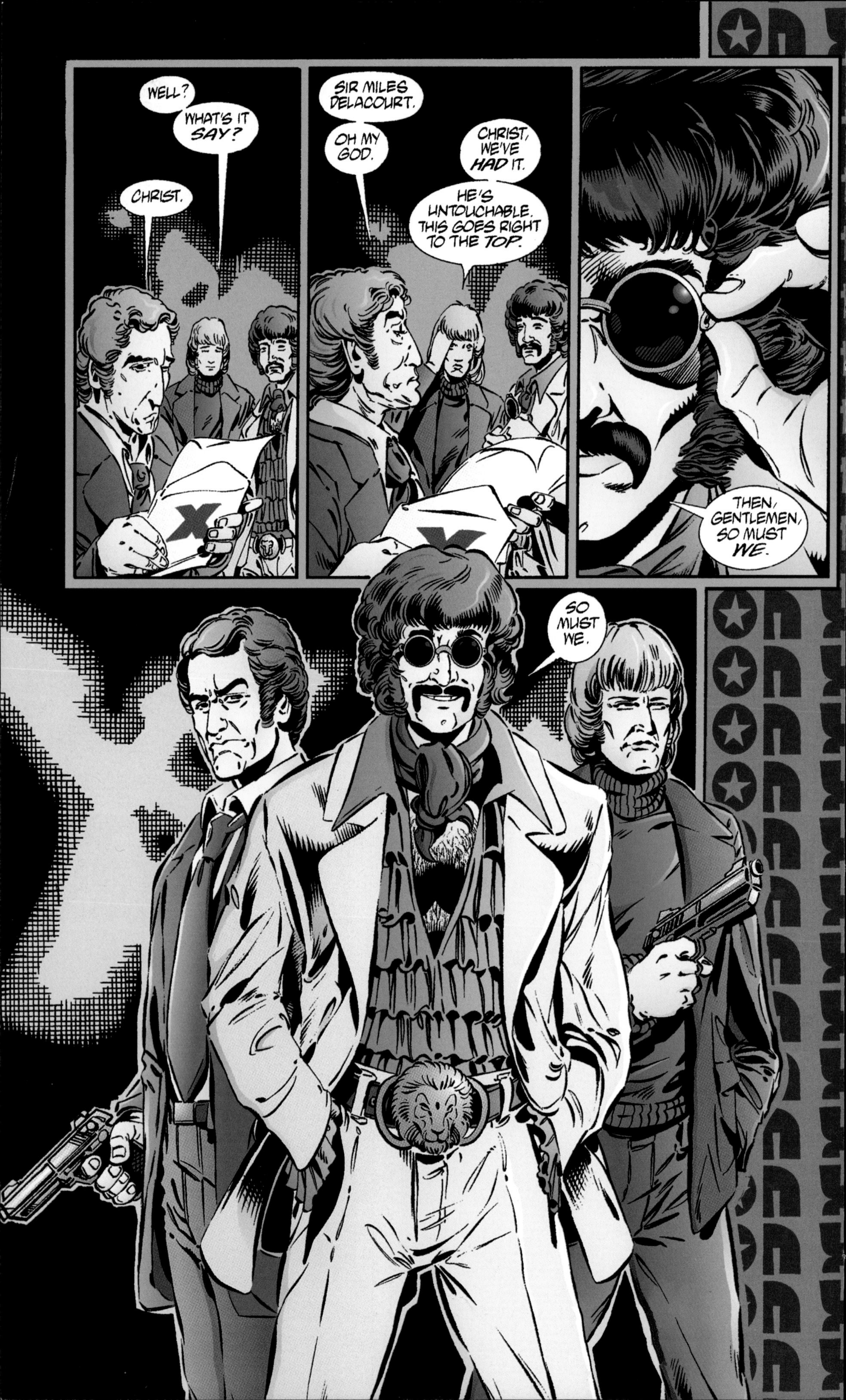
WELL?
WHAT'S IT SAY?
CHRIST.
SIR MILES DELACOURT.
OH MY GOD.
CHRIST, WE'VE HAD IT.
HE'S UNTOUCHABLE. THIS GOES RIGHT TO THE TOP.
THEN, GENTLEMEN, SO MUST WE.
SO MUST WE.

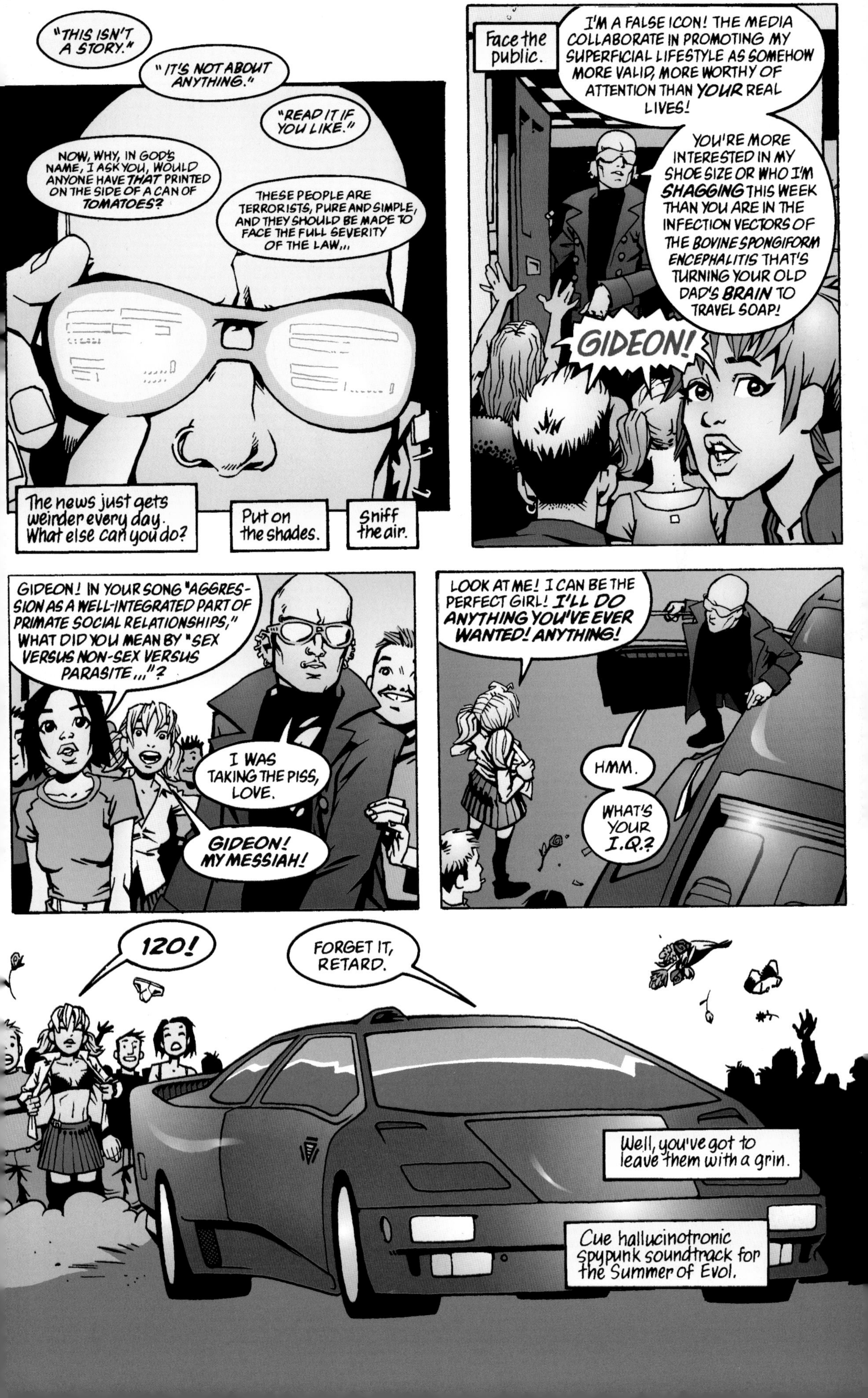

"THIS ISN'T A STORY."
"IT'S NOT ABOUT ANYTHING."
"READ IT IF YOU LIKE."
NOW, WHY, IN GOD'S NAME, I ASK YOU, WOULD ANYONE HAVE THAT PRINTED ON THE SIDE OF A CAN OF TOMATOES?
THESE PEOPLE ARE TERRORISTS, PURE AND SIMPLE, AND THEY SHOULD BE MADE TO FACE THE FULL SEVERITY OF THE LAW...
The news just gets weirder every day. What else can you do?
Put on the shades.
Sniff the air.
Face the public.
I'M A FALSE ICON! THE MEDIA COLLABORATE IN PROMOTING MY SUPERFICIAL LIFESTYLE AS SOMEHOW MORE VALID, MORE WORTHY OF ATTENTION THAN YOUR REAL LIVES!
YOU'RE MORE INTERESTED IN MY SHOE SIZE OR WHO I'M SHAGGING THIS WEEK THAN YOU ARE IN THE INFECTION VECTORS OF THE BOVINE SPONGIFORM ENCEPHALITIS THAT'S TURNING YOUR OLD DAD'S BRAIN TO TRAVEL SOAP!
GIDEON!
GIDEON! IN YOUR SONG "AGGRESSION AS A WELL-INTEGRATED PART OF PRIMATE SOCIAL RELATIONSHIPS," WHAT DID YOU MEAN BY "SEX VERSUS NON-SEX VERSUS PARASITE..."?
I WAS TAKING THE PISS, LOVE.
GIDEON! MY MESSIAH!
LOOK AT ME! I CAN BE THE PERFECT GIRL! I'LL DO ANYTHING YOU'VE EVER WANTED! ANYTHING!
HMM.
WHAT'S YOUR I.Q.?
120!
FORGET IT, RETARD.
Well, you've got to leave them with a grin.
Cue hallucinotronic spypunk soundtrack for the Summer of Evol.

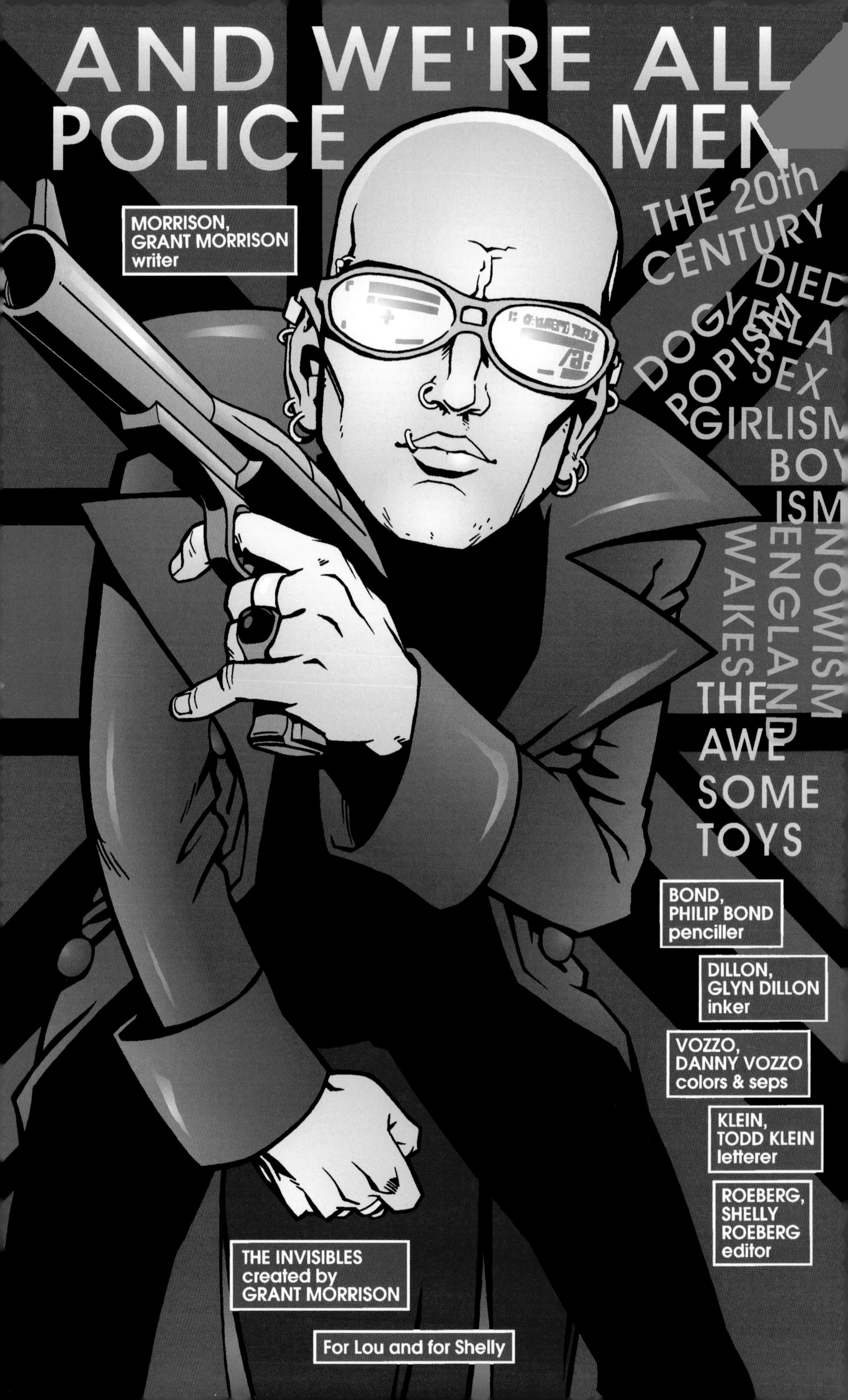
AND WE'RE ALL POLICE MEN
MORRISON, GRANT MORRISON writer
THE 20th CENTURY
DIED
POPISM
SEX
GIRLISM
BOY
ISM
WAKES
ENGLAND
NOWISM
THE AWE SOME TOYS
BOND, PHILIP BOND penciller
DILLON, GLYN DILLON inker
VOZZO, DANNY VOZZO colors & seps
KLEIN, TODD KLEIN letterer
ROEBERG, SHELLY ROEBERG editor
THE INVISIBLES created by GRANT MORRISON
For Lou and for Shelly

The new model Lamborghini ripples in the heat. Its optically-sensitive reflective chassis can record and play back visual images. Its quantum-polaroid engines, designed by Buddhist monks, extract virtually limitless energy from raw photons... so fucking what?

I LOVE THE CAR ADS. THEY MAKE ME FEEL LIKE I'M TRIPPING.

DON'T THINK FOR YOURSELVES! THINK FOR GOD! LET'S START MAKING THAT MOTHERFUCKER'S DECISIONS FOR HIM, HUH?...

THANKS FOR... AH... THANKS, CHET, FOR THAT VERY UNUSUAL AND INDEED, MOVING LOOK AT TOMORROW'S WEATHER...

PORNOPLASM TURN ON. MODEM THE FOLLOWING TO MY WORLD-WEB HOTEL PAGE.

THE UNDERLYING MOTIF OF HUMAN CIVILIZATION IS NO LONGER SUFFERING BUT PLAY.

THE CRUCIFIED GOD-IMAGE HAS BEEN REPLACED BY THE NEW AEON'S DOMINANT RELIGIOUS MOTIF--A CHILD FUCKING ABOUT WITH THE BUILDING BLOCKS OF REALITY ITSELF, RESTLESSLY DESTROYING TO CREATE.

It was the best he could think of in a hurry; let's face it, the Samaritans should have asked someone else to compose the message for their new "Sorry! We're at a party!" answering machine service.

Pornoplasm:

MY FAVORITE AD'S THE ONE FOR PORNOPLASM.

WHEN WE SAY LAPTOP, WE MEAN LAPTOP!

HE PUTS THE HARD INTO HARD DRIVE, SHE'S THE PERSONAL COMPUTER WHO LIKES TO GET REALLY PERSONAL!

Here's the pitch: the Stepford Wives with Terminator II technology. A programmable sex doll with six gender options, hands-on identikit function and a data storage capacity of 250 billion MB. It can give you head and e-mail your boss at the same time...

THIS?

NNMM. ENHANCE TITS 20%. I WANT L.A. PORN.

"I WANT THE NERDIEST GUY IN SCHOOL TRANSFORMED BY A GIFTED SURGEON'S KNIFE INTO A BEAUTIFUL, SEXY GIRL AND EXHIBITED AS A LIVING EROTIC SCULPTURE AT DIONYSIAN CEREMONIES OF HEATHEN BONDAGE..."

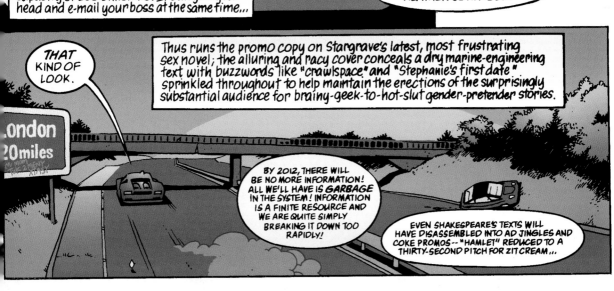

Thus runs the promo copy on Stargrave's latest, most frustrating sex novel; the alluring and racy cover conceals a dry marine-engineering text with buzzwords like "crawlspace" and "Stephanie's first date" sprinkled throughout to help maintain the erections of the surprisingly substantial audience for brainy-geek-to-hot-slut gender-pretender stories.

THAT KIND OF LOOK.

London 20 miles

BY 2012, THERE WILL BE NO MORE INFORMATION! ALL WE'LL HAVE IS GARBAGE IN THE SYSTEM! INFORMATION IS A FINITE RESOURCE AND WE ARE QUITE SIMPLY BREAKING IT DOWN TOO RAPIDLY!

EVEN SHAKESPEARE'S TEXTS WILL HAVE DISASSEMBLED INTO AD JINGLES AND COKE PROMOS-- "HAMLET" REDUCED TO A THIRTY-SECOND PITCH FOR ZIT CREAM...

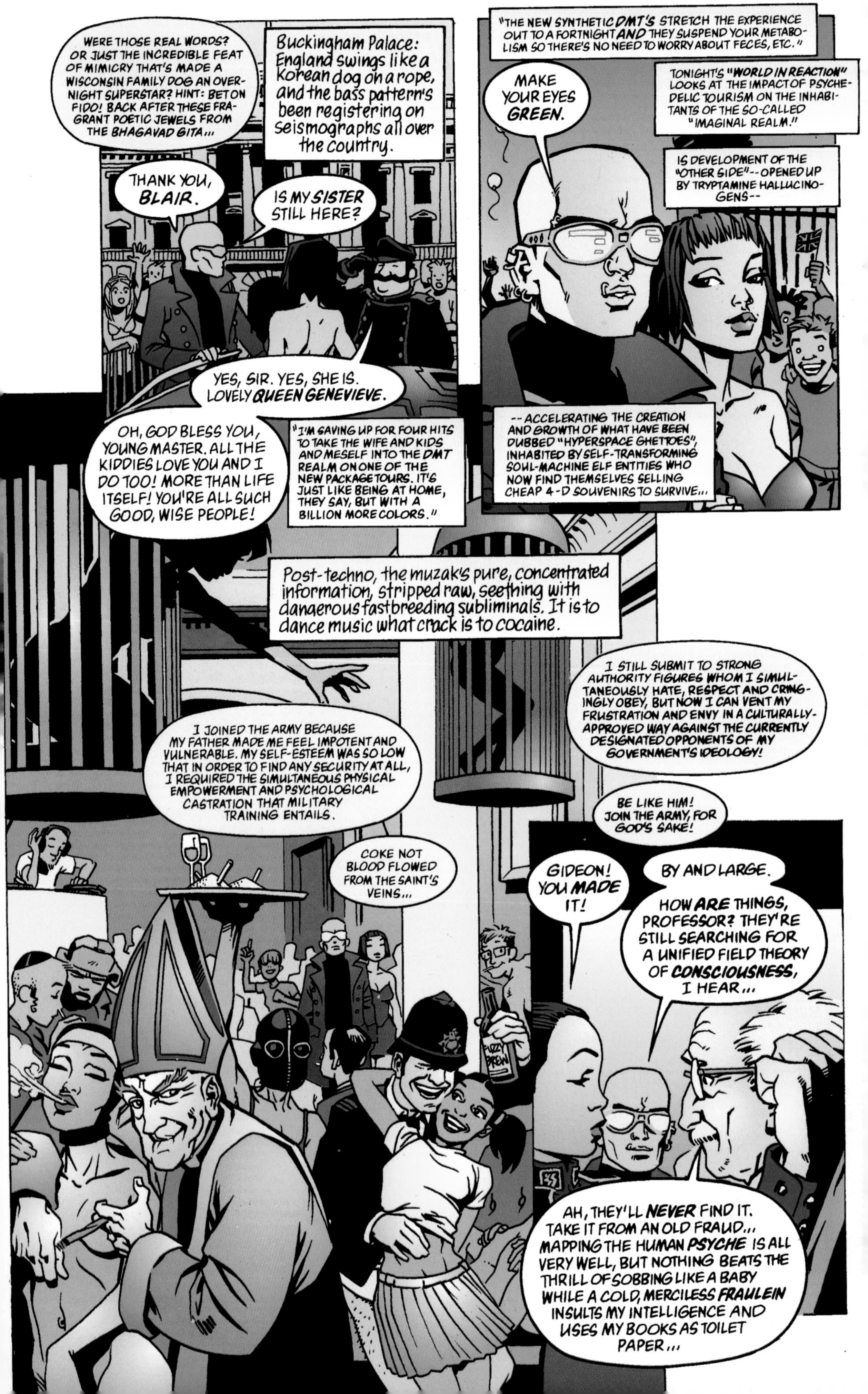
WERE THOSE REAL WORDS? OR JUST THE INCREDIBLE FEAT OF MIMICRY THAT'S MADE A WISCONSIN FAMILY DOG AN OVERNIGHT SUPERSTAR? HINT: BET ON FIDO! BACK AFTER THESE FRAGRANT POETIC JEWELS FROM THE BHAGAVAD GITA...
Buckingham Palace: England swings like a Korean dog on a rope, and the bass pattern's been registering on seismographs all over the country.
THANK YOU, BLAIR.
IS MY SISTER STILL HERE?
YES, SIR. YES, SHE IS. LOVELY QUEEN GENEVIEVE.
"THE NEW SYNTHETIC DMT'S STRETCH THE EXPERIENCE OUT TO A FORTNIGHT AND THEY SUSPEND YOUR METABOLISM SO THERE'S NO NEED TO WORRY ABOUT FECES, ETC."
MAKE YOUR EYES GREEN.
TONIGHT'S "WORLD IN REACTION" LOOKS AT THE IMPACT OF PSYCHEDELIC TOURISM ON THE INHABITANTS OF THE SO-CALLED "IMAGINAL REALM."
IS DEVELOPMENT OF THE "OTHER SIDE"--OPENED UP BY TRYPTAMINE HALLUCINOGENS--
--ACCELERATING THE CREATION AND GROWTH OF WHAT HAVE BEEN DUBBED "HYPERSPACE GHETTOES", INHABITED BY SELF-TRANSFORMING SOUL-MACHINE ELF ENTITIES WHO NOW FIND THEMSELVES SELLING CHEAP 4-D SOUVENIRS TO SURVIVE...
OH, GOD BLESS YOU, YOUNG MASTER. ALL THE KIDDIES LOVE YOU AND I DO TOO! MORE THAN LIFE ITSELF! YOU'RE ALL SUCH GOOD, WISE PEOPLE!
"I'M SAVING UP FOR FOUR HITS TO TAKE THE WIFE AND KIDS AND MESELF INTO THE DMT REALM ON ONE OF THE NEW PACKAGE TOURS. IT'S JUST LIKE BEING AT HOME, THEY SAY, BUT WITH A BILLION MORE COLORS."
Post-techno, the muzak's pure, concentrated information, stripped raw, seething with dangerous fastbreeding subliminals. It is to dance music what crack is to cocaine.
I STILL SUBMIT TO STRONG AUTHORITY FIGURES WHOM I SIMULTANEOUSLY HATE, RESPECT AND CRINGINGLY OBEY, BUT NOW I CAN VENT MY FRUSTRATION AND ENVY IN A CULTURALLY-APPROVED WAY AGAINST THE CURRENTLY DESIGNATED OPPONENTS OF MY GOVERNMENT'S IDEOLOGY!
I JOINED THE ARMY BECAUSE MY FATHER MADE ME FEEL IMPOTENT AND VULNERABLE. MY SELF-ESTEEM WAS SO LOW THAT IN ORDER TO FIND ANY SECURITY AT ALL, I REQUIRED THE SIMULTANEOUS PHYSICAL EMPOWERMENT AND PSYCHOLOGICAL CASTRATION THAT MILITARY TRAINING ENTAILS.
BE LIKE HIM! JOIN THE ARMY, FOR GOD'S SAKE!
COKE NOT BLOOD FLOWED FROM THE SAINT'S VEINS...
FUZZY BREW
GIDEON! YOU MADE IT!
BY AND LARGE.
HOW ARE THINGS, PROFESSOR? THEY'RE STILL SEARCHING FOR A UNIFIED FIELD THEORY OF CONSCIOUSNESS, I HEAR...
AH, THEY'LL NEVER FIND IT. TAKE IT FROM AN OLD FRAUD... MAPPING THE HUMAN PSYCHE IS ALL VERY WELL, BUT NOTHING BEATS THE THRILL OF SOBBING LIKE A BABY WHILE A COLD, MERCILESS FRAULEIN INSULTS MY INTELLIGENCE AND USES MY BOOKS AS TOILET PAPER...

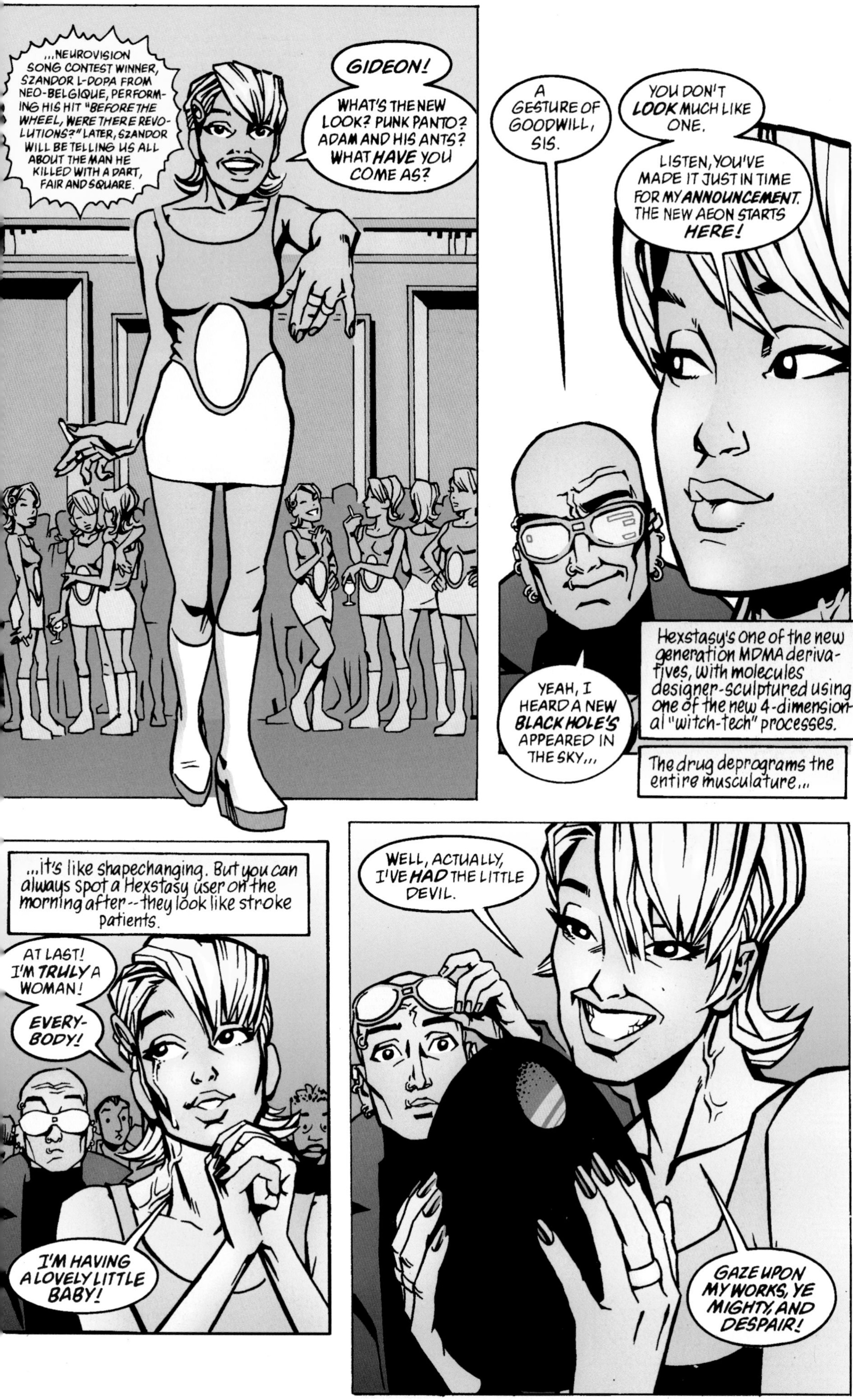
...NEUROVISION SONG CONTEST WINNER, SZANDOR L-DOPA FROM NEO-BELGIQUE, PERFORMING HIS HIT "BEFORE THE WHEEL, WERE THERE REVOLUTIONS?" LATER, SZANDOR WILL BE TELLING US ALL ABOUT THE MAN HE KILLED WITH A DART, FAIR AND SQUARE.
GIDEON!
WHAT'S THE NEW LOOK? PUNK PANTO? ADAM AND HIS ANTS? WHAT HAVE YOU COME AS?
A GESTURE OF GOODWILL, SIS.
YOU DON'T LOOK MUCH LIKE ONE.
LISTEN, YOU'VE MADE IT JUST IN TIME FOR MY ANNOUNCEMENT. THE NEW AEON STARTS HERE!
YEAH, I HEARD A NEW BLACK HOLE'S APPEARED IN THE SKY...
Hexstasy's one of the new generation MDMA derivatives, with molecules designer-sculptured using one of the new 4-dimensional "witch-tech" processes.
The drug deprograms the entire musculature...
...it's like shapechanging. But you can always spot a Hexstasy user on the morning after--they look like stroke patients.
AT LAST! I'M TRULY A WOMAN!
EVERY-BODY!
I'M HAVING A LOVELY LITTLE BABY!
WELL, ACTUALLY, I'VE HAD THE LITTLE DEVIL.
GAZE UPON MY WORKS, YE MIGHTY, AND DESPAIR!

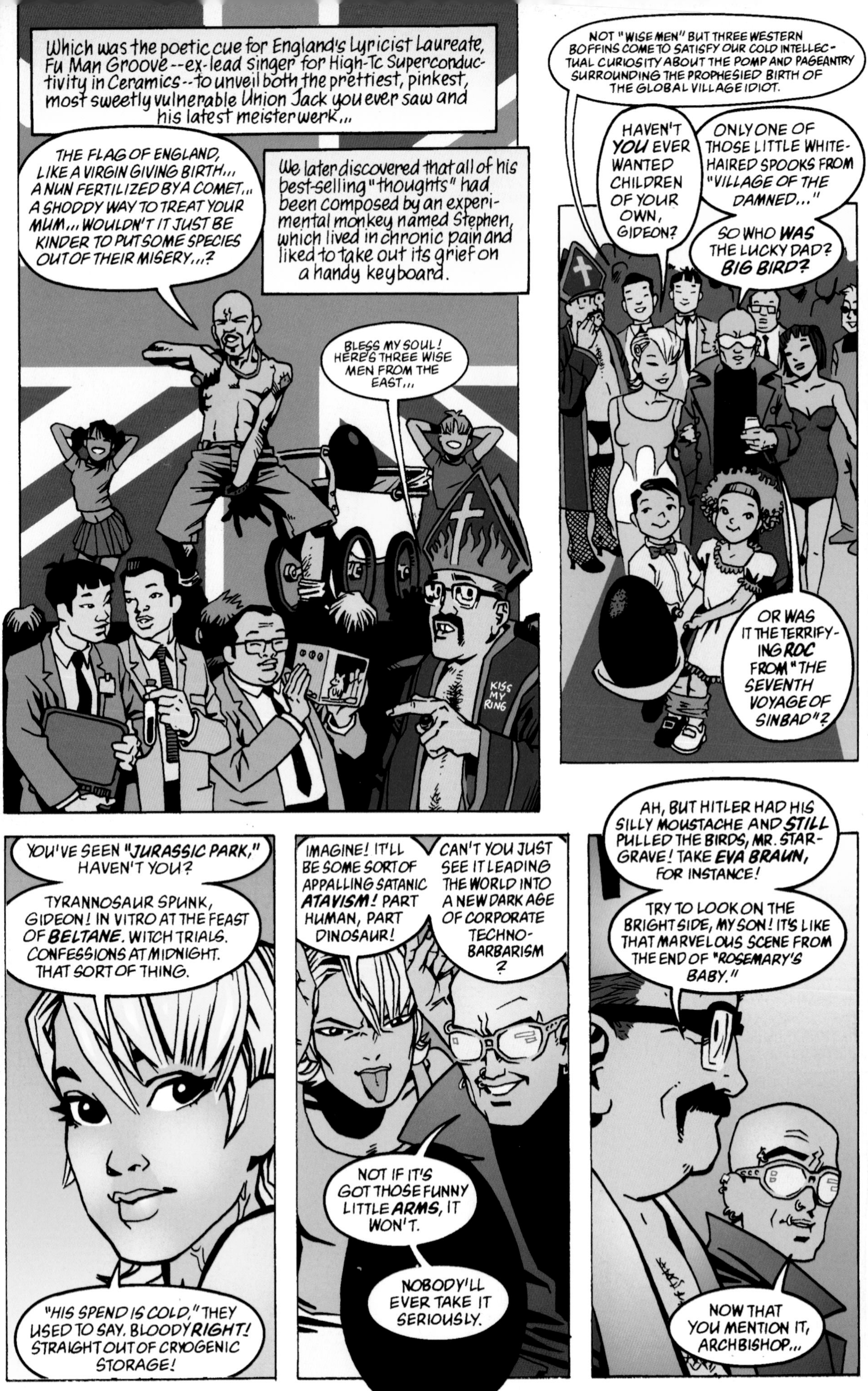

Which was the poetic cue for England's Lyricist Laureate, Fu Man Groove --ex-lead singer for High-Tc Superconductivity in Ceramics--to unveil both the prettiest, pinkest, most sweetly vulnerable Union Jack you ever saw and his latest meisterwerk...
THE FLAG OF ENGLAND, LIKE A VIRGIN GIVING BIRTH... A NUN FERTILIZED BY A COMET... A SHODDY WAY TO TREAT YOUR MUM... WOULDN'T IT JUST BE KINDER TO PUT SOME SPECIES OUT OF THEIR MISERY...?
We later discovered that all of his best-selling "thoughts" had been composed by an experimental monkey named Stephen, which lived in chronic pain and liked to take out its grief on a handy keyboard.
BLESS MY SOUL! HERE'S THREE WISE MEN FROM THE EAST...
KISS MY RING
NOT "WISE MEN" BUT THREE WESTERN BOFFINS COME TO SATISFY OUR COLD INTELLECTUAL CURIOSITY ABOUT THE POMP AND PAGEANTRY SURROUNDING THE PROPHESIED BIRTH OF THE GLOBAL VILLAGE IDIOT.
HAVEN'T YOU EVER WANTED CHILDREN OF YOUR OWN, GIDEON?
ONLY ONE OF THOSE LITTLE WHITE-HAIRED SPOOKS FROM "VILLAGE OF THE DAMNED..."
SO WHO WAS THE LUCKY DAD? BIG BIRD?
OR WAS IT THE TERRIFYING ROC FROM "THE SEVENTH VOYAGE OF SINBAD"?
YOU'VE SEEN "JURASSIC PARK," HAVEN'T YOU?
TYRANNOSAUR SPUNK, GIDEON! IN VITRO AT THE FEAST OF BELTANE. WITCH TRIALS. CONFESSIONS AT MIDNIGHT. THAT SORT OF THING.
"HIS SPEND IS COLD," THEY USED TO SAY. BLOODY RIGHT! STRAIGHT OUT OF CRYOGENIC STORAGE!
IMAGINE! IT'LL BE SOME SORT OF APPALLING SATANIC ATAVISM! PART HUMAN, PART DINOSAUR!
CAN'T YOU JUST SEE IT LEADING THE WORLD INTO A NEW DARK AGE OF CORPORATE TECHNO-BARBARISM?
NOT IF IT'S GOT THOSE FUNNY LITTLE ARMS, IT WON'T.
NOBODY'LL EVER TAKE IT SERIOUSLY.
AH, BUT HITLER HAD HIS SILLY MOUSTACHE AND STILL PULLED THE BIRDS, MR. STARGRAVE! TAKE EVA BRAUN, FOR INSTANCE!
TRY TO LOOK ON THE BRIGHT SIDE, MY SON! IT'S LIKE THAT MARVELOUS SCENE FROM THE END OF "ROSEMARY'S BABY."
NOW THAT YOU MENTION IT, ARCHBISHOP...

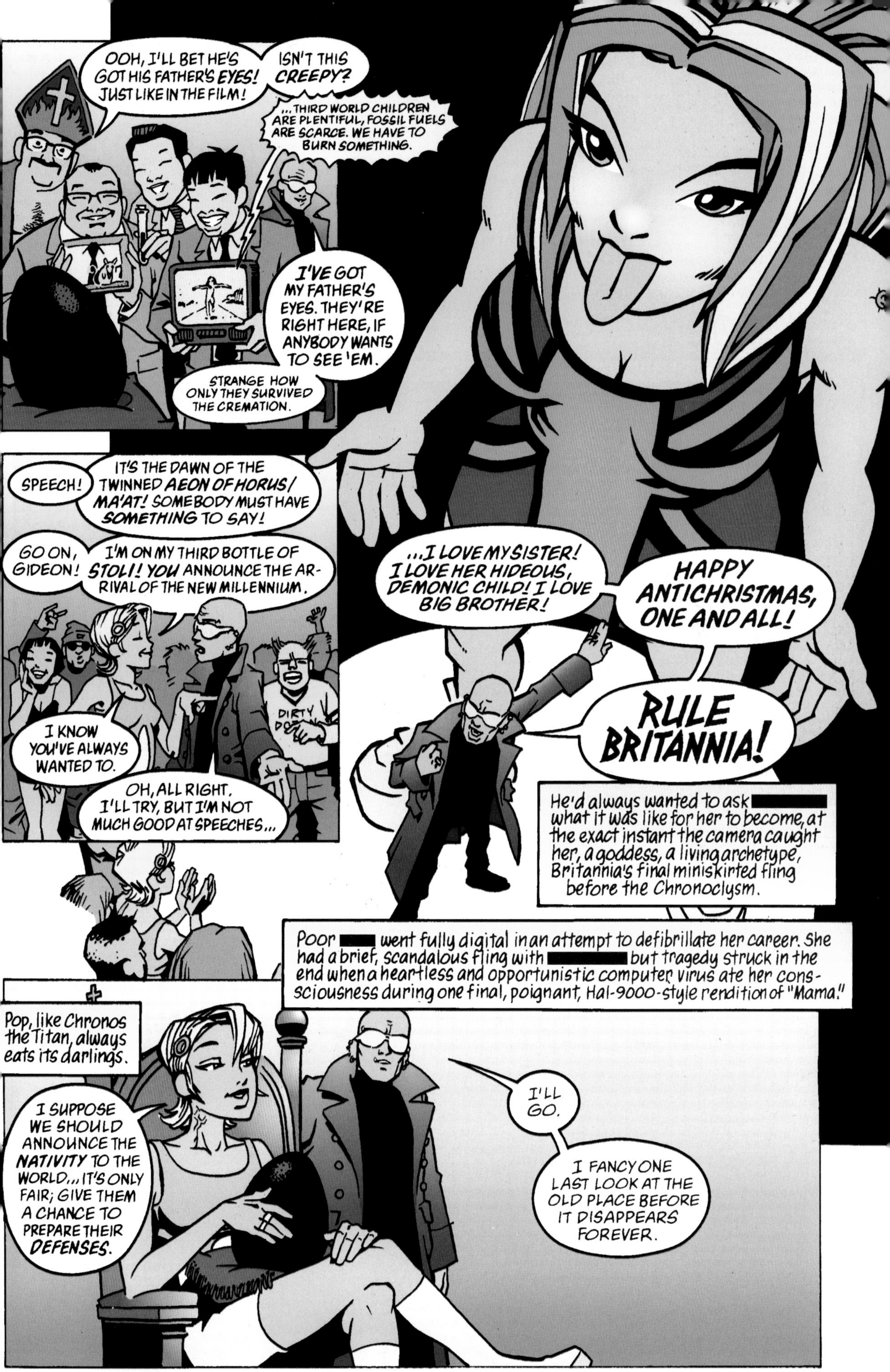
OOH, I'LL BET HE'S GOT HIS FATHER'S EYES! JUST LIKE IN THE FILM!
ISN'T THIS CREEPY?
...THIRD WORLD CHILDREN ARE PLENTIFUL, FOSSIL FUELS ARE SCARCE. WE HAVE TO BURN SOMETHING.
I'VE GOT MY FATHER'S EYES. THEY'RE RIGHT HERE, IF ANYBODY WANTS TO SEE 'EM.
STRANGE HOW ONLY THEY SURVIVED THE CREMATION.
SPEECH!
IT'S THE DAWN OF THE TWINNED AEON OF HORUS/MA'AT! SOMEBODY MUST HAVE SOMETHING TO SAY!
GO ON, GIDEON!
I'M ON MY THIRD BOTTLE OF STOLI! YOU ANNOUNCE THE ARRIVAL OF THE NEW MILLENNIUM.
I KNOW YOU'VE ALWAYS WANTED TO.
OH, ALL RIGHT. I'LL TRY, BUT I'M NOT MUCH GOOD AT SPEECHES...
...I LOVE MY SISTER! I LOVE HER HIDEOUS, DEMONIC CHILD! I LOVE BIG BROTHER!
HAPPY ANTICHRISTMAS, ONE AND ALL!
RULE BRITANNIA!
He'd always wanted to ask [redacted] what it was like for her to become, at the exact instant the camera caught her, a goddess, a living archetype, Britannia's final miniskirted fling before the Chronoclysm.
Poor [redacted] went fully digital in an attempt to defibrillate her career. She had a brief, scandalous fling with [redacted] but tragedy struck in the end when a heartless and opportunistic computer virus ate her consciousness during one final, poignant, Hal-9000-style rendition of "Mama."
Pop, like Chronos the Titan, always eats its darlings.
I SUPPOSE WE SHOULD ANNOUNCE THE NATIVITY TO THE WORLD... IT'S ONLY FAIR; GIVE THEM A CHANCE TO PREPARE THEIR DEFENSES.
I'LL GO.
I FANCY ONE LAST LOOK AT THE OLD PLACE BEFORE IT DISAPPEARS FOREVER.

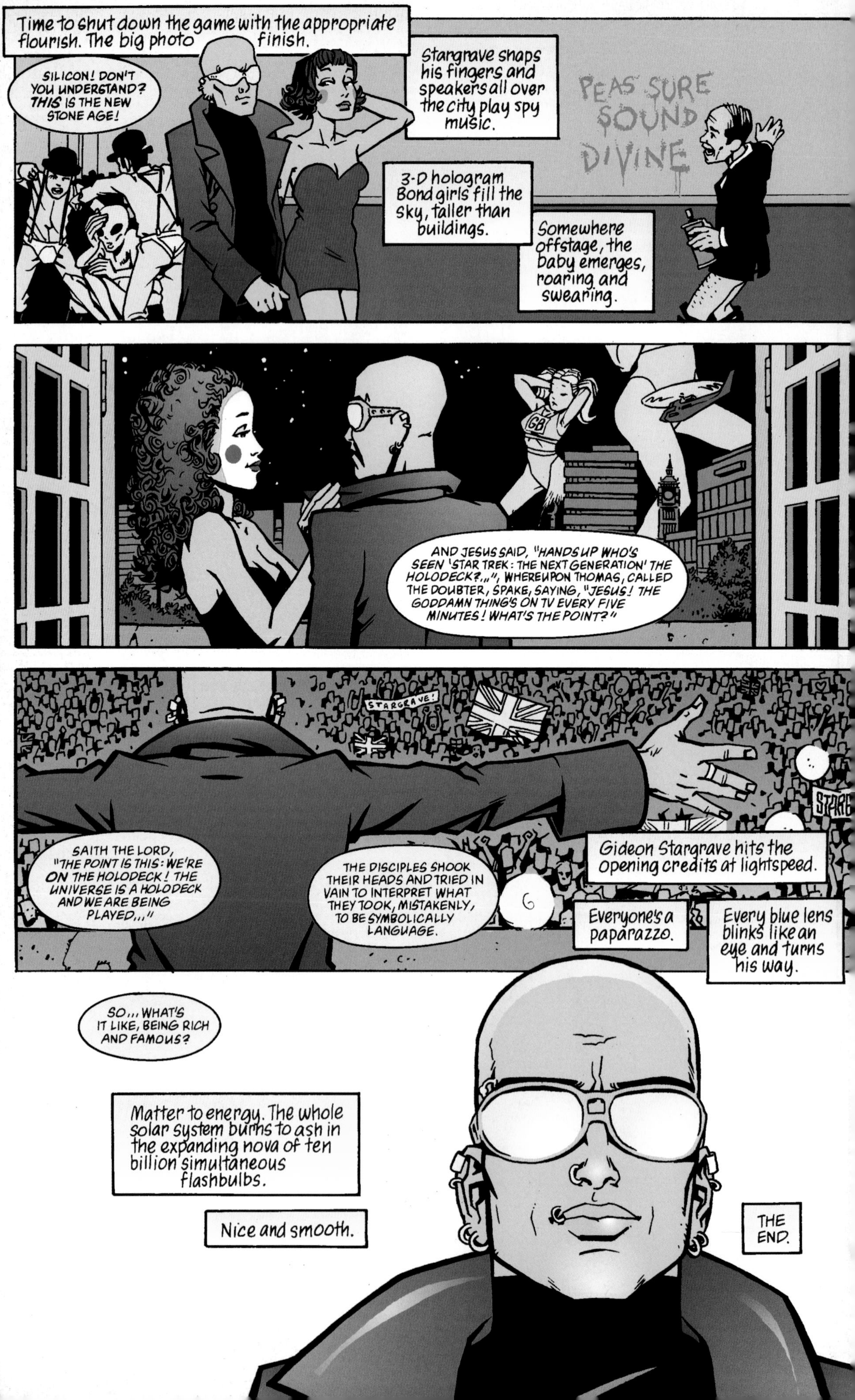

Time to shut down the game with the appropriate flourish. The big photo finish.
SILICON! DON'T YOU UNDERSTAND? THIS IS THE NEW STONE AGE!
Stargrave snaps his fingers and speakers all over the city play spy music.
PEAS SURE SOUND DIVINE
3-D hologram Bond girls fill the sky, taller than buildings.
Somewhere offstage, the baby emerges, roaring and swearing.
GB
AND JESUS SAID, "HANDS UP WHO'S SEEN 'STAR TREK: THE NEXT GENERATION' THE HOLODECK?..", WHEREUPON THOMAS, CALLED THE DOUBTER, SPAKE, SAYING, "JESUS! THE GODDAMN THING'S ON TV EVERY FIVE MINUTES! WHAT'S THE POINT?"
STARGRAVE!
SAITH THE LORD, "THE POINT IS THIS: WE'RE ON THE HOLODECK! THE UNIVERSE IS A HOLODECK AND WE ARE BEING PLAYED..."
THE DISCIPLES SHOOK THEIR HEADS AND TRIED IN VAIN TO INTERPRET WHAT THEY TOOK, MISTAKENLY, TO BE SYMBOLICALLY LANGUAGE.
Gideon Stargrave hits the opening credits at lightspeed.
Everyone's a paparazzo.
Every blue lens blinks like an eye and turns his way.
SO... WHAT'S IT LIKE, BEING RICH AND FAMOUS?
Matter to energy. The whole solar system burns to ash in the expanding nova of ten billion simultaneous flashbulbs.
Nice and smooth.
THE END.

BEHIND THE INVISIBLES' CURTAIN

Preliminary text and art for THE INVISIBLES

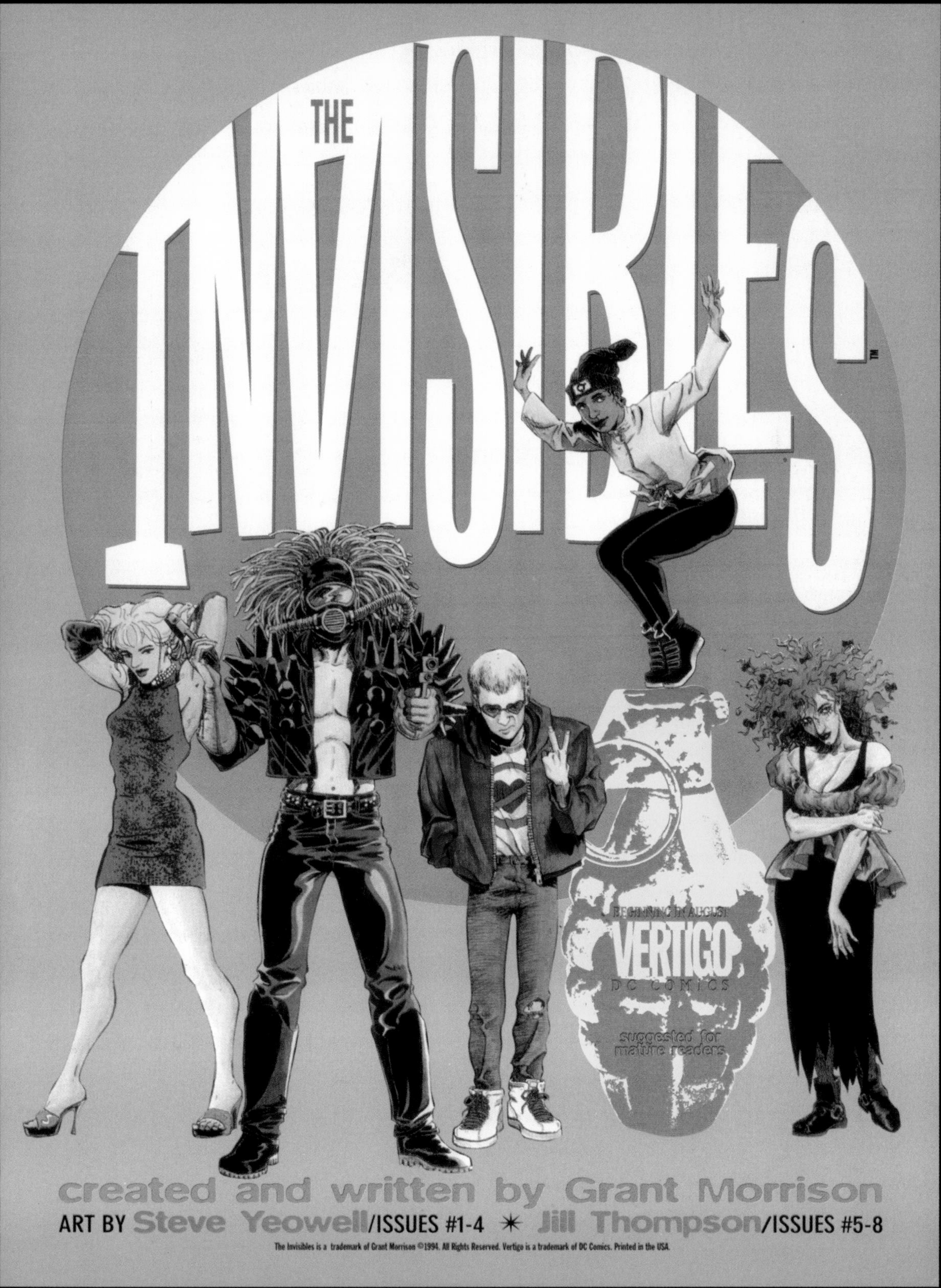

THE INVISIBLES™
BEGINNING IN AUGUST
VERTIGO
DC COMICS
suggested for mature readers
created and written by Grant Morrison
ART BY Steve Yeowell/ISSUES #1-4 ✶ Jill Thompson/ISSUES #5-8
The Invisibles is a trademark of Grant Morrison ©1994. All Rights Reserved. Vertigo is a trademark of DC Comics. Printed in the USA.

A promotional poster featuring art by Jill Thompson.

THE INVISIBLES
SERIES PROPOSAL

Grant Morrison

THE CONCEPT

After a year in the Wilderness, I've realised to my *horreur* that I'm bored and I like the idea of working on a regular book again. Working for Todd McFarlane pays more than the rent but I've a hankering to do some ...er... *serious* work again. I want to do something which gives me the opportunity to air my personal philosophies and unique viewpoint on the human condition. I've come to realise that, being of limited attention span, I lose interest fairly rapidly when I'm working on a monthly book, mainly because these things tend to have a distinctive style which is established early on. What I really want is to do a comic in which I can tell any story I want, in which I'm not shackled by a completely regular cast of characters and settings. One of the few things I truly admire about SANDMAN is the way in which it functions as a vehicle for any old thing Neil wants to say. He's able to focus on the Sandman character if he wants but he's also able to spin off in all directions and tell all kinds of stories, some of which don't have to involve his core cast in any way. This seems like the ideal environment in which to cultivate a long-running series which doesn't become boring and/or repetitive. So, taking a perfectly-formed leaf from the book of the Meister of Dark Fantasy, I think I've finally come up with a structure which accommodates all the stories I've ever wanted to tell. I want to create a radical new mix of historical stuff, biography and bizarre fiction and to create a series which acts as a home for all my stray plots and strange notions, things I've seen on my world travels, theories I've developed, occult stuff, fringe science, adventures, meditations, you name it, it'll be here. Some stories can be straight, down-to-earth social realist items, others can spin off into wild and outlandish worlds of occult horror. In addition, and staying with SANDMAN for a while, I'm convinced that one of the reasons for that book's success is, quite simply that it's a superhero book which doesn't come across as a superhero book. Neil has a cast of distinctive characters, each with their own powers, codenames and even a headquarters. I really feel that Vertigo is making a mistake by publishing stuff which isn't superhero or fantasy related in some way and, to be frank, I feel that books like my own MYSTERY PLAY and the various other 'real world' projects are actually undermining the viability of Vertigo. Ultimately, there's no audience out there for comics which simply try to be like mainstream films or novels and we should be concentrating instead on the stuff which comics does best, namely superheroes. Which is not to say that we can't do subtle and intelligent work but that we should be doing it within a structure which is recognisably a comic book structure - i.e. strong characters with unusual abilities and/or lifestyles. Look at the most popular and successful of the Vertigo titles and you will see superheroes of one kind or another. Our core audience is interested in fantastic and unusual ideas, so if we really want to consolidate the Vertigo identity this should be at its core a superhero comic, even though I'll be describing it as a character-driven Occult Thriller filled with new mindbending ideas. For me, the rationale is that, instead of spreading myself thinly through endless one-offs and miniseries, I'd like to refine all the ideas I've toyed with in things like Kid Eternity, Animal Man, Doom Patrol etcetera and concentrate everything into one ultra-groovy monthly book - THE INVISIBLES. It's the next stage in the evolution of what I want to do with comic books.

Grant Morrison's original series proposal for THE INVISIBLES.

The basic premise is this:

We have five core characters, male and female and stations between, who belong to an organisation which exists simultaneously at all points in space and time. This organisation is dedicated to subversive activity in all its forms and is seen to be implicated in everything from the French and American Revolutions to weird graffiti on toilet walls. It may be connected to the fabled Illuminati, it may not even exist in anything but conceptual terms but all of its members know that they belong in its ranks, even if they have never met any other members. ('The Invisibles' was an old term used to describe the shadowy adepts of the Rosicrucian order or indeed any other esoteric group.) The only rule of the organisation is disobedience. If you're driven to disrupt the structure of your office or school or of large scale Dominator culture itself (in the form of governments, dogmatic religions, big business), you may be contacted. The ultimate aim of the Invisibles is the Immanentisation of the Eschaton, to use Robert Anton Wilson's phrase - the End of the World as we know it and the inauguration of Cosmic Humanity, of Will made manifest. Imagination unbound, total freedom, the next step in evolution.

There are divisions of the organisation which employ only shamanic transvestite assassins; others which specialise in psychic time travel and the manipulation of Reality; maverick scientists; orders and ranks of rebellious schoolchildren and PTA housewives, who secretly work to undermine the values of middle class suburbia etc. Basically, as you can see, there's scope here for any kind of character to tell his or her story as the book progresses.

THE CHARACTERS

KING MOB

King Mob is the main character for this series, though he doesn't necessarily appear in every issue. He's the ultimate product of Invisibles training - skilled in psychic and occult techniques, a martial arts and Tantric sex expert and a devotee of Wilhelm Reich's Orgone theories. He is one of the front line troops for the Invisibles. King Mob is funny and charismatic and relies on his native charm to get him through life. He has a shaved head and wears hard cyberfetish style clothing - Craig Morrison heavy rubber spiked jackets, data gloves and sometimes a big industrial/ceremonial gas mask which makes him look like the shaman of some technopagan cult.

JACK FROST

Jack Frost is the reader identification figure for the first few issues. Through him, we learn what it's like to be plucked from obscurity and trained as an Invisible. he knows no more than we do and, as we witness the rigours of his initiation and instruction, we too should experience the same confusion and enlightenment and reconfusion that he does. Through him, we may begin to wonder just whose side the Invisibles are on and, indeed, if there are any sides at all.

BOY

Boy is a black New York street girl. She's small tough and perfectly-formed, being a body builder and dancer. Pint-sized with attitude. She's from a poor family, the only girl among several brothers, most of whom are involved in crime in some way. Boy's original intention was to join the police force and this desire led her into contact with hidden conspiratorial forces within the Police department. The

Myrmidon enemies of the Invisibles attempted to recruit her but she was rescued from their clutches by members of the Invisibles within the Police, who convinced her to join their ranks as protection against the Myrmidons. (Or perhaps, the Invisibles themselves set up the whole thing as a charade to convince Boy she was in sufficient danger to need their help. These suspicions should be ever in the mind of the reader.)

RAGGEDY ANN

Raggedy Ann is, I must admit, fairly undeveloped at this stage but basically she's going to be kinda neurotic, witchy and...um...'alternative', with hennaed hair and raggedy skirts and Doc Marten boots etc. She's the Death/Crazy Jane type of female figure beloved of boys who read Vertigo comics.

LORD FANNY

Lord Fanny is a glamourous transvestite shaman, a stalwart of the New York gay nightclub scene. She divides her time between the techno disco scene and magical work for the Invisibles. She's a tall and overwhelming Hispanic Queen, originally from South America where as an only child and as a boy, she received from her grandmother the magical instruction that's supposed to pass down through the female children of a family. Imagine Doctor Strange in full drag and you may get the picture. She's named after Lord Hervey, a nobleman in the reign of George II of England, who was nicknamed Fanny for his 'effeminate and foppish manners'.

THE PLOTS

As usual, when I really get into something, I've come up with years' worth of material but, in the interests of brevity, I'll just run through some of the stuff I'm thinking of for the first twelve or so issues. A lot of this may change as I actually get to work (some of the four issue story arcs may be expanded if need be) and become more familiar with the characters but this should provide some flavour of what I want to do. Rather than go into the boring details of the stories, (which I hate anyway because it kills all the fun of actually writing the thing), I'll simply suggest some of the ideas and concepts I'll be playing with.

ISSUE ONE - DEAD BEATLES

This first issue would be a double length intro. We begin with King Mob in some dazzlingly bizarre, action-packed scene and then cut to the grim reality of an English school as we meet the youth who is to become Jack Frost of the Invisibles. A surly adolescent outsider with a grudge against authority who, unknown to him, has been selected for induction into the order. Through him we meet some of the other core characters as they lead him into the world of mystery and wonder which exists at right angles to everyday reality.

[handwritten margin note: LENNON --OR LEGALLY?]

The story then spirals off into a scratch mix of Egyptian Mythology, school rebellion and the early lives of John Lennon and Stu Sutcliffe. (The Beatles' original bass player who died at the age of 21 on the eve of a promising career as a painter.) My forays into the world of Chaos Magick have shown me how absolutely *anything* can be used in a magical context and, most importantly for this story, how cultural figures can be transformed into godforms in magical rituals. Recently, I used John Lennon as a godform and got very interesting results. I'd like to explore this stuff in this story - the idea of dead stars becoming Gods in a new pantheon for the modern age, the God Lennon and his connection to the Egyptian scarab beetle as a symbol of rebirth which also symbolises the rebirth of Jack Frost as a fully-fledged Invisible, following the rigorous and unusual initiations and disorienting ordeals which occur across the next couple of issues.

At the end of this issue, Jack has been abandoned by King Mob in London. With no money and with his memory selectively removed, Jack is left to wander the cruel streets.

ISSUES TWO - THREE - DOWN AND OUT IN HEAVEN AND HELL

Jack is lost and homeless and his situation is growing worse by the minute. He's sleeping rough, getting sick and all seems lost until he meets a seemingly crazy old beggarman who calls himself Tom O'Bedlam. Tom begins to teach Jack how to survive and suddenly we find ourselves in a strange, urban version of Carlos Castaneda as Tom is revealed to be a shaman, who uses the secret power points of the city itself in his magical work. He leads Jack through a series of delirious adventures in the eerie byways of London. Tom's places of power are not mesas and sacred burial sites but tower blocks and garbage dumps and he opens up for Jack the occult heart of the city and reveals to him what cities *really* are. (What they really are, according to Tom, are viral organisms which use human beings as host bodies in order to reproduce themselves. The virus entered the human mind early in man's development and through man, the cities were able to grow and expand. When they have grown to cover the Earth, man will die and the virus will migrate once more to colonise other worlds. True or false ? You decide.) We learn also that Jack will shortly be required to undergo some life-threatening initiation. (Throughout this story, we meet the other core members of the Invisibles, who appear in disguise, as players in the psychodrama of Jack's initiatory journey.)

Part two takes Jack deeper into the mysteries and he must face mortality in the form of Tom, his by-now-beloved mentor, who is dying. Jack's final ordeal involves climbing to the top of the Canary Wharf Tower and stepping off into space. His survival of this and his facing the death of Tom provide his entry into the world of the Invisibles as King Mob returns to complete Jack's induction.

ISSUES FOUR - EIGHT - ARCADIA

The first major story arc 'ARCADIA' involves all of our core group in a story which takes place simultaneously in the present day, 1790 and a swirling combination of both time periods. In this one I want to take a look at the inbuilt self-destruct mechanism which seems present in all Utopian systems. The key image is Poussin's famous painting which shows two shepherds in a paradisical landscape. One of the shepherds points off to a misty and mysterious castle on a distant rock, the other leans against a gravestone whose inscription reads 'ET IN ARCADIA EGO' or 'EVEN IN PARADISE, I AM THERE'. The painting is believed to contain clues to all kinds of oddball occult secrets and will appear as a recurring motif throughout this story. In this storyline, we learn a little more about the forces which oppose the Invisibles - the Lost Ones, the Dark Gods, are all names to describe the powers of restriction and negativity which seek to dominate our planet. (However, as we progress through this series, things become more baroque, more elaborate and conspiracies turn on one another, eating themselves, until we're not sure whose side anyone is on and whether or not the Lost Ones are as black as they are at first painted.) The Lost Ones employ human servants, from all walks of life, known as Myrmidons. Many of these Myrmidons pull the strings of Government and are behind the activities of the world's secret services and intelligence agencies. They are slaves and agents of Control and throughout history have sought to enslave humanity and annihilate all creative thought.

Part One - **BLOODY POETRY** - introduces the mystery of Poussin's painting and gives us our first look at how the Myrmidons operate. We drop in on a heated conversation between Shelley and Byron, concerning the poet's responsibility towards initiating social change. Intercut with the talking, we get King Mob and the others in violent action against the Myrmidon forces.

Part Two - **MYSTERIES OF THE GUILLOTINE** - sees King Mob and Boy in Revolutionary France, witnessing the way in which revolutionary, Utopian ideals always end up being enforced by violent murder and cruelty. We are present as Donatien Alphonse Francoise de Sade, the notorious Marquis is freed from the Bastille, where he has languished for years writing his monumental, notoriously obscene books. He joins forces with King Mob.

Part Three - **120 DAYS OF SOD ALL** - takes King Mob and DeSade into Poussin's Arcadian landscape, where the mysterious Castle on the horizon becomes the infamous Castle of Silling described by DeSade in his 120 Days of Sodom. Silling was the apocalyptic retreat of the Duc de Blangis and his fellow libertines. The castle where, in Sade's novel, all moral laws are abrogated and people become mere possessions to be used and abused by these wicked aristos. We begin to learn some of the secrets that lie encoded in Poussin's painting and open up a few plot strands which will be explored later on down the line.

Part Four - **H.E.A.D.** - moves the action to modern day California where the current Utopian ideal finds its expression in the whole *'Mondo 2000'* culture of smart drugs, Virtual Reality and hedonism. DeSade drives down the Pacific Coast highway to investigate LA sex clubs and produce new forms of writing which assault the taboos of the modern world and provide the same scathing critique of the hypocrisies of our society as he once provided for the *ancien regime* of pre-Revolutionary France. Through him, we are forced to confront the failure of the lofty ideals behind the American revolution and, by extension, all revolutions. Meanwhile, the occult action element of the story ends with a confrontation between the forces of This and That at Rennes-le-Chateau in France. (Like I said, this rundown of what I want to accomplish is purposely short on plot - I'm more interested here in getting across the themes and ideas I want to work with. The plot stuff is more mechanical and will come as the stories are written. Trust me, I know what I'm doing, as Custer said just before Little Big Horn.)

ISSUE NINE is **MYSTERE ARAIGNEE**, which deals with some of the weird shit that's happening on the fringes of the new cybernetic voodoo cults, which have been inspired by the outré work of occultist Michel Bertiaux. The new voodoo, or Voudou, as it's now called, is introducing some mindwrenchingly far-out concepts into the occult world and I'd like to deal with some of this material in a story. Here, we also meet Jim Crow of the Invisibles, a Jamaican *Houngan*, or voodoo priest.

ISSUE TEN is **ROYAL MONSTERS**, which serves to open up a plot strand which will lead us into the later **SATANSTORM** arc. This one concerns the legendary creature which is allegedly locked up in Scotland's Glamis Castle and is said to be a hideously deformed member of the Royal Family, kept hidden out of sight for years. I want to tie this into some very strange evidence which is beginning to come to light concerning the Royals' involvement in ritualistic magical practices. (I've read claims that one of the reasons behind Princess Diana's mental problems and her rejection by the Royal family is that she was called upon to bear a magical

'Moonchild' and was unable to go through with it. All sort of curious allegations are being made - about how Buckingham Palace is on a major leyline and how the huge pyramid-topped Canary Wharf development was built, at Margaret Thatcher's instructions, to focus and control the ley energy. In a recent TV show, The Royals were even suggested to have been implicated in Satanic child sex abuse cases. It's all very odd stuff and I intend to incorporate it all into a scathing dissection of the British aristocracy.) Later in the series, the monster will assume its rightful place on the throne of England, the ascendant heraldic beast.

ISSUE ELEVEN - **THE DEVIL'S WALK**, is a modern version of the old Romantic conceit of the Devil taking a stroll through the world and finding it much to his liking. The original was written by Coleridge and Southey and influenced similar poems by Byron ('Devil Drive') and Shelley. The simple structure of the idea provides an excellent framework for a blackly horrific satire on the state of the world.

ISSUE TWELVE - **HOUSE OF CARDS** is the story of a spy, known only as The Card, who once belonged to an organisation known as The Pack. He was brainwashed and ejected from The Pack but has recently regained his memory of those events. Now, carrying a blank playing card, he searches for the House of Cards, the HQ of the pack, eager for revenge. His search leads us down existential, 'Prisoner'-esque byways of paranoia, conspiracy and counter-conspiracy and leads to a final startling revelation.

ISSUES THIRTEEN - SIXTEEN will feature either the **SHEMAN** or **BLACK SCIENCE** story arcs, depending on how I'm feeling at the time. Or perhaps it'll be something else entirely.

SHEMAN focuses on Lord Fanny and her world and explores the connections between the drag queen underworld of New York/London nightclubs and the shamanic world. In the past, I've touched upon the idea that transvestites unwittingly assume the role of shamans by the very act of putting on female clothes and assuming a feminine identity. Tribal shamans habitually wear female clothing to become hermaphroditic creatures and connect themselves with the spirit world. I'd like to point out the connections between this tribal world and the nighttime world of crossdressing

BLACK SCIENCE takes a look at the uses and abuses of technology, in particular the Bomb. We travel back to the Los Alamos Ranch School, where William Burroughs was sent as a boy and where, shortly thereafter, the government established their Atomic Bomb research facility. I want to look at the weird lives of people like Oppenheimer and Teller, the scientists who were instrumental in the creation of the Bomb. There's a lot of strange material and occult lore connected with these characters and with the Bomb itself. I'd also like to involve the magical world of the local Zuni Indians. (This is the tribe I stayed with in the San Ildefonso Pueblo outside Santa Fe.)

Completing the first run of twenty issues there will be another series of one offs dealing with various aspects of the Invisibles. If, for instance, I want to tell a gritty crime story, I can focus on a police or detective character who is either unknowingly a member of the organisation or is pursuing a member. The story possibilities are endless in an open series of this nature. The major storyline concluding the second year will probably be **KARMAGEDDON**, which travels to the weird Tibet of the turn of the century mystic Nicholas Roerich and to modern-day Nepal, in a story which takes in the life of Siddartha Buddha and an audacious plan to incarnate the final avatar of the Hindu God Vishnu.

Basically, I think I've at last found a way to do a comic about *everything* and I'm raring to go.

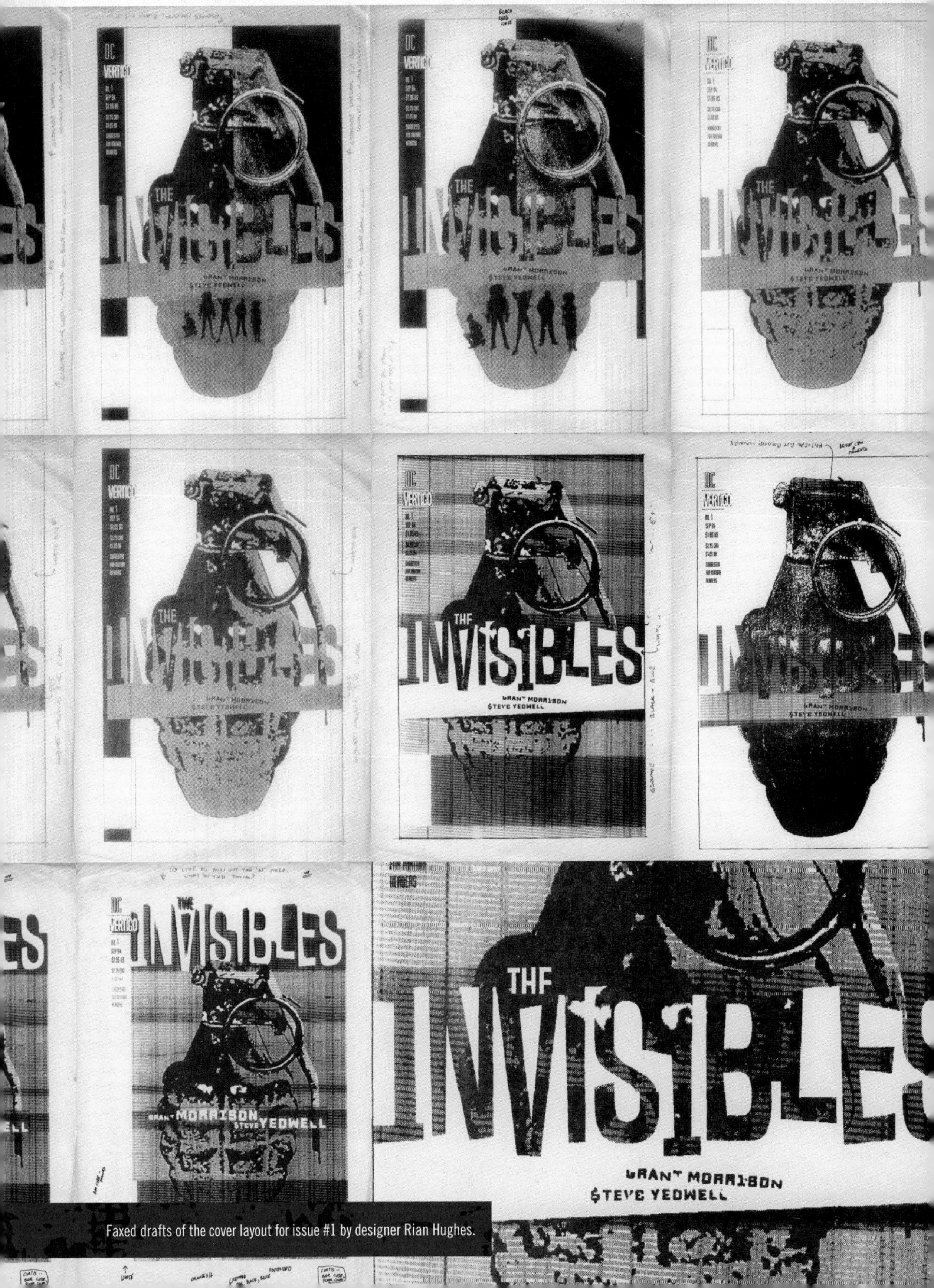
DC
VERTIGO
THE
INVISIBLES
GRANT MORRISON
STEVE YEOWELL

Faxed drafts of the cover layout for issue #1 by designer Rian Hughes.

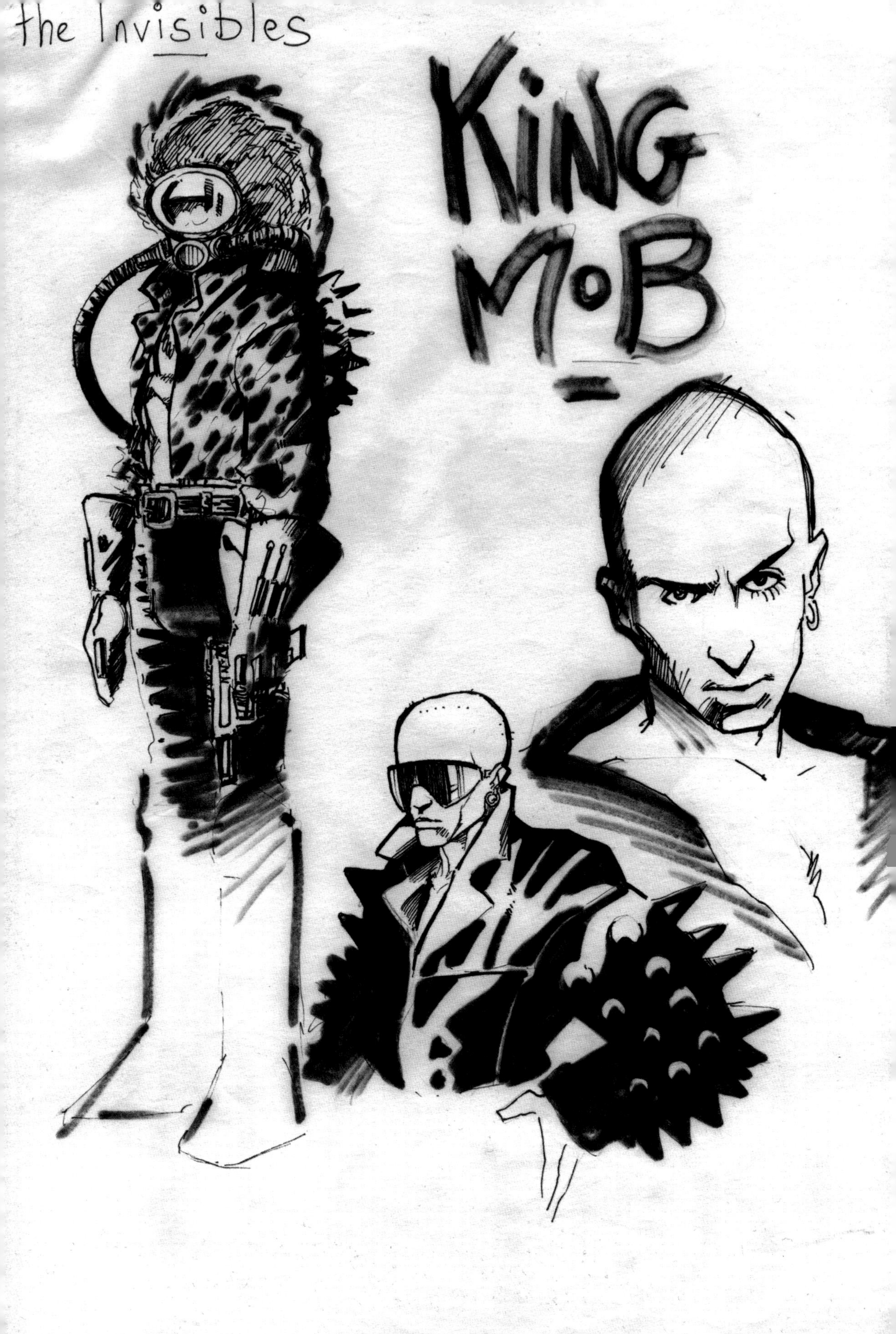
the Invisibles
KING MOB

Character sketches by Grant Morrison included with the series proposal.

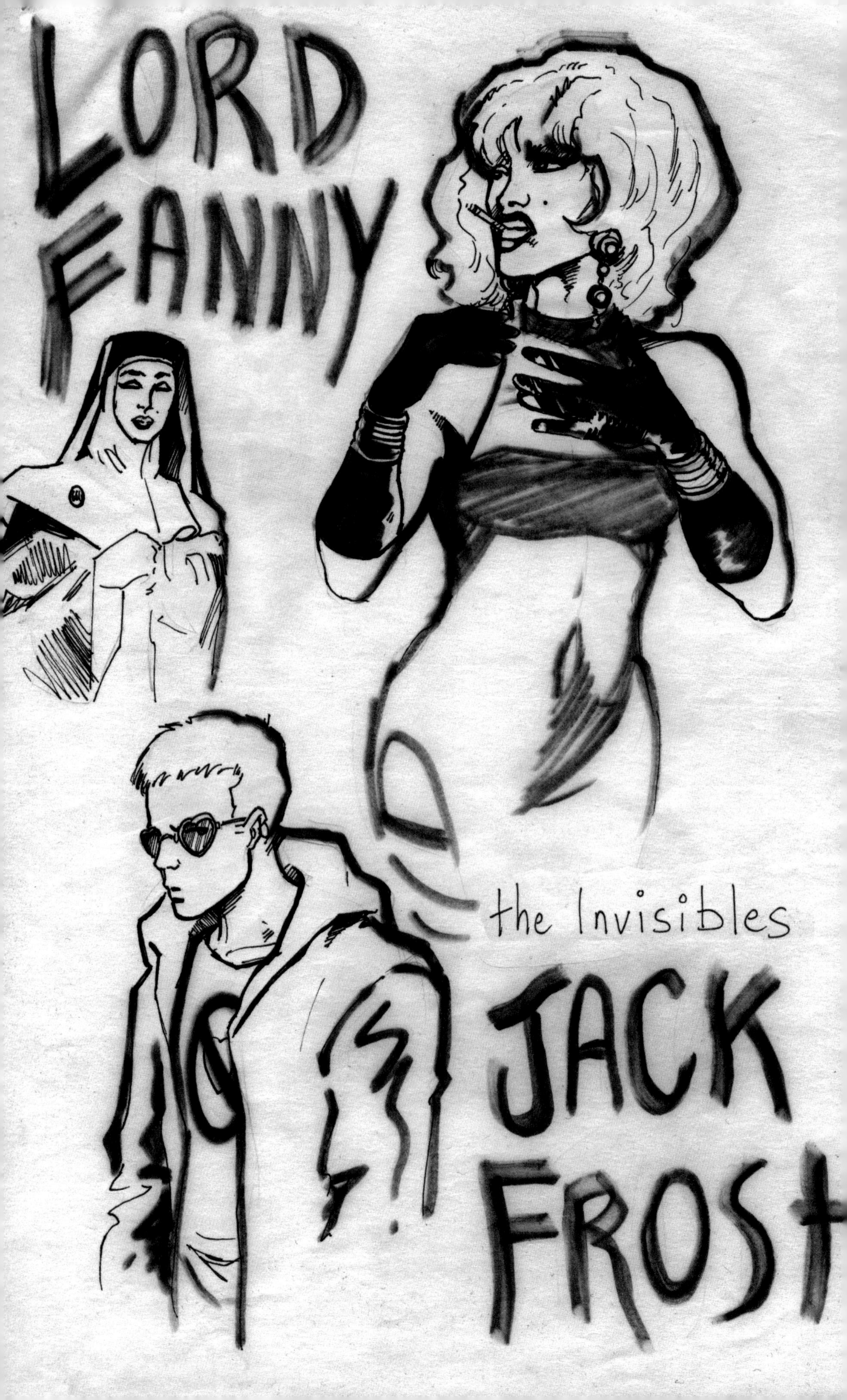
LORD FANNY
the Invisibles
JACK FROST

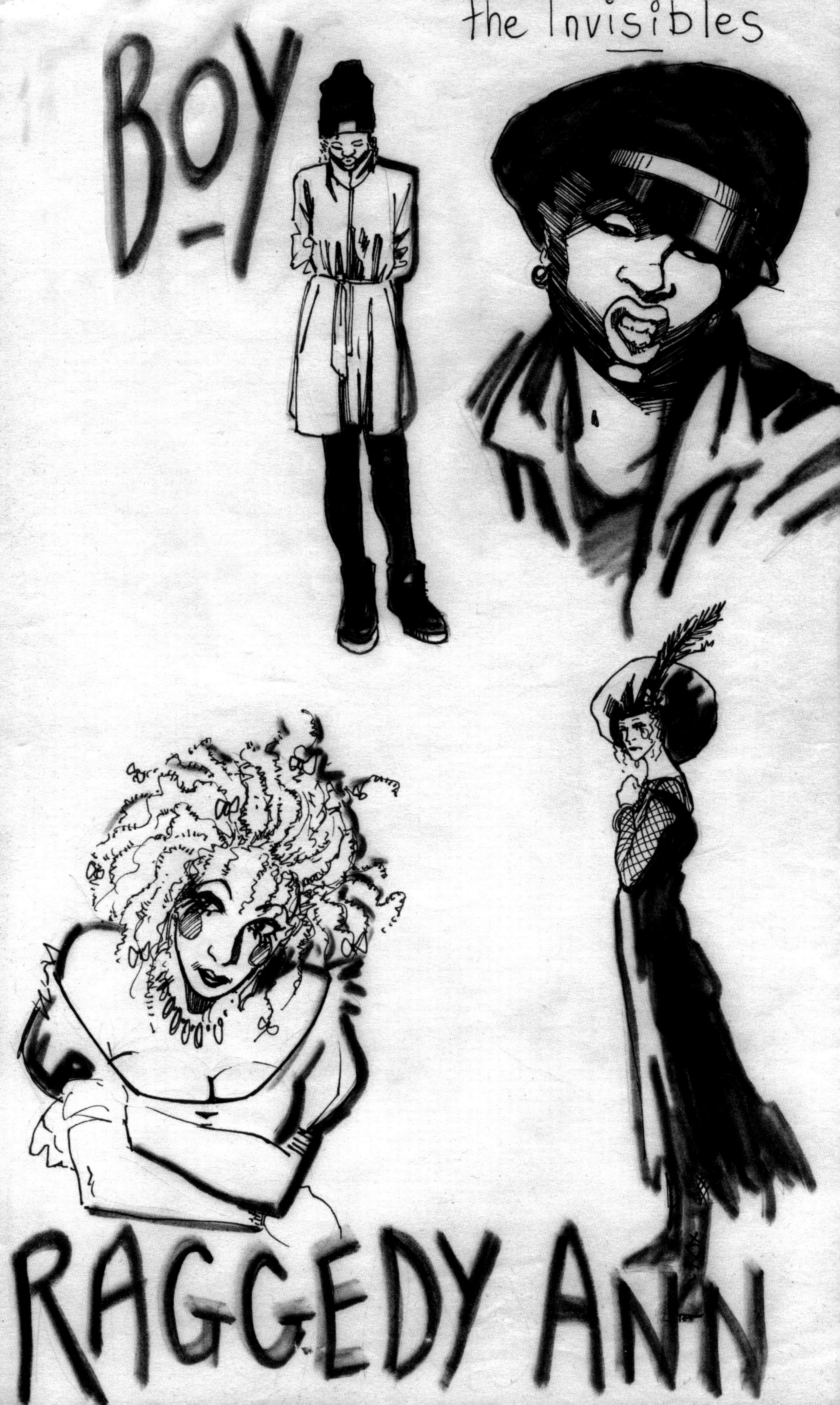
the Invisibles
BOY
RAGGEDY ANN

THE INVISIBLES

Okay, here are the additional bits and pieces which should hopefully fill the gaps in THE INVISIBLES proposal.

All comic book teams are based on some kind of structure and the five core members of the Invisibles are no exception. The Fantastic Four and the Endless, for instance, are family units, the X-Men began with a school set-up, the Avengers and Justice League are like football teams, the Doom Patrol a therapy group etc. The Invisibles, for their part, are a *cell*. Like any organised group of political subversives, The Invisibles, as a large-scale concern, are broken down into activist units or cells . These cells contain a small number of individuals who all know one another and act separately or together. The cell on which we concentrate most of our attention is made up of King Mob, Lord Fanny, Raggedy Ann, Boy and Jack Frost. (All Invisibles cells contain five members in accordance with the famous Law of Fives, as expounded in Robert Anton Wilson's books.) In the first storyline, we'll learn that Jack Frost was chosen to replace the fifth member of the cell. (This fifth member is not dead but something terrifying has happened to him/her, as we'll learn in a future storyline, when he/she comes back to kill the others.) So, the set-up is that these people have been selected to work with one another as a tightly-knit group which receives its orders from an unknown source and cannot betray any details of the large-scale Invisibles operation. Our core group will, in the course of the series, encounter other cells, (the Jim Crow character from the Voodoo story, for instance, belongs to another cell), but they tend not to have a great deal of contact with other groups. The web of conspiracy and counter-conspiracy in which they operate means that it makes a great deal more sense to trust only a few close colleagues. (There are also Solo Invisibles operatives - ultra-paranoid agents operating at the very fringes of Reality and Sanity - of course, and thousands of others who don't even know they're working for the Invisibles cause until, like Jack Frost, they may be contacted to replace a departed cell member.)

The group interactions will follow the pattern of any small gathering of people regularly exposed to intense and unusual situations. The group members are strongly bonded by trust and shared experience but they are only human and blow-ups occur as do shifting allegiances and antagonisms. It's up to the Water Master of the cell to monitor group dynamics and ensure a harmonious working environment. (The cells are structured using occult elemental symbolism - we begin with Boy in the Earth role, which includes keeping the members grounded and stable in the midst of the terrifying chaos of their lives. She also oversees the purely material aspects of the group, such as finances, proper clothing and equipment for specific situations etc. King Mob is in the Air role, concerned with the allocation of tasks, analysis of given situations, formulating plans and tactics. Raggedy Ann has the Fire Master's chores, which revolve around motivating the group and inspiring enthusiasm. Lord Fanny takes the Water role and is concerned with, as mentioned above, resolving conflicts within the group, maintaining the free flow of emotional support and empathy. Jack Frost is assigned the role of Spirit, which unifies and synthesises the other four through humour and creativity. These roles are rotated, perhaps once a year, allowing all members of the cell to experience and develop the particular mindset and abilities of each elemental role.)

Further notes on the proposed series from Morrison to editor Stuart Moore.

The High Concept for this series is the single element of the brew which is giving me the most trouble. There are so many low concepts in the mix, that I'm finding it hard to rise up and see the big picture. Someone who's not so close to the project might find it easier to condense the concept. One of the things we should be trying to bring out is the idea of The Invisibles as a group to which anyone might belong. Involve the reader in the whole process by making him/her realise that she/he too can join/has already joined the ranks of The Invisibles. Part of what I want to achieve with this title in the long-term involves actually changing the consciousness of the readers by presenting them with various techniques and concepts which will undoubtedly alter their way of looking at the world. In that sense, THE INVISIBLES isn't a comic *about* something but is the thing itself and every reader is a potential Invisible. If The Invisibles are Shamanic Terrorists, the comic itself is an act of shamanic terrorism.

If it helps to clarify things, the following description of what-it's-all-about comes from a letter I sent to a guy who wants to interview   me for the music press:

'THE INVISIBLES is the name given to a society of occult subversives which may or may not have existed for hundreds, even thousands of years. The five main characters belong to an activist cell but there are also stories dealing with people who don't even know they belong to The Invisibles. All that's required to be a member is to be involved in sustained activity against all forces which retard human development and evolution. (Or so it seems at the beginning. As the comic progresses, conspiracies and counter-conspiracies start turning on each other like hungry Moray eels until nobody can be sure who is working for whom.)'

Other than that, I'm not quite sure how to sum this up in a Hollywood-style snappy sentence.

I've also been thinking about house ads - I'd probably prefer these to be fairly mysterious and conceptual and my favourite idea is this one, suggestive of the deepest philosophical underpinnings to the series. For me, this sums the whole thing up:

'Welcome to the Ultimate Conspiracy'

then a drawing of the famous one-sided mobius strip figure and the words

'Which side will YOU be on ?'

and

'THE INVISIBLES'

Or perhaps this, referring to the soon-to-be-famous Blank Badge worn by certain members of The Invisibles. (The Blank Badge would make a great merchandising item. Just buy in a job lot of white badges and sell 'em back at outrageous prices. With me on a smart royalty, of course...)

A white circle and

'Are you ready to wear the Blank Badge ?

'THE INVISIBLES are coming.'

The order of the stories is fairly flexible and I'll try to make sure that a proper balance is maintained between the really *outré* stuff and the more down-to-earth stories. As I've said, however, the weird stuff isn't going to be like the kind of widescreen, special effects weirdness of DOOM PATROL and will be a lot more sinister and grounded. (Please please please don't make me mention David Lynch again!) Just as the 'real-life' stuff will tend to deal with those aspects of real life which are most bizarre and unexpected.

The artist situation remains a little confusing but I do want to be able to work with a variety of people on this title, so I think it's worth working things out. It would be nice to get a rotating pool of people for the multi-parters while handing out one-offs to anyone who wants to draw them - Brian Bolland's said he'd like to draw something again and he could easily be given a self-contained story which he could work on at as slow a pace as he likes. (Within reason!) Bryan Talbot's interested in doing one. Other suggestions for people who might be suitable and who I'd like to work with - Duncan Fegredo, Mark Buckingham, Glyn Dillon, Kelly Jones, Steve Yeowell, Ted McKeever, Arthur Ransom, Mike Mignola, Paul Johnson, Sean Philips, Chris Bachalo, Charles Vess and anyone else you can think of to do something, whether one-offs or longer stories. Probably the most difficult bit will be arranging the longer stories. Of course, Jill's definite for the first story and others in the future. (Perhaps she should even do the first seven issues, including the ARCADIA arc. I don't know how her schedule is with the BADGER series and other stuff she may have lined up.) Other than that, I'm open to suggestions.